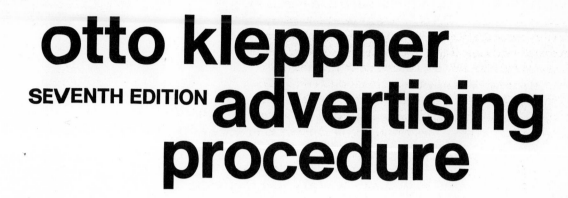

otto kleppner

SEVENTH EDITION advertising
procedure

with the
collaboration of **NORMAN A.P. GOVONI**
Professor of Marketing, Marketing Division
Babson College

prentice-hall, inc.
Englewood Cliffs, New Jersey 07632

Library of Congress Cataloging in Publication Data

KLEPPNER, OTTO (DATE).
　　Advertising procedure.

　　Includes bibliographies and index.
　　1. Advertising.　I. Govoni, Norman A. P., joint author.　II Title.
HF5823.K45 1979　　　659.1　　　78-5728
ISBN 0-13-018119-6

10　9　8　7　6　5　4　3　2　1

Cover photo by Gabe Palmer/The Image Bank.

PRENTICE-HALL INTERNATIONAL, INC., *London*
PRENTICE-HALL OF AUSTRALIA PTY. LIMITED, *Sydney*
PRENTICE-HALL OF CANADA, LTD., *Toronto*
PRENTICE-HALL OF INDIA PRIVATE LIMITED, *New Delhi*
PRENTICE-HALL OF JAPAN, INC., *Tokyo*
PRENTICE-HALL OF SOUTHEAST ASIA PTE. LTD., *Singapore*
WHITEHALL BOOKS LIMITED, *Wellington, New Zealand*

to
Beatrice

Contents

**Part Four
CREATING
ADVERTISING**

**Part Five
MANAGING THE
ADVERTISING**

**Part Six
OTHER WORLDS
OF ADVERTISING**

**Part Seven
ADVERTISING AS
AN INSTITUTION**

APPENDIX

Preface

I don't know whether this is the best of times or the worst of times," said Art Buchwald in a Vassar College commencement address, "but I do know this: It's the only time you've got." This book is about advertising for "the only time you've got."

It was in the "worst of times," during the Great Depression of the 1930s, that the first portable air-conditioner cooled a room. Cooling was made possible by the development of Freon, a gas safe for use in air-conditioners, freezers, and re-frigerators. Synthetic rubber was developed at this time, as was shatterproof glass. When nylon was announced in 1938, who would have thought it would lead to today's world of products made of synthetic materials? The first synthetic detergent (Dreft) also appeared during the Great Depression. And it was in this dreary decade that frozen foods first came into our lives.

The United States had always been an innovative and resourceful nation. New and improved products and services constantly appear, enrich our lives, change life-styles, create new industries and new jobs. And all these products and services need advertising.

This book deals with the planning, creation, use, and place of advertising in our society. The reader who is seeking a broad view of advertising will find here a comprehensive survey, crisply written. Those whose paths may lead to market-ing and advertising responsibilities will find here insights that become ever more meaningful.

I did not set out merely to update the preceding edition. Instead, I set out to review the total field and to write each chapter afresh in the light of the signifi-cant developments. In this age of anxiety about inflation and energy, we ques-tion past assumptions and strike out in new directions to solve contemporary problems. In keeping with the spirit of the times, the book offers fresh approaches to various subjects.

Advertising research, for example—traditionally treated as a special chapter or chapters in advertising texts—is presented throughout the book as *applied research*, wherever some particular form of it is indicated. The stress is on the two crucial points of research: the sharp definition of the problem and the creative interpretation of the findings, with just enough discussion of technique to show how the research is done.

In the "Print Production" chapter we enter the world of computerized photocomposition and say farewell to the age of the Linotype.

"Specific Purposes of Campaigns" is a new chapter.

In the creative chapters, the book introduces the *headline/visualization match*, leading to the *creative leap*. This discussion reflects the formation in many agencies of copy and art teams for the development of total concepts.

The media chapters discuss the use of the computer in intermedia scheduling. We present for the first time in this book—probably the first time in any advertising text—the practice of negotiation in buying time and space, so important in these days of rising media costs.

"The Story Behind" a selected campaign is presented at appropriate places throughout the book, not as a case in a casebook, but as an example of how a precept just discussed is applied to a real-life marketing situation.

The closing chapters of the book show the increasing influence of government in advertising (including the FTC's $10 million levy on Listerine, a landmark case in corrective advertising) and the crescendo voice of the consumer.

Some chapters have been pruned and combined, others have been shifted to meet teaching needs. Every chapter in the book, however, has been freshly written; even the Glossary has been revised to make way for the newest terms.

The worth of a textbook, however, lies deeper than the currency of its information. Earlier editions have left a legacy — precepts that over the years have proved valid and significant, the slow accumulation of knowledge resulting from a lifetime as a practitioner and a persistent student of advertising. I have sought to retain those qualities of presentation that have been so well received in the past.

Acknowledgments

With gratitude I acknowledge my debt to those who gave generously of their time and experience in providing major help in the chapters dealing with their respective specialties. Arthur Bellaire gave much help on the TV and radio commercial chapters, and he did so at the very time he was under pressure to complete his own book, *Controlling Your TV Commercial Costs*. Richard Briggs, vice-president, SSC&B, contributed many of the latest developments described in the outdoor advertising chapter. David H. Folkman, senior vice-president, Macys California, enriched the retail chapter. Professor Stephen A. Greyser, Harvard Business School, was helpful on consumer matters. The chapter on the advertiser's marketing and advertising operation had the benefit of help from Alfred L. Plant, vice-president, director of marketing services, Block Drug Company. The concept of teaching advertising research by presenting it in the form of applied research was born of discussions with Professor David J. Luck of Southern Illinois University, to whom I am also grateful for further suggestions. I was gratified for two reasons to have the assistance of Klaus F. Schmidt in restructuring the print production chapter: first, because of his acknowledged great expertise in the field (he is vice-president, director of creative and account support, Young & Rubicam, Inc.); second, because he still has his original copy of the fourth edition of *Advertising Procedure* (1950) from which he studied at Wayne University. Stanford B. Silverman, vice-president and managing director, Vitt Media International, brought to the media section of the book his wide-ranging experience in the planning and buying of media time and space. Once again, Frank Vos, chairman, Vos & White, brought to the direct response chapter freshness and expert knowledge.

I thank Dr. Frederick Breitenfeld Jr., Franklin Feldman, David Hymes, Professor Daniel Kleppner, Richard Manville, Milton Seasonwein, and Jules B. Singer, on whom I called recurrently to discuss specific problems in the fields of their special competence.

Insightful critiques of the manuscript were made by Professor Conrad R. Hill of the University of Rhode Island, Professor William J. Kehoe of Northwestern University, Professor Eugene A. Sekeres of Youngstown State University, and Professor Stanley M. Ulanoff of City College of New York.

For firsthand, fresh data, I went to many sources: advertisers, agencies, trade associations, media, research firms, and suppliers, to all of whom I accord credit in the text in connection with their respective contributions.

The book was fortunate in having Maurine Lewis, Prentice-Hall, Inc., as its talented and discerning editor.

For her experienced guidance through the years that I have worked with her at Prentice-Hall, in matters relating to the book, I wish to thank Judith L. Rothman.

I appreciated the dependable help in many areas of Professor Norman A. P. Govoni, professor and chairman, Marketing Division, Babson College, who collaborated on this edition.

My greatest debt of all is to those teachers who over the years have passed on reports of their classroom experiences and have made suggestions that have helped shape this book.

Wardsboro, Vermont   OTTO KLEPPNER

The place of advertising

1

Background of Today's Advertising

What does the word *advertising* bring to mind? TV and radio commercials? Newspaper ads? Magazine ads? Outdoor signs? Supermarket displays and packages? Certainly all of these are advertising. You may, however, think of all the money spent on advertising, and you wonder how it affects the already high cost of living, or whether it could better be spent on schools or in helping the poor and unemployed or for more research on disease. Or *advertising* may bring to mind a Hollywood picture of a Madison Avenue agency, where an advertising man or woman saves a million-dollar account by breathlessly phoning the client with a new slogan, just dreamed up. (It doesn't work that way.) You may recall advertisements that you liked or disliked. In any case, one cannot help being aware of the influence of advertising in our lives.

The fact is that over $40 billion a year is spent on American advertising,* which in its various forms accosts us from early morning news programs until the late shows at night. How did advertising become so pervasive in our society? We cannot find the reasons for its importance merely by studying the ads; we must, rather, understand economic and social forces producing them.

Beginnings

The urge to advertise seems to be a part of human nature, evidenced since ancient times. Of the 5,000-year recorded history of advertising right up to our present TV-satellite age, the part that is most significant begins when the United States emerged as a great manufacturing nation, about 100 years ago. The early history of advertising, however, is far too fascinating to pass by without a glimpse of it.

*By 1985 more than $76 billion will be spent. Estimate by the Television Bureau of Advertising.

It isn't surprising that the people who gave the world the Tower of Babel also left the earliest known evidence of advertising. A Babylonian clay tablet of about 3000 B.C. was found bearing inscriptions for an ointment dealer, a scribe, and a shoemaker. Papyrus exhumed from the ruins of Thebes showed that the ancient Egyptians had a better medium on which to write their messages. (Alas, the announcements preserved in papyrus offer rewards for the return of runaway slaves.) The Greeks were among those who relied on town criers to chant the arrival of ships with cargoes of wines, spices, and metals. Often a crier was accompanied by a musician who kept him in the right key. Town criers later became the earliest medium for public announcements in many European countries, as in England, and they continued to be used for many centuries. (At this point we must digress to tell about a promotion idea used by innkeepers in France around A.D., 1100 to tell about their fine wines. They would have the town crier blow a horn, gather a group—and offer samples!)

One of the oldest signs known. It identified a butcher shop in Pompeii.

Roman merchants, too, had a sense of advertising. The ruins of Pompeii contain signs in stone or terra cotta, advertising what the shops were selling—a row of hams for a butcher shop, a cow for a dairy, a boot for a shoemaker. The Pompeiians also knew the art of telling their story to the public by means of painted wall signs like this one. Tourism was one of advertising's earliest subjects.

> **Traveler**
> **Going from here to the twelfth tower**
> **There Sarinus keeps a tavern**
> **This is to request you to enter.**
> **Farewell**

Outdoor advertising has proved to be one of the most enduring, as well as one of the oldest, forms of advertising. It survived the decline of the Roman Empire to become the decorative art of the inns in the seventeenth and eighteenth centuries. That was still an age of widespread illiteracy, and inns, particularly, vied with each other in creating attractive signs that all could recognize. This accounts for the charming names of old inns, especially in England—such as the Three Squirrels, the Man in the Moon, the Hole in the Wall. In 1614, England passed a law, probably the earliest on advertising, that prohibited signs extending more than 8 feet out from a building. (Longer signs pulled down too many house fronts.) Another law required signs to be high enough to give clearance to an armored man on horseback. In 1740, the first printed outdoor poster (referred to as a "hoarding") appeared in London.

Hog in Armour

Three Squirrels

King's Porter and Dwarf

Harrow and Doublet

The Ape

Barley Mow

Hole in the Wall
"A Guide for Malt Worms"

Bull and Mouth

Man in the Moon

Goose and Gridiron

Signs outside seventeenth century inns.

The Origin of the Newspaper

The next most enduring medium, the newspaper, was the offspring of Gutenberg's invention of printing from movable type (about 1438), which, of course, changed communication methods for the whole world. About 40 years after the invention, Caxton of London printed the first advertisement in English—a handbill of the rules for the guidance of the clergy at Easter. This was tacked up on church doors. (It became the first printed outdoor advertisement in English.) But the printed newspaper took a long time in coming. It really emerged from the newsletters, handwritten by professional writers, for nobles and others who wanted to be kept up to date on the news, especially of the court and other important events—very much in the spirit of the Washington newsletters of today.

The first advertisement in any language to be printed in a disseminated sheet appeared in a German news pamphlet about 1525. And what do you think this ad was for? A book extolling the virtues of a mysterious drug. (There was no Food and Drug Administration in those days.) But news pamphlets did not come out regularly; one published in 1591 contained news of the previous three years. It was from such beginnings, however, that the printed newspaper emerged. The first printed English newspaper came out in 1622—the *Weekly Newes of London*. The first advertisment in an English newspaper appeared in 1625.

The forerunner of our present want ads bore the strange name of *siquis* (pronounced SEE-*kwees*). These were the tack-up advertisements that appeared in England at the end of the fifteenth century. Of these, Presbrey says:

Siquis, tack-up advertisements

> These hand-written announcements for public posting were done by scribes who made a business of the work. The word "advertisement" in the sense in which we now use it was then unknown. The advertising bills produced by the scribes were called "Siquis," or "If anybody," because they usually began with the words "If anybody desires" or "If anybody knows of," a phrase that had come from ancient Rome, where public notices of articles lost always began with the words "Si quis."

> First use of manuscript siquis was by young ecclesiastics advertising for a vicarage.... Soon the siquis poster was employed by those desiring servants and by servants seeking places. Lost articles likewise were posted. Presently also tobacco, perfume, coffee, and some other luxuries were thus advertised. The great percentage of siquis, however, continued to be of the personal, or want-ad, type.°

Advertising in the English newspapers continued to feature similar personal and local announcements. The British have, in fact, shown so much interest in classified advertisments that the *London Times*, until a few years ago, filled their first page with classified advertising.

° Frank Presbrey, *History and Development of Advertising* (New York: Doubleday and Company, Inc., 1929).

**Advertising comes
to America**

The Pilgrims arrived on American shores before the *Weekly Newes of London* was first published, so they had little chance to learn about newspapers; but later colonists acquainted them with the idea, and the first American newspaper to carry advertisements appeared in 1704—the *Boston Newsletter* (note the newsletter identification). It carried an advertisement offering a reward for the capture of a thief and the return of several sorts of men's apparel—more akin to the advertisement offering a reward for the return of slaves, written on Egyptian papyrus thousands of years before, than it was to the advertising printed in the United States today. By the time the United States was formed, the colonies had 30 newspapers. Their advertising, like that of the English newspapers of that time, consisted mostly of ads we describe today as classified and local.

Neither those ads, however, nor all the ads that appeared from ancient Egyptian days until the American industrial revolution explain the development of advertising in the United States. The history of advertising in the United States is unique because advertising took hold just as the country was entering its era of greatest growth; population was soaring, factories were springing up, railroads opened the West. Advertising grew with the country and helped establish its marketing system. The United States entered the nineteenth century as an agricultural country following European marketing traditions, and ended the century as a great industrial nation, creating its own patterns of distribution. A new age of advertising had begun.

We pick up the story around 1870, when this era of transition was crystallizing.

Three Momentous Decades—1870–1900

Among the major developments, transportation, population growth, invention, and manufacturing ranked high.

Transportation

Here was a country 3,000 miles wide. It had sweeping stretches of rich farmland. It had minerals and forests. It had factories within reach of the coal mines. It had a growing population. But its long-distance transportation was chiefly by rivers and canals.

Railroads today are fighting for survival, but 100 years ago they changed a sprawling continent into a land of spectacular economic growth. In 1865, there were 35,000 miles of railroad trackage in the United States. By 1900, this trackage was 190,000 miles. Three railroad lines crossed the Mississippi and ran from the Atlantic to the Pacific. Feeder lines and networks spread across the face of the land. Where railroads went, people went, establishing farms, settlements, and cities across the continent, not limited to the waterways. The goods of the North and the East could be exchanged for the farm and extractive products of the South and the West. Never before had a country revealed such extensive and varied resources. Never since has so vast a market without a trade or language barrier been opened. This was an exciting prospect to manufacturers.

In 1870, the population of the United States was 38 million. By 1900, it had **The people** doubled. In no other period of American history has the population grown so fast. This growth, which included those now freed from slavery, meant an expanding labor force in the fields, factories, and mines; it meant a new consumer market. About 30 percent of the increase was from immigrants. But all the settlers before them had been immigrants or descendants of immigrants who had the courage to pull up stakes and venture to the "New World," a land far away and strange to them, in search of a new and better life. The result was a society that was mobile, both in readiness to move their homes and in aspirations to move upward in their life-styles.

The end of the nineteenth century was marked by many notable inventions **Inventions** and advances in the manufacture of goods. Among these were the development **and production** of the electric motor and of AC power transmission, which relieved factories of

CITY HALL, LAWRENCE, MASS.

Monday Evening, May 28

THE MIRACLE

TELEPHONE

WONDERFUL   DISCOVERY

TELEPHONE

OF THE AGE

Prof. A. Graham Bell, assisted by Mr. Frederic A. Gower, will give an exhibition of his wonderful and miraculous discovery **The Telephone**, before the people of Lawrence as above, when Boston and Lawrence will be connected via the Western Union Telegraph and vocal and instrumental music and conversation will be transmitted a distance of 27 miles and received by the audience in the City Hall.

Prof. Bell will give an explanatory lecture with this marvellous exhibition.

Cards of Admission, 35 cents
Reserved Seats, 50 cents
Sale of seats at Stratton's will open at 9 o'clock.

The first telephone ad (1877).

the need to locate next to waterpower sources, thus opening the hinterland to development and growth. The internal-combustion engine was perfected in this period; the automobile age was soon to follow.

It was the age of fast communications; the telephone, telegraph, typewriter, the Mergenthaler linotype, and high-speed presses—all increased the ability of people to communicate with each other.

In 1860, there were 7,600 patent applications filed in Washington. By 1870, this number had more than doubled, to 19,000; by 1900, it had more than doubled again, to 42,000.

Steel production has traditionally served as an index of industrial activity. Twenty *thousand* tons of steel were produced in 1867, but 10 *million* tons were produced in 1900. There is also a direct correlation between the power consumption of a country and its standard of living. By 1870, only 3 million horsepower were available; by 1900, this capacity had risen to 10 million. More current being used means more goods being manufactured; it also means that more people are using it for their own household needs—all of which is a good economic index.

The phonograph and the motion picture camera, invented at the turn of the century, added to the life-style of people at that time.

The Columbian exhibition in Chicago, in 1893, was attended by millions of Americans who returned home breathlessly to tell their friends about the new products they had seen.

Media

Newspapers.   Since colonial times, newspapers had been popular in the United States. In the 1830s, the penny newspaper came out. In 1846, Hoe patented the first rotary printing press, and in 1871 he invented the Hoe web press, which prints both sides of a continuous roll of paper and delivers folded sheets. By the end of the nineteenth century, about 10,000 papers were being published, with an estimated combined circulation of 10 million. Ninety percent of them were weeklies, most of the rest dailies, published in the county seat with farm and local news. By 1900, twenty of the largest cities had their own papers, some with as many as 16 pages. Newspapers were the largest class of media at this period.

To save buying paper, many editors (who were also the publishers) bought sheets already printed on one side with world news, items of general interest to farmers, and ads. They would then print the other side with local news and any ads they could obtain (forerunner of today's color insert). Or else they would insert such pages in their own four-page papers, offering an eight-page paper to their readers.

Religious publications.   Today, religious publications represent a very small part of the total media picture; but for a few decades after the Civil War, religious publications were the most influential medium. They were the forerunners of magazines. The post-Civil War period was a time of great religious revival, marking also the beginning of the temperance movement. Church groups issued their own publications, many with circulations of no more than 1,000; the biggest ran to 400,000. But the combined circulation of the 400 religious publications was estimated at about 5 million.

Religious publications had great influence among their readers, a fact that patent-medicine advertisers recognized to such an extent that 75 percent of all the religious publication advertising was for patent medicines. (Many of the temperance papers carried the advertising of preparations that proved to be 40 percent alcohol. Today we call that 80-proof whiskey.)

Magazines.   Most of what were called magazines before the 1870s—including Ben Franklin's effort in 1741—lasted less than six months, and for a good reason. They consisted mostly of extracts of books and pamphlets, essays, verse, and communications of dubious value. Magazines as we know them today were really born in the last three decades of the nineteenth century, at a time when many factors were in their favor. The rate of illiteracy in the country had been cut almost in half, from 20 percent in 1870 to little over 10 percent in 1900. In 1875, railroads began carrying mail, including magazines, across the country. In 1879, Congress established the low second-class postal rate for publications, a subject of controversy to this day, but a great boon to magazines even then. The Hoe high-speed rotary press began replacing the much slower flatbed press, speeding the printing of magazines. The halftone method of reproducing photographs as well as color artwork was invented in 1876, making the magazines more enticing to the public. (*Godey's Lady's Book*, a popular fashion book of the age, had previously employed 150 women to hand-tint all its illustrations.)

Costly literary magazines now appeared—*Harper's Monthly, Atlantic Monthly, Century*—but the publishers did not view advertising kindly at first. Even when, at the turn of the century, Fletcher Harper condescended to "desecrate literature with the announcements of tradespeople," he placed all the advertising in the back of the book.

Inspired by the success of popular magazines in England, a new breed of publishers came forth in the 1890s to produce magazines of entertainment, fiction, and advice—forerunners of today's women's and general magazines. Magazines brought the works of Kipling, H. G. Wells, Mark Twain, and Conan Doyle to families across the face of the land. By 1902, *Munsey's* had a circulation of 600,000; *Cosmopolitan*, 700,000; *Delineator*, 960,000; while the *Ladies' Home Journal* hit the million mark—great feats for the age. The ten-cent magazine had arrived.

The number of pages of advertising that magazines carried would make some of today's advertising directors of magazines blink. *Harper's* published 75 pages of advertising per issue; *Cosmopolitan*, 103 pages; *McClure's*, 120 pages. Between 1880 and 1890, magazine advertising more than doubled. Magazines made possible the nationwide sale of products; they brought into being nationwide advertising.

Leaders in National Advertising in 1890's

A. P. W. Paper
Adams Tutti Frutti Gum
Æolian Company
American Express Traveler's Cheques
Armour Beef Extract
Autoharp
Baker's Cocoa
Battle Ax Plug Tobacco
Beardsley's Shredded Codfish
Beeman's Pepsin Gum
Bent's Crown Piano
Burlington Railroad
Burnett's Extracts
California Fig Syrup
Caligraph Typewriter
Castoria
A. B. Chase Piano
Chicago Great Western
Chicago, Milwaukee & St. Paul Railroad
Chicago Great Western Railway
Chocolat-Menier
Chickering Piano
Columbia Bicycles
Cleveland Baking Powder
Cottolene Shortening
Cook's Tours
Crown Pianos
Crescent Bicycles
Devoe & Raynolds Artist's Materials
Cuticura Soap
Derby Desks
De Long Hook and Eye
Diamond Dyes
Dixon's Graphite Paint
Dixon's Pencils
W. L. Douglas Shoes
Edison Mimeograph
Earl & Wilson Collars
Elgin Watches
Edison Phonograph
Everett Piano
Epps's Cocoa
Estey Organ
Fall River Line
Felt & Tarrant Comptometer
Ferry's Seeds
Fisher Piano
Fowler Bicycles
Franco American Soup
Garland Stoves
Gold Dust

Gold Dust Washing Powder
Gorham's Silver
Gramophone
Great Northern Railroad
H–O Breakfast Food
Hamburg American Line
Hammond Typewriter
Hartford Bicycle
Hartshorn's Shade Rollers
Heinz's Baked Beans
Peter Henderson & Co.
Hires' Root Beer
Hoffman House Cigars
Huyler's Chocolates
Hunyadi Janos
Ingersoll Watches
Ives & Pond Piano
Ivory Soap
Jaeger Underwear
Kirk's American Family Soap
Kodak
Liebeg's Extract of Beef
Lipton's Teas
Lowney's Chocolates
Lundborg's Perfumes
James McCutcheon Linens
Dr. Lyon's Toothpowder
Mason & Hamlin Piano
Mellin's Food
Mennen's Talcum Powder
Michigan Central Railroad
Monarch Bicycles
J. L. Mott Indoor Plumbing
Munsing Underwear
Murphy Varnish Company
New England Mincemeat
New York Central Railroad
North German Lloyd
Old Dominion Line
Oneita Knitted Goods
Packer's Tar Soap
Pearline Soap Powder
Peartltop Lamp Chimneys
Pears' Soap
Alfred Peats Wall Paper
Pettijohn's Breakfast Food
Pittsburgh Stogies
Pond's Extract
Postum Cereal
Prudential Insurance Co.
Quaker Oats

Reproduced from Frank Presbey, *History and Development of Advertising* (Garden City, N.Y.: Doubleday © 1929), p. 361.

Patent-medicine advertisers had been around for a long time, and by the 1870s they were the largest category of advertisers. After the Civil War, millions of men returned to their homes, North and South, many of them weak from exposure. Many needed medical aid, and the only kind available to most of them was a bottle of patent medicine. As a result, patent-medicine advertising dominated the media toward the end of the nineteenth century, its fraudulent claims giving all advertising a bad name.

Patent-medicine advertising

Meanwhile, legitimate manufacturers saw a new world of opportunity opening before them in the growth of the country. They saw the market for consumer products spreading. Railroads could now carry their merchandise to all cities between the Atlantic and Pacific coasts. The idea of packaging their own products carrying their own trademarks was enticing, particularly to grocery manufacturers; for now they could build their business upon their reputation with the consumer, and not be subject to the caprices and pressures of jobbers who, in the past, had been their sole distributors. Now magazines provided the missing link in marketing—that of easily spreading word about their products all over the country, with advertising. Quaker Oats cereal was among the first to go this marketing route, followed soon by many others.

National advertising emerges

This was the development of national advertising, as we call it today, in its broadest sense, meaning the advertising by a producer of his trademarked product, whether or not it has attained national distribution.

The words "chauffeur," "limousine," "sedan," remind us that the earliest motorcars were made in France. In the United States, as in France, they were virtually handmade at first. But in 1913, Henry Ford decided that the way to build cars at low cost was to make them of standardized parts and bring the work to the man on the assembly-line belt. He introduced to the world a mass-production technique and brought the price of a Ford down to $265 by 1925. But mass production is predicated, in a free society, upon mass selling—another name for advertising. Mass production makes possible countless products at a cost the mass of people can pay, and about which they learn through advertising. America was quick to use both.

Mass production appears

We have been speaking of the various media and their advertising. Now a word about how the media got much of that advertising—through the advertising agency, which started out as men selling advertising space on a percentage basis, for out-of-town newspapers. Later they also planned, prepared and placed the ads, and rendered further services. The story of the advertising agency is deeply rooted in the growth of American industry and advertising. Later in the book, we devote a whole chapter to the American agency, from its beginnings to its latest patterns of operation. Until then, we need keep in mind only that the advertising agency has always been an active force in developing the use of advertising.

The advertising agency

As America Enters the Twentieth Century

The moral atmosphere of business as it developed after the Civil War reflected laissez-faire policy at its extreme. High government officials were corrupted by the railroads, the public was swindled by flagrant stock-market manipulations, embalmed beef was shipped to soldiers in the Spanish-American War. Advertising contributed to the immorality of business, with its patent-medicine ads offering to cure all the real and imagined ailments of man. There was a "pleasing medicine to cure cancer," another to cure cholera. No promise of a quick cure was too wild, no falsehood too monstrous.

One of the more restrained ads in the patent-medicine category. Electricity, the new, magic power of the 1890s, was offered in a curative belt.

The Pure Food and Drug Act (1906). As early as 1865, the *New York Herald-Tribune* had a touch of conscience and eliminated "certain classes" of medical advertising—those that used "repellent" words. In 1892, the *Ladies' Home Journal* was the first magazine to ban *all* medical advertising. The *Ladies' Home Journal* also came out with a blast by Mark Sullivan, revealing that codeine was being used in cold preparations, and a teething syrup had morphine as its base. Public outrage reached Congress, which in 1906 passed the Pure Food and Drug Act, the first federal law to protect the health of the public and the first to control advertising.

The Federal Trade Commission Act (1913). In addition to passing laws protecting the public from unscrupulous business, Congress passed the Federal Trade Commission Act, protecting one businessman from the unscrupulous behavior of another. The law said, in effect, "Unfair methods of doing business are hereby declared illegal." John D. Rockefeller, founder of the Standard Oil Company, got together with some other oilmen in the early days of his operation and worked out a deal with the railroads over which they shipped their oil. They arranged not only to get a secret rebate on the oil they shipped, but also to get a rebate on all the oil their *competitors* shipped. Result: they were able to undersell their competition and drive them out of business. What was considered smart business in those days would be a violation of the antitrust laws today.

In time, the FTC (Federal Trade Commission) extended its province to protecting the public against misleading and deceptive advertising—a matter of which all who are responsible for advertising today are very much aware.

Of this period of exposure and reform, James Truslow Adams, the historian, said, "America for the first time was taking stock of the morality of everyday life."

Around 1905, there emerged a class of advertising men who recognized that their future lay in advertising legitimate products and in earning the confidence of the public in advertising. They gathered with like-minded men in their community to form advertising clubs.

Advertising comes of age

These clubs subsequently formed the Associated Advertising Clubs of the World (now the American Advertising Federation). In 1911, they launched a campaign to promote "Truth in Advertising." In 1916, they formed vigilance committees. These developed into today's Council of Better Business Bureaus, which continues to deal with many problems of unfair and deceptive business practices. In 1971, the bureaus became a part of the National Advertising Review Council, an all-industry effort at curbing misleading advertising. The main constituency of the American Advertising Federation continues to be that of the local advertising clubs. On its board are also officers of the other advertising associations.

In 1910, the Association of National Advertising Managers was born. It is now known as the Association of National Advertisers (ANA) and has about 500 members, including the foremost advertisers. Its purpose is to improve the effectiveness of advertising from the viewpoint of the advertiser. In 1917, the American Association of Advertising Agencies was formed to improve the effectiveness of advertising and of the advertising-agency operation. Over 75 percent of all national advertising today is placed by its members, both large and small.

In 1911, *Printers' Ink*, the leading advertising trade paper for many years, prepared a model statute for state regulation of advertising, designed to "punish untrue, deceptive or misleading advertising." The Printers' Ink Model Statute has been adopted in its original or modified form in 44 states, where it is still operative.

Up to 1914, many publishers were carefree in their claims to circulation. An advertiser had no way of verifying what he got for his money. But in that year, a group of advertisers, agencies, and publishers established an independent auditing organization, the Audit Bureau of Circulations, which conducts its own audits and issues its own reports of circulation. Most major publications belong to the ABC, and an ABC circulation statement is highly regarded in media circles. The ABC reports of circulation are fully accredited in most areas. (Today, similar auditing organizations are operating in 25 countries throughout the world.)

In June 1916, President Woodrow Wilson addressed the Associated Advertising Clubs of the World convention in Philadelphia—the first president to give public recognition to the importance of advertising. Advertising had come of age!

Advertising in World War I

When the United States entered World War I in 1917, a number of advertising agency and media men offered their services to the government but were turned down, for "Government officials, particularly Army chiefs, believed in orders and edicts, not persuasion."° But when these groups offered their services to the Council of National Defense, they were welcomed and became the Division of Advertising of the Committee of Public Information—the propaganda arm of the government.

Their first job, to help get all eligible men to register, resulted in getting 13 million men registered in one day without serious incident. The committee also succeeded in having advertisers use their own paid space to advertise Liberty Bonds and the Red Cross, and to carry messages of the Fuel Administration (to use less fuel), and the Food Administration (to observe its meatless and wheatless days).

The 1920s

The 1920s began with a minidepression and ended with a crash. When the war ended, makers of army trucks were able to convert quickly to commercial trucks. Firestone spent $2 million advertising "Ship by Truck." With the industry profiting by the good roads that had been built, truck production jumped from 92,000 in 1916 to 322,000 in 1920. Trucking spurred the growth of chain stores, which led, in turn, to supermarkets and self-service, because of door-to-door delivery from manufacturer to retailer.

° James Playsted Wood, *The History of Advertising* (New York: The Ronald Press Company, 1958).

From Irving Settel, *A Pictorial History of Radio* (New York: Grosset & Dunlap, 1960). © Irving Settel, 1960.

The earliest radio sets. The Aeriola Junior had heavy use in the early 1920s. Rural listeners, particularly. turned to their sets for farm information, weather reports, and even church services.

The passenger-car business boomed, too, and new products appeared in profusion—electric refrigerators, washing machines, electric shavers, and, most incredible of all, the radio. Installment selling made hard goods available to all. And all the products needed advertising.

Radio arrives

Station KDKA of Pittsburgh was on the air broadcasting the Harding-Cox election returns in November 1920, some months before its license to operate had cleared. Many other stations soon began broadcasting. There were experimental networks over telephone lines as early as 1922. The first presidential address to be broadcast (by six stations) was the message to Congress by President Coolidge in 1923. The National Broadcasting Company started its network broadcasting in 1926 with six stations and had its first coast-to-coast football broadcast in 1927. That was the year, too, that the Columbia Broadcasting System was founded, and the Federal Radio Commission (now the Federal Communications Commission) was created.

Making radio sets proved to be a boon to industry. According to Settel,

> Radio created one of the most extraordinary new product demands in the history of the United States. From all over the country, orders for radio receiving sets poured into the offices of manufacturers. Said *Radio Broadcast Magazine* in its first issue, May 1922:
>
> "The rate of increase in the number of people who spend at least a part of their evening listening in is almost incomprehensible. . . . It seems quite likely that before the market for receiving apparatus becomes approximately saturated, there will be at least five million receiving sets in this country.° [Author's note: In 1978 there were 440 million radio sets in use.]

Everything boomed in the mid-twenties—business boomed, advertising boomed. The issue of *The Saturday Evening Post* of December 7, 1929, is historic. It was the last issue whose forms closed before the stock-market crash in the fall of 1929. The magazine was 268 pages thick. It carried 154 pages of advertising. The price: 5¢ a copy. Never again would *The Saturday Evening Post* attain that record. Never again has any magazine approached it. It was the end of an era.

The 1930s Depression

The stock market crash in late '29 had a shattering effect on our entire economy. Millions of men were thrown out of work. Business failures were widespread. Banks were closing all over the country; there were no insured deposits in savings banks in those days. There was no social security, no food stamps, no unemployment insurance. Who had ever heard of pensions for blue-collar workers? There were bread lines—long ones, and well-dressed men were selling apples off the tops of boxes on street corners, for five cents. The Southwest was having its worst windstorms, carrying off the topsoil, killing livestock and crops. Farmers abandoned their farms, packed their families and furniture in old

° Irving Settel, *A Pictorial History of Radio* (New York: Citadel Press, Inc., 1960), p. 41.

SPECIAL

	PRICES TODAY	PRICES A YEAR AGO	CHANGE IN PRICE
POTATOES MAINES 100 lb. bag — PRINCE EDWARD ISLES 90 lb. bag	$2.35	3.17	—82¢
PEACHES CALIFORNIA	2 lgst. cans 25¢	2 for 46¢	—21¢
UNEEDA BAKERS MACAROON SANDWICH	3 pkgs. 25¢	NEW PRODUCT	....
STRING BEANS STANDARD QUALITY	3 No. 2 cans 28¢	3 for 30¢	— 2¢
TOMATOES STANDARD QUALITY	3 No. 2 cans 20¢	3 for 30¢	—10¢
AUNT JEMIMA **PANCAKE FLOUR**	2 pkgs. 25¢	2 for 30¢	— 5¢
AUNT JEMIMA **BUCKWHEAT FLOUR** ...	2 pkgs. 25¢	2 for 34¢	— 9¢
DEL MONTE **FRUIT SALAD**	lgst. can 29¢	41¢	—12¢
MILK WHITEHOUSE BRAND	3 tall cans 22¢	3 for 23¢	— 1¢
CATSUP BLUE LABEL	sm. bot. 13¢	15¢	— 2¢
CATSUP BLUE LABEL	lge. bot. 19¢	23¢	— 4¢
ORANGE JUICE 2 ...	15¢	2 for 20¢	— 5¢

	PRICES TODAY	A YEAR AGO	CHANGE IN PRICE
Red Circle Coffee............lb.	29c	39c	—10c
Eight O'Clock Coffee............lb.	25c	35c	—10c
Bokar Coffee............lb. tin..	35c	45c	—10c
Grandmother's Bread.........20 ounce loaf...	7c	8c	— 1c
Jack Frost Sugar.........5 lb. cotton sack...	25c	29c	— 4c
Pure Lard............lb.	15c	17c	— 2c
Nucoa............lb.	23c	25c	— 2c
Salt............4 lb. sack	8c	10c	— 2c
Pea Beans............lb. package	10c	17c	— 7c
Lima Beans............lb. package	17c	23c	— 6c
Sunnyfield Flour.........24½ lb. sack...	75c	89c	—14c
Sunsweet Prunes.........2 lb. package	15c	29c	—14c
Puffed Wheat............package	12c	13c	— 1c
Puffed Rice............package	14c	15c	— 1c

FRESH MEATS & FOWL AT A&P MARKETS

	PRICES TODAY	A YEAR AGO	CHANGE IN PRICE
PORK LOINS HALF OR WHOLE ......lb.	25¢	31c	— 6c
Prime Ribs of Beef (CUT FROM FIRST 8 RIBS) ....lb.	35c	41c	— 6c
Sirloin Steak ....lb.	49c	55c	— 6c
Loin Lamb Chops............lb...	35c	51c	—16c
Roasting Chickens (3½ to 4 lbs.) .....lb.	39c	42c	— 3c

Chain store ad, 1932

pickup trucks, and headed west. (Steinbeck wrote his *Grapes of Wrath* around this experience.) The government finally launched the Works Progress Administration (WPA) for putting men to work on public service projects, but the bread lines continued long.

Out of that catastrophe there emerged three developments that affect advertising today.

The first was the emergence of radio as a major advertising medium. In March 1933, President Franklin D. Roosevelt made the first inaugural address ever to be broadcast by radio, giving heart and hope to a frightened people. His line, "We have nothing to fear except fear itself," spoken to the largest audience that had ever at one time heard the voice of one man, became historic. In one broadcast, radio showed its power of moving a nation. Radio had arrived as a major national advertising medium. It quickly became part of the life of America. The 1930s began with 612 stations and 12 million sets; they ended with 814 stations and 51 million sets.

Second was the passage of the Robinson-Patman Act (1936) to help protect the little merchant from the unfair competition of the big store with its huge buying power. This law is operative today.

Third was the passage of the Wheeler-Lea Act (1938), giving the Federal Trade Commission more direct and sweeping powers over advertising, and the *Federal Food, Drug and Cosmetic Act* (1938), giving the administration authority over the labeling and packaging of these products. These laws, which we discuss in Chapter 26, "Legal and Other Restraints on Advertising," are a pervasive consideration in advertising today and a forerunner of the government's increasing interest in advertising.

Advertising during World War II (1941–1945)

With World War II, industry turned to production of war goods. Since all civilian material was severely rationed, many firms curtailed their advertising. Others felt that though they were out of merchandise, they were not out of business, and they wanted to keep the public good will. They applied their advertising efforts to rendering public service. The Goodyear Tire & Rubber Company's advice on how to take care of your tires in these days of product shortages, was akin to ads that were to appear in 1974–1975.

The War Advertising Council.   When the government turned to the advertising industry for help in enlisting civilian aid in the war effort, the industry organized the War Advertising Council. It was composed of media, which contributed the space; agencies, which contributed the creative talent; and advertisers, who contributed management. Among the council's succession of massive public service campaigns were those for putting workers on guard against careless talk ("The enemy is listening"), for salvaging scrap metals, purchasing war bonds, writing V-mail letters, war-time recruitment (especially of women), preventing forest fires, and planting victory gardens. More than a billion dollars' worth of space, time, and talent went into this effort. So successful was the project that it was continued after the war, to deal with public service problems. It was renamed The Advertising Council and is very active to this day.

After World War II (1945) industry went into high gear supplying the pent-up demand for cars, homes, appliances, and all the other postponed purchases. Many new and improved products appeared, made possible by the new materials and processes originally developed for war use, leading directly to the historic growth period 1950–1975.

"A surge of abundance was everywhere," wrote Manchester, in speaking of this period. "Technological change had never held a greater fascination for Americans. . . . The sheer number of innovations was bewildering. . . . One by one they appeared, were assimilated into the general experience. Millions of men and women of the swing generation realized that in countless little ways life had become more tolerable, more convenient, more interesting— in a word, more livable."° Also in discussing this era, Crichton reported:

Advertising from 1950 to 1975—the word was "growth"

> In 1950 many markets were either infantile or virtually nonexistent. Travel and leisure, second homes, food franchises, second, third, and fourth cars, many frozen and instant foods, many of the synthetic fabrics and combinations of them, many of the devices like color television, snowmobiles, the Sunfish and the Hobie Cat, mobile homes, and campers were all in the future. In 1950 the United States, untouched by the ravages of the Second World War, was embarked on a period of growth unparalleled in our history. It was a period of great buoyancy and confidence."†

The figures also said "growth."   Between 1950 and 1973‡ the population of the United States increased by 38 percent, while disposable personal income increased by 327 percent. New housing starts went up by 47 percent, energy consumption by 121 percent, college enrollments by 136 percent, automobile registrations by 151 percent, telephones in use by 221 percent, number of outboard motors sold by 242 percent, retail sales by 250 percent, families owning two or more cars by 300 percent, frozen food production by 655 percent, number of airline passengers by 963 percent, homes with dishwashers by 1,043 percent, while homes with room air conditioners rose by 3,662 percent.

Advertising not only contributed to the growth but was part of it, rising from an expenditure of $5,780 million in 1950 to $28,320 million in 1975—a growth of 490 percent. There were many developments in advertising during this time.

▲ In 1956 the Department of Justice struck down the no-rebating 15 percent commission system, which had provided the base of the agency compensation system, and made fees negotiable, encouraging the growth of media-buying services, a la carte agencies, and in-house agencies.

▲ The voice of the consumer became more powerful.

▲ Congress passed an act limiting outdoor advertising alongside interstate highways. Cigarette advertising was banned from television.

° Richard Manchester, *The Glory and the Dream* (Boston: Little Brown & Co., 1973), p. 946.

†John Crichton, "We're in the Last Quarter" (paper from the 1975 Western Region Convention of the American Association of Advertising Agencies), p. 3.

‡We select 1973 as the last full year before the oil embargo of 1974.

COAL AND CONSERVATION!

...there is now no real alternative.

JOHN DEERE CAN HELP YOU FIGHT INFLATION RIGHT IN YOUR OWN BACKYARD.

How to conserve gasoline

What appliance makers are doing to reduce your power consumption

We have enough electricity to last 200 years. But it's buried in the ground.

To Members of the Congress

You are the key to critically nee gas for jobs and a better econor

20 ways to save money on your phone bill.

Inflation Presents The Pancake

A $2.25 anti-inflation offer

The Electric Economy. We've reached a crossroads in our trip.

How to eat well while pinching pennies.

The frill is gone.

Into the last quarter of the century.

20

▲ The Federal Trade Commission introduced corrective advertising by those who had made false or misleading claims. Comparison advertising, mentioning competitors by name, was deemed an acceptable form of advertising.

▲ The magazine publishing world saw the disappearance of the old dinosaurs of publishing: *The Saturday Evening Post, Colliers, Look,* and finally *Life.* There was no vacuum at the newsstands, however; that was immediately filled by the upsurge of magazines of special interests.

▲ Newspapers felt the effect of the shift of metropolitan population to the suburbs. Free-standing inserts became an important part of newspaper billings.

▲ Radio took a dive when television came along. How it came out of that is a good example of turning disadvantages into advantages.

▲ Direct-response advertising soared from $900 million in 1950 to $6 billion in 1975, reflecting the growth of direct marketing.

▲ The two biggest developments to emerge were television and electronic data processing. TV has changed America's life as well as the world of advertising. Data processing systems have brought before the eyes of management a wealth of organized information. This, together with the syndicated research services, has revolutionized the entire marketing process and the advertising media operation.

In 1973, advertising was operating in an environment of rising expectations. The next year, its environment was clouded by energy shortage. The only thing rising was inflation. We were shocked by the realization of our dependency on foreign oil, by the awareness of the limitations of our own natural resources. Fuel prices shot up. Inflation had become a way of life.

1975—and into the last quarter of the twentieth century

Many businesses adapted their products to the times. Auto makers came out with downsized family-size cars, to consume less fuel. Food marketers ran ads like "A nutritious hot meal with meat for 25¢." Airlines created bargain package trips. Gasoline companies began advertising ways to save fuel in driving. Great changes began taking place.

As for the future . . . that's what the rest of the book is all about.

QUESTIONS

1. When someone says "advertising," what first comes to mind? Discuss.

2. Since advertising was used in England and Europe before it was used in the United States, what caused advertising usage to leap so far ahead in this country?

3. About when did publication advertising first appear in America? In what kind of medium?

4. Advertising was part of the great growth period of 1870–1900. What were the other factors that helped America's economy to grow?

5. Advertising had tremendous growth between 1950 and 1975. What were some of the causes?

6. What major changes in advertising have you observed in your lifetime?

7. Identify the Federal Trade Commission, The War Advertising Council, The Printers' Ink Model Statute.

8. Identify three significant events in our nation's history in terms of their impact on advertising as we know it today. Why single out these particular events?

9. Would you regard advertising as a modern development? Why?

READING SUGGESTIONS

BARTELS, ROBERT, *The History of Marketing Thought.* Columbus, Ohio: Grid Publishing, 1976.

CALKINS, EARNEST ELMO, and RALPH HOLDEN, *Modern Advertising.* New York: Appleton-Century, 1905.

FLEMING, THOMAS, "How It Was in Advertising: 1776–1976," *Advertising Age* (April 19, 1976), 1 ff. This is the feature article of a special Bicentennial section of *Advertising Age,* which has several other articles dealing with advertising history.

HOTCHKISS, GEORGE BURTON, *Milestones of Marketing.* New York: Macmillan, 1938.

HOWER, RALPH M., *The History of an Advertising Agency,* rev. ed. Cambridge, Mass.: Harvard University Press, 1949.

JONES, EDGAR ROBERT, *Those Were the Good Old Days: A Happy Look at American Advertising, 1880–1930.* New York: Simon & Schuster, 1959.

KETCHUM, ALTON, *Principles and Practices of Marketing Communications,* New York: Interpublic Press/Simon & Schuster, 1967. I: "A Highlight History of Advertising."

MORISON, SAMUEL ELIOT, *The Oxford History of the American People.* New York: Oxford University Press, 1965.

PRESBREY, FRANK, *History and Development of Advertising.* Garden City, N.Y.: Doubleday, 1929.

ROWELL, GEORGE P., *Forty Years an Advertising Agent.* New York: Franklin Publishing, 1926.

SAMPSON, HENRY, *A History of Advertising from the Earliest Times.* London: Chatto & Windus, 1875.

SAWYER, HOWARD G. "What It Was Like, Surviving and Thriving in the Advertising Business During the Great Depression," *Industrial Marketing,* (June 1975), 66 ff.

TURNER, ERNEST SACKVILLE, *The Shocking History of Advertising.* New York: Dutton, 1953.

WOOD, JAMES PLAYSTED, *The History of Advertising.* New York: Ronald, 1958.

saying why you you need a lipstick or another cosmetic. Food advertising is mostly competitive between products and types of products. Cosmetics are a style item with new styles always appearing, calling for more advertising than is necessary for foods. Foods are staples bought regularly. Drugs, on the other hand, are often bought when need requires, as in the case of laxatives and cough preparations. That, too, calls for more advertising than does something bought regularly, as is food. This helps explain why it takes a greater percentage of advertising to sell drugs and cosmetics than food.

Of soaps and cleansers.   No one needs to be convinced of the need for food; but when it comes to soaps and cleansers, we are dealing with a cultivated lifestyle. Generations ago housewives had a choice of two cleansing agents (toilet soap and laundry soap) and two scouring powders (exemplified by Bon Ami and Old Dutch Cleanser). When Lux soap flakes first advertised "Lux your undies every night," that was an untried routine. Today we have detergents especially formulated for a wide range of specific purposes: for different types of fabrics, for flooring, windows, woodwork, for hair, for many other purposes. To educate people in the uses of these products and to tell about improvements constantly being made in these fields takes much advertising. The average cost of advertising soap and cleanser among the 100 leading advertisers is 11.67 percent of sales. The highest is 13.3 percent; the lowest is 3.8 percent.

Of cosmetics.   Cosmetics are a style business. Its continuous flow of new colors, new make-up preparations, new vogues in packaging, keep pace with the rest of the style world. Cosmetics add an extra touch of satisfaction to life by making a woman feel that she is appearing at her best. No great harm may result from not using green eye shadow, but advertising points out how it may improve a woman's entire personality.

Advertising is essential in this industry because people tend to forget (or doubt) what beauty aids can do for them. The men's toiletry industry was created by advertising that shows how much more acceptable men are when they use toiletries. Keeping people alert to the satisfactions of toiletries is the continuing role of advertising. It is one of the reasons why a greater percentage of sales costs goes into advertising toiletries than into advertising groceries. (In the *Advertising Age* listing of expenditures, drugs and cosmetics are combined. Although we treat them separately, we will give a combination average for the two industries.)

Of over-the-counter drugs.   There is an active market for these drugs, and pharmaceutical companies are constantly trying to improve them and to develop new, more effective products. Drug companies invest much money in research and development, knowing that if they can come out with a more effective preparation, a big market may await it. They also know that to reach such a market and thereby recoup their investment, a big advertising expenditure may be needed. Confidence in advertising is a strong inducement to take big money risks in research.

Each large company already has a large following, but it needs to remind its customers of the benefits they derive from its products, to hold them against competitive claims. That, too, calls for advertising. Many products, such as those for the relief of stomach distress or headache, are used only sporadically. It is therefore important to keep the advertising of such products before the public continuously to reach those people who, at any given time, may have need of them. For all these reasons, advertising is a very important part of the marketing mix for drug products.

Among America's leading 100 advertisers of cosmetics and drugs, the average percentage of advertising to sales is 9.5; the highest is 23.6 percent; the lowest 1.4 percent.°

Differences in advertising/sales ratios within the same industry.   Among the reasons for big variations in the percentage of advertising expenditures by different companies in the same industry, these are prominent:

1. Profit goals. Some marketers are concerned about their next profit statement; others take a long-term view.
2. Use of other elements in the marketing mix; e.g., putting more money into demonstration or sales personnel.
3. Management success in generating new and improved products and marketing methods.
4. Overall management.

There are other reasons why different industries spend different percentages of sales on advertising. But our supermarket survey reveals some of the forces that lead to different levels of advertising in different industries selling their products through the same channels. We now move on to the next big step, to see where and how advertising fits into the marketing process.

The Place of Advertising in the Marketing Process

Think of a product in terms of its journey through the distributing process, from the point at which it is made to the point at which it is bought by its user. Advertising moves that product along in this journey, changing its immediate objectives along the way. This results in different forms of advertising:

Advertising to the consumer
▲ National advertising
▲ Retail (local) advertising

° *Advertising Age*, August 29, 1977.

▲ End-product advertising

▲ Direct response advertising

Advertising to business and professions

▲ Trade advertising

▲ Industrial advertising

▲ Professional advertising

▲ Corporate management advertising

▲ The advertising of services

▲ Advertising to conserve resources

National advertising.   The term *national advertising* has a special non-geographic meaning in advertising. It refers to the advertising by the owner of a trade-marked product or service sold through different distributors or stores, wherever they may be. It does not necessarily mean that the product is sold nationwide.

The purpose of national advertising is to make known to the consumer the name of the product or service, its uses, benefits and advantages, so that a person will be disposed to buy or order it whenever and wherever it is convenient to do so. It is up to the national advertiser to create the demand for the product or service. Through national advertising we have come to know products like Dial soap, Zenith TV sets, Shake 'n' Bake food mix, Avis rental cars, Suzuki motorcycles. When most people talk of "advertising," they usually refer just to national advertising.

Retail (local) advertising.   Retail advertising is that of a dealer who sells directly to the consumer. Chief among such advertisers are department stores, supermarkets, chain stores, discount stores, specialty shops. No matter how big or small the store may be, its advertising will say, "This is something you should buy *here*—today."

National advertising will say, "If you want good sheets, get Fruit of the Loom." A retail advertisement will say, "Now here! Latest patterns and colors in Fruit of the Loom sheets. Come early." Retail advertising also includes that of the many products not nationally advertised, especially the store's own brands. But whatever the message, the thrust of retail advertising is, "Buy here, now!"

F. Mayans, vice-president of Federated Department Stores, said:

> In my view, our kind of advertising does very little to create a demand for either goods or services that do not fulfill an already existing physical or psychic desire. . . . Retail advertising . . . should tell what options the retailer can offer—pricelines, sizes, colors, fabrics. . . .

Chapter 24 deals with retail advertising.

Advertising to the consumer

Electrasol.
An easy way to clean dry-hards.

Dry-hards are tough-to-clean dried-on foods... like spaghetti and sauce, meat loaf and gravy, scalloped potatoes and chocolate pudding...that dry and cake and stick. And stick.

Electrasol cleans dry-hards from plates, silverware, glasses and other tableware.

Electrasol, with its special formula, helps your automatic dishwasher give you clean, clear, bright dishes.

EL ECONOMICS LABORATORY, INC., St. Paul, Minn. 55102

CLEANS EVEN DRIED-ON FOOD SOILS

Electra Sol

for
CLEAN, CLEAR
AUTOMATIC
DISHWASHING

Approved by all leading dishwasher manufacturers

National advertising. The marketer of Electrasol tells a widespread public about the product and its chief advantages, with a view to having readers buy the product when and wherever they shop.

FedMart*
the spot for smart party shoppers

◄ *Retail advertising—supermarket. A typical supermarket ad features nationally advertised brands, private brands, and unbranded products with a common appeal—price. Purpose: to attract customers to come to the store, where they will probably buy some of the advertised items and other unadvertised ones.*

Retail advertising—department store. A department store ad features nationally advertised carpets at an attractive price. Purpose: to attract shoppers to the rug department, to buy rugs and perhaps other items in the store. ►

End-product advertising.   The Talon zipper is advertised to women for its dependability (see p. 344). They are urged to look for it when they buy zippered garments. But Talon zippers are bought mainly by garment manufacturers. The real aim in this advertising is to get garment manufacturers to use Talon zippers, because that is where the big quantity sales are. Such advertising leapfrogs over the garment manufacturer to tell its story directly to the public, so that when a woman goes to buy a garment, she will ask if it has a Talon zipper and will make sure that the one she picks has it. The ad gives a boost to the dress manufacturer, too, by saying, "Talon is known as a quality zipper and is a clue that the rest of the dress is well made, too." A Talon salesperson calling upon a dress manufacturer, does not talk about the way the zipper is made, but of the advantage of using the Talon tag on garments. This type of advertising is referred to as *end-product advertising.*

To popularize woolens in the face of the competition from synthetic fabrics, the wool industry advertises its distinguishing mark, "The Woolmark," urging buyers to look for it whenever they buy a garment, a blanket, a rug, or a fabric, to make sure it is pure wool. The consumer is not asked to buy wool, only garments and other things made of wool.

Many makers of synthetic fabrics advertise, "Look for the name ——— whenever you buy a ———." Often such ads are cooperative ads between the fabric maker and the garment manufacturer.

Behind the scenes in any such project there is considerable sales effort to induce manufacturers to buy the advertised product for use in their own product and to get the benefit of its name on their label. End-product advertising is a variant of the usual national advertising that asks the consumer to buy a product by name.

Direct-response advertising.   One of the fastest-growing sectors of our economy is direct marketing: selling a product from marketer to consumer without going through retail channels. The advertising used in direct marketing is referred to as *direct-response advertising.* This term is now the preferred one for what has long been known as "mail-order advertising," because an enormous amount of such advertising is now done through magazines, newspapers, television, and radio. Direct mail continues, however, to be the most important direct-response medium, or it was before postage rates climbed steeply.

The chief characteristic of direct response advertising is that it always bears a coupon or return card or gives a phone number or address to which to respond to a TV or radio ad. The goal of the advertiser is to get a prompt response with the name and address of the responder. Chapter 12 is a discussion of direct-response advertising.

Advertising to business and professions

There is a world of advertising that most consumers may never see. In it, one business firm tries to sell something to another. Included in this category also is advertising to professional people, like physicians and architects, who are in a position to specify the advertiser's product for others to buy. All this is in addi-

Direct-response advertising. Purpose: to obtain orders by mail. The ad is replete with a variety of offers and much specific copy, along with an order coupon.

tion to advertising products to consumers for their personal use. Advertising to business has several different forms.

    Trade advertising.   All the articles in a store must be bought by someone before they are delivered to that store. The buyer may serve a whole chain of stores, or a buying committee may have to give its approval. To reach those authorities, the marketer will advertise in the trade papers of their business, giving news about the product, especially price, special deals, packaging. The advertising may describe special consumer advertising and promotions. It may tell about the success the product is having with the public and with other retailers. The theme of all the advertising is to show the profit the store can make by stocking this product now. Such trade advertising is an important adjunct to any national advertising campaign.

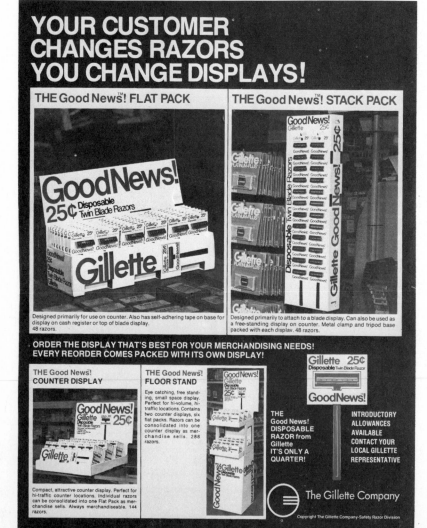

Trade advertising. Retailers are the target here—to make them aware of the product and the display material that will help produce sales and increase profits for them.

As a matter of fact seal retention is one of the best reasons to buy Timken® bearings.

Every Timken® "AP" bearing seal we make today has an elastomeric coating, right here. It gives added seal retention. And by damping vibration, guards against fretting corrosion.

The positive flare on the O.D. of the case increases the effectiveness of the interference fit and the locking bead.

The premium stock we use has been selected to reduce distortion of the seal case during installation and removal. So retention is improved.

This rib, called the locking bead, combines with the interference fit to provide retention of the seal in the cup.

Our patented three-step case provides rigidity, so you're less likely to damage the seal in removal.

Every Timken "AP" seal wears its own batch identification number to assure you of consistent product performance.

Only a Timken Company approved seal has our name, our part number, material designation and date of manufacture right here.

We have more things going for seal and lubricant retention than anybody else. So you'll keep more of your cars moving—with fewer setouts caused by leaking seals. And that's what all the improvements in our seals really add up to.
The Timken Company, Canton, Ohio 44706.

The elastomer is bonded directly to the case to reduce unsprung weight and minimize leakage.

Over 3,000,000 seal test hours in our own laboratory are behind the specs for seal compound, design, and quality control.

Mold, cavity and compound numbers—another assurance of continuous quality control.

The Bi-Rotational Elastohydrodynamic Sealing Mechanism is the most effective way found to date to minimize seal lip wear, retain lubricant and extend seal life.

TIMKEN®
REGISTERED TRADEMARK
TAPERED ROLLER BEARINGS

Business advertisement of an industrial firm. The advantage of the advertiser's product is explained to other manufacturers and users of machinery.

Industrial advertising.   A manufacturer is a buyer of machinery, equipment, raw materials, and components used in producing the goods he sells. Those who have machinery, equipment, or material to sell to other producers will address their advertising especially to them in their industry magazine. It is quite unlike consumer advertising and is referred to as *industrial advertising.*

Industrial advertising is aimed at a market that has certain characteristics: 1) sales may run into very large sums: 2) many people are involved in a decision to buy, each person a specialist or professional in some aspect of the total operation; 3) decisions on a matter may take a long time. The products are not being bought for personal use.

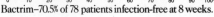

Professional advertisement addressed to physicians, to encourage them to prescribe the advertised product. Specific technical data supports its efficacy.

Advertising to the professions. The most important person in the sale of some products is the professional adviser to the buyer, as a physician or architect. The physician's recommendation is the best inducement to the patient to buy that product. In construction, the architect's specifications are usually binding. In these areas, then, advertising is frequently directed to professionals through their professional publications and by direct mail.

Corporate management advertising. Many people within a company may join in making a decision about products the company needs. If the investment is large, the highest level of management will be involved. How to reach them? Many have found the answer by advertising the broad services of a company in the publications they read, such as *Newsweek, Time, U.S. News & World Report,* and *Fortune.* Such advertising is called *corporate management advertising,* or *corporate institutional advertising* if it is addressed also to a wider audience.

Chapter 25 goes more thoroughly into advertising to business.

The advertising of services.   As examples of nationally advertised services we include airlines, rental cars, motel and hotel chains, tourist sites, tourist agencies, fast-food chains. Banks, investment houses, and insurance companies also fall

◀ (Left): **Public service (institutional) advertising. Perhaps the first ad by a utility company advocating conservation of energy. It appeared in The New York Times *two years before the oil embargo of 1974.***

(Below): **One of a series of booklets issued by Shell to encourage the conservation of gasoline.** ▼

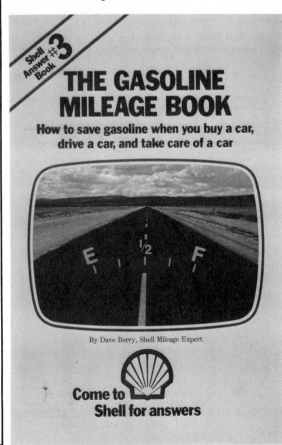

Save a watt

(it's wise to conserve energy)

Save a watt. Because New York and Westchester, and perhaps other places too, may face power emergencies this year. Because now and in future years protection of the earth's environment requires we use all kinds of energy wisely and not wastefully.

Save a watt. Because if we start conserving electricity now, *especially in day time,* we may avoid more serious problems later. Con Edison is doing everything possible to end power shortages. If new facilities can be completed on schedule, we will have one of the nation's most modern electric systems in just a few years. But even when power is plentiful it should be conserved.

Save a watt. Because with your help there's less chance of serious disruptions of electric service this summer. And using all energy wisely is essential to keeping the earth a good place to live.

10 ways to save a watt

1. During the day, when no one is home, turn the air conditioning off.

2. When using air conditioners, select moderate or medium settings rather than turning your unit on high. During the day keep windows closed and adjust blinds and shades to keep out the sun so that air conditioners won't have to work so hard.

3. Whenever possible, plan to run major appliances — and smaller appliances as well — before 8 am and after 6 pm.

4. If possible, use dishwashers just once a day — after the evening meal.

5. If possible, plan washer and dryer loads for evenings and weekends. Do one full load instead of many small loads.

6. Keep lights off when it's daylight except for safety, health and comfort reasons (the heat from lighting requires more air conditioning).

7. Never leave a kitchen range or oven on when not actually in use.

8. Turn off television and radio sets when you are not looking or listening.

9. If you can, save once-in-a-while jobs like vacuum cleaning or working with power tools until the weekend.

10. When buying an air conditioner, look for the right size unit for your needs. Select one that gives you the maximum amount of BTU's of cooling for every watt used.

Con Edison conserve energy

Shell Answer Book #3

THE GASOLINE MILEAGE BOOK
How to save gasoline when you buy a car, drive a car, and take care of a car

By Dave Berry, Shell Mileage Expert

Come to Shell for answers

into the service classification. The whole service field has been expanding greatly in recent years. The advertising of services differs from that of commodities because of the difference in the way they are marketed. The response to service advertising is meant to come directly from the prospect, or at most through one intermediary, as a travel office. One interesting development in the field of service advertising has been the proliferation of franchising. Fast-food chains, for example, will grant franchises to operators who will pay a fixed sum of money to lease or own the franchise in their own communities. The company granting the franchise will usually do national advertising to spread its fame on a broad scale. The local franchise owner can then do local advertising.

Advertising to conserve resources.   One of the great functions of advertising has evolved from an awareness of our limited resources. Although advertising is chiefly used to increase consumption, our limited natural resources have caused a surge of advertising to encourage conservation. We discuss this further in Chapter 4, "Specific Purposes of Campaigns."

QUESTIONS

1. What is the role of advertising in the marketing mix? How does advertising relate to the other functions of business?

2. How do you explain the varying amounts of emphasis different companies of similar size give to advertising? Cite specific examples.

3. Cite some products whose sales have been affected by social trends. In what ways? How has advertising been used in each case?

4. Compare and contrast the role of advertising in the following: Consumer goods companies—industrial goods companies; profit-seeking organizations—not-for-profit organizations.

5. Does advertising add value to products? If so, how? If not, why not?

6. Which is more important in achieving marketing success—the product or the advertising? Explain your answer.

7. Advertising can be effective only under certain conditions. What are conditions that are conducive to advertising? Explain why each condition is important.

8. What is meant by the "product differential"? How does it influence advertising?

9. "Advertising succeeds or fails depending upon whether or not it gets the consumer to purchase the product." Agree or disagree? Why?

10. When competing products are very similar in physical characteristics and price, what should be the role of advertising?

11. To what extent should competition dictate the amount, type, and emphasis of advertising by a particular marketer?

12. What is the relationship between self-service and advertising? Does advertising have a different role, depending upon whether or not the product is sold via self-service? Explain.

13. Define, cite the main purpose, and give two examples of the following kinds of advertising: (1) national, (2) retail, (3) end-product, (4) direct response, (5) trade, (6) industrial, (7) professional, and (8) corporate management.

14. "Advertising won't go away, because society needs it, industry needs it, the country and the world need it." (S.R. Bernstein, Crain Communications, Inc.) Agree or disagree? For what reasons?

READING SUGGESTIONS

AAKER, DAVID A., *Advertising Management: Practical Perspectives.* Englewood Cliffs, N.J.: Prentice-Hall, 1975.

BARTON, ROGER, ed., *The Handbook of Advertising Management.* New York: McGraw-Hill, 1970.

BLACK, ROBERT H., "Advertising Can Play Important Role During Economic Slump," *Industrial Marketing* (December 1975), 60–61 ff.

BORDEN, NEIL H., "The Concept of the Marketing Mix," *Journal of Advertising Research* (June 1964).

BRITT, STEUART HENDERSON, ed., *Marketing Manager's Handbook.* Chicago: The Dartwell Corporation, 1973.

BUELL, VICTOR, ed., *Handbook of Modern Marketing.* New York: McGraw-Hill, 1970

CRAVENS, DAVID W., GERALD E. HILLS, and ROBERT B. WOODRUFF, *Marketing Decision Making.* Homewood, Ill.: Irwin, 1976.

DELOZIER, WAYNE M., *The Marketing Communications Process.* New York: McGraw-Hill, 1976.

KOTLER, PHILIP., *Marketing Management,* 3rd ed. Englewood Cliffs, N.J.: Prentice-Hall, 1976.

LUSHBOUGH, C. H., "Advertising: Consumer Information and Consumer Deception," *California Management Review* (Spring 1974), 80–82.

McCARTHY, E. JEROME, *Basic Marketing,* 6th ed. Homewood, Ill.: Irwin, 1978.

MULLER, JAMES H., "Ad Communications: Where Does It Fit in the Total Marketing Mix?" *Industrial Marketing* (September 1975), 84.

"The New World of Advertising," *Advertising Age* (Special Issue, November 21, 1973).

SCHELLENBACH, BURTON, "To Have a More Effective Role in Advertising, Admen Must Know Other Functions," *Industrial Marketing* (June 1975), 78 ff.

STANLEY, RICHARD E., *Promotion.* Englewood Cliffs, N.J.: Prentice-Hall, 1977.

STAUDT, THOMAS A., DONALD A. TAYLOR, and DONALD J. BOWERSOX, *A Managerial Introduction to Marketing,* Englewood Cliffs, N.J.: Prentice-Hall, 1976.

UNWIN, S. J. F., "Where Advertising Will Fit in the Future Society," *Advertising Age* (July 8, 1974), 29–30.

VANDERMEULEN, ALICE, "Are You Welcome Where You Advertise?" *Journal of Advertising Research* (April 1976), 11–14.

WEBSTER, FREDERICK E., JR., *Marketing for Managers.* New York: Harper, 1974.

PART TWO

Planning the advertising

3

The Advertising Spiral

The following advertisement appeared in a New York newspaper. The name of the product is omitted. What would you guess the product to be?

**HAVE YOUR _____ SENT HOME
BEFORE THANKSGIVING DAY**

Add one more source of delight for the children and pleasure for the grown-ups. No home is at its best until you have a _____. Nothing else makes the home so bright and cheerful; nothing else keeps the children so lively and happy; nothing else serves so well to keep the older folks from being dull and the time from dragging. There is pleasure for all in a house that possesses a _____.

Isn't it an addition well worth having sent home before Thanksgiving Day comes with its holiday for the children and the friends who will visit you?

What product would you say was being advertised? A videocassette? No. A color television set? No. A hi-fi set? Tape recorder? Radio? Phonograph? No. It was the predecessor to all these, a Regina mechanical music box advertised by the John Wanamaker store in 1901.

The Advertising Stages

Yet there is an unmistakable similarity between the Regina music box ad and those used to introduce more recent inventions, because from the time a *new type* of product first appears on the market to the time various brands of that product are household words, the product faces similar advertising stages.

These are the

▲ Pioneering stage
▲ Competitive stage
▲ Retentive stage

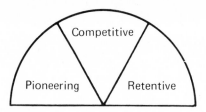

These stages depend upon the degree of acceptance accorded the products by those to whom it is being advertised. A clear understanding of these stages will be helpful in planning basic advertising strategy.

Pioneering stage

The research and development department of a large company may have been working for years on a useful new invention. When it finally succeeds and the product is ready for the market, does the public arise in elation and clamor for it? Not in most cases, because it may never have occurred to consumers to seek such a device. Until people recognize that this is something they want, a product is in the first, or *pioneering* stage.

The advertising of products in the pioneering stage (or *pioneering advertising*, as we call it) must show that previous conceptions of that field are now antiquated. Limitations tolerated as "normal" are now demonstrated to have been overcome safely. The safety razor supplanted the straight-edge razor, and the advertising said, "If you are still depending upon the barber or an old-fashioned razor, you are in the same category as a man who climbs ten flights of stairs when there is an elevator in the building. With the Gillette Safety Razor the most inexperienced man can remove without cut or scratch in three to five minutes any beard that ever grew." And when the electric shaver came upon the scene, its advertising proclaimed "no bother or fuss of old-fashioned soap and brush . . . no more shaving cuts with the new electric shaver."

Even color television was launched by the pioneering advertising of RCA Victor in the 1950s, which said:

See World Series Baseball in Living Color. . . . Rarely in a lifetime can you share a thrill like this. . . . You can see baseball's greatest spectacle come alive in your own home in color. . . . You'll sense a new on-the spot realism in every picture of the crowd, the players, the action. . . . Made by RCA—the most trusted name in electronics.

Although the music box and color television were almost two generations apart, and although the advertising techniques of their day were worlds apart, both products attacked their common problem the same way: "Add one more source of delight . . . rarely in a lifetime a thrill like this." These themes of new satisfactions in life are recurrent in pioneering advertising of new products. By "new products" we mean those which achieve a breakthrough in the principle on which the product currently operates. When the Kodak camera first came out, people had to be told, "You press the button. We do the rest." Today the

Introducing The Solar Hot Water Heater

Solar Collectors are the Look of the Future

Solar Systemizer Assembly

Solar Storage Tank

American technology presents a new generation of heating fuel... the Sun. The Sun provides more solar energy in one day than predictably can be utilized for the next ten centuries. Born of the energy crisis solar energy has become an alternate source of heating. Providing abundant, non-polluting and free energy, the technology of utilizing the Sun is right here, right now. Solar Energy Systems, Inc. has developed the contemporary system which will heat the water in your home or business...THE SUNERATOR™ SOLAR HOT WATER SYSTEM.

HOW THE SUNERATOR/SOLAR HOT WATER SYSTEM WORKS

THE SOLAR COLLECTOR

The capture of solar energy requires Solar Collectors designed to absorb and transfer solar radiation. Solar Collectors, the look of the future, each measure 35" wide and 77" high. They weigh 115 lbs. and are totally assembled.

THE SOLAR SYSTEMIZER

The Solar Systemizer consists of top grade copper and steel components which provides for the exchange of solar heating to the potable water. Solid-state thermostatic controls automate the operational functions.

THE STORAGE TANK

A thermal storage tank for the reserve of the solar heated water is located adjacent to the existing standard hot water heater. The storage tank has no fossil or electric heating element and its only source of fuel is the Sun.

AN ENGINEERING ACCOMPLISHMENT

Combining the Solar Collectors, the Solar Systemizer, and the Solar Storage Tank presents a simple and suitable efficient solar system for heating domestic water. Two Solar Collectors are usually required for an average family of four. High usage of hot water and larger families require three or four Collectors.

THE ECONOMICS

Solar energy offsets the cost of heating water by reducing the demand on fossil or electric fuels.

The SUNERATOR/SOLAR HOT WATER HEATING SYSTEM is sold as a package which includes two liquid type SOLAR COLLECTORS, SOLAR SYSTEMIZER, SOLAR STORAGE TANK and SOLAR FLUID. The price is $1095. excluding taxes, installation and shipping charges.

What you get for $1095. is an investment into an alternate source of energy fuel...the Sun. Your contribution towards resolving our energy crisis. The Government may be willing to share your investment. Home-owners may apply to their State Energy Office for a $400. grant towards the purchase of a Solar hot water system. The grants have been made available by the United States Energy Research and Development Administration.

For more information:
call (609) 424-4446

or fill out this coupon and mail to:
SOLAR ENERGY SYSTEMS, INC.
One Olney Avenue/Cherry Hill Industrial Center
Cherry Hill, New Jersey 08003

Name_____

Address_____

City_____ State_____ Zip_____
☐ Send Literature Only   ☐ Please Phone

Phone No._____ Best time to call_____

ENERGY SYSTEMS, INC.
. . .in partnership with the sun.

One Olney Avenue/Cherry Hill Industrial Center
Cherry Hill, New Jersey 08003 / (609) 424-4446

Solar heating in the pioneering stage.

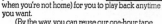
Pioneering advertising, presenting not merely a new product but a new life-style.

Kodak Ektasound camera and projector advertise, "What you hear can be as much a part of Christmas as what you see." Each of these innovations adds its touch of richness to the satisfaction of life, even changes life styles. Each represents more than a minor improvement in an existing product. Each calls for a new set of tools and dies—and it calls for pioneering advertising. It is interesting to observe how often pioneering advertising uses the terms "no more this" or "no more that," referring to existing shortcomings; also "Now you can do this" or "Now you can do that."

By the time the public accepts the idea of using the new category of product, competitors undoubtedly will have sprung up. When the public no longer asks, "What's that product for?" but rather, "Which make shall I buy?" the product enters the *competitive stage*. We speak of the advertising for a product in the competitive stage as *competitive advertising*. (This is a restrictive meaning of that term, not to be confused with the looser meaning that all advertisements are competitive with each other.)

Competitive stage

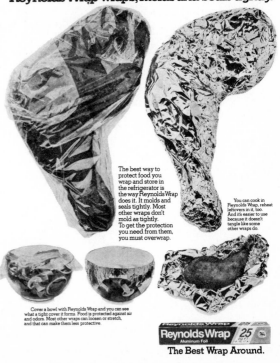

PHILCO® COLD GUARD® REFRIGERATORS CAN SAVE YOU MORE MONEY ON ELECTRIC BILLS THAN ALL THESE COMPETITORS.

Admiral	Gibson	J.C.Penney	Montgomery Ward
Frigidaire	Hotpoint	Sears Coldspot	Whirlpool
General Electric	Kelvinator	Sears Kenmore	White-Westinghouse

A bold claim. But true. And we'll send you the proof—free. Every Philco COLD GUARD Refrigerator uses less electricity than comparable models from every maker listed in the January 1976 AHAM Directory, including those with electric anti-condensation heaters.

For example, the Philco COLD GUARD Model RD16G2 (15.8 cubic feet) uses up to 55% less electricity than comparable models.

That's because only Philco COLD GUARD Refrigerators were re-engineered to give you three important energy savers: 1. Double cavity Uni-Wall Liner with no seams or joints (patented process). 2. Precision placement of insulation.

3. Completely non-electric anti-condensation system.

Another example of savings. Philco COLD GUARD Model RD19F8, the 18.9 cubic footer shown here, uses only 100 kilowatt hours a month versus an average of 145 KWH for comparable competitive models. That's

Model RD19F8

31% less. At $.04 a KWH, you'd save $21.60 a year— or $324 in an average refrigerator lifetime. Even more, if your KWH rate is higher.

So send for our free booklet that lets you fig how much money and electricity you can sav compared to the brand listed here. Learn why pays to own the refriger that helps pay for itsel Just write: Aeronutron Ford Corporation, MS Blue Bell, PA. 19422.

Actual savings may vary depen upon climatic conditions, individua and electric rate changes. Savings sent maximum economies available current performance of Philco COL GUARD Refrigerators compared w energy consumption of comparable and type models in the Januar Directory of Certified Refrigerators Freezers published by the Associati Home Appliance Manufacturers (A Comparisons for brands and model electric anti-condensation heaters based on average maximum/minim energy consumption. The average li of a refrigerator is considered to be 15 years.

THE REFRIGERATOR THAT HELPS PAY FOR ITSELF.

◀ *Philco features its competitive advantages over a dozen other refrigerators.*

Most wraps just wrap. Reynolds Wrap wraps, molds and seals tightly.

The best way to protect food you wrap and store in the refrigerator is the way Reynolds Wrap does it. It molds and seals tightly. Most other wraps don't mold as tightly. To get the protection you need from them, you must overwrap.

You can cook in Reynolds Wrap, reheat leftovers in it, too. And it's easier to use because it doesn't tangle like some other wraps do.

Cover a bowl with Reynolds Wrap and you can see what a tight cover it forms. Food is protected against air and odors. Most other wraps can loosen or stretch, and that can make them less protective.

Reynolds Wrap | 25
Aluminum Foil
The Best Wrap Around.

Reynolds demonstrates its advantages over most other wraps. ▶

A quartz watch in the competitive stage, featuring its differential.

Most products in everyday use are in the competitive stage: cars, detergents, toothpaste, headache remedies, razor blades, soft drinks, shampoos, TV sets, packaged foods. The purpose of advertising in the competitive stage is to show how unique features or *differentials* of one brand make it better than other brands. Here are some headlines.

The Sunbeam Total Clean Can Opener
It's the cleanest way we know to open cans   [Sunbeam can opener]

Get more tough steel wool in every pad   [Brillo soap pads]

Our big size is more than half-full when others are empty   [All detergent]

**The only range that cooks juicy
steaks the way they should be
cooked: on both sides at once**   [White-Westinghouse range]

**Only one electric portable typewriter
has a snap-in cartridge ribbon**   [SCM Smith-Corona typewriter]

None of these advertisements will tell you why you should use its type of product; that is taken for granted. But each sets out to tell you why you should select that particular brand from among the others in its field.

There is a third stage through which a product *might* pass—the *retentive stage.* **Retentive stage**
When a brand of a product is used by a large share of the market, the goal of much of its advertising may be to hold on to those customers. All over the world, for example, there are signs saying *Drink Coca-Cola.* They do not say what

Coca-Cola has a tremendous market, and it wants to keep its name before the eyes of its consumers. This retentive advertising reminds those who buy Coca-Cola that they are buying the real thing.

Coca-Cola is; they give no reason why you should drink it or why Coca-Cola is better than any other drink. That advertising is addressed to Coca-Cola drinkers, to reinforce, at the least cost per message, their favorable recollection of this familiar beverage.

The best-known form of retentive advertising is often referred to as *name advertising,* for that is often its chief feature. Retentive advertising, however, embraces other problems of a product in the retentive stage, such as staving off imitators, an experience faced by every highly successful advertiser. The retentive advertising will say, "Don't be fooled by imitators," or "It's the real thing," as Coca-Cola said.

Another form of retentive advertising is used when a corporation is beset by problems that affect its existence, such as product shortages or labor disputes. During the time of crisis, advertising for sales goes into limbo while the company devotes all its efforts to presenting its case to the public. This is *institutional advertising,* to be discussed in the next chapter. Here we are following the advertising stages of a product whose sales have uninterrupted, successful growth.

Shift of stage within one market

Since people may gradually change their attitudes toward a product, a product may also gradually shift from pioneering stage to competitive stage. Half the space of a movie-camera ad may be pioneering, telling of the joy of having moving pictures of children as they grow up; the other half may be competitive, explaining the special features of this particular camera. The product could be described as half in the pioneering stage, half in the competitive stage.

Product in different stages in different markets

In considering the advertising stages of a product, we think of it in terms of specific markets. A product may be in different stages in different markets at the same time. For example, typewriters are in the competitive stage in the business-office market, but the idea of giving one as a gift to college students or teen-agers is largely in the pioneering stage.

Other influences on advertising stage of product

The factor that determines the stage of a product is the attitude of the public toward it, not the recency of invention or the amount of advertising that has been done for it. Some new types of products suddenly take off like wildfire and move directly into the competitive stage—electronic calculators, as an example. There had long been much publicity about the use of calculators in the scientific, technical, and business worlds. When low-priced, pocket-size calculators appeared for general consumer use, no extensive pioneering advertising was needed to teach the public about calculators, which moved directly into the competitive stage. Public demand was so great that retailers immediately opened computer departments and began extensive advertising, each ad pointing out the competitive price and other advantages of a particular model.

Products that have a special style may catch the fancy of the public so quickly that they find themselves in a competitive price-and-style fray at an early point, without the benefit of pioneering advertising. The digital watch is a good example. Each marketer must make his own appraisal of the current attitude of the public toward his product or product class and must determine its advertising stage.

Not all products presented as "new" are new types of product. Many are familiar types of products in the competitive stage, lifted above the competition for the time being by a new innovative feature. In that event, pioneering advertising has to be done to explain the advantages of the improvement. In fact, the better part of the advertisement may be devoted to that newsworthy feature. The product, however, is still in the competitive stage; only its differential has been changed. Competitors soon come out with their versions of that improve-

Product in the competitive stage, improvement in pioneering stage

Product in the competitive stage, new feature in the pioneering stage. Sometimes a new feature of a competitive product is so radical and important that advertising attention is focused on pioneering advertising of that feature.

The only range that cooks juicy steaks the way they should be cooked: on both sides at once.

Any chef worth his sauce knows the best way to cook a steak is on both sides at once.

For a very simple reason. When you cook (or broil) a steak on just one side at a time, the natural juices seep out the other side. But cooking it on both sides at once holds them in.

So naturally the steak is juicier. And more flavorful.

You'll find it all comes true on the No-Turn Speed Broil range. Only from White-Westinghouse.

Not only do you get steak that tastes better. You get steak that cooks faster. (How about a medium steak in just 9 or 10 minutes?)

In fact, everything you cook on this broiler will cook faster. And taste better. Hamburgers, chicken, fish, hors d'oeuvres. You name it.

And to top it all off, the whole range is completely self-cleaning. So you're saved even more time and trouble.

The No-Turn Speed Broil range.

For a lot of juicy reasons, it's worth looking into.

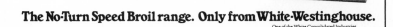

The No-Turn Speed Broil range. Only from White-Westinghouse.

One of the White Consolidated Industries.

ment, plus their own new features, forcing the originator to find some other rationale for being selected.

Change is a continuum. As long as the operation of a competitive product does not change, the product continues to be in the competitive stage, despite its pioneering improvements. When, however, the principle of its operation changes, the product itself enters the pioneering stage.

For example, a new feature in a gas oven, such as a broiler that cooks steaks on both sides at once, represents a feature in the pioneering stage, although the product is in the competitive stage. But a radar range, operating on a new principle, is in the pioneering stage among electric ovens and gas ovens.

Difference in policies

The stage of a product may be determined readily enough, but two advertisers may follow different policies in interpreting the facts. One firm may recognize that there is still a large public that buys neither its article nor any like it. That firm will continue to stress pioneering appeals, winning more customers for itself and the field. The other advertiser will take advantage of the pioneering work already done in creating a market, and will use only competitive advertising to get its brand selected.

Why be a pioneer?   Since the pioneering advertiser has the expense of educating the public to the advantages of the new type of product, and since others will then take advantage of that work, what benefits, if any, will compensate the pioneering investment? In most instances, there is little choice. One can either come into the market at the outset, with pioneering efforts, or allow someone else to step in as the first in the field. It may then cost more to enter the market later, when it will be necessary to compete with the advertising of many others.

The only sure advantage of a pioneering advertiser is a *time* advantage, the opportunity to be a leader in the field, with a head start over the followers. The leader's name will be the first to come to mind for that type of product. It will have established a following of customers before competitors get going. People will know the leader's trademark better than that of the followers; they will have more confidence in the product because they will feel that it has the benefit of longer experience.

When Hertz rental cars first appeared on the scene, they gave the impression of being taxis in which you did the driving. But the company pioneered the idea of having Hertz cars at airports, so that you could always drive a car yourself, wherever you flew in this country. And they did the pioneering advertising on that idea. Then, to popularize the concept of driving your own hired car, they ran a campaign, "Let Hertz put you in the driver's seat." Car rental companies sprang up all over the country, but Hertz was so far ahead in the public view that when Avis set out to advertise, the best they could say was "We are second." Although Avis made the best of it by adding, "We try harder," Hertz, through their pioneering advertising, had an invaluable, long-time benefit. They were first, in the public mind, for rental cars.

There is much less advertising of products in the pioneering stage than in the competitive stage, because *new types* or categories of products, not mere minor improvements on old ones, do not appear on the scene very often. Most advertising is for products in the competitive stage. Often such advertising introduces a new feature that is in the pioneering stage, and that, for a time, gets the advertising spotlight.

The least amount of advertising is for products in the retentive stage. This stage, however, represents a critical moment in the life cycle of a product, when important management decisions must be made; hence it is important to understand the retentive stage.

Comparison of stages

It appears only logical that the life of a product does not end when it reaches the retentive stage, for here it is at the very height of its popularity, where, if allowed, it can coast along. But a business that coasts can coast only downward—deceptively slowly at first, then nose-diving suddenly as the impact of more aggressive competition makes itself felt.

No business can rely on old customers only. Customers die off, their patterns of living change, they are lured away by the offerings of competitors. Just when a product is enjoying its peak years of success—when its name is the most prominent in the field—the advertising usually takes a new turn. It shows new ways of using a familiar product and reasons for using it more often. Advertising enters a new pioneering stage.

The Singer Company, whose name is synonymous with sewing machines throughout the world, is again advertising to get women to make their own clothes, showing the ease of doing so, the money they can save, and the creative enjoyment it affords. Reynolds, a name familiar to housewives for aluminum wrap, introduced the new idea of "Freezer-to-Table Cooking" and advertised "How to cook frozen meat, fish, poultry, without thawing." Johnson & Johnson's Band-Aids can be found in medicine chests throughout the country, but Johnson & Johnson wants to get the bandages out of the medicine chest more often. To do that they advertise a warning to watch out for small scratches, as they may lead to infections.

In time, other advertisers may move into the new market created by the pioneer. Other sewing-machine companies are going after the new sewing-machine prospects generated by Singer. Besides Johnson & Johnson's Band-Aids, other adhesive bandages are advertised to the public that is aware of such bandages, and the product enters a new competitive stage in that market.

The product does not actually return to the point at which it first started its career, however; instead, the market stretches out to include the additional buyers now embraced (Chart A, p. 52). After it has gone through the stages in this field, the product may repeat the movement in other fields, or with new generations, with every turn enlarging the total market of buyers, the process represented by a spiral (Chart B, p. 52).

After the retentive stage?

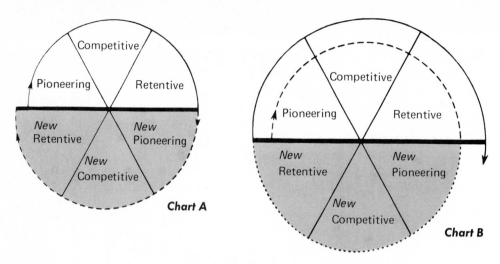

The advertising spiral.

Management decisions at the retentive stage

As a product approaches the retentive stage, management must make some important marketing decisions.

—*Can we make a significant improvement in our product, so that it is virtually a new type of product?* The new feature would get the focus of attention (until it has direct competition). It would be in the pioneering stage, though the product itself is in the competitive stage. If the new product works on a totally new principle, then the whole product will be in the pioneering stage.

—*Should we introduce a related item, the first step in creating an expanded line?* The makers of Clairol first came out with a hair rinse, then with other hair preparations, then with an ever-expanding line of cosmetics. First there was the Frigidaire refrigerator; today there are also the Frigidaire washer, Frigidaire dryer, Frigidaire food-waste disposal, Frigidaire air-conditioner, among their other products. Each shares the prestige of the original product in the line, as well as sharing the company's production resources and marketing skills and overhead expense.

—*Since our field is shrinking, can we make other things?* That's what Ronson did. Famed for its table cigarette lighters, that company used its technical competence to make other products. In one full-page ad they subsequently featured the Ronson broiler oven, the Ronson blender, the Ronson hair dryer, and the Ronson electric knife.

Thus we see that the life of a product may be affected by many conditions. If the product is to continue to be marketed, its advertising stage must be identified before its advertising goals are set.

Nothing to Watch....
but the Flowing Seam

SINGER, always the pioneer, has created a new sewing machine. You sit at ease before it, press a lever ever so gently with the knee, and while you merely guide your material, you watch a perfect seam flow forth, ruffles form like gathering foam or a tiny hem fall into place.

Tucking, shirring, binding, all those deft details of trimming and decoration, you do more perfectly than by hand—and in a tenth the time. Such is the versatile magic of this new Singer Electric that its very presence is a temptation to sew, and the creation of lovely things becomes a fascinating joy.

There is an easy way to prove to yourself what a modern Singer will do. The nearest Singer Shop will gladly send one to your home that you can use for thirty days, in doing your own sewing. You may have your choice of the widest variety of models—electric, treadle and hand machines. Any one of them may be yours on a convenient plan by which you will receive a generous allowance for your present machine, and your new Singer will pay for itself as you save.

The Famous Singer "S"

is one of the oldest of trade-marks. You will find it on the windows of 6,000 Singer Shops, in every city in the world. It is the identifying mark of sewing machines of enduring quality. It means, too, that every Singer Shop is ready always with instruction, repairs, supplies and courteous expert service.

When the Singer representative comes to your home let him tell you about this service Singer maintains in your neighborhood, wherever you live.

"Short Cuts to Home Sewing"—*free*

This interesting practical book shows you how to save time in a hundred ways on your sewing machine—how to do all the modish new details of trimming. It will help with your sewing no matter what make of machine you may have—or even though you have none now. The book is free. Simply phone or call at the nearest Singer Shop (see telephone directory) or send for a copy by mail, postpaid.

Singer Sewing Machine Company, Dept. 32A, Singer Bldg., N. Y.

SINGER
SEWING MACHINES

Entire contents of this advertisement copyright 1926-7 by The Singer Manufacturing Co.

THE
SINGER
SEWING
SPIRAL

Singer introduced the electric sewing machine with this advertisement in 1927. In true pioneering fashion, it explained a versatile, magic new way of sewing.

Meet the Dream Machine.

The new GOLDEN TOUCH & SEW* zig-zag sewing machine by SINGER

Here's the latest of the fabulous Touch & Sew sewing machines. With so many new features you can sew everything you ever dreamed of—right now.

Imagine—threading a needle with a push-button!

Basting on a sewing machine—at last!

Of course, this newest Golden Touch & Sew machine continues to bring you a built-in buttonholer, the exclusive Push-Button Bobbin and solid state speed control.

And it makes it "sew easy" to embroider, monogram, chainstitch—sew hundreds of decorative stitches. Try the Dream Machine today.

One of five new Touch & Sew machines. Prices start at $149.95.

Makes all your sewing dreams come true.

model 640

New! Speed-Basting Stitch ends tedious hand-basting forever. Easy to sew, easy to pull out.

New! Push-Button Needle Threader ends squinting; power-threads the needle!

Just set the dial and sew perfect buttonholes. It's dreamy.

SINGER
What's new for tomorrow is at SINGER today!

*A Trademark of THE SINGER COMPANY

The Singer electric sewing machine in the competitive stage. As electric sewing machines became widely accepted, different brands entered the market, and Singer came out with improvements. The product differentials that gave it an advantage over competitors were set forth in this advertisement of the late 1960s.

4

Specific Purposes of Campaigns

The advertising spiral can be helpful in setting the basic strategy of a campaign. It can identify the underlying marketing problem that a product faces at whatever stage it is in. But basic strategy has to be implemented by a specific strategy, or plan of campaign, designed to meet the immediate marketing problem. A combination of marketing and advertising thinking may tackle the problem by deciding to

▲ Increase the frequency of use of a product

▲ Increase the variety of uses of a product

▲ Add a new product to a well-known line

▲ Reinforce credibility of important claims

▲ Launch a special promotional campaign

▲ Turn a disadvantage into an advantage

▲ Dispel a misconception

▲ Enhance the image of a company (institutional advertising)

▲ Gain support for not-for-profit and public interest causes

Sometimes several purposes may be served in the same campaign.

Richard N. Oster, General Manager of Clorox, told how Clorox's market research among users showed

"that only 40 percent of total wash loads by housewives were being bleached at that time. Of those who bleached, one-third of the users bleached 80 percent of the time,

Increasing the frequency of use or replacement of product

59

Keep in touch with the whole world by telephone.

"Long Distance is the next best thing to being there."

Bell System

To increase frequency of use.

two-thirds bleached only 20 percent of the time. If we could get two-thirds of the people that were already using Clorox (the *light users*) to use it the way the other third did (the *heavy users*) we could double our business overnight without ever getting a new user.°

Another example of increasing the frequency of use is the Bell System ad which says, "Long distance is the next best thing to being there," thus increasing the frequency of making long distance calls.

Increasing the variety of uses of a product

Experience has long shown that it is easier to interest old customers in buying more of a product than to find new ones, particularly when you show them different ways of using your product. Kraft pictures different uses of Velveeta cheese to enhance dishes with which a housewife will already be familiar. The same advertising also attracts those who use other brands of this type of cheese. Food advertising thrives on offering new recipes for using the advertised product or new ways of serving it. Arm & Hammer opened new markets by recommending baking soda to absorb food odors in the refrigerator, and then pouring the baking soda down the drain as a deodorizer. Clorox, long known as a bleach, makes itself known as an efficient disinfectant, too. Every new use of a product represents a new market.

° *Business Professional Advertising Association Newsletter*, November 1975.

One of the reasons a firm will add to its line is to get benefit from the reputation it has generated for its brands. It may also want to take advantage of its expanding technical and marketing competency and facilities. Hence, Campbell's announces:

Campbell's reaches out to those who already know its quality, to tell them about its new soup. A coupon is an incentive to prompt action.

at the same time picturing it as "A great sauce and gravy maker," also as "a versatile cooking ingredient," thereby increasing the variety of its uses. While Hills Bros. introduces:

Three delicious coffee flavors
That take you away
From the same old grind

Once again, TV service technicians give these opinions about Zenith:

I. Best Picture.

Again this year, in a nationwide survey of the opinions of independent TV service technicians, Zenith was selected, more than any other brand, as the color TV with the best picture.

Question: In general, of all the color TV brands you are familiar with, which one would you say has the best overall picture?

Answers:

Zenith	34%
Brand A	21%
Brand B	12%
Brand C	8%
Brand D	7%
Brand E	4%
Brand F	2%
Brand G	2%
Brand H	2%
Other Brands	2%
About Equal	10%
Don't Know	4%

Note: Answers total over 100% due to multiple responses.

II. Fewest Repairs.

In the same opinion survey, the service technicians selected Zenith, more than any other brand, as the color TV needing the fewest repairs.

Question: In general, of all the color TV brands you are familiar with, which one would you say requires the fewest repairs?

Answers:

Zenith	38%
Brand A	18%
Brand D	9%
Brand B	6%
Brand C	5%
Brand E	3%
Brand F	2%
Brand G	2%
Brand H	2%
Other Brands	2%
About Equal	11%
Don't Know	10%

The Celebrity II, Model SH2331X, pictured here. Simulated rosewood with Bermuda Shell white front. Simulated TV picture.

For survey details, write to the Vice President, Consumer Affairs, Zenith Radio Corporation, 1900 N. Austin Avenue, Chicago, IL 60639.

ZENITH

CHROMACOLOR II

The quality goes in before the name goes on.®

Zenith chose service technicians as the most knowledgeable and credible witnesses to the quality of the sets they repair, and their testimonies enforce Zenith's claim to the best picture.

Incidentally, both advertisements offered money-off coupons to spur buyers to try the new product at once.

In all instances of expanding a well-known line, the advertising hopes to attract new customers but to reach as many of the old ones as they can, for they are the best prospects.

When an advertiser makes claim to superiority in some important respect, the public rightfully might ask, "Says who?" The costlier the product, the stronger the desire for proof. It is the burden of the advertiser to answer this question. Zenith TV did this by having a nationwide survey of independent service technicians of whom they asked these questions: "Which brand gave the best picture? Which gave the fewest repairs?" Zenith was named more than any other brand, and the report was made the basis of a continuing campaign. Considerable groundwork may be required to gather evidence that can be soundly supported and accurately presented.

Reinforcing credibility of an important claim

Television has been the great showplace of demonstrations in advertising, with one paper towel campaign showing before your eyes how this towel absorbed more moisture than a competitive one. Such dramatic demonstrations of competitive products have to meet station approval and satisfy the Federal Trade Commission's concern about unfair test presentations.

A special promotion is any idea that offers a particular inducement to bring a prospect to the store. To the marketer this is a means of stimulating business on a product. It also encourages the store to give the brand better support with good display. To the store, anything that brings in business without cost to the owner is great, because shoppers, once in a store, invariably buy other things. To the consumer, the special inducement is a spur to buy a product that he or she may or may not have thought of buying just then.

Launching a special promotional project

Promotions mostly use coupons or ask for proof of purchase for a premium, for which there may be a modest charge. Or the promotion may be an invitation to stop in for a sweepstakes ticket, without charge. Promotions are especially used to introduce a new member of a family of products, as well as a new competitive product. Promotions are also a much used competitive tool to stir things up in a quiet market or to respond to competition which is doing that.

Interestingly enough, experienced marketers run such offers not when sales are falling, with a view to attracting new users, but when sales are high, as it costs less to attract present customers to buy now than to reach out for new ones. Furthermore, when sales are going down, the problem is deep-rooted and requires probing for its real cause. This subject is further discussed in the sales promotion chapter.

"No wonder no one wants to adopt me," a mutt would say, if he could. "After all, I am a mutt. How much lower on the dog scale could I be?" That was the problem faced by the American Humane Education Society when it had an assorted collection of mongrels for which it was seeking good homes. But some

Turning a disadvantage into an advantage

A special promotion seeks to acquaint people with all members of a line. The offer of a free package spurs action.

Get the best of everything.
Adopt a mutt.

The smarts of a Lassie.

The spots of a Dalmatian.

The bark of a Shepherd.

The friendliness of a Beagle.

The heart of a St. Bernard.

The paws of a Great Dane.

Bring home a genuine All-American Mutt from your local humane society and get everything you're looking for, all in one dog. There are lots of genuine All-American Alley Kittens waiting for you too. Just come to:

Courtesy of the American Humane Education Society.

Behind this charming ad on behalf of a mutt lies a skill that is highly valuable in life as well as in advertising: the art of turning disadvantages into advantages.

thoroughbred copywriter discovered the advantages of a mutt and prepared the preceding ad, using the great technique of turning a disadvantage into an advantage.

Zenith television sells one of the highest-priced sets in the field; but instead of soft-pedalling the price, Zenith proudly says:

> **In times like these**
> **Why are so many people paying**
> **A little more to get Zenith?**

followed by a page full of copy, explaining details of its fine construction and operation.

To head off the displeasure of the public when phone rates went up, AT&T showed what a great company they are with an ad headed:

> **Why the cost of telephone service**
> **has gone up less**
> **than the cost of anything else.**

They then followed this with copy explaining the many things they have done and are doing to keep the cost down and to improve service. You ended up (if you read the whole ad) saying, "Aren't they a great company!"

Whenever you find yourself on the defensive in a situation, think of what an ad did for a mutt.

"WE'D LIKE TO TELL YOU HOW WE'RE DOING MORE BY DOING LESS."

We are coming out of the recent period of shortages with a basic change in the way we do business.

At one time, Union Carbide Chemicals and Plastics marketed some 2500 different products. Now we are narrowing our base. Because although our supply of raw materials has improved, we must be certain that we use those raw materials wisely. To keep our commitments to our

Another disadvantage turned into an advantage.

Lies, lies, lies.

"No real food value."

"Fattening"

"Few vitamins."

"Nothing but carbohydrates."

"Too many calories."

To be perfectly honest, our headline should probably say, misconceptions, misconceptions, misconceptions. But whatever you call them, there have been a lot of not-too-nice and not-too-true things said about potatoes.

Because they're a carbohydrate food, they're considered a luxury. Not true. Carbohydrates are a necessity. Nutritionists consider them basic fuel for the human body.

Potatoes are a good, economical way to get that fuel – without getting as many calories as you might think. A medium-size baked potato has just 90 calories. Add a pat of butter and enjoy that potato for only 125 calories.

It will also provide important vitamins and minerals, including about 1/3 the U.S. Recommended Daily Allowance of Vitamin C.*

As you can see, the potato is really something good that's good for you. And that's the truth.

The Potato. Something good that's good for you.

*Source: Nutritive Value of Foods, USDA #72. © 1975 The Potato Board.

An institutional ad to dispel a misconception.

Dispelling a misconception

How many times have you sat ordering a meal in a restaurant and heard one in your party say, "No potatoes, please"? Potatoes had too many calories or too little food value or were nothing but carbohydrates, they would say. Because so many people had such misconceptions, the Potato Board, trade association of the potato industry, hit the misconceptions hard in their advertisement, "Lies, lies, lies," citing figures from the *Nutritive Value of Food Report* of the U.S. Drug Administration. This is an example of the type of advertising that clearly addresses itself to dispelling a misconception that hurts the business of the advertiser.

Enhancing the image of a company (institutional advertising)

There are times when a corporation wishes to speak directly to the public to enhance the understanding and esteem with which it is regarded. Among the many forms such advertising takes are these:

To dispel a misconception (corporations have such problems, too):

**Some people think
all we have to do is stick a pin
in the earth to find oil**

[Texaco. See color plate 4]

International Paper explodes a myth about International Paper.

Because of our name, some people think all we do with our forests is make paper.

Far from it.

We make a lot of other products. Long-Bell® kitchen cabinets (like those in the picture). Lumber. Plywood. Utility poles. Pulp. Corrugated containers. Milk cartons. Hundreds of different products.

We're even taking steps to develop our petroleum and mineral potential.

But we also use our forests for things that money can't buy.

A home for wild animals.

In 1957 we started a wildlife program to make sure our forests would make the best possible home for wild animals. Here are some of the ways we help Mother Nature.

We thin the woods to encourage the growth of tender shoots, twigs and leaves that animals love to munch on.

We plant rye, chufa nuts, and wheat.

In some places we even cut down tall grasses which, oddly enough, increases the number of insects for young quail and turkeys to gobble up.

We usually harvest with an irregular border to give animals more enticing areas for browsing and better cover.

We'll spare the nesting tree of a red-cockaded woodpecker. We've restocked alligators (an endangered species) in the swamps of Arkansas. We saved 500 deer from starving during the '73 Mississippi flood.

We're rewarded. There are now more deer, quail and rabbits in our managed forests than there were 100 years ago.

More water, better air.

Forests help conserve water. In fact, three-fourths of America's freshwater supply comes from a third of her land — the forest lands.

Tree limbs, leaves and mulch help save water by slowing down the runoff of rain. This also checks erosion.

Another good thing about trees. They increase the supply of available oxygen — if they're *growing* trees. (Old trees actually use up as much oxygen as they give off.) The fact is, an average acre of vigorously growing trees can breathe in 5 to 6 tons of carbon dioxide and breathe out 4 tons of fresh oxygen every year.

Take a deep breath. Today, International Paper is reforesting its lands with five trees for every one it harvests.

A haven for Man.

We believe our forests should also be used for Man's enjoyment. Last year, over 2,000,000 people enjoyed some form of recreation on our lands.

We allow hunting and fishing on just about all of our timberlands.

We open our woods to everyone whenever we can — hikers, campers, bike riders. We even have areas with boat-launching ramps, picnic sites, and, in some cases, nature trails.

Getting the greatest use from our forests. Another example of International Paper's responsiveness to a fast-changing world.

INTERNATIONAL PAPER COMPANY

220 EAST 42ND STREET NEW YORK, NEW YORK 10017

Another misconception corrected.

To show what the company is doing for the future:

**Coal: America's
most plentiful fuel
. . . for the past ten years Exxon
affiliates have been carrying out an active program
of coal explorations and development** *[Exxon]*

*An institutional
advertisement
seeks to enhance esteem
for the company.*

The growing food problem.
What we're doing about it:

Much of the world lives on corn, soybeans and rice.

Trouble is, there just isn't enough to go around.

What can we do?

Monsanto has many ways to help produce more food per acre and more food per harvest. One way is called Lasso® herbicide, a weed control product that can help increase corn and soybean yields.

In response to the needs of rice-producing nations, we have developed Machete® herbicide for sale outside the United States. It works to increase the production of rice by reducing weed competition.

Naturally, there are many customers for products like these.

And because there are, it not only means greater crop yields, but more manufacturing plants that we're building all over the world to meet this growing need. On Lasso alone, we're working to increase world-wide production by 50%.

Because we want the world to reap the benefits of products that come from **Monsanto
the science
company.**

FREE!

Shell Answer Books have facts that can help you save driving dollars. And help keep you safer on the highway.

Get detailed information on buying and selling cars, keeping a car running for 100,000 miles, cutting your gasoline budget, and more. Free in Shell Answer Books.

They're full-color and easy-to-read. And they're just the right size to store in your glove compartment for easy reference.

Pick up Answer Books free from participating Shell stations or mail in the coupon.

1. The Early Warning Book. Learn how to spot some car problems before they cost you big money.

2. The Breakdown Book. This survival manual for car trouble on the road may come in handy some night when you need help.

3. The Gasoline Mileage Book. Pick up test-proven ways to save gasoline when you buy, drive, and take care of your car.

4. The Car Buying and Selling Book. Eleven things you should know before you make another new or used car deal.

5. The 100,000 Mile Book. Can your car make it? Six veteran mechanics share their tips on stretching the life of your car.

6. The Rush Hour Book. How some people can save up to $600 a year just by sharing their daily ride to work. And how much you can save.

Just Published!

Book #7 The Driving Emergency Book. How to react to seven dangerous surprises when you're behind the wheel and seconds count.

Shell Answer Books available for groups

You can get Answer Books for a drivers' education class, company safety department, or other organization. They're free in reasonable quantities.

A useful, free service, offered in an institutional ad, can create good will.

No lecture. No preaching. No, none of that.

Here are facts about drug laws & the system of justice overseas.

If you're traveling to Europe, the Middle East or south of our own border, here are some facts. Because a lot of people have funny ideas about foreign drug laws and justice.

Maybe you've heard possession is okay in some countries. That's wrong. Or maybe you've heard the laws aren't enforced like they are here. That's wrong, too. Really wrong.

The truth is their drug laws are tough. And they enforce them. To the letter.

Mexico, for example, demands a two to nine year sentence for possession of anything. Carrying stuff in or out of the country will put you in jail for six to fifteen years.

There's a 24 year old girl from the United States sitting in a jail outside of Rome right

now. She'll be there for six to ten months waiting for a trial. And after that she can get up to eight years.

In Spain, after you've been sentenced, you can't take your case to a higher court. You're all through. And nobody can get you out.

Those are facts. And there's no way around them. That's why over 900 Americans

are doing time in foreign jails.

Check the countries you'll be visiting. One fact will come through. Loud and clear.

When you're busted for drugs over there, you're in for the hassle of your life.

Mexico.	Sweden.	Japan.	Denmark.	Bahamas.
Possession, 2 to 9 years plus fine. Trafficking, 3 to 10 years plus fine. Illegal import or export of drugs, 6 to 15 years plus fine. Persons arrested on drug charges can expect a minimum of 6 to 12 months pre-trial confinement. U. S. Embassy: Co...	Possession or sale, up to 10 months and permanent expulsion from the country. U. S. Embassy: Strandvagen 101 S— ckholm, Sweden 63/05/20	Possession, pre-trial detention, suspended sentence and expulsion. Trafficking, maximum 5 years. U. S. Embassy: 10-5 Akasaka 1-Chrome Minato-Ku, Tokyo Tel. 583-7141	Possession, fine and detention up to 2 years. U. S. Embassy: Dag Hammarskjolds Alle 24 Copenhagen, Denmark Tel. TR 4505	Possession, 3 months to 1 year. U. S. Embassy: Adderly Building Nassau, Bahamas Tel. 21181

...ce.	Lebanon.	Turkey.	Canada.
...imum 2 years ...g, maximum ...hin's Blvd.	Possession, 1 to 3 years ...g. Trafficking, ... U. S. Embassy: Corniche at Kue Ain Mreisseh, Beirut, Tel. 240-800	Possession, 3 to 5 years. ...ears to life.	Possession, jail sentence and expulsion. Trafficking, minimum 7 years, maximum life. U. S. Embassy: ...Street

---

What About Me?

While you're opening your doors, Mr. and Mrs. America, to thousands of refugees from overseas . . . DID YOU KNOW—

*American Indian children like me are the hungriest of all your youngsters.
*We have the highest number of school dropouts.
*Our teenagers commit suicide at five times the national teenage average.

May I remind you that while you are sending huge sums of money for merciful relief to other countries . . .

*Your American Indian babies are the sickest in the nation.
*Our parents are the poorest and suffer the greatest unemployment.
*We live in the worst houses of all your citizens (some even live in old car bodies, caves, and abandoned shacks).
*Children like me suffer most and have the highest death rate.

Since these tragic facts are TRUE — while you're celebrating America's bicentennial year and being grateful for this country's blessings . . . could you find room in your heart to help a "native" American Indian child like me have a decent chance at life, too?

Mind you, we're not complaining because others are helped. But we do yearn for at least a reasonable share of

what this great country provides for its other children.

Remember, we loved this country long before 1776 or the Declaration of Independence. Our heritage stretches back thousands of years before Columbus, the Mayflower or Plymouth Rock.

WHAT ABOUT ME, MR. AND MRS. AMERICA! Will you love me and help me? Children like me are desperately hanging on the lowest rung of America's great ladder of hope. Won't you please reach down from where you are on the ladder and lift me a little closer to your heart?

*****

You can help a deserving, but needy American Indian child to a brighter future by sponsoring that child during this bicentennial year. Your sponsorship will provide love and concern which can be demonstrated in a most practical way by helping the child have healthy surroundings, medical care, shoes and warm clothing and religious strength and opportunity.

As the sponsor of an Indian child, you may exchange letters, snapshots and small gifts. Your child will know who you are, and you will receive a recent photo and history of your child. Most important, you will help your sponsored child realize and believe his own world can be changed and made better. The need is urgent and the cost is just pennies a day. Please write today.

Write to: HELP CHILDREN OF THE AMERICAS
  ℅ World Changers, International
  314 West Second Street, Tulsa, Oklahoma 74103
  Rev. Jonas Partridge, Field Director

(All gifts are tax deductible)

I wish to sponsor a needy American Indian child. Choose the ☐ boy ☐ girl who needs me the most. I will send $15 a month to sponsor this child.

I enclose $ _____ for _____ months.

I would like to contribute $ _____ to the work of World Changers.

☐ I'm interested. Please send more information.

Name _____

Address _____

City _____ Zip _____

State _____

Annual report and audit statement available on request.

Most young car thieves start your car the same way you do.

(with your keys)

Half the cars stolen last year had the keys left in the ignition. And more than half the car thieves were kids under 18. You don't have to be an "old pro" to steal a car . . . when the keys are in it.

Young car thieves need your help to steal your car. Don't give it to them.

LOCK YOUR CAR. TAKE YOUR KEYS.

Advertising contributed for the public good.

A series of ads by not-for-profit organizations.

Alerting the public to a problem.   Sometimes an industry acts through its trade association to deliver a message like this:

**The natural gas
   shortage is critical
   to you, your job,
   your way of life**   [*American Gas Association*]

**If they break up the oil companies
      You'll pay through the hose**   [*Texaco*]

To render an out-and-out public service:

**Try my do-it-yourself car check
   2 out of 3 drivers who did found dangerous
   or expensive problems in the making
   [*followed by a long explanatory ad*]** [*Shell Oil*]

Many millions of dollars are spent by corporations in sponsoring public television programs for entertainment or enlightenment or other public service projects. The only mention the company gets is its name as sponsor. The purpose: to be regarded favorably by the public.

Supporting not-for-profit and public interest causes. The plaintive cry that comes from many charitable institutions and those dedicated to medical research is, "Please help us to help the people who need our help." What these organizations increasingly need in order to operate is money. They use advertising extensively to tell of their work and their needs. Advertising is also used to advance matters of public interest, such as environmental protection, consumer education, civic affairs, health education, political causes. It is the *objective*, not the technique, that makes the difference between advertising not-for-profit enterprises and profit-oriented ones. Techniques from commercial advertising are adapted to not-for-profit causes.

In fact, the institution which is responsible for the largest expenditure in not-for-profit advertising (aside from the U.S. government) is The Advertising Council, a tripartite organization of advertising agencies, media, and advertisers. The advertising agencies contribute manpower to create ads, the media donate time and space, and advertisers donate the time of people who manage the campaigns. You have seen them:

High blood pressure—treat it and live.

Prevent Child Abuse

Let's stop handicapping the handicapped

Help show a cow a city kid.

An advertiser generates good will by donating this appeal from a not-for-profit institution.

Reduce teen-age car thefts

Food is something more than something to eat

The American economic system—your part in it.

Since 1942 over $7 billion has been donated by The Advertising Council to such causes. In addition, many business firms will underwrite advertising of a specific cause. They help the cause and spread goodwill for themselves.

QUESTIONS

1. Under what conditions might an advertiser address his or her campaign to more than one purpose?

2. In an advertising campaign designed to increase the frequency of use of a product, are there any potential dangers from an ethical point of view (for example, getting the consumer to use more of a product than is necessary or even good for the person)? Where does one draw the line between what is good for the advertiser and what is good for the consumer—or isn't such a line needed? Is what is good for one necessarily good for the other?

3. "Every new use of a product represents a new market." Explain, with special reference to the meaning of this statement for advertising.

4. If you were an advertiser with a large line of products and you were launching a new one, to which audience would you chiefly address your advertising?

5. What are the special problems associated with an advertising campaign for adding a new product to a well-known line? What is the so-called carry-over effect and how does it work?

6. The road to attracting a new generation to a product while still holding on to the long-time older customers is fraught with potential hazards. What are these hazards and how can they be dealt with?

7. When should the advertiser create a campaign to reinforce credibility of important claims?

8. Can a special promotion—say, a special inducement in the form of a free premium that the consumer receives by mailing in a proof-of-purchase label—serve as a substitute for advertising that might be done during the period of the promotion? Why or why not?

9. Can all product disadvantages be turned into advantages? If not, how should the marketer deal with such a situation?

10. What guidelines would you set to help an advertiser determine when it is time to direct advertising toward dispelling a misconception? Is it ever too early to do so? Too late?

11. Identify the conditions under which "institutional advertising" is appropriate. Can such advertising take the place of product advertising?

12. What are the major differences between commercial advertising (that done by

profit-seeking organizations) and advertising for not-for-profit or public interest causes? Is there need for different techniques in the two types of advertising?

13. Would you agree or disagree with those who contend that the best way to reverse a declining sales trend is to increase the advertising expenditure for the product? Why?

14. Advertising campaigns are designed to meet many different marketing problems. There is a great deal of skill in recognizing the problem and in creating a campaign with clearly defined purpose to overcome that problem. With this in mind, collect or cite two examples of advertising campaigns for each of the following purposes:

▲ Increase the frequency of use of a product

▲ Increase the variety of uses of a product

▲ Add a new product to a well-known line

▲ Reinforce credibility of important claims

▲ Launch a special promotional campaign

▲ Turn a disadvantage into an advantage

▲ Dispel a misconception

▲ Enhance the image of a company

▲ Gain support for not-for-profit and public interest causes

READING SUGGESTIONS

BLOOM, PAUL N., and PHILIP KOTLER, ''Strategies for High Market-share Companies,'' *Harvard Business Review* (November 1975), 63–72.

DALING, H. L., ''How Companies Are Using Corporate Advertising,'' *Public Relations Journal* (November 1975), 26–29.

DEWEY, GEORGE W., ''Advertising Is the Best Management Tool for Creating Product Preference,'' *Industrial Marketing* (August 1975), 48 ff.

DOYLE, PETER, and IAN FENWICK, ''Planning and Estimation in Advertising,'' *Journal of Marketing Research* (February 1975), 1–6.

FINN, R. H., ''Analyzing a Marketing Strategy,'' *California Management Review* (September 1975), 84–86.

GERHOLD, PAUL E. J., ''How Advertising Works,'' *Handbook of Advertising Management*, Roger Barton, ed. New York: McGraw-Hill, 1970.

''How TV Helps Corporate Giants Enhance Their Public Images,'' *Broadcasting* (November 24, 1975), 39–41.

KINDRE, THOMAS A., and PHILIP W. CALLANAN, ''Facing the Issues: Corporate Advertising's Greatest Challenge,'' *Public Relations Journal* (November 1973), 6–8.

LANE, STUART, ''Should Ads Promote Moral Values?'' *Advertising Age* (March 10, 1975), 15.

MAHANY, EUGENE, ''Boost Your Image Promoting Good Causes,'' *Advertising Age* (November 11, 1974), 46.

MARGULIES, WALTER, ''Brand Marketing Power: How to Differentiate Your Product From Competitors,'' *Advertising Age* (September 6, 1976), 45 ff.

PERRY, MICHAEL, DOV IZRAELI, and PERRY ARNON, ''Image Change as a Result of Advertising,'' *Journal of Advertising Research* (February 1976), 45–50.

5

Target Marketing

Procter & Gamble, long known for marketing capabilities in detergents and food products, entered the very competitive paper products field in the late 1950s. By the early 1970s, P&G's Bounty paper towels and Charmin toilet tissue were market leaders, each enjoying approximately a 20 percent market share in its respective field. At the same time, Pampers disposable diapers had captured nearly 75 percent of the market for disposable diapers.

P&G's ability to market new products effectively to the housewife was, as it had been in the past, a dominant factor in its success in the paper products market. The company clearly demonstrated its ability in creating products for a market and in creating markets for a product. This *target marketing* approach to advertising is the subject of this chapter.

What is a product?

To those who are buying it, a product is much more than a physical object. It represents a bundle of satisfactions. A motorcycle may be for getting a man to work. It may be a way of showing how adventurous he is. Functional and psychological satisfactions combine to make the "total" product, which is what the consumer really buys. Different people have different ideas about the satisfactions that are important to them when they consider a product. Products are designed with satisfactions to match the interests of a particular group of consumers. That is why every car company makes a wide range of cars, each with many variations. Some people may want a sporty car to establish their status; others may want a family car. Some want transportation at the lowest possible cost; others want luxury driving, regardless of cost. (Consider the advertising for the expensive BMW 3.0 Si car, which is "For those who deny themselves nothing.") Within the product class of cameras, there is equipment that is simple to operate and geared to nonexperts, and there is also sophisticated, control laden equipment for the serious photographer. (Note that cameras are not strictly divided by price, since some simple equipment can be more expensive than some of the complex designs.)

Three groups of buyers of watches can be classified on the basis of values each seeks from the product.

1. People who want to pay the lowest possible price for any watch that works reasonably well. If the watch fails after six months or a year, they will throw it out and replace it.

2. People who value watches for their long life, good workmanship, good material, and good styling. They are willing to pay for these product qualities.

3. People who look not only for useful product features but also for meaningful emotional qualities. The most important consideration in this segment is that the watch should suitably symbolize an important occasion. Consequently, fine styling, a well-known brand name, the recommendation of the jeweler, and a gold or diamond case are highly valued.[*]

When we look at a set of golf clubs in a fine bag, we do not see just a leather receptacle holding golf clubs. We try to picture the kind of person using the clubs and the persons with whom he or she might be playing. Target marketing means focusing on groups of people who seek similar satisfactions from life and from a product.

Changing product styles.   Few products are static in the wake of product development. For generations after the fountain pen had become a standard writing instrument, no up-and-coming young man would be without his Waterman pen. But after World War II, a new writing marvel appeared—the ballpoint pen, which was advertised as a pen that would write under water (even though no one explained why you should want to write under water). People stood in line to buy them at five dollars. By the 1960s, prices of ballpoint pens had come way down, and they were being sold more like long-lasting pencils than as pens. Meanwhile, fountain pens had entered a new life; they were offered as luxury items, often in gold and set in expensive desk stands, providing a set of consumer satisfactions different from those of the ballpoints. And while all this was happening, the fiber-tip pen came onto the scene and in the 1970s had achieved a substantial share of the writing instrument market. A pen is not just a pen; markets change with the product, and products change with the market.

We view a market as a group of people who 1) can be identified by some common characteristic, interest, or problem; 2) could use our product to advantage; 3) could afford to buy it; and 4) can be reached through some medium. Examples

What is a market?

[*] Daniel Yankelovich, "New Criteria for Market Segmentation," *Harvard Business Review* (March-April, 1964), 133.

Less than 240 calories with everything from sip to crunch.

That's Kellogg's® Special K® Breakfast.
A little variety, with less than 240 calories,
99% fat-free and 100% delicious.
Get your weight control program
off to a smart start every day
with Kellogg's Special K Breakfast.

The Special K Breakfast

4 oz. orange (or tomato)
    juice
1½ cups (1 oz.) Special K
    high-protein cereal
1 teaspoon sugar
4 oz. skim milk
Black coffee or tea
(less than 240 calories)

of potential markets: tennis players, mothers with young children, denture wearers, coin collectors, weight watchers, newly marrieds, physicians, outdoor sports fans, do-it-yourselfers.

The *majority fallacy* is a term applied to the assumption once frequently made that every product should be aimed at, and acceptable to, a majority of all consumers. Kuehn and Day have described how successive brands all aimed at a majority of a given market will tend to have rather similar characteristics and will neglect an opportunity to serve consumer minorities. They offer an illustration from the field of chocolate cake mixes. Good-sized minorities would make a light chocolate cake or a very dark chocolate cake, rather than a medium chocolate cake, which is the majority's choice. So while several initial entrants into the field would do best to market a medium chocolate mix to appeal to the broadest group of consumers, later entrants might gain a larger market share by supplying the minorities with their preferences.°

We will pursue the question of defining a market throughout the book. Suffice to say at this point that a market is a group of potential purchasers of our product.

What is the competition?

We speak of competition in the broadest sense, to include all forces that inhibit the sales of a product. The inhibiting forces may be products in the same subclass as your product, or in the same product class, or another product beyond your product's class. Or the forces may not be directly related to a product.

Does the 10-speed bicycle (subclass) compete primarily with 5-, 3-, or single-speed bicycles (product class) or with motorbikes (beyond product class)?

Does instant iced tea compete with non-instant iced tea, iced coffee, or soda pop? With hot tea or coffee? With fruit drinks or milk? With beer? With alcoholic beverages? Or with refreshment generally?

Does an electric shaver compete with other brands of electric shavers or, as a gift item, with pocket calculators?

The competitive array can widen even further as the basic price of the product increases. For example, in terms of the suburbanite's family budget, the real competition for a brand of riding mower (garden tractor) may *not* be other brands. Rather, for such a purchase involving over $1,500 for some mowers, the competition could be central air conditioning, a family vacation, new living room furniture, or an in-ground swimming pool. Or leave the money in the bank.

The immediate competition for a product already on the market is that of other products in its class. How does this product compare with others in differentials? In total sales? In share of the market? In the sales of this particular brand? What do consumers like and dislike about the products being offered, including the one under consideration?

°Alfred A. Kuehn and Ralph A. Day, "Strategy of Product Quality," *Harvard Business Review* (November-December 1962), 100 ff.

Market segmentation

Market segmentation means dividing a total market of consumers into groups with similar life-styles, making them a market for products serving their special needs. The fact that a market is segmented does not preclude it from being or becoming a large market.

Speaking about market segmentation, Kotler said:

> Market segmentation . . . starts not with distinguishing product possibilities, but rather with distinguishing customer groups. Market segmentation is the subdividing of a market into distinct subsets of customers, where any subset may conceivably be selected as a market target to be reached with a distinct marketing mix. The power of this concept is that in an age of intense competition for the mass market, individual sellers may prosper through developing brands for specific market segments whose needs are imperfectly satisfied by the mass-market offerings.[*]

A market can also be segmented geographically, as the accompanying table shows.

Product usage profiles (100 = average)

Product	High usage score	Low usage score
Yogurt	142 in the Southwest	68 in the Southeast
Baby food	130 in the Southwest	75 in New England
Frosting mix	116 in East-central states	75 in New England
Dips ready to serve	136 in East-central states	80 on Pacific Coast
Tuna fish	108 in New England	85 in the Southeast
Instant or freeze-dried coffee	121 in New England	84 in Southwest
Seasonings and spices	108 in Pacific states	89 in East-central

Reprinted from *Progressive Grocer*, July 1976.

Positioning

Positioning is another term for fitting a product into the life-style of the buyer. It refers to ways of segmenting a market by either or both of two ways:

▲ Creating a product to meet the needs of a specialized group.
▲ Picking the appeal of an existing product to meet the needs of a specialized group.

A product can hold different positions at the same time. Arm & Hammer baking soda is featured as a refrigerator deodorizer, an antacid, and a skin cleaner while bathing, without losing its original market as a cooking ingredient.

Creating a product for selective markets.   One of the principal ways that marketers attract a focused interest group is through variations in the conventional product. These variations are based on the idea that there exists a large enough submarket with an interest in a particular product offering.

[*] Philip Kotler, *Marketing Management: Analysis, Planning, and Control,* 3rd ed. (Englewood Cliffs, N. J.: Prentice-Hall, 1976), p. 144.

To meet the needs of the small household, as well as the "single-serving" market, foods are packed in small-sized packages. Lipton's Cup-a-Soup is soup by the single serving, four individual servings in each box; similarly, Quaker oatmeal is packed in single serving units, ten one-ounce packets in each box. Stouffer's frozen pies are packaged for the single person.

Other products are also designed to meet the needs of particular market segments. We have Honda motorcycles, whose advertising features the roadbike as "the second car for the single man." General Electric offers its Toast-R-Oven for the family that wants a second oven that "handles the small cooking jobs your big oven's too big for." Mazola Corn Oil advertising is aimed at those "concerned about cholesterol and your family's eating habits" and goes on to say "here's something you may want to discuss with your doctor," Wrigley's offers Freedent chewing gum specially for denture wearers. And there is much positioning in the toothpaste product category: Crest and Colgate, for example, are formulated to prevent cavities; Ultra-Brite and Close-up, primarily to help make teeth look brighter; Aim, to taste better to get children to brush longer and therefore acquire better brushing habits.

Positioning the product by appeal.   Sometimes you can advantageously position a product or reposition it just by changing the advertising appeal, without making any physical changes in the product.

In the mid-1960s, Sterling Drug's Lehn & Fink division considered Lysol a dying brand. The disinfectant's sales were falling. Editorial, scare advertising ("Warning: Help protect babies and new mothers against dreaded staph germs") failed to stop the decline, possibly even accelerated it. So Lehn & Fink stopped advertising, and sales increased.

Until that time, Lysol's distribution was primarily through drugstores. Yet, women were buying disinfectant cleansers in grocery stores. Research revealed that about 60 percent of homes had the product, brought into the home by new mothers and used while the children were young, but it collected dust on the shelf thereafter because the mothers became less worried about germs and stopped using the product.

By *repositioning* the Lysol as a *household cleanser* with germ-killing and odor-killing powers, *not* merely a nursery disinfectant, consumer sales response was immediate. Lysol is now a more than $20 million business, with well over 50 percent market share.

On the other hand, Clorox, long known as a liquid bleach, has been repositioned as also a disinfectant, with appeals that "you can't buy a more effective disinfectant than Clorox," and "Clorox does more than the wash." Same product, new appeals.

Johnson's Baby Oil, always known as an oil for baby's skin, is advertised also as a general cosmetic and skin care product for women, with appeals such as "It didn't start out to be an eye make-up remover, but it sure makes a great eye make-up remover."

Salada Tea has been positioned to reach coffee drinkers, as "The Coffee-Drinker's Tea." Noxzema was repositioned from a skin medication to a beauty treatment. California raisins have been repositioned to a fruit snack that is nutritionally good for children, as a substitute for candy, which is bad for their teeth.

The common thread in the foregoing examples is that no physical changes were made in the product—only different appeals were used. This is the basis for positioning by choice of appeal.

A good positioning headline.

The second car for the single man.

There are some very sound reasons for having a Honda road bike as your second car.

Great gas mileage from the famous, dependable Honda four-stroke engine.

Easy handling in traffic to help you beat the crowd to work.

The ability to park just about anywhere.

So much for the good sound reasoning that appeals to your practical side. But maybe the best reasons for owning a Honda are those that appeal to your impractical side. That part of you that always wants to get away, explore new places, experience new things.

On a weekend, a Honda becomes the ultimate sports car. Top down. Wind in your face. New country before you. The open road's never been so open.

Why go with a Honda instead of some other motorcycle?

Because no one else offers you such a choice of models. There's sure to be a Honda just right for you.

Because no one else has the Honda reputation for quality and dependability. That's probably why more people buy more Hondas than any other motorcycle.

And because near you, almost anywhere you are in the United States, there's a full-service Honda dealer. If you're in the market for a second car, drop in and see what he has to offer.

Discover why a Honda is the perfect economy car, sports car, second car...for the single man in all of us.

HONDA
Good things happen on a Honda.

Sweets make her happy. But too many sweets make you unhappy. There's one to please you both. To her it's candy. To you it's fruit. Raisins from California. Happiness by the handful.

Raisins now compete with candy for the children's trade.

How to approach a positioning problem. Trout and Ries say that the advertiser who is thinking about positioning should ask himself the following questions:

1. What position, if any, do we already own in the prospect's mind?
2. What position do we want to own?
3. What companies must be outgunned if we are to establish that position?
4. Do we have enough marketing money to occupy and hold the position?
5. Do we have the guts to stick with one consistent positioning concept?
6. Does our creative approach match our positioning strategy?°

° Jack Trout and Al Ries, *The Positioning Era* (New York: Ries Cappiello Colwell, Inc., 1972), pp. 38–41.

Mailgram is the country's first electronic mail. It grew out of the attempt to make communicating by mail speedier and more efficient. A message is given by telephone (or Telex, TWX, magnetic tape, computer, communicating typewriter or CRT terminal) to a Western Union operator and, via computer and even satellite, it is relayed to the post office anywhere in the country nearest the addressee. A regular letter carrier delivers it the next day or even the same day.

In deciding how to position Mailgram, an analysis was based on the foregoing Trout and Ries six-stage approach to positioning. The analysis asked and answered these questions.

What position do we own?   Western Union stood for the "yellow message." The telegram was firmly embedded in the minds of customers and prospects.

What position do we want?   Two possibilities arose here. Mailgram could relate to the mail or to the telegram. Both positions were explored.

Letter positioning: the theme was "Mailgram, a new high-speed service for important messages" (high-speed letter).

Telegram positioning: the theme was "Mailgram—impact of a telegram at a fraction of the cost" (low-cost telegram).

To determine which was better (the telegram or letter positioning) Western Union began a market test of both campaigns in January 1974. Six Mailgram test cities were used: Chicago and Houston, both high spending, telegram positioning markets; Philadelphia and San Francisco, both low spending, telegram positioning markets; Boston, a high spending, letter positioning market; Los Angeles, a low spending, letter positioning market. (*High* and *low spending* refer to the relative amount of dollars spent on advertising.) *Telegram positioning* was the advertising theme that related Mailgram to the "gram" portion of its name and emphasized the impact value traditionally associated with a telegram. *Letter positioning* was the advertising theme that related Mailgram to the mail or letter portion of its name. It stressed the high-speed, overnight delivery aspect of the service. The table on p. 86 summarizes the test framework.

Two test ads compare the Mailgram and the telegram—their relative speed and cost.

Courtesy Western Union.
Advertisng agency: Ries,
Cappiello, Colwell, Inc.

Mailgram positioning test

High-spending budget		Low-spending budget	
Chicago and Houston	Relating Mailgram to telegram	Philadelphia and San Francisco	Relating Mailgram to telegram
Boston	Relating Mailgram to letter	Los Angeles	Relating Mailgram to letter

Both magazines and newspapers were used in the positioning test. On a national level, *Dun's, Fortune, Forbes,* and *Business Week* were the magazines used, while *The Wall Street Journal* was used for national newspaper advertising. On a market by market basis, the metro editions of *Time, Newsweek,* and *U.S. News & World Report* were used in Chicago, Houston, Boston, Philadelphia, San Francisco, and Los Angeles. Also, the following newspapers were incorporated into the media schedule: *Chicago Tribune, Houston Chronicle, Boston Globe, Philadelphia Bulletin, San Francisco Chronicle, Los Angeles Times.*

Awareness levels in test cities. To determine awareness, research was done by the Starch-Inra-Hooper organization, using random telephone interviews with prospects in each of the test markets. In the letter positioning cities, awareness (percentage of people who could correctly describe what Mailgram was) was unchanged, statistically. In the telegram positioning cities, awareness doubled, going from 23 percent to 47 percent. Therefore, the big winner was the telegram positioning.

Mailgram volume in test cities. As measured during the 13 weeks' advertised period and 8 weeks afterward, Mailgram volume in the letter positioning cities went from plus 55 percent (during the advertising) to plus 73 percent (after the advertising). In the telegram positioning cities, Mailgram volume went from plus 62 percent to plus 100 percent. The percentage gains refer to increases over a comparable period before advertising began. Again, the big winner was the telegram positioning. Both during and after the Mailgram advertising, telegram volume remained stable in the test cities, so there was no substitution effect, as often is the case when a new product has a strong relationship to an existing product.

Recommended Standard Breakdowns For Demographic Characteristics In Surveys of Consumer Media Audiences

I. DATA FOR HOUSEHOLDS:

	Minimum Basic Data	Additional Data Highly Desired
A. County Size: (see Note 1)	A County Size B County Size C County Size D County Size	

B. Geographic Area: (see Notes 2 & 3)	Metropolitan Area
	Non Metropolitan Area
	Farm
	Non Farm
		Urban
		Urbanized Areas
		  Central Cities
		  Urban fringe
		Other urban
		  Places of 10,000 or more
		  Places of 2,500 to 10,000
		Rural places of 1,000 to 2,500
		Other rural
		
		Metropolitan Area:
		  1,000,000 and over
		  500,000 - 999,999
		  250,000 - 499,999
		  100,000 - 249,999
		  50,000 - 99,999

C. Geographic Region: (see Notes 4 & 5)	New England Metro New York Mid Atlantic East Central Metro Chicago West Central South East South West Pacific	North East North Central South West
D. Ages of Children:	No Child Under 18 Youngest Child 6-17 Youngest Child Under 6	Youngest Child 12-17 Youngest Child 6-11 Youngest Child 2-5 Youngest Child under 2
E. Family Size:	1 or 2 members 3 or 4 members 5 or more members	
F. Family Income:	Under $5,000. $5,000 - 7,999. $8,000 - 9,999. Over $10,000.	Under $3,000. $ 3,000 - 4,999. $10,000 - 14,999. $15,000 - 24,999. $25,000 and over

G. Home Ownership:	Own home
	Rent home
		Residence Five Years Prior to Survey Date
		  Lived in same house
		  Lived in different house
		    In same county
		    In different county

H. Home Characteristic:	Single family dwelling unit Multiple family dwelling unit	
I. Race:		White Non-White
J. Household Possessions:		Data on household possessions or purchases will presumably be governed by the medium's particular selling needs.

II. DATA FOR INDIVIDUALS:

	Minimum Basic Data	Additional Data Highly Desired
A. Age:	Under 6 6-11 12-17 18-34 35-49 50-64 65 and over	18-24 25-34
B. Sex:	Male Female	
C. Education:	Grade school or less (grades 1-8) Some high school Graduated high school (grades 9-12) Some college Graduated college	
D. Marital Status:	Married Single Widowed Divorced	
E. Occupation:	Professional, Semi-Professional Proprietor, Manager, Official Clerical, Sales Craftsman, Foreman, Service Worker Operative, Non-Farm Laborer Farmer, Farm Laborer Retired Student Unemployed	
F. Individual Possessions:		Data on individual possessions or purchases will presumably be governed by the medium's particular selling needs.

III. DATA FOR HOUSEHOLD HEADS:

	Minimum Basic Data	Additional Data Highly Desired
A. Sex:	Male Female	
B. Age:	34 and younger 35-49 50-64 65 and older	18-24 25-34
C. Education:	Grade school or less (grades 1-8) Some high school Graduated high school (grades 9-12) Some college Graduated college	
D. Occupation:	Professional, Semi-Professional Proprietor, Manager, Official Clerical, Sales Craftsman, Foreman, Service Worker Operative, Non-Farm Laborer Farmer, Farm Laborer Retired Student Unemployed	

IV. DATA FOR HOUSEWIVES:

	Minimum Basic Data	Additional Data Highly Desired
A. Age:	34 and younger 35-49 50-64 65 and over	18-24 25-34
B. Education:	Grade school or less (grades 1-8) Some high school Graduated high school (grades 9-12) Some college Graduated college	

C. Employment:	Not employed outside home
	Employed outside home
	  Employed Full Time (30 hours or more per week)
	  Employed Part Time (Less than 30 hours per week)	

Demographic breakdowns recommended by American Association of Advertising Agencies, Inc.

O-Vac is trying to reach males 35–49; while Rosarita Mexican Foods is interested in women 25–49. Each advertiser will seek the station reaching the sex and age bracket desired. These are standard classifications. As a product gets more costly, with a more complex demographic profile (cars, for instance), you may wish to describe not only the age bracket but the income bracket and size of the family unit of the people you are trying to reach. You may even need to know the psychographic or personality characteristics of the buyer. The key point is to have clear in your mind a profile that describes potential buyers of your product.

Heavy users.   For any product, a small percentage of users are responsible for a disproportionately large share of the product's sale. These are the *heavy users.* In the accompanying table, for example, we find that 5.6 percent of aspirin users are responsible for 29.7 percent of sales, and 17.9 percent of eye drop buyers are responsible for 55.3 percent of sales. Obviously, in defining your market it is important to determine who the heavy users are and to identify their similarities, which would define your marketing goals. Often this can be done through the nature of the appeals you use in your copy.

Portion of heavy users of ten drug products *(partial list)*

	Heavy users %	usage %		Heavy users %	usage %
Adhesive bandages			*Eye drops*		
Adult	21.2	57.3	Adult	17.9	55.3
Male	20.4	55.5	Male	11.7	43.7
Female	22.0	58.8	Female	21.9	60.9
Aspirin, headache or pain-relieving tablets			*Indigestion or upset stomach remedies*		
Adult	5.6	29.7	Adult	8.9	39.0
Male	4.2	24.3	Male	12.2	46.7
Female	6.8	33.3	Female	6.1	30.2
Cold/flu or allergy tablets			*Laxatives*		
Adult	10.1	44.1	Adult	7.3	42.5
Male	9.7	44.8	Male	6.9	41.5
Female	10.4	43.6	Female	7.5	43.0
Cough drops			*Medicated throat lozenges*		
Adult	39.1	78.6	Adult	30.2	74.9
Male	36.0	74.0	Male	30.7	75.5
Female	41.5	81.3	Female	29.9	74.4
Cough syrup			*Nasal sprays*		
Adult	32.9	76.1	Adult	18.5	58.2
Male	30.8	74.9	Male	20.3	62.0
Female	34.7	77.0	Female	16.8	54.2

Courtesy: W. R. Simmons & Associates Research, Inc.

Driving on a highway running past modest-sized backyards of middle-class homes, one is struck first by their similarity. But a longer look is more illuminating, for behind the similarity lie differences that reflect the interests, personalities, and family situations of those who live in the homes. One backyard has been transformed into a carefully manicured garden. Another includes some shrubs and bushes, but most of the yard serves as a relaxation area, with outdoor barbecue equipment and the like. A third yard is almost entirely a playground, with swings, trapezes, and slides. A swimming pool occupies almost all the space in another yard. Still another has simply been allowed to go to seed and is overgrown and untended by its obviously indoor-oriented owners.

If you wanted to advertise to this community, you would be speaking to people with different interests, different tastes. Between two groups of buyers who have the same demographic characteristics, there may still be a big difference in the nature and extent of their purchases. This fact has led to an inquiry beyond demographics into psychographics, to try to explain the significance of such differences. According to Demby:

> —psychographics seeks to describe the human characteristics of consumers that may have a bearing on their response to products, packaging, advertising and public relations efforts. Such variables may span a spectrum from self-concept and life-style to attitudes, interests and opinions, as well as perceptions of product attributes.°

People may have demographic similarities but yet perceive different benefits and satisfactions from the same product, whether it be clothing, magazines, ski resorts, or carry-out fried chicken. These variations are brought to bear in the purchase decision. The advertiser tries to reach those groups whose psychographic characteristics make them likely prospects for certain products, and to address each such group with ads appealing particularly to it. To say someone is a *single person* is talking demographics; to say a person is a *swinging single*— that's psychographics.

The Bermuda Department of Tourism used psychographics to build a tourism campaign directed at 1) "relaxers" (25 percent of those taking a vacation), the people who want to rest, loaf, read and unwind; 2) "sun and fun people" (23 percent), those who sun, swim, and play tennis by day and dress up and go out in the evening; 3) "social activists" (15 percent), primarily interested in people, gambling casinos, night life, sightseeing, and shopping; 4) "tourists" (19 percent), the sightseers, island hoppers, shoppers who want new faces and places on each vacation instead of a suntan or night life; 5) "different/exotic vacationers" (19 percent), those who want a different experience each vacation and who prefer distinctly foreign places but feel the islands are suitable for a weekend.†

The advertisers who have long made use of psychographic thinking (without being aware of the term) are those in direct-response advertising who are always

° Emanuel Demby, "Psychographics and from Whence It Came," *Life Style and Psychographics*, William D. Wells, ed. (Chicago: American Marketing Association, 1974), p.13.

† "The Campaign That Psychographics Built," *Media Decisions* (April 1974), 64–65.

New from Campbell!

The same big Chunky Soup in single-serving size.

Now four of your favorite Chunky Soups come in new single-serving cans. Just right for the times when you (or anyone in your family) would like just one bowl of Chunky Beef, Chunky Sirloin Burger, Chunky Chicken or Chunky Vegetable. They're the same big Chunky Soups with chunk after chunk of meat and vegetables. But now you can get them in convenient, new single-serving cans, too—a hearty 10¾ ounces.

So chunky you'll be tempted to eat 'em with a fork.

(But use a spoon. You'll want to get every drop.)

Campbell's goes after the singles.

buying lists of prospects from each other. They buy book-club lists, not to sell more books, but to sell some other objects or magazines for a cultured class of people. Garden-club lists are used to sell objets d'art and other fine things for the home. Psychographics—studying the life-style of a person—sharpens the search for prospects beyond the demographic data. The media are then selected, and the advertising is then directed to that special target group.

Sources of product usage and demographic data

The syndicated research services.   Among the main sources of needed information about consumers are numerous syndicated research services, such as W.R. Simmons & Associates Research, Inc., and Target Group Index (TGI). Different services specialize in different types of information. Each publishes reports, which it sells as a service to subscribers. The various reports involve questions of what type of products people buy, which brands, who buys them, their demographic status, and their psychographic distinctions; how people react to products and to ads, their styles of buying, what media reach them. In the TV and radio field, the services report their estimates of how many TV households are listening to which programs on which stations. Among the uses of such data is to help the advertiser select the target market.

THE STORY BEHIND
the Lenox China campaign

Lenox Incorporated is a leading manufacturer of quality dinnerware, giftware, jewelry, and a broad line of other related products. The company's net sales volume is over $125 million per year.

In the 1880s, Walter Scott Lenox created Lenox China. By 1887 it was being marketed by the Ceramic Art Company of Trenton, New Jersey, and was the first American china to equal European porcelains. The name Lenox China was adopted as a company name in 1906. In 1917, President and Mrs. Wilson selected Lenox for the White House. Since then, two other services were also made for Presidents Roosevelt and Truman. In 1962, the Lenox Company developed a bone china, named Oxford, for people who preferred the pure white look over ivory. In 1965, Lenox began making and marketing Lenox Crystal. In 1973, they created an informal dinnerware and began marketing that under the name Temper-ware® by Lenox.

Lenox's traditional china business and related crystal and glassware lines account for about 40 percent of total company sales. Operating in a very competitive business, Lenox can attribute its success to its ability to define target markets and develop a media plan that effectively reaches that target audience. Lenox has done this for five of its product lines.

LENOX FINE CHINA

An ivory-colored china (as opposed to the pure white of bone china), it is selected by 5 out of 10 brides who register for fine china at department and jewelry store bridal gift registries. Of total china sales, the bridal market represents approximately two-thirds, the older woman constitutes the rest, although in recent years the "mature" market has started to grow. Of the 50 top-selling fine china patterns, 27 are Lenox patterns. Lenox has about a 55 percent share of this market.

Advertising strategy is to present Lenox in an atmosphere of prestige in a manner reflective of the quality of the china. Three basic campaigns are used. All ads are in color and are full pages or spreads (see color plates 6 and 7).

Pre-bridal (early through late teens). The use of *Seventeen* magazine is to help create brand awareness among teenage girls at a time when china is a low-interest product.

Bridal (18–24). Two magazines, *Brides* and *Modern Bride,* claim to reach 8 out of 10 first-time brides. Lenox advertises in every issue of these two magazines, as well as periodically in *Glamour* and *Mademoiselle.* The objective is to give all the reasons why the bride should settle for nothing less than the finest when she registers for her china pattern. The ads are double-page spreads. Left-hand pages are full photos of things such as elegant table settings, and right-hand pages have copy on what to look for when selecting fine china and crystal patterns (product, price, where to get more information).

Mature market (women 25–55). Mass magazines such as *Better Homes & Gardens, McCall's, Good Housekeeping, Ladies' Home Journal,* and specialty publications such as *Gourmet, House & Garden,* and *The New Yorker* are used to bring the Lenox quality image to couples who are ready to replace their dinnerware, add to it, or to buy fine china for the first time. The readers of these magazines are also, of course, wedding guests who buy gifts. The objective is to make Lenox synonymous with quality and prestige in the minds of homemakers.

LENOX GIFTWARE

A line of fine china gifts, with over 100 different items ranging in price from under $10 to $100, giftware is advertised to an even broader market than dinnerware, since just about anyone can afford a bud vase or candy dish. Magazines used are *Reader's Digest, Family Circle, Woman's Day,* and others. Ads are product-oriented, with names and prices indicated, but presented in a prestigious way.

LENOX CRYSTAL

The major promotion of crystal is achieved by incorporating it into the Lenox China advertising. Just about every Lenox national ad, including those for giftware, carries the signature "Lenox China and Crystal." In addition, ads on crystal only—in *Vogue, The New Yorker,* and *Gourmet*—reach a fairly sophisticated audience.

OXFORD BONE CHINA

Oxford is the third best-selling fine china (Lenox is #1, Royal Doulton, #2). It does not carry a Lenox identification, nor does the advertising mention the fact that it is made by the same craftsmen. Retail salespeople are aware of this, however, and are urged to use this information when talking to customers. Advertising of this brand is directed exclusively to the bridal market, using *Brides, Modern Bride, Glamour,* and *Mademoiselle* magazines.

TEMPER-WARE by LENOX

This is an informal dinnerware, introduced in 1973, because of the growth of more casual entertaining. In a few years, it became the best-selling informal dinnerware (of sets costing $40 or more for service of 8). Since Temper-Ware is priced equal to, or higher than, any of the competition, this is an unusually strong success story. (A service for 8 in 1976 was $275.) Magazines used include *Woman's Day, Good Housekeeping,* and *Better Homes & Gardens.*

Advertising for Lenox China
prepared by Chirurg & Cairns, Inc.

1. What is meant when a product is referred to as a "bundle of satisfactions"?

2. Discuss how the same product can have more than one set of values. Give several examples.

3. Elaborate on the connection between the product life cycle and advertising. Cite some examples.

4. Discuss fully the meaning of the term *market*. Give examples of markets.

5. Give an example of competition (a) within the same subclass, (b) within a product class, and (c) beyond the product class.

6. What is the basic premise of market segmentation? Discuss several examples.

7. What are the ways of achieving market segmentation?

8. What is the relationship between market segmentation and advertising?

9. What is meant by positioning a product? Give several examples.

10. Compare and contrast (a) positioning by creating a product to meet the needs of selective markets and (b) positioning by changing the advertising appeal without changing the physical product. Which is the better approach? The less risky approach? The more costly approach? Why? Is one approach generally more effective? Why?

11. For which questions would you use research in market segmentation and positioning?

12. Evaluate the Trout and Ries approach to positioning problems.

13. What are the questions that are answered by a market profile? By a buyer profile?

14. What are demographic data? Who gathers such data and how do advertisers use it?

15. Explain the significance of *heavy users*. Specifically, what value is served by data such as that compiled by Simmons on usage rates of different products by consumers?

16. Explain what is meant by *psychographics*. How can a knowledge of psychographics benefit the advertiser? Give some examples.

17. Why do you think it is important to define the target market in planning advertising?

READING SUGGESTIONS

BROWN, HERBERT E., and J. TAYLOR SIMS, "Market Segmentation, Product Differentiation, and Market Positioning as Alternative Marketing Strategies," *Marketing 1776–1976 and Beyond,* Kenneth L. Bernhardt, ed., Proceedings of the American Marketing Association, Series No. 39. Chicago:American Marketing Association, 1976, pp. 483–87.

DARDEN, WILLIAM R., and WILLIAM D. PERREAULT, JR., "Identifying Interurban Shoppers: Multiproduct Purchase Patterns and Segmentation Profiles," *Journal of Marketing Research* (February 1976), 51–60.

"Demographic Analysis Service Helps U.S. Business Discover Markets Thru Census Data," *Commerce Today* (February 1975), 17.

DHALLA, NARIMAN K., and WINSTON H. MAHATOO, "Expanding the Scope of Segmentation Research," *Journal of Marketing* (April 1976), 34–41.

HURTER, ARTHUR P., and TIMOTHY J. LOWE, "Generalized Market Area Problem," *Management Science* (June 1976), 1105–15.

MAGGARD, JOHN P, "Positioning Revisited," *Journal of Marketing* (January 1976), 63–66.

PERCY, LARRY, "How Market Segmentation Guides Advertising Strategy," *Journal of Advertising Research* (October 1976), 11–22.

PERNICA, JOSEPH, "Psychographics: What Can Go Wrong," *New Marketing for Social and Economic Progress and Marketing's Contributions to the Firm and to the Society,* Ronald, C. Curhan, ed., Combined Proceedings of the American Marketing Association, Series No. 36. Chicago: American Marketing Association, 1974, pp. 45–50.

PLUMMER, JOSEPH T., "Psychographics: What Can Go Right," *New Marketing for Social and Economic Progress and Marketing's Contributions to the Firm and to Society,* Ronald C. Curhan, ed., Combined Proceedings of the American Marketing Association, Series No. 36. Chicago: American Marketing Association, 1974, pp. 41–44.

SISSORS, JACK Z., "What Is a Market?" *Journal of Marketing* (July 1966), 17–21.

SMITH, ROBERT E., and ROBERT F. LUSCH, "How Advertising Can Position a Brand," *Journal of Advertising Research* (February 1976), 37–43.

TOLLEY, B. STUART, "Identify Users Through a Segmentation Study," *Journal of Marketing* (April 1975), 69–71.

TROUT, JACK, and AL RIES, *The Positioning Era.* New York: Ries Cappiello Colwell, 1973. This is the reprint of a series of articles that appeared in *Advertising Age* (April 24, May 1, and May 8, 1972).

WELLS, WILLIAM D., ed., *Life Style and Psychographics.* Chicago: American Marketing Association, 1974.

PART THREE

Media

6

Basic Media Strategy

When we talk about media strategy, we mean the overall media plan for implementing a company's marketing strategy. Many media are available for delivering the message: television, radio, newspapers, magazines, direct mail, outdoor signs, transit advertising. In each category we have hundreds, if not thousands, of individual media from which to select. This calls for a plan.

Advertising expense is the largest variable in marketing, and media represents by far the largest part of the total advertising budget. There can be a great difference in effectiveness per dollar spent between two media plans for the same product. The development of a media plan represents a composite of many factors, including the following questions to consider:

1. What is the marketing goal?
2. What is the nature of the copy?
3. How much money is available?
4. What are the chief characteristics of people in our target market?
5. Where is the product distributed?
6. Shall we stress reach, frequency, or continuity?
7. What is the best timing?
8. What is the competition doing?
9. Are there any special merchandising plans in the offing?
10. What combination of media is best?

1. What is the marketing goal?

What does the marketer wish to attain within a given period of time? The marketing goal can be expressed in dollar amount of sales, number of units sold, share of market, or share of mind (how many more people know about our product now than before we advertised?).

The type of message the advertising is to deliver may immediately suggest certain media and preclude others. If the advertisement is to show the beautiful design and color of drapery or floor covering, we immediately think of full-color pages in magazines or the color pages of a Sunday newspaper magazine supplement. If it is desirable to demonstrate something, television is usually the best medium. If there is a special coupon offer to introduce a new product, print media suggest themselves. If a supporting campaign features a slogan, trademark, or package, outdoor or bus advertising comes to mind. Not all products have such strong media predilections, but studying the copy for ideas about the best way to present the product may suggest the medium.

2. What is the nature of the copy?

The smaller the budget, the greater the need for resourcefulness. The small advertiser looks for media that are not commonly being used in the field. One looks for special space units. Another shops intensively for television and radio spots off prime time. Such resourcefulness is good at any level; it is particularly necessary for the small advertiser. (The term *small advertiser* means small in comparison with others in his field.) The larger the budget, the greater the risk in making decisions that entail large investments, and there is no escape from the financial day of reckoning. The first judgment to make in connection with a budget, therefore, is to see whether its size permits one to think in terms of the most costly media—television networks and magazine color pages, for example—assuming that one would want to consider them. Many advertisers hold that good intermedia planning calls for concentrating on one important medium, which becomes the *primary* medium. If competition makes it necessary to advertise more often, a *secondary* medium may be used too. A goal in selecting the secondary medium is to create an interplay with the primary medium that will enhance the impression made by each (referred to as the *synergistic effect,* or $2 + 2 = 5$).

3. How much money is available?

From the profile of people who represent the target market, we want to pick out the characteristic most relevant to the use of our product. People of different ages, life-styles, and incomes buy some products more than other people do: teen-agers buy cosmetics, singles consume small servings of canned foods, young mothers buy baby food, heads of growing families purchase new cars, elderly consumers look for denture cleaners, and sports enthusiasts want tennis rackets, fishing rods, or golf clubs. What type of media would most efficiently reach such people? At a later point we can review the class of media that reach our prime target audience and select the specific medium that best meets our other qualifications.

4. What are the chief characteristics of people in our target market?

Advertising is a part of a total marketing program that prescribes the areas in which the product is sold. We now seek to coordinate the circulation of the advertising with the geographical distribution or the special interests of the market. Four basic media plans are used: a *local* plan, a *regional* plan, a *national* plan, and a *selective* plan.

5. Where is the product distributed?

Local plan.   A local plan is used when the product is on sale only in one town or community and its immediate trading zone. When a new product is being introduced, when a product is being tested in different and distant markets, or when a manufacturer is building a business town by town, a local plan is appropriate. In these situations, the medium must be confined to the specific geographic area in which the manufacturer has distribution. This applies no matter which media are used.

Regional plan.   As the sales of a product spread to larger areas, the advertiser seeks to employ media that reach that region. He uses a regional plan, a local plan grown larger. The region may cover several adjoining markets or an entire state or several adjoining states. When the sale of a product varies with sectional differences in taste or local requirements, regional plans are used. More households buy tea in New England than in the Middle West. More blended whisky is sold in the Middle Atlantic states than on the Pacific Coast. Most low-calorie soft drinks are sold in the Northeast and East Central regions. When an advertiser's product is affected by such regional preferences, he will choose media with circulations in those territories. In addition to the media used in a local plan, regional editions of national magazines and regional network television and radio can often be used successfully.

National plan.   We now jump many millions of dollars ahead to the point at which the product is in widespread distribution all over the country, in every city, town, and hamlet—Coca-Cola, for example, or Colgate toothpaste or Chevrolet cars. Here the task is to reach many different buyers of our product all over the country at the lowest cost per thousand prospects (CPM), and we embark on a *national* media plan. We can now consider network television, network radio, and full-circulation national magazines, along with the nationally syndicated Sunday supplements. Newspaper, outdoor, and transit advertising are also possibilities.

Selective plan.   We now come to a fourth plan, based not on the geographical distribution of the product but on the special interest of the users of the product *wherever they may happen to be.* Boating, tennis, art, antiques, and other crafts and hobbies whose partisans may be scattered all over the country, are special interests. The problem in such an instance is not the cost per thousand of reaching people with these interests but how the greatest number of them can be reached. Most useful in reaching these people are magazines directed at specific markets (*Sports Illustrated, Photography Today, Field and Stream*), direct mail, special sections of Sunday newspapers devoted to these subjects, and selected radio and TV programs.

A selective plan is often combined with a geographical plan. If you wanted to reach all homeowners in a certain part of the country, you might use a sectional edition of a national shelter magazine. On the Pacific Coast, you could advertise in *Sunset* magazine. The local, sectional, and national plans, along with the selective plan, provide a good media framework within which to work.

Reach refers to the total number of people to whom you deliver a message; *frequency* to the number of times it is delivered within a given period (usually figured on a weekly basis for ease in schedule planning); *continuity* is the length of time a schedule runs. Only the biggest advertisers can afford all three at once, and even they seek to spread their money most efficiently.

6. Shall we stress reach, frequency, or continuity?

The advantage of going for reach as the prime goal is that you get a message before the greatest number of people. A disadvantage is that you may not have enough time to tell your full story.

If frequency matters most, you have to decide how often you want your message to be presented. How many times do you have to tell people your story to get them to act on it? We do not have enough scientific data to make any generalizations. Admittedly, you can reach a point with an audience when just retelling your story costs more than it is worth in terms of sales. But in mass media, the fifth impression on one person may be the first impression on someone else. By the law of averages, every time the advertisement appears, it reaches some people when they are ready to buy. Furthermore, it may reach some people who had not been interested in the product before.

The third ball in this juggling act is continuity. Among the clearest examples of those who make this the prime factor are the companies that engage in long-range institutional campaigns to establish favorable attitudes toward themselves.

In the absence of more scientific data, many media directors apply the rule for competitive products: "Match competition and then some." If you don't have enough money to match competition on a national scale, you may be able to pick out a market where competition has spread itself thin and outshine it in that territory.

There is much research being done and to be done on the criteria for evaluating reach, frequency, and continuity in a given situation. One such study reached the following conclusions:

1. Advertising is quickly forgotten if the consumer is not continuously exposed to it.

2. Numerous exposures are needed to impress a message upon the memory of a large proportion of target prospects.

3. Both the number of different persons who can be made to remember a message and the length of time it can be remembered increase as the number of exposures is increased.

4. An intensive burst of exposures is more effective in making a maximum number of different persons remember advertising, at least temporarily, than spreading 13 exposures throughout the year.

5. To achieve this same goal, fewer exposures per prospect among a relatively large group are preferable to 13 exposures per prospect among a smaller group.

6. In achieving this goal, dollar efficiency of advertising decreases as additional exposures are purchased.°

° Eugene Pomerance and Hubert Zielske, "How Frequently Should You Advertise?" *Media/scope* (September 1958), 25–27.

**7. What is the
best timing?**

A decision as to *when* to spend the money in advertising is one of the key elements of media strategy. A few principal timing patterns for using media are:

Seasonal program.   Some products' sales have seasonal fluctuations—cough drops in the winter, suntan lotion in the summer, and watches at graduation time and at Christmas. In such instances, the advertising is scheduled to reflect the seasonal peaks, appearing in concentrated dosage ahead of the consumer buying season, when people might first begin thinking of such products.

Steady program.   When the sale of a product is uniform throughout the year (toothpaste, for example), the advertising could be steadily maintained. Often, however, companies choose to concentrate their advertising. Sometimes a steady schedule would have to be too thin if it were spread over twelve months, and more impressive advertising can be concentrated in shorter time periods. Sometimes money is needed to meet competitive promotional efforts or to provide for special local campaigns. During the summer, reading and watching television decrease and radio listening increases, so many television network advertisers take a hiatus or switch their advertising to radio until fall.

Pulsation.   Pulsation is a technique of having comparatively short bursts of advertising in a few markets at a time, rather than running a steady but weaker schedule of advertising simultaneously in many markets. Pulsation is usually planned in advance in connection with a sales drive and preparation of trade promotional material, which enlists stores' interest in stocking and displaying the product. *BROADCASTING* magazine, for example, reported the following forthcoming television spot campaigns:

GENERAL ELECTRIC. Hot Point products will be advertised on spot TV in long list of markets for three weeks, starting in late April.

CLUETT, PEABODY & Co. Lady Arrow shirts will be featured in spot TV campaign to begin in late April in 30 major markets, with schedules running two weeks or longer, depending on market.

GILLETTE. Various products for men and women will be promoted via spot television in extended list of markets from March 29 through June 27.

COLGATE-PALMOLIVE. Wilkinson Bonded blades will be given additional support via spot TV for one month, starting on March 22, in nine markets.°

In addition to these timing patterns, we have the campaigns of the automobile companies, in which the chief advertising effort is concentrated at the time of the annual presentation of the new models. In the first six weeks of the new-car introduction, 20 percent of the total annual budget will be spent, *half of that— 10 percent—in the first week alone!* The timing and cadence of the advertising

---

° Reprinted with permission from the February 23, 1976 issue of *BROADCASTING*.

thus has its birth in the annual marketing cycle of the product itself. In such instances, there may also be a preliminary teaser campaign to whet curiosity and excitement for the Big Moment.

In media planning, we are very much interested in what our competition is doing, especially if their expenditure is bigger than ours (as it usually seems). One popular guide is not to compete with them in media that they already dominate. Instead, it might be better to pick a medium in which you can dominate or hold your own against the advertising of similar products. There are numerous media in which your advertisement will not be overshadowed by others in your field. However, if the campaign is based on unusual copy that would be unique in any medium, go ahead and place your advertisement where you think it would be most effective, regardless of the competition.

8. What is the competition doing?

The David and Goliath story has its counterpart today among those who use the anticompetitive-media approach. Holton C. Rush reports the following:

> When our agency started handling Omega Flour, a regional brand, we faced strong competition from two national flours with multimedia programs. A careful survey showed that in outdoor and in [black] radio there was an opportunity to outadvertise our competitors. We concentrated on those media and Omega now had more sales volume in the market than either of the two big-name flours. Both we and the client give primary credit to the media strategy.[*]

By *merchandising plans*, we mean special inducements offered to the buyer—cents-off coupons, premiums, prize contests, special price reductions. These plans are usually intensive campaigns, often in special markets, designed to offset competitive pressure, to introduce new products, or intensify demand among present customers. In such cases, an entire advertising program will be built around the merchandising offer.

9. Are there any special merchandising plans in the offing?

Different media can deliver the same message in different ways to different prospects. How can we combine the media available to us in the most effective way? We've seen many of the problems entering into the formulation of a media program, and we've begun to realize the complexity of media planning. Fortunately, we have tools to help us, and one of these is the computer.

10. What combination of media is best?

By *computer thinking*, we mean the thought of the *user* of the computer, not the supposed thinking of the computer itself. Computer thinking is thereby distinguished also from the incredible tasks of computer programming and operation. The greatest contribution of the computer to media planning—even to those who do not use it—is the necessity that it imposes to think in precise terms,

Computer thinking

[*] Holton C. Rush, "Some Important Things I Believe a Young Account Representative Should Know About Media" (American Association of Advertising Agencies, Inc).

to state problems in precise form, and to base decisions on accurately gathered information.

Use of computers.   Basically, the computer speedily coordinates into a meaningful form a given set of facts from a larger set of facts. Hence the first requirement in the use of the computer for making media decisions is to define the "facts" that are fed into it. There is a familiar phrase in the computer world: GIGO (garbage in, garbage out). If you speak of "users of a product," do you mean households or individuals? If individuals, do you include children? What constitutes a user? A person who has once used the product? A person who has some on hand right now?

A second characteristic of the computer is that it deals with numbers, not adjectives. All factors for a computer, therefore, must be put in numerical form, or *quantified*. Suppose you plan to put all the data on certain magazines in a computer—their circulation, the number of readers in different age groups, and so on. These are data already offered in numerical form. In evaluating the magazines, however, you also want to consider their editorial tone, their prestige, and the environment in which the advertisement appears. Because of this, someone must go over the different magazines and form a judgment on such qualities. That judgment must be quantified by giving each magazine a rating for "editorial tone"—let us say, from 1 to 5. The computer will then be able to give an end figure in which a magazine rated 4 for its editorial tone would get twice the weight of a magazine rated only 2.

Iteration.   As one example of the use of the computer, we consider *iteration*. Iteration is a trial-and-error method of getting a mathematical solution to a problem that cannot be reduced to a formula in advance. It has been applied to determine how to get the biggest reach in a list of media at the lowest cost per thousand. Assume we use only one medium, A, which reaches one million households. We then add Medium B, which also reaches one million households. But we find there is duplication of 600,000 households reached by the two media, represented as follows:

	Circulation	
	Total	Exclusive
Medium A	1,000,000	700,000
Medium B	1,000,000	700,000
Total	**2,000,000**	**1,400,000**

Thus we are reaching a total of only 1,400,000 different households. Then we add Medium C, which also reaches one million households. Because of the duplication among the three media, however, we are not reaching 3 million different households, as the next table reveals.

Circulation

	Total	Exclusive
Medium A	1,000,000	600,000*
Medium B	1,000,000	600,000*
Medium C	1,000,000	500,000
Total	**3,000,000**	**1,700,000**

*100,000 of the former 700,000 are duplicated by Medium C.

We are paying to reach 3,000,000 households, but we are reaching only 1,700,000 *different* households. Then we begin wondering if we would be better off to

> Keep A and B, but drop C
> Keep A and C, but drop B
> Keep B and C, but drop A

As more media are added to the list, the job of picking the most efficient combination becomes even more complex. This is the kind of problem for which iteration is used. Instances are commonplace in which a medium with smaller total circulation provides greater exclusive circulation within a given list.

The following instant-coffee example shows how a list of 22 media was reduced to 10, with a loss of only 5.6 percent of the households reached. The details are provided for those who may be interested in how such problems are handled.

A MEDIA PROBLEM

Reaching heavy users of instant coffee. The problem was to determine which combination of media can reach the largest number of different households that are heavy users of instant coffee. This represents a problem for which iteration is used. You begin with the *maximum* possible list of media and whittle it down in successive steps till you get a list that gives optimum reach per dollar (in contrast to the usual way of beginning with one medium and building upon that). In computer language, each round of eliminations represents an *iteration*. *

Chart I (Preliminary Runs A and B) lists 14 eligible magazines and 17 desirable television programs, each of which might be suitable for advertising instant coffee. Alongside each medium is the number of female heads of households who are heavy users of instant coffee and whom that medium reaches exclusively (that is, who are reached by no other medium on the list).

° This case study is used through the courtesy of SRDS Data, Inc.

PRELIMINARY RUNS A and B
MEDIA EXPOSURE AMONG HEAVY INSTANT COFFEE
USING FEMALE HOUSEHOLD HEADS (in thousands)
NATIONAL

	Magazines	RUN A — Exclusive Fem. Head Heavy Instant Coffee	Network Daytime TV Shows	RUN B — Exclusive Fem. Head Heavy Instant Coffee
A	General – mass	233	TV Show – A	35
B	General – mass	198	TV Show – B	95
C	General – mass	125	TV Show – C	128
D	General – mass	543	TV Show – D	176
E	Shelter	---*	TV Show – E	---*
F	Shelter	75	TV Show – F	26*
G	Women's – mass	185	TV Show – G	35*
H	Women's – mass	110	TV Show – H	52
I	Shelter	14*	TV Show – I	130*
J	Shelter	41*	TV Show – J	164
K	Women's – mass	103	TV Show – K	60
L	Women's – mass	240	TV Show – L	730
M	General – mass	620	TV Show – M	60
N	Women's – mass	82*	TV Show – N	371
		2,569	TV Show – O	17*
			TV Show – P	373
			TV Show – Q	26
				2,478

* Eliminated for first iteration

Chart I

We review the media to see which contribute the fewest number of households not reached by other media. As a result, we drop 4 magazines and 5 television shows from this preliminary list. That leaves 10 magazines and 12 television shows, which we now combine on Chart II.

Chart II reports on the total number of female household heads who are heavy users of instant coffee; this is our goal of 15,234,000.

The total number reached exclusively by each medium in the first iteration, consisting of 22 media, is now 2,602,000.

The total unduplicated number reached by all the media (that is, if a household is reached by more than one, it is counted only once) is 12,815,000.

The percentage of the goal covered by the list is 84.1 percent.

Looking over Chart II, we again weed out those media that contribute the smallest share of exclusive households (households not reached by others, marked by *). We drop 9. That leaves 13 media.

In the second iteration, with only 13 media, the coverage of goal is now 81.1 percent.

MEDIA EXPOSURE AMONG HEAVY INSTANT COFFEE
USING FEMALE HOUSEHOLD HEADS (in thousands)
NATIONAL

Total Heavy Instant Coffee Using
Female Household Heads 15,234

Magazines & Network Daytime TV Shows	Total Audience (All Inds.)	Heavy Using Fem. Head Aud.	First Iteration Exclusive Heavy Using Fem. Head Aud.	Second Iteration Exclusive Heavy Using Fem. Head Aud.	Third Iteration Exclusive Heavy Using Fem. Head Aud.
A General - mass	29,336	3,199	176	248	319
B General - mass	24,668	2,835	213	304	375
C General - mass	22,604	2,516	74*	Dropped	Dropped
D General - mass	20,759	2,805	216	378	455
F Shelter	15,380	2,340	71	91*	Dropped
G Women's - mass	13,467	2,570	112	112*	Dropped
H Women's - mass	14,758	2,771	152	223	304
K Women's - mass	13,164	2,505	41*	Dropped	Dropped
L Women's - mass	18,038	3,259	142	294	446
M General - mass	36,356	4,518	477	649	812
TV Show - A	4,006	809	10*	Dropped	Dropped
TV Show - B	4,597	997	71	101*	Dropped
TV Show - C	5,838	1,366	20*	Dropped	Dropped
TV Show - D	11,146	2,339	177	319	461
TV Show - H	8,522	1,616	51*	Dropped	Dropped
TV Show - J	9,273	2,244	51*	Dropped	Dropped
TV Show - K	6,279	1,140	41*	Dropped	Dropped
TV Show - L	21,521	2,673	345	436	507
TV Show - M	5,328	988	61	132	183
TV Show - N	13,570	1,771	81	223	315
TV Show - P	7,521	979	20*	Dropped	Dropped
TV Show - Q	4,507	566	--*	Dropped	Dropped
Total (Exclusive Reach)			2,602	3,510	4,177
Total Unduplicated Reach			12,815	12,354	11,958
Total Goal			15,234	15,234	15,234
Per Cent Coverage			84.1%	81.1%	78.5%

* Eliminated for next iteration

Chart II

Again, we mark for elimination the media that contribute the fewest number of households not reached by other media (marked by *); this time we drop 3. In the third iteration, we have 10 media whose reach of the total goal is 78.5 percent.

The final list developed by this series of iterations consists of 10 media reaching 78.5 percent of the goal of female household heads who are heavy users of instant coffee, in contrast to the original list of 22 media reaching 84.1 percent of such households. A reduction of the media list by 55 percent resulted in a loss of only 5.6 percent of households.

Iteration is only one of four approaches to the use of the computer in building schedules.* Continuous progress is being made in the use of the computer in solving media problems.

MEDIA EXPOSURE AMONG HEAVY INSTANT COFFEE
USING FEMALE HOUSEHOLD HEADS (in thousands)
NATIONAL
FINAL SCHEDULE

Total Heavy Instant Coffee Using
Female Household Heads 15,234

Magazines & Network Daytime TV Shows	Total Audience (All Inds.)	Heavy Using Fem. Head Aud.	Exclusive Heavy Using Fem. Head Aud.
A General – mass	29,336	3,199	319
B General – mass	24,668	2,835	375
D General – mass	20,759	2,805	455
H Women's – mass	14,758	2,771	304
L Women's – mass	18,038	3,259	446
M General – mass	36,356	4,518	812
TV Show – D	11,146	2,339	461
TV Show – L	21,521	2,673	507
TV Show – M	5,328	988	183
TV Show – N	13,570	1,771	315
Total (Exclusive Reach)			4,177
Total Unduplicated Reach			11,958
Total Goal			15,234
Per Cent Coverage			78.5%

Chart III

° Jack Z. Sissors and E. R. Petray, *Advertising Media Planning* (Chicago: Crain Books, 1976), pp. 271–87.

When faced with a media planning problem for a new product, a media director has various fields from which to draw.

For a local campaign, as a test to be run in different markets:
Local newspapers
Local TV
Local radio

For a regional campaign:
Local newspapers
Newspaper magazine supplements, bought sectionally
Regional magazines
Regional editions of national magazines
Parts of regional TV networks
Spot TV; spot radio
Parts of regional radio networks
Outdoor advertising
Transit advertising

For a national campaign:
TV network
Radio network
TV and radio spots, alone or to fill gaps
National magazines
A series of selected magazines
Newspapers
Newspaper magazine supplements
Outdoor advertising
Transit advertising

Selective campaign to reach only people with special interests (such as handicrafts, tennis, photography, antiques):
Magazines devoted to that specialty
Newspapers with sections devoted to that interest (possibly on Sunday only)
TV and radio programs attracting devotees of that subject
Direct response advertising

MEDIA WORK PLAN

SECTION I -- MEDIA OBJECTIVES

*Section I must include the Creative Work Plan and a
marketing background statement.

1.   ADVERTISING PERIOD:
January-December

2.   MEDIA BUDGET:
$5,000,000

3.   KEY MARKETING OBJECTIVE: (As it relates to Media Planning)
Increase volume and share by using a product quality improvement
to attract current non-users.

4.   KEY COMPETITIVE MEDIA CONSIDERATION:

$37 million spent in this category, with 5 major brands. Tv is
primary medium, with % tv ranging from 60% to 90%. (Exhibit
attached for detailed competitive summary.)

5.   PROSPECT DEFINITION: (If more than one category assign
                                % effort for each)

A. Demographic	% U.S. Base	% Effort
women 18-24	8.6%	30%
women 25-34	10%	70%

B.   Psychographic:
Women who are more venturesome in trying new products
and concerned about approval received from family for
meals and food.

6.   KEY MEDIA OBJECTIVES & RATIONALE:
Provide continuous pressure on a predominantly national basis
to maintain an awareness level as prospects come and go out of
marketplace. New product will be distributed nationally and
continuous pressure is needed to convince prospects that
improvement is really significant.

Food product "X"		*Peter Planner*
PRODUCT	DATE	PLANNING SUPERVISOR

On this and next two pages, Y&R's work plan.

From *Media Decisions* (December 1976), 110, 112, 114. Courtesy Media Publications, Inc.

MEDIA WORK PLAN

SECTION II -- STRATEGY

1. GEOGRAPHIC: (Identify emphasis as to National, Regional,
                  Local)
Emphasis predominantly national (89% of budget). Local spending
will be placed in markets with brand development at least 20%
better than national average (11% of budget is local).

2. SEASONALITY: (Identify seasonal concentration, if any)
No seasonality for brand, but we will invest 40% of funds
during first quarter to build faster awareness of improved
product.

3. REACH & FREQUENCY GOALS:
Effective reach 5+ messages during average 4-week period in
introductory phase; 3+ thereafter (Exhibit for frequency goal
rationale attached). Anticipated reach of prime prospects
70-80% in introductory period; 50-60% thereafter.

4. OTHER STRATEGIC CONSIDERATIONS: (Include creative units
                                     if they are a strategic
(A) Environment--food prep editorial consideration)
    and high visibility positions.
(B) Commercial length--100% 60-second commercials in first
    8 weeks; 50% 60-second/50% 30-second on next 6 weeks;
    all 30's thereafter.

5. BASIC STRATEGIC DIRECTION: (Check Media classes being
                                considered)

    CLASS

    DAY NETWORK TV _____X_____   NETWORK RADIO _____
    PRIME NETWORK TV _____X_____   MAGAZINES _____X_____
    LATE NIGHT NETWORK TV _____   SUPPLEMENTS _____
    NETWORK SPECIALS ____X_____   NEWSPAPERS _____
    NETWORK SPORTS _____   OUTDOOR _____
    SPOT TV (Identify Daypart) ____   OTHER (Identify) _____

6. MEDIA RATIONALE: (Rationale for Media classes being
                       considered)
    Prime network to optimize reach, etc. Day network to provide
    efficiency against target. Specials to supply high impact
    at outset of campaign. Magazines to provide new package
    registration and strong food environment. Etc., etc.

    Food product "x"   _____   *Peter Planner*
    ---------------   -------   ------------------------
        PRODUCT   DATE   PLANNING SUPERVISOR

Second part of Y&R's work plan.

MEDIA WORK PLAN

SECTION III -- EXECUTION

*Section III must include the Media Plan Budget detail
and Flow Chart. Detail should include % Spending by
media and by quarter.

1.   MEDIA MANDATORIES & LIMITATIONS:

Avoid tv violence. Maintain competitive separation.

2.   KEY EXECUTIONAL FACTORS AND THEIR EFFECTS: (Scheduling)

Concentrate on daytime serials. Schedule primetime and daytime
activity to coincide. Heavier prime network at start of campaign,
with daytime level consistent throughout.

3.   MEDIA PURCHASE GUIDELINES: (Include techniques)

Schedule net activity on at least 2 networks to maximize reach.
Execute road-blocks wherever possible. Negotiate print positions
adjacent to high-readership, pertinent editorial. (Detailed spot
specifications in separate exhibit attached.)

4.   PERFORMANCE DATA: (How the MP accomplished strategies,
                          such as R&F, and seasonality. Identify
                          R&F period (4 wks. or quarterly) and
                          indicate national, regional if pertinent)

(Estimated performance delivery shown in exhibit attached)

5.   MEDIA TESTING ACTIVITY:

Plan for all-magazine test in two key markets as a media mix
alternative to recommended plan.

Peter Planner
PLANNING SUPERVISOR

Part 3 of Y&R's work plan.

1. The strategy of creating a media plan for a product is based upon a variety of factors. Identify these factors; what is the importance of each in the overall media plan?

2. What media strategies might best be employed by advertisers whose budget is much smaller than that of competitors?

3. Discuss the difference between a primary medium and a secondary medium. How does the synergistic effect come into play in selecting primary and secondary media?

4. What is the tie-in between development of the media plan and target market considerations?

5. Discuss the local, regional, national, and selective media plans. What type of media might be used for each plan? Why did you select them?

6. Define and analyze the significance of reach, frequency, and continuity in planning media schedules.

7. Identify and discuss the different patterns of timing in media scheduling.

8. How can a differential advantage be attained in the choice of media?

9. What is the usual benchmark for comparing costs of a publication in relation to costs in comparable media?

10. What are some of the ways in which the computer can be used in media planning?

11. Explain the impact of the company's marketing goals on its media strategy.

12. To what extent should a media plan be flexible? How does an advertiser build flexibility into his plan?

13. How does message content or the nature of the copy affect the media plan?

14. Do you think that a specific formula could be developed by which it would tell the advertiser what the most effective media plan would be under certain circumstances? State the reasons for your answer.

15. How do the merchandising plans of a company influence the media plan? Can you give some examples?

QUESTIONS

READING SUGGESTIONS

AAKER, DAVID A., "ADMOD: An Advertising Decision Model," *Journal of Marketing Research* (February 1975), 37–45.

BARBAN, ARNOLD M., *Essentials of Media Planning: A Marketing Viewpoint.* Chicago: Crain Books, 1975.

BRUNO, ALBERT V., THOMAS P. HUSTAD, and EDGAR A. PESSEMIER, "Media Approaches to Segmentation," *Journal of Advertising Research,* (April 1973), 35–42.

FITZMAURICE, ED, "We Live on Facts," *Media Decisions* (April 1976), 62 ff.

FORMAN, STAN, "A Theory of Audience Accumulation," *Journal of Advertising Research* (February 1976), 21–25.

GRASS, ROBERT C., and WALLACE H. WALLACE, "Advertising Communication: Print vs. TV," *Journal of Advertising Research* (October 1974), 19–23.

HUGUES, MICHAEL, "An Empirical Study of Media Comparison," *Journal of Marketing Research* (May 1975), 221–23.

LIEBMAN, L., and E. LEE, "Reach and Frequency Estimating Services," *Journal of Advertising Research* (August 1974), 23–25.

MANELOVEG, HERBERT D., "Media Research's Future: Is There Any?" *Advertising Age* (July 15, 1974), 23 ff.

"Media Matching Game," *Media Decisions* (November 1976), 64 ff.

"Media Research—Where It Stands Today," *Media Decisions,* a special four-part series, January through April 1977.

PAPAZIAN, ED, "Timing," *Media Decisions* (August 1975), 66 ff.

"Profile of a Creative Mediaman," *Media Decisions* (December 1976), 64 ff.

WOLFE, H. D., J. K. BROWN, G. C. THOMPSON, and S. H. Greenberg, *Evaluating Media.* New York: National Industrial Conference Board, Inc., 1966.

7

Using Television

Since the advent of the automobile, nothing has changed American family life so much as television. Nothing else has had such an impact on advertising.

In 1939, television was introduced to an incredulous public audience. On the opening day of the New York World's Fair, a giant screen on the fairgrounds showed President Roosevelt formally opening the fair via television from Washington. The skeptical crowd gathered before the screen could hardly believe what they saw and heard. There was tremendous applause, whether for the President or for television no one knows. People left saying they had seen a miracle. Newspapers prophesied that we would soon all have television in our homes; however, the fulfillment of the prophecy was delayed by World War II. It was not until 1952 that nationwide TV networks were established. In that year America saw its first TV college football and its first major league baseball game on national broadcasts.

What has happened to television since those early years is described by one advertising executive:

> The 50s could be characterized as the period of TV infancy. The impact of TV on social behavior—including purchasing habits—was stronger than any of us recognized. The viewers in the early days watched TV with little discrimination. Whatever was on the tube represented a miracle that justified sitting before the set for hours. The selling power of television advertising was felt quickly. By the mid-60s the public had become more discriminating and selective in its viewing habits. CATV (cable television) joined in reaching more people, and in improving the quality of the picture. Television advertising had to exist in a more competitive atmosphere. . . . The impact of television, however, on buying behavior, has continued to be powerful.°

° Direct communication from Alfred L. Plant, Vice-President, Block Drug Company.

Over 97 percent of all American households (more than 70 million homes) had television sets in 1977. National advertisers spend more of their money on television than on any other medium, and TV is the fastest growing local advertising medium.

Features and advantages

Television provides the most spectacular way in which an advertiser can reach the greatest number of people at one time. Almost everybody, no matter what his or her taste, watches a few favorite programs regularly. The average daily viewing time in American households is six hours, 15 minutes, a figure that would cause many parents to say, "In my house that's an understatement."

A product story can be presented in the most dramatic way on television. With the aid of live performers and appropriate settings, it provides an unmatched opportunity to demonstrate the merits of a product in the intimacy of the home. It is a fast-acting medium, especially for a new product or an important new feature of an already well-known one. Being on a popular network program is a respected argument in getting dealer support for the product.

Limitations and challenges

With all its effectiveness, television advertising has its problems.

Clutter. Nonentertainment use of the screen for announcements of forthcoming programs (*promos*), long lists of credits, and a variety of other nonentertainment presentations dilutes viewers' attention and therefore hurts advertising.

Increasing profusion of commercials. In the five-year period from 1970 to 1975, the average weekly number of commercials rose from 2,633 to 3,487.° The more commercials that are jammed on top of each other in limited broadcast time, the less attention each of them receives. The kaleidoscope of clutter and commercials produces confusion among viewers and a high rate of misidentification of brands.

Forms of television usage

An advertiser can buy television time through a network (*network TV*) or from individual stations (*spot TV*). If a national advertiser buys spots, they are strictly speaking, *national spot TV,* but they are generally referred to as *spot TV.*† When a local advertiser uses spot TV, it is, strictly speaking, *local spot TV,* but it is referred to as *local TV.* This is the standard classification established by the Federal Communications Commission and followed by the industry. In 1978, 45 percent of all television expenditure was for network; 29.6 percent, spot; 25 percent, local. In this discussion we deal chiefly with network and spot, saving our discussion of local television for Chapter 24, "Retail Advertising."

Network TV. A *television network* consists of a number of interconnected stations capable of transmitting to other stations a program originating at one of

---

° These and subsequent statistics in this chapter, unless otherwise credited, were obtained through the courtesy of Television Bureau of Advertising (TvB).

† The word *spot* is another of those terms in advertising that are used in two senses: (1) *time-buying use*—a way of buying time on a nonnetwork show, and (2) *creative use*—"We need some 30-second spots."

the affiliated stations. (*Affiliated stations* means either network-owned or the network's list of prime stations, which must be included in all network shows. Because of difference in time zones, some stations may show a network program as a delayed telecast.) The present national networks are ABC, CBS, and NBC, connected by telephone cables. (Cable TV systems are beginning to use earth satellite stations.) Each national network has arranged affiliations with stations throughout the country, specifying that these stations will carry the network's programs and commercials at certain times. The stations can sell the rest of the time independently. An advertiser placing a schedule with a national television network is obliged to use a prescribed minimum number of affiliated stations from the network's total list but may supplement this list by selecting stations from its supplementary list. (*Supplementary stations* are additional stations available to a network to meet an advertiser's marketing needs.) Thus, besides giving an advertiser the largest nationwide audience for his message, networks also offer considerable flexibility in choosing markets. (In addition to national networks, there are also regional and state networks.)

The big advantage of network advertising is the number of people it can reach at one time, at a low cost per person. A night prime-time show reaches 32 million people. In 1978 the Superbowl game reached an estimated audience of 86 million. At $350,000 per minute, the advertiser could reach 4 viewers for less than one cent.

THE TELEVISION STRUCTURE

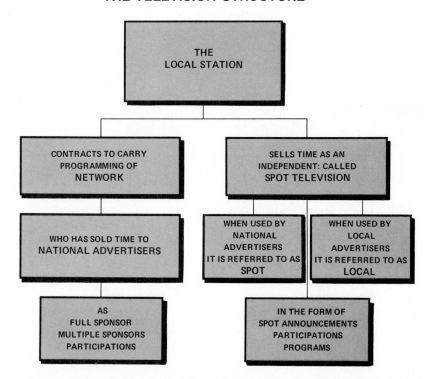

But network buying has its problems and challenges. In the first place, we are speaking of outlays of large sums of money, as we have seen above, for both time and production. These costs rule out any companies but those having a product or line of products with widespread distribution or a nationwide institutional story to tell. Most network advertisers have a whole range of corporate divisions or products to share the time and costs. Some advertisers concentrate their network effort on one- or two-hour special programs, either during periods of peak seasonal sales (Hallmark cards at holiday times) or annually (when introducing new car models).

The amount of prime time on the major networks is limited, and there is great competition for it. Some prime time, as for sports events or annual parades or other holiday features, is scheduled a year in advance.

Spot television.   Spot television advertising is time bought by advertisers from individual stations. Spot advertising is the great flexible medium of television. With it, an advertiser can choose particular cities at particular times. Often an advertiser uses TV spot schedules along with a network schedule in markets where the local affiliate of the network may not be the strongest station. Spot schedules are also useful in markets where an advertiser wants to put on a full-scale drive for a limited period of time.

The disadvantage of spot advertising has been chiefly in the problem of handling it. To place a schedule, the advertiser has had to deal with many stations in many markets. In each market, one must select a station. Then, for each station, it is necessary to: (1) determine whether the desired time is available, (2) negotiate for price, (3) place an order, (4) make sure the commercial was played as scheduled or, if preemptible, learn when it was played, (5) follow up on a make-good if it appeared at a wrong time, and (6) check the bills. In fact, paperwork has been the bane of spot television. By working with sales representatives, each of whom handles a whole list of stations and many of whom are beginning to use computerized equipment, the advertiser can now greatly simplify the whole spot-buying process. Some of the large advertising agencies have installed direct hookups with some of the major sales representatives.

Of all TV spots, 79 percent run for 30 seconds, less frequently for 60 seconds or 10 seconds. The 10-second spot, just long enough for a short message identifying the product, was born of the FCC requirement that every station identify itself every hour. It is usually referred to as an ID (short for identification) or station-break, announcement. The visual part of the commercial may last 10 seconds; the audio 8 seconds. When an advertiser sponsors a special two-hour performance, 6 two-minute announcements are usually made.

UHF stations

As you glance over the accompanying chart of the electromagnetic spectrum through which all electronic communication by air takes place, you will see that television and radio are only two of many claimants for frequency allocations. They have competition from other users. When television came along, the Fed-

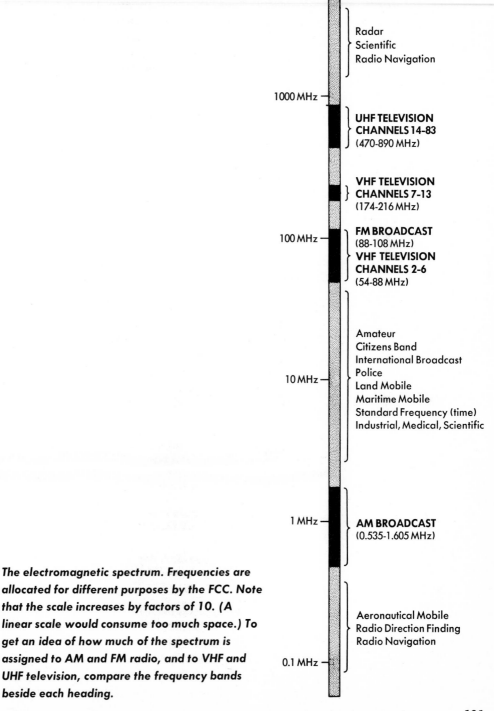

Radar
Scientific
Radio Navigation

1000 MHz —

**UHF TELEVISION
CHANNELS 14-83**
(470-890 MHz)

**VHF TELEVISION
CHANNELS 7-13**
(174-216 MHz)

FM BROADCAST
(88-108 MHz)
**VHF TELEVISION
CHANNELS 2-6**
(54-88 MHz)

100 MHz —

Amateur
Citizens Band
International Broadcast
Police
Land Mobile
Maritime Mobile
Standard Frequency (time)
Industrial, Medical, Scientific

10 MHz —

AM BROADCAST
(0.535-1.605 MHz)

1 MHz —

Aeronautical Mobile
Radio Direction Finding
Radio Navigation

0.1 MHz —

The electromagnetic spectrum. Frequencies are allocated for different purposes by the FCC. Note that the scale increases by factors of 10. (A linear scale would consume too much space.) To get an idea of how much of the spectrum is assigned to AM and FM radio, and to VHF and UHF television, compare the frequency bands beside each heading.

eral Communications Commission (FCC), which is the responsible government authority, assigned to it what were then the best available channels, now known as Channels 2 through 13. These twelve channels are in the very-high-frequency band of the spectrum and are referred to as VHF stations. Today they are the TV stations most people get on their sets.

But the demand for more television frequencies grew faster than had been anticipated. The FCC did not want to repeat its mistake of not allowing room for expansion. They leapfrogged into the ultrahigh-frequency band, where they made room for 70 channels—channels 14 to 83, referred to as UHF. But it takes a different type of receiving set to tune in on these channels. Since 1965, by law, all new TV sets have had to be capable of receiving UHF as well as VHF.

UHF stations usually offer programs of selective quality to attract specific audiences, rather than trying to compete with the entertainment fare of the VHF stations. They are popular in the Middle West and especially popular in the far West.

Elements of TV planning

Since television schedules can run into a lot of money, and since there are many alternate choices available for use in television, it is important to start with a plan, embracing considerations such as the following.

Establish the budget.   The budget tells us whether we can think in terms of network, spot, or a combination of the two.

Set a goal: reach or frequency.   The TV advertising plan is a projection of the marketing plan. What is the goal of that plan? To introduce a new product? To get a greater share of the present market? To keep our product before the many who know it (retentive advertising)? Is there anything newsworthy about the product? Is there a special promotion program being planned to run at the same time? The answers to these questions are translated into terms of *reach* and *frequency*. *Reach* refers to getting a message before as *many* people as possible. *Frequency* refers to getting a message before people as *often* as possible. (A commercial must run at least six times to be regarded as representing *frequency*.) Reach is used most often when there is something newsworthy to report about a product. Frequency is used most often for well-known repeat products without new benefits; soft drinks, for example.

Determine duration of flights.   The duration of a television advertising effort is referred to as a *flight*. Most television advertising is done in a series of flights of different duration during the year, expressed in terms of weeks, not months, as illustrated by the accompanying reports.

Define the TV territory.   Before the advent of television, a company traditionally established sales and advertising territories by state boundaries and arbitrary geographical areas within them. But a TV transmission wave goes in many directions for varying distances; it is no respecter of man-made maps. How to

Business Briefly

General Foods □ Corporation has bought full sponsorship in Wednesday's (Dec. 8) 60-minute ABC-TV special "Christmas in Disneyland" (8-9 p.m., NYT) starring Art Carney. Special was conceived by General Foods and agency, Benton & Bowles, and put on tape at Disneyland by Marty Pasetta Productions. General Foods also has 13-week selected-market spot-TV flight, through Grey Advertising, New York, ready for kick off Dec. 27. Various products in this flight will appeal to women, 25-54, and children, 6-11.

Avis □ Rent-a-car company, through Doyle Dane Bernbach, New York, is readying major-market first-quarter TV-spot buy. Thirty-second spots will be placed in sports adjacencies to reach men, 18-49.

Borden □ Various products, through Campbell-Ewald, Detroit, will receive various multi-week spot-TV flights throughout first quarter. Markets include New York, Chicago and Philadelphia. Ten- and 30-second spots will be aimed at women, 18-49.

Colgate □ Company will promote various products in 13-week selected-market spot-TV buy beginning Dec. 27. Women, 18-49, are demographic target for 30-second spots, which will be placed in daytime and early fringe. William Esty, New York, is agency.

Magnavox □ Company, through William Esty, is putting 30-second spots for various products into selected-market spot-TV campaign to begin Jan. 10 and run for five weeks. Adults, 25-54, are target for fringe-time buys.

Ralston Purina □ Company's special dinners' products, through D'Arcy-MacManus & Masius, New York, will be accorded four-week spot-TV campaign, to begin Dec. 27. Adult women are demographic target.

Western Auto □ Retail chain set to launch spot-TV drive for 12 weeks starting in early January. Barickman Advertising, Kansas City, Mo., is slanting its commercials toward adult men and women via schedules on daytime and fringe periods and on news programs.

U.S. Navy □ Forty-two week spot radio campaign is planned during 1977 to run in about 100 markets on stations of Broadcast Marketing System's off-line network. First flight is set for Jan. 16 start for eight weeks. Ted Bates, New York, is setting its sights on men, 17-22.

Hershey □ Company's San Giorgio Macaroni subsidiary, based in Lebanon, Pa., has two-week multi-market spot-TV flight ready for December launching. Agency, Creamer, Fuller, Smith & Ross.

Reprinted with permission, from the December 6, 1976 issue of *Broadcasting*.

Reports of spot schedules. Note differences in length of flights, selection of markets, audiences, and times.

coordinate sales territories with television planning for advertising was the problem on which two major research firms worked.

The A.C. Nielsen Company developed a marketing map based upon important (designated) marketing areas. It selected stations that reached those areas best and referred to these selections as Designated Marketing Areas, or DMA.

The Arbitron Company based its solution on its concept of Areas of Dominant Influence (ADI). The ADI, as the bureau defines it, "is a geographic market design which defines each market, exclusive of another, based on *Measurable View-*

ing Patterns. The ADI is an area that consists of all counties in which the home market stations receive a preponderance of viewing. Each county in the U.S. (excluding Alaska) is allocated exclusively to only one ADI. There is no overlap." (The ADI system has also been adopted by newspapers and other media to describe which part of the television ADI their circulation covers.) It is used also for radio, outdoor, and magazine scheduling.

Determine the profile of our audience. Having determined which geographical area we want to work in, the next step is to make a broad determination of what sex or age group we wish to reach. Once we know that, we have the best time to get our message across.

Profile of television day based on estimated averages for TV time segments (*prime time = 100*)

Ratings	Hours	Time designation	Audiences	Type of program
49	6:00 A.M.–noon	Morning	Women, pre-school children	Juvenile, games, news
60	Noon–4:30 P.M.	Afternoon	Women	Soap operas
68	4:30–7:30 P.M.	Early fringe	Women, men, school children	News, games, variety
80	7:30–8:00 P.M.	Access	Adults	
100	8:00–9:00 P.M.	Prime	Family viewing	Serials, sit-coms
94	9:00–11:00 P.M.	Late prime	Teen and adult	Serials, sit-coms
79	11:00–11:30 P.M.	Late fringe	Younger adults	News
60	11:30–end	Late late	Younger adults, singles, mobiles, white-collar businessmen	Talk shows, movies

The rating point system

When we have determined whom we want to reach and the best time of day to reach them, we are faced with another question. Which of the several programs presented at the same time will be seen by the largest audience? Fortunately, a system has been devised that mathematically determines the answer.

The unit of measurement determining the size of an audience is the *rating point.* A rating point is 1 percent of the total number of households who have TV sets in a specified area. A rating of 12 for a program means that 12 percent of all the TV households in a particular area have their TV sets tuned to that program.

NATIONAL *Nielsen* TV AUDIENCE ESTIMATES — DAY MON.-FRI. OCT. 24-28

TIME	7:00	7:15	7:30	7:45	8:00	8:15	8:30	8:45	9:00	9:15	9:30	9:45	10:00	10:15	10:30	10:45	11:00

WEEK 1

ABC TV

TOTAL AUDIENCE (Households (000) & %): 2,840 / 3.9 .... 2,550 / 3.5

Good Morning, America — (Co-op) (Participating) (Co-op) (Participating)

AVERAGE AUDIENCE (Households (000) & %): 2,260 / 3.1 / 22 ... 2,040 / 2.8 / 20
SHARE OF AUDIENCE %
AVG. AUD. BY ¼ HR. %: 2.9 / 3.2 ... 2.8 / 2.8

CBS TV

TOTAL AUDIENCE (Households (000) & %): 2,410 / 3.3 ... 3,750 / 5.2 ... 2,410 / 3.3 ... 4,080 / 5.6

CBS Morning News — (Co-op) (Participating) — *Captain Kangaroo* — Here's Lucy | Price is Right 1

AVERAGE AUDIENCE (Households (000) & %): 1,600 / 2.2 / 18 ... 2,410 / 3.3 / 22 ... 2,040 / 2.8 / 18 ... 3,500 / 4.8 / 29
SHARE OF AUDIENCE %: 2.2* / 3.0* / 3.6* (17* / 20* / 24*)
AVG. AUD. BY ¼ HR. %: 2.1 / 2.2 / 2.2 / 2.7 / 3.3 / 3.5 / 3.6 ... 2.7 / 2.9 / 4.6 / 5.1

NBC TV

TOTAL AUDIENCE (Households (000) & %): 3,430 / 4.7 ... 3,790 / 5.2 ... 3,650 / 5.0 ... 3,650 / 5.0

Today Show — (Co-op) (Participating) (Co-op) (Participating) — Sanford And Son | Hollywood Squares (1)

AVERAGE AUDIENCE (Households (000) & %): 2,770 / 3.8 / 27 ... 2,990 / 4.1 / 29 ... 3,060 / 4.2 / 27 ... 3,060 / 4.2 / 25
AVG. AUD. BY ¼ HR. %: 3.7 / 3.9 ... 4.1 / 4.0 ... 4.0 / 4.4 / 4.1 / 4.4

WEEK 2

ABC TV

TOTAL AUDIENCE (Households (000) & %): 3,350 / 4.6 ... 3,060 / 4.2

Good Morning, America — (Co-op) (Participating) (Co-op) (Participating)

AVERAGE AUDIENCE (Households (000) & %): 2,550 / 3.5 / 21 ... 2,480 / 3.4 / 20
AVG. AUD. BY ¼ HR. %: 3.5 / 3.6 ... 3.2 / 3.5

CBS TV

TOTAL AUDIENCE (Households (000) & %): 2,700 / 3.7 ... 4,520 / 6.2 ... 2,700 / 3.7 ... 4,590 / 6.3

CBS Morning News — (Co-op) (Participating) — *Captain Kangaroo* — Here's Lucy MTI WF (2) | Price is Right 1 MTUWF (2)

AVERAGE AUDIENCE (Households (000) & %): 1,750 / 2.4 / 16 ... 2,840 / 3.9 / 22 ... 2,260 / 3.1 / 18 ... 3,790 / 5.2 / 28
SHARE OF AUDIENCE %: 2.5* / 3.7* / 4.1* (15* / 21* / 24*)
AVG. AUD. BY ¼ HR. %: 2.4 / 2.4 / 2.5 / 3.5 / 3.8 / 4.2 / 4.1 ... 2.8 / 3.3 / 4.9 / 5.5

NBC TV

TOTAL AUDIENCE (Households (000) & %): 3,860 / 5.3 ... 4,300 / 5.9 ... 3,860 / 5.3 ... 4,160 / 5.7

Today Show — (Co-op) (Participating) (Co-op) (Participating) — Sanford And Son | Hollywood Squares (1)

AVERAGE AUDIENCE (Households (000) & %): 2,990 / 4.1 / 25 ... 3,500 / 4.8 / 28 ... 3,280 / 4.5 / 26 ... 3,500 / 4.8 / 27
AVG. AUD. BY ¼ HR. %: 4.1 / 4.1 ... 4.7 / 4.8 ... 4.2 / 4.8 / 4.8 / 4.9

TV HOUSEHOLDS USING TV (See Def. 1)

	7:00	7:15	7:30	7:45	8:00	8:15	8:30	8:45	9:00	9:15	9:30	9:45	10:00	10:15	10:30	10:45	11:00
WK 1	5.2	7.7	10.1	11.6	13.4	14.3	14.4	14.2	14.7	15.7	15.7	16.1	15.4	16.1	16.4	17.4	
WK 2	7.4	10.0	12.1	13.9	15.4	16.5	17.3	17.5	17.6	17.4	17.2	17.2	16.8	17.8	17.9	18.5	

U.S. TV Households: 72,900,000   *Half-hour ratings (for immediately preceding and subject quarter-hours).   (R) Repeat, see page B.   (OP) See Other Programs Section: Page A-36

(1) "NBC NEWS UPDATE-10:57AM", NBC, (10:57-10:58AM)(SUS.).
(2) MAGAZINE, CBS, THU., (10:00-11:00PM), FOR RATINGS, SEE OP PAGES(S).

DAY MON.-FRI. OCT. 31-NOV. 4

You may have read in the newspapers that a popular TV program has reached "a new high rating." Ratings are of the essence in the TV world; the entire business hinges on them. They determine the price of the time sold to advertisers; they give advertisers a basis for comparing the audience size of their program and competitive programs. They also provide signals to all concerned when a program's popularity is slipping or holding firm.

A number of research firms specialize in gathering ratings and demographic information on a syndicated basis, which means that at their own, considerable expense they gather audience viewing data from all the markets all over the country and publish it promptly. These firms sell their reports on an annual subscription basis, and they are closely followed because they are the basis for mak-

The syndicated research services

125

Weekly Programming — Time Period Averages

Courtesy ARB (American Research Bureau, Inc.) ©

TOTAL SURVEY AREA, IN THOUSANDS (000)

DAY AND TIME · STATION · PROGRAM	WK1 4/27 (58)	WK2 5/4 (59)	WK3 5/11 (60)	WK4 5/18 (61)	ADI RTG (1)	ADI SH (2)	FEB '77 (62)	NOV '78 (63)	MAY '78 (64)	METRO RTG (3)	METRO SH (4)	TV HH (5)	W TOT 18+ (10)	W 18-49 (11)	W 18-24 (12)	W 18-34 (13)	W 25-49 (14)	W 25-54 (15)	WKG WMN 18+ (16)	M TOT 18+ (17)	M 18-49 (18)	M 18-34 (19)	M 25-49 (20)	M 25-54 (21)	TEENS 12-17 (22)	CHILD 2-11 (24)
▲RELATIVE STD-ERR 25-49%	10	11	10	10	2					4		9	10	11	12	12	10	9	12	11	11	13	10	10	12	24
(1S.E.) THRESHOLDS 50+%	2	3	2	2	-					1		2	3	3	3	3	2	2	3	2	3	3	2	2	3	6
SATURDAY																										
6.30A-7.00A																										
KMOL BETTER WAY	-	-	-	1								1													1	2
KENS N.O.A.	-	-	-	-																						
COMDY CAPERS	1	-	2	1	1	99						4	1												1	7
--4 WK AVG--					1	99		99	99			4	1												1	7
KSAT N.O.A.	-	-	-	-																						
MEDITATION	-	1	-	-								1			1					1	1	1			3	1
--4 WK AVG--												1			1					1	1	1			3	1
HUT/PVT/TOT	1	1	1	1	1			1	2	1		6	1		1					1	1	1			5	10
7.00A-7.30A																										
KMOL WDY WDPECKER	2	1	1	1	1	17	17	33	14	2	33	7	1		3	1	2	2		2	1		1		3	10
KENS SYLVSTR-TWTY	4	1	3	3	3	50	50	44	71	3	50	13	4	3	1	2	2	2	2	3	3	2	2	2	2	12
KSAT TOM JRRY MUM	2	2	-	3	2	33	17	22	29	1	17	8	2	2	2	2	1	1		1	1	1			7	13
HUT/PVT/TOT	9	4	4	8	6			6	9	7	6		28	7	5	3	4	3	3		6	5	4	2	2	12	42
7.30A-8.00A																										
KMOL PINK PANTHER	6	5	1	6	4	40	42	33	15	5	45	20	5	3	3	3	1	1	1	6	4	4	1	1	8	27
KENS CLUE CLUB	5	2	4	4	4	40	25	33	77	4	36	16	5	4	1	3	3	3	1	4	4	2	3	3	5	26
KSAT JABBERJAW	2	2	1	2	2	20	25	20	15	2	18	9	2	2	2	1	1	1	1	1	1			6	16
HUT/PVT/TOT	13	10	6	12	10			12	15	13	11		45	12	9	6	7	5	5	2	11	9	7	4	4	19	69
8.00A-8.30A																										
KMOL PINK PANTHER	6	5	2	3	4	18	17	19	18	5	20	18	9	6	5	5	2	2	2	8	6	6	1	1	7	22
KENS BUGS-RD RUNR	15	7	11	12	11	50	50	54	65	14	56	51	11	9	4	6	6	6	5	13	10	9	5	7	18	64
KSAT SCOOB DOO SH	6	5	4	8	6	27	25	27	12	6	24	27	6	5	7	4	2	3	1	5	4	4	2	2	17	49
HUT/PVT/TOT	29	18	18	24	22			24	26	17	25		96	26	20	16	15	10	11		26	20	19	8	10	42	135
8.30A-9.00A																										
KMOL PINK PANTHER	5	6	3	4	4	17	17	18	27	5	19	20	9	7	5	6	3	3	3	9	7	7	2	2	8	24
KENS BUGS-RD RUNR	16	7	14	12	12	50	50	46	59	15	58	55	12	10	5	7	6	6	5	12	9	8	5	7	17	71
KSAT SCOOB DOO SH	5	6	5	7	6	25	29	32	9	6	23	28	7	6	8	5	3	4	1	6	5	5	2	2	19	47
HUT/PVT/TOT	28	20	23	24	24			24	28	22	26		103	28	23	18	18	12	13	9	27	21	20	9	11	44	142
9.00A-9.30A																										
KMOL SPEED BUGGY	5	6	5	5	5	20	28	21	24	5	19	24	7	7	7	5	3	3	2	4	4	3	2	2	13	33
KENS TARZAN-LORD	15	12	14	11	13	52	48	48	40	16	62	58	14	10	12	8	3	4	4	15	13	11	7	7	23	82
KSAT SCOOB DOO SH	6	5	5	7	6	20	28	24	5	5	19	24	7	4	1	3	4	5	2	5	4	3	4	4	7	34
HUT/PVT/TOT	28	23	25	24	25			25	29	25	26		106	28	21	20	16	10	13	8	24	21	17	13	13	43	149
9.30A-10.00A																										
KMOL MONSTR SQUAD	5	3	2	4	3	13	20	21	24	4	15	15	4	4	3	2	2	2	2	6	6	5	2	2	9	20
KENS ADV BATMAN	15	12	14	13	14	58	48	39	40	16	62	60	14	10	10	8	4	5	5	12	10	8	7	7	17	85
KSAT KROFFTS SHOW	6	3	9	4	5	21	28	32	28	5	19	26	8	7	4	5	6	6	3	7	6	3	6	6	15	30
HUT/PVT/TOT	27	20	26	23	24			25	28	25	26		101	26	21	19	16	12	13	9	25	22	16	15	15	39	135
10.00A-10.30A																										
KMOL SPACE GHOST	7	4	6	7	6	24	23	30	25	7	26	28	7	6	3	5	5	5	5	8	7	5	4	4	8	27
KENS SHAZAM-ISIS	19	11	12	7	12	48	42	30	38	14	52	55	22	19	15	16	9	9	9	17	15	14	7	7	20	72
KSAT KROFFTS SHOW	3	2	9	6	5	20	31	33	29	6	22	24	5	5	5	4	4	4	3	4	4	3	4	4	13	35
HUT/PVT/TOT	30	19	28	22	25			26	27	24	27		107	34	30	23	25	18	18	15	29	26	22	15	15	41	134
10.30A-11.00A																										
KMOL BG LTTL JOHN	5	2	3	4	4	18	25	38	18	4	16	16	6	5	5	4	1	1	1	3	2		2	2	6	23
KENS SHAZAM-ISIS	15	10	11	6	11	50	33	35	41	13	52	48	20	17	12	14	11	11	11	15	14	12	7	7	22	54
KSAT SUPERFRIENDS	4	4	10	9	7	32	38	27	36	8	32	33	9	9	7	8	4	4	3	6	6	6	3	3	13	40
HUT/PVT/TOT	25	16	26	20	22			24	26	22	25		97	35	31	24	26	16	16	15	24	22	18	12	12	41	117
11.00A-11.30A																										
KMOL ARAS SPORTS	5	1			3	15				3	13	15	6	3			3	3	3		7	6	2	5	5	3	9
LAND OF LOST			3	3	3	14				4	15	14	1	1	1	1				7	7	2	7	7	5	15
--4 WK AVG--					3	14	13	15	29	4	16	15	4	3	1	3	2	2		7	7	2	6	6	4	13
KENS FAT ALBERT	18	10	10	7	11	52	57	46	48	13	52	49	23	19	15	15	11	11	8	12	11	10	6	6	26	54
KSAT SHORT STORY	1				1	4				2	7	8														
ODD BALL		4	12	6	7	37				9	38	36	17	16	7	15	10	11	6	7	6	5	4	4	9	48
--4 WK AVG--					6	29	26	38	24	7	28	29	13	12	5	11	8	8	5	6	5	4	5	5	8	39
KWEX COCODRILLA	-	1										1	1													
HUT/PVT/TOT	25	16	26	16		21			23	26	21	25		94	41	34	21	29	21	21	13	24	23	16	17	17	38	106
11.30A-NOON																										
KMOL OUTDOORS	5	-			2	10				3	13	12	7	5	2		5	3	3		9	6	2	5	5		4
ARAS SPORTS			1	3	2	10				2	8	8								3	2	1	1	1	4	5
--4 WK AVG--					2	10	8	11	4	2	8	10	4	3	1	3	2	2		6	4	2	3	3	2	5
KENS ARK II	14	7	7	5	8	38	33	39	40	10	42	38	18	13	11	11	7	7	5	9	8	7	3	3	17	42
KSAT AM BANDSTAND	7	9	15	11	11	52	54	43	39	12	50	50	36	32	19	26	21	23	14	15	13	10	10	10	26	22
KWEX COCODRILLA	-	1					**	**	**			1														1
HUT/PVT/TOT	25	17	23	20		21			24	28	23	24		99	59	48	31	40	30	32	19	30	25	19	16	16	45	69
NOON-12.30P																										
KMOL TV-4 JOBS	3	-	1	1	1	5				1	5	6	2	2		2	2	2	1	3	1		1		1	2
KENS CHLD FLM FST	14	10	7	4	9	43	36	47	52	9	45	42	20	13	10	8	9	11	4	12	8	4	6	6	18	39
KSAT AM BANDSTAND	6	11	12	7	9	43	50	44	38	10	50	43	33	26	19	21	15	16	12	15	10	8	6	6	25	12
KWEX COCODRILLA	-	1					**	**	**			1														
HUT/PVT/TOT	24	24	21	14		21			22	32	21	20		92	56	41	29	31	26	29	17	30	19	12	13	13	43	53
12.30P-1.00P																										
KMOL THE RACERS	1	4	4	4	3	18	21	9	28	3	19	16	6	5	2	4	4	4	4	13	7	5	4	5	3	3
	58	59	60	61	1	2	62	63	64	3	4	5	10	11	12	13	14	15	16	17	18	19	20	21	22	24

‡ TECHNICAL DIFFICULTY
◄ M-F PROGRAM AIRED LESS THAN FIVE DAYS
* PARENT/SATELLITE RELATIONSHIP
* SAMPLE BELOW MINIMUM FOR WEEKLY REPORTING
▲ SEE TABLE ON PAGE iii

ing media plans. These reports include the Nielsen Station Index (NSI), the Nielsen Television Index (NTI) covering national advertising, the Nielsen TV Local Market Reports, and the Arbitron Television Audience Estimate. Available in the field of radio are the Arbitron Radio Market Reports, the Pulse and the Axiom Market Reports. TGI (Target Group Index), a division of the Axiom Company, and The Simmons Report also go into the demographic studies of TV audiences and magazine readers.

All audience research is based on established principles of sampling, culling from a carefully planned sample of the total audience information that can then be extrapolated to a larger audience.

Nielsen Storage Instantaneous Audimeter.   This is an exciting development in the field of ratings. It is an electronic device stored in closets or attics of homes of people who give their permission for a fee. The meter records changes in frequencies. In fact, it records every change in the set's condition (on-off, channel setting) to the nearest minute each day for each set in the household. A number of times each day, a central office computer makes quick electronic check of these recordings in each sample household. The next day the completed results are available in the offices of clients.°

Research techniques

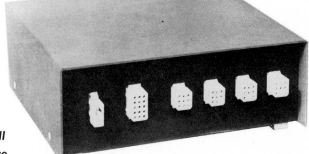

The Nielsen Storage Instantaneous Audimeter is accompanied by a small box that holds the transmitting device.

Obviously, this is an expensive process, and so far it has been found practicable only in large markets where the TV investment stakes are high, such as in New York, Chicago, Los Angeles and San Francisco. But other methods are also widely used by syndicate research services. These include:

The telephone coincidental method.   Calls are made to a preselected sampling of people who are asked, "Do you have a television set? Is it on? How many people are watching it? What channel? What program?" (Nielsen makes about 750,000 calls per year.)

° Source: A.C. Nielsen Company.

◀ (Opposite): *Arbitron television program audience estimates (San Antonio).*

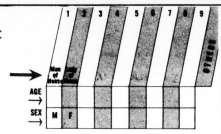

Here's how to keep your TV Diary:

In columns 1, 2, 3 . . . at the right, **please fill in the NAMES, AGE and SEX** of all household members (whether they watch TV or not). Include persons temporarily away, such as on trips or vacations. See Example below for typical entries. If no Man or Lady of House, write NONE in that column.

If you have several TV's, you probably received several diaries. Please write names in same order in each diary, and keep one diary with each TV. (If you didn't receive a diary for each TV, see instructions inside back cover.)

(A) WHEN THE TV IS "OFF"

Draw a line down the "OFF" column for all quarter-hours the TV is off.

(B) WHEN THE TV IS "ON"

> **Important:** If your TV is broken, or won't be used at all in the diary week, **please answer the questions** on the next page . . . and return your diary immediately.

- Put an X in the "ON" column for each quarter-hour the TV is turned on for six minutes or longer. Please be especially sure to show all **late-evening** TV use.
- Write in Station Call Letters, Channel Number, and Name of Program. For Movies, please write "Movie" and Name of Movie. (See Example, below.)
- Put an X in the column under the name of each person watching six minutes or longer during each quarter-hour the TV is "ON."

(C) If an entry in a column does not change from one quarter-hour to the next, DRAW A LINE down that column to show entry did not change. (See Example, below.)

(D) If the TV is "ON" but no one is watching, fill in the station and program information and put "0" in the first person column.

(E) If you have a visitor watching this TV, write "VISITOR" in one of the blank name columns along with visitor's age and sex. (If exact age is not known, put in approximate age.) If you do not have room to write in any more names, write in the *number* of other persons watching in the column marked "OTHERS."

Example

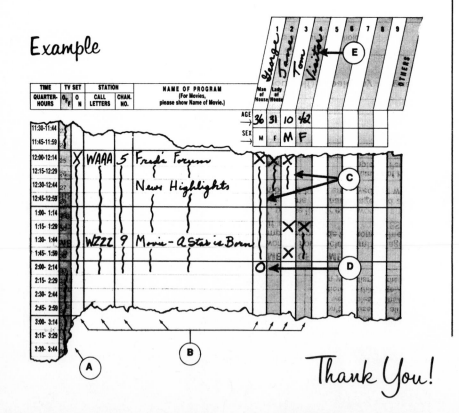

A Nielsen diary, opened to instruction pages.

Thank You!

The diary method.   Having been selected according to a carefully planned sampling pattern, families agree for a fee to keep a notebook next to their television sets. Members of the family record the stations and programs they watch and answer questions about themselves as current purchasers. The diaries are returned regularly to the research firm, and results are tabulated and reported to subscribers.

Gross Rating Points (GRPs)

Media schedules are often spoken of as "light" or "heavy," descriptions attributing to the schedules a sense of weight, or impact, on a market. To translate that feeling into mathematical form useful in planning media schedules, the Gross Rating Point (GRP) system has been evolved. In television one rating point represents 1 percent of the total households with TV within a specified area as defined by the rating service used. One percent in Duluth means 1 percent of TV households in Duluth.

A *gross rating point* is the rating a program gets (reach), multiplied by the number of times the program is played (frequency). Usually this is figured over weekly periods. Thus, if a commercial runs on a program with a rating of 10 once a week for 4 weeks, it has a GRP of 40. If it also runs 4 times on another program with a rating of 8, it would have a GRP of 40 + 32, or 72. These relationships can be expressed mathematically:

$$R \times F = GRP$$
$$\frac{GRP}{R} = F$$
$$\frac{GRP}{F} = R$$

where R = reach and F = frequency.

One of the principal merits of the GRP system is that it provides a common base that accommodates proportionately markets of all sizes. One GRP in New York has exactly the same relative weight as one GRP in Salt Lake City.

The cost for time varies by the city and by the time of day. The cost per TV rating point in different cities has been worked out, and the accompanying list is typical (see pp. 130–31).

The advertiser has to decide how much weight (how many GRPs) he wishes to place in his markets and for how long a period. This is a matter of experience and of watching what the competition is doing. Say he selects 100 to 150 per week as his GRP figure (considered a good working base). Within this figure, the advertiser has great discretion in each market. How shall he allocate the time: put it all on one station? Divide it among all the stations? With what yardstick? The answers depend on whether his goal is *reach* or *frequency*. (In the next chapter we shall see how the computer is used to present the various alternatives possible with a given number of GRPs.)

Television cost-per-rating-point trends,

	Daytime M—F 9 A.M.– 4:30 P.M.		Early evening M—F 5–7:30 P.M.	
	FL. '75	SP. '76	FL. '75	SP. '76
1. New York	$97	$115	$112	$146
2. Los Angeles	63	70	88	100
3. Chicago	62	68	75	82
4. Philadelphia	50	67	65	80
5. Boston	42	50	65	73
6. San Francisco	45	60	64	78
7. Detroit	25	36	45	52
8. Washington	30	41	44	52
9. Cleveland	22	27	35	42
10. Pittsburgh	20	25	30	42
TOP 10	**456**	**559**	**623**	**747**
11. Dallas-Ft. Worth	20	22	32	36
12. St. Louis	19	21	25	34
13. Minneapolis-St. Paul	18	23	28	32
14. Houston	20	22	28	30
15. Miami	20	24	28	34
16. Atlanta	16	18	22	27
17. Tampa-St. Petersburg	14	15	18	20
18. Seattle-Tacoma	19	23	27	33
19. Baltimore	18	22	34	35
20. Indianapolis	15	18	18	24
21. Hartford-New Haven	30	31	36	41
22. Milwaukee	14	18	19	24
23. Kansas City	13	16	20	24
24. Portland, Ore.	15	17	18	23
25. Sacramento-Stockton	16	18	20	26
TOP 25	**723**	**867**	**996**	**1,190**

Courtesy *Television/Radio Age*, April 12, 1976.

women 18–49, top 25 ADIs (Spring, '76 vs Fall, '75)

Prime time Sun.–Sat. 8–11 P.M.		Late news M—F 11–11:30 P.M.		Late evening M—F 11:30 P.M.— 1 A.M.	
FL. '75	SP. '76	FL. '75	SP. '76	FL. '75	SP. '76
$315	$364	$310	$310	$155	$190
192	245	150	183	95	115
158	220	138	158	90	102
123	160	94	133	83	95
95	110	88	100	75	90
115	135	100	120	70	85
85	95	55	70	55	60
80	95	71	81	63	67
70	85	50	62	44	51
60	75	50	59	35	45
1,293	1,584	1,106	1,316	765	900
64	70	41	52	33	43
60	60	46	46	29	36
52	55	34	35	30	34
53	60	30	35	30	32
55	70	43	55	32	44
55	55	44	45	30	36
36	46	33	35	22	24
43	50	40	50	28	34
55	66	50	64	40	41
43	48	27	32	22	28
65	67	60	62	40	45
34	36	25	29	21	25
38	40	23	28	20	24
35	35	30	30	20	24
35	41	25	35	22	30
2,016	2,383	1,657	1,949	1,184	1,400

4 WEEK TIME PERIOD AVERAGES | SPOT BUYING GUIDE

DAY, TIME, AND STATION	CHILD 6-11	ADULTS 18+	PERSONS 15-24	PERSONS 12-34	PERS 15-24	PERS 12-34	W TOT	W 18-49	W 15-24	W 18-34	W 25-49	W 25-54	M TOT	M 18-49	M 18-34	M 25-49	M 25-54	TNS TOT	CHD TOT	TIME	ADI HH RTG	MET HH RTG	TV HOUSE-HOLDS	W TOTAL	W 18-49	W 18-34	W 25-49	M TOTAL	M 18-49	M 18-34	M 25-49	CHD TOT
(col #)	25	6	7	8	31	32	33	34	35	36	37	38	41	42	43	44	45	46	47		1	3	5	9	10	12	13	17	18	19	20	24
THRESHOLDS 25-49%	17	12	15	14	6	3	2	4	12	8	6	5	3	5	8	6	5	10	12		2	4	9	9	10	12	9	10	11	14	10	23
THRESHOLDS 50+%	4	3	4	3	1	-	-	1	3	2	1	1	-	1	2	1	1	2	3		-	1	2	2	3	3	2	2	3	3	2	6
SUNDAY																																
7.00A																				6.45A												
KMOL		6			1																											
KENS																																
KSAT																																
H/P/T		6			1	1		1	1		1	1	1																			
7.30A																				7.15A												
KMOL		6			1																1	1		3	4			1	2			
KENS	3	3	1	2	1	1		1	1			1	1					1	1		1	1	2	1				1				1
KSAT																																
H/P/T	3	11	1	2	2	1		1	1		1	1						1	1		2	1	6	6	1		1	4				1
8.00A																				7.45A												
KMOL		5			1																3	4						2				
KENS	16	7		6		1	1	1		1	2	2	1	1		1	1	1	10		3	3	14	4	3	2	3	2	1	1	1	17
KSAT	1	17	1	1		3	1	1		1	1	1						1	1		1	1	5	6	1	1	1	3				1
H/P/T	17	29	1	7	1	2	5	2	1	2	3	3	2	1	1	1	1	2	10		6	4	22	14	4	3	4	7	1	1	1	18
8.30A																				8.15A												
KMOL		9	1	1		2	1														1	1	5	5	1	1		2				
KENS	18	9	1	11	2	1	2	2		1	2	2	1	1	2	2	3	11			5	6	22	5	5	3	5	3	3	2	3	30
KSAT	1	32	3	5	1	4	2	1	1	2	2	2	1	1	2	2					4	2	16	16	4	1	3	9	3	2	2	1
H/P/T	19	50	5	17	1	3	7	4	2	3	4	4	4	3	3	4	4	3	11		10	9	43	26	10	5	8	14	6	4	5	31
9.00A																				8.45A												
KMOL		6			2			1	1	1	1	1		1	1						1	1	5	5	1	1	1	3	1	1	1	1
KENS	4	4	2	6	1	1		1	1	1	1	1	1	1	1	2	2	2	2		3	4	15	3	3	2	3	3	3	3	3	18
KSAT		32	3	6		1	4	2	1	1	2	2	2	1	1	2	2				5	4	21	20	5	2	4	13	6	4	4	1
H/P/T	4	42	5	14	1	3	5	2	2	3	4	4	4	3	3	5	4	2	2		9	8	41	28	9	5	8	19	10	8	8	20
9.30A																				9.15A												
KMOL		5			2			1	1	1	1	1		1	1						1	1	6	3	1	1	1	3	2	1	2	2
KENS	4	4	1	7		1	1		1	1	1	1	1	1	1	1	2	2			1											
KSAT	4	27	2	5	4	1		1	2	2	2	1	1	2	2	2	2				5	3	19	18	5	2	4	11	6	4	4	6
H/P/T	4	36	3	14	1	3	5	3		3	4	4	4	3	3	4	4	2	2		7	6	29	23	8	5	7	17	11	7	9	8
10.00A																				9.45A												
KMOL	13	30	10	30	3	5	5	4	4	5	4	3	4	4	6	5	8	9	4		4	4	15	9	7	5	6	9	7	4	6	12
KENS	2	3		3		1				1							1	1			1	1	5	2	2	2	2	2	2	2	2	4
KSAT		20		3	4	1		1	2	2	1					1					3	3	16	16	4	2	4	8	4	3	3	
H/P/T	15	53	10	36	4	7	6	4	4	7	7	5	5	5	7	6	9	10			9	8	36	27	13	9	12	19	13	9	11	16
10.30A																				10.15A												
KMOL	12	32	10	29	3	5	5	4	4	5	4	4	4	4	6	5	8	8			7	8	29	16	14	9	11	16	13	8	11	22
KENS	1	18	4	4	1	1	2	1	1		1	1	2	1	1	1	1				2	2	8	6		3	2	6	3	2	1	1
KSAT		18		3		3	1		1	1	1	1	1				1				3	3	14	2	2	2	2	5	1	1	1	
H/P/T	13	68	14	36	5	7	8	7	5	5	7	7	7	6	6	7	7	9	9		12	13	50	34	16	11	13	27	17	11	13	23
11.00A																				10.45A												
KMOL	10	35	10	30	3	5	4	5	4	4	6	5	3	4	5	5	8	7			7	8	30	18	14	8	11	16	13	8	11	16
KENS																																
KSAT	2	10	2	2	1	1	1	1	1		1	1	1	1	1	1	1		1		3	3	11	7	2	2	3	7	3	2	2	2
		13		2		2					1						1				3	3	11	11	2	2	2	5	1	1	1	1
H/P/T	12	58	12	34	5	6	7	6	5	5	7	7	7	6	5	7	7	8	8		13	13	52	36	18	11	14	28	17	11	13	18
11.30A																				11.15A												
KMOL	1	39	3	8	1	1	4	2	1	2	3		5	3	3	4	4		1		7	8	30	18	11	5	9	19	11	7	9	8
KENS																																
KSAT	10	41	15	35	5	6	4	6	5	6	5	5	5	6	7	6	5	6			5	5	20	12	9	6	6	11	11	8	6	9
		10		1		1					1										2	2	8	7	1	1	1	5	1	1	1	
H/P/T	11	90	18	44	7	8	10	8	6	7	8	9	11	10	10	10	10	5	7		14	14	58	37	21	12	16	38	23	16	16	17
NOON																				11.45A												
KMOL																																
		19	8	9	3	2	1	1	2	1	1	1	3	3	3	1	2	1			5	5	21	13	5	2	4	17	9	6	5	1
KENS	7	49	20	42	7	7	5	6	6	7	5	5	7	7	8	7	7	7	4		8	8	33	20	17	12	11	24	20	15	13	13
KSAT		9		4		1				1	1	1	1	1	1	1	1				2	2	7	6	2	2	2	4	1	1	1	
H/P/T	7	77	28	55	10	10	8	8	8	9	8	8	11	11	13	10	10	8	4		15	15	61	39	24	16	17	45	30	22	19	14
12.30P																				12.15P												
KMOL	1	21	10	14	3	2	1	1	2	1	1	1	3	4	4	2	3	2			3	3	13	6	2	1	1	14	9	7	3	1
KENS	4	45	18	39	6	7	5	6	7	6	6	6	6	7	7	6	5	6	3		8	8	35	21	18	13	11	26	21	15	12	8
KSAT		16	1	9		1	2	2		2	3	3	2	2	2	2	2				2	2	10	7	4	3	4	6	3	2	3	
H/P/T	5	82	29	62	10	10	7	10	7	10	10	10	11	12	13	10	10	10	3		14	14	58	34	24	17	16	46	33	24	18	9
1.00P																				12.45P												
KMOL	1	32	11	20	4	4	2	2	2	2	3		5	5	7	4	5	2			4	4	17	9	5	3	3	19	14	12	6	1
KENS	4	53	20	40	7	7	4	6	5	6	5	5	7	7	8	6	6	5	2		8	9	35	21	18	13	12	28	21	16	12	7
KSAT																																
H/P/T	5	19	4	13	2	2	3	3	1	3	4	4	1	1	1	2	2	3	2		4	3	15	10	7	4	6	7	4	3	4	3
	10	104	35	73	13	13	11	11	8	12	12	12	14	15	17	13	14	11	5		17	16	67	40	30	20	21	54	39	31	22	11
1.30P																				1.15P												
KMOL	1	32	13	25	5	5	2	3	2	4	2	3	5	5	8	4	5	3			6	6	22	11	7	6	4	21	15	14	7	1
KENS	2	47	15	30	5	5	3	3	3	4	3	4	8	8	8	8	7	4	1		9	9	37	19	13	9	9	33	23	17	14	4
KSAT																																
H/P/T	3	25	6	16	2	3	4	4	3	4	5	4	2	2	2	2	3	3	1		4	4	17	14	9	6	8	8	5	4	5	4
	6	104	34	71	13	13	10	10	8	12	11	11	15	15	18	14	14	10	3		19	18	76	44	29	21	21	62	43	35	26	9

‡ TECHNICAL DIFFICULTY
+ PARENT/SATELLITE RELATIONSHIP

DAILY

Important though the GRP is, however, it has its limitations. Consideration must be given to the number of prospects for the product that are being reached by a program, regardless of rating. But the GRP concept provides a unified dimension for making scheduling judgments.

Additionally, GRPs alone cannot tell how effectively a broadcast schedule is performing. If an advertiser's target audience is women aged 18 to 49, for example, it is often the case that 5 GRPs will deliver more women 18 to 49 for the advertiser than will 10 GRPs. This, as you would suspect, is a function of where the GRPs are scheduled. Five GRPs scheduled during a Sunday Night Movie will almost always deliver many times more women 18 to 49 than will 10 GRPs scheduled on a Saturday morning.

One method that appears well received among advertisers whose products have wide appeal (such as packaged goods) is arbitrarily to determine the number of GRPs required to make an impact on a market. If the budget cannot accommodate the cost of providing this number of GRPs, the schedule may be reduced to the desirable level of frequency. Or the budget may be reexamined to determine additional dollars needed to increase frequency to desired level.

The television day. Television has many audiences, differing in character and size according to the time of day. The cost for that time will vary with the size of the audience. The first question to ask is what time of day can you reach the people in whom you are most interested?

Preemption rate. A considerable proportion of spot television advertising time is sold on a preemptible (lower rate) basis, whereby the advertiser gives the station the right to sell his time slot to another advertiser who may pay a better rate for it or who has a package deal for which that particular spot is needed. Although some stations offer only two choices, nonpreemptible and preemptible, others allow advertisers to choose between two kinds of preemptible rates. If the station has the right to sell your spot to another advertiser any time up until the time of the telecast, your rate is called the *immediately preemptible (IP)* rate. (This is the lowest rate.) If the station can preempt only if it gives the original advertiser two weeks' notice, the rate is designated *preemptible with two weeks' notice* and is sold at a higher rate; the highest rate is charged for a *nonpreemptible* time slot; the two weeks' preemptible rate is the next highest, and the immediately preemptible rate is the lowest. Preemption rates are listed on the rate card, along with the basic rate for 30 seconds. Following is a quotation from a rate card. The three columns show the preemption rates, the first listing the nonpreemptible rate, the second the rate for preemption on two weeks' notice, and the third the rate for preemption without notice. Observe how the rate goes down.

Specifics of buying TV time

	I	II	III
Tues. 8–9 A.M.	$135	$125	$115

◀(Opposite): *Spot buying guide for a specific area.*

MICHIGAN

Grand Rapids-Kalamazoo-Battle Creek—Continued

WOTV
GRAND RAPIDS
(Airdate October 19, 1951

NBC Television Network

 KATZ TELEVISION AMERICAN

 TvB

A Time-Life Broadcast Station
Subscriber to the NAB Television Code
Media Code 6 223 0500 1.00

Time-Life Broadcast Division, Box B, 120 College St. S. E., Grand Rapids, Mich. 49501. Phone 616-459-4125, TWX 810-273-6920.

1. PERSONNEL
President—Willard Schroeder.
Vice-Pres. & Gen'l Mgr.—Thomas M. Girocco.
Station Manager—Marvin Chauvin.

2. REPRESENTATIVES
Katz Television, American.
Canada—Andy McDermott Broadcast Sales, Ltd.

3. FACILITIES
Video 316,000 w., audio 56,200 w.; ch 8.
Antenna ht.: 970 ft. above average terrain.
Operating schedule: 6:30-2 am. EST.

4. AGENCY COMMISSION
15% to recognized advertising agencies on time charge for transmitter and film service.

5. GENERAL ADVERTISING See coded regulations
General: 1b, 2a, 3a, 4a, 5, 6b, 7b, 8.
Rate Protection: 14f, 16, 16a, 17.
Contracts: 20c, 21, 22a, 23, 24a, 26, 27a, 30, 31c, 32a, 32d, 33, 34.
Basic Rates: 40a, 41a, 41d, 42, 43a, 45a, 46, 47a, 49, 51, 52, 52a.
Comb.; Cont. Discounts: 60a, 60f, 61a, 62a.
Cancellation: 70a, 70i, 70j, 71, 73a.
Prod. Services: 80, 83, 84, 86, 87a, 87b, 87c.
Affiliated with NBC Television Network.
Time Change: Station reserves the right to adjust rates or rate classifications, without normal rate protection, because of time changes occasioned by governmental change in local time observance.

6. TIME RATES
No. A40 Ann rates eff 3/29/76—Rec'd 4/12/76.
No. P21 Prog rates eff 6/5/72—Rec'd 8/9/72.

7. SPOT ANNOUNCEMENTS
DAYTIME & FRINGE 30/20 SECONDS

MON THRU FRI, AM:	F1	F2	F3
7-9, Today Show. H & V	65	55	45
9-10, Buck Matthews/Not Women Only.			
H & V	55	35	25
10 am-noon, NBC Morning Rotation.			
H & V	60	45	30
PM:			
Noon-12:30, Local News. H & V	85	65	45
12:30-1:30, Mike Douglas. H & V	85	65	45
1:30-4, NBC Afternoon Rotation.			
H & V	105	85	65
4-5, Gilligan's Island/Partridge Family.			
H & V	115	95	75
5-6, Ironside. H & V	115	95	75
6-7, Early Report. H & V	180	150	125
11-11:30 Mon thru Sun, 11 PM Report.			
H & V	200	175	150
11:30 pm-1 am, Tonight Show.			
H & V	100	80	65
1-2 am Mon thru Thurs, Tomorrow.			
H & V	45	35	25
1-2:30 am Fri, Midnight Special. V	50	25	25
WEEKEND			
SAT:			
7:30 am-1 pm, Kid's Rotation. V	100	80	60
PM:			
1-2, Soul Train	65	55	45
2-5, NBC Baseball	105	85	65
5-6, Mission Impossible. V	85	65	45
6-7, Ironside. V	115	95	75
11:30-concl, Saturday Late Show. V	100	80	65
SUN:			
10-10:30 am, Cartoon Carnival	75	60	45
PM:			
Noon-12:30, Hogan's Heroes	75	60	45
12:30-1, Meet The Press	65	55	45
1-3, Various	65	55	45
3-4, Mission Impossible	85	65	45
4-6, Family Theatre	105	85	65
6-7, Brady Bunch/Squares	105	85	65
11:30-concl, Sunday La	90	70	55

Package: M...

WUHQ-TV
BATTLE CREEK
(Airdate July 24, 1971.)

ABC Television Network

 NAB

Subscriber to the NAB Television Code
Media Code 6 223 0525 8.00

Channel 41, Inc., Box 1616, Battle Creek, Mich. 49016; Phone: 616-968-9341, TWX 810-276-2201
Studio: 5200 Dickman Rd., Battle Creek, Mich. 49016.

1. PERSONNEL
General Manager—Lee G. Stevens.
Program Manager—Charles Alvey.
General Sales Manager—Ernest W. Hill.

2. REPRESENTATIVES
The Meeker Company.

3. FACILITIES
Video 3,140,000 w., audio 314,000 w.; ch 41.
Antenna ht.: 1,073 ft. above average terrain.
Operating schedule: 8-1 am.

4. AGENCY COMMISSION
15% on time & talent. No cash discount. Bills payable 15th of month.

5. GENERAL ADVERTISING See coded regulations
General: 1b, 2a, 3a, 4a, 5, 6a.
Rate Protection: 10m, 11m, 12c, 13d, 14c, 16.
Contracts: 20a, 21, 22a, 22c, 23, 24a, 25, 26, 27c, 28, 29, 30, 31c, 32a, 32c, 32d, 34.
Basic Rates: 40b, 41a, 41b, 41d, 42, 43a, 43b, 44b, 45a, 46, 47a, 49, 50, 51, 52
Comb.; Cont Discounts: 60a, 60f, 61b, 61c, 62b.
Cancellation: 70a, 70b, 70e, 70h, 71, 72, 73a, 73b.
Prod. Services: 80, 82, 83, 85, 87b, 87c.
Affiliated with ABC Television Network.

6. TIME RATES
No. 12 Eff 4/12/76—Rec'd 4/15/76.

7. SPOT ANNOUNCEMENTS
PRIME TIME

	Section I	Section II	Section III
MON:			
8-8:30	135	125	115
8:30-concl, Baseball	*150	*125	NA
TUES:			
8-9	195	185	175
9-10	135	125	115
10-11	125	115	105
WED:			
8-9	195	185	175
9-10	195	185	175
10-11	195	185	175
THURS:			
8-9	145	135	125
9-10	175	165	155
10-11	165	155	145
FRI:			
8-9	155	145	135
9-11	175	165	155
SAT:			
8-9	125	115	105
9-10	125	115	105
10-11	115	105	95
SUN:			
7-8	115	105	95
8-9	165	155	145
9-11	165	155	145

9-midnight Mon, NFL:
Less full season .... 225 Full schedule 175
8-11 Mon thru Sun, Prime ROS 95
(*) Less than full season buy.
60 sec: double the 30 sec.
10 sec: 50% of 30 sec.
Section I—Fixed.
Section II—Preemptible with 14 days notice.
Section III—Immediately preemptible.

8. PARTICIPATING ANNOUNCEMENT PROGRAMS
Rec'd 4/15/76.
30 SECONDS

MON THRU FRI:	F	P
Good Morning America—8-9 am	15	10
Dick Van Dyke—10:30-11 am	15	10
11, 11:30 am, noon	25	20
PM:		
ABC Afternoon Rotation—12:30-4	15	10
Speed Racer—4-4:30	30	25
Green Acres—4:30-5	30	25
Mod Squad—5-6	30	25
ABC News Agencies—6 or 6:30, flat	40	NA
Cinema 41—6:30-8	60	50
SAT:		
ABC Cartoons—8 am-12:30 pm	20	15
PM:		
American Bandstand—12:30-1:30	20	15
Western Theatre—1:30-3	25	20
Greatest Sports Legends—3-3:30	20	15
Bill Dance Fishing—various, flat	25	25
Wide World of Sports—5-6:30, flat	75	NA
Space 1999—7-8	100	80
Wide World of Entertainment—11:30-		
concl Mon thru Fri	20	15
Shock Theatre—11:30-concl Sat	30	25
Rock Concert—12:30-2 am Fri	15	10
Western Theatre—10-11:30 am Sun	20	15
ABC Sports—2-4:30 pm Sun, flat	75	75
National Geographic—6-7 pm Sun, flat	60	60
Mary Hartman—11-11:30 pm Mon thru	50	40

11. SPECIAL FEATURES

Partial page of TV rates from Standard Rate & Data Service. Here all rate cards are published in full, giving information in standardized numerical sequence for each medium.

Sometimes a station offers only two choices: nonpreemptible and preemptible. When a spot is preempted, an advertiser must be given a spot of equivalent value, known as a *make-good.*

Special features.   News telecasts, weather reports, sports news and commentary, stock market reports, and similar programming are called *special features.* Time in connection with special features is sold at a premium price.

Run of schedule (ROS).   An advertiser can earn a lower rate by permitting a station to run his commercials at its convenience whenever time is available, rather than in a specified position (comparable to ROP in printed advertising).

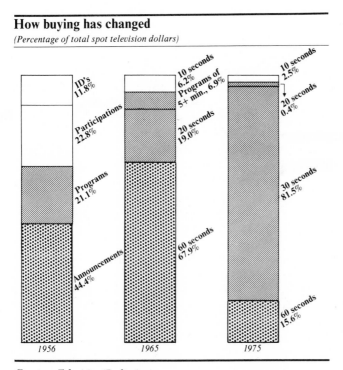

How buying has changed
(Percentage of total spot television dollars)

Courtesy *Television/Radio Age.*

Package rates.   Every station sets up its own assortment of time slots at different periods of the day, which it sells as a package. The station creates its own name for such packages and charges less for them than for the same spots sold individually. The package rate is one of the elements in negotiation for time.

Rate negotiation.   At this point it is opportune to bring up the recognized trade practice of negotiation between buyers of TV or radio spots and the broadcasting stations for better rates than those published on the rate cards. This practice is nurtured by the fact that the only asset a broadcaster has for sale is time— a most ephemeral asset indeed. Every second during the broadcasting day or night for which there is no commercial buyer means a dollar loss to the station. The station must broadcast continually during its allotted broadcast time to keep its license. The stations know this; the time buyers with big schedules know this as they bargain for a better deal than on the rate card. It may be for a lower rate, beginning with the package deals that stations always offer, or for better time slots for a given rate, or for more spots for the same money. Much depends on how much open time the station has, as well as on the expertise of the buyer. But there is never any harm in asking, "What's the best package you can work out for X dollars?" or "I may be interested in buying X rating points in your market. What's your best proposal?"

Scheduling time

Rotation: horizontal and vertical.   Rotation of a schedule refers to the placement of commercials within a schedule to get the greatest possible showing. If you bought two spots a week for four weeks on a Monday to Friday basis, but all the spots were aired only on Monday and Tuesday, your rotation would be poor. You would miss all the people who turn to the station only on Wednesday, Thursday, or Friday. Your *horizontal rotation* should be increased.

Vertical rotation assures differences in time at which a commercial is shown within the time bracket purchased. If we bought three spots on the "Tonight Show," which runs from 11:30 p.m. to 1:00 a.m., but all our spots were at 12:45 a.m., we would be missing all the people who go to sleep earlier than that. To avoid this situation, we schedule one spot in each half hour of the program, vertically rotating our commercial to reach the largest possible audience.

Other trade practices

Closing time.   Tapes and films that are to be part of a commercial must be in the station's hands 72 hours in advance, although stations are usually capable of accommodating a request for a shorter closing time in special instances. To be sure that the right commercial goes on in the right sequence, agencies' traffic departments issue standard coded instructions on the sequence in which films are to be run.

Certificate of performance.   Station invoices for spot television time include a *certificate of performance* (station affidavit) attesting to the fact that the commercials were run on the days and time enumerated. (A similar statement appears on network bills, too.) A system for electronically coding TV commercials has been developed that, with the help of computer tape, provides an exact record.

Product protection.   Every advertiser would like to keep the advertising of competitive products as far away as possible. That brings up the question of what "protection" (against competition) an ad will get. Although some stations

PETRY TELEVISION INC.

AGENCY	BUYER	ADVERTISER	PRODUCT	SCHEDULE DATES	MARKET BUDGET
Vitt Media	Alice Benson	ITT Cont Bkg	Various	Cal Yr 1977	

STATION/MARKET	CHANNEL/NETWORK	RATING SERVICE	SALESMAN	TEL. NO.	DATE
KSAT/San Antonio	CH 12/ ABC	NSI, Nov'75,F/M'76,May'76	Gene McHugh	688-0200	10/8/76

AG'Y USE	DAY	FROM	TO	TYPE	PARTICIPATION OR ADJACENCY	CODE	DMA RATING	W18-49 HOMES	W25-	W35+	W50+	K6-11	FIXED	PREEMPTIBLE	IDENT.	AG'Y USE
	M-F	7	9A	30	Good Morning America	N	3	6	7	10	6		$30			
						F/M	4	8	9	8	5					
						M	5	8	12	14	9					
	M-F	9	1030A	30	Mike Douglas	N	8	22	21	18	8		$50			
						F/M	7	17	16	16	9					
						M	7	14	15	15	10					
	M-F	1030	330P	30	ABC Rotation	N	7	22	16	13	8		$65			
						F/M	8	23	19	16	10					
						M	8	22	19	13	8					
	M-F	330	4P	30	Mickey Mouse	N	7					24	$95(TP=Merv)			
						F/M/tp6	7					3				
						M/tp	7					1				
	M-F	4	5P	30	Emergency	N/tp 6		13	9		9		$135(TP=Adam 12/FBI)			
						F/M/tp6		11	13		3		(TP=Merv)			
						M/tp 7		12	16		2					
						E	9	22	21		24					

The popular Emergency comes to daytime this fall. With the additional kids programming, there will be an increased number of available kids, and Emergency will pick them up and maintain the kids from Mouse. May'76 prime shrx Nov'75 HUT=9 rtg/32 shr. Demos to Emergency May'76.

AG'Y USE	DAY	FROM	TO	TYPE	PARTICIPATION OR ADJACENCY	CODE	DMA RATING	W18-49 HOMES	W25-	W35+	W50+	K6-11	FIXED	PREEMPTIBLE	IDENT.	AG'Y USE
	M-F	5	530P	30	Partridge Family	N/tp 4		12	8	7	4	6	$125(TP=FBI)			
						F/M/tp6	14	12	10	16	3		(TP=Adam 12)			
						M/tp 7		17	14	10	6	8				
						E	13	21	17	19	12	24				

(R) = ROTATION   * = NO PIGGY BACK

TP = TIME PERIOD   PT = PARTIAL TIME PERIOD
ES = ESTIMATED   PR = PROGRAM
ALL HOMES AND DEMOS IN THOUSANDS

A A A A-SRA RECOMMENDED FORM

AGENCY COPY

ALL AUDIENCE MEASUREMENT DATA ARE ESTIMATES ONLY—SUBJECT TO DEFECTS AND LIMITATIONS OF SOURCE MATERIAL AND METHODS, HENCE MAY NOT BE ACCURATE MEASURES OF THE TRUE AUDIENCE

Courtesy Petry Television Inc., and Vitt Media International, Inc.

Availability chart.

say that they will try to keep competing commercials 5 or 10 minutes apart, most say that while they will do everything possible to separate competing ads, they guarantee only that they will not run them back to back.

The station representative system. Persons with offices in the main advertising centers act as sales and service agents for stations around the country. These *station representatives* provide the time buyer with data about the market, the station's programming, and the audience of the station. They find out for the time buyer (often by computerized hookup, otherwise by phone or teletype) what spots are available, and they help set a firm schedule. A number of representatives, each handling many stations, have lined up their stations into *transcription networks* to handle spot sales. From their list, an advertiser can select the stations of his choice. The advertiser supplies one transcription of his commercial, and the representative makes duplicates as needed, sending them to all the scheduled stations. The advertiser places only one order and receives only one bill—an expedient way of handling a big spot list.

Barter.   Besides purchasing television time directly from the station, many advertisers make a practice of purchasing it through *barter* houses. We discuss this practice in Chapter 21, "The Advertising Agency, Media Services, and Other Services."

THE TV PLANNING CHECKLIST

The basic plan

▲ What is the budget?

▲ What is the relative importance of reach and frequency?

▲ What geographic area (ADI or DMA) do we want to cover? Over what period of time?

▲ What audience do we want to reach? Sex? Age?

▲ What is the weight in GRPs we want for a market?

▲ Shall we use network and/or spot? What proportion of each?

The network buying plan

▲ What are the availabilities of each network for the time we want? What programs?

▲ What are the ratings of available programs? Cost per point per program?

▲ What is the share of market of individual stations in their respective markets?

▲ What is the reputation of the network for product protection? For other helpful services?

Network programs must be planned well in advance—often a year ahead.

The spot buying plan

▲ How do stations compare in share of audience?

▲ What are station ratings by quarter-hour periods?

▲ Which single program best reaches the audience we are seeking?

▲ What are all the programs that best reach the audience we are seeking?

▲ What is the station's history of reliability for handling spots, product protection, make-goods?

▲ What is the best deal we can work out to get the spots we want at the least cost?

These are among the considerations in making a television spot schedule.

VITT MEDIA INTERNATIONAL, INC.

DATE:_____

AUTH.#:_____

PART I - BUYING AUTHORIZATION FORM
BUYING SPECIFICATIONS

Parent Company: _____ Agency: _____ Product: _____

Dates: Start: _____ End: _____ No. of Wks: _____ No. of Markets _____ (Attach Part III)

_____ _____ _____ _____

_____ _____ _____ _____

Target Audience: Primary _____ Secondary _____

Weekly GRP's _____ Total GRP's _____ ☐ ARB ☐ NSI _____ Month(s)

Weekly Gross Budget _____ Total Gross Budget _____

APPROXIMATE % OF GRP'S BY DAY PARTS AND COMMERCIAL LENGTHS

DAYPARTS	EASTERN AND PACIFIC TIME ZONES*		60's	30's	10's	OTHER
Daytime:	Sign on to 4:30P	Mon. - Fri-				
Early Fringe:	4:30 to 7:29P	Mon. - Fri.				
	12N to 7:29P	Sat. - Sun.				
Prime:	7:30 to 11:00P	Mon. - Sun.				
Late Fringe:	11:01 to Sign Off	Mon. - Sun				
	TOTALS					

*Adjusted for Central and Mountain Time Zones

INCLUDE ONLY THOSE SPECIFICS THAT ARE REQUIRED FOR THIS BUY

Days of the Week Preferred_____ Maximum No. of Spots in one Program per week _____

Adjacency Exceptions _____ Station Exceptions _____

Desired No. of Stations per Mkt. _____ Min. Rating/Spot _____ Min. No. Spots/Wk._____

Tags Required? ☐ YES ☐ NO Bill Tags to: _____ Salesman's Sheets ☐ YES ☐ No (Attach format)

Makegood Policy : _____

_____

Rotation Policy : _____

_____

Cancellation Policy: _____

_____

Traffic Instructions: _____

_____

Schedules ☐ FORMS SUPPLIED ☐ VMI FORMS (Sample Attached)

Other Requirements: _____

_____

_____ _____ _____ _____

APPROVED VMI   DATE   APPROVED CLIENT   DATE

Notice how this chart asks key questions for planning and purchasing time.

Cable TV   Cable television is the term used in advertising to describe what is technically known as Community Antenna Television (CATV). It is a paid subscriber system whereby one antenna serves a community of households that cannot get reception or get only poor reception because of interference from their surroundings. It began in the mountains of Pennsylvania, to bring television reception to homes from which it had been blocked by those mountains. Cable television spread to the cities, where residents were beset by the same problems because of the steel structures that surrounded them. The thin coaxial cables by which subscribers are connected are strung on either telephone or light poles by leasehold arrangement, or in cities they may be carried through conduits. An important feature of cable TV is that its reception is usually far better than that of direct transmission, because the height of the antenna puts it above electronic disturbances from many sources. Furthermore, though many home sets can normally receive only one or two stations between Channel 2 and Channel 13, cable TV can easily provide a choice of 20. Cable systems are expandable to 40 or even 60 channels, which they can use for various purposes. They can broadcast their own programs, including local events. Beyond that, they open the way for two-way communication between the subscriber and a system hookup, by means of which some day you will be able to watch a demonstration of a product and then order it by pressing a button. They also open the way for paid TV showings of programs not otherwise available on regular commercial TV.

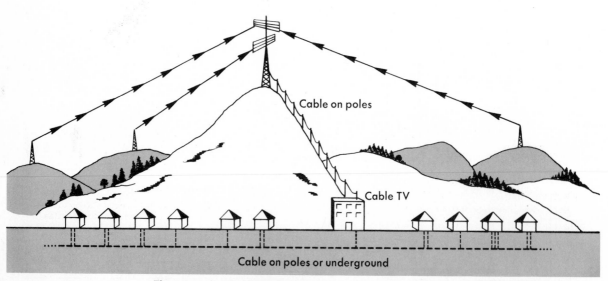

Cable on poles

Cable TV

Cable on poles or underground

The principle of cable television.

At the present time about 15 percent of the homes having television have cable TV (10,800,000 subscribers). California has the greatest number—about 1.5 million. The cost of installing lines ranges from $3,500 per mile in sparsely populated rural areas to $10,000 per mile in urban areas. Where cables must be laid underground, the costs may run up to $80,000 per mile. In 1977 the installation charge ranged from $10 to $15, with the national average monthly fee running from about $7 to $10.

At this time, Pennsylvania, where cable TV was born, has the greatest number of cable systems (301), because of the many small towns lying among its hills.°

Pay TV by satellite via domestic earth stations

On September 30, 1975, two cable companies in Florida turned on their new satellite receivers in time to beam a live telecast of the Ali–Frazier championship fight in Manila, direct to cable subscribers in Jackson, Mississippi and in Fort Pierce and Vero Beach, Florida. In the words of Monroe Rifkin, chairman of American TV and Communications, in Barron's Weekly "This was the single most important development in the cable industry since I've been in the business."

Referred to as *cablecasting*, this new system will take programs sent by satellite to earth stations and send them to cable TV subscribers. In this process, they completely bypass commercial networks and have the freedom to pick or create the kind of program for which cable TV subscribers will be glad to pay.

Trends

We start with the television network situation as it was in January 1977, of which Jim Barker, a veteran media man, said:

> Network '77 is for all practical purposes sold out, and, depending upon who you are and when you bought it, cost increases range from 50 to 60 percent. . . . There is a bigger demand for commercial time than there are units available."

Many advertisers who had planned to use network TV but were unable to find available time or to face the ever-rising costs have begun looking for alternate media, a term increasingly employed.

Cablecasting and pay TV pose a challenge. Cablecasting will never be in direct competition for today's mass TV audience, but potentially it offers such a variety of programs and services that it may have an eroding effect on network program ratings. It may be a long time until the earth satellite station makes an impact on network broadcasting, but it is being developed and therefore poses a potential threat to network TV and to local stations. The National Cable Television Association expects 20 million to 26 million homes to have cable TV by 1982.

Of all forms of television—network, spot, local—local has had the most rapid rate of growth in the past decade. This promises to be the direction of television's greatest growth.

Video cassettes will potentially affect the entire program rating system. On

From tiny acorns

Last month's 15-system hockey cablecast via satellite may be the first sign that cable tv has advertising possibilities on a multi-market basis. In 1977 commercial tv stations could be sitting up and taking notice.

Courtesy Media Decisions.

° Source: National Cable Television Association, 1977.

them, owners may record any program from TV sets, even when they are not at home, and play them whenever they wish.

Another trend in the television industry is the increase in government regulations concerning different industries. Directly and indirectly (by threatening the major networks with antitrust legislation and by regulating industries that do business with television), the government affects the television industry. The Federal Communications Commission has also exercised its authority on programming practices by establishing a "Fairness Policy" for political candidates, creating a family hour, and regulating children's programs.

To local advertisers, television will continue to be of ever growing importance. And despite all its problems, national television will continue to be the giant advertising medium. The Television Bureau of Advertising, looking toward 1980, foresees more than $10.4 billion spent that year on TV advertising, and $17 billion by 1985.

QUESTIONS

1. What are the chief advantages of television for the national advertiser? Its chief limitations? How about for the local advertiser?

2. What is network TV? Spot TV? Local TV? What are the advantages and limitations of each?

3. Define DMA and ADI. How do they apply to television advertising?

4. Explain the value of syndicated research services.

5. Describe the telephone coincidental, diary, and mechanical reorder methods of television audience research. What are the advantages and limitations of each?

6. What are the major questions you would ask when buying (a) network TV time and (b) spot TV time?

7. What is the difference between spot television and a television spot?

8. Give a brief definition, explanation or description of the following:

a) CATV
b) clutter
c) prime time
d) reach
e) frequency
f) flight
g) rating point
h) gross rating point (GRP)
i) preemption rate
j) run of schedule (ROS)
k) frequency discount

l) package rate
m) rate negotiation
n) rotation: horizontal, vertical
o) closing time
p) certificate of performance
q) product protection
r) station representative
s) barter
t) ID
u) special features

9. Why does a station have different time classifications?

10. What is your assessment of the impact television has had on American life? What has been TV's impact on advertising? How about advertising's impact on TV?

11. Cite five products which are ideally suited for advertising via television. What type of advertising does not lend itself to television advertising? In each case, state why you selected that particular product.

12. Do you think advertisers should have any voice in determining the content of television programs? Why or why not?

READING SUGGESTIONS

''Advertisers Put Over Big Ideas in 10-Second Spot Commercials,'' *Advertising Age* (July 21, 1975), 32 ff.

CATER, DOUGLAS, and others, *Television as a Social Force*. New York: Praeger, 1975.

''Daytime Net TV: Pricing Paradox,'' *Media Decisions* (April, 1976), 68 ff.

FRIENDLY, FRED W., ''Television and the First Amendment,'' *Saturday Review* (January 8, 1972), 46 ff.

''How (and How Not) to Solve TV Clutter,'' *Advertising Age* (April 4, 1975), 57 ff.

''Shrink the 30-Second Spot? No! Here Are Better Ways to Get Your Money's Worth,'' *Advertising Age* (February 10, 1975), 40 ff.

SISSORS, JACK Z., and E. REYNOLD PETRAY, *Advertising Media Planning*. Chicago: Crain Books, 1976, pp. 105–28, 192–93.

''TV: Bill Paley Remembers How It Was,'' *Madison Avenue* (December 1976), 26 ff.

8

Using Radio

Radio was the bright star of the media world from the early Twenties to the early Fifties. It had created network shows, soap operas, and nighttime shows, which became part of the American scene. Sunday night shows, particularly, provided the country with conversation pieces for the week. Radio also became the favorite source of news, particularly during World War II, when many people kept the radio on all day to catch the latest war news. Then in the early Fifties, television came upon the scene and took away big parts of the radio audience—and the advertisers. Radio was hurt. But soon, working on the old principle, "Sell what you've got," the industry realized that it still had opportunity as a daytime medium, with its news and daytime entertainment, and it need not try to compete with television nighttime shows. The accompanying chart shows what has happened since radio made itself the prime daytime medium.°

Radio has been called the ubiquitous medium. It seems to be everywhere, go everywhere. It is estimated that there are about 400 million radio sets, three-quarters of them in homes. One-quarter are battery-operated, pocket-size, carrying sets that accompany people wherever they go. The greatest advantage of radio is that people can listen to it whatever else they are doing. The radio is a presence to housewives going about their daily chores, to teenagers while they are studying. It plays in the householder's workshop, and many a farmer drives his tractor with a radio beside him. It is a companion on all trips. Ninety-five percent of all cars have radios; 92 percent of new cars are equipped with them. The second thing a driver does, getting into the car, to drive to and from work, is to turn on the radio. It has indeed become the big daytime medium.

° All data in this chapter, unless otherwise credited, are used through the courtesy of the Radio Advertising Bureau.

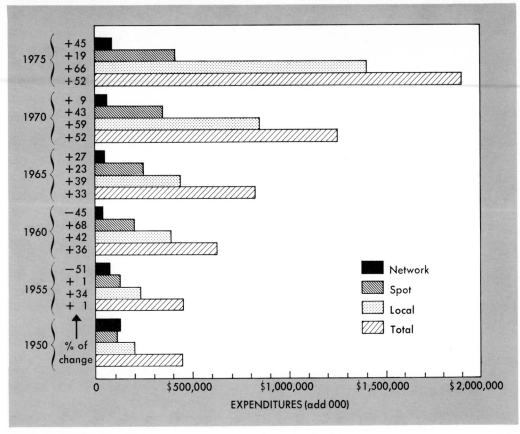

Source: Radio Advertising Bureau.

Radio expenditures. A lot of history in a little chart: the big drop in network expenditures in 1955, after TV networks had come in; the growth of spots, especially local, since that time; and the resurgence of network ads by 1975. For 1980, the Radio Advertising Bureau estimated expenditures to exceed $3.2 billion excluding production.

Radio is a personal medium. When you listen to a voice on the radio, you are hearing it on a one-to-one basis. Usually you are alone with it. Someone is speaking directly to you. Many people have a close rapport with a radio personality to whom they listen faithfully. Radio also brings a wide range of sound effects to involve the listener's imagination in the script. You can hear a plane leave the airfield as vividly as if you saw it off. A majority of Americans—men, women and teenagers—have transistor sets for personal use, which goes way up in the summertime, when people are outdoors.

Radio is broadly selective. There are more than 10 times as many radio stations as TV stations (8,300 commercial radio stations to 730 commercial TV stations).° That means a greater choice of stations from which to select. Even in

Features and advantages

° BROADCASTING, July 11, 1977, p. 47.

Radio is almost always accompanied by some kind of activity

© 1974 ARB (American Research Bureau). Reprinted by permission.

small towns there are more radio than TV broadcasts available. Each station will seek to acquire a loyal following by virtue of its programming, its announcer, its talk shows, or other program qualities. Because different programming attracts different types of audiences, the advertiser can pick the stations that attract the kind of audience desired, such as housewives, men or women of different age groups, teenagers, farmers, ethnic groups. Radio is a friendly, warm way of delivering a message at a low cost per thousand.

Limitations and challenges

Because there are so many radio stations, with many cities of under 300,000 population having 8 radio stations each, the audience is highly fragmented. It may take a number of stations to cover a market.

Since radio is an aural medium, you cannot use it for couponing, showing styles or picturing new models. You cannot show a package or trademark to help a shopper quickly identify your product on the shelf.

The chief complaint about radio is that it has too many commercials per hour. This frequency lessens the impact of all commercials and makes it much more difficult to position a commercial away from that of a competing product, even though stations try to separate them. The need for getting immediate attention in commercials, however, has inspired some of the most imaginative writing in the field of mass communication.

146

The paperwork in putting through a schedule of national radio spots, as in television, can be quite overwhelming, involving checking and gathering availabilities, confirming clearances, ordering, checking appearances and makegoods, approving bills for payment, and billing to clients with proper credits, as in the case of TV spots. But great advances have been made in computerizing the entire operation.

Yet, with all its limitations, radio ad expenditures almost tripled between 1965 and 1976.

The signal.   The electrical impulses that are broadcast, whether by radio or television, are called the *signal*. If a certain station has a good signal in a given territory, that means its programs and commercials come over clearly in that area.

A few useful technical points on radio

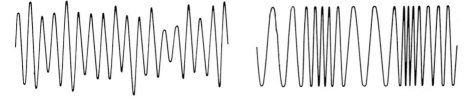

In amplitude modulation (left), waves vary in height (amplitude); frequency is constant. Frequency modulation (right) varies the frequency but keeps the height constant. These drawings, however, are not made to scale, which would reveal that width is the significant difference between AM and FM. The FM wave is 20 times wider than the AM wave. That fact helps to explain how FM captures its fine tones.

Frequency.   All signals are transmitted by electromagnetic waves, sometimes called radio waves. These waves differ from each other in *frequency* (the number of waves that pass a given point in a given period of time). Frequencies are measured in terms of thousands of cycles per second (*kilohertz, kHz,* formerly called *kilocycles, kc*) or millions of cycles per second (*megahertz, MHz,* formerly called *megacycles, mc*). Every station broadcasts on the frequency assigned to it by the Federal Communications Commission (the FCC), so that it does not interfere with other stations. The FCC, in fact, acts as the traffic director of the air, assigning frequencies to all users of broadcasting, including television, police radio, citizens' band, navigational aids, and international radio. The diagram on page 121 shows present usage. A radio station assigned a frequency of 850,000 cycles per second, or 850 kHz (kilohertz), is identified by 85 on the radio dial. (The final zero is dropped for convenience.)

Differences between AM and FM radio.   There are 4,497 commercial AM stations and 2,873 FM stations. Each system offers different values to the viewer and to the advertiser. It's all a question of waves. All waves have height, spoken of as *amplitude,* like the difference between an ocean wave and a ripple in a pond; and they have speed, measured by the *frequency* with which a succession of waves pass a given point per minute or per second. If a radio station operates on a frequency of 1580 kilohertz, for example, it means that 1,580,000 of its waves pass a given point per second.

Based upon these two dimensions—amplitude and frequency—two separate systems have been developed for carrying the sound waves. The first system carries the variations in a sound wave by corresponding variations in its amplitude; the frequency remains constant. This is the principle of *amplitude modulation* (AM).

The second system carries the variation in a sound wave by corresponding variations in its frequency; the amplitude remains constant. This is the principle of *frequency modulation* (FM).

AM (amplitude modulation).   In AM broadcasting, the radio waves are primarily *ground waves*, which travel along the surface of the earth and are relatively unaffected by obstacles or even the earth's curvature. They lose energy to the ground as they travel, finally fading out. Good ground-wave reception can extend up to 200 miles, so that the listening area could be a circle 400 miles in diameter. Certain antennas, called *directional antennas*, can be arranged to give a stronger signal in certain areas, to prevent interference in other areas, and to direct the signal away from uninhabited areas, such as an ocean. The higher the antenna, the bigger the size of the area reached.

AM waves also shoot out to the sky (*sky waves*). Have you ever tuned in a radio program late at night and discovered that the station is a thousand or more miles away? The great distances from which programs may be received by AM radio at night, but not during the day, are due to the *ionosphere*, the deep curtain of electric particles that surround the earth's atmosphere. When the waves from an AM station hit this layer they bounce back to the earth at a more distant point where they can be picked up by radio sets in that vicinity; the waves bounce back again from the earth to the ionosphere and repeat the performance until their power is dissipated. During the day, however, the layer becomes less dense, and the sky wave disappears.

Although sky waves are helpful in transmitting AM signals over great distances, they actually can be detrimental at intermediate distances. If the sky wave returns to earth before the ground wave has been dissipated, the two signals interfere and cause distorted and unpleasant reception. This starts perhaps 40 to 60 miles from the transmitter.

The result is that night AM reception is clear 40 to 60 miles from the antenna, usually weak or poor for the next 100 to 200 miles, and then intermittently good and bad for anywhere up to several thousand miles. AM is used for more car radios because AM ground waves carry better and further than do FM ground waves.

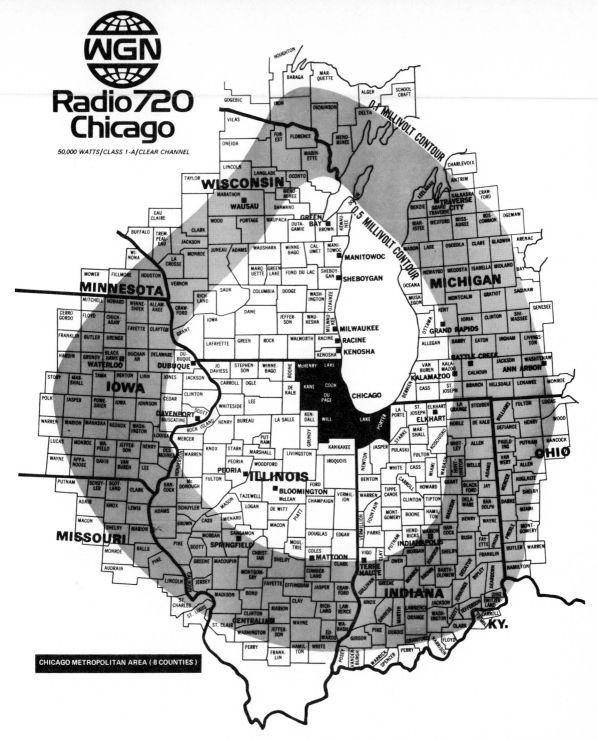

A contour map showing areas reached by a station. The dark area around Chicago represents the region receiving the strongest signal; the white area receives the next strongest; the gray area receives the weakest.

149

Allocation of AM stations.   AM stations broadcast on frequencies in the range of 535 kHz to 1605 kHz (53 to 160 on your dial—the last digit is dropped). Each AM station uses about 10 kHz of bandwidth. A station at 650 kHz, for instance, actually broadcasts over the range of 645 to 655 kHz.

To make the best use of the frequencies, without interference, within the limited confines of the AM band, the Federal Communications Commission has established four classes of stations:

Class I.   Clear channel, 50,000 watts (maximum power AM radio). (These are the giant stations found in major cities.)

Class II.   Clear channel, 250 to 50,000 watts.

Class III.   Regional channel, 500 to 5,000 watts. (A regional channel station shares its frequency with other stations far enough away not to interfere.)

Class IV.   Local channel, 1,000 watts maximum daytime to 250 watts at night, sharing frequencies with distant local stations.

Most stations are in Classes III and IV. Almost half operate during daytime only, to prevent nighttime interference. All rate cards state hours of operation, frequency, and class.

FM (frequency modulation).   FM broadcasting started about 1940, fifteen years after AM. Recently its growth has been rapid, from 678 stations in 1960 to 2,636 in 1975. It is the fastest-growing sector of the radio industry. FM first became famed because of its beautiful tone and its freedom from noise. The secret of the fine tonal reception of FM lies chiefly in the fact that the FM wave is *20 times as wide* as the AM wave. That alone produces better transmission and reception. To accommodate a wave of that width, however, a large band on the spectrum is needed, and FM was assigned one so high that its frequency is measured in megahertz (MHz) rather than kilohertz (kHz), in which AM is measured. At that height, the FM wave is above static, fading, background noises, and interference from stations at lower levels. The result of all this is sound pure enough for stereophonic reception of music, to the great joy of FM listeners.

FM, however, has its limitations. Unlike AM waves, FM waves travel in straight lines only. They cannot go around obstacles nor beyond the horizon, which limits their usefulness for car radios. To the advertiser seeking the drive-time audience, that is the present disadvantage of FM, which it is trying to overcome.

**Structure of
radio advertising**

Radio time is sold in three broad categories—*network, spot,* and *local*—like television time, but the percentages are different, as the pie chart at the top of the opposite page shows.

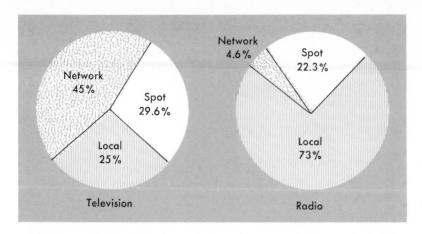

Comparison of network, spot, and local advertising on radio and TV.

Radio networks.   There have long been three national AM radio networks—CBS, NBC, ABC—but there is a possibility that ABC may divide into four networks, each with a different type of programming. All networks offer a long list of stations with which they are, or can be, interconnected, in combinations designed to reach all parts of the country and flexible enough to meet the adverti-

THE RADIO STRUCTURE

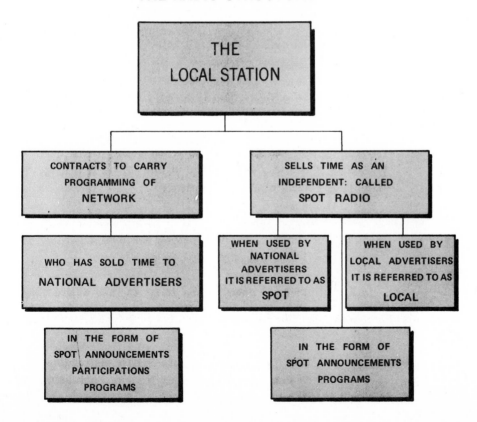

ser's marketing map. As in TV, there are also state and regional networks, interconnected but not part of a national network.

We also have *transcription networks*, formed by leading stations' representatives, who line up a large number of stations from which the advertiser can pick. The advertiser supplies one transcription and a schedule to the network, which handles all details of ordering the time, delivering the commercial, and handling the billing.

Spot radio.   When an advertiser buys time on an individual station, the usage is called *spot radio*. The program originates at the station from which it is broadcast; it is not relayed from a network broadcast. As in television, when a national advertiser uses spot radio, it is, strictly speaking, *national spot radio;* however, by FCC usage and trade custom it is called simply *spot radio*. Similarly, when a local advertiser uses spot radio, it is, strictly speaking, *local spot radio;* but it is referred to as *local radio*. (We discuss local radio in Chapter 24, "Retail Advertising.")

Spot radio represents the height of radio flexibility. An advertiser has 8,240 stations from which to tailor a choice to fit the market, for as long or short a flight as desired. The schedule can be pinpointed to the weather (for suntan lotion) or to house paint or to holiday seasons (for gift suggestions). Spot radio is often used to build the frequency of a campaign running locally in other media or to reach specific demographic segments. An advertiser can move fast with spot radio. Although some stations ask for two weeks' closing, most specify 72 hours' closing for broadcast materials. When asked his closing time, one candid station manager replied, "Thirty minutes before broadcast!"

Time classifications—dayparts. The broadcast day is divided into time periods called *dayparts*, as follows:

Daypart	*Name*
6 A.M.-10 A.M.	Drive time, breakfast audience, interested chiefly in news.
10 A.M.- 3 P.M.	Daytime, dedicated largely to programs for housewives. Serials, games, talk.
3 P.M.- 7 P.M.	Afternoon, drive time. This is radio prime time. Same as morning drive time.
7 P.M.-12 mid.	News, music, talk shows.
12 mid.- 6 A.M.	Music, talk shows.

Weekends are regarded as a separate time classification. Most radio spot time is sold in 60-second units. The cost varies with the daypart.

Types of programming.   Because there is great competition among the radio stations in a town, each station, by means of its programming, tries to reach a certain type of audience. Programs are addressed to men or to women of different age groups and to teenagers. The magnet for drawing the desired audiences is chiefly music, but it is also the personality of a particular announcer who becomes popular with an audience. Talk shows and local sports events are other program features through which various stations seek to be identified. When it comes to music, it is the type of music that attracts different age groups, as the accompanying table shows.

Index of listening by men to various radio station types
(Total listening for all men per type = 100)

Type	By age of listener				
	18–24	25–34	35–49	50–64	65+
Heavy rock	304	127	38	19	6
Top hits	209	154	68	36	14
Golden oldies	123	143	88	80	47
Pop. music	98	119	124	87	45
Standards	50	83	144	136	53
Instrumental	48	90	146	124	62
Classical & semiclassical	62	83	124	127	94
Mod. country music	54	113	141	99	68
Talk	61	67	125	130	116
News	26	49	111	156	184

Courtesy Media Publications, Inc.

Rate classifications. Every station establishes its own classifications and publishes them on its rate card. The negotiated cost of time depends on those classifications, which are typically:

Drive time. The most desired and costly time on radio, it varies by the community and usually has the highest ratings.

Run-of-station (ROS). The station has a choice of moving the commercial at will, wherever it is most convenient. Preemptible ROS is the lowest on the rate card.

Special features. Time adjacent to weather signals, news reports, time signals, or traffic or stock market reports usually carries a premium charge.

Package plans. Most spot time is sold in terms of weekly package plans, usually called *Total Audience Plans,* or *TAP.* A station offers a special flat rate for a number of time slots divided in different proportions over the broadcast day. A typical TAP plan distributes time equally through the broadcast day.

> 25%— 6 A.M.-10 A.M. (morning drive time)
>
> 25%—10 A.M.- 3 P.M. (housewife time)
>
> 25%— 3 P.M.- 7 P.M. (afternoon drive time)
>
> 25%— 7 P.M.-midnight (night time)

Courtesy S.R.D.S.

WFMB (FM)
1965

AVERY-KNODEL, INC.

WALTON FARM RADIO

Modern Country

Media Code 4 214 9130 9.00
Capital Broadcasting Co., 819-820 Meyer's Bldg.,
Springfield, Ill. 62701. Phone 217-528-3033.

STATION'S PROGRAMMING DESCRIPTION
WFMB (FM): MUSIC: top 75 country western M-F
6 am-12 M; Sat 6-1 am. Weather on hour and at
:30 throughout day. Contact Representative for further
details. Rec'd 11/30/72.

1. PERSONNEL
General Manager—H. J. Hoskins.
Station Manager—William K. Wheeler.

2. REPRESENTATIVES
Avery-Knodel, Inc.

3. FACILITIES
ERP 20,000 w. (horiz.), 20,000 w. (vert.); 104.5 mc.
Stereo.
Operating schedule: 6 am-midnight. CST.
Antenna ht.: 250 ft. above average terrain.

4. AGENCY COMMISSION
15/0 time only.

5. GENERAL ADVERTISING See coded regulations
General: 1a, 2b, 3b, 4a, 4d, 5, 6a, 7b, 8.
Rate Protection: 10b, 11b, 12b, 13b, 14b, 15b.
Basic Rates: 20b, 21a, 24a, 25a, 26, 28c, 29b.
Contracts: 40a, 42a, 42c, 43, 44a, 45, 46, 47a,
48, 51c.
Comb.: Cont. Discounts: 60e, 61a, 62b.
Cancellation: 70a, 71a, 73b.
Prod. Services: 80.
Affiliated with American Information Network.
Member: Illinois Radio Network.

TIME RATES
No. 6 Eff 3/1/74—Rec'd 2/11/74.
AAA—Mon thru Sat 6-10 am & 3-7 pm.
AA—Mon thru Sat 10 am-3 pm & 7-10 pm.
A—All other times.

6. SPOT ANNOUNCEMENTS

	AAA		AA		A	
	1 min	30 sec	1 min	30 sec	1 min	30 sec
1 ti	15	12	14	11	12	9
6 ti	14	11	13	10	11	8
12 ti	13	10	12	9	10	7
18 ti	12	9	11	8	9	7
24 ti	11	8	10	7	8	6
30 ti	10	7	9	7	7	5

10 sec ID's: 50% of 1-min.

7. PACKAGE PLANS
TOTAL AUDIENCE PLAN—1/2AAA, 1/2AA

EA:	6 ti	12 ti	18 ti	24 ti	30 ti
1 min	12	11	10	9	8
30 sec	9	8	7	7	6

10 sec ID's: 50% of 1-min.

DISCOUNT
26 wk—5%   52 wk—10%

8. PROGRAM TIME RATES

	1x	52x	104x	156x	260x
1/2 hr	50	45	40	38	35
5 min	25	22	20	17	15

WMAY
1950

Stuart Broadcasting Company
Subscriber to the NAB Radio Code
Media Code 4 214 9185 3.00
Springfield Broadcasting Co., Inc., Box 460, 525 W.
Jefferson St., Suite No. 111, Springfield, Ill. 62705.
Phone 217-525-0200.

STATION'S PROGRAMMING DESCRIPTION
WMAY: Programmed for adults, 18-49.
MUSIC: adult contemporary, current popular & gold
hits. AIR PERSONALITIES hrs. NEWS: 10 min
at :60   min   noon & pm

Contracts: 40a, 41, 42a, 42c, 43, 44a, 45, 46, 47a,
48, 49, 51b.
Comb.: Cont. Discounts: 60b, 60d, 61a, 61b, 62a.
Cancellation: 70a, 70e, 71a, 72, 73a, 73b.
Prod. Services: 80, 81, 82.
Affiliated with NBC.
Member: Stuart Broadcasting Company.

TIME RATES
No. 10 Eff 8/1/75—Rec'd 9/2/75.
AA—5:30-10 am, noon-1 pm & 3-7 pm.
A—All other times.

6. SPOT ANNOUNCEMENTS

1 MIN:	1x	52x	104x	156x	260x	312x	520x
AA	18	17	16	15	14	13	12
A	16	15	14	13	12	11	10

30 sec: 80% of 1-min. 10 sec: 50% of 1-min.

7. PACKAGE PLANS
SATURATION PACKAGE

1 MIN, PER WK:	6 ti	12 ti	18 ti	24 ti	36 ti
AA	16	15	14	13	12
A	14	13	12	11	10

30 sec: 80% of 1-min. 10 sec: 50% of 1-min.

WTAX
1930

Subscriber to the NAB Radio Code
Media Code 4 214 9240 6.00
Sangamon Broadcasting Co., Box 3166, 712 S. Dirk-
sen Pkwy., Springfield, Ill. 62708. Phone 217-
522-44441.

STATION'S PROGRAMMING DESCRIPTION
WTAX: Programmed for general interest.
MUSIC: Adult MOR. Talk programs 9-10 am M-F.
NEWS: network at :60, followed by local news.
News blocks 7-8:15 am M-Sat & 5-7 pm M-F.
SPORTS: programs daily. Play-by-play all sports.
FARM: Farm director 5-7 am & 10:30 am-1 pm
M-F & 5-9 am Sat. Farm block noon-1 pm M-F.
Farm reports, features, commodities, weather, grain
& livestock reports daily on scheduled basis. Con-
tact Representative for further details. Rec'd 10/1/75.

1. PERSONNEL
General Manager—Shelby T. Harbison.
Sales Manager—Edward J. Mahoney.

2. REPRESENTATIVES
Eastman Radio, Inc.

3. FACILITIES
1,000 w. days, 250 w. nights; 1240 kc.
Non-directional.
Operating schedule: 24 hours daily. CST.

4. AGENCY COMMISSION
15/0 time only.

5. GENERAL ADVERTISING See coded regulations
General: 1a, 2a, 3a, 3b, 4a, 4d, 5, 6a, 7b, 8.
Rate Protection: 10b, 11b, 14b, 15b.
Basic Rates: 20a, 20b, 21a, 22b, 23a, 25a, 29a.
Contracts: 40a, 41, 42a, 45, 46, 47a, 48.
Comb.: Cont. Discounts: 60b, 60d, 61a, 61d.
Cancellation: 70e, 71a, 72, 73a.
Prod. Services: 80, 81, 82.
FM facilities WDBR (FM).
Affiliated with CBS.
Affiliated with Eastman Radio Network.

TIME RATES
WTAX/WDBR (FM) COMBINATION
No. 27 Eff 10/1/75—Rec'd 12/31/75.
I—Mon thru Sat 5:30-9:30 am & 11:30 am-1 pm.
II—All other times.

6. SPOT ANNOUNCEMENTS

			I				II	
WK:	6 ti	12 ti	18 ti	24 ti	6 ti	12 ti	18 ti	24 ti
1 min 30	28	26	24	24	23	22	20	
30 sec 24	22	20	18	19	18	17	15	

10. SPECIAL FEATURES
FARM TIME—5:30-7 AM OR LATER &
11:30 AM-1 PM

	6 ti	12 ti	18 ti	24 ti
1 min	22	20	18	16
30 sec	18	16	14	12

Commodity reports—at 9:30, 10:30, 11:30 am & 1
pm, 1-min farm rates apply.

DISCOUNT
26 wk—deduct per spot 1.00.
52 wk—deduct per spot 2.00.

WTAX only: Deduct 1 min 8.00; 30 sec 6.00.
Submitted by Edward J. Mahoney.

WVEM

---

*Part of a page of
radio rates from
Standard Rate &
Data Service.*

WEDNESDAY

TUESDAY

MONDAY

SUNDAY

SATURDAY

FRIDAY

PLEASE START RECORDING YOUR LISTENING ON THE DATE SHOWN ON THE FRONT COVER.

THURSDAY

TIME		STATION		PLACE	
(Indicate AM or PM)		WHEN LISTENING TO FM, CHECK HERE (✓)	FILL IN STATION "CALL LETTERS" (IF YOU DON'T KNOW THEM, FILL IN PROGRAM NAME OR DIAL SETTING)	CHECK ONE (✓)	
FROM —	TO —			AT HOME	AWAY-FROM-HOME (INCLUDING IN A CAR)

PLEASE CHECK HERE ◯ IF YOU DID NOT LISTEN TO A RADIO TODAY.

An Arbitron Radio Diary

STARTING—

A pocket-size Arbitron radio diary for recording time spent in listening. It is to be carried around all day and returned at the end of a week, when it will be replaced by a new diary.

Average Quarter-Hour

STATION CALL LETTERS	ADULTS 18 +						ADULTS 18-34						ADULTS 18-49					
	TOTAL AREA		METRO SURVEY AREA				TOTAL AREA		METRO SURVEY AREA				TOTAL AREA		METRO SURVEY AREA			
	AVG. PERS. (00)	CUME PERS. (00)	AVG. PERS. (00)	CUME PERS. (00)	AVG. PERS RTG.	AVG. PERS. SHR.	AVG. PERS. (00)	CUME PERS. (00)	AVG. PERS. (00)	CUME PERS. (00)	AVG. PERS RTG.	AVG. PERS. SHR.	AVG. PERS. (00)	CUME PERS. (00)	AVG. PERS. (00)	CUME PERS. (00)	AVG. PERS RTG.	AVG. PERS. SHR.
*WAIT	105	3104	79	2460	.2	.9	27	830	25	720	.1	.7	64	1746	52	1388	.2	1.0
WBBM	785	15474	608	11724	1.2	7.2	56	2199	50	1938	.2	1.5	216	6150	171	4909	.5	5.2
WBBM FM	207	4568	193	4082	.4	2.3	165	3061	165	3009	.8	4.9	185	3723	185	3649	.6	3.4
*WBEE	34	818	34	818	.1	.4	9	358	9	358		.3	23	635	23	635	.1	.4
WBMX	296	3915	263	3706	.5	3.1	234	2855	203	2702	1.0	6.1	282	3640	249	3431	.7	4.6
WCFL	381	7434	287	6040	.5	3.4	126	2013	84	1502	.4	2.5	239	3956	163	3232	.5	3.0
WCLR	291	3970	291	3970	.6	3.4	106	1428	106	1428	.5	3.2	217	2951	217	2951	.6	4.0
WDAI	169	4191	160	3845	.3	1.9	151	3370	142	3101	.7	4.3	166	3917	157	3648	.5	2.9
WEFM	59	1514	59	1514	.1	.7	23	555	23	555	.1	.7	33	928	33	928	.1	.5
WFMT	7	293	7	293		.1	1	57	1	57			5	169	5	169		.1
WFMT FM	148	2119	147	1928	.3	1.7	43	724	42	682	.2	1.3	108	1475	107	1360	.3	2.0
TOTAL	155	2199	154	2008	.3	1.8	44	745	43	703	.2	1.3	113	1521	112	1406	.3	2.1
WFYR	227	4294	205	3852	.4	2.4	205	3642	183	3219	.9	5.5	218	4006	196	3564	.6	3.7
WGCI	245	3085	239	3024	.5	2.8	199	2210	194	2178	1.0	5.8	240	2898	235	2850	.7	4.4
WGN	1726	24395	1310	17533	2.5	15.4	240	5323	188	3979	.9	5.6	721	11513	581	8724	1.7	10.8
WIND	346	8510	330	7817	.6	3.9	165	4572	152	4139	.7	4.6	260	6408	246	5929	.7	4.6
WJEZ	152	2272	124	2114	.2	1.5	27	526	22	493	.1	.7	72	1153	48	1074	.1	.9
*WJJD	174	3607	152	2897	.3	1.8	40	655	40	583	.2	1.2	70	1600	61	1279	.2	1.1
WJOB	38	880	38	861	.1	.4	4	214	4	195		.1	15	417	15	398		.3
WJOL	38	678	38	678	.1	.4	2	140	2	140		.1	22	460	22	460	.1	.4
*WJPC	80	1778	75	1746	.1	.9	53	1234	48	1202	.2	1.4	72	1675	67	1643	.2	1.2
WKQX	260	4424	255	4190	.5	3.0	237	3902	233	3734	1.1	7.0	251	4250	246	4016	.7	4.6
WLAK	506	6704	497	6367	.9	5.9	82	1146	81	1096	.4	2.4	225	3056	220	2894	.7	4.1
WLOO	647	8416	639	8208	1.2	7.5	103	1765	101	1700	.5	3.0	298	4125	295	4041	.9	5.5
WLS	936	21434	497	12103	.9	5.9	667	14009	345	7640	1.7	10.3	861	18933	449	10646	1.3	8.4
WLUP	172	3821	150	3499	.3	1.8	165	3221	143	2899	.7	4.3	170	3668	148	3346	.4	2.8
WMAQ	965	19517	531	10511	1.0	6.3	319	6812	152	3147	.7	4.6	660	12655	324	6423	1.0	6.0
WMET	198	4307	197	4228	.4	2.3	166	3352	165	3273	.8	4.9	193	4145	192	4066	.6	3.6
*WMPP	30	558	30	558	.1	.4	17	317	17	317	.1	.5	28	498	28	498	.1	.5
WVON	216	4205	215	4160	.4	2.5	97	2023	96	1991	.5	2.9	156	3159	155	3127	.5	2.9
WWCA	33	764	33	764	.1	.4	10	339	10	339		.3	21	515	21	515	.1	.4
WXFM	31	942	31	907	.1	.4	7	266	7	266		.2	13	521	13	502		.2
WXRT	95	1892	90	1748	.2	1.1	83	1635	79	1532	.4	2.4	87	1727	83	1624	.2	1.5
WYEN	86	1294	86	1294	.2	1.0	68	931	68	931	.3	2.0	84	1199	84	1199	.3	1.6
METRO TOTALS			8495	50021	16.2				3340	19971	16.4				5365	32426	16.0	

Footnote Symbols: (*) means audience estimates adjusted for actual broadcast schedule

ARBITRON

and Cume Listening Estimates

STATION CALL LETTERS	ADULTS 25-49 TOTAL AREA		ADULTS 25-49 METRO SURVEY AREA				ADULTS 25-54 TOTAL AREA		ADULTS 25-54 METRO SURVEY AREA				ADULTS 35-64 TOTAL AREA		ADULTS 35-64 METRO SURVEY AREA			
	AVG. PERS. (00)	CUME PERS. (00)	AVG. PERS. (00)	CUME PERS. (00)	AVG. PERS RTG.	AVG. PERS SHR.	AVG. PERS. (00)	CUME PERS. (00)	AVG. PERS. (00)	CUME PERS. (00)	AVG. PERS RTG.	AVG. PERS SHR.	AVG. PERS. (00)	CUME PERS. (00)	AVG. PERS. (00)	CUME PERS. (00)	AVG. PERS RTG.	AVG. PERS SHR.
*WAIT	53	1546	41	1188	.2	1.1	56	1706	43	1313	.2	1.0	70	1920	46	1420	.2	1.1
WBBM	203	5535	158	4294	.7	4.3	289	7272	220	5633	.8	5.0	447	8853	342	6743	1.4	3.4
WBBM FM	100	2034	100	1951	.4	2.7	106	2277	102	2001	.4	2.3	31	1187	24	863	.1	.6
*WBEE	21	515	21	515	.1	.6	26	571	26	571	.1	.6	23	371	23	371	.1	.6
WBMX	134	1949	132	1893	.6	3.6	140	2063	138	2007	.5	3.1	58	1023	56	967	.2	1.4
WCFL	161	3211	118	2637	.5	3.2	213	4237	160	3514	.6	3.6	232	4640	182	3948	.7	4.5
WCLR	186	2501	186	2501	.8	5.1	202	2772	202	2772	.7	4.6	163	2302	163	2302	.7	4.0
WDAI	40	1176	38	1154	.2	1.0	41	1273	39	1174	.1	.9	18	788	18	711	.1	.4
WEFM	23	706	23	706	.1	.6	27	818	27	818	.1	.6	30	748	30	748	.1	.7
WFMT	5	148	5	148		.1	6	169	6	169		.1	5	169	5	169		.1
WFMT FM	99	1342	98	1227	.4	2.7	119	1660	118	1469	.4	2.7	97	1260	97	1111	.4	2.4
TOTAL	104	1367	103	1252	.4	2.8	125	1685	124	1494	.5	2.8	102	1285	102	1136	.4	2.5
WFYR	110	1930	101	1774	.4	2.8	114	2046	105	1890	.4	2.4	20	585	20	566	.1	.5
WGCI	120	1738	120	1722	.5	3.3	122	1830	121	1801	.4	2.8	44	816	43	787	.2	1.1
WGN	669	9660	544	7260	2.3	14.8	919	12380	696	8966	2.5	15.8	1128	13869	857	10310	3.5	21.1
WIND	184	4326	176	4013	.8	4.8	210	4812	202	4499	.7	4.6	155	3069	154	3023	.6	3.8
WJEZ	66	976	47	930	.2	1.3	82	1134	63	1088	.2	1.4	94	1310	74	1237	.3	1.8
*WJJD	53	1376	44	1055	.2	1.2	72	1724	57	1302	.2	1.3	98	2251	80	1748	.3	2.0
WJOB	12	283	12	264	.1	.3	18	332	18	313	.1	.4	22	466	22	466	.1	.5
WJOL	22	410	22	410	.1	.6	30	498	30	498	.1	.7	29	442	29	442	.1	.7
*WJPC	41	1012	41	1012	.2	1.1	43	1046	43	1046	.2	1.0	25	533	25	533	.1	.6
WKQX	81	1132	80	1066	.3	2.2	82	1194	81	1128	.3	1.8	23	474	22	408	.1	.5
WLAK	201	2694	196	2532	.8	5.3	272	3383	267	3221	1.0	6.1	345	4249	337	4039	1.4	8.3
WLOO	256	3636	253	3552	1.1	6.9	340	4754	333	4566	1.2	7.6	425	5201	419	5058	1.7	10.3
WLS	466	10615	261	6363	1.1	7.1	485	11247	278	6766	1.0	6.3	247	6657	139	4061	.6	3.4
WLUP	53	1254	49	1180	.2	1.3	53	1263	49	1189	.2	1.1	7	567	7	567		.2
WMAQ	571	10448	275	5319	1.2	7.5	651	11816	330	6138	1.2	7.5	514	9566	302	5881	1.2	7.4
WMET	87	1873	87	1857	.4	2.4	87	1894	87	1878	.3	2.0	31	923	31	923	.1	.8
*WMPP	15	319	15	319	.1	.4	16	328	16	328	.1	.4	13	226	13	226	.1	.3
WVON	111	2281	111	2281	.5	3.0	129	2634	129	2621	.5	2.9	106	1964	106	1951	.4	2.6
WWCA	14	308	14	308	.1	.4	15	335	15	335	.1	.3	19	317	19	317	.1	.5
WXFM	11	405	11	386		.3	15	519	15	484	.1	.3	17	559	17	524	.1	.4
WXRT	32	549	32	549	.1	.9	39	610	38	569	.1	.9	12	257	11	216		.3
WYEN	48	755	48	755	.2	1.3	49	796	49	796	.2	1.1	18	352	18	352	.1	.4
METRO TOTALS			3666	22606	15.6				4399	26557	16.0				4056	23596	16.5	

(+) means AM-FM Combination was not simulcast for complete time period.

Courtesy Arbitron.

An advertiser can buy the total plan or parts of it. In all instances there is a quantity or dollar discount plan, depending upon the total number of spots run during a given period of time, thus:

Total Audience Plan

Number of times	Per week (¼ A.M., ¼ P.M., ¼ hw., ¼ night)				
	8	12	20	32	40
1 min.	$110	$100	$92	$86	$79
30 sec.	88	80	74	69	63

Negotiation.   In buying spot radio time, as in buying spot TV time, negotiation is the rule rather than the exception.

Gross rating points (GRP) in radio

One rating point represents one percent of the total potential audience within a specified area as defined by the rating service used. A gross rating point is the rating a program gets (reach), multiplied by the number of times the program is played (frequency).

If, in a community of 10,000 people, research indicates that 160 are listening to one particular program on a certain station, that station is given a rating of 1.6 for that time period. If you were to run a commercial 5 times per week in that same daypart, the gross rating point (GRP) would be represented by the following formula:

$$\text{Rating (1.6) frequency (5)} = \text{GRP (8)}$$

National advertisers planning to enter markets across the country can determine how many GRPs they plan to buy in each market and use that as a yardstick in actually scheduling stations and programs in a city.

Cumes

A *cume* represents the accumulated number of people who have been exposed to a commercial that ran more than once. Say a commercial runs on a station 3 times a week for a 4-week period. It reaches 10,000 listeners each time it appears. That does not mean that it has reached 120,000 people; for every time it appeared, some of the previous audience were listening, and some new listeners joined the audience. The actual cume of an audience is computed by the audience measurement services, based on research and statistical experience, and is available to the advertiser. The cume, in the instance above, is figured at 15,000, which means that 15,000 different households listened to that program over a 4-week period.

At this point we again take a good look at the copy to be broadcast. Will the product be familiar to most people? Are you chiefly interested in telling one sharp story, as in a slogan, to as many customers as possible? Then you will be interested in *reach*. If you have a product or a feature of a product to be carefully explained, *frequency* may be preferable. In either case, the problem of how much time and frequency is required to establish a message in a person's mind determines the proportion of reach and frequency that is best for you.

Planning reach and frequency schedules in a market

NUMA PROGRAMMING

Radio planning by computer.* An advertiser with a budget of $500,000 for advertising is interested in reaching women in the 25- to 49-year-old age group. It has been determined that copy is most adaptable and effective in a one-minute form broadcast on weekdays and Saturday before 7:00 P.M., to coincide with shopping hours. Advertising will therefore spread over the period of 6:00 A.M. to 7:00 P.M., Monday through Saturday. What is the best pattern of reach and frequency?

These are oversimplified decisions for the sake of illustration, but they do reflect the kinds of choices that are made.

Four factors have to be established . . . namely, reach, frequency, number of markets, and number of weeks of advertising. Each of these is directly related to the others; and the choice of one will greatly affect the other. Using a computer program, it is possible to establish a variety of criteria and then make a selection from the alternatives, depending upon which element is most important.

Choice 1. The advertiser wants to *reach* at least 75 percent of the target group in any market over the course of four weeks. He then has a choice of these alternatives:

Reach	Frequency	Number of markets	Number of weeks
75	6.8	Top 10	13
75	4.2	Top 20	13
75	Cannot be achieved	Top 50	13
75	11.2	Top 10	8
75	7.6	Top 20	8
75	4.2	Top 50	8

*Developed by, and published through the courtesy of, the Westinghouse Broadcasting Company.

Choice 2. The advertiser wants an average *frequency* of 8.0 over a 4-week period. In this case the alternatives would be as follows:

Frequency	Reach	Number of markets	Number of weeks
8.0	68.8	Top 10	13
8.0	51.5	Top 20	13
8.0	33.2	Top 50	13
8.0	89.9	Top 10	8
8.0	71.4	Top 20	8
8.0	51.5	Top 50	8

Choice 3. The campaign must cover the *top 20 markets for a period of 13 weeks*. The advertiser then can select from the 4-week reach and frequency alternatives available.

Number of markets	Number of weeks	Reach	Frequency
Top 20	13	17.5	31.7
Top 20	13	42.9	10.4
Top 20	13	65.8	5.6
Top 20	13	78.2	3.9

To demonstrate how any of the alternatives in Choice 3 can be implemented, the summary table below shows the average number of stations per market to be used and the average number of announcements to be used on each over a period of time, depending on the degree of importance of reach, frequency, number of stations, and frequency in each situation.

Reach	Frequency	Average number of stations	Average number of announcements per station
17.5	31.7	1 or 2	100
42.9	10.4	3 or 4	27
65.8	5.6	7 or 8	11
78.2	3.9	12 to 15	5

This system does not tell you which plan to use. That depends on your own judgment of what is most important to you—reach, frequency, number of markets. But under this system, rather than buying an arbitrary number of stations and number of announcements in each market, the program provides a far more precise figure, which indicates the number of stations to be used in each specific market and the number of announcements to be made per station, once the buying policy has been established.

(Opposite and on p. 162): **Comparing intermedia strategies.** ▶

ALL-RADIO MARKETING STUDY

COMPARISON OF 3 MEDIA STRATEGIES TO REACH...

NEW CAR BUYERS

HOW 3 MEDIA STRATEGIES COMPARE IN TOTAL IMPRESSIONS DELIVERED AS WELL AS REACH AND FREQUENCY

STRATEGY 1	STRATEGY 2	STRATEGY 3
ALL TV BUY COMBINING NETWORK AND SPOT TV	NET TV REMAINS SAME: 50% OF SPOT BUDGET IN TV, 50% RADIO	NET TV REMAINS SAME: 100% OF SPOT BUDGET TO RADIO

Target audience measured: Men who purchased new car in past 4 model years
<u>Equal</u> weekly budget for all strategies

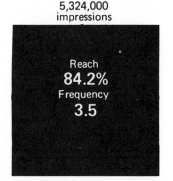

3,304,000 impressions

Reach
72.8%
Frequency
2.5

5,324,000 impressions

Reach
84.2%
Frequency
3.5

6,221,000 impressions

Reach
85.4%
Frequency
4.0

HOW 3 MEDIA STRATEGIES COMPARE IN DELIVERING NEW CAR BUYERS WHO ARE LIGHT, MEDIUM AND HEAVY TELEVISION VIEWERS

NEW CAR BUYERS REACHED WHO ARE:	REACH	FREQUENCY	IMPRESSIONS	% IMPRESSIONS GAINED WITH RADIO
● <u>LIGHT</u>-VIEWERS OF TELEVISION				
Strategy 1—Network Tv & Spot Tv	51.9%	1.5 times	476,000	**+221%**
Strategy 3—Network Tv & Spot Radio	77.9	3.3 times	1,526,000	
● <u>MEDIUM</u>-VIEWERS OF TELEVISION				
Strategy 1—Network Tv & Spot Tv	76.9%	2.3 times	1,110,000	**+101%**
Strategy 3—Network Tv & Spot Radio	86.9	4.1 times	2,228,000	
● <u>HEAVY</u>-VIEWERS OF TELEVISION				
Strategy 1—Network Tv & Spot Tv	89.2%	3.2 times	1,718,000	**+ 44%**
Strategy 3—Network Tv & Spot Radio	91.4	4.5 times	2,467,000	

DETAILS OF 3 MEDIA STRATEGIES AND CUSTOM TAB COSTS

In each strategy the network Tv schedule was 9 participations in prime and late night. A $22,600 weekly spot budget was used in the New York ADI. Strategy 1 is spot Tv in early and late fringe and was an actual buy by an automotive advertiser. In Strategy 2, $11,300 of original spot budget remains in Tv, $11,300 goes into morning and afternoon drive Radio. In Strategy 3, Radio gets total $22,600 spot budget. In Tv 30's are used, in Radio 60's. Further details available from Radio Advertising Bureau Research Department. Cost of reach/frequency analysis only (top half of page): $35. Cost of full analysis including light, medium and heavy viewers breakdown (entire page): $100.

HOW 4 MEDIA STRATEGIES COMPARE IN TARGETING WOMEN 25-49

The analysis below is from ARMS II for the Los Angeles ADI. The first table shows varying combinations of Reach and Frequency achievable on a $13,300 weekly budget. The second shows how frequency distributes and how ability to achieve more frequent repetition of the advertiser's message improves with changes in media strategy.

Strategy	Net Reach	Average Frequency	Total Impressions
All TV	45.9%	2.1 Times	1,531,000
2/3 TV, 1/3 Radio	62.1%	2.5 Times	2,412,000
1/3 TV, 2/3 Radio	60.0%	3.1 Times	2,925,000
All Radio	48.3%	4.4 Times	3,336,000

HOW REACH DISTRIBUTES AMONG WOMEN 25-49 BY FREQUENCY

Strategy	1 or More Times	2 or More Times	3 or More Times	4 or More Times	5 or More Times
All TV	45.9%	24.4%	14.9%	7.0%	3.8%
2/3 TV, 1/3 Radio	62.1%	38.4%	24.2%	14.7%	8.5%
1/3 TV, 2/3 Radio	60.0%	40.1%	27.0%	17.6%	12.8%
All Radio	48.3%	35.8%	27.1%	20.9%	16.6%

ALTERNATIVE WAYS TO REACH PRESTIGE STORE SHOPPERS

What happens if a newspaper advertiser puts half his weekly budget into Radio? Tabulation of New York ADI ARMS II data, given a weekly budget of $7,500 and a target audience of prestige department store shoppers, shows Reach, Frequency and total impressions.

REACH/FREQUENCY/TOTAL IMPRESSIONS (PRESTIGE STORE SHOPPERS)

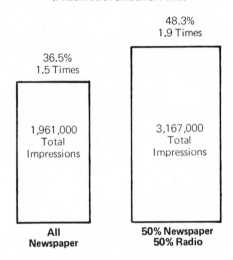

All Newspaper: 36.5% 1.5 Times — 1,961,000 Total Impressions

50% Newspaper 50% Radio: 48.3% 1.9 Times — 3,167,000 Total Impressions

HOW 3 MEDIA STRATEGIES COMPARE IN TARGETING MEN 18+

The analysis below is based on a computer run of ARMS II data for the New York ADI. A weekly budget of $10,000 was available to reach the target audience.

Strategy	Net Reach	Average Frequency	Total Impressions
All TV	26.7%	1.2	1,689,000
Half Radio, Half TV	41.0%	2.0	4,478,000
All Radio	49.2%	2.4	6,464,000

Note: Frequency distributions are also available for all above cross-tabs where only Reach and Frequency are shown.

HOW 4 MEDIA STRATEGIES COMPARE IN TARGETING TEENAGE GIRLS

Here is an analysis of ARMS II data for the Los Angeles ADI. A weekly budget of $6,600 was available to reach girls 12-17.

Strategy	Net Reach	Average Frequency	Total Impressions
All TV	27.7%	1.3	193,000
2/3 TV, 1/3 Radio	46.8%	1.8	464,000
1/3 TV, 2/3 Radio	50.3%	2.6	715,000
All Radio	50.6%	3.6	986,000

For information on other available customer and demographic audience cross-tabulations, contact RAB Research Department or ARMS II subscribing radio stations.

Comparing intermedia stragies

One important question in scheduling a campaign in a market is whether the advertising can get better results by using a combination of media than just one. If a combination is used, what media and what proportion will give the best results per dollar? In response to this question, the Radio Advertising Bureau has done considerable research on the use of radio network and radio spots in conjunction with TV network and TV spots and/or newspapers, in different combinations. More than that, it studied different classifications of buyers, because the formula that worked for one group would not necessarily work for other groups. This is the ARMS II study, ARMS being an acronym for All Radio Marketing Study. The research was conducted equally in New York and Los Angeles, with a total of 10,000 respondents.

The scope and complexity of this thoroughly computerized study are considerable. The project has generated 145 million bits of information that have been stored on 56 reels of computer tape prepared from over 570,000 IBM punch cards. It now can make available over 4,000 tables of information to supply advertisers with information they need to pick the best combination of media for their purposes. They do not have to work on hunches or precedent. The pages reproduced here are exhibits of the type of information gathered.

Intermedia scheduling in a market

Radio as a whole will continue to rise—AM particularly at the local level, because it offers news and local announcers who are favorite personalities. Yet FM will continue to show the greatest gains in advertising because of its fine tonal qualities, which appeal to today's sophisticated young listeners, the broadening of its programming, and its lighter load of commercials.

AM is working hard on a new technical system, to overcome the FM stereophonic superiority. FM is developing a quadraphonic system, further to strengthen its claim to the finest tone on the air. A second generation brought up on FM tone will soon be coming along, strengthening the position of FM in the future.

Trends in radio advertising

1. What are the major advantages of radio for the national advertiser? Its limitations?

2. Why is radio called the ubiquitous medium?

3. About how many radio stations can you get? How does the number of radio stations in a market affect the use of radio as a medium?

4. Why are AM stations assigned to different classes? What are these classes?

5. Why is FM reception better than AM reception? You can hear AM stations from far distances at night; why not FM stations?

QUESTIONS

6. Into what time periods is the broadcast day usually divided? Rank them as to size of audience.

7. Explain why radio stations have different program formats. Can you name five formats in general use? How would you characterize the formats of major stations in your area?

8. What are the four factors that were considered in Westinghouse's Numa analysis and what value does this analysis have for the advertiser?

9. Discuss the major considerations involved in buying radio network time and radio spot time.

10. What types of products and services does radio best serve as an advertising medium?

11. Compare and contrast radio with television in terms of potential effectiveness for an advertiser.

12. How important is radio's basic inability to create visual impact in advertising messages?

13. What do you see as the future of radio, both as an entertainment and as an advertising medium?

14. One important question in scheduling a campaign in a market is whether the advertising can get better results by using a combination of media rather than by using just one. Explain fully.

15. Describe the following:

a) signal
b) frequency
c) FCC
d) AM, FM
e) transcription networks
f) dayparts

g) preemptible vs. nonpreemptible time
h) ROS
i) drive time
j) Total Audience Plans
k) cume
l) reach

READING SUGGESTIONS

"ARMS II: Will It Lift Radio in the Media Mix?" *Media Decisions* (June 1976), 60 ff.

"Here Are Six Things Wrong with National Spot Radio," *Advertising Age* (December 9, 1974), 49 ff.

MAYER, G. A., "It's That Extra Thought and Planning That Make a Winning Radio Campaign," *Broadcasting* (July 29, 1974), 12–13.

Radio Corporation of America, *The First 25 Years of RCA.* New York: Radio Corporation of America, 1944.

"Radio's Ugly Duckling," *Media Decisions* (April 1976), 56 ff.

SISSORS, JACK Z., and E. REYNOLD PETRAY, *Advertising Media Planning.* Chicago: Crain Books, 1976, pp. 193–95.

"Using TV Market Areas to Buy Radio Audiences? It Can Lead You Astray," *Advertising Age* (June 30, 1975), 38 ff.

VITT, SAM B., "Uses of Broadcast Media," *Handbook of Advertising Management,* Roger Barton, ed. New York: McGraw-Hill, 1970.

9

Using Newspapers

Think of the United States not as one big market but as 1,600 individual markets. The focal point of each market is a city or town where one or more newspapers are being published. At the editorial desk of each paper sits someone who has lived in that community for many years; someone who was probably born in that region and who knows its people, their ethnic background, where they live, how they make a living, how they live, and what kind of news interests them most. No wonder 77 percent of the population over the age of 18 reads a daily newspaper. The average newspaper is read by slightly more than two people.° More advertising money is spent in newspapers than in any other medium.

Newspaper readership goes up with educational level, from 75 percent who attended high school, to 88 percent among college graduates. It also rises with income.

People go through a newspaper in a news-seeking frame of mind—a good environment for any advertisement.

Background

In the United States there are over 1,750 newspapers. About 1,400 are evening papers, 350 morning papers, and within both groups about 190 are both morning and evening papers. There are also 640 Sunday newspapers. These are in addition to weekly papers, which we consider separately.

Changes in the newspapers. Newspapers follow the population, and the city's population has been moving to the suburbs. As a result, metropolitan or "central city" circulation has been losing ground—14 percent in the 50 biggest daily markets between 1960 and 1975, and 10 percent in the Sunday paper mar-

° Unless otherwise stated, the source of statistical data in the chapter is the Bureau of Newspaper Advertising.

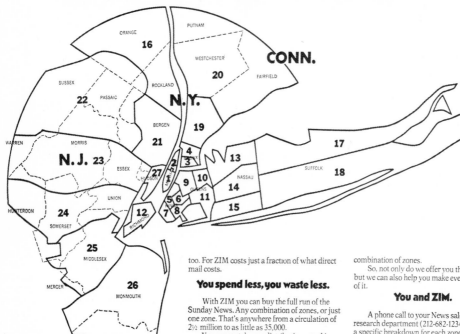

kets. To build circulation, city papers have been publishing for the outlying regions special sections or editions in which space is sold to local advertisers.

Meanwhile, suburban newspapers have been thriving. Between 1960 and 1975, the total circulation of dailies increased 45.2 percent and Sunday papers increased 240 percent. One big lesson to be learned from this is that newspapers are very close to the lives of the people, wherever they live.

Categories of Newspaper Advertising

The two major categories of newspaper advertising are:

▲ Classified advertising

▲ Display advertising

Classified advertising

Who has never looked at a "Help Wanted" column of a newspaper to see what the future might hold? The want ads constitute an important part of a publication's income. They include situations wanted, apartments for rent, houses for sale, lost and found ads, legal notices. Each category has a column heading describing its special offering; all are set in uniform type without illustrations. These are the classic examples of *classified advertising*.

In addition, papers set aside special classification sections, similarly labeled at the top, for used cars, amusements, restaurants, offices, gardening—each paper makes up its own categories. They may carry illustrations of the product and have a variety of typographic effects. All come under the head of *classified advertising*, which has its own rate card and is usually a department unto itself.

Display or general advertising

All newspaper advertising except classified falls into two classes: *local (retail)* advertising and *national (general)* advertising.

Local (retail) advertising.   This refers to all the advertising placed by local businesses, organizations or persons. Chief among them are the department stores and supermarkets; but the local category includes all other local stores and service operations—banks, beauty shops, travel agencies, morticians. Strictly speaking, *retail advertising* is only one form of local advertising, but the terms are frequently interchanged. *Local* is more inclusive.

It is the local advertising offerings, prices, and coupons that shoppers scan before going to the supermarket or the department store; and the nearer their decision to buy, the more carefully they search the local ads.

Local advertising represents 86 percent of all newspaper advertising. Classified advertising is usually included as part of the local advertising figure when media comparisons are made.

◀ (Opposite): *How metropolitan newspapers reach into the suburbs.*

National (general) advertising.   *National* newspaper advertising refers to the advertising done by any marketer who seeks to send readers to ask for a branded product or identified service at any store, showroom, or agency office dealing in such products or services.

National advertising is used to tell the latest news about a new product, a new model, a new style, an improvement in the product, a new service. The spirit of all newspapers ads, local or national, is news. The ad may combine these announcements with cents-off coupon promotions, usually for a short time, to get quick action in a market. Often coupons are offered in response to a competitor's sales drive. Such promotional drives often are inherent parts of a widespread marketing plan.

The term *general* (instead of *national*) is vestigial, found mostly on some rate cards. National newspaper advertising represents 14 percent of all newspaper advertising.

Local rates vs. national rates.   A different set of rates prevails for local advertising and for national advertising; each has its own rate card. (Only a handful of newspapers do not follow this practice.) Since retail advertisers have traditionally been the steadiest and largest newspaper advertisers, and since their advertising is placed directly, without agency commission or the need for special representatives in the major advertising centers, they are charged less than national advertisers. In fact, in the largest cities, national rates are as much as 60 percent higher than local ones. (This difference has nurtured cooperative advertising, which we discuss in Chapter 13.)

Features and Advantages

Newspapers are a basic local medium, with all the advantages of local media for the national advertiser: freedom to advertise to a widespread audience, when and where desired; the ability to conduct a national campaign, adapting the headline to each city market or to run test ads in a number of markets. Reading newspapers is a daily ritual in most homes and on commuter trains. Family shoppers carefully read supermarket ads for prices, cents-off coupons, and offerings. They study department store ads not only for planned purchases but to keep abreast of fashion and life-style trends. While reading world and local news, financial pages, and sports and entertainment sections, newspaper readers may stay to look at ads for cars, household and sports equipment, family purchases, and clothing. The fact that all these can be illustrated and described in detail is one of the great advantages of newspapers. Even full-page, beautiful color reproductions can be carried.

A national advertiser can get his ad in a newspaper quickly—overnight if necessary—an advantage much prized by advertisers who sometimes have to act very fast to get a special announcement in the paper.

Free-standing (loose) inserts which we discuss later, have become increasingly important to local advertisers, national advertisers announcing news and promotions, and to direct-response advertisers.

Limitations and Challenges

Newspapers are not suitable for reaching specific, limited target audiences; readership is low, for example, among those under 18. Newspapers are read hurriedly; their life is short. Creating an ad that can compete for attention with news headlines and other ads can be a challenge!

In operating a large newspaper schedule, many problems arise. Newspapers are printed on high-speed presses on cheap paper. Thus, special art work must be designed for newspaper reproduction. Among the 1,750 or so newspapers, there are over 200 different formats, using different numbers and widths of columns.

There is evidence that people scan the paper by opening every page or almost every page up to the classified ads, but the fact remains that the first few pages are usually preempted by the department stores.

Newspapers are overcrowded Wednesday, Thursday, and Friday with local ads. But people read papers on Monday and Tuesday as well. If what you are selling is not a supermarket product, reaching for the big shopping days, it has less advertising competition on Monday and Tuesday.

How Newspaper Space Is Bought

Measuring space. The width of newspaper space is measured in terms of *columns.* The depth from top to bottom is measured in agate lines per column, referred to just as *lines,* of which there are 14 to the inch. The size of an ad is specified in terms of lines × columns. An advertisement 5 inches deep by 2 columns wide is written "70 × 2," spoken of as "70 on 2," and is a 140-line ad. *The width of the column varies from paper to paper but has no bearing on the line rate of display advertising.* (Want ads, however, are sold per line or per word of copy.) Nor does the number of lines of type in a display ad have anything to do with the measurement of space in terms of lines. Rates are usually quoted by the line. (In small-town papers of low circulation, space may be sold by the column inch.) Just remember: 14 lines to the column inch.

The rate structure. Publishers set their own rates. About 75 percent of the papers offer a uniform *flat rate* to all national advertisers. Other newspapers offer a *quantity* discount or an alternative *time* or *frequency* discount. The advertiser elects whichever discount structure is best for him.

Published Morning, Evening, Sunday
Publication Address
Telephone Number

NAME OF NEWSPAPER

Rate Card Number
Issue Date
Effective Date

1—PERSONNEL

a. Name of publisher.
b. Names of advertising executives.
c. Name of production supervisor.

2—REPRESENTATIVES

a. Names, addresses, and telephone numbers of advertising representatives.

3—COMMISSION AND CASH DISCOUNT

a. Agency commission.
b. Cash discount.
c. Discount date.

4—GENERAL

a. Policy on rate protection and rate revision notice.
b. Regulations covering acceptance of advertising.
c. Policy regarding advertising which simulates editorial content.

5—GENERAL ADVERTISING RATES

a. Black and white rates for standard space units. Bulk and/or frequency discounts.
b. Starting date if sold in combination.

6—COLOR — ROP

a. Color availability — days of week and number of colors available.
b. Minimum size for ROP Color advertisements.
c. Rates for standard units — 1 page, 1500 lines, 1000 lines — with black and white costs as base for comparison.
d. Rates for non-standard units—black and white line rate plus applicable flat or % premium.
e. Closing dates for reservations and printing material.
f. Cancellation dates.
g. Leeway on insertion dates, if required.

h. Number of progressive proofs required.
i. Registration marks on plates and mats.
j. Full page size for direct casting, in inches.
k. Number of mats required for direct casting.
l. Running head and date line for direct casting, if required.
m. Bulk or frequency discounts on color.

7—MAGAZINE SECTIONS
(Name of Section and when issued)

a. Rates for letterpress — black and white, color.
b. Rates for rotogravure — monotone, color.
c. Minimum depth and mechanical requirements.
d. Closing and cancellation dates.

Anatomy of a rate card. This is a model rate card, widely used by newspapers and based on the recommendation of the American Association of Advertising Agencies. The chief feature of the card is that all information is given in standardized numbers and is listed

8—COMIC SECTIONS (When issued)

a. Rates for color units.
b. Minimum depth and mechanical requirements.
c. Closing and cancellation dates.

9—CLASSIFICATIONS

a. Rates for special classifications
(amusements, financial, political, etc.,
and special pages.)

10—SPLIT RUN

a. Availabilities and rates.

11—POSITION CHARGES

a. Availabilities and rates.

12—DAILY COMIC PAGES

a. Rates.
b. Minimum requirements.
c. Regulations covering acceptance of
advertising.
d. Closing and cancellation dates.

13—CLASSIFIED

a. Rate per word, line or inch; number of words
per line.
b. Minimum requirements.

14—READING NOTICES

a. Available pages.
b. Rates and requirements.

15—CONTRACT AND COPY REGULATIONS

a. Regulations not stated elsewhere in rate card.

- -

16—CLOSING AND CANCELLATION DATES (Black and White)

17—MINIMUM DEPTH ROP

18—MECHANICAL MEASUREMENTS

a. Type page size before processing —
inches wide by inches deep.
b. Depth of column in lines.
c. Number of columns to page.
d. Number of lines charged to column and to page.
e. Number of lines charged to double-truck and
size in inches.
f. Requirements as to mats, originals and
electros.

g. Screen required.
h. Address for printing material.
i. Other mechanical information.

19—CIRCULATION INFORMATION

a. Circulation verification (details in Publisher's
Statement and Audit Report).
b. If unaudited, basis for circulation claim.
c. Milline rates, if desired. Daily .... ,
Sunday ....

20—MISCELLANEOUS

a. Year established.
b. Subscription price; single copy price.
c. News services, e.g. AP, UP.
d. Other information not listed elsewhere.

(Standard Form Rate Card recommended by the American Association of Advertising Agencies, Inc.).

*in standardized sequence. All newspapers follow the same
numbering system and sequence of information. If they have
no information under some classification, they skip the number
but do not change the numbering of the rest of the card.*

NEWSPAPER CIRCULATION/MARKET DATA APPLIED TO TV MARKET AREAS

(Newspaper Group circulation is not included in any total)

MARKET DATA & DEMOGRAPHIC SUMMARY

CLEVELAND

		Households	Percent of ADI	Consumer Spendable Income (000)	Percent of ADI	Total Retail Sales (000)	Percent of ADI	Women 18+	Men 18+	Teens 12-17	Children 2-11	White
CLEVELAND	SMSA	668,250	50.5	11,578,251	54.0	5,652,710	50.2	748	654	237	334	1,579
AKRON	SMSA	221,120	16.7	3,536,806	16.5	1,937,947	17.2	248	223	82	115	605
CANTON	SMSA	133,990	10.1	1,984,477	9.3	1,145,083	10.2	144	128	47	67	379
LORAIN-ELYRIA	SMSA	82,400	6.2	1,337,158	6.2	722,138	6.4	90	83	35	50	247
MANSFIELD	SMSA	44,150	3.3	633,261	3.0	417,161	3.7	44	42	16	22	122
SANDUSKY, OHIO	SMSA	26,100	2.0	388,536	1.8	261,363	2.3	27	24	10	14	73
BALANCE NON-SMSA COUNTIES		146,030	11.0	1,987,552	9.3	1,117,526	9.9	154	139	55	78	435
TOTAL FOR MARKET AREA		1,322,040	100.0	21,446,041	100.0	11,253,928	100.0	1,455	1,293	482	680	3,440
RANKINGS			5		9		9					

DAILY CIRCULATION AND COVERAGE / SUNDAY OR WEEKEND

Metro Area Name of Newspaper(s)	Daily Open Line Rate ($)	Total Circ (000)	Within Home County Circ (000)	To H/H %	Within SMSA In ADI Circ (000)	Percent %	In Non-SMSA Counties In ADI Circ (000)	Percent %	Total ADI Circ (000)	Percent %	Sunday Open Line Rate ($)	Total ADI Circ (000)	Percent %
CLEVELAND													
CLEVELAND P DEA	1.80	395.8	284.7	51.2	315.5	47.2	10.7	7.3	373.4	28.2	2.22	468.0	35.4
CLEVELAND PRESS	1.68	361.6	312.3	56.2	344.9	51.6	2.6	1.8	359.8	27.2		.0	.0
MEDINA CO GAZETT =	.30	13.6	13.3	43.4	13.4	2.0	.0	.0	13.4	1.0		.0	.0
PAINE/ME/C TE TL =	.31	24.2	15.7	25.4	23.9	3.6	.1	.1	24.0	1.8	.35	43.0	3.2
WILLOUGHBY/M N-H =	.27	28.0	25.0	40.4	27.7	4.2	.0	.0	27.7	2.1	.27	26.9	2.0
AKRON BEACON JOU					9.7	1.5	.0	.0	***			***	
ASH/CO/G SB NH P =					.4	.1	.0	.0	***			***	
CANTON REPOSIT					.0	.0	.0	.0	***			***	
ELYRIA CHRON-TE =					2.5	.4	.0	.0	***			***	
HORVITZ NEWS IN	{these newspapers spill-over from another area in this TV Market}				27.8	4.2	.0	.0	***			***	
KENT-RAVENNA R-C =					.0	.0	.0	.0	***			***	
LORAIN JOURNAL					.1	.0	.0	.0	***			***	
ROWLEY NWSP NTWD					24.3	3.6	.0	.0	***			***	
ROWLEY NWSP NTWW					2.5	.4	.0	.0	2.5	.2			
ROWLEY NWSP NTWC					26.8	4.0	.0	.0	***			***	
SANDUSKY REGIST =					.1	.0	.0	.0	***			***	
WOOSTER RECORD =					.5	.1	.0	.0	***			***	
METRO TOTAL					738.8	110.6	13.4	9.2	798.3	60.4		537.8	40.7
AKRON													
AKRON BEACON JOU	1.22	170.4	144.7	79.2	152.4	68.9	2.3	1.6	169.9	12.8	1.38	208.5	15.8
KENT-RAVENNA R-C =	.26	24.7	22.4	58.5	24.0	10.8	.0	.0	24.0	1.8		.0	.0
ALLIANCE REVIEW =					.3	.1	.0	.0	***			***	
CLEVELAND P DEA	{these newspapers spill-over from another area in this TV Market}				20.2	9.2	.0	.0	***			***	
CLEVELAND PRESS					6.5	2.9	.0	.0	***			***	
MASSILLON INDEP =					.0	.0	.0	.0	***			***	
WOOSTER RECORD =					.0	.0	.0	.0	***			***	
METRO TOTAL					203.5	92.0	2.3	1.6	193.9	14.7		208.5	15.8

Courtesy Standard Rate & Data Service.

To simplify multimedia scheduling, newspaper circulation in geographical markets is converted into ADI territories and used in television scheduling.

The highest rate, against which all discounts are figured, is called the *open* rate or *basic* rate or *one-time* rate, as shown in the following examples:

Quantity discounts		Time discounts	
Open rate .... 78¢		Open rate .... 78¢	
2,500 lines within one year.............. 74		13 times within one year................. 74	
5,000 lines within one year.............. 68		26 times within one year................. 68	
10,000 lines within one year.............. 62		52 times within one year................. 58	
20,000 lines within one year.............. 56		156 times within one year................. 56	

ROP and preferred-position rates.   The basic rates quoted by a newspaper entitle the advertisement to a *run-of-paper* (abbreviated *ROP*) position anywhere in the paper that the publisher places it, although the paper will be mindful of the advertiser's request and interest in getting a good position. An advertiser may buy a choice position by paying a higher, *preferred-position rate*—similar to paying for a box seat in the stadium instead of general admission. A cigar advertiser, for example, may elect to pay a preferred-position rate to be sure of getting on the sports page. A cosmetic advertiser may buy preferred position on the women's page. There are also preferred positions on the page itself. An advertiser may pay for the top of a column or the top of a column next to news reading matter (called *full position*). Each paper specifies its preferred-position rates; there is no consistency in this practice. (A familiar position request for which you do not have to pay extra is "Above fold urgently requested.")

Combination rates.   In a number of cities, the same publisher issues a morning paper and a separate evening paper, in which you can buy space individually or at a better combination price for both. The same space and copy must be used in both papers. In some instances, however, the papers are sold on a *forced combination basis.* Such publishers usually require the ads to be run the same day, but you may be able to get them to run the ads a few days apart, to get the advantage of a wider time spread.

The Rate Card

A publisher's rate card contains more than rates; on it is all the information that an advertiser needs to place an order, including copy requirements and mechanical requirements, set in a standardized, numbered sequence. Most advertising offices subscribe to the Standard Rate & Data Service, which publishes in full all the rate-card information in monthly volumes, kept up to date by monthly supplements.

Atlanta Suburban—Continued
NEIGHBOR NEWSPAPERS, INC.—Continued

Color
The following rates apply to Units 2, 3 and 4.
Use b/w line rate plus the following extra charges:

	b/w 1 c	b/w 2 c	b/w 3 c
Extra	85.00	135.00	200.00

Process color (separations furnished by advertiser)
extra 187.50
Process color (1 set of separations furnshed by
newspaper), extra 225.00
The following rates apply to Units 5, 6, 7, 8 and
9.
Use b/w line rate plus the following extra charges:

	b/w 1 c	b/w 2 c	b/w 3 c
Extra	110.00	175.00	250.00

Process color (separations furnished by advertiser)
extra 250.00
Process color (1 set of separations furnshed by
newspaper), extra 300.00
Rates above apply to standard red, yellow, blue.
Extra 15.00 per color for color not listed.
Minimum color space, 1/2 page.

Classifications
Political—general rates apply.
Classified
1.20 per line; min. 3 lines, 2 times.
Classified Display .38 per line; min. 42 lines.
Minimum Depth R.O.P.
As many inches deep as columns wide.
Closing Time
3:00 p.m., Monday before publication.
Mechanical Measurements (Offset)
8/9-6/12—8 cols/each col. 9-6 picas-pts/12 pt. rule.

page depth		—lines charged to—		double truck width
inches	col.	page dbl truck	picas	inches
21-1/2	301	2408 5117	168-6	28-1

Circulation—C.A.C. 3-31-75 (Consolidated)

	Non-Paid	Paid	Total
Wednesday/Thursday	86,023	11,235	97,258

U. S. SUBURBAN PRESS INC.
SUBURBAN ATLANTA

Includes:
DECATUR NEWS PUBLISHING CO. INC.
Southside Sun (w)   Decatur DeKalb
                          News (w)

TIMES JOURNAL INC.
Marietta Journal (d)   Powder Springs
East Point Neighbor (w)   Neighbor (w)
North Atlanta   Roswell Neighbor (w)
  Neighbor (w)   Smyrna Neighbor (w)
Doraville Neighbor (w)   Austell Neighbor (w)
Clarkston Neighbor (w)   Sandy Springs
Stone Mtn. Neighbor (w)   Neighbor (w)
Woodstock Neighbor (w)   Southside Neighbor (w)
Chamblee Neighbor (w)   West End Neighbor (w)
Kennesaw Neighbor (w)   Tucker Neighbor (w)
Acworth Neighbor (w)   Alpharetta Neighbor (w)
Vining Neighbor (w)   College Park
Mableton Neighbor (w)   Neighbor (w)
North Side Neighbor (w)   Hapeville Neighbor (w)
                          Dunwoody Neighbor (w)

Lawrenceville Gwinnett Daily News (d)
WOODPRINT, INC.
News Daily (d)
Mailing Instructions
Send all orders to U. S. Suburban Press Inc., 262
E. Illinois St., Chicago, Illinois 60611. Phone 312-
321-0275. Send 6 repro proofs.
Representatives
U. S. Suburban Press Inc.
Commission and Cash Discount
15% of gross to advertising agencies; cash discount
2% of net to advertising agencies on all bills paid by
10th of month following publication.
General Rate Policy
Alcoholic beverage and tobacco advertising accepted
(except Woodprint News Daily).
ADVERTISING RATES
Received August 5, 1975.
Combination Rates
Flat, per line, zone combination.......................... 1.65
Color
Available.
Special Days/Pages/Features
Best Food Days: Wednesday and Thursday.
Inserts
Available on CPM basis.
Minimum Depth R.O.P.
As many inches deep as columns wide.
Ads over 266 lines charged 300 lines (full col.)
depth. Minimum size 10

SOUTHSIDE SUN
1614 Thompson Ave., Atlanta, Ga. 30044.

Published weekly—Thursday.
Established 1967. Per copy .10.
Member: Suburban Newspapers of America.
Personnel
General Manager—Gerald W. Crane.
Advertising Manager—Carvill F. Worrell.
Representatives
U. S. Suburban Press, Inc.
Commission and Cash Discount
15% to agencies; 2%—10th following month.
General Rate Policy
60-day notice given of any rate revision.
Alcoholic beverage advertising accepted.
ADVERTISING RATES
Effective January 1, 1975.
Black/White Rates
Open, per inch.. 4.58

YEARLY BULK CONTRACT PLAN

Per inch		Per inch	
100 inches	3.88	2,500 inches	3.47
250 inches	3.80	5,000 inches	3.35
500 inches	3.71	7,500 inches	3.23
1,000 inches	3.59	10,000 inches	3.11

WEEKLY MINIMUM PLAN

Within 1 year: Per inch		Per inch	
2 inches	3.64	43 inches	3.34
4 inches	3.52	86 inches	3.28
8 inches	3.47	129 inches	3.22
20 inches	3.39	172 inches	3.16

Weekly Minimum Plan based on minimum insertion
per week for 52 consecutive weeks. On weekly con-
tract, publisher reserves right to print previous week's
copy if replacement copy not received by final dead-
line:
Alternate A: 26-week (minimum insertion), add .10.
Alternate B: 13 week (minimum insertion), add .20.
Combination Rates
Sold in combination with Decatur, Ga., News. Same
copy must appear within 7 days. No minimum size.
Inch Rate:
Open, per inch.. 9.31
Circulation C.A.C. 3-31-75: Non-Paid 68,171; Paid
4,877; Total 73,048.

YEARLY BULK CONTRACT PLAN

Within 1 year: Per inch		Per inch	
100 inches	7.48	2,500 inches	6.77
250 inches	7.35	5,000 inches	6.56
500 inches	7.19	7,500 inches	6.39
1,000 inches	6.98	10,000 inches	6.29

WEEKLY FREQUENCY PLAN

Within 1 week: Per inch		Per inch	
2 inches	7.00	43 inches	6.58
4 inches	6.88	86 inches	6.46
8 inches	6.77	129 inches	6.34
20 inches	6.65	172 inches	6.22

Weekly Minimum Plan based on minimum insertion
per week for 52 consecutive weeks. On weekly con-
tract, publisher reserves right to print previous week's
copy if replacement copy not received by final deadline.
Alternate A: 26 week (minimum insertion), add .10
Alternate B: 13 week (minimum insertion), add .20
Color:
B/w 1c & 2c no minimum; b/w 3c 86 inch minimum
Use b/w inch rate plus the following applicable costs:

	b/w 1c	*b/w 2c	*b/w 3c
Per page (comb.)	225.00	300.00	465.00

(*) Plus separation when required.
Color
B/w 1c & 2c minimum; b/w 3c 86 inch minimum.
Use b/w inch rate plus the following applicable costs:

	b/w 1c	*b/w 2c	*b/w 3c
Per page (Sun only) extra	120.00	180.00	260.00

(*) Plus separations, when required.
Closing time: 7 days before publication.
Classifications
Political—general rate applies.
Position Charges
Specified position, extra 20%. No minimum.
Classified
Classified Display, open 5.44.
Minimum Depth R.O.P.
As many inches deep as columns wide.
Closing Time
Noon, Tuesday before publication.
Mechanical Measurements (Offset)
8/11/12—8 cols/each col. 11 picas/12 pt. col. rule.

page depth		—lines charged to—		double truck width
inches	col.	page dbl truck	picas	inches
21-1/2	301	2408 4816	372	31

Circulation—C.A.C. 3-31-75

	Non-Paid	Paid	Total
Thursday			35,780

In comparing the cost of newspaper space, two variables enter: the rate per line and the circulation. To provide a clear basis for computing comparative costs, a hypothetical figure called the *milline* rate is used. *A milline is what it would cost per line to reach a million circulation of a paper, based upon its actual line rate and circulation.* Since virtually all newspapers have either more or less circulation than an even million, the milline (pronounced **mill**-line) was created to put them on a comparable basis.° The formula is:

The Milline Rate

$$\frac{1,000,000 \times \text{rate per line}}{\text{Quantity circulation}} = \text{milline}$$

as shown in this example:

What is the milline rate of a newspaper with 2 million circulation and a rate of $2.00 per line?

$$\frac{1,000,000 \times \$2.00}{2,000,000} = \$1.00 \text{ milline rate}$$

As a rule, the smaller the circulation, the higher the milline rate. You cannot buy a milline of advertising. It is merely a basis of comparing rates of papers having different rates per line and different circulations.

The Space Contract; The Short Rate

If a paper has a flat rate, all you need do is send in an insertion order, specifying the space, date, and rate. But if the paper gives a scale of discounts depending on the amount of linage run during the next 12 months, you must first enter upon a *space contract*. Such a *space contract* is not a guarantee for the amount of space you will run but an agreement of the rate you will finally pay for any space that has been run during the year in question. It involves two steps: first, you estimate the amount of space you think you will run and agree to any rate adjustments needed at the end of the year. You are then billed during the year at the selected rate. Second: at the end of the year, the total linage is added. If you ran the amount of space you had estimated, no adjustment is necessary. If you failed to run enough space to earn that rate, you have to pay at the higher rate charged for the number of lines you actually ran. That amount is called the *short rate*. For example, a national advertiser plans to run advertising in a paper whose rates are as follows:

Open rate	$1.45 a line
1,000 lines	1.42
5,000 lines	1.39
10,000 lines	1.36

° The milline was the brainchild of Benjamin Jefferson, then advertising manager of the Lyon & Healy Piano Co., Chicago, in the early 1920s.

The advertiser expects to run at least 5,000 lines and signs the contract at the $1.39 (5,000 line) rate (subject to end of year adjustment). At the end of 12 months, however, only 4,100 lines have been run; therefore, the bill at the end of the contract year is as follows:

Earned rate	4,100 lines @ $1.42 per line = $5,822
Paid rate	4,100 lines @ $1.39 per line = 5,699
	Short rate due $123

If the space run had reached the 10,000 line rate ($1.36), the advertiser would have received a rebate of $300. Some papers charge the full rate and allow credit for a better rate when earned.

The Audit Bureau of Circulation (ABC)

Publishers list their rates on a standardized rate card, which includes a statement of circulation. Since advertising rates are based on circulation, verification of circulation statements is at the heart of the publisher-advertiser relationship. As long ago as 1914, the industry recognized the problem by forming an independent auditing group representing and supported by the advertiser, the agency, and the publisher. The Audit Bureau of Circulation (ABC), whose members include only paid circulation newspapers and magazines, audits the complete circulation methods and figures of each publication member. Rate cards marked "ABC" are accorded top confidence by the industry.

Over 95 percent of the daily papers and most of the significant magazines belong to the ABC. Available to all advertisers, the ABC circulation statement of a newspaper contains much other useful information, including:

'Net paid circulation

Amount of circulation in city zone, trading zone, other

Number of subscribers obtained through cut prices, contests, premiums

Number of papers sold at the newsstands, sent by mail, home delivered. (Home or mail distribution is considered advantageous to advertisers because it promises leisurely reading by several members of the family.)

The ABC reports have nothing to do with the rates a paper charges. They deal with circulation statistics only. Publishers will be glad to supply demographic data of their users. The ABC, however, now has a separate division giving demographic data for many of the markets in the United States. All data are computerized and quickly available as their accompanying ad reports. The ABC also audits paid subscription magazines, a service we will discuss in the next chapter.

Now you can get demographic information on newspapers, too.

A new service from the Audit Bureau of Circulations.

The ABC Newspaper Audience Research Data Bank is now operational. It is providing advertisers and agencies information on not only how many copies of each newspaper are bought, but also what their readers are like, in specific demographic terms. These custom reports save countless hours of work.

The new data bank contains not only "hard" circulation figures, it also contains demographic data, comparable from market to market, for many major and smaller markets throughout the United States. It answers an industry need for standardized measurements in the newspaper medium.

Demographic information includes age, education, household income, size of household, marital status and color. All studies meet industry standards and pass review by the Committee on Newspaper Research of the Advertising Research Foundation before being included.

Grey Advertising was one of the first to use Newspaper Data Bank. A researcher at Grey wanted to know the demographic profiles of 77 newspapers in 40 markets for a project involving its client, Columbia Pictures. ABC set its computer to work, analyzing the 84 demographic cells stored for each participating newspaper, collapsing and sorting to meaningful combinations. The 119-page report was on its way within two days after the initial query. The cost? Comfortably under $100. Advertisers, like General Foods, have also used the computerized data bank to solve a media problem.

Other Services. ABC provides 55 other valuable services for members in the advertising and publishing industries. Everything from on-the-spot examination of publisher-members' records and special audit of research surveys to numerous training and educational aids.

 A Basic Tool for Advertisers, Agencies and Publishers Since 1914

The scope of available information is ever widening.

(Blank No. 4)

CHECKING RECORD

MONTH	1	2	3	4	5	6	7	8	9	10	11	12	13	14	15	16	17	18	19	20	21	22	23	24	25	26	27	28	29	30	31	TOTAL

TO PUBLISHER OF   ORDER NO.

CITY AND STATE   DATE

PLEASE PUBLISH ADVERTISING OF (advertiser)
FOR (product)

┌─── SPACE ───┐ ┌─── TIMES ───┐ ┌─── DATES OF INSERTION ───┐

POSITION

COPY   KEY   CUTS

ADDITIONAL INSTRUCTIONS

RATE

LESS AGENCY COMMISSION   PER CENT ON GROSS | LESS CASH DISCOUNT   PER CENT ON NET

PER - - - - - - - - - - - - - - - - - -

MONTH	1	2	3	4	5	6	7	8	9	10	11	12	13	14	15	16	17	18	19	20	21	22	23	24	25	26	27	28	29	30	31	TOTAL

A record of the published advertisement. After an ad is published, the advertiser or agency receives a copy of the page or issue containing the advertisement. This "checking copy" or "tear sheet" is recorded on a form like this.

Tear Sheets and Checking Copies

When a national advertisement has been run in a newspaper or magazine, the publisher forwards to the agency a copy of the page bearing the advertisement. Torn out of the newspaper, this page is called a *tear sheet;* the magazine page is called a *checking copy.* To *check a tear sheet* is to examine the page and record on a form whether the advertisement ran according to the instructions and standards of the agency, particularly in respect to position in paper, position on page, and reproduction quality. If the ad is satisfactory, payment is approved. If not, the advertiser may be entitled to an adjustment. Should there be a serious error, the publisher may agree to a correct rerun of the advertisement, called a make-good, without additional cost.

Most newspapers forward their sheets through a private central office, the Advertising Checking Bureau.

Newspaper Space Restrictions

Most newspapers require an advertisement to be at least 14 lines deep for every column width. They set a break point in column depth, beyond which the advertiser must pay for the full column depth, even though the ad may not use all of it. Each paper sets its own break point, usually about 270 lines on a 300-line page. If you run 280 lines, you are charged for a full column (300 lines). On a 200-line tabloid page, you are charged the amount of a full column for any ad over 175 lines. Newspapers insist on this provision because they would have a hard job selling a small fringe of unused space.

Between 1973 and 1975, the whole newspaper world was shaken by a 50 percent increase in paper costs—and they have continued going up. Among the steps many papers have taken to meet costs is the reduction in width of their columns, so that they now get 9 advertising columns on a page that formerly had 8 columns. The smaller column costs as much as the larger one did. Although column width has never been standard, recent reductions have resulted in so much disparity that the American Association of Advertising Agencies and the American Newspaper Publishers Association are making an effort to standardize a limited number of column widths.

To have an advertisement dominate a page without having to pay for a full page ad, advertisers often will run an ad to its break point. Instead of taking all 9 columns on a page, they will take only 8 columns on a 9-column page, saving the cost of the space they haven't bought, but nevertheless dominating the page.

For example:

$$300 \text{ lines} \times 9 \text{ columns} = 2700 \text{ lines}$$
$$270 \text{ lines} \times 8 \text{ columns} = 2360 \text{ lines}$$
$$\text{Saving} = 340 \text{ lines}$$

On a large schedule, in large markets, that may mean a lot of money.

To avoid paying for space you don't need, remember that on papers still printed by letterpress, mats shrink in the printing process. The rule of thumb is that they shrink one line in depth in a 50-line advertisement. In an advertisement 100 × 2, a loss of 4 lines will ordinarily occur. Such losses are real, and newspapers charge for space ordered, not for space filled. The best thing to do is to make the mats longer; they will shrink to the correct size.

Newspaper Marketing and Merchandising Services

To show what an attractive market their paper offers the national advertiser, most newspapers, especially in the larger cities, can usually provide helpful marketing and demographic data about their city and its people. Lured by the prospect of a large schedule, newspapers may also be helpful in preparing material to send out in advance to the trade. This material tells about the forthcoming schedule and can help "merchandise the advertising." (Put "merchandising" down among the words that have many meanings.) The *Milwaukee Journal,* for example, has for years published an annual household inventory of consumer product usage. In addition to showing the total usage of each type of product studied, it shows the rank of different brands in each category.

Newspaper-distributed Magazine Supplements

How could we be sure it was a weekend if we didn't have newspaper magazine supplements? When we open our Sunday papers, many of us find two kinds of supplements: *syndicated* and *local.* Syndicated supplements are published by an independent publisher and distributed to papers throughout the country with the publisher's and local paper's logotypes printed on the masthead. Best known are *Family Weekly,* with a national circulation of about 20 million, sold through 300 newspapers; *Parade,* with a national circulation of about 19 million, distributed through about 110 newspapers; and *Sunday Metropolitan's Sunday Newspaper Group,* with about 22 million circulation. The various supplements differ in respect to the proportion of big cities and smaller cities in which they are distributed. The advertiser can select the combination that best fits his marketing plan.

Magazine supplements in newspapers reach a large audience that many magazines do not reach. They offer beautiful color reproductions comparable to those of magazines, and they provide a medium for distributing cents-off coupons. Another great advantage to the advertiser of a campaign in a syndicated magazine supplement is that the campaign involves only one order and the handling of only one bill for all the markets in which the ad appears.

There are also local magazine supplements printed by a newspaper or group of papers in the same locality. These supplements concentrate on the advertising of department stores and other local advertisers. Many newspapers have both a syndicated and a local magazine supplement. Of the Sunday magazine supplements published, 29 million copies are syndicated, and 26.6 million are locally published.

Newspaper Color Advertising

Two broad categories characterize color advertising in newspapers. In one, the color is printed by the newspaper on its own presses as a part of the regular

(Opposite): **A HiFi newspaper ad, originally in full color. The design, like that of wallpaper, repeats itself. The other side of the page was blank, so that the newspaper could use it to print its own material.** ▶

press run. This is referred to as ROP color, meaning that it is printed on the same presses that print the rest of the paper. In the second category are preprinted, roll-fed color pages. An advertisement printed in black ink is referred to as a black-and-white ad. If one color is added, it is a two-color ad (black is counted as one of the colors). If a second color is added, it is a three-color ad, and so forth. In ROP color, the color is used mostly for attracting attention by a mass effect, as a background, border, or a strong design or headline, rather than for a picture of the product (unless it is a flat-colored package).

Preprinted roll-fed color pages.   If, while going through a newspaper, you come upon a full-page ad in many colors, chances are that you are looking at either a Hi-Fi ad or a Spectacolor ad. The advertiser had the ad printed in advance by specialists in this kind of printing. The full-color ad was printed on one side of a roll of newsprint paper. That roll was then shipped to the newspaper, which put it on its regular presses and printed the obverse side with black-and-white editorial matter and ads.

The unique feature of *Hi-Fi* is that it is printed like wallpaper. The art work must be created as a repetitious and continuous design, with the whole ad slightly longer than the page size, so that no matter where it is cut off, the area will contain a complete message. *Spectacolor* ads are precisely placed one-page ads. They also require a special paper. Whether Hi-Fi or Spectacolor is used depends on cost and availability of paper. The advertiser pays for the plates, paper, printing, and freight, in addition to the space charge of the newspaper. Space reservations and printing plans must be made well in advance. Some firms specialize in handling such production assignments.

Free-standing (preprinted loose) Inserts

Since the early 1970s, the free-standing, preprinted insert (also known as a loose insert) has zoomed in importance as a medium for advertisers and a source of income for newspapers. Ranging from a single card to a tabloid-size enclosure running to 32 pages or even more, it is prepared by an outside printer and delivered to the newspaper before the newspaper itself is printed. Then it is loosely inserted in the regular edition of the paper.

Because of postal regulations, the words "Supplement to (logotype)" must appear on the masthead. It is the advertiser's responsibility to supply these printed inserts to the newspaper. In some cities, an advertiser can buy circulation in specific sections of the city at a fixed cost per thousand.

The loose insert is designed for quick response. It is being used widely by retail stores, by national advertisers in promotions with coupon redemption offers, and by direct response advertisers as a reaction to increasing postal rates for direct mail. Some now have a reply card tip-in, which is mechanically affixed to the advertising page. Loose inserts must be planned and scheduled well in advance.

*Full section,
newspaper page size.*

*Folder with
gatefold reply card.*

Men's fashion catalog.

*Multiproduct co-op sheet,
perforated coupons.*

Courtesy Newspaper Advertising Bureau, Insert Division.

Free-standing newspaper inserts are available in a variety of formats.

Black Newspapers

There are about 350 newspapers published specifically for black readers. Their circulation totals over 6 million, 71 of these papers reaching more than 25,000 people each, and 4 with a circulation of over 90,000 each. Weekly newspapers make up 84 percent of the black newspaper field; others are published monthly, biweekly, or 3 to 5 times a week. Two are published daily. Whether they are published frequently or infrequently, black newspapers have high readership.

Weekly Newspapers

America was a country of weekly newspapers before it became a daily newspaper land, and to this day there are about 3,000 weekly newspapers listed in the Standard Rate & Data Service. (A "weekly" paper is sometimes published twice a week.) About two-thirds of the papers are urban-oriented, published in communities in the metropolitan areas or in the suburbs and in the satellites of the suburbs; one-third are published in farm communities. Ranging from paid subscriptions to partially paid or even free circulation, weeklies have high readership because they offer so much local news. They also have local shopping information; in fact, many are known as shopping newspapers because they contain less than 25 percent news.

National advertisers often use suburban papers to round out a promotion they are running in the dailies of the nearby cities. Weeklies are often offered as part of a group of papers within the same geographical market. The Pioneer Press of Chicago, for example, offers a flat rate for a group of 17 separate suburban papers with a combined circulation of more than 90,000.

National advertisers usually buy weekly newspapers through representatives who specialize in weeklies and who are located in the chief advertising centers. They represent long lists of papers. Advertisers choose their territories, place one order, get one bill, and pay one check—an easy way to handle a medium that reaches into the homes of so many different communities.

Comics

The Sunday comic supplement that comes with most weekend newspapers is a family institution. An estimated 111 million people read the comics, a figure that may not surprise you until you discover that 72.4 percent of them are adults 18 years or older. (Children from 7 to 12 make up 16.5 percent, and teenagers 11.1 percent of the audience.)

Comics are syndicated, and space in the comic supplement is sold by national or sectional groups of papers, although space is also sold by individual papers. The chief national comics are *Puck*, in 141 papers with a national circulation of

21 million, and *Metro* comics, in 71 papers with 21 million circulation. The advantage of the group purchase is that the advertiser places only one order and receives one bill. Space in the comic publications is usually sold in terms of a page or fraction of a page.

Split Runs

For advertisers who would like to test different ads for the same product, Sunday magazine supplements offer a *split run*. By this method, an advertiser prepares plates of two or more ads of the same size to be run on the same day, each representing a different appeal. Each ad calls for a reply and includes a coupon with the ad's key number. The plate for one ad is included on the pages printed on press A; the plate for the second ad is included on the pages printed on adjacent press B. Both presses feed alternately into a common stacking of newspapers; hence will all be delivered to the same neighborhoods. The only difference will be the content of the ads. By the number of responses each receives, the advertiser can judge which is better. This is only one of a number of split-run tests that can be conducted in newspapers and magazines.

Trends in Newspaper Advertising

To make up for their circulation losses in the central cities, metropolitan newspapers will continue to expand their penetration of outlying areas, to include local editions with local editorial matter, to attract local advertisers. To compete with other newsgathering media, they will carry more in-depth articles and more articles of general interest like those in magazines. Free-standing inserts will be an important part of the newspapers' income. Letterpress printing will be replaced by offset and phototypesetting.

Because of their many advantages, newspapers will continue to be the backbone of media for local advertisers and a continuing medium for national advertisers with news announcements. The Newspaper Advertising Bureau foresaw $13.5 billion in newspaper advertising (not including production costs) for 1980.

QUESTIONS

1. What are the differences between the two major categories of newspaper advertising, classified and display?

2. Compare and contrast local (retail) advertising with national (general) advertising. Include in your analysis the difference in rates and the reasons for the difference.

3. Discuss the advantages of newspaper advertising. What are the limitations?

4. What is the difference between a milline rate and a short rate? How is each computed?

5. What is meant by an ABC newspaper report? What is special about it? What is the importance of the ABC report for an advertiser? How does he use it? How does it differ from a Standard Rate & Data Service report?

6. What are some of the various marketing and merchandising services that newspapers normally provide for large national advertisers?

7. What are the two types of newspaper magazine supplements? What is their chief difference as far as the advertiser is concerned?

8. How do you explain the increased usage of free-standing preprinted inserts? What kind of advertising do they normally carry?

9. What considerations enter the choice of one newspaper in a two- or three-newspaper city?

10. How is newspaper display advertising space measured?

11. What are the chief things to know regarding the advertising rate structure of newspapers?

12. Who are the biggest users of weekly newspapers?

13. Give a definition, explanation, or description of the following:

a) open rate   f) tear sheet
b) flat rate   g) make-good
c) ROP   h) loose insert
d) preferred-position rate   i) split run
e) space contract   j) rate card

14. What changes have you observed in your local newspapers in the past few years?

READING SUGGESTIONS

"Five Criteria for Newspaper Ads—and How They Work," *Advertising Age,* (November 17, 1975), 54 ff.

"How 12 Agencies View Newspapers," *Media Decisions* (September, 1976), 124–40.

JAIN, CHAMAN L., "Newspaper Advertising: Preprint vs. R.O.P.," *Journal of Advertising Research* (August, 1973), 30–32.

"Newspapers' ABC Data Bank: What It Isn't . . . What It Is," *Media Decisions* (February, 1976), 58–59.

"Newspapers: Now It's 'Target Market Coverage,'" *Media Decisions* (September 1976), 64–65 ff.

SISSORS, JACK Z., and E. REYNOLD PETRAY *Advertising Media Planning.* Chicago: Crain Books, 1976, pp. 188–90, 191–92.

10

Using Magazines

National advertising first became possible in the 1870s, when railroads opened the West. Trains carried magazines to people all across the country, telling them of the new products made in the East. In the hundred years since then, magazines have continued to be a major advertising medium. But when television came along in the 1950s, people's reading habits became viewing habits, and national magazines had to change to survive.

National advertising in the days before television meant advertising in *Life, Look,* or the old *Saturday Evening Post,* the traditional, big-page general magazines designed to appeal to everyone. But people began turning to TV by the millions, and advertisers followed the crowd. After spending years and fortunes to hold their audiences and advertisers, the big giants of the general magazine world folded, one by one, victims of television and of rising paper and postage costs, which particularly hurt the large-size, enormous circulation magazines. By coincidence, the demise of *Life* magazine, the last of the old giants, occurred at the end of 1972, just when the sixth edition of this book went to press. No single event could have more clearly marked the turning point in the revolution that had been taking place in the magazine world since the advent of television.

Meanwhile, a new generation of now successful magazines had appeared on the scene: *Playboy, Psychology Today, Money, Rolling Stone, Ms., Smithsonian, Apartment Life,* and others. They all have one thing in common: each appeals to a specific group of people who share the same interest, taste, hobby, or special point of view. The older magazines that survive appeal also to people who share a common interest. *Good Housekeeping, Vogue, Seventeen, House Beautiful,* and *Cosmopolitan* all go to women, but each stresses different aspects of women's lives. Also among today's older successful magazines are *Time, Fortune, Popular Mechanics, Field and Stream, Ebony,* and *National Geographic,* each appealing to a specific economic, social, or cultural level, or special interest. The only general mass-circulation magazine surviving from pretelevision days is small-sized *Reader's Digest*. About the only new general magazine to take hold since then is *People*.

Magazines reflect changes in life styles. Greater sexual freedom, greater interest and participation in sports, more women in the work force, more and easier traveling—all find expression in today's magazines. On the desk of every magazine editor are manuscripts to be read with one question in mind: "Is this for my readers?"

Features and Advantages

High selectivity

Each magazine represents a target market whose demographic and psychographic characteristics can be identified; each offers a sharp target for advertisers seeking a particular type of buyer.

Leisurely reading

When you get a magazine, you look forward to reading it at leisure. You have plenty of opportunity to select ads of interest and to read all their details, no matter how much copy is involved. You have a chance to study a picture along with the copy and become familiar with the appearance of the product or the package. Time for leisurely reading is particularly important for new pioneering products, for products with new features, and for other products about which the advertiser has an important story to tell. Your leisurely reading time is also valuable to the advertiser offering suggestions for wider uses of the product. The more you read about a product in an ad, the better are chances that you will remember the brand name. All this adds up to the cumulative value of magazine advertising.

Some years ago General Foods ran a massive series of tests of 5 products in 6 cities and compared the effects of magazine advertising with those of TV advertising. One outstanding finding was the high memorability of brand names among magazine readers as opposed to the high misidentification among TV viewers. Result: a major shift to magazine advertising, doubling General Foods' magazine investment from $6 million to $12 million.

Quality of controlled color reproduction

Some of the most outstanding contemporary color work appears in magazines. When color is important in depicting or enhancing a product (carpets, drapes, printed sheets, lipsticks, and nail polish for example), exquisite color work is significant. Color work is so common these days that not using color may put a product at a disadvantage with competitive products that do use color advertising.

Coupon and direct response advertising

Magazines are an excellent medium for ads calling for a coupon or card response with coupon. Since a magazine will probably be around the house for days, weeks, or even months, it is a good place to put a color photo of a product, with ample space for copy. The reader will have time to read the ad and cut out a coupon. For these reasons magazines are a favorite medium for direct response advertisers.

Limitations and Challenges

It is a costly process to provide a selected audience, as magazines do. The value of this service is lost if all you want to do is get a short message about a familiar product before the widest possible audience. Magazines are most economical in sending a message about a specialized product to a specialized audience. They are usually least economical in delivering to the general public just the name and a short message about a widely distributed type of product.

Most magazines have closing dates long before publication, so they may not be the best medium for making news announcements, such as a change in an airline schedule. Many magazines close 5 to 7 weeks before publication for black-and-white ads, 8 weeks for color ads. The closing date is even farther ahead for special editions. With the latest phototype printing developments, improvements can be made in this time schedule. *New York*, a weekly magazine, announced a 5-day closing.

Geographic and Demographic Editions

One of the great recent developments in magazines has been the ability, using a computer, to split the nationwide circulation of a magazine into geographic and demographic classifications.

Geographic editions   In more than 100 of the largest-circulation national magazines you do not have to buy the entire national circulation to run an ad. In their *sectional* or *regional* editions, you may buy circulation in whatever markets you wish to select. The tremendous advantage is that you do not have to pay for running the ad in markets that are of no interest to you. *Time*, for example, has divided its circulation into 127 separate markets from which the advertiser can make up his own list. The special edition usually consists of a special section inserted as a part of the magazine. Schedule for a minimum number of markets is required.

Among its many other advantages, the geographical edition

▲ Permits a marketer to relate advertising to territories in which the product is sold.

▲ Supports promotions being run in different parts of the country.

▲ Tests a campaign in various markets before embarking on a national campaign.

▲ Reaches a scattered set of markets with one order.

▲ Encourages local retail support, since retailers' names are listed as distributors in their home markets.

▲ Is ideal for local and sectional advertisers.

There are some disadvantages to contend with in the geographical edition, however:

▲ Cost per thousand is higher than in a national edition.

▲ Forms close much sooner.

▲ Ads for a given market may not run in every issue.

▲ Orders must be placed well in advance.

▲ All local ads may be run back-to-back in an insert—a situation not conducive to high readership. (It is better to place an ad in one of the regional editions with a special localized editorial section for each major split.)

Demographic editions   There is another type of split, the demographic edition, for subscribers who have similar life-styles and can be identified from a subscription list as belonging

Introducing:

A new idea in metro market selectivity.

Golf Digest and Tennis, publications of The New York Times Company, have joined seven magazines from the Ziff-Davis Publishing Company to form what we refer to as SIM, Special Interest Metros.

This unique combination of nine leading magazines reaches the largest active leisure market anywhere on a local level.

A full page ad, for example, in every one of these nine major magazines reaches over 2.9 million above-average people* who live in New York, Chicago and Los Angeles. SIM lets you also select from two media plans including combinations of six or nine magazines, which enable you to isolate top prospects in any one, two or all three markets.

Not just any people. But discriminating, successful young adults who live the active lifestyle. They earn more. Do more. Entertain more. Spend more. Not only on their active leisure interests, but on all those quality products and services that go to make up the good life. Everything from cameras to cars to cordials.

Special Interest Metros. It took the combined efforts of two major publishing companies to bring you this unique new idea for penetrating the uppermost segments of America's top three markets.

For full details, write or call Bob Golden, Advertising Director, Special Interest Metros, One Park Avenue, New York, N.Y. 10016; (212) 725-8705.

Ziff-Davis/ Golf Digest & Tennis

SPECIAL INTEREST METROS

Where leisure means business... in America's top three markets.

*Estimate of adult impressions delivered assuming one insertion in each SIM magazine.

New groupings of magazines are constantly being offered to advertisers.

to a particular group. *Time* is an outstanding example. It has special editions for business people, for subscribers living in 144 top income zips in 158 markets, for doctors, and for students. In the demographic edition the special insert will be heavily weighted editorially toward topics of interest to the target group.

The proportion of geographic and demographic editions in relation to the total circulation has been around 20 percent for a number of years. These editions are now referred to as *less than full run.*

Magazine Elements

Sizes

The *page size* of a magazine is the type area, not the size of the actual page. For convenience, the size of most magazines is characterized as *standard size* (about 8″ × 10″, like *Time*) or *small size* (about 4 3/8″ × 6 1/2″, like *Reader's Digest*). When you are ready to order plates, you must get the exact sizes from the publisher's latest rate card, as sizes keep changing.

Space-buying designations

The front cover of a magazine is called the *first cover page.* This is seldom if ever sold in American consumer magazines (though it is sold in business magazines). The inside of the front cover is called the *second cover page,* the inside of the back cover the *third cover page,* and the back cover the *fourth cover page.* For the second, third, and fourth cover positions, you must pay a premium price and may have to get your ad on a waiting list.

Space in magazines is generally sold in terms of full pages and fractions thereof (half-pages, quarter-pages, three columns, two columns, one column). Small ads in the shopping pages in the back of many magazines are generally sold by the line. Most magazines are flexible in allowing one-page or double-page ads to be broken up into separate units.

Gatefolds

Sometimes when you open a magazine, you find that the cover or an inside page opens to reveal an extra page that folds out and gives the ad a big spread. Advertisers use these *gatefolds* on special occasions to make the most spectacular presentation in the magazine, usually to introduce a colorful product like a new model car. Not all magazines offer gatefolds, because plans for them must be made well in advance, and they are expensive.

Bleed ads

When an ad runs all the way to the edge of the page, leaving no margin, it is called a *bleed ad.* Designed to get extra attention, the ad may bleed on only three sides or it may bleed on two sides, leaving the white space on the other two sides open for copy, if desired. Although some publications, especially new ones, do not charge for bleeds, usually you must pay an extra 15 to 20 percent whether the ad bleeds on one, two, three, or four sides.

Inserts

These are the return cards, coupons, recipe booklets, and other kinds of outside material bound into magazines in connection with an adjoining ad. They are

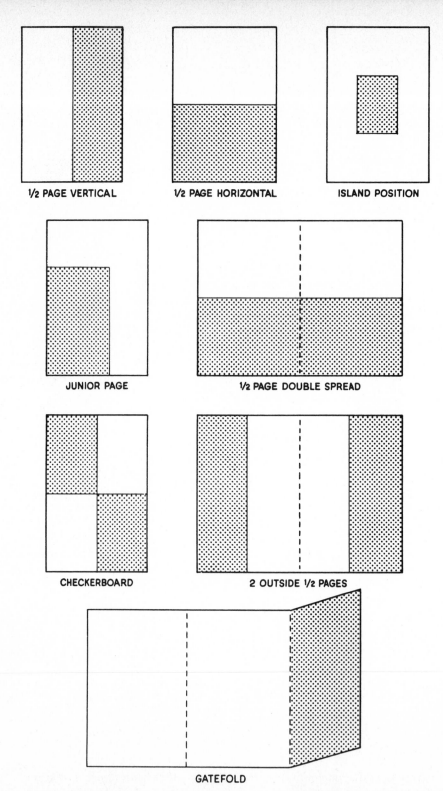

1/2 PAGE VERTICAL

1/2 PAGE HORIZONTAL

ISLAND POSITION

JUNIOR PAGE

1/2 PAGE DOUBLE SPREAD

CHECKERBOARD

2 OUTSIDE 1/2 PAGES

GATEFOLD

▲ *Various ways of using magazine space.*

(Opposite:) *A full-page bleed ad.* ▶

never sold separately. Return cards, effective in getting prompt response from an advertisement, are widely used in direct response advertising; they are also an effective way of distributing coupon offers. As we shall see in Chapter 12, when we discuss magazine inserts, they can be an effective part of a sales promotion campaign. We mention magazine inserts here to recognize that they are an important feature of magazine advertising.

Magazine inserts.

On the question of position in magazines, no one has more accurate information than the direct response advertisers. They know exactly what response they
get from each advertisement. Bob Stone, an authority in that field, reports:

> Decades of measured direct response advertising tell the same story over and over
> again. A position in the first seven pages of the magazine produces a dramatically
> better response (all other factors being the same) than if the same insertion appeared
> farther back in the same issue. . . .
>
> Here is about what you may expect the relative response to be from various page
> positions as measured against the first right-hand page arbitrarily rated at a pull of
> 100:

Position	Ranking
First right-hand page	100
Second right-hand page	95
Third right-hand page	90
Fourth right-hand page	85
Back of book (following main body of editorial matter)	50
Back cover	100
Inside third cover [inside of back cover]	90
Page facing inside third cover	85

> Right-hand pages are more visible than left-hand pages; right-hand pages pull better
> than left-hand pages—by as much as 15 percent. Insert cards open the magazine to
> the advertiser's message, and thereby create their own "cover" position.[*]

Exceptions: A position in front of any article relevant to your product is good.
A page facing reading matter is better than an ad facing an ad.

In many magazines only the cover positions and possibly the pages facing
them are preferred positions that can be reserved at a premium. This need not
prevent you, as an advertiser, from letting your view on positioning up front be
known to the publisher.

There are three sets of dates to be aware of in planning and buying magazine
space:

1. *Cover date,* the date appearing on the cover.
2. *On-sale date,* the date on which the magazine is issued. (The January issue
   of a magazine may come out on December 5, which is important to know
   if you are planning a Christmas ad.)
3. *Closing date,* the date when the print or plates needed to print the ad must
   be in the publisher's hands in order to make a particular issue.

---

[*] Bob Stone, *Successful Direct Marketing Methods* (Chicago: Crain Books, 1975), p. 78.

Dates are figured from the cover date and are expressed in terms of "days or weeks preceding," as in the following example:

New Yorker
Published weekly, dated Monday
Issued Wednesday preceding
Closes 25th of 3rd month preceding

How Space Is Sold

Magazine rate structure

Publishers issue rate cards quoting the costs of advertising space in their magazines. The rate card of one weekly reads like this:

Black/White	
1 page (3 columns)	$7,750
Double column (⅔ page)	5,500
Single column	2,750
½ column	1,375
Agate line	20

The listing above is the one-time rate. The card continues to give the rates for 13, 26, 39, and 52 insertions and the corresponding rates for color. (Weeklies' rates are quoted in units of 13.)

Whereas newspaper rates are compared by millines, magazine rates are compared by *cost per page per thousand circulation* (CPM).

The formula is

$$\frac{\text{cost per page}}{\text{circulation (in thousands)}} = \text{cost per thousand (CPM)}$$

Discounts

The one-time, full-page rate of a publication is referred to as its *basic* or *open rate.* All discounts are computed from that. There are two familiar types of discounts:

The frequency discount.   Not to be confused with "frequency" in scheduling an advertisement, a frequency discount results in a lower cost per unit, the more often the advertiser runs ads within the contract year. Thus:

13 pages or more	7%
26 pages or more	12%
39 pages or more	16%
52 pages or more	20%

Newsweek

A Newsweek, Inc., Publication

Media Code 8 572 0500 9.00

Published weekly by Newsweek, Inc., 444 Madison Ave., New York, N. Y. 10022. Phone 212-350-2000. **For shipping info., see Print Media Production Data.**

PUBLISHER'S EDITORIAL PROFILE

NEWSWEEK surveys the world's news for people with an abiding interest in the week's events, departmented into 20 sections, from National Affairs to Movies, Music, Books, and Art. Periscope includes behind-the-scene highlights, plus forecasts of things to come. Also featured are distinguished columnists writing on national and international developments, on the Washington scene, on the economy. (Rec'd 10/31/73).

1. PERSONNEL
Vice-Pres. Mktg. & Adv. Sales—John E. Mandable.
National Adv. Sales Mgr.—Eugene W. Mac Millin.
Administrative Adv. Mgr.—Richard F. Bausch.
Advertising Make-Up—Richard M. Suhr.

2. REPRESENTATIVES and/or BRANCH OFFICES
New York 10022—John G. Alexander, Mgr., Arthur E. Karlan, Mgr., 444 Madison Ave. Phone 212-350-2000.
Boston 02199—J. Devereux de Gozzaldi, 1935 Prudential Center. Phone 617-267-6677.
Chicago 60611—Paul C. Bowman, Erich W. Bruhn, 430 N. Michigan Ave. Phone 312-467-5000.
Cleveland 44113 — William E. Nieman, 1 Public Square. Phone 216-696-3565.
Southfield (Detroit) Mich. 48076—James W. Allbaugh, Willard W. Holman, 1218 Travelers Tower. Phone 313-355-3333.
Atlanta 30303—James Baillie, 1206 Peachtree Center South. Phone 404 577-6943.
Washington, D. C. 20006—Douglas P. Jeppe, 1750 Pennsylvania Ave. Phone 202-298-7880.
St. Louis 63101—Robert M. Hawkes, 1139 Olive St. Phone 314-231-4525.
San Francisco 94111—Huntley Bennett, 735 Montgomery St. Phone 415-982-2645.
Los Angeles 90010—Lemuel C. Hall, Rm. 711, 3810 Wilshire Blvd. Phone 213-384-2161.
London—Michael G. Conroy, 80 Haymarket.
Paris—Michael Boutin, 90 Champs Elysees.
Tokyo—Keiichi Kato, 1, 6-4, 1-chome Marunouchi, Chiyoda-ku.
Sydney—Ian Leonard, 55 Elizabeth St.
Manila—Julie Carpenter, Sabas-Almeda Bldg., 505 A Flores St.
Brussels—Hubert de Micheoux, Ave. Mollere 307a.
Frankfurt/Main—Wittigo Graf Einsiedel, Beethovenplatz 9.
Geneva—Hans Fluijt, 6 Place des Eaux-Vives.
Hong Kong—Peter Luffman, 1521 Central Bldg.

3. COMMISSION AND CASH DISCOUNT
15% of gross. Cash discount 2% of net for payment on or before due date. Payments due on or before 10th day of month following issue date. Date of payment, if mailed, is date of postal cancellation. Charge may be made on any outstanding amount.

4. GENERAL RATE POLICY

ADVERTISING RATES
Rates effective January 5, 1976.
Rates received November 4, 1975.

5. BLACK/WHITE RATES

	1 pg	2 cols	*1/2 pg	1 col	1/2 col	Line rate
1 pg	22.650.					
2 cols		16.875.				

	1 ti	13 ti	17 ti	26 ti	39 ti	52 ti
1 pg	22.650.	21.745.	21.405.	20.840.	20.385.	20.025.
2 cols	16.875.	16.200.	15.945.	15.525.	15.190.	14.920.
*1/2 pg	13.815.	13.260.	13.055.	12.710.	12.435.	12.210.
1 col	8.835.	8.480.	8.350.	8.130.	7.950.	7.810.
1/2 col	4.530.	4.350.	4.280.	4.170.	4.075.	4.005.
Line rate	67.30	64.60	63.60	61.90	60.55	59.50

(*) Limited availability.

DISCOUNTS
FREQUENCY DISCOUNTS
Rates determined by number of insertions contracted for and used during a 12 month period. Schedules composed of mixed space units of 1/2 column or larger entitled to standard frequency discounts except when use of smaller units lowers cost of campaign below amount which larger units would reach at their earned rate. Schedules composed of National and Regional and/or Executive Newsweek insertions may be combined to earn frequency discounts except when use of Regional and/or Executive Newsweek space lowers cost of campaign below amount which National insertions cost at their earned rates.
Schedules composed entirely of regional advertising

national Editions of Newsweek. Frequency discounts earned by insertions in the American or its Regional and Group I Market Editions will also be granted on insertions in any edition of Newsweek International. Newsweek International insertions, however, will not contribute toward earning frequency discounts in the American Edition.

6. COLOR RATES
Black and 1 color:

	1 ti	13 ti	17 ti	26 ti	39 ti	52 ti
1 pg	28.630.	27.485.	27.055.	26.350.	25.765.	25.310.
2 cols	21.760.	20.890.	20.565.	20.020.	19.585.	19.235.
*1/2 pg	17.465.	16.765.	16.505.	16.070.	15.720.	15.440.
1 col	11.415.	10.960.	10.785.	10.500.	10.275.	10.090.
1/2 col	5.980.	5.740.	5.650.	5.500.	5.380.	5.285.

4 color process:

	1 ti	13 ti	17 ti	26 ti	39 ti	52 ti
1 pg	35.335.	33.920.	33.390.	32.510.	31.800.	31.235.
2 cols	27.325.	26.230.	25.820.	25.140.	24.595.	24.155.
*1/2 pg	22.085.	21.200.	20.870.	20.320.	19.875.	19.525.
2 pg sprd	70.670.	67.840.	66.780.	65.020.	63.600.	62.470.

(*) Limited availability.

7. COVERS
4 color process:

	1 ti	13 ti	17 ti	26 ti	39 ti	52 ti
2nd or 3rd cover	35.335.	33.920.	33.390.	32.510.	31.800.	31.235.
4th cover	45.455.	43.635.	42.955.	41.820.	40.910.	40.180.

8. INSERTS
Insert Cards: Units consisting of a minimum of a page and a 2 color insert card are available, on a limited basis, in National, Regional and Metro Group I Editions. Minimum size: 6" x 4-1/4".
Rates for National card, 35,335.00 plus applicable supporting space rate. Rates for other than minimum size, Regional Editions and other situations are available. Note: a 5% margin must be allowed in the distribution of insert cards. Closing: 10 weeks. Insert Stock: Black and white, black and 1 process color, 2 process colors, 3 process colors, and 5 process colors (4 process) ads are available on 4-color insert stock for special purposes. Prices are available and are subject to frequency discounts. Contract must be received 9 weeks prior to issue date. Closing date for plates is the same as standard 4-color units.
Gatefolds: 1/2 page and full page gatefolds are available, as well as other special ads. Mechanical details and dimensions should be confirmed with Newsweek prior to preparation of original art for engraving. Premium charges for these units are available
Closing 9 weeks prior to issue date

9. BLEED
Bleed pages, 2 Columns, 1 column and 1/2 page horizontal accepted at earned rates plus 15%. No charge for bleed across gutter in 4 column and larger ads.

12. SPLIT-RUN
On a limited basis, advertisers, purchasing national or regional circulation may tailor copy to different geographical areas. Split runs should follow state lines, except when influenced by regional edition distribution patterns. States are to be contiguous. Premiums vary according to number of geographical splits, coloration and regional unit boundaries that are followed. On cycle of Student Editions, a limited number of advertisers may purchase the non-student portion of the National Edition at a special rate. 5% margin for distribution error required on all split-run contracts. Send for premium charges and issue availabilities. Closing: Regional close required on regional and national split runs. All premiums on split-runs, gatefolds, etc., are non-commissionable.

13a GEOGRAPHIC and/or DEMOGRAPHIC EDITIONS
Issue Dates:
1st Cycle: Jan. 5, Feb. 2, Mar. 1, Mar. 29, Apr. 26, May 24, June 21, July 19, Aug. 16, Sept. 13, Oct. 11, Nov. 8, Dec. 6.
2nd Cycle: Jan. 12, Feb. 9, Mar. 8, Apr. 5, May 3, May 31, June 28, July 26, Aug. 23, Sept. 20, Oct. 18, Nov. 15, Dec. 13.
3rd Cycle: Jan. 19, Feb. 16, Mar. 15, Apr. 12, May 10, June 7, July 5, Aug. 2, Aug. 30, Sept. 27, Oct. 25, Nov. 22, Dec. 20.
4th Cycle: Jan. 26, Feb. 23, Mar. 22, Apr. 19, May 17, June 14, July 12, Aug. 9, Sept. 6, Oct. 4, Nov. 1, Nov. 29, Dec. 27.

DEMOGRAPHIC EDITIONS
STUDENT EDITION
Available in 2nd cycle.

1 page:	1 ti	13 ti	17 ti	26 ti	39 ti	52 ti
B/w	5.165.	4.960.	4.880.	4.750.	4.650.	4.565.
B/1c	6.530.	6.270.	6.170.	6.010.	5.875.	5.775.
4 color	8.055.	7.735.	7.610.	7.410.	7.250.	7.120.

Publisher states: Effective January 5, 1976 issue. "Circulation rate base 400,000."
Circulation: A.B.C. 12-31-75—480,015.

Volume (dollar) discount. The more total space an advertiser uses within a contract year, measured in dollars, the lower the rate. For example:

13 pages or more	7%
26 pages or more	12%
39 pages or more	16%
52 pages or more	20%

Sometimes frequency and volume discounts are combined to give the advertiser the best possible rate, but this must be planned and contracted for in advance.

Other discounts. Publishers are always alert to give special rates to large advertisers and to other advertisers they are anxious to attract. Among different magazines we find various special discounts: *mail order* discount, *travel* discount, *trade book* discount, *multiple page* discount, *seasonal adjustment* discount, *consecutive page* discount. Blanketing all these is a *corporate* or *total dollar* discount. This overall discount, above all the others earned, is based on the total dollars spent by all of a corporation's divisions in a year. There is obviously no such thing as a standard trade discount or standard use of terms. It pays to ask a lot of questions when buying space.

Remnant space. A number of publishers, especially those with geographic or demographic editions, find themselves with extra space in some editions when they are ready to go to press. Rather than run an empty space, the publisher often offers this *remnant space* at a big discount. For direct response advertisers, whose ads are not part of a continuing campaign but stand on their own, remnant space is an especially good buy. Of course, material for the ad must be ready for instant insertion.

The magazine short rate

When an advertiser and a publisher sign a noncancellable, nonretroactive space contract at the beginning of the year, they agree to make adjustments at the end of the year if the advertiser's estimates are off. If the advertiser uses less space than estimated, the publisher charges more. If more space is used, the publisher gives a rebate.

Take a magazine with these page rates:

1 time	$2,000
3 times	1,975
6 times	1,950
9 times	1,925
12 times	1,900

The advertiser believes ads will be run 12 times during the year, qualifying for the $1,900 rate, and the contract is entered tentatively at that figure. If ads are run 12 times, all is well; there is no problem. But if the ads run only 10 times, the advertiser would get a bill like this:

Ran 10 times. Paid the 12-time rate of $1,900 per page,	$19,000
Earned only the 9-time rate of $1,925 per page,	19,250
(There is no 10-time rate)	
Short rate due	$250

If the advertiser had earned more than the rate contracted for, the publisher would give a rebate.

Some publishers charge the top (basic) rate throughout the year but state in the contract, "Rate credit when earned." If the advertiser earns a better rate, the publisher gives a refund. If the publisher sees that an advertiser is not running enough pages during the year to earn the low rate on which the contract was based, the publisher sends a bill at the short rate for space already used. Further ads are billed at the higher rate earned. Failure to keep short rates in mind when you reduce your original schedule can lead to unwelcome surprises.

Placing the Order

Placing advertising in a magazine on a 12-month schedule may entail two steps: the *space contract* and the *insertion order*. An advertiser who plans to advertise in a particular magazine during the coming 12 months will sign a *space contract* in order to get the best rate. This is not an order for a specific amount of space but merely an agreement to pay at the current rate schedule for whatever space is used. The advertiser estimates how much space might be run during the year and is billed for the discount rate charged for that amount of space. The contract usually allows the publisher to raise the rates during the contract year with, however, a two- or three-months' notice. The advantage to the advertiser is that during those months no increase in rates is permitted. When the advertiser is ready to run an ad, he or she sends an *insertion order* to the publisher, specifying date of issue, size of ad, and contract rate.

Magazine Networks

A publisher may gather into one selling group a number of publications, his own and those of other publishers reaching readers with similar general interests and life-styles. Space in groups of these publications (usually three or more) is then sold at lower rates per publication than for any single member of the network. Ziff-Davis, for example, offers an advertiser a choice among seven magazines—*Flying, Car and Driver, Boating, Popular Mechanics, Stereo Review, Skiing,* and *Cycle.* Publishers who offer their magazines through a network are still free to pursue any other circulation and advertising sales effort they wish to make. Magazine networks offer publishers an efficient way to build circulation and sell advertising space, and they offer advertisers an economical way to buy space. Because of these advantages, the use of magazine networks has been spreading.

Split-Run Advertising

Just as Sunday newspaper magazine sections offer split-run advertising, so do many magazines, and for the same purpose: to test different ads against each other. Many magazines also have *split-run* editions, or more specifically, they divide a geographic edition for testing purposes. In the simplest of such tests, the advertiser supplies two different ads of the same size and shape, each running in the same position in half an edition, and each calling for a coupon response. The publisher arranges to distribute both sections equally in the same territory or in two adjacent territories with the same demographics. The advertiser can then readily compare results. The basic principle is that there is to be no difference whatever between places where the ad is run; the only difference is in the two ads. In our discussion of split-run tests in Chapter 12, we will see how this principle can be applied to test six advertisements at one time.

Magazine Circulation; the Audit Bureau of Circulation (ABC)

When advertisers buy space in magazines, they are really buying the delivery of their ad to as many people as possible, expressed in terms of circulation. All rates are based on the circulation that a publisher promises to provide, referred to as *guaranteed circulation.* How many copies of the magazine were really distributed, and how was that circulation obtained? These are key questions every space buyer asks. To help answer these questions, the Audit Bureau of Circulation collects and evaluates data about magazines just as it does about newspapers. Briefly, the bureau audits the magazine's books, checks how many copies were printed, sold at newsstands, and returned; how many were sold by subscription; how the subscriptions were obtained, measured in terms of cut-rate sales and delinquent subscribers. It also determines the rate of renewal. These vital facts all help evaluate the worth of the magazine as a medium.

Primary circulation vs. pass-along circulation

Advertisers are also interested in how many copies of the magazine are read by *primary* (original) buyers and how many copies are passed along from one friend to another or read in beauty parlors or doctors' waiting rooms. The assumption is that the person who buys a magazine is more affluent and more interested than the reader who is next in line. But sometimes pass-along circulation is especially valuable. Circulation to beauty parlors is just what advertisers want if they are selling hair and beauty preparations. The woman who gets *Good Housekeeping* from a friend may be watching her budget more closely than her friend, but she may be all the more avid a reader for money-saving suggestions.

Magazine Merchandising Services

Magazines offer a variety of services to help advertisers *merchandise°* their advertising. They may prepare mailings and counter display cards for advertisers to send to dealers. With this service, advertisers profit because dealers are notified of forthcoming advertising, and magazines profit because display cards often include lines like "As advertised in _____ Magazine." The service may extend to store promotions. In its "Fashion Locator," *Esquire* lists department stores carrying fashions featured in the current issue. The August issue of *Mademoiselle* is famous for its back-to-school fashion predictions, and the magazine holds a fashion show in New York in June, attended by stores' buyers and fashion coordinators. *Reader's Digest* has a computerized marketing service that helps readers find local outlets via a single nationwide phone number. Many a magazine campaign has been successful because the manufacturer's salespeople could present the advertising to buyers and show them the advantage of building their merchandising efforts around it.

Merchandising services vary from magazine to magazine; their scope depends upon the size of the advertiser's schedule. Because of ever-rising costs, magazines have greatly reduced their expenditures for merchandising aids.

Criteria for Selecting Magazines

If answers to the following questions show gaps in a magazine's coverage, it might be wise to look at other media.

Does the magazine reach the type of reader to whom we are trying to sell our product?

How does distribution of the circulation compare with our product's distribution?

What is the cost of reaching a thousand prospects (not merely the cost per thousand readers)?

How do readers regard the magazine?

Will the advertisement be in acceptable company?

How cooperative is the publisher in giving good position?

° This is one of the many uses of the term. In this context it means the action and materials supplied by the publisher to help the dealer get direct benefit from magazine advertising.

How important are merchandising aids, and what aids are available?

How do other magazines compare with this one with respect to the above points?

Other Magazines

Farm magazines

We have a big farm population, and it has its own, special magazines. These may be classified as *general farm magazines, regional farm magazines,* and *vocational farm magazines.* These classifications do overlap, however, because a number of the larger magazines have geographical and demographic splits.

General farm magazines.   The largest of these is *Farm Journal,* with a circulation of about 3 million. Two-thirds of its editorial content is devoted to farm production, management, and news; one-third to the needs of women and families. It is published in a series of regional editions.

Regional farm magazines.   These publications specifically aim at farmers in different regions of the country. They discuss problems relating to farmers' chief crops, their general welfare, and governmental activity affecting them. Publications such as *Ohio Farmer, California Farmer,* and *Dakota Farmer* are obviously regional.

Vocational farm magazines.   Many farm publications are devoted to certain crops or types of farming. They are really vocational papers and include such publications as *The Dairyman, American Fruit Grower, Poultry Press,* and *Better Beef Business.* Classifications overlap in magazines like the *New England Dairyman, Washington Cattleman,* and *Gulf Coast Cattleman.* Whatever the farmer's interest may be, there are a number of publications edited for him. Many farm homes get several publications.

Business magazines

In addition to consumer magazines, other magazines are used as trade papers and for industrial audiences. Because of the specialized nature of these publications, we treat them separately in Chapter 25, "Advertising to Business."

Trends in Magazine Advertising

We can expect a continuing flow of new magazines, each devoted to a specialized interest that its publishers think has not been reached effectively.

The major problems facing all magazines are the rising costs of printing, paper, and postage. To offset high paper costs, magazines that have not already done so will trim their size, but this is a limited solution. To meet rising printing costs, magazines will continue to raise per-copy prices and will use newer, less expensive composition and printing methods. The magazines face continuing postal increases, which may affect circulation methods, advertising costs, and the very character of magazines. Publishers are finding ways of reaching consumers without having to pay high postal costs. Some deliver their magazines in bulk to distributors, who put the magazines in plastic bags and hang them on subscribers' doorknobs. (They are prohibited by law from using the mailbox.) Others have discovered the importance of supermarket distribution. And magazines have a continuing competitive problem of establishing their importance on every media schedule.

Cable television (CATV) is a potential threat, for like magazines, it can reach selected audiences. Only 15 percent of TV households have cable TV now, however, and there will probably always be a great many advertisers and consumers who do not use cablecasting.

Despite their problems, the number of magazines will increase, total circulation will increase, and the total volume of advertising they carry will increase, probably to $2.6 billion or more, not including production costs, by 1980.

QUESTIONS

1. What are the major advantages and limitations of magazines for the national advertiser?

2. What are the reasons for the recent upsurge in geographic and demographic editions of magazines? What are their advantages? Limitations?

3. "Back cover" is one of the various magazine space-buying designations. How many more can you name and describe?

4. What is the relationship between page positions in magazines and the relative response an advertiser may expect from the advertisement?

5. There are three sets of magazine dates one must be aware of in planning and buying space. What are they?

6. Explain in detail the magazine rate structure. Include identification and discussion of the various special discounts that publishers normally offer to various classes of advertisers.

7. How does the magazine short rate work? Can you give an example?

8. Outline and discuss the steps involved in placing an advertising schedule in a magazine.

9. In the past 10 years, geographic and demographic editions of magazines have become widely used by most large circulation magazines. What brought this about?

10. What is "split-run" advertising as it pertains to magazines? Who uses it and why?

11. Explain the difference between primary and pass-along circulation.

12. Describe the various ways in which magazines merchandise the advertising they carry.

13. What are the major criteria you would use for selecting a consumer magazine?

14. Distinguish among general, regional, and vocational farm magazines.

15. What are the chief trends in magazines?

16. How would you explain the following?

a) page size
b) standard size
c) small size
d) fourth cover page
e) gatefolds
f) bleed ads
g) inserts
h) closing date
i) rate card
j) basic rate (open rate)
k) CPM
l) remnant space
m) short rate
n) space contract
o) magazine network

READING SUGGESTIONS

"A.R.F. Study Aims to Clarify Magazine Research Quandary," *Advertising Age* (August 18, 1975), 20 ff.

CHOOK, PAUL, "Magazine Audience Research: Does Politz Hold the Key?" *Media Decisions* (April 1976), 66 ff.

FORD, JAMES L. C., *Magazines for Millions: The Story of Specialized Publications.* Carbondale, Ill.: Southern Illinois University Press, 1969.

"Magazine Audience Data Today: Let's Get Those Numbers Right," *Advertising Age* (October 13, 1975), 51 ff.

"Magazine Publishing," special section in *Advertising Age* (November 18, 1974), 31 ff.

"Magazine Research Could Be Marching Off in the Wrong Direction," *Advertising Age* (January 6, 1975), 29 ff.

MOTT, FRANK LUTHER, *A History of American Magazines,* 3 vols. Cambridge, Mass.: Harvard University Press, 1930–1938.

SISSORS, JACK Z., and E. REYNOLD PETRAY, *Advertising Media Planning.* Chicago: Crain Books, 1976, pp. 129–48 and 190–91.

WOOD, JAMES PLAYSTAD, *Magazines in the United States,* 3rd ed. New York: The Ronald Press Company, 1971.

11

Outdoor Advertising
Transit Advertising

Much of America is on wheels today, going to and from work, shopping, visiting, weekending, touring. As people drive, they are greeted on different parts of their trip by out-of-home advertising, one of today's major advertising media.

Outdoor Advertising

It is appropriate that the oldest form of advertising, outdoor advertising, should have the oldest trade association in the industry. The Associated Bill Posters formed in 1891 "to establish standards and adopt uniform practice as far as possible." The association has functioned continuously since that time and is known today as the Outdoor Advertising Association of America. Through sustained activity, the association has established standardized types and sizes of outdoor structures and standard trade procedures for handling business all over the country, so that a national advertiser can plan an outdoor campaign for any of 8,000 markets across the country[*]

Most of our attention in this chapter is devoted to standardized outdoor advertising. We do not deal with the myriad identification signs of varying sizes, shapes, and colors that mark eating places, bowling alleys, motels, movies, used car lots, shops, and almost every other public place.

Outdoor advertising provides the largest and most colorful display for an advertiser's trademark, product, and slogan. It offers the most spectacular use of

Features and advantages

[*] Unless otherwise identified, information in this chapter is from the Outdoor Advertising Association of America, Inc.

lights to attract attention and has shown special effectiveness in getting a name known.

It is geographically flexible; and for its more than 8,000 markets computerized market data are available. An advertiser can reach his market nationally, regionally, and locally. In many cities, advertisers can reach special ethnic neighborhoods. Outdoor advertising offers both frequency and reach at low cost.

Used with other media, outdoor advertising can round out a campaign by providing extra frequency or reach. Local advertisers, especially those handling institutional or service accounts, blanket their markets with outdoor ads.

Limitations and challenges

Since cars pass outdoor signs quickly, copy is limited to a message that can be told in a few words. Creating a design that can tell its story in pictures is the greatest challenge for outdoor advertisers. Not all messages are suited to such compression. Although outdoor advertising reaches a wide audience, an advantage for a product in widespread sale, its use is limited for advertisers trying to reach a segmented market, such as women 25–49.

The outdoor plant

The basic business unit of the outdoor industry is the local outdoor company, the *outdoor plant*. Its stock in trade is the location it has leased or bought under local zoning regulations permitting the erection of signs. Having acquired a location, the plant operator builds a structure at his own expense, sells the advertising space on it (technically he leases the space), posts or paints the advertiser's message, and is responsible for maintaining the board and the ad in good condition during the life of the advertiser's contract.

The two forms of standardized outdoor advertising handled by outdoor plants are the poster panel and the painted bulletin.

Poster panels

Frequently called *posters*, these outside structures have blank panels on which preprinted advertisements can be gummed. Posters can be illuminated (for the more important locations) or unilluminated (for the less costly ones). A standard size poster panel is 12′ × 25′. (In outdoor advertising, the height is given first, then the width.) It has a standard construction and frame. A distinguishing feature of poster panels is the ease and simplicity of replacing the message. They are the lowest-cost method of buying outdoor advertising and are the most widely used form.

Poster sizes.   Poster sizes are measured in terms of *sheets*. The term originated in the days when it took 24 of the largest sheets the presses could hold to cover a sign 12′ × 25′. The presses have become much larger, but the designation has stuck. Today all poster ads are still mounted on standard 12′ × 25′ boards. The most popular size is the *30-sheet poster*, which consists of a metal frame around the outside, a margin of blank paper acting as a mat or border, and the message mounted on a standard size panel in the center. If the artwork extends all the way to the metal frame, without a margin, it is called a *bleed poster*. (Since it costs the least, a *24-sheet poster* is generally used for noncommercial purposes.)

FOSTER and KLEISER

Sunkist

Eat a best seller.

Courtesy Foster and Kleiser.

24 SHEET

30 SHEET

BLEED

The standard size structure, 12 ft high by 25 ft long, is the most popular size. Within this framework are ads in three sizes, depending upon how much white space is left between the ad and the frame. There is no difference in cost among any of these sizes. The most popular is the 30 sheet; the bleed is second.

OUTDOOR RATES AND MARKETS

Florida

PLANT	MARKET-COUNTY		POP.	EFF. DATE	GRP	POSTERS NON ILL.	ILL.	COST PER MONTH	DISC.	CRO REN
4550.0	MADISON (TAL)	MADISON	3.7	07-15-6	*100	2		170.00		
					* 50	1		85.00		
9179.0	MARIANNA (DOT)	JACKSON	11.8	07-15-6	*100	4		340.00		
					* 50	2		170.00		
9182.0	MARINELAND (ORL)	ST JOHNS	1.1	07-15-6	*100	1		85.00		
9296.0	MARTIN COUNTY MKT (WES)	MARTIN	40.7	01-01-7	*100	2	2	360.00	D	
					* 50	1	1	180.00	D	
9182.0	MELBOURNE MKT (ORL)	BREVARD	111.2	07-15-6	*100	8	4	1425.00		099
					* 50	4	2	710.00		
9182.0	MELBOURNE-TITUSVILLE COCOA (ORL) BREVARD	METRO MKT	249.9	07-15-6	*100	12	10	2830.00		
					* 75	9	7	2140.00		
					* 50	6	5	1475.00		
					* 25	4	3	935.00		
1972.2	MIAMI METRO MKT (MIA)	DADE-BROWARD	1615.9	12-20-6	100		120	20280.00	D	
					75		90	15210.00	D	
					50		60	10140.00	D	
					25		30	5070.00	D	
9294.0	MIAMI METRO MKT (MIA)	DADE-BROWARD	1871.2	01-01-7	*100		100	14850.00	D	
					* 75		75	11137.00	D	
					* 50		50	7425.00	D	
					* 25		25	3712.00	D	
4531.0	MILTON (MOB)	SANTA ROSA	14.5	07-15-6	*100	3		255.00		122
					* 50			170.00		
9484.0	TAMPA MKT (TAM)	HILLSBOROUGH	574.0	07-01-6	*100		53	5194.00	D	
					* 75		43	4214.00	D	
					* 50		30	2940.00	D	
					* 25		20	1960.00	D	
5055.2	TAMPA METRO MKT (TAM) MANATEE-PASCO-POLK	HILLSBOROUGH	766.3	12-20-6	*100	8	50	5982.00		
					* 75	6	40	4764.00		
					* 50	4	30	3528.00		
					* 25	2	20	2298.00		
4540.0	TAVARES (ORL)	LAKE	3.9	07-15-6	*100	1		85.00		
9182.0	TITUSVILLE (ORL)	BREVARD	34.8	07-15-6	*100	4		470.00		099
					* 50	2		235.00		
1893.4	TRENTON (GAI)	GILCHRIST	1.1	06-01-6	*100	1		65.00	D	
4540.0	UMATILLA (ORL)	LAKE	2.3	07-15-6	*100	1		85.00		
4532.0	WAKULLA (TAL)	WAKULLA	.2	07-15-6	*100	1		85.00		
4535.0	WAUCHULA (TAM)	HARDEE	4.6	07-15-6	*100	3		255.00		
					* 50	2		170.00		
9296.0	W PALM BEACH METRO MKT (WES) PALM BEACH		405.9	01-01-7	*100		28	3080.00	D	
					* 75		21	2310.00	D	
					* 50		14	1540.00	D	
					* 25		7	770.00	D	
4550.0	WHITE SPRINGS (JCV)	HAMILTON	.8	07-15-6	*100	1		85.00		
4535.0	WILDWOOD (ORL)	SUMTER	2.5	07-15-6	*100	2		170.00		
					* 50	1		85.00		

Buyer's Guide to Outdoor Advertising, Outdoor Advertising Association of America.

Page from outdoor advertising rate book. All stations offer 100 GRPs and smaller units, but the number of posters in a 100 GRP and the price vary by community. The number of GRPs per dollar is easily calculated.

In addition to the standard 24-sheet poster operation we have been discussing, there is another sector of the industry, which deals in 8-sheet posters, 6' high and 10' wide, often called *junior posters*. These are used mostly to reach ethnic groups in neighborhoods where pedestrians will see them on walls adjacent to stores. Usually 8-sheet posters are handled by special poster plants and frequently appear concurrently with 24-sheet showings in a market.

Buying poster advertising; GRP units

Until 1973 the traditional way of selling outdoor posters of uniform size was in a *showing*, a package or assortment of different poster locations. The price of a showing depended on the number of posters and the quality of the locations. There was a 100 showing; there was a 50 showing and a 25 showing. Obviously the 25 showing was half the 50 showing, and the 50 showing was half the 100 showing. What then, you might ask, was a 100 showing? A 100 showing was each plant owner's private opinion of what would make an excellent impression on that particular market. Obviously, this system caused advertisers problems. How could they compare the values of showings in different markets when different plant owners did the rating?

Because of these problems, in 1973 the industry moved to the practice of selling posters in *GRP units*, preselected by the plant owner. The showing is priced according to its *Gross Rating Points (GRPs)*. (Posters are never sold individually.)

A rating point is equivalent to the exposure of an ad to 1 percent of the population of a market per day. A 100 GRP package consists of the number of poster panels required to deliver exposure opportunities to 100 percent of the population of the market in one day; a 50 GRP buy offers exposure opportunities to 50 percent of the population of a market. A 100 GRP showing in one city may

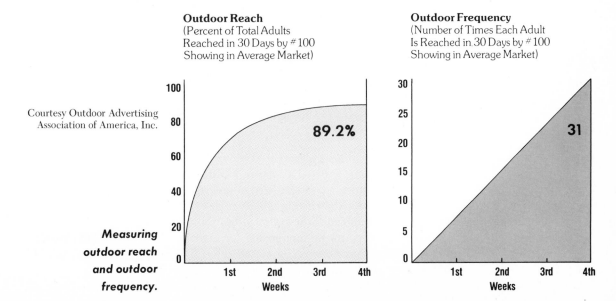

Outdoor Reach
(Percent of Total Adults Reached in 30 Days by #100 Showing in Average Market)

Outdoor Frequency
(Number of Times Each Adult Is Reached in 30 Days by #100 Showing in Average Market)

Courtesy Outdoor Advertising Association of America, Inc.

89.2%

31

Measuring outdoor reach and outdoor frequency.

1st   2nd   3rd   4th
Weeks

1st   2nd   3rd   4th
Weeks

include fewer posters than in another larger city, but it will provide the same intensity of market coverage. A study of the accompanying page of the *Outdoor Buyers Guide* shows you the difference in the number of posters in a 100 showing in different cities.

When the time comes actually to purchase posters, the outdoor space buyer rides through the area with a plant operator or his representative, who has a map spotting the prepared sites included in a package. Posters are sold on a monthly basis, and copy can be changed monthly.

The Traffic Audit Bureau

The sale of space in the outdoor advertising industry is based on a count of automobile traffic passing a sign every day. The traffic count ignores duplication (people who pass a sign twice a day) but it does provide a yardstick for comparing values of different locations. The central source of all such information is the *Traffic Audit Bureau*, a tripartite organization formed years ago by the advertisers, agencies, and plant owners who constitute its membership. Its field employees are continually gathering the latest traffic data from local, state, and federal authorities, and they make their own checks as well. (The TAB audits some 100,000 panels per year.) TAB reports are a key part of all outdoor buying because they accumulate and update market information as well as mass traffic statistics in all markets where outdoor advertising is being used.

Inspecting the outdoor signs

After the outdoor signs are up, the advertising agency is notified. A representative of the agency drives around to inspect the signs (called *riding a showing*) to make sure that all boards are in proper working order. The boards are inspected regularly to make sure the traffic flow has not changed, that no obstruction (such as the foliage of a tree or new construction) impedes the view of the sign, and—if posters are used—that the posters are not peeling, and all flashing and lighting arrangements are working properly.

Just what may be involved in an inspection of outdoor signs was revealed by Richard L. Briggs in *Media Decisions:*

> We insisted on a number of quality controls. We reviewed materials and construction, elevation of structure, spacing and individuality, lumen output, pictorial reproduction, size of display as related to impact, copy flexibility as related to repaints, space costs as related to circulation, and audience demographics of traffic passing the location.

Painted bulletins

Painted bulletins are permanent structures, larger (usually 14′ × 48′) and costlier than posters. Erected at choice locations, these structures are made of prefabricated steel with a standardized or specially constructed border trim. The advertisements are either hand-painted or mounted on separate panels in the shop and then assembled at the bulletin site.

Painted bulletins can be illuminated for night traffic. Often extending from them are clocks, thermometers, or electric time and temperature units known as *jump clocks*. Some signs have revolving units or rotating panels to attract attention. Others display three-dimensional styrofoam structures or enlarged, extend-

"I want 50 GRP's a day against men 18 to 34 in Peoria.

Dan F. Pearson
Media Director
R. J. Reynolds Tobacco
Company

How much Outdoor do I buy?"

Dan Pearson, Media Director of R. J. Reynolds, had a problem. He knew how many people he wanted to reach in a number of key markets. What he didn't know—because the figures were simply not available at that time—was how much Outdoor he had to buy to obtain those audiences. Now he *does* know, thanks to AMMO, Phase II. (AMMO stands for Audiences Market by Market for Outdoor.)

Recently, in response to advertiser and agency requests, the Institute of Outdoor Advertising has improved AMMO. We added Phase II. Essentially what Phase II does is reverse the original AMMO computer program introduced

last year by the IOA. Instead of telling you how many people you'll reach with, let's say, a #75 Outdoor showing in New Orleans, it lets you know how big a showing to buy in New Orleans if you want 100 female rating points a day. Or 75. Or 52 or 29 or 7 rating points.

For additional information about AMMO, in any of its phases, please contact Edward MacDonald, Vice President and Marketing Director, Institute of Outdoor Advertising, 485 Lexington Avenue, New York, N.Y. 10017, or order your AMMO runs directly from AIS/Marketronics, 100 Park Avenue, New York, N.Y. 10017, attention David Grossbard.

Institute of Outdoor Advertising

The modern way of buying outdoor advertising.

Painted bulletins. (Above): **With extension. ▲**
(Below): **Illuminated at night, sold on a rotary plan. ▼**

ing cutouts of packages or trademarks displayed in lights. Local ordinances limit the size of extensions allowed.

Buying painted bulletins.   Painted bulletins are bought individually, unlike posters, which are bought by GRP units. Contracts run for a year or more, especially if the bulletins require extra construction. The advertiser or a representative visits a territory to inspect each location offered by the local plant operator, who supplies a traffic flow map of the locations. The advertiser judges the ad's circulation, the distance from which it is visible, the amount of traffic, competing signs and distractions, and any special features affecting its visibility. If shortcomings are found, the price quoted for the individual painted bulletin may be subject to negotiation. About three times a year, the advertiser can change the copy and supply the design and art work to the plant operator, who is responsible for reproducing it and maintaining the sign in good condition.

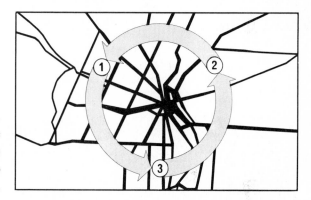

Rotary plan map. Every 30 or 60 or 90 days, painted bulletin 1 is moved to site 2; bulletin 2 is moved to site 3; bulletin 3, to site 1. Later the process is repeated, but bulletin 1 is moved to site 3.

Rotary plans.   With a *rotary plan,* an advertiser may buy painted bulletins in three different favorable locations. The faces of the boards are removable, and the copy is different on each one. Every 30, 60, or 90 days the bases of the boards are rotated in sequence, so that each board gets a different audience each time, and each audience gets a different message. The panels may even be moved to different markets.

Criteria for selecting painted bulletins.   Among yardsticks besides circulation to take into consideration in picking a location are:

▲ *Length of unobstructed approach*—the distance from which the location first becomes fully visible to people driving.

▲ *Type of traffic*—the slower the better. Is it all auto, or is it also pedestrian, bus, or a combination of these? Is the traffic toward the location or away from it, as happens on a one-way street?

▲ *Characteristics of placement*—angled, parallel to line of traffic, or head-on. *Angled* is easily seen as cars approach in one direction; *parallel* can be viewed by traffic traveling in both directions but better by people sitting in the car at the near side; *head-on* is viewed by traffic approaching a location on the outside of a curve or where traffic makes a sharp turn.

▲ *Immediate surroundings*—Is it close to a shopping center? Is there competition from surrounding signs? Is the sign by a traffic light? Red lights give people more time to read the sign.

▲ *Size and physical attractiveness of the bulletin.*

▲ *Price*—an area of comparative values and negotiation.

Comparison of outdoor advertising

	Poster panels (Standardized)	Painted bulletins	Spectaculars (not standardized)
Description	Permanent structure, 12' x 25', on which preprinted advertisements are mounted. Most frequent size of poster panel is 30 sheet, with small white margin or bleed, with no margin.	Permanent structure, usually 14' x 48', on which the message is painted or mounted.	Special steel construction, built or altered to order.
Chief characteristics	Least costly per unit of standardized outdoor advertising. Standard size, nationwide. Most popular form of standardized outdoor advertising.	Placed in higher traffic locations. No uniform size, but proportion is always 1:3½.	Placed only in busiest locations. Each one is specially fabricated. The costliest and most conspicuous form of outdoor advertising.
How bought	By ready-made assortments, according to the size of GRP units, as 100 GRP units, 50 GRP units, 25 GRP units. Bought by the month.	Individually. Price individually negotiated. Bought on 1- to 3-year basis.	Individually. Price of construction, rental, and maintenance individually negotiated. Usually bought on 3- to 5-year basis.
Special features	Illuminated or unilluminated boards. Illuminated ones are in best locations.	Illuminated. Jump clock, oversize bottle, scenes that rotate, neon-lit trademarks, and many other extra construction features possible.	Everything is constructed to order.
Comments	Formerly sold as arbitrary *showings.* Practice changed since 1973. Copy changeable monthly.	Placed in more important locations. Costlier per unit than posters. Copy usually repainted every 4 to 6 months.	Change of copy difficult and costly.

The outdoor advertising of a national advertiser is usually part of a campaign appearing also in other media. The problem is to create an effective tie-in with the total campaign theme. Whether you are adapting copy to tie in with other advertising or creating copy to stand on its own, it is well to remember that outdoor advertising should contain no more than three elements:

Adapting and creating copy for outdoor advertising

1) *Clear product identification.* The trademark may appear alone or on a package. Can it be immediately recognized? How clear is it at a distance?

2) *Large illustration size.* Size gets attention. The picture should tell the story. Colors should be bold and bright, not pastel. Figures should be distinct and silhouetted (backgrounds usually interfere with illustrations).

3) *Short copy.* The copy, if any, should be concise, the words short, the message unambiguous. Read the copy out loud. If it takes more than eight seconds, it's too long. The typography should be large, preferably heavy sans-serif, liberally spaced. The best color combination for legibility is black on yellow.

The secret of outdoor advertising design is simplification.

In an industry with its own special jargon, it is refreshing to come upon a word that literally means what it says—the outdoor *spectacular* sign. This is not a standardized sign; it is made by specialists in steel construction. Spectaculars are the most conspicuous and the costliest in terms of cash outlay (but low cost per person reached) of all outdoor advertisements. Placed in prime day-and-night locations and designed to attract the greatest number of passers-by, they are built of steel beams, sheet metal, and plastics. They utilize bright flashing lights and technically ingenious designs. (Everything is subject to local zoning laws and limitations on energy use, of course.) Spectaculars are individually designed; the cost of space and construction is individually negotiated. Changes are costly be-

Spectaculars

Courtesy Foster and Kleiser.

A spectacular, built to order.

◀ (Left): *When space is scarce, a one-pole bulletin like this special construction can be erected at a good traffic point.*

A well-designed poster. ▶

◀ *An early appearance of litre on an outdoor poster.*

cause they may entail reconstruction of steelwork and neon lighting, so new advertisers often use the construction of existing spectaculars to erect their own designs. Because of the high cost of construction, spectaculars are usually bought on a three- to five-year basis. It takes an experienced and skilled buyer to handle negotiations involving engineering and legal problems as well as the usual advertising considerations. Large outdoor advertisers often use poster displays, painted bulletins, and spectaculars in large cities.

Since outdoor joined other media in adopting the GRP system, advertisers have a better base for intermedia cost comparison. The industry's huge investment in outdoor research and computerization, along with the adoption of the GRP system, will greatly expand the stature and use of outdoor advertising planning. **Trends in outdoor advertising**

The Federal Highway Beautification Act of 1968, banning outdoor signs within 660 feet of a federally financed highway, permits signs within that area if it is locally zoned for business and industrial use. The act was revised in 1976 to permit identification, directional, and distance signs for services. Most states and municipalities also have laws restricting outdoor advertising to business and industrial areas, a policy the Outdoor Advertising Association of America has long supported. The trend is toward fewer signs in appropriate locations and better art work, probably requiring expenditures of $580 million or more, exclusive of production, by 1980.

Transit Advertising

As we travel in buses, commuter trains, or subways, we find ourselves reading and rereading the overhead advertising cards facing us. As we wait for a train at the station or walk to a plane through the airport, we glance at the posters and displays. All of these are *transit advertising*.

Forty million people, including many who have their own cars, now travel in buses. The biggest gains have been in cities of over 500,000 with bus lines reaching ever outward. The average ride is 22 minutes; the average rider takes 24 rides a month. **Importance**

In the New York City subways, 5.3 million different adults are exposed to subway ads more than 160 million times a month, and now the passengers of the Washington subway and the Bart subway in San Francisco must be added to the roster of those exposed to transit advertising. When we include suburbanite commuters and airline passengers, we have listed the markets that advertisers are investing about $50 million per year to reach. Fifty-eight percent of that huge sum is invested in local advertising; 42 percent in national.

Bus advertising, the most widely used form of transit advertising, actually in-

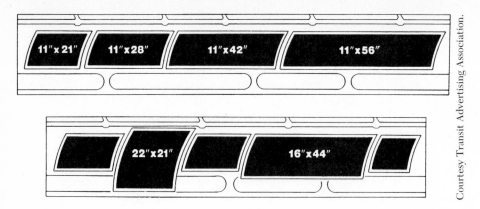

Courtesy Transit Advertising Association.

(Above): **Standardized sizes of interior bus cards. ▲**

Interior bus cards. Sunshine logotype at the bottom of posters puts it close to eye level. Because all ads are those of the same company, this is known as a basic bus.

cludes two separate transit media: *interior transit advertising* (28 percent of ad expenditures) and *exterior transit advertising* (72 percent).°

Interior transit advertising

Card sizes. We speak of interior bus advertising in terms of the cards on which the ads are printed. The standard sizes are:

Overhead rack card	11″ high × 28″ wide*
Overhead rack card	11″ × 42″
Overhead rack card	11″ × 56″
A large unit near the door	22″ × 21″

*In transit advertising, as in outdoor advertising, the height is given first, then the width.

° This and the following data in this section, unless otherwise credited, are from the Transit Advertising Bureau.

8. MECHANICAL REQUIREMENTS
King Size, Queen Size and Taillight Spectaculars posters must be produced on minimum 70 lb. opaque posting paper and varnished. Allow 1-1/2″ all sides as margin covered by frame.
Headlight and Traveling Displays: Produce on 14-ply waterproof stock, horizontal grain and varnish, 1″ margin on all sides.
Inside Cards: Produce on 4 or 5-ply stock, coated one side, horizontal grain, 1/2″ margin on all sides. Poster Requirements: Service plus 15%.
Shipping Information
Shipping dates: Ship posters, displays and cards prepaid to arrive minimum 10 days before commencement date.
Ship to: Mark DeHaven, Fort Wayne PTC, 801 Leesburg Rd., Fort Wayne, Ind. 46808.

9. MONTHLY ESTIMATED RIDES
TAA—3/31/75
Monthly rides (12 month average)............ 231,467

GARY

TAA   CERTIFIED **TAA** CIRCULATION

Gary Transit Company.
Operated by The Batchelder Co., 502 E. War Memorial Dr., Peoria, Ill. 61614. Phone 309-688-8508.

1. PERSONNEL
B. J. Batchelder.

2. REPRESENTATIVES/BRANCH OFFICES
New York, Chicago, Detroit, Cleveland, Philadelphia, Los Angeles—Metro Transit Advertising (Div. of Metromedia).

3. AREAS SERVED
Gary.
Number of vehicles operating: 100.

4. AGENCY AND CASH DISCOUNT
15% to agencies; cash discount 0%. Terms: Bills issued monthly in advance and payable at the first of the month after received.

5. ADVERTISING RATES
Eff 1/1/76.
Rec'd 10/10/75.
Outside Rates
KING SIZE POSTERS (street and curb)
30″ x 144″:

Showing:	Units	1 mo.	3 mos.	6 mos.	12 mos.
Intensive..	60	3,150.00	2,992.50	2,835.00	2,520.00
100	40	2,100.00	1,995.00	1,890.00	1,680.00
50	20	1,050.00	997.50	945.00	840.00
25	10	525.00	498.75	472.50	420.00

QUEEN SIZE POSTERS (curb)
TAILLIGHT SPECTACULARS (rear)
30″ x 88″/21″ x 72″:

Showing:	Units	1 mo.	3 mos.	6 mos.	12 mos.
Intensive..	60	2,362.50	2,244.37	2,126.25	1,890.00
100	40	1,575.00	1,496.25	1,417.50	1,260.00
50	20	787.50	748.13	708.75	630.00

HEADLIGHT DISPLAYS
TRAVELING DISPLAYS
21″ x 38″/21″ x 44″:

Showing:	Units	1 mo.	3 mos.	6 mos.	12 mos.
Intensive..	60	945.00	897.75	850.80	756.09
Unit rate............		15.75	14.96	14.18	12.60

Inside Rates
Service values:
Full 60 vehicles.
11″ x 28″:   Per month
Full service 135.00
Unit rate 2.25

MOODS IN MOTION
(All inside cards)
Minimum 3 months, per bus.................... 40.00

8. MECHANICAL REQUIREMENTS
King Size, Queen Size and Taillight Spectaculars posters must be produced on minimum 70 lb. opaque posting paper and varnished. Allow 1-1/2″ all sides as margin covered by frame.
Headlight and Traveling Displays: Produce on 14-ply waterproof stock, horizontal grain and varnish, 1″ margin on all sides.
Inside Cards: Produce on 4 or 5-ply stock, coated one side, horizontal grain, 1/2″ margin on all sides. Poster Requirements: Service plus 15%.
Shipping Information
Shipping dat... ... ... prepaid ... arrive min...

5. ADVERTISING RATES
Eff 1/1/76.
Rec'd 10/10/75
Outside Rates
KING SIZE POSTERS (street and curb)
30″ x 144″:

Showing:	Units	1 mo.	3 mos.	6 mos.	12 mos.
Intensive..	120	6,300.00	5,985.00	5,670.00	5,040.00
100	80	4,200.00	3,990.00	3,780.00	3,360.00
50	40	2,100.00	1,995.00	1,890.00	1,680.00
25	20	1,050.00	997.50	945.00	840.00

QUEEN SIZE POSTERS (curb)
TAILLIGHT SPECTACULARS (rear)
30″ x 88″/21″ x 72″:

Showing:	Units	1 mo.	3 mos.	6 mos.	12 mos.
Intensive	120	5,400.00	5,130.00	4,860.00	4,320.00
100	80	3,600.00	3,420.00	3,240.00	2,880.00
50	40	1,800.00	1,710.00	1,620.00	1,440.00

Add 1/3 for upper 21″ x 72″ London Roof Taillight Spectacular.

HEADLIGHT DISPLAYS
TRAVELING DISPLAYS
11″ x 42″/21″ x 44″:

Showing:	Units	1 mo.	3 mos.	6 mos.	12 mos.
Intensive..	120	1,890.00	1,795.00	1,701.60	1,512.00
100	80	1,260.00	1,196.80	1,134.40	1,008.00
50	40	630.00	598.40	567.20	504.00

Inside Rates
Service values:
Full 185 vehicles.
11″ x 28″:   Per month
Full service 370.00
Unit rate 2.00
22″ x 21″:
Unit rate 3.00

MOODS IN MOTION
(All inside cards)
Minimum 3 months, per bus.................... 40.00

7. RESTRICTIONS
No liquor ads on curb side.

8. MECHANICAL REQUIREMENTS
King Size, Queen Size and Taillight Spectaculars posters must be produced on minimum 70 lb. opaque posting paper and varnished. Allow 1-1/2″ all sides as margin covered by frame.
Headlight and Traveling Displays: Produce on 14-ply waterproof stock, horizontal grain and varnish, 1″ margin on all sides.
Inside Cards: Produce on 4 or 5-ply stock, coated one side, horizontal grain, 1/2″ margin on all sides. Poster Requirements: Service plus 15%.
Shipping Information
Shipping dates: Ship posters, displays and cards prepaid to arrive minimum 10 days before commencement date.
Ship to: Preferred Advertising, 217 E. St. Joseph, Indianapolis, Ind. 46202.

9. MONTHLY ESTIMATED RIDES
TAA—3/31/75
Monthly rides (12 month average)................1,089,756

SOUTH BEND-Mishawaka

TAA   CERTIFIED **TAA** CIRCULATION

South Bend Public Transportation Corp.
Operated by The Batchelder Co., 1127 W. Central Ave., Toledo, Ohio 43610. Phone 419-243-1241.

1. PERSONNEL
Regional Manager—Joe Conway.

2. REPRESENTATIVES/BRANCH OFFICES
New York, Chicago, Detroit, Cleveland, Philadelphia, Los Angeles—Metro Transit Advertising (Div. of Metromedia).
Branch Office
Peoria, Ill. 6'614—502 E. War Memorial Dr. Phone 309-688-8508.

3. AREAS SERVED
South Bend, Mishawaka.
Number of vehicles operating: 57.

4. AGENCY AND CASH DISCOUNT
Agencies 15%; cash discount 0%. Bills issued monthly in advance and payable at the first of the month after received.

Transit rates from Standard Rate & Data Service. Note terms used.

Service values.   We now meet a new term in the space-buying world. *Service values* are units for buying interior transit space. Each plant owner decides how many cards will give an advertiser excellent coverage in a market. That number of cards are "full service," and have a certain price. *Half service* and *quarter service* may command correspondingly lower prices. All this is published on the rate card. Prices are quoted on a one-month-per-card basis with discounts for longer contracts. Because each plant owner sets the terms, there is no such thing as a "standard service value" in transit advertising. Plant owners give individual rates for their cards on their own rate cards. An advertiser buying card space in interior transit advertising specifies the card size, the service unit, the length of time the ad will run, and the price.

Figuring circulation.   The key questions in buying any medium are, "How many people will this message reach, and am I getting the circulation I'm paying for?" To answer these questions the industry has established a system of measuring inside audience by a fare-box count, defined as "one person riding a display-carrying vehicle for one trip." All references to circulation are in terms of *estimated monthly rides*. This does not mean that all riders see every card or that riders are different people each trip. The Standard Rate & Data Service Transit Section reports whether or not it has received certified or notarized figures from the different transit operations. Special research services are available in some markets to judge how many riders see and remember specific advertisements.

Take one.   A special card called a *Take One* has a pad of direct-response return cards attached. The rider is invited to take one and mail it in for further information or for an application blank to join something. This is an effective way for direct-response advertising to reach many prospects.

Features and advantages.

▲ Because of the length of the ride, a rider gets a chance to read the copy in the ad. The cards permit more copy than do exterior cards or outdoor signs.

▲ A rider can usually see and read three adjacent ads. During rush hour, attention may well be fixed on one ad.

▲ Because the rider goes back and forth on the same route, an ad may make two impressions a day, expanding the frequency of the ad in another medium.

▲ In large cities, advertisers may be able to choose buses that pass supermarkets or travel through neighborhoods with the ethnic audience they particularly want to reach.

Limitations and challenges.

▲ Bus riders present a wide audience, but it is nonselective. Ads for everyday products suited to middle-class life-styles can reach a fine concentration of consumers.

▲ It takes time to produce the cards needed in transit advertising. Furthermore, there must be plenty of time to put the cards where they belong. Plans for this type of advertising must be made well ahead.

▲ Costs must be compared with other local media.

Ads carried on the outside of buses are the most conspicuous form of transit advertising and the largest part of bus advertising.

Exterior transit advertising

Forms of exterior transit advertising.   Exterior space comes in various sizes:

King size	30″ × 144″	(side of bus)
Busorama	22 × 144	(side of bus)
Queen size	30 × 88	(side of bus)
Traveling display	21 × 44	(side of bus)
Taillight spectacular	21 × 72	(rear of bus)
Headlights	21 × 44	(in front)

King size, traveling display, headlights, and taillight spectacular are more widely used than queen size. Next time a bus passes by, see how many of these different forms you can recognize.

Standardized sizes for exterior bus signs.

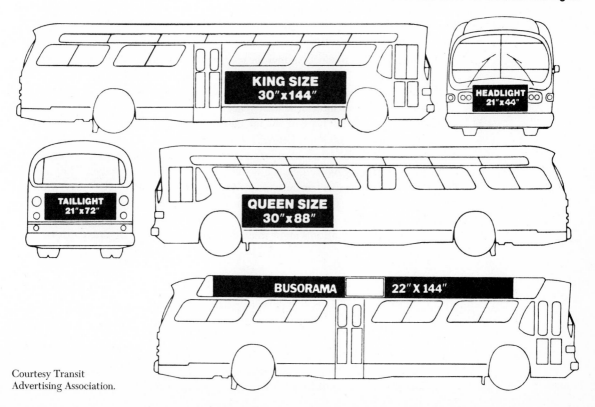

Courtesy Transit
Advertising Association.

The important thing to carry away from this discussion of sizes is the resourcefulness of the transit advertising operators in creating standard sizes to fit the different available areas of a bus. Among the options offered, the advertiser may choose those that best fit the message to the budget.

Features and advantages.

▲ Buses pass through the neighborhoods where people live, shop, and work.

▲ They provide great reach for any message.

▲ Ads are seen by passersby on the street and by riders in passing cars and buses.

▲ In larger cities, the advertiser can select routes that best reach particular demographic groups.

▲ The ads are virtual traveling outdoor signs, reaching many who never travel inside buses. They represent media values different from those of interior advertising.

Limitations and challenges.

▲ Exterior ads must be limited in copy, usually to brand names, package, and slogan.

▲ They reach a wide, unclassified audience; consequently, they are not suitable for a segmented market.

▲ Time is needed to prepare and schedule them, so they are not appropriate for news flashes. Good location on buses must be scheduled well in advance.

▲ Circulation is estimated.

▲ Cost (including production) must be compared with other available local media.

How exterior space is sold.   Exterior space is sold on a basis completely different from that of interior transit space. Exterior space is sold by the number of cards or "units." Each plant owner determines how many cards would make a strong impression on a market (a *100 showing*) and sets a price. Then *half showings* are offered for sale and in large cities even *quarter showings,* as outdoor advertising formerly offered. Space is sold in terms of such packages. The rate card tells how many "units" go into a showing. Since some advertisers may want two cards on opposite sides of one bus, space is not sold in terms of numbers of buses. In smaller markets, the price is also quoted in terms of a number of units.

The chief information sought in exterior transit advertising rate cards is:

1. Number of cards
2. Availability of one or two side panels
3. Quantity of units per 100 showing
4. Basis for charging (showings or number of units)
5. Cost

The basic bus; the total bus; the total total bus.   Instead of selling all their advertising space to different advertisers, transit companies have developed the

Exterior of this "total bus" shows advertising of only one company.

idea of selling all advertising space in one bus to one advertiser at a time. Advertisers may use the space to sell different products made by a company, or they may concentrate all the ads on one product. No rider leaving that bus, no matter how long or short the ride, will be unmindful of the advertiser's product or products. The use of an entire bus interior by one advertiser is referred to as a *basic bus.* (One of the large national outdoor companies calls these interior ads Moods in Motion.) Basic buses are not available everywhere, but more and more cities are selling the arrangement.

An advertiser may also buy all the advertising space on the exterior of a bus—front, back, sides, and top. This is called a *total bus* and is also sold on an exclusive basis to one firm in an industry at a time. If you combine a basic-bus buy with a total-bus buy, you are said to have bought a *total total bus.* You can't buy more advertising on a bus than that.

Commuter trains and stations; air terminals

One sector of the transit advertising industry specializes in commuter trains and terminals. There are such train stations in about 50 cities, serving over 400 communities.

In New York, Philadelphia, and Chicago, two out of three executives commute from home to office by train. The level of affluence of commuters is higher than that of riders in subways and buses, and the average length of rides is 44 minutes. Usually, commuters have seats and plenty of opportunity to see the signs in the trains or stations. Since most commuters ride five days a week, there is also the advantage of frequency of exposure to the signs.

In the sale of station and platform advertising, the number of posters is identified in terms of showings, but here they are called *intensive showings, representative showings,* and *minimum showings.* In each instance, the plant operator announces how many posters are involved in each bracket.

Courtesy Transit Advertising Association.

A suburban station transit sign.

Airline terminals provide another opportunity for reaching a large upper-income audience. Eighty-six percent of all airline passengers are executives, businesspeople, or professionals on business trips. And to the airports come not only passengers but people seeing them off or awaiting their arrival. Advertising space and display unit space in terminals are sold on a per-unit basis.

A characteristic of major train and airline terminals is the variety of advertising forms: floor exhibits, two-sheet posters, dioramas (three-dimensional scenes), island showcases, illuminated signs, and clocks. If ever you find yourself in an air terminal with time on your hands (that does happen), you can make good use of it by seeing how many different forms of advertising you can spot.

Station and platform posters. Poster space is available on the walls of many bus, train, and subway stations, where passengers have time to read while waiting for transportation. They can read all the copy on these posters; and since people pass through these stations regularly, advertisers can build the frequency of their ads.

The New York subway system, the largest user of station posters, has reduced the number of one-sheet posters. Now advertisers can use a smaller number of two-sheet posters and get better exposure with improved overall appearance.

Copy for transit advertising

Because passengers have time to read signs in a bus, copy for interior bus signs can be fuller—more like magazine copy than outdoor copy. It is a good idea, though, to place the name of the product on the lower part of the card, close to the rider.

Copy for exterior bus advertising is similar to outdoor advertising, except that the shape is different and units are more compressed (since they are read at closer range).

226

An overhead door card in a subway train.

It must have been 3:00 Sunday morning when this round island display at an air terminal was photographed. That is about the only time a terminal is not busy.

Trends in transit advertising

The major force that promises to increase the importance of transit advertising is the pressure for more public transportation, particularly around large cities. Increasing gasoline prices have popularized riding the bus. Within the industry, the trends will be to create more attractive cards and to encourage the use of more scientific data for making buying decisions. By 1980, transit advertising (excluding production) will probably exceed $60 million.

QUESTIONS

1. Identify and discuss the advantages and limitations of outdoor advertising.

2. Identify the main forms of standardized outdoor advertising. What are their distinguishing characteristics? How are they bought?

3. What is the size of a standard sized poster panel?

4. What is a Gross Rating Point Buy in buying outdoor advertising? What are its advantages over the previous way of buying poster advertising?

5. What are the considerations to have in mind when selecting outdoor advertising locations? Which factors do you consider most important (rank them in order of importance)? Why did you rank them that way?

6. What is involved in inspecting outdoor signs?

7. What are the three main copy considerations recommended for designing outdoor advertising?

8. "The great art of outdoor advertising design is simplification." Discuss.

9. What do you consider to be the advertiser's responsibility with respect to the impact outdoor advertising has on the environment?

10. What is meant by:
    a) outdoor plant
    b) 30-sheet poster
    c) a 100 GRP buy
    d) junior-size poster
    e) jump clock
    f) rotary plan
    g) riding a showing
    h) bleed poster
    i) TAB
    j) spectacular sign

11. Name all the places and vehicles where transit advertising can be found.

12. What are the two major forms of transit advertising?

13. Discuss the advantages and limitations of transit advertising, for both interior and exterior advertising.

14. Explain "service value" as it applies to transit advertising.

15. How is interior transit advertising circulation computed? Exterior transit advertising?

16. What are the forms of exterior transit advertising? Which are most widely used?

17. How is exterior transit advertising sold? What is meant by a "Basic Bus"?

18. Discuss fully the idea of a "Take One." Include in your discussion the advantages and limitations.

19. What do these terms mean in transit advertising?

a) card size

b) 100 showing

c) basic bus

d) total bus

e) intensive showings

READING SUGGESTIONS

"Outdoor's AMMO," *Media Decisions* (August 1976), 72–74.

PRASSE, HENRY, "Don't Miss the Bus," *Media Decisions* (March 1976), 86.

SISSORS, JACK Z., and E. REYNOLD PETRAY, *Advertising Media Planning*. Chicago: Crain Books, 1976, pp. 196–98.

STOLBOF, BERNIE, "Plant Operators Are Missing Their Opportunity to Match the Medium to Marketing Needs," *Media Decisions* (April 1976), 78–80.

12

Direct-Response Advertising
Direct-Mail Advertising

Who, at one time or another, has not sent in a coupon from an advertisement for a book or record album or a bird feeder or some other item of interest? The firm which ran the advertisement was engaged in the business of selling by *direct marketing*. The advertising used in direct marketing is called *direct-response advertising*, a field in which it is very easy to confuse terms. It is a commingling of distributive methods, media, trade practices, and tradition. Hence we begin with some definitions.

Definitions

Direct marketing

In this form of marketing, the marketer sells directly to the end user of the product, without recourse to a dealer. It uses direct mail, magazines, television, newspapers, and radio satellite cablecasting. It is one of the fastest-growing sectors of the American economy, one of the favorite areas of acquisition by big companies seeking to diversify. In fact, out of the 50 leaders in the Fortune 500 list of leading American companies, half have acquired direct marketing divisions. General Mills alone has 4 direct-response operations. American Express does $70 million a year in its Giftwares Direct-Marketing Division.

The term *direct marketing* is being used to supplant the term *mail-order* business because today so much of the business is initiated or shipped by means other than mail.

Direct-response advertising

Any form of advertising done in direct marketing is direct-response advertising. The well-known term *mail-order* advertising is also giving way to *direct-response advertising*. At present the two terms are often used interchangeably.

This is a medium, one of many used in direct-response advertising. Expenditures for direct-response advertising in 1976 amounted to $43 million in newspapers, $56 million in television, and most of the $4,725 million spent on third-class mail. By 1980, the volume of direct mail will exceed $7.4 billion.° According to Maxwell Sroge, the authority on direct-selling figures which we use in this chapter, 65 percent of all direct-mail promotional advertising material is opened and read by a member of the household. The terms *direct-mail advertising* and *mail-order advertising* are often confused. Just remember that mail order is a method of bringing goods from seller to buyer, whereas direct mail is an advertising medium for delivering messages.

Direct-mail advertising

If a recipe booklet is sent through the mails, it is direct-mail advertising. If, however, the same booklet is sent to dealers to put on their counters for their customers to pick up, it is regarded as *sales promotion* (discussed in the next chapter, "Sales Promotion"). In this chapter we deal with direct mail as a direct-response medium.

Difference between direct mail and sales promotion

Growth of Direct-Response Advertising

Direct marketing, with its direct-response advertising, has zoomed since 1960, spurred by changes in living patterns and new technology. Electronic data processing makes it possible to put names on magnetic tape. Credit cards simplify payment and encourage purchases of expensive items. Toll-free telephone numbers invite people to pick up the phone and order. Working women, who have money to spend but little time to shop, are another boon to direct marketing.

The computer can instantly produce stored lists of people with their special interests and preferences, so an advertiser can extract names of those most likely to be interested in a particular service or product. This capacity has spawned a profitable practice among noncompetitive direct-response advertisers: they rent one another's lists.

In all this, one point bears repetition: *direct mail is a medium,* one of several used in *direct-response advertising,* a method of selling goods and services by *direct marketing.*

What Makes a "Good" Direct Response Product

Not every product is suitable for direct-response advertising. Broadly speaking, it should not be the usual product available at a neighborhood store, unless it is offered at a very special price. It should have some distinguishing quality or render a useful service not generally convenient to buy. It should be small, for mailing, unless it is a costly purchase. It should open the door to repeat business.

°Estimate, courtesy Maxwell Sroge Company, Inc., is based on a 6 percent rate of inflation yearly between 1978 and 1980. It does not take into consideration any major increases in postal rates.

If it comes with a well-known name back of it, so much the better. Above all, it should be a good value. The advertiser must be geared to handle repeat business, for it is on repeat business that the total direct-marketing business rests.

Unique Features of Direct-Response Advertising

Every direct-response advertisement is financially on its own; it is not part of a campaign. Although many different types of offers are made, a distinguishing feature of every form of direct-response advertising is that it always calls for a prompt reply, giving the name and address of the sender. Since the direct-response advertiser knows exactly how many dollars come back for every dollar spent, it is the most scientific of all forms of advertising. The ad is judged only by the number of coupons returned in relation to cost per order (CPO) and the number and quality of its responses requesting further information—cost per inquiry (CPI). Scorekeeping is strict. There is no credit for cumulative effect. "The art of direct response advertising is getting an order," said Frank Vos, an authority in the field.

Types of Direct-Response Offers

One-step purchase of specific product

The simplest examples of this type of direct-response advertising are the small ads one sees in the back of the shopping section of many magazines or in the Sunday newspaper's shopping section supplement.

Whoever responds to a mail-order advertisment will probably receive the product with one or more circulars in the package, offering other merchandise of related interest. *Bounce back* circulars, as these are called, often produce as much as 20 to 40 percent additional sales from the same customers and often launch the buyer on the path to becoming a steady customer.

The two-step sales operation

Another form of direct-response advertising is the two-step sales presentation, frequently employed by firms selling costly products or services, such as encyclopedias and study courses. The prospect may want to discuss the project with a salesperson who can answer questions relating to the prospect's special interests. In that case, the direct-mail operation is broken into two parts: the first to attract people who may have any interest in the subject. That represents a lead which, second, a salesperson can follow up to complete the sale. A close record is kept of how many responses were received and how many of those inquiries were converted into sales. One of the largest classes of direct-response advertisers—insurance companies—uses advertising to get leads on a "no salesman will call" promise, however; but then they proceed to do a thorough selling job, anticipating all questions, by mail.

(Below): *A one-step, straightforward offer.* ▼

▲ (Above): **A two-step offer to enroll in a service that may involve considerable expense. The first step is to generate inquiries. The second step is to follow up with mailings designed to complete the selling process.**

Any 4 for $1 with The Literary Guild's no-time-limit membership.

(Left): *The basis of book-club operation is to make a generous offer of books at a very low price, in order to reach people who are interested in books and who will permit themselves, as a rule, to buy a number of books over a certain period of time. The proposal is made in various forms, but most book clubs operate on the same principle.*

(Right): *Catalog buying is popular in many fields. Firms specialize in becoming the center for certain types of merchandise presented in their catalogs, which become steady salespeople for them.* ▶

**Book clubs;
record and
cassette clubs**

These utilize still another form of direct-response selling. They offer the buyer a great bargain now, in exchange for the promise to buy a certain quantity later. In offers of this type, advertisers do not expect to break even on the original offer. Their profit lies in subsequent paid purchases. Book publishers are among the top users of direct-response advertising. (It is estimated that more books are being sold through book clubs than through bookstores; it is also held that book-club advertising develops bookstore business.)

Catalog selling

Another important way of using direct-response advertising is to issue catalogs of special classes or types of product, such as gift items, gourmet foods, sports clothing, tools, housewares, seeds. The advertising is directed toward getting the prospect to send for the catalog. Of course, the name of the sender is added to the list for further follow-up.

This is aside from the massive mail-order catalogs of Sears and of Wards, which offer items of every kind and are sent in split sections to people who have shown interest in some particular category.

Timing of Direct-Response Advertising

Direct-response advertising has its good months and poor months for getting responses. For most (not all) offerings, the best months are January and February. Other good months are August, September, October, November, and December. The low months for most products are June, March, April, May, and July. Direct-response advertisers always plan their tests well in advance, to be able to come out strong with their best mailings and ads in the best months of their sales calendars.

TIME SCHEDULE FOR A TYPICAL PROMOTION MAILING

PROJECT: **ABC MAILING**   REVERSE TIME SCHEDULE   PROJECTED DROP DATE: **January 15th**

	Creative			Production				Mailing			
ELEMENT	LAYOUT DUE	COPY DUE	TYPE DUE	FINAL ART DUE	SEPARATIONS DUE	PRINTING DUE	DELIVERY TO MAILING SERVICE	LABELS TO BE AFFIXED BY MAIL SERV.	AFFIXING TIME	PRE-ADDRESSED MATERIAL	DROP DATE
CIRCULAR 17 x 11—4/c-2/s Fold to 8½ x 5½	11/20	11/25	11/29	12/5	12/19	1/4	1/5				J A
BONUS SHEET 8½ x 5½—2/c-1/s	12/1	12/7	12/10	12/8	12/26	1/4	1/5				N
LETTER 17 x 11—2/c-2/s Fold to 8½ x 5½	12/1	12/7	12/10	12/18		1/4	1/5				U A
ORDER CARD 11½ x 5½—2/c-2/s Die-cut fold to 8½ x 5½	12/1	12/5	12/8	12/14		1/4	1/5				R Y
OUTER ENVELOPE 9 x 6—2/c-1/s Open side die-cut perforated cellophane window	11/20	11/25	12/2	12/4		1/3	1/4				15
REPLY ENVELOPE 6¾ x ?—1/c-1/s	11/20	11/25	12/2	12/4		1/3	1/5				
ADDRESSING MATERIALS								12/30	1/5-1/7	1/5-1/7	

Bob Stone, *Successful Direct Marketing Methods* (Chicago: Crain Books, 1975).

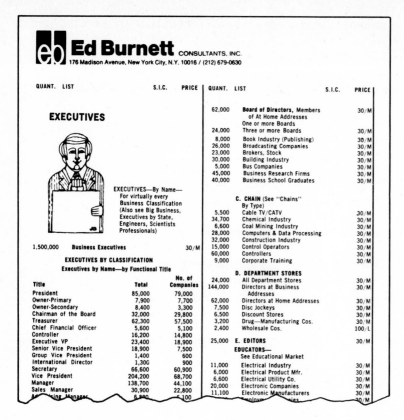

EXECUTIVES

EXECUTIVES—By Name—
For virtually every
Business Classification
(Also see Big Business,
Executives by State,
Engineers, Scientists
Professionals)

QUANT.	LIST	S.I.C.	PRICE
1,500,000	Business Executives		30/M

EXECUTIVES BY CLASSIFICATION
Executives by Name—by Functional Title

Title	Total	No. of Companies
President	85,000	79,000
Owner-Primary	7,900	7,700
Owner-Secondary	8,400	3,300
Chairman of the Board	32,000	29,800
Treasurer	62,300	57,500
Chief Financial Officer	5,600	5,100
Controller	16,200	14,800
Executive VP	23,400	18,900
Senior Vice President	18,900	7,500
Group Vice President	1,400	600
International Director	1,300	900
Secretary	66,600	60,900
Vice President	204,200	68,700
Manager	138,700	44,100
Sales Manager	30,900	22,800
Advertising Manager	6,900	6,100

QUANT.	LIST	S.I.C.	PRICE
62,000	Board of Directors, Members of At Home Addresses One or more Boards		30/M
24,000	Three or more Boards		30/M
8,000	Book Industry (Publishing)		30/M
26,000	Broadcasting Companies		30/M
23,000	Brokers, Stock		30/M
30,000	Building Industry		30/M
5,000	Bus Companies		30/M
45,000	Business Research Firms		30/M
40,000	Business School Graduates		30/M
	C. CHAIN (See "Chains" By Type)		
5,500	Cable TV/CATV		30/M
34,700	Chemical Industry		30/M
6,600	Coal Mining Industry		30/M
28,000	Computers & Data Processing		30/M
32,000	Construction Industry		30/M
15,000	Control Operators		30/M
60,000	Controllers		30/M
9,000	Corporate Training		30/M
	D. DEPARTMENT STORES		
24,000	All Department Stores		30/M
144,000	Directors at Business Addresses		30/M
62,000	Directors at Home Addresses		30/M
7,500	Disc Jockeys		30/M
6,500	Discount Stores		30/M
3,200	Drug—Manufacturing Cos.		30/M
2,400	Wholesale Cos.		100/L
25,000	**E. EDITORS**		30/M
	EDUCATORS— See Educational Market		
11,000	Electrical Industry		30/M
6,000	Electrical Product Mfr.		30/M
6,600	Electrical Utility Co.		30/M
20,000	Electronic Companies		30/M
11,100	Electronic Manufacturers		30/M

Part of a compiled list in a catalog that lists thousands of classifications.

Using Direct Mail

The biggest medium used in direct-response advertising is *direct mail,* an institution built on a structure of mailing lists, which the advertiser has to gather. This is the only medium for which the advertiser must provide the circulation. There are two types of lists: *compiled* and *mail-derived.*

Compiled lists

Lists of names are gathered from published sources, such as lists of car owners, people recently married, new home buyers, boat owners, lists of people by trade or profession. The Standard Rate & Data Service reports over 27,000 compiled lists for sale by *mailing list houses* all over the country who specialize in assembling them from many sources, and who sell them at so much per thousand. The catalog of a list house, Zeller Lists, Inc., sets forth a good description of its offerings:

> Our scope is the total field of compiled lists . . . all business, manufacturers, wholesalers, retailers, contractors, finance, service firms . . . executives in all categories . . . professions . . . institutions . . . residents . . . consumers . . . and all the echelons, functions, disciplines, specialties, ratings, SICs,[°] demographics which allow us to refine lists for all your special requirements.

° See Glossary.

There are changes taking place in every list all the time. One of the first questions to ask about any list is "How old is it?" or more specifically, "When was the last time it was used?" because presumably it would have been corrected at that time for all returned mail.

Many mailing list houses sell lists of names of people who have ordered something by mail or have responded to an ad for further information. People on mail-derived lists are those who are prone to order by mail; therefore, these lists are more productive than compiled lists. A mail-derived list can be your own house list or a response list that you rent from some other advertiser.

Mail-derived lists

House lists. The finest asset that any direct-marketing firm can have is its own list of customers. These customers have shown that they buy by mail, that they have had dealings with the house, and have confidence in its integrity and wares. By the nature of the purchase they have made they reveal what type of product might hold further interest. Besides, there is no extra cost for the use of their names.

Renting lists from other advertisers. Next best to one's own list of customers' names are those of people who have bought from other establishments. This fact has led to the creation of an industry within an industry, each direct advertiser setting up a profit center with a sales department for selling lists or renting them to noncompetitors.

Doubleday Mailing Lists, a subsidiary of Doubleday & Company, publishers of a long list of book clubs, is offering at this writing a list of garden club members and lists of members of its many other special interest clubs. Diner's Club offers different segments of their total list of nearly one million names (with good credit). Columbia House (an affiliate of CBS) offers a choice of 15 lists of "Proven Mail Order Buyers" from among its different cassette and record club members. Every issue of *Direct Marketing* magazine carries advertisements of many firms who offer their own lists to other firms.

List brokers. Another important industry within an industry is that of the *list broker*, who acts as a clearing house of lists and as a consultant. Rose Harper, president of the Kleid Company, one of the leading brokers in the field, describes the list broker's work in this way:

> Our office registers some 15,000 different lists. We merely act as agents and negotiate the rental or exchange of names. These lists run from approximately $35 per M up to $40 per M. At the lower end of the scale we have inquiry names, contest names, premium names, and at the other end there are subscriber lists, members of record clubs, buyers of financial services, etc.
>
> Our commission (20 percent) is paid by the owner of the list, so that the user gains our knowledge, experience and advice without a surcharge.
>
> It would be hard to define all the possible types of lists used for any specific mailing, since it is a matter of constant testing (trying out a small part of the list before buy-

238

ing the whole list). For example, a magazine like *Saturday Review* would test lists of people who have bought records by mail, books by mail, people who have attended concerts, people who have been abroad, and almost any other list which has a cultural mail order qualification. Such lists are not sold, but rented for one-time use.

Usually these rented lists do not actually come into the advertiser's possession. A third party, such as a *lettershop*, which we shall discuss later, undertakes to address Company A's mailing pieces with the names on Company B's list. Company A, therefore, never actually sees the mailing list it uses. Only those names that respond ever become known to the mailer.

Almost 95 percent of the available lists are now being reproduced on labels and magnetic tape. The magnetic tape is also used for computer letter writing and for eliminating duplication among the lists being mailed.

List brokers can supply their own collections of choice lists; or they may serve as consultants to list buyers, participate in the planning, prevent the use of lists that do not appear appropriate, and bring to bear the latest experiences in the field.

Merge/Purge. One of the big problems involved in using a number of lists is that the same name may be on several of them. One person may receive two, three, or even four copies of the same mailing, an annoyance to the recipient, an extra cost to the advertiser, and perhaps the loss of a prospective customer. To advertisers who send out millions of pieces a year, this loss and expense is considerable.

To offset duplication, computerized systems have been developed whereby all lists for a mailing are sent directly to a central service equipped to handle what is known as a *merge/purge* operation. This results in having all duplicates removed from the list, so that the recipient gets only one mailing. Numerous firms are equipped to handle a merge/purge operation, but it can be used only on response-derived lists with names on magnetic tape.

The constant increase in postal cost has inspired different ways of getting a message to a list of prospects. Among them are the following:

Other direct-mail techniques

Package inserts.   It has long been the custom to enclose a *bounce-back* circular when an order is filled. The circular advertises another of the firm's products that might interest the purchaser. But in recent times it has become possible to contract for package inserts in the shipments of other companies, much as one would buy space in a magazine. There are usually severe restrictions on size and weight, but package inserts are a significant direct-response medium. They are another approach to the high cost of list rental, also.

Cooperative (joint) mail advertising.   There are firms who specialize in sending out mailings to selected lists, each mailing carrying the offer and return-order form of a group of direct marketers who want to reach the described audience. The joint mailing may be made in an envelope, or it may be a full-page

Do you have a choice about which types of duplication to eliminate?
For DIAL·A·DUPLICATE users, the answer is always yes!

The rapid growth in the usage of Merge/Purge systems has created a widespread increase in interest among mailers about how such systems **really** work.

What types of duplicates are being eliminated?

What forms of duplicates are being missed?

Characteristically, service bureaus have answered these and many other pertinent questions with vague references to overkill percentages, hit ratios, match code formulation techniques or mathematical probability routines. Unfortunately, these answers don't provide mailers with the information they really need.

We are attempting to change all that.

You deserve to know in detail how your Merge/Purge processor decides what names to kick out and which ones to keep. We give you that information with our new **Dial-A-Duplicate** Merge/Purge system. Not only will we show you how dupes are identified but **Dial-A-Duplicate** lets you choose which categories of duplicates you want eliminated from your mailings. We think you should insist on the same information from anyone else you may consider for Merge/Purge processing.

For comparison, here are the various forms of duplicates which our **Dial-A-Duplicate** system can find and eliminate. Each Merge/Purge, **you** decide which ones you want eliminated.

DUPLICATION CATEGORIES	Would you call these dupes?		Will your current supplier call these dupes?		Will DIAL·A·DUPLICATE call these dupes?
	Yes (✓)	No (✓)	Yes (✓)	No (✓)	
Group A. Identical Name and Address: Mr. Charles Callahan Mr. Charles Callahan 92 Thorndike Street 92 Thorndike Street Palmer, Mass. 01069 Palmer, Mass. 01069 *"Are these duplicates?"*	☐	☐	☐	☐	Yes, if you say so.
Group B. Same Name and Address · Minor Errors: Mr. C. Edwin VanAuken Mr. C. Edwin VanAuken 411 Deerfield Road 811 Deerfield Road East Syracuse, N.Y. 13057 East Syracuse, N.Y. 13057 *"Are these duplicates?"*	☐	☐	☐	☐	Yes, if you say so.
Group C. Same Name and Address · Multiple Errors: Mr. Roger E. Winters Mr. Roger E. Wintors 1662 East Berks 1626 East Berks Philadelphia, Pa. 19125 Philadelphia, Pa. 19125 *"Are these duplicates?"*	☐	☐	☐	☐	Yes, if you say so.
Group D. Two In Same Household: Ms. Helen T. Bertram Mr. C. E. Bertram 108 Aucilia 108 Aucilia Cocoa Beach, Florida 32931 Cocoa Beach, Florida 32931 *"Are these duplicates?"*	☐	☐	☐	☐	Yes, if you say so.
Group E. Same Person · Major Name Misspelling: R. Langford R.W. Lagfard 3030 Sherwood Drive 3030 Sherwood Drive Brunswick, Georgia 31520 Brunswick, Georgia 31520 *"Are these duplicates?"*	☐	☐	☐	☐	Yes, if you say so.
Group F. Same Person, Completely Different Address: A. M. Prigge, Jr. A. M. Prigge, Jr. 102 Spruce 412 Seeds Avenue Sarasota, Florida 33577 Sarasota, Florida 33578 *"Are these duplicates?"*	☐	☐	☐	☐	Yes, if you say so.
Group G. Two In Same Household · Address Errors: Robert Mulligan Katie Mulligan 31252 North Shore 31257 Norshore Sedalia, Mo. 65301 Sedalia, Mo. 65301 *"Are these duplicates?"*	☐	☐	☐	☐	Yes, if you say so.
Group H. Two People, Same Company: John Abercheck Robert Wilkinson Merchants Grocery Mer. Groc. 204 Nalle Place 204 Nalle Place Columbia, Missouri 65201 Columbia, Missouri 65201 *"Are these duplicates?"*	☐	☐	☐	☐	Yes, if you say so.

Wiland&AssociatesInc.

219 East Davis Street ■■■ Culpeper, Virginia 22701 ■■■ Telephone (703) 825-5100

A firm in the merge/purge field illustrates pitfalls in recognizing a duplicate name.

240

Every mailing you make has a <u>potential for profit</u>
...when you pass along to your members or customers a

Substantial Group Discount on
Britannica 3

Do yourself a favor!

No one has to tell you how expensive it is to mail out bills, statements and other regular communications today—and the cost is rising rapidly!

BUT...when you insert a colorful Encyclopaedia Britannica brochure and business reply card in your mailing, you've turned your mail room into a real Profit Center!

Because for every inquiry card returned—*whether or not* the people on your list ever buy an encyclopaedia— you'll receive a generous cash reward!

Already one major bank has earned over $100,000 by inserting Britannica 3 flyers in statements—and you can do as well or possibly even better!

These are just a few of the well-known participants in our Encyclopaedia Britannica endorsement program— you'll see that you'll be in good company!

Fingerhut	Amoco
Unity Buying Service	Exxon
Parents' Magazine	Continental Bank
Doubleday	Bankers Trust of New York

Help your customers or members!

As you've no doubt read in the nation's leading magazines and newspapers the revolutionary new Britannica 3 is more than a new encyclopaedia—it's a complete Home Learning Center that every member of every family can use to their benefit.

This all new Britannica 3 is, without a doubt, the most-wanted encyclopaedia in America—and you can be sure that your customers and members are would-be Britannica owners too!

When you include an Encyclopaedia Britannica flyer and business reply card in your mailbox, you're giving them a chance to Preview the exciting new Britannica ABSOLUTELY FREE, and WITHOUT THE SLIGHTEST OBLIGATION.

Once they've seen what Britannica can offer—and heard the full story on all the benefits of Britannica 3 ownership, they're entitled to take advantage of the Group Discount Program—and, thanks to you, SAVE a substantial amount of money! They'll have *you* to thank for it!

And...if you qualify, solo mailings are also available in the all new Encyclopaedia Britannica "3rd Party" program—find out more about them today!

One-Volume Outline of Knowledge ▶

▲ 10-Volume Ready Reference   ▲ 19 Volumes of Knowledge in Depth

Mail this coupon for full information on the
Britannica 3 Discount Program

**Encyclopaedia Britannica
Group Discount Program**

Attention: Charles E. Brocker
425 N. Michigan Ave., Chicago, Ill. 60611

☐ YES! Please have one of your representa- tives contact me with full details on your Britannica 3 Group Discount Program, along with actual case histories showing the profit potential for me.

NAME _____ TITLE _____

COMPANY _____

ADDRESS _____

CITY _____ STATE _____ ZIP _____

YOUR PHONE NUMBER: _____

Inviting others to use your insert in their mailings.

ad in a magazine, the page consisting entirely of coupon-like ads of different firms. The arrangement divides postage and mail handling costs.

Syndicate mailings.   Here a marketer prepares a direct mailing piece offering a product or service; but instead of mailing it himself, he makes financial arrangements with other mail-order companies to mail his offer under their letterhead. The marketer supplies material that the mail-order people can use to sell his product under the name of the mail-order house. Thus, Meredith Publishing Company, who publishes the *Better Homes & Garden Family Medical Guide*, might syndicate it to Doubleday Book Clubs, Encyclopaedia Britannica, and others who may be able to sell it to their lists of prospective customers. Each of these direct marketing companies might adapt the syndicator's letter copy to some extent. Most of them will use his circular without change. An important factor in such arrangement is to keep down the weight of the mailing piece.

What Makes a Good Name?

Some people are more responsive to mailings than are others. Among the more responsive are

▲ Customers who have recently ordered or who order frequently

▲ Buyers of similar products

▲ Volume buyers

▲ People who have shown interest in a related product; e.g., book-club members, record and tape buyers

▲ People who have a demographic interest in a product; e.g., parents, who buy encyclopedias, young marrieds, who buy insurance

▲ Those who are known to reply to direct mail (in contrast to those whose response is unknown)

Direct-Response Copy

The difference between direct-response copy written for direct mail or for publication advertising is chiefly in format, not in substance. Because we have already become familiar with preparing print publication copy, we shall discuss the subject in that framework. Then we shall discuss the special needs of the direct-mail format and how to adapt copy for it.

Direct-response publication copy invariably has a strong promise-of-benefit headline to attract immediate attention. It is usually news of a special value, to attract a certain type of audience. This is not the place for subtlety or a play on words; seldom for humor. Subheads appear frequently, describing the offer in a different way. This is immediately followed by an abundance of clear copy, spelling out details of the offer. This is the place for all forms of evidence available to give assurance to the reader, specify money-back guarantees, and close with a special bonus for promptness in replying. All this will be recognized as following the PAPA formula: Promise, Amplification, Proof, Action.

The order form should be big enough for the reader to fill out easily. Terms should be clearly presented, including handling and shipping charges, approval offers or money-back guarantees, and use of credit cards.

The formula is applied in a different way to direct-mail pieces, especially if they are not single cards but part of a package of different pieces sent in the same envelope.

The Direct-Mail Package

All the different pieces that go out in one mailing are referred to as its *package*. When you get a direct-mail envelope, you may think someone had an envelope addressed, then stuffed a lot of various advertising into it. But the chances are that it was all one unit of carefully selected pieces, each with its purpose. It may include the following elements.

Envelope

The selling effort begins on the outside of the envelope. Everything depends upon rousing interest and curiosity, so that the recipient will open it. In fact, 15 percent of people who receive unsolicited mail coming in an envelope throw it away because they think they already know what is inside, and they are not interested. The message should not make any false pretense; otherwise, the reader will feel tricked, and toss the whole mailing away. The envelope must break through that barrier by what it says.

Letter

The addressee's name may be computerized on it, but it is usually a personal letter, establishing contact directly with the reader. It explains the importance of getting the full details given on the handsome brochure enclosed. The job of the letter is to interest the reader in such an enclosure.

Brochure

This is the big selling part of the mailing—a booklet, folder brochure, or broadside, perhaps with color pictures and charts to illustrate everything discussed. This is the workhorse of the team.

Order form

Requirements for this form are the same as those for the publication advertisement. The order form may, however, be considerably larger and may have the addressee's name computerized on it, needing only a signature.

ACT NOW

The ACT-NOW enclosure may be a different-colored slip, offering a special bonus for a prompt reply.

Reply envelope

A very important, standard practice, based on experience, is to enclose a return envelope when an order is requested. Convenience encourages the reader to reply.

WORKSHEET FOR PLANNING PROFITABLE MAILINGS

Date: _Date_

PROPOSITION _Practical Mathematics_ KEY _64_

1 - Price of Merchandise or Service	**$25.00**

2 - Cost of Filling the Order

a) Merchandise or Service	5.00	
b) Royalty	—	
c) Handling Expense	.75	
d) Postage and Shipping Expense	.60	
e) Premium, including Handling and Postage	.30	
f) Use Tax, if any (1 x **3** %)	.75	
TOTAL COST OF FILLING THE ORDER		7.40

3 - Administrative Overhead

a) Rent, Light, Heat, Maintenance, Credit Checking, Collections, etc. (**10** % of # 1)	2.50	
TOTAL ADMINISTRATIVE COST		2.50

4 - Estimated Percentage of Returns, Refunds or Cancellations	10%

5 - Expense in Handling Returns

a) Return Postage and Handling (2c plus 2d)	1.35
b) Refurbishing Returned Merchandise (**10** % of # 2a)	.50
TOTAL COST OF HANDLING RETURNS	1.85

6 - Chargeable Cost of Returns (**10** % of $ **1.85**)		.19
7 - Estimated Bad Debt Percentage	10%	
8 - Chargeable Cost of Bad Debts (# 1 x # 7)		2.50
9 - Total Variable Costs (# 2 plus # 3, # 6, and # 8)		12.59
10 - Unit Profit after Deducting Variable Costs (# 1 less # 9)		12.41
11 - Return Factor (100% less # 4)	90%	
12 - Unit Profit Per Order (# 10 x # 11)		11.17
13 - Loss Per Unit Profit Due to Returned Merchandise (**10** % of # 2a)		.50
14 - Net Profit Per Order (# 12 less # 13)		10.67
15 - Cost of Mailing per 1,000	96.03	
16 - NUMBER OF ORDERS PER 1,000 NEEDED TO BREAK EVEN		9.0

For additional copies of this form, contact Marketing Services Manager.
BOISE CASCADE ENVELOPES, 313 Rohlwing Road, Addison, Illinois 60101 - Tel. 312, 629-5000

Form No. 8-9

A mail-order cost worksheet, showing how quotas for mailings are established.

Copy Testing

Direct-mail tests

One of the great advantages of direct-response advertising is that you can test everything on a small but meaningful scale before proceeding on a very large scale. Testing is especially simple in direct mail. You may want to test which of two propositions or two appeals or two different formats is better. You prepare the materials to be tested the way they are to go out. Every other name on a list is sent mailing A; the other half is sent mailing B. All order cards have a code or key number by which replies are identified and tabulated. But to get statistically meaningful differences, you must use a big enough sample of a mailing list. You must receive enough responses to show clearly which is the better ad. If mailing piece A produces 14 orders while mailing piece B produces 11, the result of the test is meaningless. And in order to make our test beds, or mailings, large enough, we have to have some idea of the percentage of response to expect. This will vary enormously by medium and by proposition. You must make sure that the names chosen for a direct-mail test are a fair sample of the rest of the list.

Split-run tests

For magazine ads, split-run tests are used. We met them briefly in Chapter 10, "Using Magazines." By this method the advertiser runs two different advertisements in the same position, on the same date, in alternate copies of the same publication. Ads in newspapers are placed in papers distributed equally in the same area. Magazine ads may appear in geographic editions split for testing or in mailings to different but equivalent areas. Each advertisement carries a coupon with its own key number. The advertiser can then tell whether ad A or ad B brings in more responses.

As a practical matter, advertisers usually will test a number of ads at one time, in the hope of finding at least one real jewel among them. The one-at-a-time system is a very slow one. Therefore, in conducting such tests, advertisers will pick out one of the successful ads they already have and regard that as a *control* against which all their other ads are separately tested. You can plan a series of tests such as these:

Ad A vs. control ad

Ad B vs. control ad

Ad C vs. control ad

Ad D vs. control ad

They will then run the series in one of the magazines with geographic editions that accept split-run advertising, running different sets of ads (new vs. control) in various editions at the same time. Thus an advertiser can test four, six, or any number of ads at one time, a great saving in the total time taken for testing.

Free advice
...to help you get ahead

Sending for the opportunity booklet of your choice could be one of the smartest moves you make this year.

Sometimes free advice can be mightly valuable. So, if you're not satisfied with your progress, send for a free LaSalle booklet in your field of interest.

We've been helping ambitious people improve their knowledge and skills for over 60 years. We have home study programs to upgrade your present job skills . . . or for self-enrichment . . . or to completely change your career direction. Any one could make a big difference in your life.

LaSalle home study is such a pleasant way to learn. Lessons come to your home, so you can set your own pace as a *class of one.* In spare time to suit your convenience. Experienced instructors guide you by mail — correct and grade your assignments — every step of the way.

Get the facts without obligation. For free booklet that interests you most, check name of program in coupon below and mail it today. There's no obligation.

1 **Interior Decorating** A fascinating field where you can put your creative talents to practical use. Turn your home into a showcase. Help your friends with their decorating problems. Or even start a full or part time career. Send for free booklet.

2 **Accounting** Accounting is an interesting and growing profession. The study of accounting is not only helpful in preparing for a career, but it can also be a personal asset. Ambitious people have used their grasp of accounting principles to get ahead in many fields. Send for free booklet.

3 **Business Management** If you seek advancement with your present employer, or a bigger opportunity in another company, or plan a business of your own some day — you can be greatly helped by studying the principles of business management. LaSalle's program includes finance, marketing, organization, executive skills, and much more. Send for free booklet.

4 **College Degree at Home** Now you can earn a college degree in your spare time at home. Choose from five practical programs: Associate in Business Degree with a major in Business Management, Accounting, Banking and Finance or Hotel/Restaurant Administration, or a Bachelor of Science Degree in Commerce and Social Studies.

5 **Dental Office Assistant** Dental Office Assistants enjoy the satisfaction of helping people. LaSalle training includes receptionist duties, personality development, office records, lab and X-ray theory, patient psychology, many other subjects. Send for free booklet.

6 **Secretarial Careers** Choose from three business programs: Secretarial — learn speed-shorthand, typing & office skills, to prepare for this popular career field; Stenotype — the modern machine shorthand that's easier to take, read, transcribe; Administrative Assistant — prepares you for more responsible executive duties, such as handling employees, supervising work.

7 **You'll find a choice** of other LaSalle programs listed on the coupon below. We'll be glad to send you a free booklet and full information on the one that interests you. Simply check coupon below and mail.

Do yourself a big favor. Send for the free booklet that could help you most now.

©1975 LA SALLE EXTENSION UNIVERSITY • A CORRESPONDENCE INSTITUTION

1

This ad and those following are five sets of split-run tests. The better ad of each set was used as the basis for extensive campaigns. After you have judged which you consider the better ad of each pair, turn to p. 265 for the results, then try to analyze the qualities that made the winning ads successful.

Free advice
...to help you get ahead

Sending for the opportunity booklet of your choice could be one of the smartest moves you make this year.

Accounting

Business Management

Secretarial

Hotel/Motel Management

Drafting

Traffic Management

Banking & Finance

Supervisory Management

Art Training (no submissions required)

Sometimes free advice can be mighty valuable. So, if you're not satisfied with your progress, send for a free LaSalle booklet in your field of interest.

We've been helping ambitious people improve their knowledge and skills for over 60 years. We have home study programs to upgrade your present job skills . . . or for self-enrichment . . . or to completely change your career direction. Any one could make a big difference in your life.

LaSalle home study is such a pleasant way to learn. Lessons come to your home, so you can set your own pace as a *class of one*. In spare time to suit your convenience. Experienced instructors guide you by mail—correct and grade your assignments—every step of the way.

Get the facts without obligation. For free booklet that interests you most, print name of program in coupon below and mail it today.

©1975 LA SALLE EXTENSION UNIVERSITY • A CORRESPONDENCE INSTITUTION

Interior Decorating

Dental Office Assistant

Administrative Assistant

Real Estate

Stenotype Machine Shorthand

Personnel Management

Writing

High School

Associate Degree Programs in
Business Management
•
Accounting
•
Banking/Finance
•
Hotel/Motel Administration

**LA SALLE
EXTENSION
UNIVERSITY**
A Correspondence Institution
417 S. Dearborn Street, Dept. 00-0000,
Chicago, Illinois 60605

Please send me, without cost or obligation, FREE booklet and full information on the field I have written below:

_____
(write field of interest here)

Mr.
Mrs.......................................Age........
Miss   *(circle title & please print)*

Apt.
Address....................................No..........

City...

State...Zip..........
D70

2

Courtesy LaSalle Extension University.
Advertising agency for all ads: Vos & White Incorporated.

Why 30,000 air travelers show this card wherever they go.

(And save hundreds of dollars!)

It looks like a credit card. It even feels like one.

But instead of making it easy for you to spend money (like a credit card) . . . this one makes it easy for you to *save* money. And enjoy V.I.P. privileges wherever and whenever you travel.

Because this is the card that identifies you as an important traveler. An experienced traveler. A member of the Airline Passengers Association.

1. Low cost travel/accident insurance at special member rates.

As an APA member, you get up to $400,000 of travel accident coverage for just a few dollars a month *(tax deductible* if you travel for business). This is more than just "flight" insurance too. Your APA policy covers you *on the job or off* . . . at home or abroad . . . on ANY licensed common carrier in the world. You're covered while riding, boarding or alighting—yes, even if you're struck by ANY common carrier, including planes, buses, trains, even taxis. You're even covered while on the *premises* of any airport, bus or train station, or any other facility for licensed common carriers. And your APA policy, which is issued by Lloyd's of London, pays *in addition* to any and all other insurance you may have.

2. Hotel and Motel Discounts— and V.I.P. benefits.

Show your APA Privilege card and you'll enjoy preferred rates (and service) at more than 4,100 hotels and motels, including participating Sheratons, Rodeway Inns, Holiday Inns, Howard Johnson's, Hyatt Hotels, Ramada Inns and many others.

3. Car rental discounts.

Show your APA Privilege Card and save a full 20% at all National Car Rental agencies. Use your APA Privilege Card at all Econo-Car and American International offices for a full 10% discount there. Going abroad? Be sure to pack your APA Privilege Card—it gets you a 10% discount at more than 1,400 InterRent and 1,000 Europcar rental agencies throughout Europe and the Mediterranean. Only APA offers you this unique combination of car rental discounts . . . to save you money wherever and whenever you travel.

4. First Class vacations at "coach" prices.

Through APA's own Travel Service, you can participate in group trips to some of the world's finest resorts . . . at surprising savings. We'll get you there the most economical way possible—without sacrificing convenience or comfort. If you're making travel plans for business or pleasure, APA Travel Service can handle all the details, including ticketing.

5. Luggage Protection.

As an APA member, your luggage is protected by our exclusive Bag-Guard luggage retrieval and protection system. With Bag-Guard luggage tags and pressure-sensitive labels on and/or inside your luggage, brief cases and other personal property, they're never completely lost. If your property is misplaced, just call APA at the special toll-free WATS number you receive to report the loss and your itinerary. When your property is located, we arrange for its rapid return.

6. Flight Log and Credential Case.

Handsome credential case contains your valuable Airline Passengers Association membership card, Flight Log and Handbook—an easy-to-use directory of airport, customs, and local accommodations data and information. Ideal for carrying tickets, passports, and other documents.

7. Got a gripe? Now you've got "clout".

More than 30,000 seasoned travelers belong to APA. They give us a voice that carries important weight with airlines, hotels and regulatory agencies. (We were instrumental in repealing the infamous passenger "head tax" and are constantly campaigning for greater passenger safety measures.)

We'll see your opinions get to the right people with the full force of your 30,000 fellow APA members behind them.

8. 90-Day Money-Back Guarantee.

Now you can join Airline Passengers Association with this money-back guarantee: If at any time you feel that APA membership is not worth the annual fee, let APA know within 90 days and we'll return your membership fee in full.

Just select the membership class that best serves your needs, fill out and mail the card facing this page. You can even charge your membership fee (and any insurance coverage you wish to purchase) on your credit card. If the postage-paid card has been detached, WRITE for your FREE Privilege Package, plus full details of APA membership and travel insurance. The address is AIRLINE PASSENGERS ASSOCIATION, P.O. Box 2758, Dallas, Texas 75221

3

Whether you travel once a year or once a week... Airline Passengers Association may well be the most important investment you've ever made.

249

5

250

Pick your Beauty Profile Stamps and place on card to get a lavish $15.00* 'Beauty Kit'† for only $1

What a beautiful way to discover the wonderful World of Beauty! It's fun, exciting—because each money-saving Beauty Kit brings you a different assortment of famous-name cosmetics and beauty aids. Mail your card today and get in on a beautiful thing—the World of Beauty!

†'Beauty Kit' is a trademark of the World of Beauty Club® for its cosmetics package.

Get kit after kit of costly fragrances . . . lipsticks . . . eye make-up . . . bath oils . . . blushers . . . creams . . . colognes . . . from world-famous cosmetics makers.

One dollar lets you enter the World of Beauty. And here's what you get . . .

A Fabulous $15.00* Beauty Kit, brimming with famous-name cosmetics and beauty aids—products you've always wanted to try—from companies you know and trust. $15.00 worth of luxury cosmetics for just $1. *At least seven prestige cosmetics in your first Beauty Kit . . . and not just sample sizes!*

Plus A Beauty Guide Magazine packed with "how to" articles by renowned beauty experts to help you make yourself even more attractive!

Plus A Bonus Coupon entitling you to extra beauty products at significant savings!

How Can We Make This Fabulous $1 Offer? Because the world's great cosmetics makers want you to discover and try their finest creations, they make them available to you at far less than their value through the World of Beauty Club.

And That's Just The Beginning! After your Introductory Beauty Kit, you'll go on getting similar kits of prestige beauty products about every two months, automatically, for as long as you want . . . plus, once a year, a deluxe men's kit of famous grooming aids and an exclusive Springtime Fragrance Kit, ideal for gift giving—*all on approval.*

Each kit will be worth far more than the member's money-saving price—many as much as $15.00, some even more. Yet you pay only $5.98 per kit plus shipping and handling for those you choose to keep. No obligation to continue. If you don't find your Introductory Kit or any other Beauty Kit completely irresistible, you may cancel your membership at any time. Yet your $15.00 Introductory Kit for just $1 is yours regardless.

$15.00 Worth Of Famous-Name Cosmetics . . . Beauty Guide Magazine . . . Bonus Offer . . . mail the card today and see what a dollar can do for you!

World of Beauty Club, 623 S. Wabash Ave., Chicago, Illinois 60605.

Over 10,000,000 women have already discovered the World of Beauty Club®. Shouldn't you?

Ask your friends! They'll confirm that World of Beauty Club—the *original* beauty club—brings you kit after kit of famous-name cosmetics—at far less than their value. Since 1965, more than 10 million beauty-conscious women have discovered the fun, excitement, convenience and savings of World of Beauty. Join the Club today!

"I'm sure I will be able to use every single item. I feel prettier just trying all the new things. My husband says I seem to have a glow that he hadn't noticed before—that's great!"
Sandi Dunnagan, East Alton, Illinois

"I would like to thank everyone who has made the World of Beauty Club possible. I am very happy to be a member. The kits that are sent every two months are terrific! I thoroughly enjoy all the latest make-up hints and the fantastic lines of make-up available! I simply couldn't find a better way to get so much for so little!"
Patricia Najjar, Fort Lee, Virginia

"Thanks for making my make-up problems simple ones. I enjoy the kits and also the books included. What fun it is to receive such wonderful items at such a moderate price. Every woman should join your club! I love it!!"
Donna Mann, Rancho Cordova, California

"I just can't believe the generous assortment of beauty aids I've been receiving! The last one was super! This has to be the best thing I've ever done for myself! The beauty guides have helped so much too. Thanks and keep those kits coming!"
Sue Courtney, Tiffin, Ohio

*Based on manufacturers' suggested retail prices.

SOME WOMEN WILL NOT ACCEPT THIS OFFER OF A $15.00* BEAUTY KIT FOR ONLY $1 -- EVEN THOUGH THEY ARE NOT OBLIGATED TO BUY ANOTHER THING.

WHAT WILL YOU DO?

Dear Friend:

I'm puzzled! If your favorite cosmetics boutique offered you $15.00 worth of their finest beauty products for only $1, wouldn't you accept the offer? That's exactly what we offer you, yet some women will pass up this chance.

Perhaps you think this offer is a "gimmick." Let me reassure you -- you are under no obligation to buy another thing -- you may cancel your membership at any time after examining your first kit.

If you decide you don't want any more Beauty Kits, just tell us. That will end the matter. The $15.00* kit is yours to keep for only $1, regardless.

Eve Marshall
World of Beauty Club

P.S. If you don't like the kit, simply return it. We'll refund your dollar or give you full credit for the total amount billed.

75W-I-18

6

CHEESELOVERS OF THE WORLD, *UNITE!*

ENJOY YOUR FAVORITE CHEESES FOR AS LOW AS 3¢ TO 7¢ ABOVE WHOLESALE BY ORDERING DIRECT THROUGH THE WORLD'S LARGEST CHEESE CLUB.

● *Prize French CAMEMBERT*, smooth and creamy gold. Perfect "love-match" for fruit & red wine. Price this month only 4¢ over wholesale—so hurry!

● *Zesty Italian BEL PAESE*, a princely dessert cheese at our "pauper's price"—recently just 3¢ over wholesale!

● *Golden French PORT SALUT*, luscious with Beaujolais on crusty bread—our last price only 7¢ over wholesale!

● *Mellow Norwegian JARLSBERG*, full of "Swiss" holes—our last price only 3¢ over wholesale!

● *Tangy WHITE CHEDDAR* from Belgium—no colors or chemicals added. A brand new taste adventure!

● *Snowy white CAERPHILLY* from Wales—favorite of poet Dylan Thomas on crusty black bread with foamy ale!

PLUS all your special favorites (as well as delicious new discoveries) from every country of the world!

Our famed "Super Cheddar" — only members can get it!

Ever taste fabulous Irish "Swiss"? Our members love it!

YOU GET ALL THIS . . . FREE!

FREE Concise Encyclopedia of the World's Great Cheeses. Every cheese displayed by country, flavor, size, aroma, shape, usable life, how to serve, store, buy, match with food & wine, much more!

FREE How to Hold a Successful Cheese & Wine Tasting

FREE How to Love & Care for Fine Cheeses

FREE How to Throw a Fondue Party at Home

FREE Cooking with Cheese "Recipe Guides"

FREE Gourmet Consultation

Entertain graciously with cheese & wine—we show you how!

PLUS Cheese & Wine Tasting Invitations, Holiday Gift Giving Privileges and Much More!

NO OBLIGATION TO BUY ANYTHING . . . EVER

To join, mail coupon with Membership Fee of only $6—**good for life.** (Never another Club fee EVER.) We do not profit from this fee; it helps offset member cost. Fee refunded in full if not delighted. But hurry, Cheese season just getting into full swing **now.** Send to: CHEESELOVERS INTERNATIONAL, Dept. D114, Cheeselovers International Bldg., Freeport, N.Y. 11520.

FREE BONUS GIFT if you act promptly

$6.00 WORTH OF CHEESES—FREE!

Join promptly and get $6.00 in Cash Certificates you can use for **any** Club cheeses—Port-Salut, Swiss, Cheddar, Brie—whatever you desire. It's like getting your Club membership FREE. What's the catch? No catch. I just know that after your first taste of our marvelous cheeses, **you're bound to want MORE!** And you keep this free gift even if you later decide to cancel!
—Gerard Paul, *Directeur*

8

Courtesy Cheeselovers International.

PLAY IT.
DON'T "FAKE IT"

Free Booklets reveal the secret of teaching yourself to play the guitar, the piano, or the spinet organ – *the "right" way.*

Many people are content to "fake their way" through the tunes they love. Strumming a few chords or pecking at a few keys. And it's such a pity.

Your fingers could make beautiful music...if you gave them the chance.

They could be playing folk or rock. Classical or pop. Hymns or spirituals. Jazz or ballads. All your favorite songs.

So why miss out on the thrill of making your own music? Give yourself a chance to become as good as you *really* could be! You can teach yourself to play the "right" way – at home – in much less time than you might imagine.

Play "right" from the start

Thousands of people just like you have gained new pleasures by learning to play with the enjoyable self-teaching lessons we give by mail. You can too. *Even if you've never had a music lesson before!*

The secret lies in our *clear*, step-by-step,

word-and-picture instruction method. It teaches you to play the *right* way. Without gimmicks. You learn to read and play notes . . . so you'll be able to play practically any song, merely by looking at its sheet music.

A lot of the songs you practice first are tunes you've heard many times. And since you already know how these tunes are supposed to sound, you can tell immediately when you've "got them right."

Then you go on to more advanced pieces. By this time you can tell if your

notes and timing are right, even without ever having heard the songs before. Sooner than you might think possible, you'll be able to play the kind of music you like.

You learn in spare time, in the privacy and comfort of your own home. There's no one standing over you to make you nervous. And because you teach yourself, you can set your own pace. There's no clock-watching private teacher at $4 to $10 per hour to worry about. You take as much time mastering any lesson as you wish.

It's really such a marvelous way to learn. In fact, graduate Mrs. Norman Johanson wrote to tell us, "My daughter has taken lessons for 8 years from a private teacher, and now she asks *me* questions."

Send for FREE Booklet

If you've ever dreamed of being able to play the piano, the guitar or the spinet organ, why not learn more about our convenient, low-cost way to learn? Mail coupon for free booklet today. With it we'll include a free "Note-Finder." There's no obligation. U.S. School of Music, A Home Study School Since 1898, 417 S. Dearborn St., Chicago, Illinois 60605.

9

The secret of teaching yourself music

It's just organized common sense, says this 75-year-old home-study school. Their step-by-step word-and-picture instructions take the mystery out of learning to play the piano, the guitar, or the spinet organ.

It may seem odd at first—the idea of teaching yourself music. You might think you need a private teacher at $4 to $10 an hour to stand beside you and explain everything you should do—and tell you when you've made a mistake.

But surprising as it seems, you need no such thing. Thousands of people just like you have taught themselves to play with the U.S. School of Music courses. By mail. And you can too.

The secret lies in the step-by-step way our lessons teach you. Starting from scratch, they show you with simple words and pictures exactly what to do. You learn to play correctly—by note, from sheet music. Without gimmicks.

But how do you know you're doing it right? Easy. A lot of the tunes you'll practice first are simple songs you've heard before. And since you already know how they're supposed to sound, you can tell right away when you've "got them right."

By the time you go on to more advanced pieces, you'll be able to tell if your notes and timing are right, even without ever having heard the songs before. Sooner than you might think possible, you'll be able to play different kinds of music: ballads, old favorites, show tunes, or hymns.

Convenient and Economical
You learn in your spare time, in the privacy and convenience of your own home.

There's no one standing over you to make you nervous. And because you teach yourself, you set your own pace.

And you'll be delighted to discover how economical it is. The cost comes to less than you'd have to pay a private teacher.

There Are So Many Rewards
How effective are the lessons? Ask Jeffrey Livingston of York, Pa. "I thought the organ course was excellent," he writes. "I knew almost nothing about playing an instrument before I enrolled. Now I can play not only the organ, but the piano too. My new music ability has enabled me to play at churches and small conventions. I am even considering making music my career."

Another recent graduate, Cecelia Feeney of Vineland, N.J. reports: "It's like a dream come true. Knowing how to play the piano and read music has given me new self-confidence."

Mail Coupon Today
If you'd like to learn more about this convenient, pleasant way to teach yourself music, send for our free booklet "Be Your Own Music Teacher." With it, we'll include a free "Note-Finder."

There's no obligation. Just mail the coupon today to U.S. SCHOOL OF MUSIC. *A Home Study School Since 1898.*

494 ©1975 U. S. SCHOOL OF MUSIC

Advertising Agency: Vos & White Incorporated.

Courtesy U.S. School of Music.

10

Guidelines for copy testing

Here are a few guidelines for copy testing, whether for publication advertisements or for direct-mail use.

▲ Test most important differences first, such as offers, prices, formats, appeals, Then, if you have time, patience, and money, test small refinements.

▲ There should be a conspicuous difference between new ads or elements being tested against each other.

▲ Set a quota of replies-per-dollar before you start.

▲ Keep careful records of replies.

▲ Test only one variable at a time. Make sure that ads or mailings are identical in every respect except the one being tested. Don't try to test several variables at one time to save time or money. Neither is saved.

▲ Make no final judgments based on small percentage differences. They may represent simply a normal statistical variation.

▲ Do not change or attempt to improve the mailing or condition of the ad or mailing, once a test has proved satisfactory. If any improvement suggests itself, test it out before using it further. The test may show that it is no improvement at all.

Planning the Direct-Mail Pieces

The creator of direct mail has a wide latitude in format. It may be a single card encompassing a coupon. It may be a letter with a return card, a small folder, a brochure or a folded broadside with an order form and return envelope. Each has a different function and use depending on (1) the cost of the product being sold, (2) the importance of pictures, (3) the nature and length of the copy. As a rule, a warm letter, even if not personalized, should accompany any request for the order, stressing the benefits, describing the key features and importance, and asking for the order. No matter what material is to be sent, there is always the possibility of presenting it in a more interesting form, within postal limitations.

Producing the Direct Mail

What a different world direct-mail production is, compared with that of magazine ad production! In production for magazine ads, the publisher is responsible for the total printing and delivery of the publication. In direct mail, however, the advertiser has the complete burden of having all the material printed, which involves selecting the paper, the type, establishing prices, and selecting the printer. It involves also selecting a letter shop, whose functions we discuss below. All this is the burden of direct-mail production.

A mail production program

Perhaps the clearest way to see what is involved is to see a work schedule and touch upon some of the key points.

Checking weight and size with post office.   Everything begins upon receipt of a complete dummy of the mailing unit, including copy and artwork from the creative department, along with quantities and mailing dates. First, and most important to do, is to check with the post office on weight and size.

Selecting the printing process.   In Chapter 17, "Print Production," we discuss the three major types of printing: letterpress, offset, gravure. For the time being, we can say that most direct-mail advertising is printed by the offset method, except very big runs, which may use rotogravure.

Selecting the paper.   Here we have to pause to become familiar with some important things about the choice of paper, as this is not covered elsewhere in the book.

The three chief categories of paper used in advertising are:

> Writing stocks
> Book stocks
> Cover stocks

Writing stocks. These cover the whole range of paper meant to write or type on. Quality varies from ledger stock, used to keep records, to bond stock for top level office stationery, to utility office paper, to memo paper. If you wanted to include a letter in a mailing, you would find a paper stock in this class.

Book stocks. With many variations, book stocks are the widest classification of papers used in advertising. Chief among them are:

▲ *News stock.* The least costly book paper, built for a short life; porous, so it can dry quickly. Takes line plates well. Used for free-standing inserts in magazines. Not very good for offset.

▲ *Antique finish.* A paper with a mildly rough finish. It is a soft paper, widely used for offset. Among the antique classifications are: *eggshell antique,* a very serviceable offset paper; *text,* a high-grade antique, used for quality offset books, booklets, brochures. It is often water-marked and deckle-edged.

▲ *Machine finish.* Most books and publications are printed on machine-finish paper. It is the workhorse of the paper family.

▲ *English finish.* Has a roughened nonglare surface. Widely accepted for direct mail and sales promotion printing. Especially good for offset lithography and gravure.

▲ *Coated.* This is a paper that is given a special coat of clay and then ironed. The result is a heavier, smoother paper. Not for offset. It can take 150-screen halftones very well for letterpress printing and is therefore frequently used in industrial catalogs, where fine sharp reproduction is important and where there will be continuous usage over a period of time.

Cover stocks. Here is a strong paper, highly resistant to rough handling, used not only for the cover of booklets but sometimes by itself in direct-mail work. Although it has many finishes and textures, it is not adaptable for halftone printing by letterpress, but reproduces tones very well in offset.

There are many other types of papers used for many purposes, but writing, book, and cover are the chief ones in advertising. The printer will submit samples of paper suitable for a given job.

Basic weights and sizes. Paper comes off the machine in large rolls. It is then cut into large sheets in a number of different sizes. In that way, many pages can be printed at one time. Paper is sold by the ream of 500 sheets, and its grade is determined by weight. To meet the problem of trying to compare the weight of paper cut to different sizes, certain sizes have been established for each class as the basic ones for weighing purposes. These are:

For writing paper	17 x 22 inches
For book paper	25 x 38 inches
For cover stock	20 x 26 inches

Hence, no matter how large the sheet may be into which the paper has been cut, its weight is always given in terms of the weight of that paper when cut to its basic size. Thus one hears a writing paper referred to as a *20-pound writing paper*, a book paper referred to as a *70-pound paper*, a cover stock identified as a *100-pound cover*.

Paper has to be selected in relation to the printing process to be used and the plates to be used.

Paper is usually procured by the printer, after a specific choice has been made. In large cities it may also be bought directly from paper jobbers. Each will be glad to submit samples. Before paper is finally ordered, check once more with the post office for weight, shape, and size of envelope. Check the total package.

In planning direct mail, it is important to know basic paper sizes and plan all pieces so that they may be cut from a standard sheet size without waste. Before ordering envelopes, be sure to check with the post office to learn of their latest size restrictions. These are subject to change.

Selecting the printer.   The big problem in selecting a printer is, first of all, to consider only those printers who have the type of presses and the capacity to handle the operation that you have in mind. They may not be located near you. In any case, experience has shown it is always best to get three estimates. Of course, in selecting a printer, the reputation of the firm for prompt delivery is important.

Have finished mechanicals, with type and illustrations, or else photographic negatives ready to turn over to the printer. Proofs should be carefully checked and returned promptly to the printer.

Selecting the letter shop (mailing house).   Once all the material has been printed—including the envelope, which has to be addressed, a letter possibly calling for a name fill-in, a folder that has to be folded, a return card, also perhaps with the name imprinted—it goes to a mailing house (called in many quarters a *letter shop*). Many letter shops are mammoth plants where everything is done by computer. Their computerized letters not only mention the addressee's name, but include a personal reference. The name is also printed on the return order form. Machines automatically address various units, fold all pieces that need to be folded, collate all material and insert it in the envelope, which is sealed, arranged geographically for postal requirements, and delivered to the post office. There is always a question of which is more wonderful, the machines with their swinging arms that do all these things or the production director who has all the material ready in one place, on time.

Since the letter shop and the printer must work closely together, it is desirable to have them near each other.

Timing in scheduling. The direct-mail production manager has special scheduling problems to solve in preparing direct-mail advertising. First of all, a mailing date deadline must be met. This date will be determined by the availability of list rentals at a particular time, the seasonality of the offer, and the wishes of the advertiser. Certain parts of the mailing piece are going to take much longer to produce than others. Envelopes must be ordered.

Mechanical artwork for the circular is usually next to be released. The order card and the letter are usually simpler, and thus they require less time between the release of the mechanical and the delivery of the finished work by the printer.

The mailing pieces sent to different lists will have to be keyed separately, so that the advertiser can tell exactly how many orders are produced by each list. The production manager must determine the exact quantities of each key and issue precise instructions to the printer and to the letter shop.

Using Magazines for Direct-Response Advertising

Magazines are the second largest medium used by direct-response advertisers, but the direct-response advertisers' approach to buying space in them is different from that of national advertisers. Many magazines have mail-order sections in the back of the book; and judging by advertisers' continued use of them, we can assume that results on the whole are good. Many a small business has grown to be a big one through these ads. In direct-response advertising, the question is not what is the cost per thousand of the magazine, but what will be the cost per order or inquiry. You work both for good position and for good prices.

This means at the outset a very close matching of the media to the type of person you want to reach. *House and Garden* is a good magazine for seeds and plants; *Popular Mechanics,* for a new wrench set. Any promising magazine is worth testing if the space cost is low enough.

In direct-response magazine advertising, small ads have paid because it does not take too many orders to show a profit. Big ads have paid because of the attention they get and also, very important, because of the position they get. But

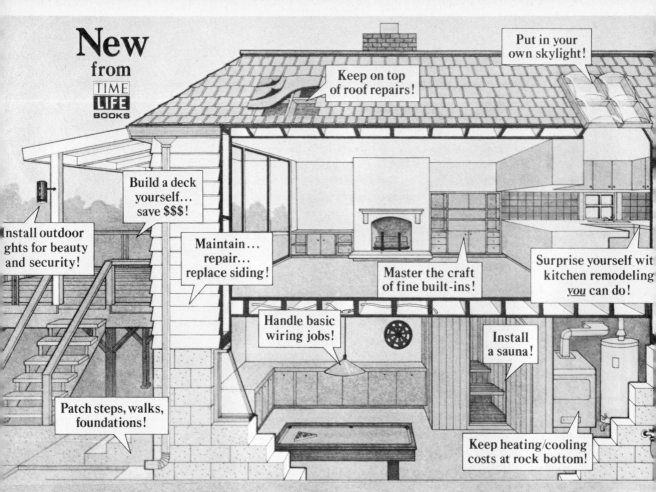

This illustration, in color, was on the back of a mailing envelope that contained
the enclosures pictured on the facing page. The run has exceeded 10 million
mailings.

260

medium-size ads can be expensive. You lose priority in negotiations when you reduce from full-page to smaller than full-page ads. You no longer can bargain for position in the book, and you cannot bargain for position on the page. You not only pay a higher premium for the smaller space, but you lose any bargaining power you might have.

Some publications will accept a *per inquiry* (PI) space ad, to run at no initial cost. The publisher charges for the ad at so much per response received, whether the respondents buy or just make an inquiry.

Most direct-response advertisers expect a full-page magazine ad to pull from 0.05 percent to 0.20 percent of circulation; in other words, from one-half of a response per thousand to 2 responses per thousand. This is a typical range of figures, but results vary enormously. According to Frank Vos, an authority on the subject, direct-mail results will usually range between 0.7 percent and 5.0 percent of names mailed; in other words, from 7 orders per thousand to 50 orders per thousand. You will notice that the ratio of response per thousand between direct mail and magazine space is roughly on the order of 10 or 20 to 1. However, the same ratio applies to the cost per thousand of the two kinds of media. Therefore, many advertisers find that their *cost per order* for both space and direct mail is about the same.

Importance of position in magazines

Direct-response advertisers are particularly fussy about position in the regular part of the magazine, for one good reason: they are the only advertisers who can figure exactly what the differences are in various positions (see Stone's precise figures in Chapter 10, p. 197).

Inserts

One of the important features of magazines is the fact that an advertiser can have a special insert bound into the magazine opposite his page, greatly increasing the response from an ad. The trend to physical flexibility is pronounced. There are bound-in response cards, full-page inserts, and multi-page inserts of various kinds provided by the advertiser, who pays an extra space charge and possibly a charge for binding. The insert might also be a recipe booklet or a miniature catalog. Position in the magazine, again, is of great importance. Here is Stone's ranking of effectiveness of position on the pull of inserts.

First insert card position	100
Second insert card position	95
Third insert card position	85
Fourth insert card position	75 (if after main editorial)
Fifth insert card position	70 (if after main editorial)

Source: Stone, *Successful Direct Marketing Methods*, p. 78.

It is important to make sure that your coupon ad is not backed up by another. Publishers usually watch out for this.

Before placing an ad, ask whether there is a special mail-order rate or a special mail-order section. Rates can be substantially lower than for other classes of advertising. Also ask if they have remnant space, which we discussed in Chapter 10, "Using Magazines." Check all other discounts offered. If your advertising is for a company that is an affiliate of a large advertiser, see if you can get in under "corporate discounts." Also look into the question of barter space, which we discuss in Chapter 21.

Discounts

Using Other Media for Direct-Response Advertising

Newspapers are the third largest medium in the use of direct response advertising. The Sunday magazine supplements have long been a favorite medium for direct marketers. They are also ideal for split-run testing, with the supplements being distributed in cities all over the country. The use of free-standing inserts is an important medium for direct-response advertising, with the use of devices borrowed from direct mail: business reply envelopes, die cuts, punch-out tokens.

Newspapers

TV is a natural for any product you can demonstrate, including recordings of music. The way you buy TV space is quite different from the way a national advertiser buys it, which is by ratings. You can buy off-spots at off hours at low cost; all you want is good returns per dollar.

Television

Innovative marketers have found new methods of using TV that produce cost-per-thousand responses comparable to direct mail. Direct-response advertisers have found that television expands their markets by reaching prospects who were missed by traditional media. High ratings are not necessary; low cost spots can be very profitable. Record and book clubs, insurance companies, and direct marketers are among TV's biggest users. One of the innovations that has helped make TV a great direct-marketing medium has been the introduction of the toll-free phone number for getting immediate responses.

Like TV, radio for direct-response advertising is bought by cost per order, not by ratings, as national advertisers buy it. Hence there is always a search for a good time buy. Direct-response advertisers can be more venturesome in radio than can national advertisers. They can test their commercials at low cost. And at those low nighttime rates you can afford to take 60-second spots to deliver your story.

Radio

One of the greatest contributions that radio makes to direct-response advertising lies in connection with a massive mailing that a firm is going to make in the area reached by the radio station. *Reader's Digest,* for example, has an elaborate sweepstakes package with a computerized letter, computerized check, and mailing form. Just prior to the mailing, a heavy radio schedule is launched, telling people to be sure to watch for this mailing. The technique, though costly on the face of it, has been so effective that this plan has been repeated in *Reader's Digest's* drives for subscribers. Radio has proven to be of great value as a back-up for direct-mail campaigns, as well as in getting orders by mail and by toll-free telephone, directly.

Barter

There is a trade practice called *barter* through which you can buy time, but not prime time, at low cost. We discuss this in Chapter 21, but keep it in mind when you wonder how to buy time at low cost.

Trends in Direct-Response Advertising

In 1976, for the first time, direct-response advertisers reported that responses were coming in at a slower rate. But publicly owned companies, whose profits are published, showed continued increases in responses.

The computer continues to be of ever-expanding usefulness. Direct marketers are seeking ways other than the post office for reaching the public. Direct marketing has become a fixed part of the American way of life.

Direct-response advertisers have shown great ingenuity and resourcefulness in continuing to create effective ideas for profitably reaching an enormous and still-expanding market.

The next step may be electronic in-home ordering. Your cable-TV screen will show you a range of men's neckwear or ladies blouses. If you see something you like, you'll simply push a few buttons on your set, the order will be received instantly and electronically, and somewhere a computer will be making this note: "Mr. Jones likes red neckties" or "Ms. Smith likes print blouses."

QUESTIONS

1. Distinguish among direct marketing, direct-response advertising, mail-order advertising, and direct-mail advertising.

2. In terms of consumer response, what differentiates direct-response advertising from most other advertising?

3. What characteristics make a product suitable for direct-response advertising?

4. Direct response advertising has certain unique features. How many can you describe?

5. Identify the types of direct-response offers.

6. Distinguish between compiled lists and mail-derived lists; between house lists and outside lists.

7. Describe the role and functions of the list broker.

8. Explain the difference between cooperative mail advertising and syndicate mailings.

9. Discuss some of the criteria for good names for direct response advertising.

10. Compare direct response copy for direct mail and for publication advertising.

11. Explain how a split-run test works.

12. What are the guidelines for copy testing for publication advertisements and for direct-mail advertisements?

13. Describe some of the special scheduling problems faced by the direct-mail production manager.

14. Discuss several ways in which direct-response advertisers use media (direct mail, magazines, newspapers, television, and radio) differently from most other advertisers.

15. Why is direct-response advertising usually more wordy than other advertising?

READING SUGGESTIONS

CAPON, NOEL and JOHN U. FARLEY, "The Impact of Message on Direct Mail Response," *Journal of Advertising Research* (October 1976), 69–75.

Direct Mail Manual. New York: Direct Mail/Marketing Association, 1975.

FABIAN, MICHAEL R., "Media Interrelationship: Maximizing Sales Impact," *Direct Marketing* (October 1976), 26 ff.

GROSSMAN, GORDON, "Conceptions, Misconceptions About Direct Marketing Today," *Direct Marketing* (August 1976), 43–47.

HODGSON, RICHARD S., *The Dartnell Direct Mail and Mail Order Handbook,* 2nd ed. Chicago: The Dartnell Corporation, 1974.

PATTY, C. ROBERT, ALBERT HARING, and HARVEY L. VREDENBURG, *Selling Direct to the Consumer.* Fort Collins, Colo.: Robinson Press, 1973.

RANEY, THOMAS, "Direct Mail Is True Medium for Targeting Your Customers," *Direct Marketing* (August 1976), 36–42.

SEVIER, HELEN, "What Is Invasion of Privacy? Are Mailers Invading Privacy?" *Direct Marketing* (January 1976), 24–25.

SROGE, MAXWELL, "Direct Marketing Relates to the Consumer Market," *Direct Marketing* (November 1976), 24 ff.

STONE, BOB, "Co-op Mailers Grow in Stature; Unique Medium Can Boost Sales," *Advertising Age* (January 3, 1977), 27.

———, "Direct Marketers Need to Look Under the Tip of the Iceberg," *Advertising Age* (March 17, 1975), 44–45.

———, "How You Can Maximize Profits From Your Current Customer List," *Advertising Age* (September 13, 1976), 76–78.

———, *Successful Direct Marketing Methods.* Chicago: Crain Books, 1975.

"Survey Reveals Consumer Attitudes on Direct Mail," *Publishers Weekly* (May 20, 1974), 56 ff.

WEINTZ, WALTER, "Ideas in Copy and Creativity Change Only With Environment," *Direct Marketing* (January 1976), 31–32.

SPLIT-RUN WINNERS: 2, 3, 6, 7, 9.

13

Sales Promotion

 𝒜 salesperson for a new spray oven cleaner walks into a store and says, "Good morning, I have a new spray oven cleaner I would like to show you."

"Have enough oven cleaners."

"But this one is different—it does a much better job than anything now on the market."

"Never heard of it."

"Soon this advertising campaign will appear; and when it does, you will have many calls for this cleaner—it's such a fine product."

"Well, maybe so. Just as soon as I get any calls for it, I'll call you."

What is the salesperson supposed to say?

Here is another problem: The sales representative of a well-known product is called in by the buyer of a chain carrying that product.

"We have just completed an analysis of all items in your category, and we are planning to drop those making the poorest showing; we just haven't got room for them all. You are on the list to be dropped unless you do something to change the sales picture quickly. Have you any plans?"

In both instances, the salesperson is faced with the problem of presenting a program through which the dealer can expect fast sales action. Creating and producing such programs, as a part of the basic sales presentation, is standard operating procedure for any advertiser selling through distributors. These projects are variously known as *promotions, dealer programs, merchandising plans,* and *sales-promotion plans.* More than $30 billion is spent on sales promotion activities.

FORMS OF SALES PROMOTION

The most frequently used forms of sales promotion (sometimes used in combination) are:

▲ Point-of-purchase advertising

▲ Premiums

▲ Coupons

▲ Sampling

▲ Deals

▲ Contests and sweepstakes

▲ Advertising specialties

▲ Cooperative advertising

▲ Booklets, brochures, mailing pieces

Point-of-Purchase Advertising

Point-of-purchase advertising displays are placed in retail stores to identify, advertise, or merchandise a product. The effective use of point-of-purchase advertising is based on an understanding of:

Shopping habits of the consumer

Needs of the retailer

Forms of displays

The display idea

Ways to the display used

Shopping habits of the consumer

Of 6,795 shoppers interviewed in mass merchandising stores (discount stores), 30 percent (2,038) made a total of 3,144 unplanned purchases (1.5 + items per shopper). Unplanned purchases, or things that shoppers did not intend to buy when they came into the store, are often called impulse purchases. Eighty-one percent of the unplanned purchases were manufacturers' brands, as opposed to store brands. Shoppers most frequently said that they made unplanned purchases because they "saw it displayed." That was the primary reason for 50 percent of the unplanned purchases and the secondary reason for 30 percent of them. Approximately 4 out of every 5 shoppers relied on point-of-purchase displays.°

Another study, this one involving first-time purchases by shoppers in supermarkets, revealed that 38 percent of the shoppers purchased some brand or item

° "Why Shoppers Make Unplanned Purchases in Mass Merchandising Stores," Point-of-Purchase Advertising Institute, Inc., 1973.

that was new to them, and 54 percent of the first-time purchases were unplanned. The primary reason for a first-time purchase was, most frequently, "saw it displayed." More than 25 percent of the shoppers responded this way, and about 86 percent of the brands they purchased were manufacturers' brands.[*]

In still another study in 7 types of retail outlets, 60 percent of the shoppers reported that point-of-purchase material was an aid in shopping. In supermarkets the figure was 73 percent.[†]

Which items should be promoted with point-of-purchase advertising? The retailer uses the following criteria:

▲ Sale of product accounts for a good dollar volume.
▲ Theme of the display is exciting (often it is one used in mass media).
▲ Appropriate display is well-adapted to the character and size of the store.
▲ Related items may be sold by the promotion.
▲ Promoted merchandise has a good markup.
▲ The promotion fits in with the retailer's own schedule of promotions.[‡]

Needs of the retailer

The manufacturer and retailer can make the most out of point-of-purchase materials when they realize that advertising at the point of sale is part of the total advertising program. A study made for Campbell Soup Company indicated that by tying in point-of-purchase advertising to related television advertising, display productivity (in terms of sales) could be increased significantly. Point-of-purchase displays that were tied in with TV advertising sold 15.5 percent more soup than did similar displays without the TV tie-in.

Forms of displays

If someone has not thought of a display for every dimension and area, someone will. Maybe you will. There are signs for outdoors, indoors, windows, and overhead. Merchandisers or floor displays include jumble displays, modular displays, and those for counters, shelves (shelf extenders), walls, and checkout counters. Display cards hold merchandise, too.

Permanent signs.   A sign in front of a gas station, one surrounding a clock in a restaurant, and a glass sign that frames an expensive watch are familiar examples of permanent displays. If they are illuminated, they attract more attention and are reserved for good spots, since they are usually designed to be effective even when they are not lighted.

Motion displays.   In a succession of tests, displays with motion were favored by 70 percent of the dealers, were given 88 percent of the prime in-store loca-

[*] "Motivations Which Impel First-Time Purchase Decisions," Point-of-Purchase Advertising Institute, Inc., 1973.

[†] "Consumer Reaction to Point-of-Purchase Advertising in Seven Major Types of Retail Outlets," Point-of-Purchase Advertising Institute, Inc., 1971.

[‡] "The Value of In-Store Support," The Point of Purchase Advertising Institute, Inc., 1971.

Displaying merchandise is not a new idea.

tions (compared with 47 percent for nonmotion displays), and produced an 83 percent average gain above normal shelf sales. Motion displays are especially effective in attracting the consumer's attention.

Permanent merchandise trays, racks, and cases. Many dealers welcome displays that will occupy little space on a counter or floor, will serve as a showcase for merchandise, and provide a self-service feature. The display may be an open-face stand from which merchandise such as paint brushes can be picked out. Small, costly items such as watchbands or lipsticks may be displayed to the customer but made accessible only from the dealer's side of the counter, in a pilfer-proof arrangement. In recent years there has been a trend toward display of hard goods, such as electric irons and washing machines.

The heart of the display is the campaign selling idea, designed to generate purchases. Here, we can think in terms of three dimensions, and—subject only to outer-size limitations and need for construction simplicity and cost—the creative person has the world of shapes and materials with which to work. Among the directions we can go are these:

The display idea

The product itself. The most important display piece in a store is the product itself, and any idea that focuses attention on it is helpful. The solution may be a large stack of the packaged product on the floor, with a sign stating an ad-

269

Courtesy Superior Display, Inc.

Flat cartons are easily mounted on a metal frame that stands on a counter. The cartons hold different types of pens, which they display to advantage.

Permanent displays.

Courtesy Thomson-Leeds Company, Inc.

The permanent part of this floor display is a bracket holding the tires and the overhead frame. The tires and the message in the frame can be changed to meet the current merchandising program.

vantage and the price. Or the merchandise can be tumbled in a large box from which the shopper is invited to pick one (a relic of our childhood grab-bag days, no doubt), likewise with a sign stating an advantage.

The current advertising theme. Point-of-purchase advertising is a projection of the current advertising theme, whatever it may be. The challenge is to reduce it to its simplest elements, then dramatize it in three dimensions.

Tie-in with other products. This idea promotes other products, related to the one advertised, that the store also sells. A display of beer suggests pretzels and potato chips. Cold cereal displays feature appetizing dishes of cereal with berries and other fruit on sale in the store.

Storewide promotion. Some displays are based on a storewide promotion, as Back-to-School, Cook-Out, Spring Cleaning, Fall Festival, and Vacation Needs.

▲ The problem was to make a floor display that a salesperson could transport, set up, and place in a variety of locations. It had to be useful for selling soap and flexible enough to hold the many different sizes of packages in the Dial toiletries line. This display could be set up in one minute. (It won a silver prize in POPAI's annual display awards.)

(Right): **A compact display of variety was the problem solved by this floor stand. It occupies little floor space and is easily accessible to the customer, whom it invites to pick up a package or a jar.** ▶

Floor coverings can be difficult to handle. They may take up too much floor space, and numerous patterns can require huge inventories. But this display unit holds about sixty samples, easy to reach and to handle, large enough to show the patterns. It requires a minimum of floor space. ▼

Customers attracted by this Plexiglas display can test and compare variations and combinations in the product line. It is also a convenient total-line merchandiser that salespeople can easily maintain and keep up-to-date with new products. ▼

Display solutions to merchandising problems.

Here, the manufacturer provides thematic point-of-purchase material that can apply to all departments in the store, with special emphasis, of course, on his own products.

Tie-in with national advertising.   For the smaller independent stores, window displays based on the national advertising theme may be particularly helpful in reminding the passerby that here is the place to get the product she saw advertised.

Demonstrating the product.   Often the display can invite the shopper to try out features of the product by pressing a button, looking through an opening, or turning a knob. This is especially good for new types of products.

In summary: point-of-purchase advertising displays can help create an atmos-

A working counter display. Texas Instruments' marketing objective was fourfold: to (1) gain valuable counter space for the new Programmable calculator models, (2) make Texas Instruments' professional models interesting to customers in calculator departments, (3) create a silent salesperson, and (4) project a quality image for Texas Instruments' professional calculator line. The display features sample problems that customers can use in working their own problems on four operating demonstrator models.

Courtesy POPAI.

phere conducive to buying, and they can reinforce an advertising campaign at the retail level.

One of the main problems with displays is in getting them used. There should be a plan, and the retailer should know about it in advance. In the majority of cases, whether in independent or chain stores, the store manager authorizes the use of point-of-purchase display materials, and the manager's cooperation must be enlisted by the manufacturer's salesperson. Usually display materials come with the order, and store personnel set them up. But many displays are not used because they are not in accordance with promotion or merchandising policy of the store. Sometimes tailor-made displays are needed to fit the store's requirements.

Getting displays used

Products displayed by major users of point-of-purchase materials

Apparel	Drugs	Recreational
Automobiles	Food	products
Automotive parts and	Hardware and paints	Services
accessories	Home furnishings	Soaps and
Beer	Household appliances	detergents
Confectionary products	Notions and sundries	Soft drinks
Cosmetics and toiletries	Office supplies and stationery	Tobacco

Source: *POPAI News*, Point-of-Purchase Advertising Institute, Inc., June 29, 1976 and September 24, 1976.

Firms that create and manufacture displays sometimes specialize according to the materials used for those displays: cardboard, metal, wood, plastic, or glass. Some companies combine these materials or subcontract parts of the work. A display company will usually submit a sketch that portrays an idea. Then a handmade model, or dummy, follows with an estimate of complete costs of production.

Having displays made

Many firms serve as consultants and brokers in the sale of displays. They supply the idea; and if they get the order, they will have the display produced through a manufacturer.

Before you deal with either type firm, you must have a clear understanding about the conditions under which you are doing business. You may, for example, be presented with an idea that you like but find too expensive. Perhaps the creating firm will agree to manufacture the first run at their price but allow you to get competing bids for reruns. Whatever the deal, it must be made before any work is done.

Most large firms that continually require displays create ideas for them in their own display departments. Manufacturing, however, is done elsewhere, and the costs are handled through the advertiser's purchasing department.

get rich on peanuts

...and pretzels
...and potato chips
...and Holland House

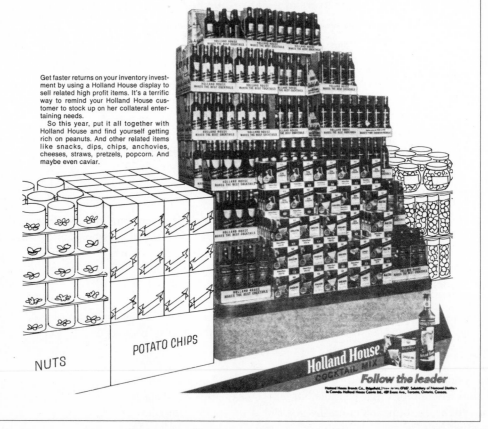

Get faster returns on your inventory investment by using a Holland House display to sell related high profit items. It's a terrific way to remind your Holland House customer to stock up on her collateral entertaining needs.

So this year, put it all together with Holland House and find yourself getting rich on peanuts. And other related items like snacks, dips, chips, anchovies, cheeses, straws, pretzels, popcorn. And maybe even caviar.

NUTS   POTATO CHIPS

Holland House
COCKTAIL MIX   *Follow the leader*

To encourage dealers to use this display, a trade paper ad shows them how it can also increase the sale of pretzels and potato chips.

Premiums

A *premium,* as the term is used in advertising, is an item offered as an inducement to buy the advertised product. Among the most popular of the various types of premium plans are *self-liquidators, direct premiums, free mail-ins, continuity coupon premiums,* and *free giveaways.*

A *self-liquidating premium* is one offered upon proof-of-purchase and payment of a charge (usually handled by mail). Self-liquidators are best used when the advertiser wants to give some new excitement to a mature brand and when the objective is to pick up new or occasional users of his product or to reward loyal users. Examples of self-liquidating premiums:

Self-liquidating premiums

▲ Nabisco Premium Saltine Crackers offers a West Bend Slo-Cooker for one Premium Saltines boxtop and $12.99.

▲ Campbell's Soup offers a knitted winter cap for two labels and $1.25.

▲ Scotties facial tissues offers an HO electric train set for five proof-of-purchase seals and $13.99.

Sometimes, the premium offer gives the consumer a choice in obtaining the incentive item. For example,

▲ Chicken of the Sea tuna offers a *free* tuna cookbook with any 10 Chicken of the Sea labels *or* $1.30 with three labels.

▲ Chun King offers a *free* Chinese checkers set with 20 proofs of purchase *or* $7.25 and one proof.

These premium offers are actually a combination of self-liquidators and free mail-in premiums, which will be discussed shortly.

Direct premiums are usually free, given to the consumer at the time of purchase. There are several types of direct premiums, including *on-pack, in-pack, near-pack,* and *container* premiums.

Direct premiums

On-pack premiums. On-pack premiums are affixed to the outside of the package or may be part of a double package to hold both the advertised product and the premium. On-packs have the advantage of getting fast consumer reaction because they can generate instant response. Consider the following:

▲ Sta-Puf fabric softener has two magnetic note holders attached to the package, free of charge to the purchaser.

▲ Gillette affixes a Trac II razor to its Trac II brand shaving cream.

▲ Purina Dog Chow has a feeding dish accompanying the Dog Chow package.

▲ A Bic ball point pen is attached to a can of Folger's regular grind coffee.

In-pack premiums.   In-pack premiums are those packed in the packages that are purchased. The enclosure can be either the premium itself or a coupon that can be redeemed. Like the on-pack premiums, in-packs can promote fast action by the consumer because they provide immediate rewards. Additionally, they might serve as an effective substitute for "cents-off" deals. In-packs such as the following have been found to be effective:

▲ Dolly Madison Zingers packages containing free Snoopy inflatables.

▲ Maxim brand freeze-dried coffee offering a hardwood cutting board with a 40¢ coupon.

▲ Cheerios packages with Carefree sugarless chewing gum inside.

Near-pack premiums.   Near-pack premiums are items offered by the advertiser, but they are located in a separate display, usually adjacent to the product. Such inducements have good display potential; and since they are usually distributed by the retailer, they help to increase the store's business. Examples:

▲ Pampers disposable diapers offering a child's pail and shovel, free.

▲ Spic 'N Span offering 2 goldfish free with the purchase of the Giant Size package. The goldfish are in a tank at the end of the supermarket aisle. The consumer uses a fish net to catch the goldfish and puts them in a special container for the trip home.

▲ Mr. Clean in the 28 oz. size entitling one to an issue of the monthly Disney magazine.

Container premiums.   Container premiums, the final form of direct premiums, are reusable containers that serve as the package for the product. It is a good way for the advertiser to increase consumer trials of his product, and the containers act as a constant reminder of the brand. For example:

▲ Cool Whip's nondairy whipped topping in a container that, after use of the product, serves as a one-quart measuring cup complete with handle.

▲ L'eggs stockings, in Christmas-colored metallic egg-shaped packages that can be used as Christmas tree ornaments or stocking stuffers.

▲ Mrs. Filbert's soft margarine in a container that can be used as a flowerpot.

Free mail-ins

Free mail-ins are premiums that the consumer gets by mailing in to the advertiser a request for the premium and some proof of purchase. Since most free mail-ins require several proofs of purchase, the advertiser uses such premiums to stimulate product (or product line) sales. And the consumer benefits, since there is no payment involved. Colgate-Palmolive offered a free basketball to consumers who accumulated 35 points with proof of purchase from several products in the Colgate-Palmolive line, including Fab laundry detergent, Irish Spring soap, Baggies (sandwich bags), Colgate toothpaste, and Palmolive dishwashing liquid. A free mail-in offered jointly by Viva paper towels and Pine-Sol liquid cleaner required 5 Viva "Seals of Quality" and 3 Pine-Sol "Marks of Quality" for a free 2-gallon utility pail. A free designer T-shirt was given when a proof of purchase for the Free Spirit Back Buckle Bra was mailed in to Playtex.

Continuity coupon premiums are those that the consumer gets by saving coupons or special labels that come with the product. It is an on-going program, and the premiums normally are selected from a catalog. Premiums vary according to the number of coupons redeemed. General Mills, with Betty Crocker coupons on all its products, is a good example of continuity coupons. The main purpose underlying such premium plans is to build customer loyalty, because the consumer has to stay with the product for an extended period in order to accumulate enough coupons to get a worthwhile premium.

Continuity coupon premiums

Sometimes the premium is given to the consumer directly by the dealer at the time of purchase. This is known as a *free giveaway,* and it is used to build store traffic. A sporting goods store might give a baseball bat to those who buy a set value of other sporting goods, or a fast food outlet might hand out glasses to people who buy a certain item or amount of food.

Free giveaways

The basic purpose of a premium is to get an immediate increase in sales. It may help to introduce new products. It may be used nationally or in a local territory where strong competitive pressure has developed. It may be an effort to increase the unit of sales or to get traffic into the store. It may be used to offset seasonal slumps and to attract repeat purchasers. It can get people to try a product or to use it more often.

Use of premiums

Premiums are not normally appropriate, however, for products that are bought only occasionally, as people buy tires, or for products like cough preparations, bought only when a special need arises. Premiums are not helpful when a product's sales have been steadily declining, because the cause for such a downtrend is usually far too critical to be offset by premiums.

Among the types of premiums used most are games, toys, sporting goods, appliances, general kitchenware, wearing apparel, silverware, and glassware. A wide variety of marketers use premiums, the biggest users including those in: food products; retail grocery; toiletries; insurance; radio and TV; banks, savings and loans; detergents and cleansers.

For maximum effectiveness, a premium should be

What makes a good premium?

Useful

Glamorous

Something of which the consumer seldom has too many

Not on sale elsewhere, or of limited availability

A real value in quality and price

Noncompetitive with another product regularly sold in the same store, unless it is in the advertiser's family of products

Simple to handle and to mail

Tied in with the company's advertising program

The trend in premiums is to offer products of better quality and higher price.

A symposium of the Premium Advertising Association made the following suggestions:

Give complete specifications about your premium in the advertising. Give sizes, colors, and any other details that will help visualize what you are offering.

Deliver premiums as quickly as possible; this applies especially to children's premiums.

If you charge anything at all for your premiums, be sure that your customer will feel that his money was well spent.

Be sure that premiums offered to children will have the approval of the parents.

If it is necessary that a coupon be filled out in order to get a premium, provide room enough for writing in an average name and address.

Different premium offers will frequently be tested in various markets to determine which holds the most promise.

But premiums have their problems, too. An in-pack premium in a package of food must meet the requirements of the Food and Drug Administration, to make sure it does not impair the foodstuff. In-pack coupons must meet the regulations of the Federal Trade Commission. On-pack premiums are not favored by the trade on account of pilferage.

There is one guide that should be followed in advertising premiums. *The advertising must so clearly and correctly describe and picture the premiums, and must state the terms so clearly, that the person receiving it will not be disappointed.* This applies to prompt delivery, too. If a child, especially, has been disappointed, the whole family feels his sadness.

Fulfillment firms.   The physical work of handling premiums, including opening the mail, verifying payment, packaging, addressing, and mailing, is often handled on a fee basis by firms who specialize in "premium fulfillment." They also handle contest responses and prizes.

Premiums as trade incentives

Premiums are also used as incentives for salespeople to reach certain sales goals, obtain new accounts, or introduce new products. They may even boost morale. As dealer incentives, premiums are designed to increase sales volume, stimulate sales for the full product line, and move new items. Their purpose may be to offset competition, bolster a slow season, support a consumer promotion, or to secure store displays.° Giving premiums to salespeople and the trade usu-

---

° *Marketing with Premiums* (New York: Premium Advertising Association of America, Inc., 1975), pp. 14–15.

Coupons, coupons, coupons! A cooperative mailing. All these coupons came in one envelope.

ally falls within the province of the sales department, but any advertising person sitting in on the conference that is establishing an entire sales and advertising promotion should be aware of them. They are referred to as the *incentive* end of the premium business.

Cents-off Coupons

Manufacturers distribute "cents-off" coupons, which can be redeemed at a retail store, entitling the consumer to a specified price reduction on a specific product. The manufacturer reimburses the retailer (about 5¢ per coupon redeemed) as a handling fee above his normal profit. Couponing can be thought of as a massive sampling campaign, supported by the advertising done in behalf of the product featured.

Couponing is done for a variety of reasons. It attracts new users and brings back previous users who have switched brands. The desirability of the product is reinforced for present users, while competition is reduced. Coupons complement the regular advertising done by the manufacturer.

With roughly two out of every three households using them, over 2 billion coupons are redeemed, for a saving to the consumer of about $300 million.° It is also estimated that nearly 1,000 companies regularly use cents-off coupons, distributing approximately 40 billion coupons (not counting retailer in-ad coupons in newspaper advertisements, especially those for food). Coupons are being used by an increasing variety of products, but consumers redeem them most frequently for buying food (99 percent), household products (90 percent), toiletries (73 percent), and drugs (37 percent).†

Coupons are distributed in a number of ways. They appear in the daily newspaper (lowest average redemption rate of all media carrying coupons). They appear in the Sunday supplements, the syndicated or independent magazine sections included with the newspaper. Many advertisers distribute their coupons through free-standing inserts that contain several different coupons on the sheet, which is inserted in the Sunday newspaper. Often, coupons are issued through magazines, as a magazine on-page (a coupon printed as part of the ad) and a magazine pop-up (a coupon bound into the magazine separately, on heavier stock, and usually facing an advertisement). Many coupons are of the in-pack or on-pack variety. Here the coupons are either in the product package or imprinted on it and redeemable on a later purchase of the same product or a different product *(a cross coupon)*. Package coupons have the highest redemption rate: 17 percent. Finally, coupons may be sent by direct mail. Because of the high postage costs, those advertisers using direct mail often share in a joint mailing with coupons for noncompetitive products.

° *Advertising Age* (October 25, 1976) 112.

† "A New Look at Coupons," *The Nielsen Researcher,* No. 1 (1976), 3.

The accompanying table compares the various couponing media according to distribution and redemption.

Comparison of couponing media

Medium	Total coupon distribution (%)	Total coupon redemptions (%)	Average redemption rate (%)
Newspapers	55.9	29.6	2.4
Magazines	13.8	14.0	6.3
Sunday supplements	11.6	7.9	3.1
Package	8.0	30.0	17.0
Free-standing inserts	6.5	7.7	5.4
Direct mail	4.2	10.8	11.7

Source: adapted from *The Nielsen Researcher*, No. 1 (1976), 5–6.

Advertisers have a choice of distributing coupons by themselves, without cooperative efforts of other couponers (individual placement), or they can participate in a joint program in which several national advertisers get together and place the coupons via one of the couponing media (called *multibrand* couponing). The sheer size of multibrand couponing efforts normally impresses the consumer and tends to have a synergistic effect. Regardless of which way an advertiser chooses to distribute coupons, one thing is certain: the advertised product should be in the store when the customer redeems the coupon. Otherwise, you have an angry customer on your hands.

Sampling

Way back in the first chapter of this book, there is a report of the way the French innkeepers around 1100 A.D. attracted trade to their taverns. They had the town crier go out, blow his horn, attract a crowd, and give samples of the wine of the inn. That is the first recorded use of sampling. Giving the consumer a free trial of a product, or sampling, has today become an established technique of promoting sales, along with the use of advertising. The sample is often a smaller version of the product—say a 4 oz. bottle of dishwashing liquid or a 3 oz. tube of toothpaste.

While sampling can be very effective, it is an expensive form of sales promotion (national sampling campaigns can run up to $5 million for a single product). Sampling generally is most effective in introducing a new product when some or all of the following conditions exist:

▲ The product has demonstrable superiority.

▲ The product concept is difficult to communicate by advertising alone.

▲ There is a sizable budget for use in a broad usage category.

▲ Dominance is sought in a particular product category.°

Sampling is usually done by door-to-door delivery through distributing firms geared to handle such assignments. Or samples may be mailed (the expensive way, especially in light of escalating postal rates). Sometimes the sample is provided in a magazine, or a coupon is to be sent in for a free sample. A sample might be attached to another package. A sampling strategy can even be combined with an in-store demonstration. For example, General Electric gives department store shoppers free samples of food cooked in GE microwave ovens right in the store.

A trade practice has developed whereby an advertiser's product is sold in sample size mini-packages through retail stores. To the consumer, it is a good value and minimizes the risk of trying a heretofore unknown or untried product. To the store, it is a high-margin profit. To the advertiser, it is an economical way of distributing the sample. But the value of the sample package contents lies in the reputation the product has built through customer usage and advertising. (Regardless of how the sample is distributed, it is common for sample packages to be miniatures of regular product packages, thereby allowing greater package recognition.)†

Retailer support, in the form of adequate inventory and special displays, can go a long way in determining the success of an advertiser's sampling campaign.

The basic philosophy underlying sampling of a repeat product is rather simple: the best advertisement for a product is the product itself.

Deals

There are two types of deals: *consumer deals* and *trade deals*.

Consumer deals

A consumer deal is a plan whereby the consumer can save money in the purchase of a product. It may be a direct price reduction, of which the cents-off deal is the most familiar form. Or it may be a merchandising deal, in which three bars of soap are wrapped together and sold at a reduced price. Or a package of a new member of the product family is attached to a package of the older product, at little or no extra cost—an effective way of introducing a new product.

Sometimes the advertiser uses a deal to spread out the buying season for certain products, such as the annual "Early Bird" sale of Scotts Fertilizer, allowing the consumer to save up to $3.00 on a bag of lawn fertilizer if purchased before the normal buying season. Another type of deal is illustrated by this headline: "Buy three Firestone steel-belted radials and get the fourth tire at half price." Or the deal might be a straight "20 percent off" on a Sears Craftsman tool kit.

° Eugene Mahany, "Package Goods Clients Agree: Promotion Importance Will Grow," *Advertising Age* (April 14, 1975), 46–48.

† Richard E. Stanley, *Promotion* (Englewood Cliffs, N. J.: Prentice-Hall, Inc., 1977), p. 328.

In a study of price deals, Hinkle reports:

▲ The closer deals are to each other, the less effective they are. Brands which deal frequently encourage even regular customers to stock up and wait for the next deal.

▲ The majority of annual price reductions occur in high-volume periods, but off-season deals are more effective.

▲ Dealing is more effective for newer brands than for old.

▲ Deals are as much as two to three times more effective when a brand's advertising share level is maintained.

▲ Deals are fruitless for products whose sales have been going off steadily. "An assessment should be made of the more basic corrective measures."°

Deals may provide the theme for a strong local advertising campaign. Cents-off deals must meet Federal Trade Commission requirements.

Trade deals

A trade deal is a special discount to the retailer for a limited period of time. It may involve free goods or a minimum purchase. It may be a sliding scale of discounts, depending on the size of the purchase. It may be in connection with a consumer merchandising deal, offering a discount on the purchase of a given number of consumer deals and size assortments. Counter displays may be included to help sell the product to the consumer. (All trade deals are subject to the Robinson-Patman Act, which we discuss in Chapter 26.)

Trade deals, which are extensively advertised in the trade papers, are used to achieve or expand distribution of the advertiser's product. And because the retailer stands to gain from trade deals, they are usually effective (although rather expensive) in enlisting merchandising support of retailers.

Contests and Sweepstakes

Somewhere in every discussion of a consumer promotional plan, the idea of a contest or a sweepstakes is likely to come up. A "Backyard America" sweepstakes promotion for Hefty utility bags distributed over 100 million entry blanks. A Coca-Cola "Tour the World" contest brought in more than 9 million entries. Not many firms can embark on promotions of this magnitude, but the fact that the public responds in such numbers gives contests and sweepstakes a permanent place for consideration in major advertising plans. The prize value of such promotions exceeds $50 million each year.

A typical promotion prize structure (normally a "pyramid" structure) might be: a grand prize of $10,000 plus a new automobile; 2 first prizes—new cars; 20 second prizes—2-week, all-expenses-paid vacations; 50 third prizes—color TV sets; 80 fourth prizes—digital watches; 100 fifth prizes—AM-FM radios; 200 sixth

---

° Charles L. Hinkle, "The Strategy of Price Deals," *Harvard Business Review* (July-August 1965) 75–84.

Win your dog's weight in gold up to $100,000 from Chuck Wagon.

*Price of gold subject to fluctuation.

You could win your dog's weight in pure gold in Chuck Wagon dog food's Win Your Dog's Weight In Gold contest. With gold selling for about $2,000* a pound, even a five-pound Chihuahua could win you $10,000! (Maximum prize: $100,000.)

How do you get a chance to win all this gold? Just carefully read the rules on the adjoining page or on specially marked packages of Puppy Chuck Wagon® or Chuck Wagon at your grocer. Enter today. It's your golden opportunity.

©1976 Ralston Purina Co.

For your pet's health . . .
See your veterinarian regularly.

Even dogs get into contests.

prizes—electric toasters; and 300 seventh prizes—one-year subscriptions to a magazine.

In a highly competitive, highly advertised field, prize promotions may be a welcome change of pace from head-on competitive claims. They bring fresh interest in the product to its present customers. They reach out for new customers. Promotions may be run locally to meet competition or to serve as a test before expanding the program regionally or nationally. They may generate new interest among dealers by bringing traffic into their stores. As in the case of other inducements, contests and sweepstakes are not the solution to a company's steadily declining sales picture; something more basic requires correction.

In a contest, entrants are asked to purchase the advertised product, then compete with other entrants in order to win a prize. Winners are determined strictly on the basis of skill. In a sweepstakes, by contrast, winners are selected on the basis of chance, and chance alone. (The advertiser may urge entrants to buy the product to get a proof of purchase, but he cannot make this a requirement for participation in the sweekstakes.)

Historical trends in prize promotions

There are vogues in forms of promotions that award prizes. In 1950, most contests were for trademarks and slogans. In 1966, sweepstakes were 65 percent of all contests; 23 percent required explanations such as "Why I like . . . " In 1971, *Incentive Marketing* magazine reported that 84 percent of all contests were sweepstakes. Completing statements were not even mentioned. By 1975, the preference for sweepstakes over contests had increased still further to the point where, according to Thomas J. Conlon, president of D. L. Blair Corporation, the world's largest sales promotion agency, sweepstakes represented 89 percent of all prize offers, with skill contests accounting for only 11 percent.

A contest or a sweepstakes may provide a theme for the whole advertising and sales promotion program. Each must be planned well in advance. All contests and sweepstakes are subject to federal and state laws (discussed in Chapter 26).

Handling contests and sweepstakes replies

Firms that specialize in the design and execution of contests and sweepstakes (fulfillment firms) are equipped to handle every detail of the promotion, including receiving entries, selecting and notifying winners. But the success of the contest or sweepstakes greatly depends on advertising support.

Advertising Specialties

An *advertising specialty* is a useful object bearing the advertiser's name or message. It is given to carefully defined recipients as goodwill offerings, without any cost or obligation to them. The category includes calendars, pens, matchbooks, and thousands of other things. The industry claims that there are more than 10,000 advertising specialties.

An advertising specialty differs from a premium in that a premium requires a proof of purchase, often accompanied by a charge. The advertiser's name, as a rule, does not appear on the premium. An advertising specialty is an advertising medium carrying a name and a message. It is given free and is usually quite inexpensive. It is a useful, goodwill gift that keeps the advertiser's name before selected recipients for a long time.

Limitations of the advertising specialty are the shortness of the message it can deliver, the problem of getting it into the right hands, and checking the results. Advertising specialties are not a substitute for advertising in the mass media. Each of these serves different functions.

Planning the use of specialties—

Specialties may well be considered when there is a specific, limited group of people whose goodwill you wish to develop. The group may be prospective customers, present customers, or those in a position to influence important sales—like architects, physicians, and certain corporate officials. The use of the specialty should be part of an organized plan for reaching these defined audiences.

The following guidelines for an effective specialty promotion are recommended by the Specialty Advertising Association:

▲ Define the objectives—know what the program is expected to accomplish.

▲ Identify the target audience.

▲ Develop a suitable distribution plan.

▲ Choose an advertising theme that will reflect the product or service being offered.

▲ Develop a message to support the theme.

▲ Select the specialty advertising article, preferably one that bears a natural relationship to the product, service, or advertising theme.°

Cooperative Advertising

In cooperative advertising, a national advertiser reimburses a retailer or local distributor for an ad placed in local media. The repayment may be 100 percent, 50 percent, based on the volume of business, or whatever terms are agreed upon. But *whatever the terms are, they must be available to all other distributors in the market on the same proportionate basis.* That is the crux of the federal Robinson-Patman Act governing cooperative advertising and enforced by the Federal Trade Commission. (We discuss this at greater length in Chapter 26.)

The major media used in cooperative advertising are newspapers (about 75 percent of cooperative advertising), radio, and television. Usually the national advertiser will provide reproduction proofs for newspaper advertising, videotape for television, scripts and recordings for radio, and printed matter for any direct mail, in each instance allowing room for the dealer's name. More than 50 percent of all department-store newspaper advertising is cooperative, but the

---

° "Specialty Advertising vs. Direct Mail," Specialty Advertising Information Bureau (March, 1975).

287

store may not use advertisers' reproduction proofs. Instead, it uses its own logo and receives a cooperative allowance. In an *omnibus* advertisement, a store uses reproduction proofs from different manufacturers and creates a full-page ad over its own name. Each manufacturer then pays a pro rata share of the total cost.

The idea for cooperative newspaper advertising was originally spawned by the fact that in many papers the local rate was much lower than the national rate, so that even if the national advertiser reimbursed the retailer 100 percent, money might still be saved.

The retailer might also be disposed to provide room for store displays for the product if it is advertised over his name, and to make sure the item is in stock if a special cooperative ad on it is run.

Retailers are paid for advertising when they submit documentation or proof of performance. For newspaper advertisements, they show tear sheets giving the name of the newspaper, the date the ad ran, and the exact ad copy as it ran. This can be matched with the newspaper invoice stating its cost. For radio and TV cooperative advertisements, proof of performance used to be a perennial problem until the Association of National Advertisers and the Radio and TV Advertising Bureaus developed affidavits of performance that document in detail the content, cost, and timing of commercials as discussed in Chapter 24, "Retail Advertising."

Among the advantages of cooperative advertising are that it helps defray selling costs and creates local prestige by additional advertising. Furthermore, space used by a manufacturer's cooperative advertising may help to earn a better rate for all of that firm's advertising. The disadvantage is that even if a store has to pay only 50 percent of the cost, that sum may not be justified by the profits on the sale of that product, or the manufacturer's ads may not meet the special style of the store.

What's the catch to all this? There are a number. There are often difficulties and disparities for the advertiser in the store's billing procedure. Stores may not use the manufacturer's ad; rather, they may prepare an advertisement in the store style, charging the manufacturer the production cost, and changing the image of his advertising. An advertisment may be placed in the weaker paper in town to help the store earn a quantity discount there. As a result, the manufacturer may lose strict control over the format of the advertising, as well as over the choice of media.

WARNING ON TV AND RADIO COOPERATIVE ADVERTISING

Dealers who want to make sure they are paid should check with stations about new Association of National Advertisers' form.

When a manufacturer plans a budget for advertising, cooperative advertising is also budgeted. Most of it is expected to appear as part of a store's effort to build the consumer's image of the brand. Each store, however, decides for itself whether or not it will run the ad and how much of that cooperative advertising it will use. Therefore the manufacturer never has complete control over how much of his name advertising will be seen by consumers.°

Booklets, Brochures, Mailing Pieces

In the sale of household appliances, cars, motorcyles, and other costly items that give the customer a choice of models or styles, the manufacturer will usually supply colorful booklets or other descriptive pieces printed for distribution by the dealer. Such material, with clear technical information, is especially helpful to distributors who have a high turnover in personnel and a consequent lack of experienced help. Some sales promotional material will also be offered in connection with do-it-yourself equipment sold in hardware stores, where there may be special racks to hold it. In some specialized fields, producers may offer booklets: recipe booklets, for example, to liquor stores, or booklets on planting or lawn care, where seed and garden equipment is sold. Often, such booklets have space for the dealer's imprint, becoming a part of the cooperative advertising plan. Counter space for booklets is a problem for stores that are offered such material, and waste is a problem for the producer who offers the material without charge. The quantities supplied must be distributed and used as planned.

Trade Shows and Exhibits

Trade shows and exhibits, effective complements to a regular advertising program, are particularly important in industrial fields, but they are also staged by manufacturers of consumer products. A trade show is a particularly good forum in which to demonstrate new products and to interest prospective buyers. At a boat show, for example, consumers and dealers both see the latest innovations in marine craft and equipment; advertisers develop sales leads (see Chap. 25).

Cash Refunds

Money refunds primarily encourage people to try a particular product. The refunds are sent by mail to consumers from whom the advertiser has received (by mail) proof of purchase. Although most refunds for package goods items are $1 or less, it is not uncommon to find some for $2 or $3. Rebates of larger sums are given for appliances; and for automobiles, $200 to $500 have been paid back to buyers. It is a way of cutting price without affecting the dealer's discount structure.

° In Chapter 23, there is a special case on the controlled use of cooperative advertising.

Concluding thoughts

"It is important to recognize what promotion can and cannot do. It cannot overcome either too little or poor advertising. It is best used as an adjunct to brand-sell advertising, not as a replacement."° Among the valuable characteristics of sales promotion, however, is its power to inspire the marketer to keep thinking of fresh ways to stir special interest in a product.

QUESTIONS

1. The text describes eleven major categories of sales promotion. How many can you name and describe?

2. What is the relationship between advertising and sales promotion?

3. Explain the benefits to be derived from the effective use of point-of-purchase advertising—from the viewpoints of the advertiser, the retailer, and the consumer.

4. What are the criteria a retailer normally uses in selecting products for which point-of-purchase advertising will be used?

5. Explain the philosophy underlying the use of premiums.

6. Distinguish clearly among the following types of premiums: self-liquidators, direct premiums, free mail-ins, continuity coupons, and free giveaways (include in your discussion the several types of direct premiums). Give two examples of each type of premium.

7. What comprises a "good" premium?

8. For what reasons might an advertiser use cents-off coupons?

9. Explain how cents-off coupons are distributed.

10. Discuss in detail (a) why sampling has become an established way of promoting sales, (b) the product-market conditions under which sampling is most effective, and (c) how sampling can be integrated with media advertising.

11. Distinguish between consumer deals and trade deals.

12. What are the similarities and differences between contests and sweepstakes?

13. What are the principal benefits to the advertiser in conducting a contest?

14. What are the chief benefits that advertisers may derive from conducting sweepstakes?

15. What are the major advantages and limitations of advertising specialties?

° Eugene Mahany, "Package Goods Clients Agree: Promotion Importance Will Grow," *Advertising Age* (April 14, 1975), 48.

16. How does an advertising specialty differ from a premium?

17. Discuss the concept of cooperative advertising, and explain the advantages and limitations of cooperative advertising for the advertiser and for the retailer.

18. "The manufacturer never has complete control over the actual use of cooperative advertising." Comment. Is there anything the manufacturer can do to assure its use?

19. Explain the uses of booklets, brochures, and mailing pieces.

20. For what types of products are trade shows and exhibits best suited?

21. "It is important to recognize what promotion can and cannot do." Comment.

22. What are the factors that determine how much money an advertiser should allocate to sales promotion activities?

READING SUGGESTIONS

BROWN, R. G., "Sales Response to Promotions and Advertising," *Journal of Advertising Research* (August 1974), 33–38.

CHEVALIER, MICHAEL, "Increase in Sales Due to In-Store Display," *Journal of Marketing Research* (November 1975), 426–31.

HERPEL, GEORGE L., and RICHARD COLLINS, *Specialty Advertising in Marketing.* Homewood, Ill.: Dow Jones-Irwin, 1972.

HOPPER, L. C., "How Advertising and S. P. Can Make or Break Your New Product," *Industrial Marketing* (September 1976), 132–35.

LEWIS, HERSCHELL GORDON, *The Businessman's Guide to Advertising and Sales Promotion.* New York: McGraw-Hill, 1974.

MAHANY, EUGENE, "Package Goods Clients Agree: Promotion Importance Will Grow," *Advertising Age* (April 14, 1975), 46–48

Marketing with Premiums. New York: Premium Advertising Association of America, Inc., 1975.

McELNEA, J. K., "How to Buy Promotion Efficiently When Budget Control Is Tight," *Advertising Age* (October 27, 1975), 58 ff.

"A New Look at Coupons," *The Nielsen Researcher,* Chicago: A. C. Nielsen Company (No. 1), 1976.

"Premium and Incentives Section," *Advertising Age* (October 11, 1976), 17–31.

PRENTICE, ROBERT M., "How to Split Your Marketing Funds Between Advertising and Promotion," *Advertising Age* (January 10, 1977), 41 ff.

Retailers' Attitudes Toward P-O-P. New York: Point-of-Purchase Advertising Institute, Inc., 1976.

ROBINSON, WILLIAM A., "12 Basic Promotion Techniques: Their Advantages—and Pitfalls," *Advertising Age* (January 10, 1977), 50–51.

——, "Test Your Promotion Savvy with Student Exam from MSU," *Advertising Age* (December 6, 1976), 45–46.

STANLEY, RICHARD E., *Promotion.* Englewood Cliffs, N. J.: Prentice-Hall, 1977, pp. 308–32.

STRANG, ROGER A., *The Relationship Between Advertising and Promotion in Brand Strategy.* Cambridge, Mass.: Marketing Science Institute, 1975.

——, "Sales Promotion—Fast Growth, Faulty Management," *Harvard Business Review* (July-August 1976), 115–24.

TURNER, HOWARD M., *The People Motivators: Consumer and Sales Incentives in Modern Marketing.* New York: McGraw-Hill, 1973.

WILLIAMSON, JOHN H., "Think Co-op on Advertising and S. P. Pieces—and Then Merchandise for All It's Worth," *Industrial Marketing* (September 1976), 142–45.

PART FOUR

Creating advertising

14

Use of Behavioral Sciences

𝒜 person's decision to buy a product or service is influenced in many ways. The behavioral sciences—anthropology, sociology, and psychology—attempt to determine what these influences are and how they work. Although the behavioral sciences are not concerned solely with consumer behavior, they can help us understand why people buy what they do. Anthropology studies the way people are influenced by their cultural heritage, as they might be when they prefer one kind of food to another. Sociology, the study of people in groups, may show how our friends influence what we buy. Psychology determines how people's needs and drives influence their buying habits. Although these behavioral sciences often overlap, they are all of interest to the advertiser. The field of consumer behavior brings together all the behavioral sciences in the study of how and why we make buying decisions. Understanding consumer behavior is the key to learning what makes advertising work.

Anthropology and Advertising

The word *anthropology* usually brings to mind the study of primitive societies. But anthropologists study the cultures of all societies, and from their work they have found that certain needs and activities are common to people wherever they are. Bodily adornment, cooking, courtship, food taboos, gift giving, language, marriage, status, sex, and superstition are practiced in all societies, although each attaches its own values and traditions to them.

The anthropologist sees the United States as a pluralistic society made up of an array of subcultures. In each subculture lives a different group of people who share its values, customs, and traditions. The 500 radio stations that broadcast programs in 50 languages, and the 400 with black-oriented programs, bear witness to the strength of cultural identification in the United States. Even if we move into another culture later, the one we were brought up in permanently influences our tastes and behavior.

Anthropologists make major contributions to advertising through their study of the distinctive living patterns of cultural groups and subgroups. Ethnic, religious, and racial subgroups all have identities that can affect food preferences, language, customs, styles of dress, and roles of men and women. All of these preferences may in turn affect the advertising addressed to members of the subgroup.

One exploration of comparative household expenditures by black vs. white families showed distinct differences, amounting to 6.6 percent of all spending, between them. Black families spent more on clothing, personal care products, household furnishings, and alcoholic beverages than did whites.[*]

Some ethnic groups prefer highly spiced foods (Polish or Italian sausage) or distinctively flavored foods (Louisiana chicory-flavored coffee). Indeed, many dishes favored in certain parts of the country identify people in that area with their cultural past. Pennsylvania Dutch cookery, with its fastnachts and shoofly pie, has roots mainly in the valley of the Rhine. In North Carolina, the serving of lovefeasts (sugar cake, Christmas cookies, and large white mugs of coffee) reflects people's Czechoslovakian heritage: in Rhode Island, tourtière (meat pie) reflects the French Canadian influence. Mexico's influence is revealed in the tamale and other Mexican-style foods served in southern California and the Southwest.

There are regional variations in the American language, too. A sandwich made of several ingredients in a small loaf of bread is a *poor boy* in New Orleans, a *submarine* in Boston, a *hoagy* in Philadelphia, a *hero* in New York City, and a *grinder* in upstate New York. A soft drink in Boston is a *tonic*, while in Syracuse it is a *soda*, and in Phoenix it is a *pop*. Creamed cottage cheese is known as *schmierkase* around Cincinnati, while what is cottage cheese to most Americans is *cream cheese* in New Orleans. *Salad* in Virginia means *kale* and *spinach*. In Key West, evaporated milk is referred to as *cream,* and sweetened condensed milk is called *milk*. In Minnesota a *rubber band* is a *rubber binder*. Advertisers make use of their knowledge of cultural differences in food preferences, terminology, and subgroup identities when they advertise their products.

Rites of passage   Every society celebrates certain milestones of life. In ours we mark births, birthdays, confirmations, bar mitzvahs, graduations, weddings, and anniversaries, usually celebrating them with appropriate gifts. Marketers often relate their advertising to these milestones.

---

[*] Raymond A. Bauer and Scott M. Cunningham, *Studies in the Negro Market* (Cambridge, Mass.: Marketing Science Institute, 1970), p. 22.

Does an Italian wine go with Noël, La Navidad, Hanukkah and Weihnachten?

Bolla does.

It has a gift for celebration.

A handsome wooden-rack filled with 6 bottles of delightful Bolla wine imported from Italy.* About $20. Feel free to give the Bolla Gift Selection to anyone, any time. It will be the nicest compliment a holiday ever had. No matter what language you feast in.

Bolla
Gift Selection

*2 bottles each of Soave and Bardolino, 1 each Valpolicella and Rosé.

Appealing to different ethnic groups.

How the quick-food business has been affected by the working woman.

Food products	Female heads; heavy users	
	Working	Not employed
Frozen meat or poultry pies	109	94
Frozen complete dinners	108	94
Frozen prepared vegetables	118	87
Soup (prepared, canned)	102	92
Tuna	108	94
Yogurt	123	85
Ice cream	103	98
Salad dressing, diet liquid	115	87
Packaged dry sauces	120	88
Mayonnaise	112	93
Pizza mix	113	91

The changing role of women

In the past few years, there has been an astounding change in the way women perceive their role in life.

"First off, we can't compare today's working woman with the woman we knew 5 or 10 years ago. Today her needs and motivations for working are vastly different. She works because she wants to improve the quality of her personal life as well as her family life. This thought is key to understanding why more and more women are choosing to work. . . . The working woman, and specifically the married working woman has become the most significant segment of the consumer market."[*]

Because women have access to higher job levels and a greater variety of jobs, they have more discretionary income than ever before. From truck driver to company president, from jockey to federal judge, the American woman is playing an ever-increasing role in society. *Glamour* magazine points out in an ad how young women (18–35) have changed their life styles and goals.

Young women are Deciding for Themselves—Everything

They're marrying later

They're having fewer children

They're expecting to work nonstop

They're handling their own money

With more options than ever before, the contemporary woman continues to search for a better quality of life, one that allows her to be an individual in her

[*] *Woman's Day,* 1977.

I had a great game, Mom. I went 3 for 4, threw out a runner
at home plate and I think the shortstop likes me.

Kodak film. For the times of your life.

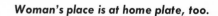

Woman's place is at home plate, too.

own right. Women's new attitudes and roles represent a basic cultural change in
our society, and advertising reflects that change.

Anthropology helps sharpen our understanding of, and insights into, differences in cultural heritage, regional variations, rites of passage, and changing cultural roles. Because it does, anthropology has great relevance for marketing and
advertising.

297

Sociology and Advertising

Sociologists view people in relation to others. They observe our identification with a group, the group's influence on us, and our influence on the group. Whenever, as consumers, we ask ourselves, "What will *they* think?" or "How will this appear to *them?*" we are behaving according to one or more reference groups. These reference groups can be face-to-face (family, friends, neighbors, fellow workers) or impersonal groups with which we identify (professional athletes, TV stars, weight watchers).

Social class and stratification

Just about any society is clustered into classes, which are determined by such criteria as wealth, income, occupation, education, achievement, or seniority. We sense where we fit into this pattern; we identify with others in our class ("these are my kind of people") and we generally conform to its standards. People's aspirations often take on the flavor of the social class immediately above their own; experienced advertisers do not go above that.

An understanding of social-class structure helps explain why data on income, occupation, education, and other demographic categories sometimes fail to provide meaningful insights into consumer characteristics. Although a young professional couple may have the same family income as a senior factory foreman, their interests in products may be worlds apart. A rich man is not simply a poor man with more money. Given the same income, a poor person would not behave exactly as a rich one does. Furthermore, people's attitudes in the lower class differ profoundly from those of people in the middle class. Where and what they buy differ not only in economics but in symbolic value.°

How different people view new products

Extensive research has been done on the ways people learn about and accept new products. Generally, consumers can be divided into five groups:

1. *Innovators:* highly venturesome, cosmopolitan people who are eager to try new ideas and willing to accept the risk of an occasional bad experience with a new product.

2. *Early adopters:* people in the community with whom the average man or woman checks out an innovation; a successful and *careful* innovator, the early adopter is influential with those who follow.

3. *Early majority:* a group that tends to deliberate before adopting a product; its members are seldom leaders, but they are important in legitimizing and innovating.

4. *Late majority:* a cautious group that adopts ideas after the bulk of public opinion is already in favor of an innovation.

5. *Laggards:* past-oriented people who are suspicious of change and of those

---

° Pierre Martineau, "Social Classes and Spending Behavior," *Journal of Marketing,* 23 (October 1958), 122–23.

who bring it; by the time they adopt a product, it may already have been re-placed by yet another.°

Early buyers tend to be venturesome, cosmopolitan, socially integrated within the community, financially secure, and self-confident in problem solving. Advertising appeals to the innovator to be the first in his group to have a particular product. Urging consumers to "be the first on your block" to use its yeast, Fleischmann personalized the attraction:

> Make your husband glad he's yours. Be the only wife on your block to make a beautiful whole wheat bread loaf. . . . Let him brag about you.

American Airlines' advertisement for its four-week Pacific Islands tour called the consumer's attention to "the last great area to explore. Before everybody else does."

Opinion leaders

Although not every early buyer of a new product is considered a reliable source of new-product ideas, those people whose ideas and behavior do serve as models to others are of special interest to advertisers. These *opinion leaders* can speed the acceptance of new products by their own purchases. Of course, opinion leaders in one field are not always influential in others. The friend whose opinion you value when buying new clothes may not be much help when you're shopping for an air conditioner.

> General Motors, like all motor companies coming out with a new line, will promote its wares in the so-called buff books for automobile enthusiasts. "Buffs are important to the manufacturers," Mr. Smith said, "because they are usually respected for their knowledge by their friends and neighbors, who frequently seek their advice on new car buying."†

Traditionally, advertisers have used opinion leaders to give testimonials: movie stars endorse cosmetics and perfume; television personalities promote soft drinks and cars; politicians, socialites, and business people ask you to donate to charitable causes. There are, however, Federal Trade Commission restrictions on the use of testimonials.

An ad may also seek status for a product or service through association with the institutions that use it. A United Airlines ad read:

> United Airlines flies more twenty-game winners, more .300 hitters, more RBI leaders, more southpaws, knuckleballers and relief hurlers, more bonus-babies and bullpen firemen, more pinch-hitters, clutch-hitters and switch-hitters than any other airline. In fact, United flies 19 out of the 24 major league baseball teams.

American Express card ads point out that the credit card is welcome at

---

° Everett Rogers, *Diffusion of Innovations* (New York: The Free Press, 1962), pp. 168–71.

† *The New York Times* (September 24, 1976), 31.

Loew's hotels all over the world, and eleven specific jewelry, gift, and clothing stores worldwide honor it.

Family life cycle and buying behavior

The basic unit of buying behavior is the family. As the following table shows, most households pass through an orderly progression of stages, and each stage has special significance for buying behavior. Knowledge about the family life cycle permits you to segment the market and the advertising appeal according to specific consumption patterns and groups.

An overview of the life cycle and buying behavior

Stage in life cycle	Buying behavioral pattern
1. Bachelor stage: young, single people not living at home	Few financial burdens. Fashion opinion leaders. Recreation-oriented. Buy basic kitchen equipment, basic furniture, cars, vacations.
2. Newly married couples: young, no children	Better off financially than they will be in near future. Highest purchase rate and highest average purchase of durables. Buy cars, refrigerators, stoves, sensible and durable furniture, vacations.
3. Full nest I: youngest under six	Home purchasing at peak. Liquid assets low. Dissatisfied with financial position and amount of money saved. Interested in new products. Buy washers, dryers, TV, baby food, chest rubs and cough medicines, vitamins, dolls, wagons, sleds, skates.
4. Full nest II: youngest child six or over	Financial position better. Some wives work. Less influenced by advertising. Buy larger-sized packages, multiple-unit deals. Buy many foods, cleaning materials, bicycles, music lessons, pianos.
5. Full nest III: older couples with dependent children	Financial position still better. More wives work. Some children get jobs. Hard to influence with advertising. High average purchase of durables. Buy new, more tasteful furniture, auto travel, nonnecessary appliances, boats, dental services, magazines.
6. Empty nest I: Older couples, no children living with them, head in labor force	Home ownership at peak. Most satisfied with financial position and money saved. Interested in travel, recreation, self-education. Make gifts and contributions. Not interested in new products. Buy vacations, luxuries, home improvements.
7. Empty nest II: Older married couples, no children living at home, head retired	Drastic cut in income. Keep home. Buy medical appliances, medical-care products that aid health, sleep, and digestion.
8. Solitary survivor, in labor force	Income still good, but likely to sell home.
9. Solitary survivor, retired	Same medical and product needs as other retired group. Drastic cut in income.

Source: William D. Wells and George Gubar, "Life Cycle Concept in Marketing Research," *Journal of Marketing Research* (November 1966), 355–63. Reprinted with permission.

Psychology and Advertising

One of the most effective tire advertisements in recent times showed a woman on a lonely road gazing forlornly at the flat tire on her car. "When there's no man around, Goodyear should be," said the caption of the advertisement, which went on to say:

> She'll never have to change tires with Goodyear Lifeguard Safety Spare. Stranded. Helpless. Alone. You'd help her if you were there—but you're not. . . .

A psychologist could explain why the advertisement did so well. First, there was a sense of *self-identification* by women readers with the woman in the advertisement; a woman could easily picture herself in such a predicament. Second, there was a clear understanding of the woman's feelings and *motivation*— the desire to avoid danger. A man reading the advertisement could see his wife or daughter in that predicament, so that he, too, was compelled to identify with it. It made him aware of his responsibility toward them; he was motivated by his *desire to protect those he loves.* These interpretations represent insights that advertising has gained from psychology. In fact, the language of psychology has become a part of the advertiser's vocabulary—self-identification and motivation, status symbol, ego-involvement, self-image, appeals, attitudes, perception.

Psychology, the branch of the behavioral sciences that is particularly interested in motivation, studies all the inner strivings variously described as needs, wants, desires, wishes, urges, and all the drives that initiate a series of events known as behavior. What are these drives? One classification divides drives into *physiological* motives (those, like hunger, thirst, and mating, whose satisfaction is essential to survival) and *secondary* or *social* motives (those whose satisfaction is unrelated to survival: the desire to be socially accepted, to win a tournament, to get a promotion).

The nature of motivation

Another classification describes motives in terms of people's needs:

Affectional—the need to form satisfying relations with others

Ego-bolstering—the need to enhance one's personality

Ego-defensive—the need to protect one's personality

Still another lists motives based on 28 attitudes, including:

Acquisitive—to gain possession of property ("Sometimes Bank Americard can make all the difference.")

Conserving—to protect against damage (Prestone Coolant ads say, "A summer boilover can do more than ruin a trip. It can ruin your engine.")

Constructive—to organize and build ("With Kirsch kits and components you can assemble complete entertainment centers in minutes.")

Achievement—to overcome obstacles (If you're all thumbs when it comes to things like paneling, here's a helping hand from Masonite.")

Recognition—to gain praise and commendation ("No wonder Downy-rinsed clothes have earned a lot of mothers a lot of compliments.")

Dominative—to influence or control others ("When your kids ask for a goodie, give them something that's good. Give 'em a Chiquita banana instead. Give them something that's nutritious. . . . ")

Other lists contain as many as 60 separate motives. Although no single set of classifications has been recognized as a standard in the field, the point is clear. At all times man is crying (even though the world does not often hear him), "Please understand me!" The advertiser has to *understand the buyer*, not merely the product. To be successful, advertising must empathize with the goals, needs, wants, desires, drives, and problems of the people it's addressing. AT&T tells customers it understands their needs: "We hear you." Bufferin does the same when it advertises, "No headache seems small when it's yours."

Differences in motivation

The reason a person *says* he buys a certain product may have nothing to do with his *real* reason for buying it. A man may say he bought a car because he likes its looks; the real reason may be that he likes the youthful way it makes *him* look. A woman may say she took up tennis for its health benefits; perhaps she really took up the game because it provided her entry into the "in" crowd of her neighborhood.

The same experience may mean different things to different people. Consider the ways men and women view fishing. Men fish primarily for the thrill of catching fish; success is measured in terms of the catch. Women, on the other hand, see fishing as an opportunity to enjoy the peaceful atmosphere, the beautiful scenery, and male companionship; whether they catch any fish is secondary, often irrelevant. Men select their equipment for practical reasons, while women think the appearance of the gear is more important. Generally, men are unconcerned about their appearance when they're fishing; often they delight in wearing old, sloppy clothes. Women tend to be more concerned about being well dressed. Both men and women, however, agree that fishing provides a way to "get away from it all."°

Self-images and roles

Our motivations are closely related to the way we see ourselves—our self-images and the different roles we play. Through the products we buy, we tell the world how we would like to have it think of us. In this way, products serve as symbols of who and what we think we are. A Drexel furniture advertisement dwells on the symbolic significance that furniture may have: "In subtle ways it can speak volumes about you and your taste . . . reflect who you are and where you are going."

All of us have a number of roles, many of which we play at the same time. The same 35-year old man may be a husband, a father, an employee, and a youth baseball team manager. Advertising addresses each of these roles when it urges

° Ernest Dichter, *Handbook of Consumer Motivations* (New York: McGraw-Hill, 1964), pp. 246–47.

gifts for his wife, toys for his children, furniture for his office, equipment for his team. Just as we buy products that serve our self-image, our buying behavior tends to be consistent with our roles.

Consumer Life-Styles

Each of the behavioral sciences we have touched upon offers its own contributions. They can also work in combination, as is the case in the study of consumer life-styles. Advertisers are interested in life-styles as they reflect the ways individuals see themselves and their living patterns. Life-style research is linked to social trends and how people fit themselves into them. Since the future of virtually any consumer product is affected by one or more of these trends, they can also affect the direction and tone of advertising.

Daniel Yankelovich, who has extensively studied American life-styles, has identified 31 social trends that he believes can change the overall patterns of American life and of buying behavior.° These trends do *not* push in a single direction, and they do *not* affect all people. They have been categorized into five major groupings:

1. Trends that are effects of the psychology of affluence, particularly felt among consumers who seek fulfillment beyond economic security. Included are trends toward personalization (expression of one's individuality through products), new forms of materialism (deemphasis on money and possessions), and more meaningful work (work satisfactions aside from money).

2. Trends that reflect a quest for excitement and meaning beyond the routines of daily life. Included are trends to novelty (constant search for change), to sensuousness (emphasis on touching and feeling), and to mysticism (new spiritual experience).

3. Trends that are reactions against the complexities of modern life. Included are trends toward life simplification, toward return to nature (rejection of the artificial and chemical in dress and foods), toward stronger ethnic identification (new identification in one's background), and away from bigness.

4. Trends that reflect new values pushing out traditional ones. Included are trends toward pleasure for its own sake and living for today, toward blurring of the sexes (and their roles), and toward more liberal sexual attitudes.

5. Trends reflecting the personal orientations of those now in their teens and twenties. Included are trends toward tolerance of disorder (such as against fixed plans and schedules, affecting shopping and eating habits), toward rejection of hypocrisy (affecting attitudes toward exaggeration in communication), and toward female careers (away from traditional home-and-marriage roles as sufficient for women).

°"What New Life Styles Mean to Market Planners," *Marketing/Communications* (June 1971), 38 ff.

"...our parents lived to work, we work to live."

"For dad, being away from work was harder than being at work.

Even when he was on vacation.

Because to our parents, working was a way of life.

For us, it's a way *to* life.

A way to experience new places. New people. New ideas.

Now don't get us wrong, we enjoy working. It's just that we enjoy the rewards of work even more.

Like taking more than one 2-week vacation a year. Getting into new sports. Experimenting with new hobbies. Buying the things that let us get the most from life.

Just making every day count.

You see we know what we want from life. And when you know that, you don't have to wait for tomorrow to live the good life.

You live it today.**"**

The way Warren and Judy feel about work is an example of the new values many young adults share today.

And because Psychology Today responds to those values, it attracts over four and a half million people every month.

People who believe in living their dreams today, not tomorrow.

For example, according to Simmons, more of PT's readers travel, own a car and entertain, than the readers of just about every other major magazine.

Our readers are young, affluent and always in the market for quality products and services.

And PT readers set the trends others follow.

PT readers live their dreams today, not tomorrow.
Psychology Today

A Ziff-Davis Publication

Different times, different ways.

To reflect these changing trends and values *and* their effect on marketing and advertising, Yankelovich offers two vignettes:

> An older married couple whose children are grown move from their big home to a smaller, brand-new apartment. With fewer home repairs, with more labor-saving appliances, they have more time and money for leisure pursuits. Their efforts at "life simplification" are relevant to marketers of such products as home appliances, prepared and frozen foods, and travel.

> A young professional, about 30, married, with two children, wonders about how meaningful his job really is, how important the traditional home-family-job "rat race" is. He buys new stereo equipment, trades in his American sedan for a foreign car, and is an avid reader of publications about how people are changing their lives.

Dramatically different life-styles are reflected in the two accompanying advertisements, both of which appeal to young, single people. One (the De Beers diamond ad) is oriented to the traditional pattern of finding the ideal mate and a happy marriage. Although the couple is pictured with the hairstyles and informal attire of the Seventies, the text evokes the traditional life pattern: "He lives with his parents and I live with mine. And so to be alone to talk, to dream, to scheme, we take aimless drives to no place special. Then he said, 'Isn't it time we stopped driving nowhere and started our lives going somewhere.' And I said yes."

How different an orientation to life from the advertisement in behalf of Club Méditerranée, a vacation resort emphasizing an informal, antistatus manner of living. "Last names, job titles, and related trivia couldn't matter less. . . . Ties and jackets, never. . . . the whole atmosphere is free, and the people are free with each other. . . . We impress each other with each other."

The difference between the two ads is not mere advertising technique; it is in the life-styles they picture.

In their responses to a survey, company presidents showed how important they consider life-style research. Asked the specific purpose of their companies' formal or informal "early warning system" of monitoring changes in social attitudes and opinions, 73.1 percent answered, "to evaluate changes in consumer attitudes and life-styles."*

Although new social values and life-style trends can change the overall patterns of American life and buying behavior, they do not affect everyone equally. Indeed, many Americans are not caught up in patterns of change at all. Some people cling to the old value system. One study of a broad sample of married middle-class Americans shows that this "large segment of U.S. society portrays itself as happy, home-loving, clean and square. . . . For most Americans it is indeed a Wyeth, not a Warhol world."†

* *The Gallagher Report*, XXIII, 22, Supplement to June 2, 1975 issue.
† William D. Wells, "It's a Wyeth, Not a Warhol World," *Harvard Business Review* (Jan.-Feb. 1970), p 26.

He lives with his parents and I live with mine. And so to be alone to talk, to dream, to scheme, we take aimless drives to no place special.

Then he said "isn't it time we stopped driving nowhere and started our lives going somewhere."
And I said yes.

Photographed for De Beers Consolidated Mines, Ltd. by Peter Vaeth.

A diamond is forever.

"The Day You Buy a Diamond," a free booklet with the answers to any questions you may have about buying an engagement diamond, is available at many retail jewelers, or you may write for a copy to: The Diamond Information Center, 260 West Lehigh Ave., Philadelphia, Pa. 19133.

The traditional life-style.

Understanding People—a Continuing Study for Advertising

All advertising seeks to influence people's behavior. Sometimes its goal is simply to reinforce a consumer's existing pattern, to encourage the repurchase of a frequently bought brand. Sometimes the goal is to modify a consumer's behav-

ior, to bring about a switch in brands or to replace an older model of a product with a newer one. Sometimes, especially in the case of truly new products, it can be to change a behavior pattern, to get someone to substitute a new way of doing something for an old one. All this points up the most important element of effective advertising—understanding people.

THE STORY BEHIND
Welch's Sparkling Grape Soda campaign

Welch's Sparkling Grape Soda, one of the most successful new soft drinks ever marketed, was introduced in May in the New York market. Its distribution carried out by the Coca-Cola Bottling Company of New York, the brand achieved almost instant success in both retail acceptance (including introductory display and featuring) and consumer take-out.

Introductory advertising began in late May and ran through the peak summer selling months to the end of August. The schedule utilized a multimedia effort, which included prime-time television and radio for the mass consumer audience. A follow-up wave of advertising ran from early October to mid-November.

Research indicated that the user profile of grape soda is skewed toward the lower socioeconomic groups. Incidence of consumption among nonwhites is approximately one-third higher than among whites. In order to reach this all-important consuming group most effectively, the brand utilized ethnic media as an integral part of its mix. Heavy schedules ran on Spanish TV and radio and black radio. To maximize impact against the trade, introductory newspaper advertising ran in all markets in the New York ADI.

The user profile research was also extremely valuable in the development of creative executions for the various media. Particularly noteworthy is the fact that the introductory television commercial developed for the general viewing audience (prime time) represents a substantial departure from Welch's traditional approach to broadcast advertising. Traditionally, Welch advertising has been targeted to female head of household between the ages of 25 and 49. Grape Soda advertising, however, is targeted toward all members of the family, including children 6 to 11, teens, and parents. Additionally, in the general audience commerical, special emphasis is given to blacks and Spanish-speaking people. To communicate most effectively with the black and Spanish segments of the brand's target audience, special creative executions were developed for both television and radio. A Spanish TV commercial emphasized the family orientation prevailing in the Spanish-speaking community; and black and Spanish radio commercials included music specially written in the idiom of these demographic groups.

To measure advertising awareness and brand usage among the various target groups, the agency undertook a consumer research study. Results were even more startling than was predicted, as shown by the following table.

	Ethnic Group (%)		
	White	Black	Spanish
Awareness	49	88	79
Trial	14	55	36
Aware of and tried	29	63	46
Tried and repeated	79	86	90

Initial research also confirmed a well-known fact about both Welch and the entire spectrum of grape-flavored products. Welch's name, already associated with grapes, almost instantly provides a new product with a preemptive market position. Using this name association to advantage, the introductory TV commercial for markets outside New York carried the theme line, "You've never really tasted grape soda before till you've tried Welch's." The theme is repeated in the photoscript on the next page.

Welch's Grape Soda, one of the leading items handled by Coca-Cola of New York, reports excellent sales as it continues to expand its national market.

Courtesy Welch Foods, Inc.
Advertising Agency: Richard K. Manoff, Inc.

Welch's
Sparkling Grape Soda

Introductory :30 Commercial

"Street Scene"

Who's new grape soda bubbles with zip?

Whose bubbly grape taste will make you flip?

Whose new grape has bubbles to tickle your lip?

Who but Welch's!

ANNCR: Introducing Welch's new Sparkling Grape Soda!

Who took grape taste and gave it a zing?

Whose bubbly grape flavor'll make you sing?

And who let grape bubbles do their own thing? Who but Welch's!

ANNCR: Try Welch's new Sparkling Grape Soda. It's the grapest!

1. How does the anthropologist view people's behavior? How is this viewpoint applicable to advertising? Cite an example from current advertising.

2. Find and discuss an example of current advertising illustrating two of the following: subcultural identities, a milestone of life, changing role of women.

3. How does the sociologist view people's behavior? How is this viewpoint applicable to advertising? Cite an example from current advertising.

4. Find and discuss an example of current advertising illustrating two of the following: reference group, social class, innovators, opinion leaders.

5. Of what significance in advertising is the family life cycle?

6. How does the psychologist view people's behavior? How is this viewpoint applicable to advertising? Select an example from current advertising. How does this perspective differ from that of the sociologist?

7. Explain the differences (a) between physiological and social motives, and (b) among affectional, ego-bolstering, and ego-defensive needs.

8. Find and discuss an example of current advertising illustrating any four of the following: affectional needs, ego-bolstering needs, ego-defensive needs, acquisitive attitude, conserving attitude, constructive attitude, achievement attitude, recognition attitude, dominative attitude.

9. What is meant by life-styles? Find two examples of current advertising reflecting different life-styles.

10. "A product may mean different things to different people." Comment.

11. "The goal of marketing and advertising is to provide consumer satisfaction." Discuss this statement.

12. What were the special marketing problems facing the launching of Welch's Sparkling Grape Soda?

13. The company embarked on research. For what were they looking?

14. When they had the results of the research, what did they do with that information? What were the results of what they did?

READING SUGGESTIONS

AAKER, DAVID A., and GEORGE S. DAY, "Dynamic Model of Relationship Among Advertising, Consumer Awareness, Attitudes and Behavior," *Journal of Applied Psychology* (June 1974): 281–86.

ARMSTRONG, GARY M., and LAURENCE P. FELD-MAN, "Exposure and Sources of Opinion Leaders," *Journal of Advertising Research* (August 1976): 21–27.

BELK, RUSSELL W., "Situational Variables and Consumer Behavior," *Journal of Consumer Research* (December 1975): 157–64.

BLOCK, CARL E., and KENNETH J. ROERING, *Essentials of Consumer Behavior.* Hinsdale, Ill.: Dryden, 1976.

CUMMINGS, WILLIAM H., and M. VENKATESAN, "Cognitive Dissonance and Consumer Behavior," *Journal of Marketing Research* (August 1976): 303–08.

DAVIS, HARRY L., "Decision Making Within the Household," *Journal of Consumer Research* (March 1976): 241–60.

ENGEL, JAMES F., DAVID T. KOLLAT, and ROGER D.

BLACKWELL, *Consumer Behavior,* 2nd ed. Hinsdale, Ill.: Dryden, 1973.

FABER, RONALD, and SCOTT WARD, *Consumer Socialization of Young People: a Bibliography.* Cambridge, Mass.: Marketing Science Institute, 1976.

GREEN, ROBERT T., and ISABELLA C. M. CUNNING-HAM, "Feminine Role Perception and Family Purchasing Decisions." *Journal of Marketing Research* (August 1975): 325–32.

HANSEN, FLEMMING, "Psychological Theories of Consumer Choice," *Journal of Consumer Research* (December 1976): 117–42.

HENRY, WALTER A., "Cultural Values Do Correlate With Consumer Behaviour," *Journal of Marketing Research* (May 1976): 121–27.

KERBY, JOE KENT, *Consumer Behavior.* New York: Dun-Donnelley, 1975.

PETERSON, ROBERT A., *Trends in Consumer Behavior Research.* Chicago: American Marketing Association, 1977.

PRASAD, V. KANTI, "Socioeconomic Product Risk and Patronage Preferences of Retail Shoppers." *Journal of Marketing* (July 1975): 42–47.

REYNOLDS, FRED D., and WILLIAM D. WELLS, *Consumer Behavior.* New York: McGraw-Hill, 1977.

WELLS, WILLIAM D., "Psychographics: a Critical Review," *Journal of Marketing Research* (May 1975): 196–213.

WRIGHT, PETER, "Factors Affecting Cognitive Resistance to Advertising," *Journal of Consumer Research* (June 1975): 1–9.

15

Creating the Copy

The remarkable thing about advertising is that it can prompt people to buy a specific product voluntarily. Advertising has no authority to compel a person to buy anything; it exercises no mystical power. To the most vigorous exhortation of an advertiser, the meekest of us can yawn and say, "No, thank you!" Nevertheless, people do buy specific goods and services because of advertising. Since it has neither the power nor the authority to compel a person to do anything, one may ask just how does advertising do its work?

Not Millions, Just One

In discussing advertising we deal with big numbers: billions of dollars, millions of television sets, thousands of radio stations. But whether it's directed toward a reader, a viewer, or a listener, an advertisement deals with only one person at a time. If a housewife feels an ad is speaking directly to her, she pays attention; otherwise she does not. In either case, she is indifferent to the fact that the advertisement is addressing millions of others at the same time. Her interest depends upon the degree to which the ad speaks to her about her interests, her wants, her goals, her problems.

The Nature and Use of Appeals

An appeal is any statement designed to motivate a person to action. To motivate anyone to action, the statement must relate to that person's interests, wants, goals or problems. The reason anyone buys anything is for the benefit he or she expects to derive from it. Perhaps a homemaker wants the satisfaction of providing a nutritious meal for the family on a limited budget. Both men and women may buy clothes and jewelry to make them look their best. One consumer responds to the joy of being able to take the whole family off on a trip in a trailer, another is attracted by the freedom of riding a motorcycle. Regardless of the product, it is the benefit the buyer will receive that prompts him or her to buy it. The life-giving spark of an advertisement is its promise of the special significant benefit the product will provide—a promise the product must be able to fulfill. That special significant benefit becomes the *appeal* of an advertisement. For example:

West Bend Slo-Cookers are Fast Cleaners

Selecting the Appeal

Many appealing things can be said about any product, but we want to put our effort behind the appeal that has the most significance. Since selecting the appeal is a key decision in any campaign, many research techniques have been developed to find out which appeal to use. These techniques usually fall into two categories:

▲ Structured research

▲ Unstructured research

Structured research

In structured research, the inquirer prepares a list of questions and choices and asks the respondent to select the choice that appeals most to him or her. The consensus of findings serves as a base for deciding which appeal to use.

A company planning a promotional campaign for a new house plant food listed seven appeals that might influence growers of house plants to try the product:

1. A complete feeding program for your plants
2. A uniform timed-release application that keeps feeding your plant for three months
3. Just the right amount of nitrogen, phosphorus, and potassium
4. No danger of burning or overfeeding
5. No mess, no waste
6. No mixing or measuring
7. Quick-starting nitrogen for immediate benefit

The question was: which advantage meant the most to house plant owners? Research revealed that two benefits stood out: no danger of burning or overfeeding and no mixing or measuring.

The advantages of structured research are that it is clear, simple, easy to administer, and it can be mathematically computed. The disadvantages are that the research is limited to the predetermined questions of the investigator and does not invite the respondent to stray outside those questions with other views relevant to the use of the product. To be meaningful, the selected appeal must also be tested against the appeals of competitors.

Unstructured research, also known as *motivational research* or *depth interview* research, is undertaken in a relaxed interview in the respondent's home. Not confining themselves to "yes" or "no" answers, the interviewer and the respondent discuss attitudes about the use of the product. From such conversations a true picture of the respondent's feelings about the product may emerge. The interviewer often discovers the best appeal and may even elicit suggestions for a product change. Because it is very costly to conduct such research on a one-to-one basis, researchers sometimes gather into one room a group of people who could be, or are, purchasers of the product under study—a group of housewives or mothers of young children, for example. These are called *focus groups*, and many techniques for conducting discussions in them have been developed. Such an indirect approach takes more expertise and more planning time than does structured research, however.

Unstructured research

Whit Hobbs reports an experience with the S.C. Johnson Company, makers of furniture wax, when the account was first assigned to his agency. The product had clear advantages over competition, but sales had been sliding. Instead of embarking on a campaign to stress product differentials, the agency conducted unstructured research to find out why the sales were declining. He reports:

> It wasn't a healthy market. . . . What was the problem? The problem was that women hated to wax their furniture. It was a chore and a bore. They did it once or twice a month and wished it were even less often than that. On the other hand, research pointed out that women *dust* their furniture nearly every day. And this fact led to a strategic question: What would happen if you could get that once-a-month furniture wax onto the dust cloth?
>
> What happened was a remarkable sales success. The creative team took this get-it-on-the-dust-cloth creative strategy and came up with the promise of "waxed beauty instantly as you dust." The Johnson product, Pledge, did not merely stop the decline; it doubled the market.°

Sometimes a project starts off as structured research but evolves into unstructured research—with interesting results. In one such project, the Cy Chaikin Research Group was given a proposal for structured research limited to three questions.

> The product class was a liquid dishwashing detergent. The objective of the research was to ascertain which of three proposed copy themes would be the most effective in

° Whit Hobbs, "Copy Strategy," in *Handbook of Advertising Management,* ed. Roger Barton (New York: McGraw-Hill, 1970), p. 14–1.

developing interest and action on the product. Each theme began and ended with:

"This Amazing Dishwashing Discovery
[*new line to come here*]
and is extra kind to hands."

The three themes being considered were:

Gets you away from the sink faster.
Keeps your hands out of greasy dishwater.
Powerful, effective, gets it all out.

We raised the question of where would we be if all we learned was that none of these themes appealed to the consumers. We recommended that we approach the problem, instead, via depth interviews; the proposal was accepted.

We undertook a series of depth interviews and focus group discussions and learned there was confusion and some misunderstanding in the consumers' minds on each of the three proposed themes. Some said, "How can you get away from the sink faster if the dishes are stacked a mile high?" Others wondered how they could possibly keep their hands out of greasy dishwater. With respect to the third theme, homemakers wondered how a powerful product could be "extra kind to hands." The conclusion of this research was that none of these three themes was effective.

At this point intuition suggested a different approach. In the course of the study many questions were discussed. One of them was, "What do you find easiest to do?" Consumers generally replied, "The dishes and the glasses." That led to another question: "And what do you find most difficult to do?" The response was, "The greasy pots and pans."

These answers led to the creative leap that resulted in a new appeal:

This Amazing Dishwashing Discovery
Does Pots and Pans as Easy as Glasses
—and is extra kind to hands.

The theme was further tested against those used by leading competitors. It was also tested for believability with respect to all themes under consideration. The findings showed that the "Pots and Pans as Easy as Glasses" approach in the slogan scored best with housewives and had a high credibility quotient.

This copy strategy was adopted in all media, particularly TV and radio. The theme appeared on the facing of the package, and the share-of-market increased from 3 percent to nearly 9 percent.°

The most important part of any research, structured or unstructured, is interpreting the findings. In making interpretations, intuition and creative imagination often play vital parts. Support for the role of intuition in this scientific age

---

° Direct communication with Cy Chaikin, Cy Chaikin Research Group, New York, N.Y.

comes from Lord Brain, late president of the British Association for the Advancement of Science, who said:

> The contributions which science can make to the interpretation of something as complex as human nature are at present limited, and in unscientific theories, as in art, there may be insights, intuition, and illuminations, which are of value for practice as well as for theory.°

It is good that we begin our creative work with the "insights, intuitions and illuminations" of which we are possessed, and which "are of practical value."

It was an intuitive idea, not the result of research, that prompted the Doyle Dane Bernbach Agency to use Volkswagen's small size as the appeal for an advertising campaign to launch the car nationwide. While all the other cars were outdoing each other in size, this agency made a creative leap to the headline "Think small," and a new car with a new size was launched across America.

Whether created by research or in other ways, the appeal provides the basis of the advertising structure. That appeal can be expressed in words, a picture, or both. In this chapter we discuss how to make use of words, called copy, in presenting the appeal.†

Structure of an Advertisement

In some instances the promise is the whole advertisement.

Freedent gum won't stick to most dentures.

Usually, however, a fuller exposition is required, in which case the promise can act as the headline—the first step in the structure of the advertisement. Most ads are presented in this order:

- ▲ **Promise** of benefit (the headline)
- ▲ **Amplification** of story (as needed)
- ▲ **Proof** of claim (as needed)
- ▲ **Action** to take (if not obvious)

° Lord Brain, F.R.S., "Science and Behavior," *The Listener*, LXXII, 1848 (August 27, 1964), 294.

† The term *copy* is a carry-over from those days in printing when a compositor, given a manuscript to set in type, was told to copy it. Before long, the manuscript itself became known as *copy*. In the creation of a printed ad, *copy* refers to all the reading matter in the ad. However, in the production of printed ads, *copy* also refers to the entire subject being reproduced—words and pictures alike. This is one of the instances in advertising when the same word is used in different senses, a practice that all professions and crafts seem to enjoy using as a way of bewildering the uninitiated.

If you like acronyms, PAPA may help you remember the order. Unlike a cookbook recipe specifying what ingredients must go into every dish, however, this list serves only as elements at your command in writing copy.

The headline

The headline is the most important statement in an advertisement. The first thing a person reads, it relates the product to the consumer's life. It's the headline's responsibility to arouse the interest of the particular group of readers you want to reach; if it doesn't, the rest of the ad has little chance of being read.

The major forms of headlines fall into the following classes:

▲ Headlines that present a new benefit.
▲ Headlines that directly promise an existing benefit.
▲ Curiosity invoking and provocative headlines.
▲ Selective headlines (often combined with one of the others).

Headlines that present a new benefit.   The moment of peak interest in a product is when it first offers a new benefit. That is why, in our innovative society, you often see headlines such as these:

**The First Dishwasher Detergent
for Dry-hards**   [Electrasol cleanser]

**On April 6 Swissair Begins Regular Service
To the People's Republic of China**   [Swissair]

**New!
The Ultimate Cooking Center:
Microwave. Self-Cleaning. Smoothtop.**   [Litton microwave stove]

**It's Here!
The Kodak Instamatic**   [Kodak cameras]

Headlines that directly promise an existing benefit.   Products can't be offering new benefits all the time, of course, so headlines often remind consumers of existing features about their products.

**Keep a Spill
From Becoming
a Stain**   [Scotchgard spray]

**A Good Hot Dish with Meat
Now About 23¢ a Serving**   [Chef Boy-ar-dee Italian food]

It's Always a Pleasure   [I. W. Harper bourbon]

Most Wraps Just Wrap
  Reynolds Wrap Wraps, Molds and Seals Tightly   [Reynolds Wrap]

Curiosity-invoking and provocative headlines.   As a change of pace from the direct-promise headlines, an advertiser may challenge the curiosity, prompt the reader to read further, and lead to the key message. Tacitly, the message promises helpful information for the reader.

If a Fire Broke Out
  In Your Home Tonight   [General Electric new home
Could You Get Your Family Out in Time?   sentry smoke alarm]

How to Help Save Gasoline   [Delco Electronics]

20 Ways to Save Money on Your Phone Bill   [AT&T]

Remember, however, that readers should not feel tricked into reading something that fails to answer the question or relate the challenge to their self-interest.

Selective headlines.   Readers scanning a publication are more likely to read an advertisement that seems to concern them personally, rather than one that talks to a broad audience. For this reason, the *selective* headline, addressed to that particular segment of the total readership that would be most interested in the product, is often used.
  Here are four headlines:

  To All Men and Women

  To All Young Men and Women

  To All College Men and Women

  To All College Seniors

The first headline is addressed to the greatest number of readers, but it would be of least interest to any one of them. As each succeeding headline reduces the size of the audience it addresses, it improves the chances of attracting that particular group.
  Besides addressing them directly, headlines can appeal to a particular group by mentioning a problem they have in common:

How High on Your Agenda
  Is Lowering Your Serum Cholesterol?   [Fleischman's margarine]

Colors You
  Could Never
  See Before
  in 60 Seconds   [Polaroid camera]

**Great News for Mothers of
Cavity-Prone Children**   [Aim toothpaste]

**If the Yarn You're Knitting
With Now Can't Pass These   [Coats & Clark's
Tests, You're Wasting a Lot of Time**   Red Heart Wintuk Yarn]

Lips Too Sore for a Stick?   [Blistex salve]

Another vital quality in headlines is that they be specific. "A sewing machine that's convertible" is better than "A sewing machine with an unusual feature." In fact, being specific is vital not only in headlines but in the rest of the copy as well.

The subcaption (subcap).   A headline must say something important to the reader. The actual number of words is not of the essence; long headlines have been known to work as well as short ones. If the message is long, it can be conveyed with a main headline and a *subheadline* (more frequently called *subcaption* or *subcap*). The subcaption can spell out more specifically the promise presented in the headline. It can be longer than the headline. It can invite further reading, and it serves as a transition to the opening paragraph of the copy. As examples:

Headline

**NOW SALTON TURNS YOUR FREEZER
INTO A LITTLE ICE CREAM FACTORY**

Subcap

**The Ice Cream Machine Makes Ice Cream in Your
Freezer Without Rock Salt or Ice**   [Salton ice cream machine]

Headline

**HALLELUJAH!
A DRAIN OPENER THAT
WORKS WHERE LIQUIDS
AND CRYSTALS FAIL**

Subcap

**Amazing Drain Power! It opens over 9 out of 10
clogged and sluggish drains that liquids and
crystals fail to open . . . and it works
instantly without lye or acid.**   [Drain Power]

HALLELUJAH! A DRAIN OPENER THAT WORKS WHERE LIQUIDS AND CRYSTALS FAIL

Amazing Drain Power! It opens over 9 out of 10 clogged and sluggish drains that liquids and crystals fail to open ...and it works <u>instantly</u> without lye or acid.

Drain Power® isn't like any other kind of drain opener you've ever used.

It works by using pressure instead of lye or acid so it loosens clogs—even grease and hair—and pushes them out in one second flat.

Drain Power is better. We proved it.

While no household drain opener will solve every prob-

lem all the time, tests in household drains just like yours have proved that Drain Power works where other drain openers have failed.

In fact, Drain Power opened over 9 out of 10 sinks, showers and tubs that liquid and crystal drain openers couldn't open. *9 out of 10!*

Costs no more than the leading liquid.

When used according to directions, you can get only two uncloggings from a bottle of the leading liquid drain opener.

The average cost per use for unclogging a drain is 40-50 cents.

But you can get *five* uncloggings from a can of Drain Power. Average cost per use? 40-50 cents.

No worry about your hands.

Since Drain Power contains no harsh chemicals, you don't have to worry about burning your hands.

However, because Drain Power is unlike any other drain opener you've ever used, be sure to read the accompanying instruction booklet carefully.

Buy Drain Power first.

Try Drain Power *before* you use the others...and you won't *want* the others.

Amazing Drain Power. It works where liquids and crystals fail. Or you'll get your money back.

A LIMITED WARRANTY TO CONSUMERS
Good Housekeeping
PROMISES
REPLACEMENT OR REFUND IF DEFECTIVE

DRAIN POWER

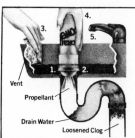

Drain Power is easy to use.
1. Fill sink with 1 to 2 inches of cold standing water. **2.** Remove strainer or stopper from drain and quickly insert nose of Drain Power can into drain opening. **3.** Hold wet cloth firmly over vent to prevent splashback. **4.** Push bottom of can firmly downward for one second. **5.** Run hot water for one minute to flush loosened particles down drain.

Important: do not use in clogged drains where lye or acid may still be present.

A promise-of-performance headline that is clear, direct, and enthusiastic.

321

Headline

WE'D LIKE TO TREAT YOU
TO 150 CUPS
OF GREAT TASTING COFFEE

Subcap

Buy Any GE Immersible Coffeemaker Now
And Get 3 Cans of Max-Pax Electra-Perk
Blend Coffee Free   [GE immersible coffee maker]

Amplification

After the headline comes the body of the advertisement, where we present our case for the product and explain how the promise in the headline will be fulfilled. What we say and how deep we go depend upon the amount of information an interested reader seeks at this point of the buying process. A new high-cost product, such as a new type of range, calls for more explanation than does a low-cost product, such as a soup with a new flavor. When a product results from technical advances, there may not be room to give a detailed explanation of all the features; the thing to do is explain in detail a few salient features and invite the reader to go to the dealer for further elaboration.

Technical features of a product should be presented in terms of what they will do for the user. A Litton Microwave oven advertisement described its features in this manner:

Microwave speed.
Cook a complete meal or a quick snack in the eye-level microwave oven. Or rely on automatic defrost to thaw frozen foods fast. Either way, you save time and energy with microwave speed.

Self-cleaning ease.
Save clean-up time, too. Litton Micromatics have a self-cleaning oven system that removes even the toughest baked-on stains. And a one-piece smoothtop that keeps spills from dripping away.

Cooks four ways.
So now there's always time for complete meals. Cook with microwave speed in the eye-level oven. Bake or broil in the conventional oven. Stir up something saucy on the smoothtop. Or prepare one dish or a complete meal using both ovens for a combination of conventional browning and microwave speed.

Before we conclude this section of the ad, it is wise to offset any potential objections that might inhibit a prospect from buying the product. Hair preparation ads say, "Leaves the hair soft, not sticky." Janitor-in-a-Drum cleanser advertised, "Contains no concentrated phosphates, and is biodegradable so that it will not pollute water."

Before coloring the hair became stylish, many women hesitated for fear their friends would know they were dying their hair. Clairol Shampoo built a multi-million dollar business with the slogan:

**Does she or doesn't she?
Only her hairdresser can tell for sure.**

There comes a point in the consideration of a new product or costly purchase when the prospective buyer wonders, "But how much can I count on all these claims?" Proof supporting the promises made are especially important for high-priced products, health products, and new products offering a special feature. The reputation of the maker is very important. Other evidence, however, is often necessary too.

Proof

Warranties.   Especially when consumers cannot tell how good the product is until they have used it, warranties are reassuring. Scotts anti-crabgrass preparation advertises:

**We'll Keep the Crabgrass from Growing
in Your Lawn
and We Put That in Writing**

Car and tire companies continually seek to outdo each other with their warranties. We discuss the legal aspects of warranties in advertising in Chapter 26.

Trial offers.   Widely used for such low-cost, nonconsumable products as books and small tools, trial offers show consumers that the company is confident about its product.

Money-back guarantees.   These are the basic assurance for lower-priced products.

Seals of approval.   From accredited sources, such as *Good Housekeeping, Parents' Magazine,* the American Medical Association, and Underwriters Laboratories, seals of approval allay consumers' fears about product quality.

Demonstrations.   Simple demonstrations, like those for paper towels, can be performed live on TV. When demonstrations are performed outside the field, under impartially controlled conditions (tests of car brakes, for example), they can be shown on TV and in print ads. It is important to show convincingly that such tests were fairly conducted. Of course if the product was used in a public competition, as is the case when tires are used in the Indianapolis 500, excellent evidence is automatically available.

Testimonials.   Testimonials should come from persons competent to pass judgment on the subject or whose judgment, for other reasons, is respected. A golf champion's opinion of a golf ball is meaningful; but on the fine-tuning of a TV set, his or her opinion is of little worth. Health testimonials are unacceptable to the government.

The entire ad as dramatic proof.   Although we have listed *proof* as third in the hierarchy of elements of a comprehensive ad, often whole campaigns are devoted to establishing the validity of one important claim. We have discussed this strategy in Chapter 4, "Specific Purposes of Campaigns."

Action

Before you begin to write an advertisement, ask yourself exactly what you want the readers to do. Whatever you may want them to do must be consistent with their normal procedures in buying a product like the one you are advertising. Sometimes you simply want to dispose consumers favorably toward the product, so that when next they are in the market, they will turn to your brand.

For most lower-priced products widely sold in supermarkets, you want consumers to buy them next time they go shopping. Lest they forget the name, an urge line may be added: "Enjoy _____ for dinner tonight." Many advertisers include a cents-off coupon as an incentive to buy the product on the next shopping expedition.

For more costly products, such as household appliances, there is more deliberating, more shopping. The advertisement aims to get the reader to visit a dealer. "See your dealer" or, "Visit your dealer for demonstration or trial run" are familiar closing lines. The advertisement may also invite the reader to send for a booklet giving more information; that inquiry can then be passed on to the local dealer for follow-up by a sales representative.

Copy Style

Like people, advertisements have personalities all their own. Some say what they have to say in a fresh way. They make an impact. Others, although they try to say the same thing, are boring. Unfortunately, while many of us may be polite to a dull person, no one is polite to a dull ad. We simply pass it by.

Up to now we have been discussing how the building blocks of copy are put together. We now discuss how the way we say what we have to say can lift it out of the humdrum. That's style. The creative essence in writing copy is to see a product in a fresh way, to explore its possible effects upon the reader, to explain the product's advantages in a way that causes the reader to view the product with new understanding and appreciation.

Most advertisements end in the same way, by asking or suggesting that the reader buy the product. The difference between a lively advertisement and a dull one lies in the *approach* to the message at the outset.

The lens through which a writer sees a product may be the magnifying glass of the technician, who sees every nut and bolt and can explain why each is important. It may be the rose-colored glasses of the romanticist, who sees how a person's life may be affected by the product. Therefore we speak of *approaches of ads,* rather than types of ads. The chief approaches in describing an article may be characterized as:

▲ The factual approach
▲ The emotional approach

In the factual approach we deal with reality, that which really exists. We talk about the product—what it is, how it's made, what it does. Focusing on the facts about the product that are of most importance to the reader, we explain the product's advantages. An interesting thing about a fact, however, is that it can be interpreted in different ways, each accurate, but each launching different lines of thinking. The most familiar example is that of the eight-ounce glass holding four ounces of water, of which it could be said:

The factual approach

This glass is half full.
This glass is half empty.

Both statements are factually correct. The difference is in the interpretation of the reality and in the viewpoint projected, as the Chivas Regal ad so aptly illustrates. The skill in presenting a fact is to interpret it in the way that means most to the reader.

The Volvo ad that could have said, "You can always depend upon Volvo" asked instead, "Did it ever occur to you that your car might panic in a crisis?"

A White-Westinghouse washer ad could have said only, "Announcing the full-size washer that saves space. But the headline said:

White-Westinghouse Brings the Laundry Room
Up Out of the Basement

An advertisement for the John Deere Snow Blower could have said, "Blow heavy snow away quickly with a John Deere." Instead it said:

Blow Away a Blizzard Before Breakfast

Imaginative copy can be used to sell more than products. Facts about services, ideas, places—anything an ad can be written for—can be presented with a fresh point of view. The Economic Development Department of Memphis, Tennessee, ran an advertisement to encourage industries to move there. The writer could have said, "Memphis—a city of 650,000"; but the writer interpreted the city's size this way:

Memphis—a city of manageable size

DID IT EVER OCCUR TO YOU THAT YOUR CAR MIGHT PANIC IN A CRISIS?

The 1975 Volvo 240 series was planned with the unexpected in mind.

Because, while it's human to err, driving errors can be fatal. Volvos are designed to compensate.

Jamming on the brakes may make them work too well.

When a car stops fast, its weight shifts forward. The rear wheels tend to lock before the front ones. This can cause a skid.

Volvo's 4-wheel power disc brake system has a pressure-proportioning valve on each rear brake line. It minimizes premature rear wheel lock-up, and helps keep you on the straight and narrow.

Road debris could damage a brake line. So Volvo has two independent braking systems. Each works on *three* wheels—two front, one rear. (According to Volvo's math, you could lose 50% of your braking system, and have about 80% of its effectiveness left.)

If you can't stop, you've got to go around. Volvo's rack and pinion steering is similar to a racing car's. It's extremely quick. And even in high speed dodging, Volvo's new suspension holds you steady, smooth and flat.

No matter how good your reflexes are, you have to rely on your car's reactions. And when it comes to avoiding accidents, Volvo thinks you can't go too far.

VOLVO
The car for people who think.

There is always a fresh way of saying something.

WHITE-WESTINGHOUSE BRINGS THE LAUNDRY ROOM UP OUT OF THE BASEMENT.

Announcing the full-size washer that does what no other full-size washer can do.

It saves space.

Because our washer is a front-loading washer, you can stack it under our dryer in a closet. Without having to pull out the washer each time you put in a load.

It can be built in anywhere.

Stacked or side by side, this full capacity washer can fit in lots of places no other full-size washer can.

Because all you need is a space 27" wide by 27" deep by 35" high. (With stacked matching dryer 70" high.)

Or you can install them side by side to fit into places like under a kitchen counter. Under a bath vanity. Or even built right into your wall.

So when you're building or remodeling, remember: you don't need a whole laundry room to do your laundry anymore.

It saves work and footsteps.

Bringing the washer up out of the basement means that now you can bring the washer to where the laundry is, instead of bringing the laundry to where the washer is. And that saves you a lot of running up and down stairs with baskets of clothes.

It saves money.

Since our washer is tumble-action, it uses less water to clean an average load of clothes than other full-size washers. And you need less soap to get the clothes just as clean. And less gas or electricity to heat the water.

In short, you're saving money each time you do your wash.

It circulates your wash better.

A tumble-action washer works like heavy-duty commercial washers work. Effectively and efficiently. Yet it's gentle enough to handle your most delicate fabrics.

It tumbles clothes through the water instead of just sloshing them around. So, unlike an agitator washer where only the clothes near the centerpost get the full benefit of the agitator action, all your clothes get washed thoroughly and evenly.

Our tumble-action washer and matching clothes dryer. **Another quality product from White-Westinghouse.**

WHITE-WESTINGHOUSE CORPORATION
One of the White Consolidated Industries.

The factual approach. A factual statement, made in an interesting way, reaching the life of the reader.

328

A fact is no less a fact if it is presented with imagination. The art of creating copy lies in saying a familiar thing in an unexpected way.

The emotional approach

There is a world of values that have no yardstick, that can never be weighed, that can only be experienced. It is a world of inner experiences, of feelings. People often buy products for the satisfaction and joy to be experienced from their use. We cannot find these qualities by cutting the product apart and seeing what is inside it. Rather, we must look into the readers' lives to perceive how their lives, or those of people in whom they are interested, somehow, somewhere, will be enriched through this product. That launches us on the *emotional approach.*

Certo is a pectin from which jams and jellies are made. An ad for Certo could have said, "Here is a pectin with which you can make jam or jelly." Instead it said:

**Spread a Little Happiness
With Your Own Homemade Jam**

It pictured a smiling family gathered around a table.

Campbell's Soups could have said, "When you have guests, serve Campbell's Soup." Instead, they said:

**Give Me the Campbell Life
It's an Informal Party
Where Guests
Help Themselves
to a Good Time**

Both these ads appeal less to our reason than to our emotions. Like ads taking a factual approach, they tacitly make a promise, but the promise is emotional satisfaction.

Although people may become interested in an advertisement because of the emotional approach of its headline, they may also want to know some specific facts about a product before deciding to buy it. Often, therefore, the copy approach of an advertisement begins with an emotional presentation and ends with a factual one. Some of the most effective ads have combined an emotional headline and picture with factual copy. A factual statement interpreted imaginatively, backed up by factual copy, can also be persuasive. We avoid speaking of *factual advertisements* or *emotional advertisements;* we say ads are using a factual *approach* or an emotional *approach.*

Emotional approach backed by factual copy

Much advertising is devoted to people who have specialized interests—tennis, cars, gardening, hunting, sailing, photography. In ads for special interest groups, the copy promises to solve specific problems common to members of the group.

Copy for special interest groups

Spread a little happiness with your own homemade jam.

Put it up in minutes. Eat it up for pennies.

THERE'S NO COOKING.

All you do is mix.
And all it takes is about 30 minutes.
And you've got 5 jars of
your very own homemade jam.
Better jam. (Just ask those
families who make their own!)

The recipe on the right will do it.
Or, look for other fruit jam and
jelly recipes with the package,
when you buy Certo® fruit pectin.
(Or Sure-Jell®). It's the very ingredient
you need to help make it jam.

It makes good time.
It makes good sense.
And it makes the kind of jam
you'll be proud to put your name on.

The powder way or the liquid way

AND, IT'S EASY TO DO.

> **STRAWBERRY JAM RECIPE**
> 1¾ cups crushed strawberries (about 1 qt.)
> 4 cups sugar
> 2 tablespoons lemon juice
> ½ bottle Certo® fruit pectin
>
> Thoroughly mix fresh, crushed strawberries
> with sugar, and let stand for 10 minutes.
> Combine lemon juice with Certo® and add
> to fruit mixture. Stir the whole thing for
> 3 minutes. And that's it for 5 cups of jam.
> Ladle your fresh homemade jam into any 5
> scalded jars, (8 oz. or smaller, with screw
> tops). Or use plastic containers (with
> snap lids). Cover right away and then let
> stand at room temperature for 24 hours to set.
> Keep what you can eat in the refrigerator.
> And freeze the rest for sweeter days.

*The emotional approach. Presenting the
advantages of a product in terms of happiness.*

330

WITHOUT BREAKING ANY RULES, WE BROKE ALL THE RULES.

With the help of Howard Head, we've created a tennis racket with a 50% larger hitting area. This new racket weighs no more and offers no more wind resistance than an ordinary racket. What's more it is entirely acceptable to both the USPTA and USTA.

This ingenious new racket is called the Prince. Here are just a few of its advantages:

A LARGER SWEET SPOT.

A sweet spot, as if you didn't know, is the high response zone of the strings. A sweet spot 3½ times as large as that of an ordinary racket has an obvious and enormous benefit for any player—from a rank beginner to a Wimbledon champion.

MORE ACCURACY. LESS EFFORT.

The shape of the Prince racket places more of the head's mass further from the center of the racket. This makes the

racket less vulnerable to twisting in a player's hand. Which in turn leads to truer, more controlled shots with less effort.

MORE UNIFORM BALL RESPONSE.

The cross strings and the main strings of the Prince have much less proportionate variation than a conventional racket. This consistency of length, offers a more consistent ball response off the strings.

IT'S EASIER TO HIT THE BALL HARDER.

Because there's a much larger high velocity zone on the strings you nat-

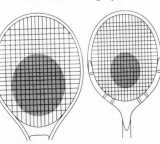

urally hit more high velocity shots. In short, you'll find you get more pace on the ball, more often.

GUT-LIKE RESPONSE WITH NYLON.

Conventionally, nylon strings are less responsive than gut. But by stringing nylon over greater lengths

at slightly higher tensions, it becomes a different animal. The increased stretch allows the strings to bend back like a drum head and offers better contact with the ball—which means better control.

THE IDEAL RACKET HAS AN IDEAL PRICE.

Not only will the Prince give you a competitive advantage, it's also competitively priced. It sells for $65; a price no higher than that of some ordinary rackets. And now that we've told you a little about the Prince you probably want to see our amazing new tennis racket for yourself.

Toll free, call (800) 257-9480 or, in New Jersey, (800) 792-8697, for the pro shop or tennis shop nearest you.

Discover the many advantages of the Prince racket—before your opponent does.

prince TENNIS RACKET

Prince tennis rackets promise more controlled shots, more consistent ball response, better contact with the ball. Big Tomato ads assure the reader smog-free vegetables 365 days a year, no weeding, more nutritious produce. You may also have noticed that the language in the ads is aimed directly at connoisseurs. Prince's "sweet spots," "high velocity zones," and "USPTA and "USTA" would probably be nearly unintelligible to people who know nothing about tennis; and Big Tomato assumes the reader understands "fertilizer loss" and "the 16 basic nutrient elements." As we said when we discussed selective headlines, these ads are not expected to appeal to a broad audience—but members of the particular group an ad is addressed to are very likely to read it.

Comparison Advertising

The term *comparison advertising* (also called comparative advertising) means advertising in which the advertiser's named product is directly compared with one or more competitive named or readily identified products. It was long held by most advertisers that naming competitive products was just giving free advertising to the competitor. Moreover, the networks banned its use until in 1973 the Federal Trade Commission held that naming competitors' brands was not unfair competition, provided the statements made were all supportable. Since that time comparison advertising has become a familiar technique. There are legal problems in comparison advertising, however, as we shall see in Chapter 26.

"How good is comparison advertising, anyway?" The question will be answered only with time and experience. As of now, we have learned these things:

1. The leader in a field has never embarked on such campaigns.
2. The most successful comparison ads are those comparing the advertised product with products identical in every respect except for the specific differential featured in the ad. The stronger the proof that products are otherwise identical, the better.
3. The differences featured should be of importance to the consumer.

One unexpected advantage that comparison advertising has brought to consumers is this: when Product A comes out with an advantage over Product B, the makers of Product B often set out to improve their product, so that it may be even better than Product A. That is the creative competitive impact of the free enterprise system at work.

Slogans

Originally from the Gaelic *slugh gairm*, meaning "battle cry," the word *slogan* has an appropriate background. Slogans are used to sum up the theme of a company's advertising, to deliver an easily remembered message in a few words.

(Opposite): ***Knowing how to talk to your customers.*** ▶

Grow Smog-Free Vegetables.

(On your patio or backyard.)

Hydroponics (hi-dra-pon-iks) n. The growing of plants in nutrient solutions with or without an inert medium (soil) to provide mechanical support.

Now anyone with an 10'x12' patio or back yard can grow beautiful, smog-free hydroponic vegetables. 365 days a year! The easy, enjoyable and economical hydroponic gardening way.

Hydroponics eliminates virtually 99% of the work and risks that come with soil-grown gardening. (No more weeding. Or hoeing. Or dog damage. Or bird damage. Or fertilizer loss. Or too much water or too little water. Etc., etc.)

Feed a family of 5 with the minimum average fresh vegetable diet (recommended by U.S. Gov't. Agricultural Dept.) at a cost *less than* most families are now paying for supermarket produce.

200% more nutritious.

Because hydroponically grown plants are raised in a controlled environment and are fed the 16 basic nutrient elements (plus trace elements), your new patio garden will produce vegetables 200% more nutritious than soil-grown, supermarket produce. A delicious fact.

Your tomatoes will drive you mad.

Many people still call tomatoes "fruit" rather than "vegetable." (A carryover from the 16th century when tomatoes *were* considered "fruit.") In fact, many stories of their aphrodisiac qualities caused tomatoes to be called "love apples" and "passion fruit" before the U.S. Government took both the fun and promise out of it by officially declaring tomatoes a vegetable in 1893.

Nevertheless, when you see the beautiful, luscious, firm, red, appetizing, tantalizing tomatoes your back yard or patio hydroponic unit grows, you'll drive yourself, and your neighbors, mad. Absolutely *mad*.

Three portable kits: Very Small; Small; Bigger.

Our new back yard and patio hydroponic kits are designed to fit into the smallest do-it-yourself gardener's space. And into anyone's budget.

Our mini unit is 18" x 25". A real charmer at $65. Our mobile patio/indoor unit is 3' x 5'. A hobbyist's delight at $195. And our 10'x12' "biggie" is the delux, greatest-thing-to-happen to grow-your-own vegetables since high super market prices. With automatic controls (so you can take your two-week vacation without worrying), only $1685.

They're almost a snap to put together.

As you probably know, "how-to-install" instructions are almost always written in Mongolian code. Ours are not. So you shouldn't have much trouble putting your kit together. ("If *we* can, *you* can," is our motto.)

Here's how to order: First, be sure you've got a 6' vertical clearance for the indoor unit; 8' clearance for the patio and delux units. Then identify the size kit you want: Very Small, Small, Bigger.

After we receive your check (Calif. residents, add 6% sales tax) we'll organize your kit and ship right away. (Shipping charges, C.O.D.) Allow about 30 days for delivery.

By Christmas you'll be growing your own incredibly delicious vegetables. Now, who says miracles don't happen?

BIG TOMATO

Experienced commercial growers.
700 W. First Street, Tustin, Ca. 92680,
(714) 838-3060

"IT'S EASY AND FUN."
"RIPE TOMATOES IN NINETY DAYS."

©Copyright 1975 Garden Resources, Inc.

Used even more often on television and radio than in print, slogans may be combined with a catchy tune to make a *jingle*. They are broadly classified as either institutional or hard-sell.

Institutional

Institutional slogans are created to establish a prestigious image for a company. Relying on this image to enhance the company's products and services, many firms insist that such slogans appear in all their advertising and on their letterheads. An entire advertisement may feature the slogan. Some institutional slogans are familiar:

You're in good hands with Allstate.   [Allstate Insurance Company]

The quality goes in before the name goes on.   [Zenith television]

Where science gets down to business.   [Rockwell Industries]

Such policy slogans are changed infrequently, if at all.

Stating the platform or virtues of the candidate in a few words, slogans used in political campaigns likewise fall into the institutional slogan classification. Such campaigns expire on Election Day (regrettably, so do many of the promises).

Hard-sell

These capsules of advertising change with campaigns. They epitomize the special, significant features of the product or service being advertised, and their claims are strongly competitive.

Built better, not cheaper   [Kitchen Aid Dishwasher]

The refrigerator that helps pay for itself.   [Philco refrigerator]

The gutsy little import.   [Ford Courier]

Charcoal mellowed, drop by drop.   [Jack Daniels whiskey]

Slogans are widely used to advertise groceries, drugs, beauty aids, and liquor. All are repeat products of comparatively low price, sold amidst direct competition, without great deliberation at the time they are bought. If at that moment a slogan can remind a shopper of the special features of the advertised product, it will have served its purpose. Also popular for advertising appliances, slogans can remind shoppers of the name of a product of which they have a good opinion. Not all advertising needs a slogan, however; high style ads, one-shot announcements, and sales ads, for which price is the overriding consideration, generally don't use slogans. But when called for, creating a good slogan is one of the fine arts of copywriting.

Elements of a good slogan

A slogan differs from most other forms of writing because it is designed to be remembered and repeated word for word, to impress a brand and its message on the consumer. Ideally, the slogan should be short, clear, and easy to remember.

Rhyming helps:

A title on the door rates a Bigelow on the floor.

[Bigelow Carpets]

Parallelism helps:

Put it up in minutes.
  Eat it up for pennies.   [Certo Pectin]

Aptness helps:

The canned dog food without the can.   [Gainesburger Dog Food]

Alliteration helps:

Progress for People.   [General Electric Company]

The name of the product in a slogan is a great advantage:

Datsun Saves   [Datsun]

The way to create a slogan is to collect a group of marketing and creative people and begin to discuss the special significant features of the product on which a campaign can be based. During the discussion someone with a keen ear will say, "That's it; that's our slogan!"

Reviewing the Copy

After the copy has been written, review it with these questions in mind:

▲ Is it arresting?
▲ Does it clearly state a promise of a significant benefit?
▲ Is the ad clear?
▲ Does it give the information that the prospective buyer would seek at that point in the buying process?
▲ Are all factual claims supportable?
▲ Is it believable?

We have seen how advertisements are built on an appeal, using a headline to present a concept of the product. We now will discuss how, by using a visualization along with a headline, we can emerge with a strong total concept.

THE STORY BEHIND
the Smith-Corona cartridge ribbon typewriter campaign

Smith-Corona's Research and Development Group had developed a unique new typewriter with the ribbon encased in a single cartridge.

PROBLEMS

The main questions that the company and its advertising agency wanted to answer were:

1. How would consumers react to this product?
2. Which creative strategy would be the most effective in generating interest in the product?
3. In view of the importance of the introduction and the large budget for print and TV advertising, which specific appeals would be the most productive?

SOLUTION

1. Initial consumer reactions   One of the earliest research projects, focus group sessions, allowed a skilled moderator to demonstrate the typewriter and discuss it in depth with several small groups of people. These sessions provided the initial insights into how consumers reacted to the product.

Exploratory in nature, this research enabled the moderator to probe the participants on all possible areas of importance. The research generated a wide range of perceived consumer benefits, which were used in drafting alternative creative strategies for consideration.

2. Alternate creative strategies   The product's features and benefits were listed on separate cards, which were used by a group of trained interviewers in extensive personal interviews. To simulate the manner in which advertising would ultimately be seen, interviewers showed the consumers four-color pictures of the typewriter, rather than the machine itself. A few of the benefits and features evaluated were:

- ▲ Speed in changing ribbons
- ▲ Simplicity in changing ribbons
- ▲ Color flexibility
- ▲ Eraser cartridge
- ▲ Capacity to switch to carbon film ribbon (offered by no other portable)

The primary conclusion of this research was that no single feature or benefit should be stressed alone. Analysis of the research showed that the most exciting aspect of the new typewriter was the actual cartridge itself because of its very high inherent interest. Most respondents were able to read into the cartridge idea that specific benefit they considered most important. In addition, research showed that although the eraser feature was more important than anticipated, response to the carbon film ribbon was limited.

3. The most productive commercials   To determine which television commercials scored highest in "interest," "attitude-shift," and "purchase intent," SCM showed four roughly finished versions to hundreds of viewers on closed circuit TV. Using the diagnostic data from this research, advertisers "fine-tuned" the finished production of the three best commercials and prepared the magazine ads.

RESULTS

The introduction was an enormous success. Eight weeks after the advertising campaign had started on television and in magazines, consumer and dealer demand had already exceeded expectations by a wide margin. Today, the Smith-Corona cartridge ribbon typewriter is the largest selling portable typewriter in the country.

Courtesy SCM Corporation
Advertising Agency: Richard K. Manoff, Inc.

Smith-Corona introduces the 3-second ribbon change.

Time it yourself on our new cartridge ribbon typewriter.

First it will amaze you. Then it will impress you.

The amazing part is that we succeeded in putting a typewriter ribbon in a cartridge for the quickest, simplest typewriter ribbon change imaginable. Also, the cleanest.

The impressive part is that Coronamatic™ Ribbon Cartridges come in nylon <u>and</u> carbon film (the kind usually available only with expensive office typewriters).

STANDARD NYLON
ribbon

CARBON FILM
ribbon

So in the same 3 seconds it takes to change a cartridge, you can now change to carbon film for typing that looks like printing.

It's like having two typewriters in one. One for day-to-day use. One for more professional-looking correspondence or reports.

CORRECTION RIBBON

And in case you make a mistake, we put a correction ribbon in a Coronamatic cartridge so you can correct errors, in seconds.

We also put an assortment of colors into the cartridges—so you can add a little (or a lot of) color to your typing if you feel like it.

Smith-Corona's new cartridge ribbon typewriters. In electric portable and office models.

Now you have a lot of reasons to <u>want</u> to change typewriter ribbons.

SCM **SMITH·CORONA**
SCM CORPORATION

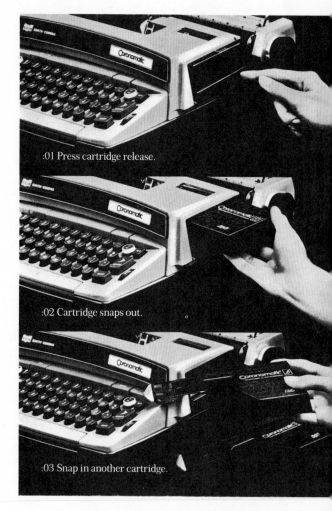

:01 Press cartridge release.

:02 Cartridge snaps out.

:03 Snap in another cartridge.

1. What is an advertising appeal? On what is it based? What is the appeal supposed to do?

2. Select a product category in which there are several competing brands. From current advertising, see how many different specific appeals are used by the various brands. In each case what is the advertiser trying to accomplish?

3. What do you see as the qualities of an effective advertising appeal?

4. The most important part of any research is the way the findings are interpreted, often a blend of facts, intuition, and creative imagination. Discuss how these were used in the examples cited in this chapter.

5. Advertising copy generally has a basic structure. What are the elements of that structure?

6. Why is the headline the most important statement in an advertisement? What are the major forms of headlines? Find two examples illustrating each type. What is the function of the subcaption?

7. What does amplification specifically seek to accomplish? What determines the extent of amplification?

8. When is proof important in an advertisement? Describe the various ways to substantiate claims. How much proof is required in an advertisement? Can you suggest some guidelines for deciding how much proof to include?

9. Distinguish between the factual and emotional copy approaches. Find three examples of each.

10. What is the emotional approach backed by factual copy? Illustrate with two examples.

11. Describe situations in which slogans are particularly useful.

12. Identify and discuss (including an example of each) the major types of slogans.

13. What are the elements of a good slogan?

14. What are the questions you should keep in mind when reviewing the copy?

15. From current advertising, find and analyze the copy approaches used by two different brands of the same product.

16. Identify what you think are the most desirable qualities of good copy. Select an ad that illustrates some of these qualities and explain why.

17. What kind of background and training do you think a copywriter should have?

READING SUGGESTIONS

BARBAN, ARNOLD M., STEPHEN M. CRISTOL and FRANK J. KOPEC, *Essentials of Media Planning.* Chicago, Ill.: Crain Books, 1976.

BOGART, LEO, "Mass Advertising: The Message, Not the Measure," *Harvard Business Review* (September-October 1976): 107–16.

BOYD, HARPER W., JR., RALPH L. WESTFALL, and STANLEY F. STASCH, *Marketing Research.* Homewood, Ill.: Irwin, 1977.

BURTON, PHILIP WARD, *Advertising Copywriting.* Columbus, Ohio: Grid, 1974.

CAPLES, JOHN, *Tested Advertising Methods,* 4th ed. Englewood Cliffs, N. J.: Prentice-Hall, 1974.

Do's and Don'ts in Advertising Copy. Washington, D.C.: Council of Better Business Bureaus, undated.

The Effects of Comparative Television Advertising that Names Competing Brands. New York: Ogilvy & Mather, 1975.

GREENBERG, ALLAN, "Copy Research," *Handbook of Advertising Management,* ed. Roger Barton. New York: McGraw-Hill, 1970.

HOBBS, WHIT, "Copy Strategy," *Handbook of Advertising Management,* ed. Roger Barton. New York: McGraw-Hill, 1970.

HOPKINS, CLAUDE, *Scientific Advertising.* New York: Crown, 1966.

KEISER, STEPHEN K., "Awareness of Brands and Slogans," *Journal of Advertising Research* (August 1975): 37–43.

LEAVITT, CLARK, "Information Processing Theory: New Ideas for Copy Testing," *Marketing in Turbulent Times and Marketing: The Challenges and the Opportunities.* Combined Proceedings of the American Marketing Association, 1975.

LUCK, DAVID J., HUGH G. WALES, DONALD A. TAYLOR, and RONALD S. RUBIN, *Marketing Research,* 5th ed. Englewood Cliffs, N. J.: Prentice-Hall, 1978.

MCMAHAN, HARRY WAYNE, "Alltime Ad Triumphs Reveal Key Success Factors Behind Choice of '100 Best,'" *Advertising Age* (April 12, 1976): 74–78.

PRASAD, V. KANTI, "Communication-Effectiveness of Comparative Advertising: a Laboratory Analysis," *Journal of Marketing Research* (May 1976), 128–37.

RINEY, HAROLD, *How to Write Advertising and Stay Out of Jail.* New York: American Association of Advertising Agencies, 1975.

SCHWAB, VICTOR O., *How to Write a Good Advertisement.* New York: Harper, 1962.

TANNENBAUM, STANLEY I., and ANDREW G. KERSHAW, "For and Against Comparative Advertising," *Advertising Age* (July 5, 1976), 25.

TYLER, WILLIAM D., "Universal Key to Ads That Work: Good Old-fashioned Simplicity," *Advertising Age* (June 28, 1976): 44–46.

ZALTMAN, GERALD, and PHILIP C. BURGER, *Marketing Research.* Hinsdale, Ill.: Dryden, 1975.

16

The Headline/Visualization Match Layouts

Up to now we have been speaking of ideas in terms of copy. Now we want to enlarge the scope of our effectiveness by thinking of copy and visualization at one time, as a total concept.

Concept is defined as "an idea of something, mentally combining all its elements." In creating an advertisement, the chief elements with which we deal are headlines and visualization. Sometimes the headline and picture need each other to make sense. Or the visualization gives a realistic picture of what the headline says, each reinforcing the other. Often the picture interprets imaginatively what the copy says, the combined effort of matching headline and copy being referred to as a *total concept.*

The importance of thinking of ideas in terms of a total concept was emphasized by an advertising agency seeking two art directors. Its ad in *Advertising Age* read:

> We want total concept people who believe they can write as good a headline as some of our writers (because our writers, more often than not, have great visual ideas).

Often an agency art director will be teamed up with a copywriter in developing a concept for a new campaign, ending up with the art director suggesting a headline and the copywriter suggesting a visualization for it, so closely is their thinking intertwined. When such teams are asked, "How do you create your ideas?" their invariable answer is, "We go off in all directions, and—flash!—there

341

*"We're at the edge of a concept, Miss Lawrence.
Rush in a fresh cassette."*

it is!" That was the creative leap! Which is the same answer you get when one person alone comes up with such ideas. But behind that creative leap is disciplined thinking. Therefore, instead of thinking of headlines and visualization as separate elements, we will now think of them together in creating one striking concept to meet a marketing problem.

What is visualizing an idea?

To visualize an idea is to form a mental picture of it. You do not have to be an artist to visualize an idea and to think in terms of pictures. Suppose you were asked to suggest a visualization of golfing. You might think of a player blasting out of a sand trap or completing a beautiful swing. You might show a locker room scene. The scope of visualizing is boundless. (Just for fun, how would you visualize Success?) In creating an advertisement, you can describe your visualizing idea in words or in the crudest sketch for an artist to carry out—unless you are the artist creating the ad. The important thing in visualizing is to imagine the kind of picture you think would express your idea.

A marketing approach to visualizing

Before you embark on any creative project, spend time with the marketing department and get agreement on:

▲ the special, significant benefit the product offers

▲ the marketing problem to be overcome with the competition and in getting acceptance of the public

When you have this information, write a statement of the one thing you would say about the product if that were all you could say. This is your basic statement or theme.

The creative leap

Try making different types of headlines out of that statement, in as many ways as you can. Suggest any visual ideas you may want to go with the headlines, or try a reverse deal: think of a picture in which the product would fit and try writing a headline to go with it. You will find that ideas beget ideas. Make as many versions of the basic idea as you can. Be as imaginative as you want to be, provided the end result delivers the basic message. Take from this collection the concept that delivers the message best. That is the concept for the ad.

You might say that's a lot of work. You have now learned the first lesson in creating a total concept for a good ad on which the copy can be written and an illustration prepared. You have made the creative leap.

The entire purpose of this approach is to guide your thinking, so that whatever creative ideas you offer will be respected as being in the direction of helping to solve the marketing problem. They will make good "selling" ads. Some good examples follow.

Talon zipper

Special significant benefit: the Talon zipper is dependable.

Marketing problem: To make women aware of the importance of having dependable zippers on the garments they buy and to look for a Talon zipper.

Basic statement: You can depend upon Talon zippers to stay closed at all times.

The Breaks of the Game.

You couldn't resist that adorable little tennis dress. But how were you to know that when you attacked at the net, your zipper would be the one to surrender?

You should have made sure the dress had a zipper you could rely on. Like the Talon Zephyr® Nylon zipper.

Its performance has been proven for years on tennis courts all over the world.

That's why Talon is known as a quality zipper. And why it's your clue that the rest of the dress is well-made, too. The next time you buy a tennis dress (or any active sportswear), look for the Talon name.

Even if you have an undependable volley, at least you'll have a dependable zipper.

Talon THE WORLD'S QUALITY ZIPPER

The Talon Zephyr Nylon Zipper says a lot about what it's in.

TALON. A textron COMPANY © 1970

THE CREATIVE LEAP: *Instead of showing the advantage of using the Talon zipper, this ad shows the great disadvantages of not having one on a garment. Observe the excellent placement of the subject in the foreground, in a natural situation. An example of headline and illustration needing each other.*

LOOK WHAT YOU CAN DO WITH ONE CAN OF SPAM®

(1)

(2)

(3)

(4)

(5)

(6)

A lot of meat. But not a lot of money.

SPAM is a special blend of pork shoulder with ham. It makes a great sandwich with (1) cream cheese and scallions on white bread, (2) sweet pickle relish on sesame bun, (3) grilled Cheddar cheese on pumpernickel, (4) baked beans on wiener bun, (5) tomato, lettuce and mayonnaise on white bread, (6) sauerkraut and Swiss cheese on dark rye.

Best of all, when you have a hungry family to feed, you can make them all the way we did here. With just one, 12-ounce can of SPAM.

≋Hormel≋
FINE FOOD PRODUCTS

SPAM is a registered trademark for a pork product packed only by Hormel.

PLATE 1. The headline offers a benefit and a challenge. Sandwiches are stacked to attract attention and tell the whole story quickly, without confusion. Numbered and identified below the picture, the sandwiches tempt the reader to try them soon. (See discussion, p. 353.)

Bacardi rum mixes with everything.

Except driving.

Courtesy Bacardi Imports, Inc. Advertising agency: Ross Roy of New York Inc.

PLATE 2. An ingenious, striking arrangement of bottle caps shows the variety of mixers with which the product may be used. (See discussion, p. 353.)

MGB sports car

SPECIAL SIGNIFICANT BENEFIT: An open sports car which is unique among hard-top cars.

MARKETING PROBLEM: To reach a sports-loving audience who would like the freedom of an open car, with lively performance.

BASIC STATEMENT: This car is especially made for people who like the feeling of great freedom when driving.

THE CREATIVE LEAP: *This startling picture of a hang glider above a headline and a car quickly attracts youthful, adventurous people most likely to be interested in this sports car. It sets the tone for the description of the car.*

Hanes pantyhose

SPECIAL SIGNIFICANT BENEFIT: Makes women's legs look attractive.

MARKETING PROBLEM: To takes Hanes out of price competition by showing how it offers qualities that cheaper pantyhose cannot supply.

BASIC STATEMENT: Men like the way Hanes looks.

THE CREATIVE LEAP: *Observe how the slogan has been interpreted in head-line form and how headline and picture need each other.*

Lysol spray disinfectant

SPECIAL SIGNIFICANT BENEFIT: A household disinfectant that also kills unpleasant odors.

MARKETING PROBLEM: To increase frequency of use. The specific goal here was to get people to carry Lysol with them when they go away for the summer.

BASIC STATEMENT: You need the protection of Lysol when you go away this summer.

THE CREATIVE LEAP: *A literal photographic interpretation of headline, suggesting a family on a summer vacation. A mother and daughter entering a public restroom subtly hints of sanitary problems that may be encountered in a strange environment.*

Pan Am airline

SPECIAL SIGNIFICANT BENEFIT: The American airline that can take you to 98 cities in 65 countries.

MARKETING PROBLEM: To dispose American travelers to use Pan Am whenever they go abroad, wherever they want to go.

BASIC STATEMENT: Whenever you intend to travel to any foreign country, think of Pan Am, with its worldwide experience.

It's easier to remember where we don't go.

Our apologies to the Antarctica Tourist Board.

For despite the fact we have the world's largest fleet of 747s.

And despite the fact we have 28,000 people who've made a profession out of taking Americans to foreign lands.

And despite the fact we have a route structure that takes in 98 cities in 65 countries.

There's still one continent we don't fly to.

Of course, tastes may change radically.

In which case, we'll open

Antarctica to air travel.

Even as we opened every other continent.

And take the apology back and start taking tourists.

America's airline to the world.

See your travel agent.

THE CREATIVE LEAP: *A reverse twist, supported by a dramatic and unexpected picture, drives home a fact that would otherwise be dull.*

Red Wing trail boot

SPECIAL SIGNIFICANT BENEFIT: A boot especially designed for the hiker, shooter, camper, anyone who likes the outdoors.

MARKETING PROBLEM: To point out specific qualities and distinguishing details.

BASIC STATEMENT: Here is a boot with many special features designed to meet the requirements of any outdoor person.

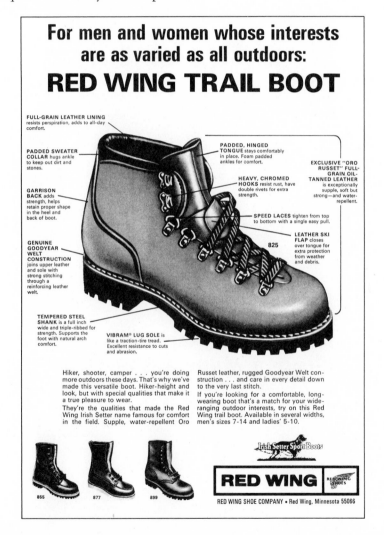

THE CREATIVE LEAP: *The headline reaches a selected audience, the visualization and copy are clearly related, and specific advantages are labeled on the well-drawn shoe. A good example of directly matching visualization with copy.*

Dynamo® laundry detergent

SPECIAL SIGNIFICANT BENEFIT: Saves money by using a smaller quantity than other detergents per wash.

MARKETING PROBLEM: Direct competition of giant advertisers who spend a lot of money on full-page ads in full color.

BASIC STATEMENT: Use less, get better results than with other detergents.

THE CREATIVE LEAP: *The quarter-cup of Dynamo® that will clean a whole wash is colored blue and effectively shown in a quarter-page space. Who says you need elaborate four-color artwork to visualize an idea?*

Spam® Luncheon Meat

SPECIAL SIGNIFICANT BENEFIT: SPAM® Luncheon Meat is a well-known and well-liked meat preparation,—appetizing, convenient, versatile, and economical.

MARKETING PROBLEM: SPAM® Luncheon Meat has long been on the market. Many users have become accustomed to serving it in just a limited number of ways. The problem was to increase the variety of its uses. The creative problem was to do so in a distinctive way and to encourage immediate use.

BASIC STATEMENT: "There are many kinds of sandwiches you can make with SPAM® Luncheon Meat."

For the creative leap, see color plate 1, following page 344.

Bacardi rum

SPECIAL SIGNIFICANT BENEFIT: Whatever mixer you use, you can enjoy Bacardi with it.

MARKETING PROBLEM: To increase use of the product by getting people to use rum with their favorite mixer.

BASIC STATEMENT: It mixes with everything.

For the creative leap, see color plate 2 in the preceding color insert.

Top Choice dog food

SPECIAL SIGNIFICANT BENEFIT: All dog lovers look for food that their dogs will like and that have high nutritional value. Here is a dog food made with real beef and beef by-products, in addition to vegetables and vitamins.

MARKETING PROBLEM: To differentiate Top Choice's benefits from those of other dog foods and to show that it is enticing to the dog.

For the creative leap, see color plate 3 in the preceding group.

Texaco

A PUBLIC AFFAIRS PROBLEM: Among the public affairs problems besetting oil companies is the public's lack of comprehension of the cost of finding oil. Added to this is the general lack of interest in reading about oil companies' problems, especially when they involve many technical difficulties in finding oil. How, in one ad, you can say something to get attention, make a point clear, and help change public opinion is a challenge indeed.

The creative leap can be seen in color plate 4 in the preceding color pages.

Nice'n Easy hair coloring

SPECIAL SIGNIFICANT BENEFIT: Nice'n Easy results in beautiful coloring, healthy-looking hair, and honest colors that beam.

MARKETING PROBLEM: In a very competitive field, each brand offers to beautify hair in its own special way. The problem is to come up with an altogether different type of appeal.

BASIC STATEMENT: Clairol is good for your personality as well as for your hair.

For preliminary layouts leading to the ad, see pp. 371–72. For the creative leap, see color plate 8.

Layouts

An advertisement is made up of parts: headline, illustration, copy, logotype. There may be a subheadline, several different illustrations of varying importance, long or short copy, a coupon, an infinite variety. We shall now discuss putting these together in an orderly form called the *layout* of the advertisement. The term *layout* is one of the many used in advertising in two senses. First, it means the total appearance of the advertisement, its design, the composition of its elements. You will hear it said (we hope), "That is an attractive layout." The term *layout* also means the physical rendering of the design for the ad, its blueprint for production purposes. You will hear someone say, "Here's the copy and the layout," as he hands another person a typed page and a drawing. Right now we are talking about the layout as the overall design of an advertisement.

The layout person as editor

Although the person who created the visual idea may be the same as the one who makes the layout, the two functions are different. The visualizer designs the furniture to go into a room; a layout person arranges it. The visualizer translates an idea into visual form; a layout person takes that illustration and all the other elements that are to go into the ad and makes an orderly, attractive arrangement.

Before putting pencil to paper, however, the layout person—usually an art director—reviews all the elements. The first task is to decide what is most important. Is it the headline? The picture? The copy? How important is the package? Should the product itself be shown and, if so, should it be shown in some special environment or in use? Is this essentially an ad to tell a fast story with a picture and headline, or is it a long copy ad with illustration only an incidental feature? The importance of the element determines its size and placement within the advertisement. The layout person picks the most important feature and builds the ad around that.

Getting meaningful attention

Every advertisement in a publication directly competes for attention with every other advertisement and with the editorial matter. It is axiomatic in advertising that a person must first pay attention to your advertisement, if it is to be

Fedders heat pump air conditioner cuts winter fuel bills

Saves on summer cooling, too!

The money you save operating your Fedders Flexhermetic II heat pump air conditioner to warm your home in the winter can pay for the cost of operating the Flexhermetic II heat pump air conditioner to cool your home in summer.

The Flexhermetic II heat pump air conditioner is a single system that performs like two...to provide comfort all year long. In summer it's a super efficient central air conditioner that removes heat from your home at an exceptionally low operating cost and leaves it comfortably cool and dry. In winter the Flexhermetic II heat pump air conditioner is reversed automatically and it becomes a heating system...a heating system that uses the natural heat always present in the outdoor air (82 percent of heat in the air that was available at 100°F is still available at 0°F).

Because it uses this natural heat, the Fedders heat pump air conditioner can achieve dramatic savings in winter fuel bills when compared to straight electric heat. Electric heat has a C.O.P.* of 1.0 and provides 3413 BTUs of heat per kilowatt hour. Fedders Flexhermetic II model CKH024B7A outdoor unit and CFJ024CQA indoor unit provide a C.O.P. of 2.6 at 47°F outdoor temperature or 8874 BTUs of heat per kilowatt hour. It is easy to see how savings can quickly add up to offset the low operating cost of Flexhermetic II heat pump cooling.

The Fedders heat pump air conditioner is exceptionally reliable and efficient because of the Fedders Rotor-H compressor that was specifically designed for heat pump operation. Its smooth rotary motion with only three basic moving parts (less to wear out, less to go wrong), its solid construction, its special low-friction Carblucon™ bearings (this a spectacular engineering achievement in its own right) set new high standards of reliability.

So reliable in fact is the Rotor-H compressor that Fedders makes available a four-year extended full warranty in addition to the one year standard parts warranty. The super-efficient Rotor-H compressor is the heart of a system designed and constructed to match its unparalleled reliability and performance.

So no matter if you're adding on or replacing, Fedders makes central air conditioning and heating more affordable. For more information on how you can save with Fedders, write Fedders Air Conditioning Sales Co., Dept. HB, Edison, New Jersey 08817.

*C.O.P. stands for Coefficient of Performance, the ratio of heat output to energy consumed.

FEDDERS
the most comforting name in air conditioning

Some advertisements are chiefly copy.

Good news travels fast.

And it travels in masterful style. Introducing the new Honda CB-400F. The power and smoothness of a mighty 408cc four-cylinder, overhead cam engine. The versatility of a slick six-speed transmission which makes the most of this power.

The CB-400F is a fabulous road bike. Thanks to handling features that include a long-travel free valve front suspension, new riding position, handlebars, footpegs and shift pedal. And how about those four-into-one pipes? Purring power! Naturally, there's a burly disc brake up front.

Plus a whole array of other features you'd expect with your Honda. Like the electric starter interlock. The engine emissions control system. The combination ignition/front fork locking system. And much more. See the new CB-400F at your Honda dealer's.

And be ready to take power—in style!

HONDA
Good things happen on a Honda.

Some advertisements are chiefly picture, but this picture is alive with action.

read. Many sins have been committed in the name of this oversimplified directive, because you can use an odd device or a freak drawing that will catch a person's eye long enough for him to discover that it was only a lure that mislead him. The real art in getting attention in advertising is to get meaningful attention to an idea that immediately relates the product to the reader's life.

The skill in making a layout is to assemble all elements of the ad into one pleasing arrangement. Here are some guides that may be helpful.

Composing the elements

Unity. All creative work begins by seeing a subject as a whole unit. A face is more than eyes and nose and mouth; it is a complete expression of personality. People smile not only with their mouths but with their eyes. Thus a layout must also be conceived in its entirety, with all its parts related to each other, to give one overall, unified effect.

Balance. By balance, we mean the relationship usually between the right-hand side and the left hand side of the advertisement.

When objects to the right and left sides of the page match each other in size, shape, and intensity of color and are placed opposite each other, the balance is called *formal* balance. This kind of balance is the easiest to achieve. It makes the easiest reading, but it tends to be static.

Informal balance. The optical center of a page, measured from top to bottom, is ⅝ths of the way up the page, thus differing from the mathematical center. (To test this, take a blank piece of paper, close your eyes, then open them and quickly place a dot at what you think is the center of the page. The chances are that it will be above the mathematical center.) Imagine that on the optical center, a seesaw is balanced. We know that a lighter weight on the seesaw can easily balance a heavier one by being farther away from the fulcrum. The "weight" of an element in an advertisement may be gauged by its size, its degree of blackness, its color, or its shape. Objects are placed seemingly at random on the page, but in such relation to each other that the page as a whole feels in balance. This type of arrangement requires more thought than the simple bisymmetric formal balance, but the effects can be imaginative and distinctive.

Flow. We speak now of that quality in an ad that causes the reader's eyes to flow naturally through the advertisement. In formal balance, that is no problem; the reader begins at the top and goes toward the bottom. But in informal balance, the art is to attract attention to a clear focal point, and by having optical stepping stones leading from there to the end, hold the ad together and lead the reader through the copy. Flow may also be helped by the line of direction of the artwork sweeping across the page. It may be helped by *gaze motion;* that is, having people in the picture look toward the center of attention or perhaps leading the eye to it by means of other elements of the ad. (One basic rule: never have a person look out of an ad.)

Color is a great enhancer of print advertising. It can bring brightness and attractiveness to any ad, and it is particularly important for ads of products that are sold because of color—cosmetics, drapery, jewelry, fashion, carpeting, appe-

Color in advertising

While the price of food is going up, the price of cooking it is going down.

While the price of food is going up, the price of cooking is going down.

We're not going to let a little inflation keep you from becoming a great cook.

So to show you that there are other ways to save money besides macaroni and cheese, we're giving you 4 special offers. On 4 incredible Farberware appliances that can turn an unaccomplished cook into an accomplished one. Without cooking lessons or practice.

Three of our specials cost $29.99 each; the fourth is $49.99. They'll all have you cooking like you've never cooked before and saving money before you make your first dish.

Our big 10" x 15" Open Hearth® Broiler/Rotisserie,* for $49.99, will broil anything from hamburgers to scampi. And rotiss things like turkey and roast beef. While the

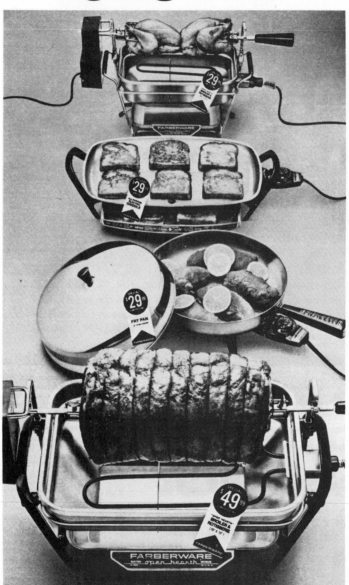

*U.S. Pat. No. 3,240,147

food cooks, the cook will stay cool.

Our Farberware Griddle and Hot Plate, will help you cook a family-full of french toast, without using all 4 burners and the oven, too. Or 10 fried eggs. All at once.

Our 8½" x 12" Open Hearth® Broiler/Rotisserie makes juicy, evenly browned everything. With no smoke, and just a little help from you. In the kitchen or out.

When you get tired of the kitchen, you can plug our Electric Fry Pan into the dining room and serve sukiyaki. Or curry. Or beef bourgignon.

Before our special ends, your new Farberware appliance will have you cooking like the born cook you always thought you weren't. And no one will ever believe you got so much talent for so little. We're certainly not going to tell.

FARBERWARE®
AN LCA DIVISION

Formal balance. Also an example of an ad that is half illustration and half copy.

Hunt's Prima Salsa.®
"It's thicker and zestier than Ragú."

We're delighted when spaghetti sauce lovers like Boston's Mr. Frank Gagliardi tell us, "Hunt's Prima Salsa® is thicker and zestier than regular Ragu* Spaghetti Sauce." That's because he's pretty fussy about his spaghetti sauce. If Hunt's Prima Salsa pleases him, imagine how it will please you!

The fact is, among people who really like their spaghetti sauce, most preferred Hunt's Prima Salsa to Ragu.

Next time you're looking for spaghetti sauce, try delicious Hunt's Prima Salsa. You'll find it thicker and zestier than Ragu.

Frank Gagliardi
3 North Square
Boston, Mass.

UNRETOUCHED PHOTO SHOWS THE DIFFERENCE.

RAGU—See how the regular Ragu Spaghetti Sauce begins to come through the strainer in a matter of a few seconds.

HUNT'S PRIMA SALSA—It's thicker and zestier than Ragu. It even <u>looks</u> better—it stays in the strainer.

© 1977 Hunt-Wesson Foods, Inc.

*Ragu is a trademark of Ragu Foods, Inc.

Available in Three Flavors: Regular, With Mushrooms, and Meat Flavored.

Informal balance.

359

Gaze motion at work. Everything points to baby's tooth.

tizing foods. With most full-page and many half-page advertisements in magazines in color, there is great pressure on the competition—and from the advertiser's own trade—to use color for ads that can be enhanced by it. Color talks its own psychological language. To make a drink look cool, there will be plenty of blue in the background; to make a room look warm (for heating advertisements), there will be plenty of red in the background. Springtime suggests light colors; autumn, the dark tones. Thus, a clue to the choice of the dominating color may often be found in the mood in which the product is being shown.

One goal in creating a layout is to have the ad stand out among all the ads in a medium, particularly all ads for similar products. The first step in creating national advertising (there are different rules of the game for other forms of advertising) is to break away from whatever is the layout trend among others in the same field. Yes, there are styles in layouts and great waves of follow-the-leader take place. Result: all ads in the field are in the same mold. Make believe you are the first person in your field to advertise. Create a layout to fit the mood and nature of your message.

The search for distinction

Among the techniques for creating distinction, size is a familiar one. You will get more attention if you take a full-page rather than a half-page ad in a newspaper. A double-page spread in a magazine is obviously more attractive than a single page. The great problem is cost. Twice as much space does not give you twice as much attention, and it soon chews up the budget. The only time such use of space may be worth the cost is on those exceptional occasions when you have a special announcement to make, as for a new car model.

Other techniques may use an extra large headline or the reverse; and when everyone is using large-size type, set the headline smaller with lots of white space around it. You can establish a different style of art work or establish a distinctive art subject. Marlboro cigarettes were once known as a lady's cigarette. They came in white boxes with delicate lettering. The positioning was changed to make it a man's cigarette, and the company reached out for the most masculine type of man, the cowboy who rides around in what is now "Marlboro Country"—a valuable visual property, setting Marlboro apart from other cigarette advertising. Another example of breaking away from tradition is found in the liquor field, for which four-color pages are the standard magazine formula. Yet Jack Daniels broke away from that tradition by running all their ads in black and white. Those ads not only stand out among all the four-color liquor ads but represent a tremendous saving in costs. Sometimes a product will become known for always having a fresh-looking ad, each clearly delivering the same story in a different way. But at least the reader will not confuse the brand with others in the field.

This is not meant to be a catalog of techniques for achieving distinction. It merely lists a few of the myriad devices for making layouts distinctive.

Happy Mother's Day.

A day like today can be Mother's Day.
And the best gift you can give is a gift
of yourself. Dial Long Distance.
It's the next best thing to being there.

Distinction in size of lettering.

362

The businessman's best friend... ADT's Electronic Watchdog System.

His bark is his bite.

Because ADT Electronic Watchdog Systems sound the early alarm to protect you from fire, burglary and theft.

No one has credentials like ADT. We manufacture over 40,000 separate components for systems designed to prevent loss of life and property. Even the most advanced electronic circuits, minicomputers and microprocessors are designed or programmed by our engineers, assembled in our plants, and tested by our own quality control experts. Since most ADT systems are operated and maintained by us, we're our own biggest customer. Biggest and toughest.

To service this equipment, we have over 5,500 people in the field. By far the largest field force in the industry.

And 130 central monitoring stations cover the nation. Over 100 years experience qualifies us better than anyone else to help you choose what kind of systems you need — for homes, retail stores, commercial buildings, and manufacturing plants.

For your own peace of mind, talk to an ADT consultant about our Electronic Watchdog Systems for your home or your business.

ADT. One World Trade Center, N.Y., N.Y. 10048.

Call toll-free 800-821-2270. Ext. 704.
In Missouri, 800-892-7655. Ext. 704.

ADT

DANSKINS ARE NOT JUST FOR DANCING

THEY'RE FOR WISHMAKING, BIRTHDAY PARTYING, AND FOR LOOKING VERY CHIC ON THE FIRST DAY OF SCHOOL. ZIPPY ZIP-UP-THE-FRONT JUMPSUIT WITH U-NECK, 2T-4T 13.75, 4-6X 14.75; WITH CLASSIC, TURTLENECK SWEATER 2T-4T 6.00, 4-6X 8.00. BOTH OF 100% NYLON. LEARN-TO-COUNT T-SHIRT OF NYLON AND POLYESTER, 2T-4T 6.50, 4-6X 7.50; MATCHING STRAIGHT-LEG PANTS, 2T-4T 7.50, 4-6X 9.75. ALL ARE KNIT FULL-FASHIONED. AVAILABLE AT BLOOMINGDALE'S, B. ALTMAN & CO., MACY'S (NEW YORK), ABRAHAM & STRAUS, GERTZ, MARTIN'S, MARSHALL FIELD, WOODWARD & LOTHROP, JOSKE'S (SAN ANTONIO), IVEY'S (FLORIDA), DONALDSON'S (MINNEAPOLIS) AND OTHER FINE STORES. FOR 96 PAGE CATALOG, SEND 25¢ TO DANSKIN, INC., DEPT. NY8, 1114 AVE. OF THE AMERICAS, N.Y., N.Y. 10036.

DANSKIN®

Distinction by unusual use of white space.

From the Monet summer White Enamel Collection. At fine stores.

Monet®

Master Jeweler

© Monet

Distinction through design. The ad ran as a bleed on all sides.

**Preparing
the layouts**

We now refer to layouts as the actual drawings used in planning the final design of the advertisement. Different types of layouts represent different stages in the development of the advertisement. For the first ad of an important new campaign for a big schedule of color magazine ads, an elaborate step-by-step series of layouts may be prepared, identified as follows:

▲ *thumbnail sketches:* miniature drawings trying out different arrangements of the layout elements. The best of these will be selected for

▲ *rough layouts:* drawings, the actual size of the ad. All elements are presented more clearly, to simulate the way the ad is to look. The best of these will be chosen for

▲ *the comprehensive* or *mechanical layout* (often just called *the comp* or *the mechanical:* all the type set and pasted in place exactly as it is to appear in the printed advertisement. Because art work is drawn 1½ times the actual size it will be in the ad (for sharper reproduction) and is prepared separately, it is precisely indicated on the comprehensive by blank boxes of the exact final size. This layout will be used not only for client approval but also for making the final print or plate.

Once a basic ad for a campaign has been approved, layouts for subsequent ads usually consist just of a rough layout and a finished layout.

**Layouts for small
advertisements**

Small advertisements are usually one-column ads up to four inches deep. They appear in many magazines, and numerous businesses have been built by them. Successful small advertisements usually have a strong promise in a selective headline with a functional picture. The eye takes in all of a small advertisement at one time, so that a liberal part of the space is used merely to be noticed. A small advertisement is not a big advertisement reduced; it is created by abstracting the one or two most essential elements of a big advertisement (if one has already been created) and emphasizing one of them.

**The artist's
medium**

The tool or material used to render an illustration is the artist's *medium,* the term *medium* being used in a different sense than it is in *advertising medium* (as TV or magazines). The most popular medium in advertising is photography. Other popular ones are pen and ink, pencil, crayon, and wash. Perhaps a photograph may be used as the main illustration for an ad, but for the smaller secondary illustration, pen and ink will be used. The choice of the artist's medium depends upon the effect desired, the paper on which it is to be printed, the printing process to be used, and most important, the availability of an artist who is effective in the desired medium.

**Trade practice
in buying
commercial art**

Creating an advertisement may require two types of artistic talent: one, the imaginative person who helps create the visual idea, with a copywriter or alone, and who makes the master layout; two, an artist who does the finished art of the illustrations. In larger cities, agencies have staff art directors and layout people who visualize and create original layouts. Agencies also have studios and artists to handle routine work.

DOES MORE JOBS IN *LESS* TIME

The red handle with the black head —exclusively Plumb.

You'll find many uses for this Plumb hatchet. It chops, pounds, pulls nails and cuts. Handiest of hand tools, it does better work faster, in the home or work shop.

PLUMB
HAMMERS
HATCHETS
AXES
FILES

HOW TO GET THE MOST OUT OF AN OUTBOARD

FREE BOOK for outboard skippers

This 64-page handbook, written by a staff of experts, tells you all you need to know to get the most out of your outboard. Neat Nautical Tricks, Safety Afloat, Navigation, How to Select a Boat and Motor, many more subjects. Practical, authoritative, generously illustrated. Write for free copy now: Dept. SI49, Scott-Atwater Mfg. Co., Inc., Minneapolis 13, Minn.

- How to have more fun afloat
- How to make an 'eggshell landing'
- How to rig remote controls
- Trouble shooting made easy

Hook 'em and cook 'em the Indian way

● Sneak up on the deep, dark pools where the big ones hide. It's easy in a perfectly balanced Old Town Canoe. This modern birch-bark is built for sportsmen. Steady and strong, yet light to carry. Made with Old Town skill to last for many a moon.

FREE CATALOG shows all kinds of canoes for paddling, sailing or outboards. Also outboard boats, including big all wood family boats. Sailboats. Rowboats. Dinghies. Address Old Town Canoe Company, 562 Elm Street, Old Town, Maine.

"Old Town Canoes"

New IMPROVED *Electric* MOTO-SAW

Only $5.85 (with 3 Saw Blades) Postpaid

SAFE AS A HAND SAW JUST GUIDE IT!

More like magic than any tool you ever saw. Imagine an electric scroll saw only slightly heavier than a hand coping saw . . . a tool that takes no effort to run, no pressure to feed. Works at any angle—on big assembly jobs or on the tiniest piece you can hold in your fingers. Runs 7200 strokes a minute . . . so fast the blade seems to stand still. Sturdily built . . . only two moving parts . . . never needs oiling. Easily cuts intricate designs —so smooth it eliminates sanding. Novice or craftsman, a thrill awaits you when you get a Moto-Saw in your hand. Thousands of satisfied users.

Patented
No Limit to Length of Stock it Will Cut. Saws to Center of 19″ Widths.

It's fast . . . Cuts on an average of 1 ft. per minute up to ¾″ medium hard wood. Operates on 110-120 v. 50 or 60 cycle alternating current. **MONEY-BACK GUARANTEE:** Buy Moto-Saw from your dealer. If he cannot supply you, send only $5.85 (check or M.O.) and we will ship postpaid; or send only $1 now, and pay postman balance plus postage. Your MONEY-BACK if not delighted after 5 days' trial.

DREMEL MFG. CO., Dept. S319-D, Racine, Wis.

Advertisements this size, from 28 to 50 lines, are the backbone of many advertising campaigns. Copy and layout are planned at the same time to achieve these strong promise headlines, the variety of illustrative effects, the ingenuity and simplicity of layouts, the clarity of typography.

Before they can even tell time they're always reminding you how quickly it passes

Metropolitan

From thumbnail sketch . . .

Before they can even tell time, they're always reminding you how quickly it passes.

🟊**Metropolitan**
Where the future is now.

. . . to rough layout . . .

Before they can even tell time, they're always reminding you how quickly it passes.

If you're like most parents, you measure time in outgrown sneakers and jackets.

Children are a constant reminder of the obvious: that time waits for no man, or woman, or wardrobe. And while you and your family are racing toward the future, it helps to take a moment to consider what it might be like once you arrive. That's where Metropolitan Life can help.

We think insurance should be more than just security for your family. While one third of all the money Metropolitan pays out goes to beneficiaries, *the other two thirds goes to living policyholders.* And that's money you can use to help pay for your future.

Take the time to listen when a Metropolitan representative calls. We can help design not just an insurance program for you, but a secure future. And it's never too soon to begin.

Because your Size-2 will soon be Size-4.

Then a Size-6. Then a Size-8. Then...

✻ Metropolitan
Where the future is now

. . . and the finished ad.

Courtesy Clairol, Inc.
Advertising agency: Doyle Dane Bernbach, Inc.

Thumbnail for Clairol ad.

It lets me be me.

In hair color, as in make-up, clothes, love, work...a woman wants to be herself. Not somebody else's idea of what she is, or should be. That's what women like about Nice 'n Easy.® Whether you want to

color or conceal, to change a little or a lot, Nice 'n Easy assures you of beautiful coverage, healthy-looking hair and honest color that becomes part of you.

No wonder, now more than ever, it sells the most. Nice 'n Easy. From Clairol.

Finished layout and type proof for Clairol ad. See color plate 8 for finished ad.

In the largest advertising centers—New York, Chicago, Los Angeles, San Francisco—a host of free-lance artists and photographers specialize in certain fields—fashion, sports pictures, cartoons, food, character studies. They may be called in for preparing the final art of such subjects. In fact, agencies in many other cities often go to one of the major art centers to buy their graphic art work for special assignments.

There are two important points to observe in buying art work, especially photographs. First is the *legal release*. You must have written permission from anyone whose picture you will use, whether you took the picture or got it from a publication or an art file. (In the case of a child's picture, you must have a release from the parent or guardian.) The second point to have in mind is to *arrange all terms in advance*. A photographer may take a number of pictures, from which you will select one. What will be the price if you wish to use more than one shot?

"How are we doing?" Starch Reports

In our next chapter, we shall get back to ads, but now we are going to leapfrog into the future. The new ad on which we have been working is appearing in a magazine, and everyone connected with the ad—management as well as the creative team—asks, "How are we doing?" especially against competition. One method of obtaining answers to that question is through the Starch Reports.

Starch is the pioneer service for appraising magazine ads at the primary level of effectiveness, to see how many people noted the ad, associated it with who was doing the advertising, and read most of it. Starch publishes these results for all ads in the magazine issue being researched, so advertisers can make comparisons, especially with the competition. Starch gets its information through personal interviews. A large staff of women call upon householders, by appointment, and go through copies of the magazines with them, page by page. This method of research is called *aided recall*. The information compiled is published in reports such as the one on page 374, which are issued to subscribers. To illustrate, here are two competitive products on the report.

	PERCENTAGES			READERS PER DOLLAR		
	Noted	Associated	Read most	Noted	Associated	Read most
Magnavox color TV	38%	35%	10%	76	70	20
Zenith Chromacolor TV	60	58	15	120	116	30

The Starch Reports are limited to just one aspect of advertising effectiveness: how well does the ad get attention and get the reader into the ad. The total effectiveness of the ad depends at the outset on its performing well on this level.

Studies such as those reported on the accompanying chart are made separately for each issue of each magazine on the list to be studied. Before drawing any conclusions about the effectiveness of a campaign in getting attention and readership, one waits for a number of successive reports.

READERSHIP REPORT

PAGE 3

83 ADS 1/2 PAGE AND OVER
READER'S DIGEST   NOVEMBER 1976

MEN READERS

PAGE	SIZE & COLOR	PRODUCT CATEGORIES — ADVERTISER	COST PENNIES PER READER	RANK IN ISSUE BY NUMBER OF READERS	RANK IN ISSUE BY COST PER READER	PERCENTAGES NOTED	PERCENTAGES ASSOCIATED	PERCENTAGES READ MOST	READERS PER DOLLAR NOTED	READERS PER DOLLAR ASSOCIATED	READERS PER DOLLAR READ MOST	COST RATIOS NOTED	COST RATIOS ASSOCIATED	COST RATIOS READ MOST
		(CONT.) CAMERAS/PHOTOGRAPHIC SUPPLIES												
100	1P4B	KODAK EK4 INSTANT CAMERA	1.0	12	6	56	50	20	112	100	40	187	200	400
213	V1/2P4	EASTMAN KODAK COMPANY G P	.9	33	3	36	31	13	131	112	47	218	224	470
		LUGGAGE/LEATHER GOODS												
238	1P4B	AMERICAN TOURISTER LUGGAGE	1.4	28	22	38	35	12	76	70	24	127	140	240
		PETS/PET FOODS/PET SUPPLIES												
77	1P4B	TABBY CANNED CAT FOOD OFFER	2.6	49	58	30	19	2	60	38	4	100	76	40
		BUSINESS PROPOSALS/RECRUITING												
282	V1/2P	QSP INC BUSINESS PROPOSITION	1.8	64	34	17	13	5	74	57	22	123	114	220
		FLOOR COVERING												
267	1P4B	CONGOLEUM SHINYL VINYL FLOOR	2.0	40	41	34	25	9	68	50	18	113	100	180
		MAJOR APPLIANCES												
8	1P4	SEARS KENMORE COMPACTORS	2.2	45	50	27	23	5	54	46	10	90	92	100
40 X	1S4B	WHITE-WESTINGHOUSE RANGE	4.0	48	71	31	21	4	36	25	5	60	50	50
55	1P4B	K-MART/WHIRLPOOL WASHER & DRYER	1.6	32	27	41	32	1	82	64	2	137	128	20
206	1P	WHIRLPOOL CORPORATION G P	2.4	58	55	19	17	*	46	41	*	77	82	*
248	1P4	KITCHENAID DISHWASHER	3.1	60	65	20	16	2	40	32	4	67	64	40
		SMALL HHLD. APPLIANCES/EQUIP.												
7	1P4	WESTCLOX CLOCKS	1.5	30	25	39	33	2	78	66	4	130	132	40
48	1S4B	K-MART/SMALL APPLIANCES	2.0	17	45	52	46	6	56	49	6	93	98	60
287	1P4B	MR. COFFEE BREWER/FILTERS	1.4	27	20	39	36	8	78	72	16	130	144	160
		RADIOS/TV SETS/PHONOGRAPHS												
20	1P4B	MAGNAVOX TOUCH-TUNE COLOR TV	1.4	28	22	38	35	10	76	70	20	127	140	200
51	1P4B	K-MART/CAPEHART STEREO SYS	1.1	17	10	52	46	11	104	92	22	173	184	220
53	1P4B	K-MART/CAPEHART 1000 STEREO ENSEMBLE	1.0	14	8	54	49	18	108	98	36	180	196	360
57	1P4B	K-MART/PORTABLE RADIO & CASSETTE RECORDER	1.1	19	11	48	45	13	96	90	26	160	180	260
89	1P4B	ZENITH CHROMACOLOR II TV	.9	6	2	60	58	15	120	116	30	200	232	300
229	1P4B	ZENITH ALLEGRO CONSOLE	1.2	22	13	46	43	16	92	86	32	153	172	320
		BUILDING MATERIALS												
17		OWENS-CORNING FIBERGLAS INSULATION/AMERICAN GAS ASSOCIATION SEE COMMUN/PUBLIC UTILITY												
		BLDG. EQUIP./FIXTURES/SYSTEMS												
90	1P4	GE HOME SENTRY SMOKE ALARM	1.0	14	8	51	49	27	102	98	54	170	196	540

* LESS THAN 1/2 OF ONE PERCENT.

| | | MEDIAN READERS/DOLLAR | | | | | | | 60 | 50 | 10 | | | |

READERS PER DOLLAR ARE BASED ON 12,965,000 MEN READERS AND PUBLISHED ONE-TIME SPACE RATES. READER FIGURES
ARE OBTAINED FROM 18,006,799 U.S. A.B.C. CIRC. TIMES MEN PRIMARY READERS PER COPY FROM STARCH ESTIMATES.

A Starch report, showing how well ads get attention and readership.

Once again, TV service technici[ans] give these opinions about Zen[ith]

I. Best Pict[ure]

Again this year, in a na[tional survey] of independent TV service t[echnicians,] selected, more than any other brand, as the color TV with the best picture.

Question: In general, of all the color TV brands you are familiar with, which one would you say has the best overall picture?

Answers:
Zenith 34%
Brand A 21%
Brand B 12%
Brand C 8%
Brand D 7%
Brand E 4%
Brand F 2%
Brand G
Brand H
Other Brands
About Equal
Don't Know

Note: Answers [total more than 100%] due to multiple [answers]

II. Fewest Repairs.

In the same opinion survey, the service technicians selected Zenith, more than any other brand, as the color TV needing the fewest repairs.

Question: In general, of all the color TV brands you are familiar with, which one would you say requires the fewest repairs?

Answers:
Zenith 38%
Brand A 18%
Brand D 9%
Brand B 6%
Brand C 5%
Brand E 3%
Brand F 2%
Brand G 2%
Brand H 2%
Other Brands 2%
About Equal 11%
Don't Know 10%

For survey details, write to the Vice President, Consumer Affairs, Zenith Radio Corporation, 1900 N. Austin Avenue, Chicago, IL 60639.

Th[e]
Model SH2331X,
Simulated [picture]
Bermuda She[ll]
Simulat[ed]

ZENITH
CHROMACOLO[R]
The quality goes in before the name go[es on]

A magazine page that has been through the Starch test.

QUESTIONS

1. Distinguish between visualization and layout.

2. What is meant by a "total concept"? Why is it important to think in terms of a total concept?

3. Explain what is meant by visualizing an idea.

4. What is the creative leap?

5. Name several ways in which the visualization of an idea and the headline need each other. Illustrate with examples from recent advertising.

6. Find several examples from current advertising that you think have excellent visualization. Explain why you think so.

7. What are some of the major guides to developing an effective layout?

8. From contemporary advertising, find three examples reflecting what you consider to be excellent layouts. Explain why you selected the ones you did.

9. Discuss the particular layout problems of small advertisements. From present-day advertising, can you find three excellent examples of small ads (not over four inches)?

10. Describe some of the techniques for creating distinction in advertisements. Pick out three ads with distinctive layouts. What makes them distinctive?

11. Distinguish among the following types of layouts: thumbnail, rough, and comprehensive (or mechanical). Must every advertisement have all these forms? Explain.

12. In your newspapers and magazines, find three different art media used by artists in advertisements.

READING SUGGESTIONS

Art Directors of New York, *Annual of Advertising Art.* New York: Reinhold.

BERRIEN, EDITH HEAL, *Visual Thinking in Advertising.* New York: Holt, 1963.

BURTON, PHILIP WARD, *Which Ad Pulled Best?* 3rd ed. Chicago: Crain Communications, 1975.

CAPLES, JOHN, *Tested Advertising Methods,* 4th ed. Englewood Cliffs, N. J.: Prentice-Hall, 1974.

"A Lesson for the Artist: Function of Layout Is Simple as 1, 2, 3," *Industrial Marketing* (January 1972), 21–25.

"The Measurement and Control of the Visual Efficiency of Advertisements." New York: Advertising Research Foundation, Inc., 1965.

TAYLOR, ROBERT C., and R. D. PETERSON, "A Textbook Model of Ad Creation," *Journal of Advertising Research* (February 1972), 35–41.

TURNBULL, ARTHUR T., and RUSSEL N. BAIRD, *The Graphics of Communication.* New York: Holt, 1964.

PROGRESSIVE STEPS

IN

FOUR-COLOR PROCESS

PRINTING

Four plates (yellow, red, blue, and black) combine to produce the desired colors and contrasts.

Yellow

Blue

Yellow, Red, and Blue

Red

Yellow and Red

Black

Yellow, Red, Blue, and Black

17

Print Production

skip

When the copy for an advertisement has been written, the layout has been made, and the illustrations have been prepared, the material must be assembled into a form that the printer can use for his presses. This conversion process, which is the responsibility of the advertiser or agency, is called *print production*.

The planning of print production is a management function involving much money, and many people: the production department, the copy and art departments, the media department, the account executive, and finally the management executive who will be called upon to approve all expenditures. Anyone entering the marketing and advertising world would do well to understand certain basics of print production, and this is a good time to learn.

Selecting the Printing Process

The first step in print production is to select one of the three major processes by which advertising is printed:

▲ Letterpress printing (from a raised surface)

▲ Offset lithography (from a flat surface)

▲ Rotogravure (from an etched surface)

All the work of print production depends upon the process used. In publication advertising, each publisher has already decided on the printing process, and the advertiser must plan his work accordingly.

Whoever has used a rubber stamp has applied the principle of *letterpress printing*—printing from a raised surface. The surface to be printed stands out in

Letterpress printing

377

relief from the rest of the stamp and gets the ink when pressed against the ink pad. Then, when the stamp is pressed against paper, the message is reproduced. The same principle applies to anything printed by letterpress, whether a rubber-stamped mailing piece or a book of many pages. In letterpress printing, the advertiser or agency must supply photoengravings for all artwork, or duplicates of such plates.

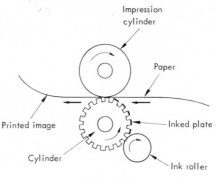

Letterpress.

For generations all presses printed from raised type and from relief plates; some still do. But in advertising and in general publication printing, letterpress has given way to offset and rotogravure.

Offset lithography

Offset is the most popular printing process in the United States. It can print illustrations on rougher paper than can letterpress, and its plates cost less than those of the other major processes. It makes the best use of the photocomposition process. Most periodicals, books, and large runs of direct mail are now printed in offset. This book was printed by offset; earlier editions were printed by letterpress.

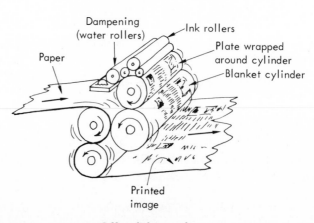

Offset lithography.

Offset printing is done on a rotary press with a thin sheet of aluminum or zinc wrapped around the cylinder. By a photomechanical process, an image is transferred to this plate. The plate is chemically treated so that the nonprinting areas accept water while the greasy printing ink adheres only to the portions to be printed. The principle of lithography is that oil and water do not mix. In *straight lithography* the printing is done directly from the plate (originally, from the stone) onto the paper. In *offset lithography* we go a step further: instead of printing the design directly onto a sheet or roll of paper, an intermediate cylinder is introduced, covered with a rubber blanket, which, in turn, *offsets* it onto the paper.

The advertiser or the agency must supply the artwork and mechanicals or films from which offset plates can be made.

Rotogravure

Rotogravure printing utilizes the photographic method of transferring the printing image to a large copper cylinder used on a rotary printing press. In this process the etching of the cells or wells (tiny depressed printing areas created by means of a screen) is only one to two thousandths of an inch deep; nevertheless, it is an etching. Rotogravure is the printing method for long-run printing, as mail-order catalogs, Sunday newspaper supplements, a growing number of consumer magazines, packaging, and other material with an abundance of photographic copy. It is characterized by relatively high preparatory costs. Yet it is economical for long runs, since it provides excellent color quality with inexpensive inks, on paper stocks usually less costly than those used for letterpress or offset. Major corrections on press, however, are expensive. Rotogravure cylinders are made by the printer, usually from films or art and copy supplied by the advertiser.

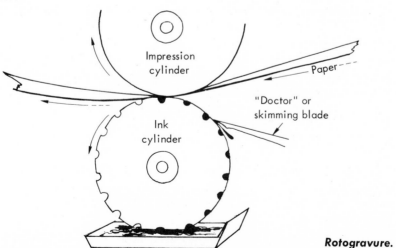

Rotogravure.

Screen printing

There is also one minor, economical process worth knowing about, especially when you work only in broad, flat colors, as for car cards, posters, and point-of-purchase displays. This is *screen printing*, also known as *silk screen printing*. It is a stencil process, especially good for short runs. The stencil of a design can be manually or photographically produced, then placed over a textile or metallic mesh screen. Ink or paint is spread over the screen and, by means of a squeegee, is pushed through screen and stencil onto the paper. This can be done by hand for short runs, or by machine.

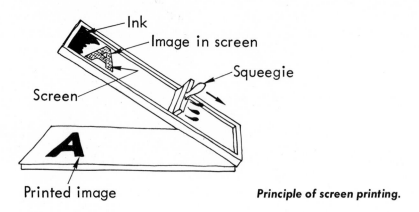

Principle of screen printing.

Planning the Typography

Typography is the art of using type effectively. It entails selecting the style (face) of type to use, deciding upon the sizes in which different elements of the copy are to be set, and preparing the specifications for the typesetter.

Typefaces

Type does not merely convey the words of a message; it can enhance and complement pictures and words. If you were advertising jewelry, you might use a light, decorative type, reflecting the beauty of the jewelry. If you were advertising chain saws, you might use a heavier, straighter type. For products and services that do not have such sharp typographic personalities, you would probably seek a type compatible with the creative tone of the ad. Yes, type talks.

The earliest type letter, now known as black-letter or text, and four other styles of type—Oldstyle Roman, Modern Roman, sans serif, and square serif—have had a lasting influence on the types of today.

Text or black-letter.   Johannes Gutenberg, in the fifteenth century, invented printing from movable type. He fashioned the letters after the hand-lettering style of the scribes in German monasteries, who used wide-pointed reed pens. These types, called *text* or *black-letter*, are seldom seen today in English-speaking countries except in diplomas or ceremonial announcements or for captions.

Oldstyle Roman.   During the Renaissance, type designers seeking to get away from black-letter, found inspiration in letter forms chiseled on old Roman stone monuments. The stone cutters had marked the top and bottom of their letters with a little bar called a *serif.* Oldstyle Roman, often called Oldstyle, is characterized by graceful serifs and by relatively little contrast between thick and thin strokes.

Modern Roman. Late in the eighteenth century there appeared another version of a Roman letter, called *Modern Roman* or just *Modern.* It differs from Oldstyle in that there is a decided contrast between the thicks and thins, and the horizontal serifs are cut sharply, as if by a pointed tool, rather than drawn gracefully by a pen.

Sans serif. This group is characterized by the absence of serifs and by relatively even weighting of the entire letter. Some common examples in this group have become associated with functional, contemporary design. The marginal heads in this book are set in a sans serif type.

Square serif. This is a group of typefaces with strongly pronounced square serifs and evenly weighted strokes.

Type font. An individual letter, numeral, or punctuation mark is called a *character.* (In copy casting, which means counting the number of characters, space between words is usually also counted as a character.) For any face and size of type, a *font* consists of all the lower-case (l.c.) and capital (caps) characters, as well as numerals (figures) and the usual punctuation marks. Some fonts also include small caps (s.c.), which are capitals in lower-case height. THIS LINE IS SET IN SMALL CAPS.

Type fonts and families

ABCDEFGHIJKLMNOPQRSTUVWXYZ
abcdefghijklmnopqrstuvwxyz
1234567890 &?/!$(""'-:;—.,)

This is a font of 10-point Helvetica roman.

A font may be roman or italic. A *roman type* (with a lower-case r) refers to the upright letter form, distinguished from *italic,* which is oblique. Roman (with a capital R) denotes a group of serified type styles, as explained earlier.

THIS LINE IS SET IN ROMAN CAPS.
This line is set in roman, initial cap and lowercase.
THIS LINE IS SET IN ITALIC CAPS.
This line is set in italic, initial cap and lowercase.
THIS LINE IS SET IN CAPS AND SMALL CAPS.

Courtesy Typographic Communications, Inc.,
who set other type specimens in this chapter.

Type family. From a single roman type design, a number of variations are possible by altering letter slant, weight (stroke thickness), and proportion. Each one, however, retains essential characteristics of the basic letter form. There may be italic, semibold, bold, bold condensed, expanded, and so forth. These variations are called a *type family.* A family of type may provide a harmonious variety of types for use within an ad.

Helvetica Thin

Helvetica Light

Helvetica Light Italic

Helvetica

Helvetica Italic

Helvetica Italic Outline

Helvetica Regular Condensed

Helvetica Regular Extended

Helvetica Medium

Helvetica Medium Italic

Helvetica Medium Outline

Helvetica Bold

Helvetica Bold Compact Italic

Helvetica Bold Outline

Helvetica Bold Condensed

Helvetica Bold Condensed Outline

Helvetica Bold Extended

Helvetica Extrabold Condensed

Helvetica Extrabold Condensed Outline

Helvetica Extrabold Ext.

Helvetica Compressed

Helvetica Extra Compressed

Helvetica Ultra Compressed

A family of type retains its basic letterform and style characteristics through all its variations. Some type families consist of only roman, italic, and bold versions. Others, like the popular Helvetica family, have many variations and different stroke thicknesses.

Type sizes are measured in *points,* 72 to the inch. They are determined by the depth of the metal body on which the type character was traditionally cast, including the metal shoulder at top and bottom. Thus, the printed letter, measured from the top of an ascender to the bottom of a descender, is slightly smaller than its point size.

SIZE of type   6 POINT

SIZE of type   8 POINT

SIZE of type   10 POINT

SIZE of type   12 POINT

SIZE of type   14 POINT

SIZE of type   18 POINT

SIZE of type   24 POINT

SIZE of type   30 POINT

SIZE of type   36 POINT

Size of type   48 POINT

You may have two lines of letters of the same point size, yet one appears larger because it has a larger lower-case or x-height (the size of the letter x) and short ascenders and descenders. It looks bigger than one with a small x-height and longer ascenders and descenders. Moral: Before you specify size of type, check a type specimen sheet to see the face in the size you require.

The size of type is determined by the height of the face (not the height of its letter x alone) and includes ascenders, descenders, and shoulders. A point measures almost exactly 1/72 inch. This word is photoset in 72-point Times Roman.

Type sizes below 18 points are normally referred to as *text types,* while sizes from 18 points up are called *display types.* In phototypesetting, the type is photographed, and its size can easily be changed; yet the traditional system of denoting type sizes has been retained.

A pica ruler. ▼

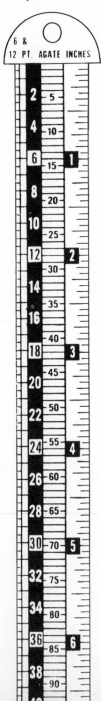

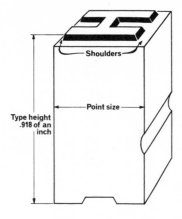

Foundry type used in hand setting. Note shoulders on type. Point size measures the whole block, which explains why a printed letter is slightly less than point size.

Relative size

Relative size

Relative size

▲ *These words are set in the 24-point size of three different typefaces: Bodoni, Century Schoolbook, and Avant Garde medium. Although the point size is identical, the relative size of these three typefaces varies substantially, owing to differences in the x-height. Relative size of a typeface influences its readability.*

Readability of fype is also affected by word spacing. If words are spaced too widely, the line lacks coherence, but they should not "hang at each other's tails." The space between sentences should be the same as the word space within that line. ▼

This line is spaced with en spaces.

This line is spaced with 4-to-the-em spaces.

This line is spaced with 5-to-the-em spaces.

The pica (the pica em).   The width of the line in which type is to be set is stated in *picas*. There are 12 points to the pica and approximately 6 picas to the inch. Areas of composition are usually given in picas (width first, then depth). Pica is the name originally given to 12-point type when all type sizes had names rather than numbers. An *em* is the square of any point size, usually formed by the capital letter M. The 12-point em (which is 12 points wide and 12 points deep) is also known as the *pica em*. An *en* is half of an em.

When lines are set to the same width, as they are on this page, they are said to be *justified.* It is necessary to specify the width only once for all type in one block of copy to be set. This paragraph is set 28 picas wide.

The agate line.   In newspaper advertising and in small-space magazine advertising, the *depth of space* (height of the ad) is measured in terms of *agate lines*, of which there are 14 to a column inch, regardless of how wide a column is. Newspaper space is referred to as depth (agate lines) and width (number of columns): for "100 × 2" read "100 lines deep by 2 columns wide."

Line spacing.   To increase the normal space between lines of metal type, a thin strip of lead, measured in points, was inserted between the metal lines, giving rise to the term *leading* for increasing line space in type. The term has spread to phototypesetting, although measurements are also made from the base of one letter to the base of the letter below. Lines are leaded, as a rule, to make the type more readable. The extra space is usually specified as "10 pt. with 2 pt. leading" or "10 on 12," denoting 10-point type with 2-point leading.

To recap:

▲ *Height (size) of type* is expressed in points, 72 points to the inch.

▲ *Width of a line of type* is measured in *picas*, 6 to the inch.

▲ *Depth of newspaper space* is measured in *agate lines* per column, 14 agate lines to the inch.

Type specifications and copy casting

The type of most national advertising is set by *advertising typographers*, firms that specialize in photo or metal composition, but generally they do not print. Recently, some advertisers and advertising agencies have installed their own photographic display or text typesetting equipment.

Copy sent to a typographer or publication carries the type specifications marked on the typescript and is usually accompanied by a rough or comprehensive layout.

Before the size of type can be chosen, the number of characters in the copy typescript must be determined (*cast off*). Published tables show how many characters of various typefaces and point sizes fit into different line widths. In advertising agencies, type specifications and casting might be handled by art directors, print production personnel, or specialized *type directors*.

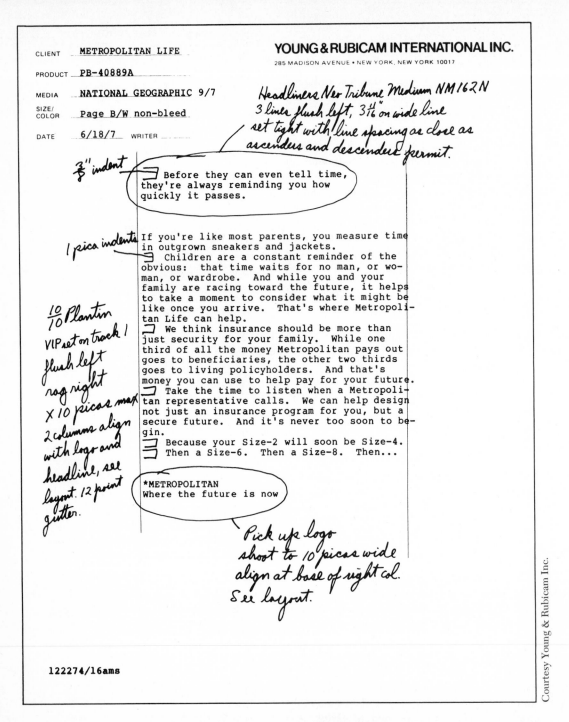

CLIENT METROPOLITAN LIFE

PRODUCT PB-40889A

MEDIA NATIONAL GEOGRAPHIC 9/7

SIZE/COLOR Page B/W non-bleed

DATE 6/18/7   WRITER

YOUNG & RUBICAM INTERNATIONAL INC.

285 MADISON AVENUE • NEW YORK, NEW YORK 10017

Headliners Neo Tribune Medium NM162N
3 lines flush left, 3½" on wide line
set tight with line spacing as close as
ascenders and descenders permit.

⅜" indent

Before they can even tell time,
they're always reminding you how
quickly it passes.

1 pica indents

If you're like most parents, you measure time
in outgrown sneakers and jackets.
Children are a constant reminder of the
obvious: that time waits for no man, or woman, or wardrobe. And while you and your
family are racing toward the future, it helps
to take a moment to consider what it might be
like once you arrive. That's where Metropolitan Life can help.
We think insurance should be more than
just security for your family. While one
third of all the money Metropolitan pays out
goes to beneficiaries, the other two thirds
goes to living policyholders. And that's
money you can use to help pay for your future.
Take the time to listen when a Metropolitan representative calls. We can help design
not just an insurance program for you, but a
secure future. And it's never too soon to begin.
Because your Size-2 will soon be Size-4.
Then a Size-6. Then a Size-8. Then...

10/10 Plantin
VIP set on track 1
flush left
rag right
× 10 picas max
2 columns align
with logo and
headline, see
layout. 12 point
gutter.

*METROPOLITAN
Where the future is now

Pick up logo
shoot to 10 picas wide
align at base of right col.
See layout.

Courtesy Young & Rubicam Inc.

122274/16ams

Copy ready for the advertising typographer. Finished ad is on p. 370.

The headline tells the story

On this page we have examples of four families of type, with the headline set in 24-point type of the family, and the body copy set in 10 point on 12 of the same family. You need not go outside a family to have an interesting, harmonious ad. Note how the number of words per line varies; see where the last word of each of the paragraphs falls. Novices are in the company of master typographers when they stay within one type family per advertisement. The sign of a real amateur is trying to use too many faces in one advertisement.

This paragraph has been set in Times Roman

The headline tells the story

On this page we have examples of four families of type, with the headline set in 24-point type of the family, and the body copy set in 10 point on 12 of the same family. You need not go outside a family to have an interesting, harmonious ad. Note how the number of words per line varies; see where the last word of each of the paragraphs falls. Novices are in the company of master typographers when they stay within one type family per advertisement. The sign of a real amateur is trying to use too many faces in one advertisement.

This paragraph has been set in Century Expanded

The headline tells the story

On this page we have examples of four families of type, with the headline set in 24-point type of the family, and the body copy set in 10 point on 12 of the same family. You need not go outside a family to have an interesting, harmonious ad. Note how the number of words per line varies; see where the last word of each of the paragraphs falls. Novices are in the company of master typographers when they stay within one type family per advertisement. The sign of a real amateur is trying to use too many faces in one advertisement.

This paragraph has been set in Souvenir Light

The headline tells the story

On this page we have examples of four families of type, with the headline set in 24-point type of the family, and the body copy set in 10 point on 12 of the same family. You need not go outside a family to have an interesting, harmonious ad. Note how the number of words per line varies; see where the last word of each of the paragraphs falls. Novices are in the company of master typographers when they stay within one type family per advertisement. The sign of a real amateur is trying to use too many faces in one advertisement.

This paragraph has been set in Helvetica

Readability
of type

The first principle of good typography is that if copy is important enough to be printed, it must be readable. Tests have proven that a line length of 1½ alphabets (or about 40 characters), regardless of the typeface, is best for easy readability. A line length of one alphabet (or about 25 characters) constitutes the lower limit for good readability, whereas the upper limit lies at 3 alphabets (or about 75 characters).

The practice of typography demands atten
5-point Grotesque Medium, No. 215J

The practice of typography demands atten
6-point Century Expanded, No. 20A

The practice of typography demands atten
7-point News Gothic, No. 206J

The practice of typography demands atten
8-point Bodoni Book, No. 875A

The practice of typography demands atten
9-point Caledonia

The practice of typography demands atten
10-point Times Roman

The practice of typography demands atten
11-point Scotch Roman, No. 36A

The practice of typography demands atten
12-point large Optima

Courtesy ATA, who set other type specimens in this chapter.

Types in eight faces and sizes set in lines of 40 characters. The difference between each of the lines demonstrates the flexibility one has in selecting a typeface to fit the requirements of copy and layout.

Words in capitals, reverse type (white type on black), or italics are harder to read than those in lower case, printed in black on white paper, or set in roman. Boldness of type does not necessarily increase its readability. A LINE IN CAPITAL LETTERS IS HARDER TO READ THAN A LINE IN LOWER-CASE LETTERS.

Every typesetting shop and every print shop has its own manual of the typefaces it has on hand. As a practical matter, you will probably confine your choice to those available in one shop.

The foregoing guide may be helpful in distinguishing one typeface from another.

ℰ	Dele, or delete: take it out.
⑨	Letter reversed—turn.
#	Put in space.
◠	Close up—no space.
⋁⋀	Bad spacing: space more evenly.
wf	Wrong font: character of wrong size or style.
tr	Transpose.
¶	Make a new paragraph.
⊓	Indent; or, put in an em-quad space.
⊏	Carry to the left.
⊐	Carry to the right.
⊓	Elevate.
⊔	Depress.
✕	Imperfect type—correct.
↧	Space shows between words—push down.
⫽	Straighten crooked line.
‖ ＝	Straighten alignment.
stet	Restore or retain words crossed out.
⌒	Print (æ, fi, etc.) as a ligature.
t. see copy	Words are omitted from, or in, copy
⑦	Query to author: Is this correct?
caps	Put in capitals.
sc	Put in SMALL CAPITALS.
lc	Put in LOWER CASE.
rom	Put in roman type.
ital	Put in italic type.
bf	Put in bold face type.

Proofreaders' marks are printers' shorthand in correcting type proofs.

Selecting the Typesetting Process

There are three methods of setting type: by hand, which has passed into history; by machine, which is passing into history; and by phototypesetting, which is now making history.

The hand-setting method. The drawing on page 390 is almost a collector's item, showing the hand-setting method used before machine typesetting was invented. The type was set letter by letter, by hand, assembled in a composing

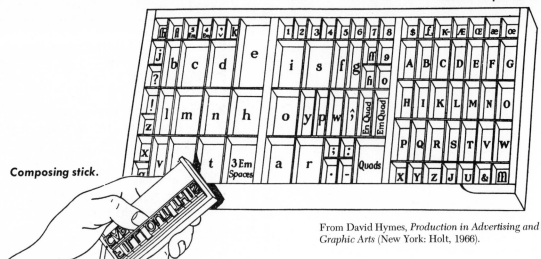

From David Hymes, *Production in Advertising and Graphic Arts* (New York: Holt, 1966).

stick, as pictured, and then placed in a long tray or *galley* until the entire passage had been set. Then it was assembled into columns and pages. After the job was done, each letter had to be returned by hand to its cubicle. It is not hard to perceive the laboriousness of this operation. And this was the only way in which type was set from Gutenberg's day until mechanical typesetting came along in the nineteenth century.

Mechanical typesetting: the Linotype. In 1886 Ottmar Mergenthaler invented a machine which not only set type but molded a whole line at one time. The *Linotype* made possible the mass production of books, newspapers, and magazines all over the world. A Linotype is operated by one person sitting at the keyboard of a machine. From a pot of molten metal attached to the machine, the type is cast. Because Linotype is being displaced by phototypeset-

Linotype slugs. Easy to handle, but to correct one letter or punctuation mark, the whole line must be recast.
Courtesy Mergenthaler Linotype Company.

ting—in fact, its manufacture has been discontinued in the United States—there is little point in describing the ingenious mechanism. But we must recognize the tremendous leap forward it gave to typesetting, helping raise the literacy of the world, the wealth of its publications, and the growth of advertising.

The development of equipment to set type photographically, having accelerated since the end of World War II, has made phototypesetting dominant in advertising. It is being further advanced by electronics and computer technology, a complex field; but those who are just beginning the study of print production enjoy the advantage of not being burdened and confused by all the limitations and problems of metal typesetting.

Phototypesetting has numerous advantages. Phototypesetting equipment, especially when computerized, works considerably faster than does metal typesetting machinery. It fits right in with all photoplatemaking processes. The image quality is excellent, and there is utmost flexibility in spacing of letters and words. Display type (18 points and up) that requires fine optical spacing is usually set on *photodisplay* equipment. Text type (below 18 points) is usually set on *phototext* equipment. However, there are exceptions: some of the phototypesetting machines normally used for phototext can set type as large as 72 points.

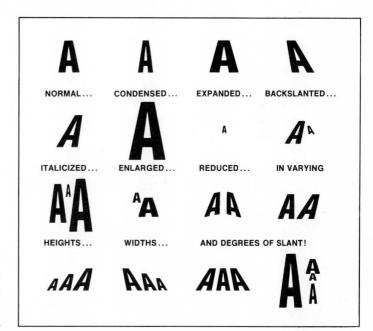

All of these were made from the same letter A, but with different positioning of the lens.
Courtesy Visual Graphics Corp.

Principle of phototypesetting. Phototypesetting machine systems consist of two units: a *keyboard* for input of the copy to be set in type, and a *photounit* for output of the copy so set. On a typewriter-like keyboard, the operator produces a perforated paper tape or magnetic tape that contains the text and all typographic instruction codes. These tapes are loaded into a separate machine, the *photounit.* The accompanying schematic drawing may help explain how everything works synchronously within the photounit.

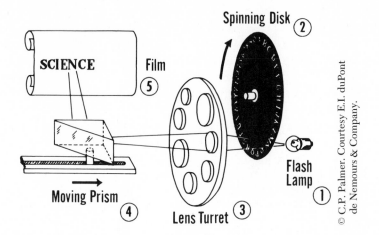

A high-intensity flash lamp that can be turned on instantly by signal from computer tape.

A spinning disc, with photographic negatives of an entire type font (or several fonts) around its rim. Any letter or other character on the disc can instantly be moved into the line of light from the lamp by instruction from perforated tape. Some machines use negative font grids or film strips instead of discs, but the principle is the same.

A lens turret with different lenses or a single zoom lens that can be moved to set that font of type in different point sizes. No need to have a different font image master for each size.

On the far left, a prism moves along synchronously with the flashes of light and casts the image onto film, so that the letters are placed in position to form lines and blocks of type. The film stays still, but the letters move.

This is the film (or photosensitive paper) onto which the copy is exposed. The film is developed in a separate processor and can be used in making photoplates and photoprints for all major printing processes.

◄ (Left): *Typical photocomposition perforated tape.*
It transmits copy and type instructions to photounit.

A Fototronic spinning type disc that contains two fonts of type, 120 characters each, 240 characters per disc. The characters can be exposed in any size from 5 points to 72 points. A punched paper tape signals the disc to spin to the required character, which is instantly photographed as positive on film or paper. The size is also determined by a punched tape signal that selects the size lens. The Fototronic photographic units (which were used for this book) each accommodate 5 discs and have output speeds of up to 150 newspaper equivalent lines per minute. The square holes on the disc are part of the computer code signaling system. No light goes through them. The spinning type disc is one kind of font image master used in phototypesetting machines. Others are rectangular grids or film strips.

Phototypesetting is a continually developing process. Advances such as the following are constantly being made. These are cited not in an effort to explain how they operate, but to show the endless possibilities now unfolding.

Computerized composition.   Some of the phototypesetting systems work with *counting keyboards*. Here the operator justifies the lines, tells the machine where to break lines and whether or not to hyphenate the last word.

Other systems operate from *noncounting keyboards* that do not justify the lines. The text is keyboarded in continuous sequence. The resulting tape is subsequently run into a computer that can be either separate (*stand-alone*) or built into the photounit.

This computer, on the basis of rather complex *software* (i.e., a program, as opposed to the machine itself, which is termed *hardware*) makes all line-end decisions and implements many other typographical instructions. Hyphenation programs can be based on logic (rules of grammar) or on dictionaries stored in the computer.

Computerized composition is particularly useful where identical (or nearly identical) text is utilized, especially for newspaper ads of different sizes. The computer can tell the photounit how to set in different point sizes and measures from a single unjustified tape.

Optical character recognition (OCR).   Recently, electronic devices have been created to "read" typewritten copy. The typewriter faces used are stylized to facilitate their recognizability by the machine. These "reading machines" produce perforated paper tape of the text, which, via computer, can be used directly for phototypesetting, thus avoiding double keyboarding.

Cathode ray tube composition (CRT).   The most advanced development in phototypesetting at this time is cathode ray tube composition. These machines can generate type characters at speeds of thousands of characters per second. It is increasingly used for books and other publications, and it is beginning to make inroads into the advertising field.

Video display terminals (VDT).   When the copy has been set, it is presented in film form or photopaper setting. If corrections have to be pasted (stripped) into the original film or paper setting, they can be slow and costly; but VDT provides a quick method for making corrections in type set on film. It accepts previously keyboarded tapes and displays sizable blocks of text on a television-like screen. The operator can insert corrections by tapping an attached keyboard. The terminal thereupon produces a new, clean, corrected tape. This tape is used for a quick resetting of the text.

This is not the time or place to elaborate on these technical developments. It is enough to know that such resources are available, along with others still on the drawing board.

Photoproofs.   Most advertising phototypesetting is done on film rather than on photopaper, especially when multiple proofs are required. For proofreading, photoproofs—also called *submission* or *reading proofs*—are usually made on sensitized paper which is chemically developed.

After the copyfit has been checked and all corrections have been made, the type shop can make reproduction-quality photoproofs *(photorepros).* They can be used in making camera-ready, paste-up mechanicals, with copy all pasted in place.

Mechanicals and artwork

Before an advertisement can be turned over to a photoplatemaker, the advertiser has to review the *mechanical* and artwork. The mechanical is the master from which the photoplatemaker works.

If a *photomechanical* (film make-up) has been made of photographically set type, illustrations may be positioned on a final photoproof of that mechanical. On a camera-ready *paste-up mechanical,* there are several ways of showing the platemaker where the illustrations must be placed. Although artwork is usually prepared larger than printing size, a photoprint or photostat of the illustration, reduced to the proper size, can be pasted on the mechanical; or the illustration can merely be indicated by lines. Scaling and cropping instructions can be given separately.

Besides the mechanical with all the type stripped or pasted in place, the photoplatemaker needs the actual artwork, unless a prescreened photoprint has been used in the mechanical. The artwork is usually prepared larger than printing size so that photographic reduction may help remove imperfections.

Typesetting is normally the first step in the production of an advertisement. The second step deals with the preparation of the artwork for the printing process. This is *photoplatemaking;* i.e., producing a printing plate or other image carrier for publication printing. In *offset and gravure,* normally *films* are sent to the publication printers, from which they will produce their own plates or cylinders. For *letterpress* printing, the advertiser will order *photoengravings* (combining photography and chemical engraving).

Photoplatemaking

The two major forms of photoengraving are *line plates* and *halftone plates.* In offset and gravure photoplatemaking, the basic principles are very similar.

Line plates (or line cuts).   The least costly form of photoengraving, these can be printed even on rough paper. How a message on a flat piece of paper can be converted into a printing block with the message standing out clearly for printing, like the letters on a rubber stamp, is indeed interesting. Typical results can be seen in the accompanying illustration.

Line tint plates.   To give a line subject some variation in shades between different areas, the photoplatemaker can break up solid areas with screen tints, for instance 20 percent black or 70 percent black, providing variations in shading. The platemaker can also take a clearly defined blank area on the artwork and, in

Line plate made from illustration with solid lines. ▶

the film stripping stage, lay over it a pattern of geometric or irregular lines and dots—often used in making subdivisions of a chart. Such plates are referred to as *line tint plates.*

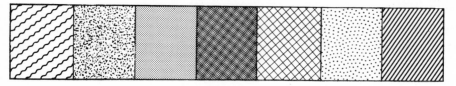

Tint patterns.

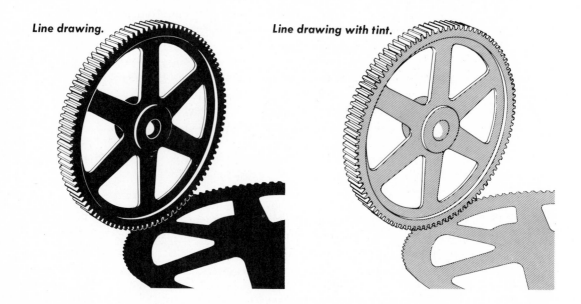

Line drawing.   **Line drawing with tint.**

Line color plates.   To produce line plates in two, three, or more flat colors, the artwork itself need not be colored. Each extra color is marked on a separate tissue or acetate overlay on the base art. The platemaker then makes a separate plate for each color. Line color plates provide a comparatively inexpensive method of printing in color with effective results.

Halftone plates.   Unlike a line drawing, a photograph or painting is a continuous blend of many tones from pure black to pure white. Such illustrations are therefore called *continuous-tone artwork.* The plates used for them are called *halftone plates.*

How can these various tones of gray be converted into a printable form? The secret lies in a *screen* that breaks up the continuous-tone artwork into dots. These dots are formed on the negative during the camera exposure when a glass

Line copy.

Halftone copy.

Magnification of a halftone plate, showing light and dark portions of the photographic copy reproduced as dots of different sizes. Lighter dots are freestanding; but at about the 50 percent value (half black, half white) the dots begin to connect. The centers of the dots are equidistant from each other.

or acetate contact screen is inserted between negative and artwork. These screens bear a crosshatch of 50 to 150 or more hairlines per square inch, forming thousands of little windows through which light can pass.

When you look through a screened window, you are aware for the moment of the screen; but soon the brain adjusts, and you become oblivious to the screen. A camera, however, records exactly what it sees through each of those windows; and what it sees is so tiny that only a dot can come through, varying in size with the blackness of the part of the picture it is seeing. Where the picture is dark, the dots are big and seem close to each other; where it is light, the dots are small. The eye sweeps over the picture and sees a whole photograph.

After photography, the picture, in the form of dots, is printed on a metallic plate, and just like a line plate, it is washed with a preparation that makes the dots acid-resistant. The letterpress plate is splashed with acid that eats away the metal except for the dots, and before long the dots stand out in relief. When a roller of ink is passed over them, and paper applied, the ink on top of the dots is transferred to the paper, producing a replica of the original picture.

Screens come in a variety of standard sizes, so that one chooses the size of dots that will reproduce best on the paper to be used, depending on its smoothness or roughness. The screens most frequently used are 55, 65, 85, 100, 110, 120, and 133 lines each way per inch. The higher the screen number, the more dots per square inch, and the greater the fidelity and detail in the final reproduction. But the higher the screen, the smoother the paper has to be, to have all the dots strike it. That is why newspapers often use a 65-line screen; magazines, a 120-line screen.

Halftone screens (left to right): *65, 110, and 165 lines per inch. The lower the screen ruling, the fewer dots per square inch. The higher the screen ruling, the more dots per square inch. The choice of screen depends on the requirements of a publication, smoothness of the paper, and the amount of detail required.*

Square halftone (background included).   *Silhouette halftone (background omitted).*

The halftone finish.   If you want to make a halftone of a photograph of a face, the platemaker can treat the background in a number of ways; that treatment is called its *finish*. All background can be retained, with the background screen extending to the edge of the rectangular plate. This is called a *square halftone,* even if the background is trimmed to some other shape. Or the photo-platemaker can cut away everything in the background, so that the face will appear sharply against the white background of the paper. This is called a *silhouette* or *outline halftone,* best for most purposes where the background is not an important feature. In a *vignette* finish, the dots fade into the background. This is good, but needs very smooth paper.

Combination plates combine continuous-tone and line artwork in the same plate. If, however, you want to print a line subject (such as a black headline) directly across the face of a continuous-tone subject (such as a photograph) that is a *surprint*. If the line is to print in white, it is called a *dropout*. If you have a halftone subject on which you want to make frequent changes (such as a change in price) in one place, you actually cut a hole in the plate to make room for that change. That is called a *mortise*.

Two-color halftone plates.   A two-color reproduction can be made from monochromatic artwork in one of two ways: (1) a screen tint in a second color can be printed over a black halftone; (2) the artwork can be photographed twice, changing the screen angle the second time, so that the dots of the second color plate fall between those for the first plate. This plate is called a *duotone*.

399

Four-color process printing.   The finest reproduction of a color print or painting is by means of a set of four color plates: red, yellow, and blue—which in various combinations produce every color—plus black, which is needed for delineation and contrast. The photoplatemaker photographs (*separates*) the original artwork through filters of different colors, resulting in four negative films. Although these separation films are black-and-white, one of them records all of the red; another one, all of the yellow; and a third, all of the blue portions of the original. A fourth film records shades of black to provide contrast and depth in the shadow portions of the picture.

The four *separation films* are subsequently screened in order to be reproduced as halftones. From each of the screened films a separate halftone plate is made. When these halftone plates are inked in the corresponding process inks and printed onto paper, a full-color reproduction of the original picture results.

The screen is angled differently for each color, so that the dots print side by side, not on top of each other. Thus the colors are not created by *physical* mixing of the printing inks but by an *optical* effect similar to the painting techniques of the nineteenth-century French pointillist painters.

The photoplatemaker will pull a separate proof of each color plate, combinations of two colors and of three colors, and finally a combination of all four colors. These proofs are assembled as a set of *progressive proofs* and sent to the printer together with the set of plates. The "progressives" or "progs" thus serve as a guide in four-color printing (see color insert before p. 377).

Offset and gravure photoplatemaking

Contrary to letterpress publication printing in which the plate has to be furnished by the advertiser or agency, offset and gravure publications require only films, because they can produce their own offset plates or gravure cylinders.

If an agency wishes to retain complete control over the preparatory steps, it usually sends the mechanical and artwork to its own supplier, to prepare for the printer. This can be an *offset separation house,* a *gravure service house,* or a *photoengraver* who has branched out into the offset and gravure preparatory fields and thus has truly become a *photoplatemaker* for all major printing processes. Such combination plants are particularly important when media lists contain publications that print by means of different printing processes. Photoengravings as well as separation films for offset and gravure can be made simultaneously in one plant from a single piece of artwork and a single mechanical.

The photographic preparatory steps in the three major printing processes resemble each other closely. In offset and gravure, the photoplatemaker produces plates merely for proofing purposes. These plates are not shown to the publications; only the final, corrected films are sent, with proofs and progs pulled from these plates. In letterpress printing, actual plates are sent.

Conversions.   In order to save time and expense, it is sometimes desirable to convert material from one printing process to another. This can be done by most photoplatemakers.

It is rather rare for a print advertisement to run in a single publication. Frequently, advertisers have different publications on their schedules, or they want to issue reprints of their advertisements or send material to dealers for cooperative advertising. There are various means of producing duplicate material of magazine or newspaper ads.

Duplicate material for magazine advertisements.   If a magazine ad for *letterpress* has to be duplicated, two methods can be employed: (1) an *electrotype* can be produced. This is a molded, electrolytically formed relief plate bearing an exact duplicate of the original plate. (2) *DuPont Cronapress plates* (called *Cronars*) can be made with DuPont Cronapress film, a pressure-sensitive material onto which an impression of the original plate is made. This material is subsequently turned into a negative film from which duplicate halftone plates can be produced, reflecting exactly what was contained in the original.

Duplicate material for *offset publications* can consist of *repro proofs* or *3M Scotchprints* (a plasticized repro proofing material) pulled with ink from the original letterpress photoengravings. Or *duplicate films* can be made from an original mechanical and artwork. For *gravure magazines* or *Sunday supplements* duplicate positive films are usually supplied. For black-and-white offset or gravure ads, *photographic prints* are often substituted for films.

Duplicate material for newspaper advertisements.   There was a time, not so long ago, when almost all daily newspapers were printed by letterpress. Duplicate material prepared for national newspaper campaigns usually consisted of *mats*. The mat was made by pressing a letterpress plate into papier-mâché. When dried, the papier-mâché formed a hard matrix. At the newspaper, molten lead was poured into the mat, forming a replica of the original plate, and called a *stereotype* or stereo. The use of mats has dwindled because of the decline in letterpress printing of newspapers.

Material for ad insertions in offset or phototype/letterpress newspapers can take on various forms. If an original photoengraving of a newspaper ad is available, inexpensive *reproduction proofs* can be pulled and sent to the newspapers. If the list contains no metal composition/letterpress newspapers, the advertiser may choose to prepare the ad photographically. A film master is produced. This serves for the quantity production of *photoprints (screened prints* or *Veloxes)* or of contact *film negatives.* Proofs are pulled via an offset plate. Usually photoprints or reproduction proofs are preferred for partial-page ads; film is often requested for full-page insertions and R.O.P. (*run of paper*) color ads in newspapers.

In order that the creative and the production work may move with the necessary precision, a time schedule is planned at the outset. The *closing date* is the date or time when all material must arrive at the publication. Then the advertiser works backwards along the calendar to determine when the work must be begun in order to meet that date.

Making duplicate material

Production planning and scheduling

Let us take a four-color advertisement to appear in several magazines for which the closing date is October 1. We must plan a production schedule like this (note that *calendar* days are not always *working* days):

Production Schedule

In order to reach publications by closing date	October 1
Duplicate material must be shipped by	September 28
Duplicate material making must be started by	September 24
Photoplatemaker should deliver final proof by	September 21
Photoplatemaker should have first proof by	September 12
Material should go to photoplatemaker by	August 27
Retouched art and mechanical should be ready by	August 24
Type and mechanical should be ordered on	August 18
Finished artwork (photograph) should be delivered by	August 17
Finished artwork (photograph) should be ordered by	August 9
Creative work (layout and copy) should be approved by	August 6
Creative work should start by	July 26

**Review
of print
production**

It may be helpful to review some of the more important technical terms we have encountered in this chapter. We discussed three major printing processes:— *letterpress* (from raised surface), *offset lithography* (from flat surface), and *gravure* (from depressed surface). The form of printing affects the way material is prepared for publication.

Typography deals with the style (or face) of type and the way in which the copy is set. *Typefaces* come in related designs called *families*. The size of type is specified in *points* (72 to the inch). The width of the line in which type is to be set is measured in *picas* (6 to the inch). The depth of newspaper space is measured in (agate) *lines* (14 to the column inch), regardless of the width of the column, which varies from paper to paper.

The chief methods of typesetting are: *metal typesetting* (usually by Linotype, which is cast one line at a time) and *phototypesetting* (type set photographically or electronically onto light-sensitive paper or film). Most phototypesetting is computerized.

If you plan to run advertisements in letterpress publications, you will have to order *photoengravings*. The two classes are *line plates* (for type and all-line artwork) and *halftones* (for continuous-tone artwork). The *screen* you specify for halftones depends on the smoothness of the printing paper's surface. The smoother the paper, the higher the screen ruling (expressed in lines per inch). You also have to specify the background finish: *square* (includes everything), *outline* or *silhouette* (everything cut away except the subject itself) or *vignette* (dots fading into the background). Vignettes are not good for newspapers.

YOUNG & RUBICAM INTERNATIONAL INC.   JOB PRODUCTION ORDER/SCHEDULE — **PRINT**   53 Rev. 6/74

Client	DISTRIBUTION	
	Name	Function
Product		Account Supervisor
Job #		Account Executive
Subject		Assoc. Creative Dir.
Description		Art Director
		Copywriter
		Art Buyer
		Print Producer

Title (Max. 22 characters)

EVENTS/ITEMS	DUE FROM	DATE	NOTES
Briefing Meeting			
Layout & Copy Due			
Layout & Copy Approved by Client			
Estimate Request Prepared			
Estimate Due			
Art Bids Due			
Type Due			
Art Due			
Final Art & Mechanical Due			
Art & Mechanical Approved by Client			
First Proof Due at Y&R			
Final Proof Approved by Client			
All (Duplicate) Materials Ready to Ship			
Materials Due at First Publication			

PUBLICATION	ISSUE	SPACE	SIZE	4/C B/W	N/B BLD.	PUBLICATION	ISSUE	SPACE	SIZE	4/C B/W	N/B BLD.

Job Quote	Job Billing Requirements		Antic. Mo. 1st Use (Impact)	Antic. Exp. Date
$				
Prepared by:		Date	Authorized by:	Date
PRODUCTION COORDINATOR			ACCOUNT MANAGEMENT AUTHORITY	

Note the number of steps involved.

403

For a full-color advertisement, you have to order *separations* and a set of plates to be printed in the four *process inks*. For letterpress ads, plates are sent to the publications; for gravure and offset lithography, films are supplied, with plates made by the photoplatemaker only for proofing purposes. Material for color ads is usually accompanied by *progressive proofs*. Both offset and gravure publications frequently also accept artwork and mechanicals.

Letterpress magazines can be sent *electrotypes* or *Cronar plates*. Duplicate material for offset publications can consist of *repro proofs, 3M Scotchprints, photoprints* (Veloxes or screened prints) or *films*. Gravure publications almost invariably require *film positives*.

In all print production work, a most important element is timing.

In publication printing, which is the kind of printing that concerns most advertisers, the publisher is responsible for supplying the paper and doing the printing. But in direct-mail advertising and other forms of nonpublication advertising, as we have discussed in Chapter 12, the advertiser has to pick the printer, buy the paper, and follow up the entire production job.

QUESTIONS

1. Identify and describe the three major printing processes.

2. What are the chief things to strive for in typography?

3. Why is the choice of a typeface so important?

4. What are four basic styles of typefaces?

5. When do you measure by points? How many to the inch? When do you measure by picas? How many to the inch?

6. How is the depth of newspaper space measured?

7. Explain the factors that influence the readability of typography.

8. Discuss the two chief methods of typesetting.

9. Describe the differences in the use of line plates and halftone plates.

10. What is the principle used in the making of four-color process plates?

11. Explain the importance of production planning and scheduling. Why is timing so critical?

12. What is meant by the following terms?

a) relief printing
b) offset printing
c) rotogravure
d) screen printing
e) typeface
f) serif
g) point
h) pica
i) em
j) agate line
k) leading
l) font
m) type family

n) character, as used in measuring type
o) galley
p) composing stick
q) Linotype
r) phototypesetting
s) justified lines
t) photoproofs
u) mechanical
v) photoengraving
w) tint plates
x) progressive proofs
y) photoprints
z) publication closing date

READING SUGGESTIONS

BAHR, LEONARD F., *ATA Advertising Production Handbook,* 4th ed. New York: Advertising Typographers Association of America, 1969.

CRAIG, JAMES, *Designing with Type: A Basic Course in Typography.* New York: Watson-Guptill Productions, 1973.

————, *Production Planning for the Graphic Designer.* New York: Watson-Guptill Productions, 1974.

GTA Gravure Copy Preparation Guide. New York: Gravure Technical Association, 1972.

LATIMER, HENRY C., *Preparing Art and Camera Copy for Printing.* New York: McGraw-Hill, 1977.

Phototypography Report No. 1. New York: American Association of Advertising Agencies, 1972.

Pocket Pal, 11th ed. New York: International Paper Co., 1976.

SCHLEMMER, RICHARD M., *Handbook of Advertising Art Production,* 2nd ed. Englewood Cliffs, N. J.: Prentice-Hall, 1976.

18

The Television Commercial

Unlike print advertisements, a television commercial enters the homes of prospective buyers and becomes alive with sound, motion, people, and the unique ability of demonstration. Although a whole new family of techniques is open to you when you create a TV commercial, your overriding consideration must be the climate in which it is expected to function effectively.

Creating the TV Commercial

Climate of the commercial

More people turn at one time to television than to any other medium (over 100 million people have watched a bowl game). In the average home, the television set is on 6 hours and 56 minutes a day.° Obviously, TV's advertising opportunities are great—but so are its challenges. Your commercial must compete for the viewer's attention not only with the commercials of similar products and services, but with all the other commercials attempting to exhort the viewer to some kind of action. In addition, the commercial has to compete with countless short messages of upcoming programs, called *promos*, or promotions. Amidst this *clutter*, as promos are also termed, your commercial may well run sandwiched among as many as five other commercials.

Where to begin

The commercial contains two elements: the *audio* part, made up of spoken words, music, and other sounds, and the *video* part, comprising the visual presentation. Creating a TV commercial usually starts with writing a script.

° *1976 Broadcast Year Book.*

406

tually every commercial should contain at least one or two closeups to show package and logo. Humor is adaptable to most other techniques. Animation and live-action make an effective mixture in many commercials, and side-by-side comparisons may be combined with almost any other technique.

With such a rich variety of techniques available, you might find it difficult to decide which to use. Answering the following questions may help:

▲ Does your promise of benefit and supporting evidence suggest a particular technique? Do you intend to demonstrate your product? Could it win in a side-by-side comparison with other brands? Is any of your copy based on reports of satisfied users? Is your sales story simple and direct enough to warrant the personal touch a speaker may provide?

▲ What techniques are your competitors using? Although no law prevents you from following their lead, you may want to choose a different direction in order to give your product its own television image.

▲ From previous advertising, has your product or service established a special personality that may suggest continuing a technique?

▲ Do consumer attitudes discovered in research interviews suggest any problems to be met or any special advantages to be stressed for your product?

▲ Does your campaign already exist in print advertisements? If so, you will probably want your television effort to bear a visual resemblance. Often the reverse is true: many print techniques follow the lead set by TV commercials.

▲ How much money is available for production of your commercial? If your budget is modest, you will want to give serious thought to closeups, artwork, simple sets, or locations with a minimum of personnel.

▲ What production facilities are available? If you plan to produce your commercial in a large city, facilities will probably be at hand. Otherwise, the nearest television station or a free-lance film maker may be your best choice.

▲ What techniques are used in other commercials? Make it your practice to view television often and to analyze techniques. This will sharpen your own familiarity with the subject, and you may see techniques that suggest new directions for your product.

Assume you have decided on your visual technique. As you write out your script in a formal structure, try to think in terms of words and pictures simultaneously. Divide your paper into two columns. In the left-hand column, state the promise of benefit and supporting evidence in actual audio copy. In the right-hand column, write a verbal description or put a picture of the video part of the commercial. Corresponding audio and video elements go right next to each other, panel by panel. If you are going to have someone speaking, write your copy story in a conversational style, indicating alongside it what the speaker will be doing at various times. If you have decided to depict your product and benefits in a series of closeup scenes, write your copy for an off-screen announcer and key the various paragraphs of your audio to their corresponding scene. Matching the audio with the video makes a cohesive commercial.

As the copywriter, you begin with the promise of the product's significant benefit to the viewer, a promise you can offer in good faith—exactly as you do in print advertising. The promise is followed by whatever amplification and proof are possible within the limited time.

If the campaign appeal has already been established in the print advertising, you should repeat it in the commercial. If a new appeal is needed, write it out in a sentence; then see if you can say the same message in a crisper, more intriguing way. Perhaps you can make it into a slogan. The important point is to have clearly in mind exactly what promise you want the viewer to remember.

Now the second hand on your watch becomes your master. Few commercials last longer than 30 seconds, the most common length for both network and local commercials. Even in this short span of time, you aim to repeat your promise and brand name at least twice and flash your logotype, either by itself or on a package held conspicuously in view.

Unlike writing a piece of copy for print advertising, your writing does not now continue to complete the story. Instead, you now stop to select the *visual technique* you will use; that will determine how you will write your copy.

Fortunately for the creative person, whether or not a beginning copywriter, a whole gamut of successful visual techniques has been gathered and categorized. These provide a fine reservoir from which to draw in creating your own original commercial.

Selecting the visual technique

Spokesperson. An announcer, or "presenter," stands before the camera and delivers your copy directly to the viewer, as a salesperson might do in a store. Displaying and perhaps demonstrating the product, the speaker may appear against *limbo* (plain white background with no set); in a living room, kitchen, or other room of a home; or in a factory, out of doors, or in any surroundings relevant to your product and product story. The problem is to cast your announcer, choosing someone who is likeable and believable but not so slick that attention is called to the person instead of the product.

Testimonial. In a testimonial, selling is attempted by a well-known personality, either an authority on the type of product being advertised or a famous name in another field such as acting, with a large and loyal following. But the product should be one on which he or she is qualified to speak. In selling a food, the person may be famous for recipes or nutrition. A sports personality's personal experience may enable him to persuade viewers to buy anything from razor blades to beer, but not qualify him to give testimony for a medical product. Even people who are unknown can give testimonials, as long as they are credible and viewers can identify with them.

Demonstration. TV is ideal for demonstrating the advantages of a product. A cleanser removing stubborn stains, a refrigerator's new shelf arrangement, and a rent-a-car company's speed in getting the customer into a car—all happen before the viewer's eyes. A word of warning, however: legally, the demonstration must correspond to actual usage.

Closeups.   Television is the medium of closeups. You may want to move in closely to depict a demonstration of your product and to show people reacting favorably to the demonstration. A fast-food outlet may use closeups to show appetizing shots of its frankfurters as they are grilled or served. With this technique, the audio is generally delivered off-screen; such a *voice-over* costs less than a presentation by someone on the screen.

Slice-of-life.   This approach is based on a dramatic formula: predicament + solution = happiness. A typical, true-to-life situation is dramatized in the hope of involving the viewer to the point of thinking, "I can see myself in that scene." Since problem solving is a useful format in almost any commercial, slice-of-life is widely used. A meets B. B has a problem. A has a solution: buy the product. Next scene: grateful B reports success. This is such a popular format that special skill is needed to achieve variety in the setting and presentation of the problem.

Story-line.   A story-line commercial is similar to a miniature movie episode, except that narration is done off screen. A typical video may show a family in their driveway, hoping to leave for vacation but unable to fit all the gear into their automobile. Camera then shifts to the family next door, also leaving on vacation, but able to pack everything and everybody into their new station wagon. During these scenes, the announcer explains the advantages of the roomy wagon.

Customer interview.   Most people who appear in television commercials are professional actors, but customer interviews also involve nonprofessionals. An interviewer or off-screen voice may ask a housewife, who is usually identified by name, to compare the advertised kitchen cleanser with her own brand by removing two identical spots in her sink. She finds the advertised product does a better job.

Vignettes and situations.   Advertisers of soft drinks, beers, candy, and other lower-priced products find this technique useful in creating excitement and motivation. A fast-paced series of scenes shows people enjoying the product as they enjoy life. Audio over these scenes is often a lively jingle with lyrics based on the situations we see and the satisfaction the product offers.

Direct product comparison.   Do you remember "Brand X," the product that was never as good as the advertised brand? Well, Brand X has gone out of style. Now the trend is to show competitive named products in direct demonstration with your own. Of course, your product comes out better. There are two problems with direct product comparisons, however. In case of a lawsuit by a competitor, you must be prepared to prove in court that your product is significantly

superior, as stated. Second, you must be credible in the way you make claim, or the commercial may have a reverse effect on your audience.

Still photographs and artwork.   Using closeup photography of still and artwork, including cartoon drawings and lettering, you can struc highly illustrative, well-paced commercial. Supplied at modest cost, t quired material may already exist, or it can be shot candid-style or be draw cifically for your use. Deft use of the camera can give otherwise static visu terial a surprising amount of movement. Either changing lenses, which p an inward or outward motion, or "panning" the camera across the photos work gives the commercial motion. (*Panning* means changing the viewp the camera without moving the dolly it stands on.)

Humor.   Combined with practical salesmanship, humor can be effect sales message. The challenge is to make the humorous copy relevan promise of benefit and not allow it to stray off the copy line. Handle manner, humor can convey a serious message. The test is whether pe member the product, not just the humor.

Animation.   As opposed to "live action," the use of real people and animation consists of artists' inanimate drawings, which are photogra motion picture film one frame at a time and brought to life with appare ment as the film is projected. Most common is the cartoon. A favorit children but popular with all ages, the cartoon is capable of creating friendly atmosphere both for product and message. Animation can als to simplify technical product demonstrations. In a razor commercial, t product may be shown as it shaves a man's face, and an animated sequ then explain how the blades of the razor remove whisker after whis much animation costs depends upon how elaborate the style. If there movement, few characters, and few or no backgrounds, the price can b the other hand, the Disney style of animation, with many character tailed and colorful backgrounds, is much more costly.

Stop motion.   When a package or other object is photographed in different positions, movement can be simulated as the single frame jected in sequence. Stop motion is like artwork photographed in With it, the package can "walk," "dance," and move as if it had come

Rotoscope.   In the rotoscope technique, animated and live action are produced separately and then optically combined. A live boy ma breakfast food while a cartoon animal trademark character jumps u on his shoulder and speaks to him.

Combination.   Most commercials combine techniques. A speake and conclude the message, but there will be closeups in between.

Which te to select?

Writing the script

The following suggestions may be helpful in writing the *audio* portion of your commercial script:

Guidelines for writing the audio portion

▲ Dedicate your efforts to conveying one basic idea; avoid running in fringe benefits.

▲ Be certain that your words as well as your pictures emphasize your *promise of benefit*. State it, support it, and if possible demonstrate it. Repeat your basic promise near the end of the commercial; that is the story you want viewers to carry away with them.

▲ Use short, everyday words.

▲ Read the audio aloud to catch any tongue twisters.

▲ Your audio and corresponding video should relate. Don't talk about one point while demonstrating another.

▲ Don't waste words by describing what is obvious in the picture. Make the words interpret the picture and thereby advance the thought.

To help you visualize your TV commercial at the same time you are writing your copy, these suggestions may be helpful:

▲ Regardless of technique, avoid static scenes. Some type of movement, either within the scene itself or toward or away from the camera, adds interest.

▲ Don't cram the commercial with too many scenes; the viewer may become confused. The only exception is the quick vignette technique, in which quick changes of active scenes are meant to give a total impression of excitement.

▲ Be sure transitions are smooth from scene to scene. Conceiving your commercial as a flowing progression of scenes makes it easier to help the viewer follow it.

▲ Avoid long shots with the camera distant from the subject. Even the largest television screens are too small to capture far-off action.

▲ Be sure that backgrounds of your scenes are kept simple and uncluttered. They should point up, rather than detract from, your subject matter.

▲ Try, if possible, to show the brand name. If it is prominent, give a shot of the package; otherwise flash its logotype.

▲ In writing your video description, describe the scene and action as completely as possible. "Open on man and wife in living room" is not enough. Indicate where each is placed, whether they are standing or sitting, and generally how the room is furnished.

Guidelines for the video portion

The question of whether the words or the picture is more important in the television commercial will probably never be answered; they are intended to dovetail in delivering a common message. Nevertheless, remember that although the pictures achieve an impact unparalleled in any other medium, the prime communicator of the message is still the words. The need for strong copy is as vital in TV as in print or in radio copy.

The art director steps in

When you have your rough script worked out, you will be joined by the art director of your agency. When the art director is very experienced—perhaps even the creative head of the agency—you should confer at the beginning of the creative work. The art director's role is to translate the written script into a visual form called a *storyboard*. The art director and the copywriter discuss exactly what meaning is to be conveyed, and parts of the script may be reshaped to allow a better video scene. Later on, the art director will serve on the production team.

The storyboard

The storyboard is the bridge that takes us from writing the script to production of the commercial. On this master chart, the various major video paragraphs of the script are roughly sketched out, scene by scene, each in a panel by itself, and the audio is typed under the corresponding picture.

Storyboard sketches need involve little more than placement of elements such as people and objects within their respective scenes; they need not attempt to show minute detail of backgrounds. Simple stick figures are often sufficient.

The storyboard is the key element around which all activity takes place. It serves as a master visualization of the video and audio makeup of the commercial. Account executives and creative management can get a good idea of what is being proposed, and they can approve or make policy corrections. The client sees what the visual will consist of and what the commercial's message will be. Upon client approval, the storyboard goes into production and the creative work is formally completed.

Copies of the storyboard are then provided to each of the studios invited to give estimates, as a base for computing their costs. Once a studio is selected, the storyboard provides the blueprint for the producer, the director, and the editor. With the completion and approval of the storyboard, we move into TV production.

Producing the TV Commercial

The task of converting the storyboard or script into a commercial that is ready to appear on the air is the province of *TV production*. In complete charge of production is the *producer*, who must combine the talents of a creator, coordinator, diplomat, watchdog, and businessperson. Some producers are on the staffs of large agencies or advertisers. Many work on a free-lance basis, subject to call when needed. The work of the producer is so all-embracing that the best way to describe it is to live through the production of an entire commercial. Let's do that now.

Elements of production

At the outset it is helpful to think of production as a two-part process: *shooting* and *editing*. Shooting encompasses the work of filming or videotaping all scenes in the commercial. In fact, several "takes" are made of each scene. Sometimes even scenes that may be promising but later deemed unnecessary are shot as well.

Editing, also known as *completion* or *finishing* or *postproduction*, includes selecting scenes that have been shot, arranging them in their proper order, inserting transitional effects, adding titles, combining sound with picture, and delivering the finished commercial. We will elaborate on all these aspects of editing. Let's begin with the problems of shooting the film, for which a director is appointed by the producer.

The director's function.   As the key person in the shooting, the director takes part in casting and directing the talent, directs the cameraman in composing each picture, assumes responsibility for the settings, and puts the whole show together. Before selecting a studio, the agency° finds out which director is available. The director may even be the owner of the studio. Because studios all provide basically the same equipment, the director is more important than the studio.

Shooting on film.   Most commercials are shot on film, the oldest form of presenting motion pictures. Although the film of finest quality is the 35mm, it is expensive. Less costly is the 16mm film, used by most local and some national advertisers. Originally there was a great difference in quality between the 35mm and the 16mm films, but the 16mm film has improved so much that today it's difficult to distinguish between the two.

Unless the action is simple and continuous from beginning to end, the film commercial is generally shot "out of sequence." All indoor scenes are shot as a group, regardless of their order within the final commercial, and closeups are also generally filmed together. They will all be put in place by the editor, whom we shall soon be meeting.

Generally a scene is shot more than once, because the first time or two the performances may be unsatisfactory. Even after the director gets an acceptable "take," one more shot may be made for protection. In a normal day's shooting, the film camera may expose from 2,000 to 3,000 feet of 35mm film (45 feet will be used in the final 30-second commercial) or 800 to 1,200 feet of 16mm film (18 feet will be used in the 30-second commercial).

Opticals.   Since most commercials contain more than a single scene, optical devices or effects between scenes are necessary to provide smooth visual continuity from scene to scene. These are inserted during the final editing stage. Among the most common are:

Other elements of the commercial

the *cut:* one scene simply abuts the next

the *dissolve:* an overlapping effect; one scene fades out and the following scene simultaneously fades in

the *wipe:* the new scene literally "wipes" off the previous scene from top or bottom, side to side, or by means of a geometric pattern

the *matte:* part of one scene is placed over another, so that the same narrator, for example, may be shown in front of different backgrounds; lettering of slogans or product names can be matted, or superimposed, over another scene

the *zoom:* a smooth, sometimes rapid move from a long shot to a closeup or from a closeup to a long shot

° Usually the agency is the originating point of the creation and production of the commercial. Some large advertisers, however, have their own production operations. Often free-lance producers are then hired for a series of commercials.

Planters Nuts
"Personality - Dry Roasted" :30

VIDEO	AUDIO
OPEN ON FRANK GIFFORD STANDING NEXT TO END OF ASSEMBLY LINE.	FRANK GIFFORD: Planters Dry-Roasted Nuts!
HE PICKS A JAR FROM THE LINE.	Wow! They're still warm...
MOVE INTO TIGHTER SHOT AS HE WALKS PAST WORKER.	Warm...because they go right from the roaster into the jar.
HE REMOVES SEAL FROM JAR.	Then they're double-sealed...
CUT TO CLOSEUP OF OPENED PLANTERS JAR IN HIS HAND.	to keep in that fresh-roasted flavor. So they sound fresh-roasted...
PULL BACK AS GIFFORD SMELLS THE FRESH-ROASTED PLANTERS NUTS.	smell fresh-roasted...
CONTINUE TO PULL BACK...	taste fresh-roasted.
...AS HE TASTES THE NUTS.	Mmmm, that Planters seasoning. Nothing like it. That's Planters.
HE TURNS TO WORKERS BEHIND HIM.	Congratulations gang.
CUT TO CLOSEUP OF OPENED JAR.	ANNCR.: (VO) Planters. Fresh-roasted.
JAR SEALS ITSELF.	Double-sealed.
PULL BACK TO JAR AND BOWL OF PLANTERS NUTS. MR. PEANUT ANIMATES ON. SUPER: THE FRESH-ROASTED, DRY-ROASTED NUTS.	The fresh-roasted, dry-roasted nuts.

(Benton & Bowles)

Courtesy Standard Brands Foods. Advertising agency: Benton & Bowles.

Script for the photoscript on the facing page. The abbreviation VO means "voice over"; the voice will be heard, but the speaker will not be seen. SFX means "sound effects."

PLANTERS NUTS
"PERSONALITY - DRY ROASTED"

Length: 30 Seconds

Comm'l No.: SBPN 6973

(SFX: ASSEMBLY LINE)
FRANK GIFFORD: Planters Dry-Roasted
Nuts!

Wow, they're still warm...

Warm...because they go right from the
roaster into the jar.

Then they're double-sealed...

to keep in that fresh-roasted flavor. So
they sound fresh-roasted...
(SFX: WHOOSH)

smell fresh-roasted...

taste fresh-roasted.

Mmmm, that Planters seasoning.
Nothing like it. That's Planters.

Congratulations gang.

(MUSICAL EFFECT)
ANNCR: (VO) Planters. Fresh-roasted.

Double-sealed.

The fresh-roasted, dry-roasted nuts.

415

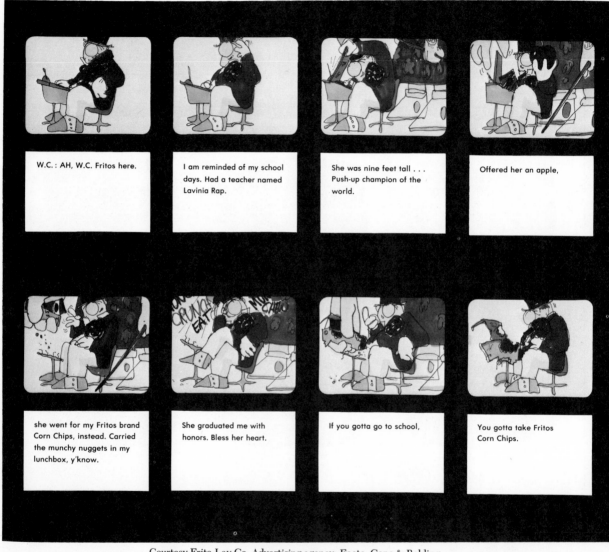

Courtesy Frito-Lay Co. Advertising agency: Foote, Cone & Belding.

Fritos Corn Chips are a light food that invites being treated in a light way. A comic cartoon character is appropriate to tell a good selling story amusingly. This storyboard is one of a series.

FOOTE, CONE & BELDING
As-filmed Photo-Script
Date_____
Producer_____

*Client*___FRITO-LAY CO._____
*Product*___FRITOS CORN CHIPS_____

*Film No.*___FL-71-269_____
*Film Title*___"LAVINIA RAPP"____
*Film Length*___30 SECONDS_____

1. ANIMATED MAN: Ah, W.C. Frito is here.

2. I'm reminded of my school days.

3. Had a teacher named Lavinia Rapp.

4. She was nine feet tall, push up champion of the world.

5. Offered her an apple.

6. She went for my Fritos Brand Corn Chips instead.

7. (SFX: CRUNCH)

8. Carried the munchy nuggets in my lunchbox, y'know.

9. She graduated me with honors.

10. Bless her heart.

11. If you got to go to school, . . .

12. you got to take Fritos Corn Chips.

Photoscript of a commercial based on a storyboard. Another script in the Fritos Corn Chips series.

Courtesy EVE Screen Gems.

Taking an interior scene.

Getting ready for an exterior shot of the Wrigley twins.

Courtesy NBE Productions.

The sound track.   The audio portion of the commercial may be recorded either during the film or videotape shooting or at an earlier or later time in a recording studio. When the sound track is recorded during the shooting, the actual voices of people speaking on-camera are used in the commercial. If the sound track is recorded in advance, the film or videotape scenes can be shot to fit the copy points as they occur; or if music is part of the track, visual action can be matched to a specific beat. If shooting and editing take place before the sound track is recorded, the track can be tailored to synchronize with the various scenes.

Music.   Music enhances the uniqueness and interest of many commercials. It is used either as *background* to the announcer's copy or as a *jingle,* usually sung off-screen over the video action. Background music is available as *stock music* (instrumental music, prerecorded and sold, usually reasonably, by stock music companies) and *original music* (composed and recorded specifically for a given commercial, most often by an independent contractor).

The jingle sets to music either the slogan or the lyrics written by the agency or by an outside music specialist. If the melody is original, you must pay a composing fee; if it belongs to a popular or once-popular song, you must get permission from, and pay a fee to, the copyright owner. Permission is generally not necessary if the song is in the public domain; but in that case, others may be using it too. Whether the tune is original or standard, the advertiser must also pay fees for musical arrangements, fees to both musicians and singers, studio charges for recording the jingle, and editing charges to complete the sound track.

Once all the scenes have been shot, the film is sent to the laboratory to be processed. Often overnight, all scenes are developed (though not all may be printed), and the film is delivered for viewing. At this point the film becomes known as *rushes* or *dailies*. Once these rushes have been viewed to make certain no reshooting will be necessary, the shooting is officially concluded, and the editing begins.

Even when the shooting has been finished, the commercial is by no means ready to be shown. Many shots have been taken out of sequence; some scenes have been reshot several times; extra shots have been taken, in case they should be necessary. A separate sound track and possibly a music track have been prepared. Which of the shots shall we use? How should they be assembled with transitional optical effects? How shall the sound track be coordinated with the rest of the commercial? The person responsible for answering all these questions is the editor, who must cut out the good shots and splice them by hand. The editor is responsible for coordinating sound and music with the video portion and for assembling and inserting optical effects so that they make sense. In fact, although the producer and the art editor may contribute ideas, it is the editor who brings to fruition the efforts of all the creative people who have worked on the commercial.

Role of the editor

The table on page 421 shows how the film passes for review from the time of the rushes to the delivery to the stations for airing.

J. WALTER THOMPSON COMPANY

PRODUCTION SCHEDULE FOR SIXTY-SECOND 35MM COLOR TELEVISION COMMERCIAL

Client approves final script and storyboard	Friday, August 4
Bids	Monday - Thursday August 7 - August 10
Client approves budget	Friday - August 11
Pre-production, Casting	Monday - Friday August 14 - August 25
Shoot	Monday - Tuesday August 28 - August 29
Edit	Wednesday - Thursday August 30 - August 31
Client approves rough cut	Friday - September 1
Record music	Friday - September 8
Client approves answer print	Friday - September 15
Ship air prints to stations	Friday - September 22

Courtesy J. Walter Thompson Company.

A TV commercial production schedule involves several activities, complete with deadline dates.

From camera to air on film

Process	What it's called
After shooting, the film is processed in a day or two and shown on screen to the producer, director, art director, and film editor.	Dailies, or rushes
The best take of each scene is selected, cut, and spliced in correct sequence by the editor. The final film is submitted for preliminary client approval.	Work print, or rough cut (Picture changes made most economically at this time.)
Once the film has been approved, the film editor prepares opticals and sound tracks on separate reels to be synchronized with the film reel.	(Still time for changes.)
Sound and film tracks are combined in one reel.	Composite print, or optical print
The optical print is approved.	Answer print
The answer print is corrected for color, quality, and synchronization.	Final print
From the final print, duplicate prints are made and sent to stations.	Release prints, or dupes

At last, the film is on the air!

Videotape

So far, we have been working in the world of film. We now enter the incredible world where everything we've said about shooting and editing is accomplished electronically, by *videotape* recording (also called *VTR* or *tape*). The videotape process, using a live television camera, carries the picture impulses through wires, and it records them on either a one-inch or a three-quarter inch magnetic tape. A process newer than film, videotape gives an excellent picture. While most viewers cannot tell whether a commercial was shot on film or on videotape, some professionals argue that videotape offers a more brilliant and realistic look; those favoring film still maintain that it offers a softer, more glamorous quality. Nevertheless, among both local and national advertisers, videotape is increasing in popularity as a method of shooting commercials.

Unique advantages of videotape.   Videotape's unique advantage is the speed with which a commercial can be produced. Whereas editing a film commercial may take weeks to complete, tape can be played back immediately after shooting. With videotape, therefore, it is possible to shoot one day and be on the air the next—a boon to many advertisers, particularly retailers who change their commercials every few days to feature timely items.

Another advantage is that studio shooting of videotape can achieve fascinating trick effects. As one camera focuses, say, on an electric range in a kitchen setting, another camera can focus on a person speaking. The two pictures can be instantly combined in such a way that the speaker, magically reduced to the size of a doll, may seem to be standing on top of the range.

Since no processing of the videotape picture is required, shooting officially ends after the tape of the dailies is played back and approved for editing. If the commercial has been shot from beginning to end and will not require editing, shooting ends after the final version has been approved.

Videotape editing.   Since the images recorded on videotape are invisible, film methods of editing cannot be employed. The tape editor, therefore, calls upon some very sophisticated equipment in combining the same basic elements into the final commercial. Although the equipment is vastly different from film, the steps are parallel. First the reel of dailies is screened on a monitor and takes are selected. The various takes are then duplicated and lined up on another monitor in their proper order. This first rough cut edit, the *work print,* is again the early stage in which the rough commercial can be visualized. Once this version is approved, opticals can be added electronically, and titles can be shot separately and matted over any scene in any position.

Tape's tremendous saving in time minimizes any possible limitations, and many people feel that videotape is the process of the future.

Role of the producer

The producer's role begins after the approval of the storyboard. Conferring with the copywriter and/or the art director, the producer becomes thoroughly familiar with every frame of the storyboard and encourages the client to make suggestions relating to the actual production (types of performers, for example). The producer:

1. *Prepares the "specs,"* or specifications, the physical production requirements of the commercial, in order to provide the production studios with the precise information they require in order to compute realistic bids. Every agency prepares its own estimate form. The accompanying estimate form from the J. Walter Thompson Company gives an excellent idea of the chief elements of such estimates. In addition, some advertisers may request a further breakdown of the cost of items such as:

Preproduction and wrapping	Equipment	Studio markup
Shooting crew labor	Film	Directing
Studio	Props, wardrobe	Insurance
Location travel and expenses	Payroll taxes	Editing

DPX No. 131

(JWT) J. WALTER THOMPSON COMPANY

TELEVISION PRODUCTION ESTIMATE

CLIENT: XYZ Corp	CC	CLIENT CODE	JOB/EST. NUMBER

CC: **N** 1 3 2 | 4 6 4 3 2 1

PRODUCT: Breakfast Cereal

TYPE	EST. DATE	REVISION DATE	REV.#
*	MO. DAY YR.	MO. DAY YR.	
	1 2 1 2 2		0

DESCRIPTION: 35mm film, color

13 | PROD. # | *DO NOT FILL IN—EDP INFORMATION / CLIENT REFERENCE NUMBER(S)

JOB ORDER NO.	COMM. CODE NO.	TITLE
		:60 commercial
		:30 commercial

DESCRIPTION OF COST ELEMENTS	CARD NO.	TC #	WHOLE DOLLAR AMOUNT ONLY
PRODUCTION RFL Productions, Inc.		40	12,400.
COLOR CORRECTION		41	300.
ARTWORK		42	550.
WARDROBE/PROPS		43	275.
EDITORIAL		44	3,250.
MUSIC Stock library score		45	500.
TALENT: PAYROLL 2 on camera performers, 1 voice over announcer		47	374.
PENSION & WELFARE (6.5 % OF TALENT PAYROLL)		47	24.
COMMISSIONABLE MISCELLANEOUS **Write-in appropriate descriptions and numbers from list given below.		**	
TOTAL COMMISSIONABLE COSTS	DO NOT KEYPUNCH		17,673.
AGENCY COMMISSION (15 % OF ABOVE COSTS)		81	2,651.
LOCATION EXPENSE (TRAVEL & MAINTENANCE)		70	
EMPLOYER'S TAX (9 % OF TALENT PAYROLL)		76	34.
SALES TAX (7 % OF TAXABLE AMOUNT $ 3,425*)		76	240.
NON-COMMISSIONABLE MISCELLANEOUS **Write-in appropriate descriptions and numbers from list given below.		**	
TOTAL			20,598.

**WRITE APPROPRIATE CODE NUMBERS AS LISTED BELOW IN THIS COLUMN

COMM. MISC. WRITE-INS
- 31 Outside Services
- 34 Other commissionable
- 39 Contingency

NON-COMMISSIONABLE MISCELLANEOUS WRITE-INS
- 70 Travel Expense
- 71 Overtime (other than location)
- 72 Telephone and Telegraph
- 73 Shipping and Delivery (Inc. postage & messenger)
- 74 Outside Services
- 75 Storage Charges
- 76 Other Non-commissionable
- 79 Contingency

NOTES: THIS ESTIMATE IS BASED ON PRESENT INFORMATION. ACTUAL COSTS OF INTANGIBLE OR UNKNOWN ELEMENTS THAT ARE PRESENTLY DIFFICULT TO ESTIMATE WILL BE REFLECTED IN OUR BILLING AND/OR IN REVISED ESTIMATES:

*New York Sales Tax

Approved By: _____	Prepared By: _R. W. Nelson_
CLIENT SIGNATURE DATE	SIGNATURE

DEPT. NO. _____

A TV production estimate.

Invariably, changes are made in the specifications, either because the producer thinks they are worth making or at the client's request. Always get a written approval of any changes at the time they are made.

2. *Contacts the studios* that have been invited to submit bids based on their specialties, experience, and reputation; meets with them either separately or in one "common bid session," and explains the storyboard and the specs in detail.

3. *Analyzes the studio bids* and recommends the studio to the client.

4. *Arranges for equipment.* The studio may own equipment such as cameras and lights, but more often it rents all equipment for a job. The crew, too, is freelance, hired by the day. Although the studio's primary job is to shoot the commercial, it can also take responsibility for editorial work. For videotape, a few studios own their own cameras and production units; others rent such facilities.

5. *Arranges the casting.* Working through a talent agency, the producer arranges, or has the production company arrange auditions. Associates also attend auditions, at which they and the director make their final choices of performers. The client also may be asked to pass on the final selection.

6. *Participates in the preproduction meeting.* At this meeting the producer, creative associates, account executive, and client, together with studio representatives and director, lay final plans for production. These include what action will take place in each scene, how the sets will be furnished or where the outdoor location will be situated, how the product will be handled, whether the label will be simplified or color-corrected for the camera, what hours of shooting will be scheduled—all logistics, in fact, relating to the shooting, which is probably scheduled for only a few days ahead.

7. *Participates in the shooting* and, on behalf of the agency and the client, is the *only* communicator with the director. On the set or location, the creative people and the client channel any comments and suggestions through the producer, in order to avoid confusion.

8. *Participates in the editing,* which begins after viewing of the dailies.

9. *Conducts the recording session.* Either before or after shooting and editing, the producer arranges for the sound track, which may call for an announcer, actors, singers, and musicians. If music is to be recorded, the producer will have had preliminary meetings with the music contractor.

10. *Schedules screenings.* The producer arranges for agency associates and client to view and approve the commercials at various editing stages and after completion of the answer print.

11. *Handles the billings;* approves studio and other invoices for shooting and editing and payment to talent.

Controlling the cost of commercial production

The cost of producing a television commercial is of deep concern to both the agency and the advertiser. The chief reason money is wasted in commercials is inadequate preplanning. In production, the two major cost items are labor and equipment. Labor—the production crew, director, and performers—is hired by

SPOT SCHEDULING INSTRUCTIONS

To: OPERATIONS DESK (station call letters)   DATE: _____

AGENCY: REVISION NO.: _____

ADVERTISER: Issued by: _____
    BROADCAST OPERATIONS DESK
FOR: _____   Telephone: _____
    (DURATION OF COMMERCIAL SCHEDULE)   (Area Code)   (Tel. #)

- -

Schedule the following commercials in accordance with facilities contract:

PRODUCT   ISCI   TITLE (Optional)   LENGTH

Inventory of Commercials:

     Prints ( )   Tapes ( ) of commercials are:

        (SUGGESTION TO AGENCY: DESIGNATE COMMERCIALS WHICH ARE
                      ON HAND, EN ROUTE OR ENCLOSED)

Disposition of Commercials:

     Following completion of schedule, prints should be:

        (SUGGESTION TO AGENCY: DESIGNATE WHETHER COMMERCIALS SHOULD BE
                      DESTROYED, RETURNED OR HELD FOR FURTHER
                      INSTRUCTIONS)

Questions regarding instructions or delivery of commercial material should be
addressed to Broadcast Operations Desk above.

These instructions do not constitute an order for time. Questions regarding time
purchase and/or product allocation should be addressed to the time buyer or your
station representative.

The agency time buyer for this schedule is: _____.

Courtesy American Association of Advertising Agencies.

Note the information contained in the instructions for scheduling spot TV.

the day, and equipment is rented by the day. If, however, a particular demonstration was improperly rehearsed, if a particular prop was not delivered, if the location site was not scouted ahead of time, the shooting planned for one day may be forced into expensive overtime or into a second day. These costly mistakes can be avoided by careful planning.

Before we can cite dollar averages for commercials, we have to recognize that there are actually two plateaus of costs. One is paid by the local advertiser, whose 30-second commercial may cost from $500 to $4,000; the other is paid by the national advertiser, whose 30-second commercial may cost from $12,000 to $25,000. (There have been cases of a national advertiser paying over $250,000 for one commercial!) This vast difference reflects the varying prices charged by studios and the ability of the local advertiser to work with fewer restrictions.

The union scale. "Restrictions" usually means *union restrictions.* One of the first facts of life one becomes aware of in television production is that it is a highly unionized business. Especially in the large TV centers, rate schedules are spelled out for every step.*

Residual fees. Another major expense is the *residual* or *re-use fee* paid to performers—announcers, narrators, actors, and singers—in addition to their initial *session fees.* Under the union rules, performers are paid every time the commercial is aired on the networks, the amount of the fee depending upon their scale and the number of cities involved. In a commercial aired with great frequency, a national advertiser may sometimes pay more in residuals than for the production of the commercial itself. This problem is less severe for the local advertiser because local rates are cheaper than national rates.

The moral is: cast only the number of performers necessary to the commercial and not one performer more.

Photoscripts

All advertisers like to be proud of their commercials, and they want to make the best sales promotion use of them. In addition, they wish to keep a record of the commercials they've made. For this purpose, advertisers often make photoscripts—series of photographic frames taken from key frames of the actual print film, with appropriate copy printed underneath.

We now move on to radio production.

---

* The major unions involved are the American Federation of Television and Radio Artists (AFTRA), the Screen Actors' Guild (SAG), the American Federation of Musicians (AFM), International Alliance of Theatrical Stage Employees (IATSE) and the National Association of Broadcast Employees and Technicians (NABET).

QUESTIONS

1. In selecting the visual technique for telling your story, you have a wide range of proven techniques from which to choose. Discuss as many as you can and indicate when you think each would be most appropriate.

2. What guidelines might be used to help in the selection of the visual technique for a given situation?

3. Describe some of the guidelines offered for writing the audio portion of the television commercial.

4. It is important to visualize the TV commercial as you are writing the copy. What are some helpful suggestions to bear in mind during the process?

5. What is the role of the TV art director?

6. Explain in detail the importance of the storyboard.

7. What is meant by TV production?

8. What is the director's function?

9. Production is a two-part process. Explain.

10. Describe the usual way of producing a commercial with a musical background.

11. What is the role of the editor in producing a television commercial?

12. What are the advantages and limitations of videotape?

13. Explain in detail the responsibilities of a TV producer.

14. What is discussed at a preproduction meeting?

15. What are some of the ways of controlling the costs of television commercial production?

16. Explain the following:

   a) promos
   b) clutter
   c) limbo
   d) voice-over
   e) slice-of-life
   f) story-line
   g) panning
   h) rotoscope
   i) promise of benefit
   j) TV production
   k) shooting
   l) editing

   m) opticals
   n) sound track
   o) stock music
   p) jingles
   q) work print
   r) composite print
   s) release prints
   t) VTR
   u) specs
   v) residual fees
   w) photoscripts

READING SUGGESTIONS

BELLAIRE, ARTHUR, *Controlling Your TV Commercial Costs.* Chicago: Crain Books, 1977.

BUCKLEY, DONALD BRIGHT, "Execution of Copy Strategy in Broadcast Media," *Handbook of Advertising Management,* Roger Barton, ed. New York: McGraw-Hill, 1970.

BYOR, T. V., "Judge Production Value by How Well It Supports Point of Copy." *Advertising Age* (September 27, 1976), 50–52.

————, "TV Clutter Makes Right Video Technique for Product a Must." *Advertising Age* (January 10, 1977), 42 ff.

HEADEN, ROBERT S., JAY E. KLOMPMAKER, and JESSE E. TEEL, JR., "Predicting Audience Exposure to Spot TV Advertising Schedules," *Journal of Marketing Research* (February 1977), 1–9.

————, "TV Audience Exposure," *Journal of Advertising Research* (December 1976), 49–52.

HEIGHTON, ELIZABETH J. and DON R. CUNNINGHAM, *Advertising in the Broadcast Media.* Belmont, Calif.: Wadsworth, 1976.

McEWEN, WILLIAM J., and CLARK LEAVITT, "A Way to Describe TV Commercials," *Journal of Advertising Research* (December 1976), 35–39.

McMAHAN, HARRY WAYNE, "So Funny It Ain't Funny: Sort of a Serious Look at Humor," *Advertising Age* (September 13, 1976), 74–75.

————, "What's Wrong With TV Commercial Research and Can It Be Improved?" *Advertising Age* (August 16, 1976), 44–45.

National Association of Broadcasters, *The Television Code.*

RAY, MICHAEL L., and PETER WEBB, *Experimental Research on the Effects of TV Clutter: Dealing With a Difficult Media Environment.* Cambridge, Mass.: Marketing Science Institute, 1976.

RESNICK, ALAN, and BRUCE L. STERN, "An Analysis of Information Content in Television Advertising," *Journal of Marketing* (January 1977), 50–53.

TERRELL, NEIL, *Power Technique for Radio-TV Copywriting.* Blue Ridge Summit, Pa.: Tab Books, 1971.

19

The Radio Commercial

Advertising may be a mass medium, but a radio commercial is from one real person, you, to another important person, the listener. In creating any advertising, you must try to picture a typical person who might buy the product; but in writing radio copy, your challenge is even greater. You also have to visualize what people are doing as you try to talk to them. They may be standing up or moving about, listening to the radio with only one ear as they go about their daily routines. They may be eating, reading, conversing, playing cards, studying, paying bills, or driving a car with an eye on the traffic. Radio reaches an audience more preoccupied than does any other medium.

Creating the Radio Commercial

As compensation, however, radio copywriters enjoy almost unlimited freedom in their choices of people and places. With no scenery or transportation costs or limitations, they can summon any characters from any part of the globe. With the aid of sound they can set any stage—a car door slamming, a phone ringing. The writer can picture 100,000 people at a bowl game with a five-second roar of the crowd. Best of all, the writer can use music, either for background to set the mood or for a jingle to popularize the advertiser's slogan. Such a jingle is called a musical logo, and it helps identify the product and make the message memorable. It is often so memorable that adults and children sing it! (Musical rights for radio are the same as for television. See Chapter 18.)

Like the television commercial, the basic ingredient of the radio commercial is the promise of a significant and distinctive benefit for the listener, on which the product can make good. Once you have determined your product's promise,

Writing the commercial

the whole world of radio imagery and technique is open to you. With voices, music, and sound effects at your command, you are free to fashion a mental backdrop of any scene, no matter how spectacular, how modest, or how far away. But you'll have to be imaginative. In radio, words and sounds comprise the copywriter's entire arsenal for communicating the copy story; these make up the entire commercial. You can vitalize the copy with:

Simplicity.   Use known words, short phrases, simple sentence structure. Build around one main point. Avoid confusing the listener with too many copy points.

Clarity.   Keep the train of thought on one straight track. Avoid side issues. Use the active voice in simple sentences. Avoid adverbs, clichés, and ambiguous phrases. Delete unnecessary words. (Test: would the commercial be hurt if the word were deleted? If not, take it out.) Write from draft to draft until your script becomes unmistakably clear and concise.

Coherence.   Be certain your sales message flows in logical sequence from first word to last, using smooth transitional words and phrases for easier listening.

Rapport.   Remember, as far as your listeners are concerned, you are speaking only to them. Try to use a warm, personal tone, as if you were talking to one or two people. Make frequent use of the word "you." Address the listeners in terms they would use themselves.

Pleasantness.   It is not necessary to entertain simply for the sake of entertaining, but there is no point in being dull or obnoxious. Strike a happy medium; talk as one friend to another about the product or service.

Believability.   Every product has its good points. Tell the truth about them. Avoid overstatements and obvious exaggeration; they are quickly spotted and defeat the whole purpose of the commercial. Be straightforward; you will convey the feeling of being a trusted friend.

Interest.   Nothing makes listeners indifferent faster than a boring commercial. Products and services are not fascinating in themselves; it is the way you look at them that makes them interesting. Try to give your customer some useful information as a reward for listening.

Distinctiveness.   Sounding different from other commercials and setting your product apart from others are never easy in a radio commercial. Employ every possible means—a fresh approach, a musical phrase here, a particular voice quality or sound effect there—to give your commercial its own character.

Compulsion.   Inject your commercial with a feeling of urgency. The first few seconds are crucial ones, for they are when you capture or lose the listener's attention. Direct every word toward moving the buyer closer to wanting the product. Repeat your promise of benefit; register the name of your product. And

```
ALLSTATE INSURANCE COMPANIES
60-Second Recorded Radio Announcement
"SOUNDS OF L.A."  (2-CAR DISCOUNT)
L.A. RADIO
AUTO


0385-AUTO-60

1  SFX:      HAMMERING AND SAWING OF HOUSE BEING BUILT--ALSO GARAGE.  ESTABLISH...
             HOLD FOR FIVE SECONDS...THEN UNDER THROUGHOUT

2  REIMERS:  I'm Ed Reimers for Allstate.  And I'm watching them build a nice little

3           house here in the (Westwood) section of Los Angeles.  Fact is, that

4           racket you hear is the garage being constructed.  It's a two-car garage,

5           naturally.  So many families need two cars today.  That's why you'll

6           find so many families have Allstate Insurance.  Because Allstate gives

7           you a two-car discount.  If you insure two or more cars with Allstate,

8           you get a discount on the liability coverage on both cars.

9           Plus a discount on the collision coverage for both.  So you save two

10          ways.  If you have two cars, you might say you're in twice as good

11          hands with Allstate.  Right?

12 MUSIC:   FADE IN TAG (10 Seconds)

13 NOTE:    WE CAN CHANGE LOCATION TO ANOTHER CITY, IF ADVISABLE.
```

This and the following scripts in this chapter appear through the courtesy of the identified companies. Advertising agency: Leo Burnett Company, Inc.

Since the sound of hammering is familiar to everyone who has a home, this commercial almost literally strikes home. Many homeowners also have two cars. Allstate's two-car discount commercial is directed toward this audience.

COMMONWEALTH EDISON COMPANY
60-Second Recorded Radio Announcement
"INTERVIEW REV."
INFORMATIVE

0196-INFO-60

1 ANNCR: Excuse me, do you know what EER is?

2 WOMAN: Oh sure. I voted for it in the last primary.

3 YOUNG   Uh, isn't that a singles bar on Rush street?
  MAN:

4 WOMAN: Oh, that's when you can read someone's mind!

5   Oh, yeah that's when you move the clock uh, I don't know.

6 ANNCR: EER really stands for Energy Efficiency Ratio. And it can help you select

7   an efficient room air conditioner. An efficient air conditioner that will

8   cost less to operate and help save critically needed fuel. To find the EER,

9   look on the metal plate attached to each model. Simply divide the watts into

10   the BTU's and you'll get the EER. If the answer is eight or more, it's an

11   energy saving unit that we would recommend. So before you buy an air conditioner

12   find out the EER. It's one of the most important things you can do about the

13   energy crisis this summer.

14 MAN: EER oh, that's the hottest stock on the market.

15 ANNCR: Commonwealth Edison is working for you.

A lively, friendly conversation introduces the Energy Efficiency Ratio and helps people select an energy-saving air conditioner, whatever brand they choose. A public service of the Commonwealth Edison Company.

don't forget to urge the listener to act without delay. (It's surprising how many commercials don't do this.)

If you were editing the following commercial, how many weaknesses could you spot? Compare your criticisms with the analysis and revision that follow.

> *Announcer:* Go to Hamburg Hut for a really great meal. Hamburg Hut has the best hamburgers and french fries in town. They cook their hamburgers rare, medium, or well done. They also offer thick, creamy shakes and have plenty of clean tables where the meal can be enjoyed. What's more, the Hamburg Hut people are courteous. Remember: Hamburg Huts are almost everywhere, and at Hamburg Hut we serve the best, bar none!

A careful rereading of this commercial shows several weaknesses. First, the copy is incoherent. Second, it contains too many ideas; no major promise of benefit comes through. Third, since the copy talks in terms of the advertiser, with never a mention of "you," there is no rapport with the listener. Fourth, it is riddled with trite phrases such as "best . . . in town," "what's more," and "best, bar none." The copy is hardly distinctive—it fails to stand Hamburg Hut apart from its competitors.

Now note how the commercial improves when we play up its promise of benefit, personalize the message, simplify the copy, and place the thoughts in a more coherent order.

> *Announcer:* How do *you* like *your* hamburgers? Nice and juicy and cooked to your special order? Well, that's the way to get 'em at Hamburg Hut—and *only* at Hamburg Hut. Rare, medium, or well-done—cooked to *your order*—topped off with our crispy french fries and thick creamy shakes. So for hamburgers the way you like 'em, bring your family to Hamburg Hut and tell us: rare, medium, or well done!

Basically a medium of words, radio—more than any other medium—relies heavily on the art of writing strong copy. But just as print advertisement and the television commercial include pictures and graphics to add impact to the copy, radio creates mental pictures with other techniques. Radio copywriters can choose among many proven techniques to give more meaning to the copy, help gain the attention of the busy target audience, and hold that attention for the duration of the commercial. Some of these techniques, you will note, parallel those in television.

Straight announcer.   In this commonly used and most direct of all techniques, an announcer or personality delivers the entire script, as in the Hamburg Hut example. Success depends both on the copy and on the warmth and believability of the person reciting the commercial.

Two-announcer.   In this format, two announcers alternate sentences or groups of sentences of copy, enabling the commercial to move at a fast pace and generate excitement. Often used to cover sale items for retail stores, this technique may give a news flavor to the commercial.

Announcer-actor.   The listener may identify still more with the situation if the writer intersperses an actor's or actress's voice reacting to, or supplementing, the message delivered by the announcer.

Slice-of-life.   Writing dialogue that reenacts a true-to-life scene involves the listener in a problem that the advertised product or service can help solve. The announcer may or may not be part of this format.

Jingle-announcer.   The jingle offers two advantages. As a song, it is a pleasant and easily remembered presentation of at least part of the copy. As a musical sound, it is the advertiser's unique property, which sets the commercial apart from every other advertisement on radio. Generally, an announcer is used in this flexible technique, which may be structured in countless ways. Most common is the jingle at the beginning of the commercial, followed by announcer copy; the commercial is concluded by a reprise of the entire jingle or its closing bars.

Customer interview.   The announcer may talk not with professional talent but with actual consumers, who relate their favorable experience with the product or service or store. As a variation, the satisfied customer may deliver the entire commercial.

Humor.   Tastefully handled, humor may be an ingredient in almost any other technique. A slice-of-life scene can have humorous overtones, and even straight announcer copy may be written in a humorous vein. Humor is often appropriate for low-priced package products, products people buy for fun, products whose primary appeal is taste, or products or services in need of a change of pace in advertising because of strong competition. Never, however, make fun of the product or the customer, or treat too lightly a situation that is not normally funny. The test of a humorous commercial is whether the customer remembers the product, not the commercial. Humor is not called for when your product has distinct advantages that can be advertised with a serious approach.

Combination.   Radio techniques may be mixed in almost countless ways. To select the right technique for a particular assignment, follow the guidelines we discussed for selecting television techniques in Chapter 18; they also apply to radio.

Timing of commercials

Most radio stations accept these maximum word lengths for *live* commercial scripts:

10 seconds	25 words
20 seconds	45 words
30 seconds	65 words
60 seconds	125 words

When the commercial is prerecorded, you may use any number of words as long as you stay within the time limit.

COMMONWEALTH EDISON COMPANY
60-Second Recorded Radio Announcement
"AIR CONDITIONER CLEANING"
INFORMATIVE

0202-INFO-60

1 SINGERS: We got ideas right now,

2   working for you

3   Got the people who know how,

4   working for you.

5   We're keeping this in view

6   In everything we do

7   We're working for you.

8   Working for you.

9 ANNCR: Commonwealth Edison reminds you that this is a good time to clean or

10   replace the filter on your air conditioner, whether you've got a

11   window unit or central air system. When the filter's dirty, your air

12   conditioner has to work harder. That takes more energy. A good periodic

13   cleaning will make your machine more efficient, and will help you save

14   on its operating costs. And the more thoroughly you clean, the more

15   money you'll save.

16 SINGERS: We're working for you.

17   We're working for you.

Singers lead to Commonwealth Edison's advice to clean or replace the filter of an air conditioner. Another public-relations commercial.

After you have written the commercial, read it aloud, not only to time it properly but to catch tongue-twisters and insure that it flows smoothly.

Musical commercials

Often commercials are set to music especially composed for them or adapted from a familiar song. A few bars of distinctive music played often enough may serve as a musical identification of the product. Such a *musical logotype* usually lasts about ten seconds. Jingles are also popular ways of making a slogan memorable.

This brings us to the question of musical rights. A melody is in the public domain, available for use by anyone, without cost, *after* the copyright has expired. Many old favorites and classics are thus in the public domain and have been used as advertising themes. That is one of their detriments: they may have been used by many others.

Popular tunes that are still protected by copyright are available only by agreement with the copyright owner. You may find a catchy, familiar tune, but it may be costly.

An advertiser can also commission a composer to create an original tune, which becomes the advertiser's property and gives the product its own musical personality.

Methods of delivery

There are two ways of delivering a radio commercial: *live* and *prerecorded*.

The live commercial. A live commercial is delivered in person by the studio announcer, disc jockey, newscaster, or other station personality, or by a sports reporter from another location. Generally read from a script prepared by the advertiser, the commercial is sometimes revised to complement the announcer's style. If time allows, the revised script should be approved in advance by the advertiser. *Ad-libbing* (extemporizing) from a fact sheet should be discouraged, since the announcer may inadvertently omit key selling phrases or, in the case of regulated products such as drugs, may fail to include certain mandatory phrases.

Some commercials are delivered partly live and partly prerecorded. The prerecorded jingle, for example, can be played over and over with live announcer copy added. Sometimes the live part (the dealer tie-up) is left open for the tie-in ad of the local distributor.

The advantage of the live commercial is that the announcer may have a popular following; listeners tend to accept advice from someone they like. Furthermore, particularly when the news announcer also delivers the commercial, some of the believability and timeliness of the news may spill over to the ad.

The prerecorded commercial. For a regional or national campaign, local announcer capabilities are not known, and it is impractical to write a separate script to fit each one's particular style. Commercials for these campaigns are therefore usually prerecorded. Not only are advertisers secure in the knowledge that the commercial is identical each time it is aired, but they can take advantage of myriad techniques impractical for live commercials.

```
UNITED AIRLINES
60-Second Recorded Radio Announcement
"MORE, MORE, MORE"
PASSENGER SERVICE


01994-PASS-60

1  MUSIC:  INTRO

2  ANNCR:  We fly to the snow.

3  SING:   HAVE YOU SEEN THE OTHER SIDE

4  ANNCR:  We fly to the sun.

5  SING:   OF WHERE YOU LIVE

6  ANNCR:  United Airlines flies more people to more of this land than anyone.

7  SING:   MOTHER COUNTRY'S GOT HER ARMS OPEN WIDE

8  ANNCR:  Feel the spirit in our people.  That's Friendship Service in the friendly skies.

9  SING:   YOUR LAND IS OUR LAND, ANYWHERE THE BIG BIRD FLIES

10 ANNCR:  We'll show you this land in a big way ... with more widebody DC-ten's and seven

11         forty-seven's than any other airline.

12 SING:   COME ALONG, SING THE SONG, PEOPLE NOW'S THE TIME

13 ANNCR:  We give people more reasons to choose us.  And they do.

14 SING:   SWEET MOTHER COUNTRY

15 ANNCR:  Because we do our best to make you feel we're flying just for you.

16 SING:   (MODULATE)  SWEET MOTHER COUNTRY

17 ANNCR:  We're Mother Country's favorite airline.  United.

18 SING:   THE FRIENDLY SKIES OF YOUR LAND
           UNITED AIRLINES.
```

Using a musical lead to establish the importance of United Airlines and their friendship service.

Producing the Radio Commercial

Although there are certain broad similarities, producing radio commercials is far simpler and less costly than producing TV commercials. First of all, the agency or advertiser appoints a *radio producer,* who converts the script into a recording ready to go on the air. After preparing the cost estimate and getting budget approval, the producer selects a *recording studio,* a *casting director* if necessary, a *musical director,* orchestra, and singers if the script calls for them.

After the cast has been selected, it rehearses in a recording studio, which can be hired by the hour. For complex productions, a rehearsal day may be scheduled ahead of shooting. Since most commercials are shot in short "takes," however, which are later joined in the editing, a formal rehearsal is usually unnecessary. When the producer feels the cast is ready, the commercial is acted out and recorded on tape. Music and sound may be taped separately, then mixed with the vocal tape by the sound recording studio. In fact, by double- and triple-tracking music and singers' voices, modern recording equipment can build small sounds into big ones. You have to pay for this ability, however. Union rules require that musicians and singers be paid extra fees when their music is mechanically added to their original recording. After the last mix, the *master tape* of the commercial is prepared. When final approval has been obtained, duplicates are made on quarter-inch tape reels or audio cassettes for release to the list of stations.

Steps in radio production

We may summarize the steps in producing a commercial.

1. An agency or advertiser appoints a producer.

2. The producer prepares cost estimates.

3. The producer selects a recording studio.

4. With the aid of the casting director, if one is needed, the producer casts the commercial.

5. If there is to be music, the producer selects a musical director and chooses music.

6. If necessary, a rehearsal is held.

7. The studio tapes music and sound separately.

8. The studio mixes music and sound with voices.

9. The producer sees that the master tape is prepared for distribution on either tape or cassettes and shipped to stations.

You are on the air!

QUESTIONS

1. Describe and explain the characteristics of effective radio copy.

2. Why is compulsion important in radio copy?

3. In attempting to create mental pictures, the radio copywriter has a choice of many proven techniques to give more meaning to the copy and to gain and keep the attention of the target audience. What are these techniques?

4. What is meant by the timing of radio commercials?

5. What are the comparative advantages and limitations of live and prerecorded radio commercials?

6. What is the role of the radio producer?

7. Identify the steps in producing a radio commercial.

8. Since radio is not a visual medium, what are the special challenges of creating effective radio commercials?

9. Describe the following:
   - a) two-announcer
   - b) jingle announcer
   - c) musical logotype
   - d) public domain
   - e) ad-libbing
   - f) master tape

READING SUGGESTIONS

BUCKLEY, DONALD BRIGHT, ''Execution of Copy Strategy in Broadcast Media,'' *Handbook of Advertising Management.* Roger Barton, ed. New York: McGraw-Hill, 1970.

HEIGHTON, ELIZABETH J. and DON R. CUNNING-HAM, *Advertising in the Broadcast Media.* Belmont, Calif.: Wadsworth, 1976.

Major Discoveries About Radio Reach and Frequency Revisted. New York: Radio Advertising Bureau, Inc., undated.

ROBINSON, SOL, *Radio Advertising: How to Sell It and Write It.* Blue Ridge Summit, Pa.: Tab Books, 1971.

TERRELL, NEIL, *Power Technique for Radio-TV Copywriting.* Blue Ridge Summit, Pa.: Tab Books, 1971.

YOUNG, LAWRENCE R., ''Estimating Radio Reach,'' *Journal of Advertising Research* (October 1972), 37–41.

20

Trademarks
Packaging

Trademarks   Never before has a good trademark been so important as in this age of self-service. The trademark directly affects the distinctiveness of the product, therefore the ease with which it is remembered and its sales. The creation of a good trademark is the biggest single contribution a person can add to the marketing success of a product. Although a product usually has only one trademark in its lifetime, companies are constantly coming out with new products for which new trademarks will be needed. An advertising person with a knowledge of people, marketing, and copy is in an ideal position to meet the challenge of creating winning trademarks.

Grooming the Product for the Market

The trademark often becomes the most important asset of a company, growing more valuable each year. A whole body of law has been developed to protect this property against infringers. Getting legal protection is the province of the attorney; however, it begins with the creation of the trademark itself. Hence, in creating or considering an idea for a trademark, it is important to understand some of the basic legal ground rules.

What is a   A trademark is any symbol, sign, word, name, device, or combination of these
trademark? that tells who makes a product or who sells it, distinguishing that product from those made or sold by others. Its purpose is to protect the public from being deceived, and to protect the owner from unfair competition and the unlawful use of his property.

A trademark invariably consists of, or includes, a word or name by which people can speak of the product—"Do you have *Dutch Boy* paint?" That word

440

or name is also called a *brand name.* A trademark may, but does not have to, include some pictorial or design element. If it does, the combination is called a *logotype.*

A *trade name,* on the other hand, is the name under which a company does business. *General Mills,* for example, is the trade name of a company making a cake mix whose trademark (not trade name) is *Betty Crocker.* The terms *trademark* and *trade name* are often confused.

A product can have several trademarks, as *Coca-Cola* and *Coke.* Chief among the basic requirements for making a trademark legally protectable are the following:

▲ *The trademark must be used in connection with an actual product.* The use of a design in an advertisement does not make it a trademark, nor does having it on a flag over the factory. It must be applied to the product itself or be on a label or container of that product. If that is not feasible, it must be affixed to the container or dispenser of it, as on a pump at a gas service station.

▲ *The trademark must not be confusingly similar to trademarks on similar goods.* It should not be likely to cause the buyer to be confused, mistaken, or deceived as to whose product one is purchasing. The trademark should be dissimilar in appearance, sound, and significance. *Cycol* was held to be in conflict with *Tycol,* for oil; *Air-O* was held in conflit with *Arrow* for shirts; *Canned Light* was held in conflict with *Barreled Sunlight* for paint, because of such possible confusion.

The two products involved need not be identical. The marks will be held in conflict if the products are sold through the same trade channels, or if the public might assume that a product made by a second company is a new product line of the first company. The name So-Soft *tissues,* for example, was held in conflict with Snow & Soft *paper napkins* for this reason. BIG BOY! powder for *soft drinks* was held in confusion with BIG BOY *stick candy.*

▲ *A trademark must not be deceptive.* It must not indicate a quality not in the product or be misdescriptively deceptive. Words that have legally been barred for this reason include *Lemon* soap that contained no lemon, *Half-Spanish* for cigars that did not come from Spain, *Nylodon* for sleeping bags that contained no nylon.

▲ *A trademark must not be merely descriptive.* "I have often noticed," the head of a baking company might say, "that people ask for fresh bread. We will call our bread *Fresh;* that's our trademark. How nice that will be for us!" But when people ask for "fresh bread," they are describing the kind of bread they want, not specifying the bread made by a particular baker. To prevent such misleading usage, the law does not protect trademarks that are merely descriptive, applicable to many other products.

Aircraft for control instruments and *Computing* for a weighing scale were disallowed as trademarks because they are merely descriptive. The misspelling or hyphenating of a word, such as *Keep Kold* or *Heldryte,* does not make a nondescriptive word out of one that, if spelled correctly, would be descriptive of the product. Although a word must not literally be descriptive, it may *suggest* certain qualities, and we will touch upon this matter shortly.

Dictionary words.   Many trademarks consist of familiar dictionary words used in an arbitrary, suggestive, or fanciful manner. *They must not be used in a merely descriptive sense* to describe the nature, use, or virtue of the product. Good examples of dictionary words that meet the foregoing requirements are

Forms of trademarks

Dial soap, *Glad* plastic bags, *Sunbeam* toasters, *Shell* oil, and *Rise* shaving cream. The advantages of using words in the dictionary are that you have so many from which to choose, and the public will recognize them. The task is to get them to associate the word with the product. If you have done that, the chances of protection against infringement are good. (A problem may arise with a manufacturer who has not had trademark experience and who asks, "But what has that to do with my product?")

A word alone, even if set in a standard type, can be a trademark. When it is formed into a design or combined with one, to add distinctiveness and memorability, it is called a logotype.

Coined words.   Most trademarks are words made up of a new combination of consonants and vowels. *Kodak* is the classic forerunner of this school of thinking. We also have *Kleenex, Xerox, Norelco, Exxon*—the list is long. The advantage of a coined word is that it is new; it can be made phonetically pleasing, pronounceable, and short. Coined words have a high rank for being legally protectable, but to create one that is distinctive is the big challenge. (One drug company tried using a computer to create coined words for its many new products. They were distinctive, but just not pronounceable.)

When coining a word from a root word associated with a product, there is danger that the basic word may be so obvious that others in the field will use it, with resulting confusion of similar names. In one issue of the *Standard Advertising Register,* there were fifteen trademarks beginning with *Flavor* or *Flava.* We also have *Launderall, Laundromat, Launderette; Dictaphone, Dictograph.* But think of a fresh root concept, and you have the makings of a good trademark.

Personal names.   These may be the names of real people, such as Sara Lee; fictional characters, like *Betty Crocker;* historical characters, as in *Lincoln* cars; mythological characters, as in *Ajax* cleanser. A surname alone is not eligible as a new trademark; others of that name may use it. Names like *Lipton's* tea, *Heinz* foods, or *Campbell's* soups have been in use so long, however, that they have acquired what the law calls a "secondary meaning"; that is, through usage the public has recognized them as representing the product of one company only. But a new trademark can have no secondary meaning.

Geographical names.   A geographical name is really a place name: *Nashua* blankets, *Utica* sheets, *Pittsburgh* paints. These names are old trademarks and have acquired secondary meaning. Often the word *brand* is offered after geographical names. The law does not look with favor on giving one person exclusive right to use a geographical name in connection with a new product, excluding others making similar goods in that area. However, a name chosen because of the fanciful connotation of a geographical setting, rather than to suggest it was made there, may make it eligible for protection, as with *Bali* bras.

Initials and numbers.   Fortunes and years have been spent in establishing trademarks such as *RCA* television, *AC* spark plugs, *J & B* whisky, *A-1* sauce. Hence, they are familiar. In general, however, initials and numbers are the hardest form of trademark to remember and the easiest to confuse and to imitate. They suggest no visual image by which they can be remembered. One issue of the *Standard Advertising Register* listed the following numerical trademarks: No. 1, No. 2, 2 in 1, 3 in 1, 4 in 1, 5 in 1, No. 7, 12/24, No. 14, 77, and 400.

Pictorial.   To reinforce their brand name, many advertisers use some artistic device, as distinctive lettering, a design, insignia, picture, or other visual device. The combination, as we mentioned before, is called a *logotype.*

Creating the trademark

The use of a word for a trademark generally gives the owner the right to express the idea in a variety of ways, as with a picture or symbol (such as the trademark *Green Giant* for frozen and canned vegetables and a picture of a green giant for the same purpose). The total design can then be carried on labels, cartons, packing cases, warehouse signs, and gasoline service stations, both here and abroad. A trademark word or name is more apt to get quick recognition if it is always lettered in a uniform style; this unit is also called a *logotype*. A test of a design is whether it is distinctive enough to be recognized immediately in any size.

Goals of a trademark

A trademark should be

Distinctive.   Its purpose is to *identify* a product. Trade directories are full of trademarks that play it safe and follow the leader, with the result that one directory listed 89 *Golds* or *Goldens*, 75 *Royals*, 95 *Nationals*, and 134 *Stars!*

There are styles in trademarks. We are now in the This 'n That stage: Fresh 'n Ready, Set 'n Go, Stir 'n Serve, Gloss 'n Toss. These may be legally eligible for protection, but do they rank as distinctive? Or simply bewildering?

The quest for distinction also applies to designs, where the use of circles, ovals, and oblongs are commonplace.

Simple, crisp, short.   Good examples: *Sanka* coffee, *Ajax* cleansers, *Ritz* crackers, *Crest* toothpaste.

Easy to pronounce, and in one way only.   The makers of *Sitroux* tissues changed their name to *Sitrue;* the makers of *Baume Bengué* changed it to *Ben Gay.* To help customers pronounce *Suchard,* the makers created a charming trade character called *Sue Shard,* and changed the name too. These companies made the best of their old trademarks. But there should be no doubt about the pronunciation of a new trademark.

The great problem with suggestive trademarks is that they may so easily go over that vague boundary that divides them from being descriptive. Even experienced advertisers have this problem. The Sun Oil Company spent upward of $30 million over a six-year period advertising its brand of gasoline called *Custom Blended,* only to have the courts finally rule that it was a descriptive term that any gasoline company could use.

A usable design.   If a design is used, will it be usable and identifiable in black-and-white when reduced to small size? It takes a long time for the public to associate a company name with a design; hence, many are meant to be used in connection with the product or company name, to help reinforce the identification. A design is especially useful on packages, shipping cartons, trucks, and letterheads.

Free of unpleasant connotations, here or abroad.   A trademark should be avoided if it can be punned unpleasantly. It should not be offensive abroad. The makers of an American car discovered its name meant "sudden death" in one Oriental country where they had been trying to do business.

If a trademark conveys some attribute of the product, so much the better. Mere description cannot have legal protection, but a suggestion can; for example, *Downy* fabric softener, *Band-Aid* bandages, *Accutron* watches, *Bisquick* biscuit mix.

Having reviewed the desirable attributes of the trademark, we come back to the first question: is it distinctive?

In the United States, the first to use a trademark for a certain category of goods has the exclusive right to it for those goods and for other goods that people might assume to be from the same producer. To let the world know who is using a trademark, and to help establish the date on which it was first used, a trademark may be registered with the Patent Office, which has a complete record of all trademarks registered. Registration is not compulsory; but through the Lanham Act, it provides 20-year protection, renewable indefinitely. Federal registration applies to goods sold in interstate or foreign commerce. If, within five years of registration, old ads or bills of sale prove that someone used a trademark before it was registered by another, the first user has rights over the person who registered it. Nevertheless, most firms apply for federal registration. There is also state registration for those seeking limited protection only.

What "registering" a trademark means

Once a trademark has been registered, it should carry a notice to that effect wherever it appears, such as ® next to the trademark, or "Registered, U.S. Patent Office" or "Reg. U.S. Pat. Office," or some similar notice. When a trademark is repeatedly used in an ad, some firms require the registration notice on the first use only, to reduce the possibility of typographic "bugs."

We now meet a paradoxical situation, in which the owner of a successful trademark suddenly discovers that anyone can use it—all because certain precautionary steps were not taken. This problem arises when the public begins using a trademark to describe a type of product, rather than just a brand of that type of product. Originally, *Thermos* was the trademark owned by the Aladdin Company, which introduced vacuum bottles. In time, people would ask, "What brand of thermos bottles do you carry?" The courts held that "Thermos" had become a descriptive word that any manufacturer of vacuum bottles could use as "thermos," with a lower case "t" and was no longer the exclusive trademark of the originator. *Victrola, cellophane, nylon, escalator, aspirin,* and *linoleum* started off as the trademark of one company, but then became generic—a word that is public property because its owners failed to take certain simple steps to put a "lock" on their property.

Putting a lock on trademarks

The steps to "putting a lock" on the ownership of a trademark are these: (1) Always make sure the trademark word is capitalized, or set off in distinctive type. (2) Always follow the trademark with the generic name of the product: Glad *disposable trash bags,* Kleenex *tissues,* Windex *glass cleaner.* (3) Don't

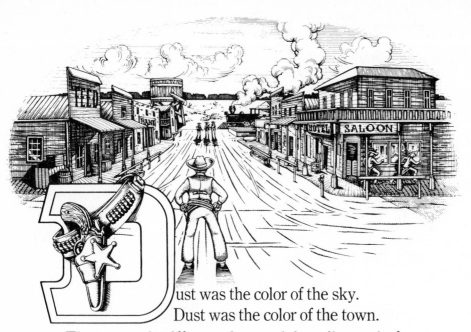

Dust was the color of the sky.
Dust was the color of the town.

The young sheriff moved toward the railway platform, pausing only to wipe his moist palms on his holsters.

He watched the Union Pacific engine hurtle around the bend and screech to a clanging, hissing stop. Silently, the Dalton boys swung from the train onto the station platform. Suddenly the sheriff found himself staring down the barrels of three shotguns. The street behind him was empty but for the dust.

There was no turning for help.

As his hands crept slowly toward his gun belt he knew he had to say it now or forever hold his peace. A crooked smile played about the corners of his mouth, as he drawled, "Boys, I want you to hear me and hear me good. Just remember, that Xerox is a registered trademark of Xerox Corporation and, as its brand name, should be used only to identify its products and services."

Xerox seeks to protect its exclusive right to its trademark.

speak of it in the plural, as three Kleenexes; rather, say three Kleenex tissues. (4) Don't use it in a possessive form—not Kleenex's new features, but the new features of Kleenex tissues—or as a verb—not "Kleenex your eyeglasses," but "Wipe your eyeglasses with Kleenex tissues." This is a legal matter, but the advertising person's responsibility to carry out in the advertisements.

Up to now, we have been speaking of trademarks that identify specific products. We now speak of the *house mark,* the primary mark of a firm that makes a large and changing variety of products. Here the house or firm mark is usually used with a secondary mark: *Du Pont* (primary), Lucite, Dacron, Zerone (secondary); *Kellogg's* (primary), Special K, Product 19 (secondary).

Many companies create a design to go with their house mark. This design alone can appear on everything from a calling card to the sides of a truck and on shipping cases going overseas. It can become an international identification. But it takes time to establish a design; hence, companies often use their name along with the house mark.

This brings us to a major marketing-policy decision on how, if at all, the relationship of all the company's products should be presented to the public. We quote from a report on the subject issued by the 4 A's:

> This is a question of policy. What may be logical for one advertiser may not be at all suitable for another. The food field offers a good example of the two philosophies at work.
>
> General Foods aims to have each of its many brands stand on its own advertising feet. In their early days they were acquiring companies at the rate of one every three months . . . in virtually every case, each was already established as an advertiser. For many years there was no family identification in the advertising. Then "A Product of General Foods" was included in small type, and more recently there has been an attempt toward family identification through the General Foods Test Kitchen . . .
>
> On the other hand, California Packing has too many products to attempt to establish brand names for each. Consequently all are carried under the house mark, *Del Monte.* They feel that the quality reputation established for the overall mark rubs off on each product. They also point out that this philosophy makes their trademark generically invincible. Who would ask for "a can of Del Monte"?
>
> Some follow a mixed course. National Biscuit has some 200 cookie and cracker packages in its line, a good many of which feature their own brands. Yet all carry the *Nabisco* trademark—usually shown on a corner of the package.
>
> In some cases the association of brand and company is deliberately omitted from advertising, usually because of product competition within the company's line itself. This is a common occurrence with these companies.
>
> This also applies when such associations reflect unpleasantly on the product or corporate image. A food company making fertilizer, for instance. The Quaker Oats "Q" trademark is not seen in connection with Puss-in-Boots cat food.
>
> Or when the association is meaningless. The *Gillette* mark is not used in advertising Paper-Mate pens.

House marks

A house mark combined with a trademark of one of the company's products.

Thus we see that a consideration of trademarks goes deep into management problems regarding the entire policy of marketing a variety of products made under the control of one company.°

Service marks; certification marks

Service mark.

People who render *services*, as an insurance company, an airline—even Weight Watchers—can protect their identification mark by registering it in Washington as a *service mark*. There is also registration for *certification marks*, whereby a firm certifies that a user of his identifying device is doing so properly. Teflon is a material sold by Du Pont to kitchenware makers for use in lining their pots and pans. *Teflon* is Du Pont's registered trademark for its nonstick finish. *Teflon II* is Du Pont's certification mark for Teflon-coated cookware that meets Du Pont's standards. Advertisers of such products may use that mark. The Wool Bureau has a distinctive label design that it permits all manufacturers of pure-wool products to use. These marks are all registered as certification marks. They have the same creative requirements as trademarks—most of all, that they be distinctive.

Certification mark.

Packaging

Whether we talk about a supermarket, hardware store, sporting goods store, hobby shop, drugstore, toy store, or department store, one thing is certain: a store's environment is an everchanging panorama, with new products, improved products, and new package designs constantly appearing on the scene. This is the arena in which consumer products have to fight for the consumer's patronage.

The package is the most conspicuous identification a product can have, and it is a major factor in the success of most consumer products. It is very persuasive in the consumer's decision to buy a product and in the retailer's decision to carry the product, but it is important to each for different reasons. With so many demands placed on the package, several people are involved in packaging decisions. The advertising director is one of them, especially because advertising and packaging complement each other.

Basic requirements

From the consumer's viewpoint.   With all the changes in packaging taking place, certain basic requirements never change. The package must protect its contents from spoilage and spillage, leakage, evaporation, and other forms of

° American Association of Advertising Agencies, *Trademarks—Orientation for Advertising People*, pp. 22–23. © 1971. Published by permission.

Evolution of the Coca-Cola bottle. The first Coca-Cola bottle (1900) had a rubber stopper, and it popped when the bottle was opened—thus the word pop for soft drinks.

Courtesy Modern Packaging Encyclopedia.

deterioration from the time it leaves the plant until the product is used up. (How long that might be is an important consideration.) It must fit the shelf of the refrigerator or medicine cabinet in which that type of product is stored. (The Vaseline bottle, which had been round for generations, was redesigned as a rectangular bottle, to save room in the crowded medicine chest.) Cereal boxes must fit pantry shelves. If the package is meant to be set on a dressing table, it should not tip easily. The package should be comfortable to hold and not slip out of a wet hand. (Note how shampoo bottles usually provide a good grip.) It should be easy to open, without breaking a fingernail, and to reclose for future use. It should be attractive.

From the store operator's viewpoint. The store manager has additional criteria for judging a package. It must be easy to handle, store, and stack. It should not take up more shelf room than any other product in that section, as might a pyramid-shaped bottle. Odd shapes are suspect; will they break easily? Tall packages are suspect; will they keep falling over? The package should be soil-resistant. Does it have ample and convenient space for marking? The product should come in the full range of sizes and packaging common to the field.

For products bought upon inspection, as men's shirts, the package needs transparent facing. (Puritan Shirts even included a plastic hanger for the store's use.) The package can make the difference in whether a store stocks the item.

Small items are expected to be mounted on cards under a plastic dome called *blister cards,* to provide ease of handling and to prevent pilferage. Often these cards are mounted on a large card that can be hung on a wall, making profitable use of that space. And at all times, the buyer judges how a display of a product will add to the store.

There are factors other than packaging that may cause a product to be selected, but poor packaging may relegate that product to a poor shelf position. Moving a product from floor level to waist level has increased sales of a product by as much as 80 percent. Good packaging can make that much difference.

Finally, the package should enhance the beauty of its surroundings at the point of use or display.

Designing a new package

Package design embraces the entire physical presentation of the package—its size and shape, the materials of which it is made, the closure, the outside appearance, the labeling.

Fitting the package to marketing goals

Walter P. Margulies, a leading package designer, stresses the fact that package thinking is first of all marketing thinking, and embraces questions such as:

▲ How much emphasis should be placed on the brand name? On the product name?

▲ Toward what segment of the market should the product's basic appeal be aimed?

▲ In what way will the packaging system best communicate product appeal?

▲ Should the graphics try to convey the size, shape, color, in-use applications? If so, how?

▲ In dealing with a food product, is it advisable to include recipes on the package? Which ones? Should they be changed in accordance with the seasons?

▲ Are all package panels being used to their best advantage? Will they effectively sell the product, regardless of the way the package is stacked on the supermarket shelf?

▲ Can the basic design be extended to encompass other items in the manufacturer's line? Is it flexible enough to permit the addition of new products at some future date?

▲ Is there ample space for the inclusion of extra copy to announce special sales offers?

▲ What about price marking? Has a specific place been set aside where the product can be priced easily by the retailer but not mar the total look of the package?

These are a mere handful of the multitudinous factors that have to be taken into consideration by those whose job it is to launch a new package.°

Time for a change?

We now jump ahead a number of years and perhaps many millions of dollars in sales for the product we so wisely trademarked and packaged and whose merits have earned it many repeat customers. "What's this?" someone exclaims some morning. "You want to make changes in our good-luck package?" There is no clock of package life that says whether or when you might want to consider a change. But there are certain telltale market indexes that say it may be time to review the situation. Among them, Margulies cites the following:

1. Innovation in physical packaging

2. Exploiting a reformulated product based on a meaningful formula change

3. The force of competitive action

4. Repositioning your product
   General Foods learned that the image of the decaffeinated Sanka brand was that of a castrated bean. The coffee-loving public avoided it. To reposition Sanka, the yellow label, which according to research, suggested weakness, was replaced with a dominantly brown label, "very strong." And the statement "97 percent caffein-free" was given a less significant spot on the label

° Reprinted by permission of The World Publishing Company from *Packaging Power* by Walter P. Margulies. Copyright © by Walter P. Margulies.

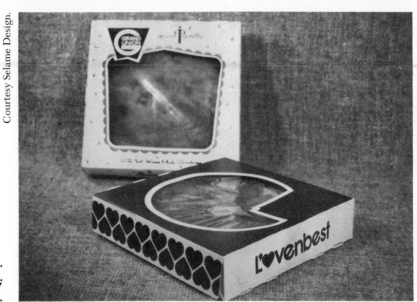

**The old vs. the new.
The old package is on top;
the new is on bottom.**

5. When effective ads force a shift in tactics
   Only when a theme has established itself as distinctive and long-lived

6. When changing consumer attitudes force a shift in marketing tactics

7. Upgraded consumer taste in graphic design

8. Changing retail selling techniques

9. When unrecognized home use determines a new marketing posture

In contrast to these reasons for considering a change, Margulies offers the following warnings:

1. Don't change because of a new brand manager's desire to innovate.

2. Don't change to imitate your competition.

3. Don't change for physical packaging innovation only.

4. Don't change for design values alone.

5. Don't change when product identification is strong.

6. Don't change if it may hurt the branding.

7. Don't change if it will weaken the product's authenticity.

8. Don't change if it will critically raise the product's price.

"A decision to stay with the status quo," he adds, "is as important as the one to innovate."[*] Some companies, however, frequently test new packaging to try to revitalize a product or turn an old product into a new one, and yet spend less money than if they had started from scratch.

When a package is to be changed, it is often done on a gradual basis, changing

[*] Ibid., pp. 62–67.

only one element at a time, so that old customers will not suddenly feel that this is no longer the product they have known and trusted.

Package design has become so important that a specialized field of package designers has developed.

Testing the package design

What research techniques can provide information that can be translated into guidelines for a sound package design program? Among the most common approaches are the following: tachistoscope tests, focus group interviews, semantic differential tests, forced choice association tests, and attitude study interviews.[°]

Courtesy International Paper Co.

The old label (left) **was redesigned** (right) **to give the name greater prominence on the store shelf.**

Tachistoscope test.   A tachistoscope is a device, similar to a slide projector, that flashes pictures on a screen for very short, controlled periods of time (usually in intervals of a fraction of a second). The respondents are exposed to pictures of a package to determine, for example, how quickly they recognize the brand name, the type of product, package size, illustration, or any other design feature of the package. The results of this test (which is best used in combination with another technique) can be a useful basis for evaluating how the package's message is being received.

Focus group interview.   In an unstructured approach, a number (usually from 5–10) of group participants are brought together under the direction of a group discussion leader. They engage in a free-wheeling, open discussion about the subject at hand, which ranges from the general ("How do you feel about breakfast in your home?") to the specific ("What do you look for in a cereal package?"). This approach can provide useful insights into packaging and comparative package designs.

Semantic differential test.   This technique uses a series of scales, with each scale consisting of two opposite adjectives; for example, expensive–cheap, natu-

° Walter Stern, "Research and the Designer," *Modern Packaging*, (April 1975), 30–31.

Packaging a complete line.

ral–artificial, modern–old-fashioned, national–local, sweet–sour, strong–weak, heavy–light. The semantic differential method of testing package designs is simple, so that several packages can be rapidly rated and compared.

Forced choice association test.   Respondents rate package attributes on a scale providing answers that most accurately reflect their opinions on certain questions. (The scale is similar to multiple-choice exams.) The test permits comparison among various packages or design elements.

Attitude study interview.   Sometimes it is advantageous to conduct interviews to determine consumer attitudes toward packaging. The interviews are normally done at the point of purchase among consumers who have purchased and used the product (or a competitive one), and the respondents are asked a variety of questions pertaining to the product and package. The result is a great deal of data that the packager can use in evaluating a package and in deciding which alternative to choose, if any, for a new package design. An important feature of attitude study interviews is that the data are usually collected in the actual buying atmosphere of the store.

Legal aspects of packaging

There are both federal and state laws that regulate packaging and labeling. The Fair Packaging and Labeling Act of 1966 says:

> Informed consumers are essential to the fair and efficient functioning of a free economy. Packages and their labels should enable consumers to obtain accurate information as to the quality of the contents and should facilitate value comparisons. Therefore it is hereby declared to be the policy of the Congress to assist consumers and manufacturers in reaching these goals in the marketing of goods.

This is the most far-reaching law affecting packaging and labeling. The Food and Drug Administration is responsible for enforcing the law as it affects foods, drugs, cosmetics, and health devices. The Federal Trade Commission has jurisdiction over "other consumer commodities."

Trends in packaging

Packagers, like most others in industry, have to deal with energy and materials shortages. Whether we talk about plastics, aluminum, glass, paper, or any other packaging material, the problem is the same—supplies are not unlimited, as we once thought. Packagers have been trying to economize by finding substitute materials and by developing simpler and more standardized packages. Alcoa has run extensive advertising to urge people to turn in old aluminum cans for recycling. To save on the more expensive metal, Band-Aid has switched to a paperboard carton for its bandages. A packaging change born of necessity very often results in a package that consumers like better than the old one, as Taylor Wines found out when it switched from scarce lead foil to PVC (polyvinyl chloride) for the overcap on its bottles—and Taylor got better color identification for the package as a bonus.

The quest continues.

QUESTIONS

1. Define a trademark. What is its purpose?

2. Distinguish between (a) trademark, (b) brand name, and (c) trade name. Give two examples of each.

3. What are the important legal requirements to keep in mind when creating a trademark?

4. Discuss the six forms of trademarks cited in the chapter.

5. What are the chief qualities desired of a trademark?

6. Discuss the importance of a trademark from the viewpoint of advertising.

7. What is meant by the registration of trademarks?

8. What are the basic requirements of a package from the consumer's viewpoint? From the retailer's viewpoint?

9. "The package is part of the total product." What is your comment?

10. How do packaging and advertising work together?

11. Explain why packaging thinking is marketing thinking.

12. What are some of the conditions that suggest a need for considering a packaging change? What are some reasons for not changing?

13. Describe the approaches used in package testing.

14. In your opinion, does packaging do a good job? Whatever your answer, justify your position.

15. What do you see as the social responsibilities of packaging? Are they being fulfilled? Why or why not?

16. Cite three examples of what you believe to be "effective" packaging and three examples of what you consider ineffective packaging. Explain the reasons for your choices.

READING SUGGESTIONS

BABCOCK, W. F., "How to Stay Out of Trouble with Your New Corporate Logo," *Advertising Age* (July 19, 1976), 43–44.

BARKER, STEVEN M., "How to Steer a New Packaging Program," *Advertising Age* (October 18, 1976), 73–74.

DICHTER, ERNEST, *Packaging: The Sixth Sense?* Boston: Cahners Books, 1975.

EVANS, E. C., "How to Design the 'Right' Package," *Purchasing* (July 23, 1974), 53–54.

"Experts Tackle Current Packaging Questions," *Advertising Age,* Packaging Section (April 28, 1975), 29–54.

MARGULIES, WALTER P., *Packaging Power.* New York: World Publishing Company, 1970.

Modern Packaging Encyclopedia. New York: McGraw-Hill.

NEUBAUER, ROBERT G., *Packaging: The Contemporary Media.* New York: Van Nostrand Reinhold, 1973.

SELAME, ELINOR, and JOE SELAME, *Developing a Corporate Identity: How to Stand Out in the Crowd.* New York: Chain Store Publishing Corp., 1975.

STERN, WALTER, "Research and the Designer," *Modern Packaging* (April 1975), 28–31.

"Technical Advances Push Packaging Forward," *Advertising Age* (April 29, 1974), 45.

Trademarks—Orientation for Advertising People. New York: American Association of Advertising Agencies. 1971.

PART FIVE

Managing the advertising

The Advertising Agency Media Services and Other Services

The Advertising Agency

The advertising agency has long played an important role not only on the advertising scene but also in American industry, and more recently in world industry. It has grown with the times; it has changed with the times.

Just what is an advertising agency? What does it do? Where does it fit into the picture? What is its role in relation to advertisers and media? How does it get paid? What changes are now taking place in the field? To understand these matters, it is well to begin at the beginning.

It is not generally known that the first Americans to act as advertising agents were the colonial postmasters.

How today's agency developed

In many localities, advertisements for Colonial papers might be left at the post offices. In some instances the local post office would accept advertising copy for publication in papers in other places; it did so with the permission of the postal authorities. . . . William Bradford, publisher of the first Colonial weekly in New York, made an arrangement with Richard Nichols, postmaster in 1727, whereby the latter accepted advertisements for the *New York Gazette* at regular rates.[*]

Space salesmen.   In 1841, Volney B. Palmer of Philadelphia became a sales agent on a commission basis, soliciting advertisements for newspapers, which, at

[*] James Melvin Lee, *History of American Journalism*, rev. ed. (Boston: Houghton Mifflin Company, 1933), p. 74.

that time, had difficulty getting out-of-town advertising. Palmer contracted publishers, offered to get them business for a 50 percent commission but often settled for less. There was no such thing as a rate card or a fixed price for space or commission. "A first demand for $500 by the papers might be reduced before the bargain was struck to $50." (Today we call that *negotiation*.) Soon there were more agents, offering various deals.

Wholesalers of space.   In the 1850s, George P. Rowell of Philadelphia became a wholesaler, buying a big block of space from publishers at a very low rate for cash (most welcome), less agent's commission. He would then sell it in small "squares"—one column wide—at his own retail rate. Rowell next contracted with 100 newspapers to buy one column of space a month and sold space in his total list at a fixed rate per line for the whole list. "An inch of space a month in one hundred papers for one hundred dollars." Selling by list became widespread. Each man's list, however, was his private stock-in-trade. (The original *media package* deal.)

The first rate directory.   In 1869, Rowell shocked the advertising world by publishing a directory of newspapers with their card rates and with his own estimates of their circulation. Other agents accused him of giving away their trade secrets. Publishers howled, too, because his estimates of circulation were lower than their claims. Nevertheless, he offered to provide advertisers an estimate of space costs based on those published rates for whatever markets they wanted. This was the beginning of the *media estimate*.

The agency becomes a creative center.   In the early 1870s, Charles Austin Bates, a writer, began writing ads and selling his services to whoever wanted them, whether advertisers or agents. Among his employees were Earnest Elmo Calkins and Ralph Holden, who, in the 1890s, founded their own agency, famous for 50 years under the name of Calkins and Holden. They did more than write ads. They brought together planning, copy, and art, showing the way to make all three into effective advertising. Not only was their agency a most successful one for half a century, but the influence of their work helped establish the advertising agency as the creative center for advertising ideas. That many of the names on the list of firms advertising in 1890 (p. 10) are still familiar today is a tribute to the effectiveness of that generation of agency people in developing the new power of advertising agency services.

The business had changed from that of salesmen going out just to sell advertising space to that of agencies which created the plan, the ideas, the copy, and the art work; produced the plates, then placed the advertising in publications from which they received commission.

Since the early days of Calkins and Holden there have been many changes in the agency world, and many new services have been, and are being, offered by

Earnest Elmo Calkins
580 Park Avenue
New York
21

Dear Mr. Kleppner:

You perhaps do not realize what a disorganized muddle advertising was in the 1880's and 1890's. Most agencies merely placed copy furnished by clients. The rate cards were farces. The average agent simply bartered with the medium, magazine or newspaper, as to cost, beating it down to the lowest possible amount by haggling.

I consider my greatest contribution as being the first agency to recognize that advertising was a profession, to be placed on a much higher plane than a mere business transaction of placing advertising -- with the copy, the art work, the plan as the important part. I wrote my first advertising while still living in my home town, won a prize for an ad, wrote copy for local business men, worked a year as advertising manager for a department store, and received an offer from Charles Austin Bates, who was the first man to make a business of writing advertising copy. There I met Ralph Holden, and from that association sprang the name of the old firm of Calkins and Holden. I am now more than 96 years old.

Cordially,

Earnest Elmo Calkins

"All of this I have seen, and part of which I have been." Calkins, a pioneer in the advertising agency business, wrote this letter three months before his death in 1964.

agencies. But the unique contribution to business for which agencies are most respected, to this day, is their ability to create effective advertising.

Agency-client relationship established. In 1875, N. W. Ayer & Son of Philadelphia (successors to Rowell, and one of our big agencies today) made a proposal to bill advertisers for what they actually paid the publishers (i.e., the rate paid the publisher less the commission) adding a fixed charge in lieu of commission. In exchange, advertisers would place all advertising through agents. This established the relationship of advertisers as clients of agencies, not merely customers who might give business to different salespeople, never knowing whether they were paying the best price.

The Curtis no-rebating rule. In 1891 the Curtis Publishing Company, the giant that published *The Saturday Evening Post* and the *Ladies' Home Journal*, announced it would pay commissions to agencies only if they agreed to collect the full price from the advertiser. This was later adopted by the Magazine Publishers Association. It was the forerunner of the no-rebating agreements, which were an important part of the agency business for over 50 years. Agency commissions, however, ranged all the way from 10 percent to 25 percent both in magazines and newspapers.

Standard commission for recognized agencies established. In 1917, newspaper publishers, through their association, set 15 percent as the standard agency commission, a percentage that remains for all media to this day (except local advertising, for which the media deal directly with the stores and pay no commission). The commission would be granted, however, only to agencies that the publishers' associations "recognized." One of the important conditions for recognition was that the agencies agree to charge the client the full rate (no rebating). Other criteria for recognition were that the agency must have business to place, it must have shown competence to handle advertising, and it must be financially sound. Those three conditions are in effect to this day. Anyone may claim to be an agency, but only those who are "recognized" are allowed a commission.

Agencies still receive commissions from the media for space they buy for clients. Art work, however, and the cost of production generally are charged by the agency to the advertiser, plus a service charge, usually 17.65 percent of the net—equivalent to 15 percent of the gross. A service charge by pre-agreement is made for other services.

The American Association of Advertising Agencies. The year 1917 also marked the date when the American Association of Advertising Agencies (the 4A's) was formed. This organization has continuously been a great force for improving the standards of agency business and of advertising practice. Its members today, large and small, place over 75 percent of all national advertising.

We can summarize the events of those years in the agency world, which have left their mark today:

Radio.   Radio came in about 1925. The main event of that year was the Scopes trial, and the main advent was radio. Both did a lot for each other. Radio added drama to evolution on trial; it brought the issue of teaching evolution closer to listeners and brought those at home closer to the radio. Tuning in became a major part of American life, especially during the Great Depression; and during World War II, it established itself as a prime news medium. It gave advertising a new medium and challenged the agencies to create a new art of advertising: the *radio commercial.* The manufacture of radio sets became a booming new industry that also needed advertising. Radio billings helped many agencies pull through those troubled years. A number of agencies handled the entire production of the program as well as the commercial. By 1942, agencies were billing more for radio ($188 million) than for newspapers ($144 million). The radio boom lasted until TV came along.

Television.   Television really got going after 1952, when nationwide network broadcasts began. Between 1950 and 1956, TV was the fastest-growing medium. It became the major medium in many agencies. National advertisers spent more on TV than on any other medium. TV expenditures grew from $171 million in 1950 to $1,225 million in 1956.

Electronic Data Processing.   The computer entered advertising through the accounting department. By 1956 it was already changing the lives of the media department, the marketing department, and the research department, all having grown in competence with the increasing number of syndicate research services. Agencies prided themselves on their research knowledge and were spending hundreds of thousands of dollars for research per year, better to serve their clients.

Business was good, and consumers were attaining a better standard of living than they had ever had before. The 1950–1956 period proved to be the beginning of the biggest boom we have ever had. Total advertising expenditures jumped from $4,570 million in 1950 to $9,910 million in 1956. Over 60 percent of this was for national advertising placed by advertising agencies. And the agency business was good, too.

The consent decrees—1956.   In this year a great change occurred in the advertiser-agency relationship. The Department of Justice held that the no-rebating provision between media associations and agencies limited the ability to negotiate between buyer and seller, that it was in restraint of trade and a violation of the antitrust laws. People involved in such a charge, however, might consent in writing to drop the unlawful practice, and the charge would be dropped. Consent decrees to stop that practice were entered into by all the media associations on behalf of their members.

This decree in no way affected the 15 percent the agencies received from the media, but it opened the way to review the total compensation an agency should receive for its services, using the 15 percent commission from the media as a basic part of the negotiations. We shall shortly see the many effects this has had on the agency-client relationship.

Work of the full-service agency

If a new account or a new product is assigned to your agency, work on it will generally proceed along these lines: first, you will ask yourself questions.

What is the marketing problem?   This will entail research to determine to whom we are trying to sell. Where are they? What are their demographic and psychographic characteristics? How does this product fit into their life style? How do they regard this type of product? This particular product? Competitive products? What one service, above all others, do consumers seek from such product? In what distinctive way can the product deliver the greatest satisfaction? What media will best reach our market?

The creative response.   Based on answers to the foregoing, your agency will set the positioning of the product, decide on the copy appeal, prepare copy, prepare rough layouts and storyboards.

The media plan.   Select media. Prepare schedules, with costs.

Total plan.   Present roughs of the copy, layout, production costs, along with media schedules and costs, leading to total cost.

When approved, proceed with production of ads, issue media orders, ship plates and prints to media, or tapes and films as required.

Notify trade of forthcoming campaign.   Inform dealers of the campaign details, giving them time to get ready.

Billing and payments.   When ads are run, take care of billing to client and payment of bills to media and to production vendors. As an example of the billing procedure, let us say that an advertiser has ordered an ad in the *Leisure-time* magazine, through your agency, for one page at $2,000. When the ad appears, your agency will get a bill from the publisher reading,

1 page, October Leisure-time magazine	$2,000
Agency commission @ 15%	300
Balance due	$1,700

(The cash discount is omitted here for convenience.)

Your agency will then bill the advertiser for $2,000, retain the $300 as its compensation and pay the publisher $1,700.

The agency commission as described above applies only to the cost of space or time. In addition, as mentioned earlier, your agency will send the advertiser a bill for production costs for items such as finished art work, typography, reproduction prints—all at actual cost plus a service charge, usually 17.65 percent of the gross (which is equivalent to 15 percent of the net).

Organization of the full-service agency

Many of today's agencies were started by two entrepreneurs, one creative, the other an account manager. At first they may have handled all the functions of an agency themselves, but soon they would have to round out their organization to handle the basic areas of full-service agency responsibility. Although agencies differ in the way they are organized, dividing these areas of responsibility into four main categories will give us a good idea of basic agency structure. For the purposes of this discussion, we put the agency under the command of four major executives: the vice-presidents for (1) the creative department, (2) account services, (3) marketing services, and (4) management and finance. We shall discuss briefly how each department is organized.

1. Creative department.   At the head, the creative director is responsible for the effectiveness of advertising produced by the agency. On this, the success of the agency depends. The creative director sets the creative philosophy of the agency, its standards of craftsmanship, and generates a stimulating environment that inspires writers and artists to do their best work, that, in turn, inspires the best people to seek work there.

At first the writers and artists will work directly with the creative director; but as the business grows, various creative directors will take over the writing and art activities of different brands. To keep the work flowing on schedule, there will be a *traffic department.*

2. Account services.   The vice-president in charge of account services is responsible for the relationship between agency and client and is indeed a person of two worlds: that of the client's business and that of advertising. The vice-president must, of course, be knowledgeable about the client's business, profit goals, marketing problems, and advertising objectives. He or she is responsible for helping to formulate the basic advertising strategy recommended by the agency, for seeing that the proposed advertising prepared by the agency is on target, and for presenting the total proposal—media schedules, budget, rough advertisements or storyboards—to the client for approval. Then comes the task of making sure the agency produces the work to the client's satisfaction.

As the business grows and the account services director has several clients, account executives will be appointed to become the continuing contact with the various accounts. Account executives must be skillful in communication and follow-up. Their biggest contribution is to keep the agency ahead of clients' needs. But the account management director will continue the overall review of account handling, maintaining contacts with a counterpart at the advertiser's office.

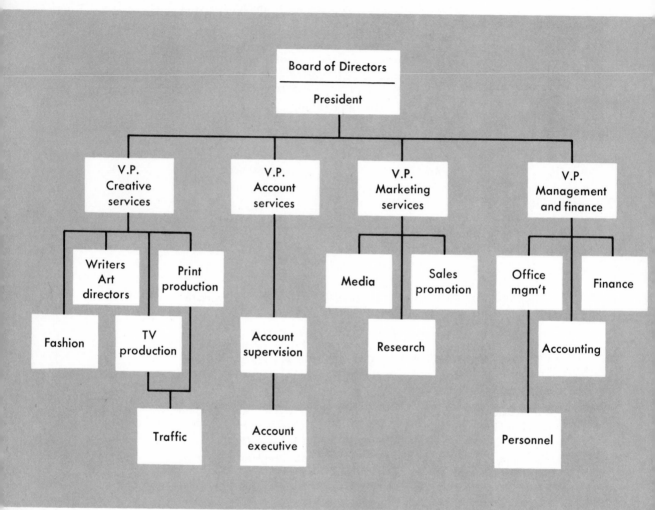

An organization chart for a typical full-service agency. It is based upon a chart from the American Association of Advertising Agencies.

3. Marketing services.   The vice-president in charge of marketing services will be responsible for media planning and buying, for research, and for sales promotion. The marketing vice-president will appoint a media director who is responsible for the philosophy and planning of the use of media, for the selection of specific media, and for buying space and time. As the agency grows, there will be a staff of media buyers, grouped according to media (print, TV or radio), accounts, or territory. The media staff will include an estimating department and an ordering department, as well as one to handle residual payments due performers. The media head may use independent media services, especially in the purchase of TV and radio time, as we shall shortly describe.

The research director will help define marketing and copy goals. Agencies usually use outside research organizations for field work; but in some agencies, research and media planning are coordinated under one person. The division of work among the executives may vary with the agency.

The sales promotion director takes care of premiums, coupons, and other dealer aids and promotions.

4. Management and finance.   Like all businesses, an advertising agency needs an administrative head to take charge of financial and accounting control, office management, and personnel (including trainees).

International agency operations

Virtually every large American agency has branch offices in the lands where its clients conduct their international business. There are such branches in 88 countries. These international branch offices serve as a defensive step; for if an agency does not have a foreign office to serve an overseas client, that advertiser will turn to the local branch of another agency. The door is then open for the competitive agency to take over the American part of the billings—the largest of all.

Setting up a foreign office, however, is more complex than opening a branch office within the United States. Each land is a different market with its own language, buying habits, ways of living, mores, business methods, marketing traditions, and laws. Most American agencies now purchase a majority or minority interest in a successful foreign agency, instead of trying to organize a new agency with American personnel. They usually do have a top management person at the head of an overseas branch. Key members of international offices regularly gather at the home office for an intensive seminar on the philosophy and operation of the agency, giving them ideas to carry back and adapt as they see fit.

Competing accounts

The relationship between client and agency is a professional one. A full-service agency will share many of the client's confidences, often including plans for new products; therefore, a full-service agency will not, as a rule, accept the advertising of products in direct competition. This practice has led to many conflicts in our age of conglomerates, when a client may buy a company, one of whose products competes with one the agency is presently handling. When two agencies consider merging, the first question is, "Will any of our accounts conflict?" This subject also presents a problem in dealing with outside creative services and is an inhibiting factor to consider.

The agency of record

Large advertisers will have a number of agencies handling the advertising of their various divisions and products. To coordinate the total media buy and the programming of products in a network buy, the advertiser will appoint one agency as the *agency of record*. It will make the corporate media contracts under which other agencies will issue their orders, keep a record of all the advertising placed, and transmit management's decisions on the allotment of time and space in a schedule. For this service, the agencies involved pay a small part of their commissions (usually 15 percent of their 15 percent) to the agency of record.

Agency networks

In the 1920s, Lynn Ellis, an advertising management consultant, saw the problem of middle-size agencies that had no branch offices to handle the regional problems of their clients. He organized a group of such agencies—one in each main advertising center—into an *agency network*, to help one another on any problem in their respective areas and to exchange ideas, experiences, and facilities. The success of this plan has prompted the formation of other agency networks.

Other developments in the agency world

New services have been springing up outside of the agency, contributing to big changes in agency structure.

Independent creative services. Because advertisers were looking around to find top creative talent whose services they could buy on a fee basis, a number of creative shops opened (often called *boutiques*). Usually they were headed by former top-level agency talent and included copywriters and artists. One creative shop won a major advertising award and got so much business that it became a full-service agency, now a very large one.

Media buying services (usually referred to as *media services*). This institution came to advertising in the late 1960s. It represents independent companies of media specialists, concentrating largely on buying TV and radio time. (We discuss it at greater length later in this chapter.)

Both of these services were born in the Sixties and Seventies—times of increasing costs and decreasing profits, which caused advertisers to look in all directions to see how they could more effectively handle advertising costs. The availability of these new independent services made possible two new forms of agency structure: the *a la carte* agency and the *in-house* agency.

The a la carte agency.   Many agencies offer just that part of their total services that the advertiser wants, on a fee basis. The a la carte arrangement is used mostly for creative services, and for media planning and placement.

The in-house agency.   When advertisers found that all the services an agency could offer were purchasable on a piecemeal fee basis, they began setting up their own internal agencies, referred to as *in-house agencies.*

Under the in-house agency operation, an advertiser can employ an agency or a creative service to originate advertising for a fee or markup. A media buying service will buy the time or space, and an agency will place it for a fraction of their 15 percent commission. Whereas the older house agency was equipped with a complete full-service staff, the in-house agency is an administrative center that gathers and directs varying outside services for its operation. It has a minimum staff.

The term *in-house* distinguishes the talent-assembling type of agency operation from the self-contained *full-service house agency* born in the earliest days, when large advertisers owned their own agencies. Even Procter & Gamble had its own Procter and Collier agency. But most such house agencies fell out of favor as the advertisers discovered that they got better advertising when they used independent agencies. Even the few such house agencies operating today may use outside services to supplement their own staffs. There is a distinction between the in-house agency (which merely calls in and supervises the work of all the services it needs), and the older full-service house agency (geared to perform most all the advertising functions itself). By people who do not sense the difference, in-house agencies are often referred to as just house agencies.

But saving money is not the only or even the chief reason for some firms to use an in-house agency. In the industrial field, dealing with highly technical matters and with constant technical changes and advances, some advertisers have found it more efficient to have their own technical people prepare the ads, to save the endless briefing necessary for outside industrial writers. But they place their ads through an agency of their choice, at a negotiated commission.

The establishment of an in-house agency operation requires careful planning. Various estimates running up to $20 million have been made on how much billing is required for a successful operation. The in-house agency is definitely not for the small advertiser.

Forms of agency compensation

Since 1972 the Association of National Advertisers has conducted biennial surveys among its members, regarding their methods of agency compensation. The purpose of the survey is twofold: to report the variations in ways of compensating agencies and to provide a basis for comparisons that might show trends.

The two broad sources of agency compensation are (1) traditional 15 percent media commission, including ways of settling on the final percentage, and (2) strictly a fee basis, whereby the agency commission reverts to the advertiser and the agency receives a fee computed on whatever basis has been agreed upon.

The following table is a summary of the reports of 257 advertisers surveyed in 1976 by the Association of National Advertisers.

Client-agency compensation arrangements

Commission-related arrangements	*Number of mentions*	*% of 275 total*
Traditional 15% media commission plus markup	168	61%
Reduced commission	11	4
Increased commission	3	1
Combination of hourly rates and commissions	4	1
Volume rebate	1	—
Minimum guarantee	12	4
Efficiency incentive compensation plan	7	3
Other	21	8
Total media commission-related	227	82%
Strictly fee arrangements		
Cost plus profit	16	6%
Fixed fee (flat fee, fixed compensation)	18	7
Flat fee plus direct costs	6	2
Supplemental fees (project fees)	3	1
Other	5	2
Total fee	48	18%
Overall total	275	100%

As indicated by the survey results, advertiser-agency compensation arrangements are, as a rule, tailored to the specific service requirements of the advertiser and the willingness and ability of the agency to fulfill those needs at a mutually agreeable cost.[*]

Just as some advertisers move their accounts from independent agencies to form their own in-house agencies, so other advertisers, having tried in-house agencies, have returned to independent agencies. The 4A's made a two-year

[*] Current advertiser practices in compensating their advertising agencies. Association of National Advertisers, Inc. 1976.

study of such shifts among its members. The accompanying table summarizes their report.

Client movement to and from in-house agencies

	Dollar volume		% of total 4As volume	
	1975	1976	1975	1976
Movement to "in-house"	$32,060,000	$11,720,000	40%	12%
Movement from "in-house"	25,408,000	52,740,000	32	55
Net movement "in-house"	$ 6,652,000	—	08	—
Net movement to 4As agencies	—	$41,020,000	—	43

Source: American Association of Advertising Agencies.

Media Buying Services

The 1960s were exciting for television, its first ten years of nationwide network TV. It was the decade of booming sales of TV sets and TV advertising; in fact, television time sales doubled during those years. Television media directors of large agencies were spending millions of dollars under great professional pressure to make the most effective use of their budgets by planning the scheduling and by negotiating for the best buys. Meanwhile, in every business office of every TV station there was always concern about unsold time—a cardinal sin, for it represented a complete, irreversible loss. The situation was ripe for time buyers, especially in large agencies with large TV schedules, to plan and to place, and to negotiate for the best deal for a schedule. Negotiating for time became an art. So much so, that some media directors decided to start their own time-buying services, performing whatever part of the total media operation an advertiser or agency might require—planning, scheduling, negotiating, verifying. The chief service featured by most of them was at the pocketbook level, in negotiating the purchase of time on behalf of the advertiser—and thus a number of today's outstanding independent media services were born.

Heads of media services believed they could save the advertiser money by operating with an experienced staff of negotiators and media technicians, concentrating on media function only. They also felt they might be able to save agencies money in handling some phases of their own media operations. Upon their ability to make good on this challenge rests the survival and success of the independent media service.

The advent of these services was also in response to the quest of some advertisers to retain specialists to handle their work, operating on an in-house-agency basis. Some advertisers also saw that competition in media negotiations would

MEDIA PLANNING

VITT MEDIA INTERNATIONAL, INC.
437 Madison Avenue
New York, N Y 10022
(212) 751-1300
TWX-710-587-4294

Sound media plans–ones which can be solidly documented by logic and media facts–are able to be constructed only where marketing objectives are explicitly clear. • The purpose of this form is to aid in the achievement of that clarity.

I. 1. **Product** _____   2. Date: _____

3. Budget: $ (M) _____ 4. Advertising Period: Start date _____ ; End date _____

II. 5. **Purpose of Plan** (Check where applicable):

a) _____ Introduction   b) _____ Annual   c) _____ Heavy-Up   d) _____ Weight test   (_____ hi; _____ low)

4) _____ Other (pls. explain): _____

_____

III. 6. **Marketing Objectives** (Pls. describe briefly the two or three objectives you feel should govern the product's strategy, e.g. a) Where advertised must use competive pressure; b) Follow brand development):

a) _____

b) _____

c) _____

IV. Target Demographics (Pls. indicate priority of target audiences by categories shown–use rank number, index, check or other):

7. Sex/Age (Yrs)

Female	Male
_____ to 6; _____ 6-11; _____ 12-17; _____ 18-34; _____ 35-49; _____ 50+ Other: _____	_____ to 6; _____ 6-11; _____ 12-17; _____ 18-34; _____ 35-49; _____ 50+ Other: _____

8. Income ($M)   : _____ Under 9. _____ 9-14.9. _____ Over 15

9. Education   : _____ Coll Grad; _____ Attend Coll; _____ HS Grad; _____ Attend HS

10. Region*   : _____ NE _____ EC _____ WC _____ S _____ P

11. County Size*   : _____ A _____ B _____ C _____ D

*Nielsen

V. Geographic Sales (Pls. first show percent of product's sales by its sales territories, secondly your best estimate of how percents would fall if best potentials by sales territories could be realized.)

%
Tot.

12. Territories: _____ _____ _____ _____ _____ _____ _____ _____ _____ _____

13. % Sales: _____ _____ _____ _____ _____ _____ _____ _____ _____ _____   100.0

14. % Potentials: _____ _____ _____ _____ _____ _____ _____ _____ _____ _____   100.0

There is much to be learned by a careful study of these forms.

V. Geographic Sales (cont.)

Markets	% Sales Brand	Industry	Markets	% Sales Brand	Industry
1-10	_____	_____	51-60	_____	_____
11-25	_____	_____	61-75	_____	_____
26-35	_____	_____	76-85	_____	_____
36-50	_____	_____	86-100	_____	_____

VI. Seasonal Sales (Pls. repeat same procedure as in V):

	1st J F M Tot.	2nd A M J Tot.	3rd J A S Tot.	4th O N D Tot.	Grand Total
15. % Sales:	__ __ __ ___	__ __ __ ___	__ __ __ ___	__ __ __ ___	___
16. % Potential:	__ __ __ ___	__ __ __ ___	__ __ __ ___	__ __ __ ___	___

VII. Copy (Pls. check copy lengths, sizes and mix available for consideration):

17.

TV %	Radio %	Mags. %	Newsp. %	Outdr. %
60" —	60" —	P-4C —	ROP —	24 —
30" —	30" —	P-BW —	Color —	30 —

Other: ____ __   ____ __   ____ __   ____ __   ____ __

Other requirements: _____

VIII. Media

18. Reach & Frequency (Pls. check the relationship of reach to frequency you feel most pertinent to this product):

_____ Reach more important _____ Reach less important _____ Reach and frequency equal

19. Competition (Pls. list share of market, advertising budgets and distribution among major media of product and its three largest competitors):

	Mkt. Share	Ad.Bud. $M	% Media Distribution TV Net	TV Spot	Radio	Mags	Newsps	Outdr	Other	Total
Prod.	•	•	___	___	___	___	___	___	___	100.00
A.	•	•	___	___	___	___	___	___	___	100.00
B.	•	•	___	___	___	___	___	___	___	100.00
C.	•	•	___	___	___	___	___	___	___	100.00

IX. 20. Other Considerations (Pls. check other items which must be considered in constructing this media plan):

a. _____ corporate network support   d. _____ dealer listings/tags

b. _____ ethnic and/or special market support   e. _____ other _____

c. _____ coupon and/or sampling promotion support

X. 21. Special Notes _____

_____   Signed: _____
                                         Client

_____   Signed: _____
                                         VMI

Courtesy Vitt Media International, Inc.

result in the best rates for the advertiser—and media services represented competition to the agency's media department.

How media services function

An advertiser retains a media service at a predetermined fee to work

1) *when initial media planning is being done.* The service may develop the plan for the agency or advertiser, or the service may counsel them in the development of the plan from its specialized knowledge of media usages and media rates.

2) *when the media plan is ready to be executed and the media buying is ready to be done.* If the media service has developed the plan, then, after approval by the agency or advertiser, it proceeds to purchase media schedules according to specifications. If the plan has been developed by the agency or advertiser, the media service reviews the specifications of the plan and agrees to accept responsibility for purchase of media schedules that will meet specifications.

3) *as a full-time media department.*

After the media buys have been made, the media service provides the agency or advertiser with summaries of the media schedules purchased and estimates of the audience delivered. Generally, the media service will also verify schedule performance (by means of television or radio station affidavits or print media checking copies), check on preemptions and make-goods, and pay the media. Some of the media services will also provide the agency or advertiser with a "post-buy analysis," documenting the audience delivery of the media schedule according to syndicated research-service measurements of the media schedule as it ran. Generally this is what agencies do also; the media services try to do it better.

Although the specialized skill offered by media services is employed by advertisers, advertising agencies frequently avail themselves of the media services to augment their own media staff. To the small-to-medium agency, a media service may also be helpful in case of a sudden increase in the work load.

Other Services

Barter

Barter is another way for an advertiser or agency to buy media below card rates, especially TV and radio time. It has nothing to do with media services, except that they often use it, too.

When the advertiser is the buyer. Long before radio and television appeared on the scene, hotels began a practice that they continue to this day: paying for advertising space in exchange for *due bills*, which were good for the payment of rooms and were transferable. They bartered their rooms for advertising space in newspapers and magazines.

Barter in broadcasting began in the early days of radio. Cash was always tight (even as it often is today), but studios would have to spend a lot of money for

on various stations, accumulating their own timebanks, then offering the
their clients at less than rate card costs. As the writer of the foregoing .
said, barter is a growing force.

Advertising Research Services

In addition to the syndicate research services previously discussed, which
regularly report the latest findings on who may buy our product—who and
where they are, how they live and buy, what media they read, watch, or listen
to—we also have a vast array of advertising and marketing research services.
These services offer custom-made research reports to marketers and their
agencies, answering their questions about their own products and their advertising. Studies cover subjects such as advertising effectiveness, television and print
pre-testing and post-testing, concept testing, market segmentation, positioning
of products, media preferences, purchasing patterns, and similar problems
directly affecting advertising decisions.

The variety of techniques used in gathering such information is fascinating. It
includes field surveys, consumer mail banks, focus groups, continuous tracking
studies, CATV testing of commercials, image studies, electronic questionnaires,
opinion surveys, shopping center intercepts, and media mix tests.

Regardless of the technique used in gathering information, when a research
report has been submitted, the real value of the effort will be made manifest by
the creative interpretation and use of its findings.

QUESTIONS

1. Define the agency commission system and explain how it works. Has it always
   been 15 percent? Who pays it? To whom?

2. What are the two main sources of agency compensation? What are some of the
   variations in the way they are applied?

3. When an agency is said to be "recognized," by whom is it recognized? What is
   the value in + being recognized?

4. Discuss how the work on a new account or a new product usually proceeds in a
   full-service agency.

5. What are the responsibilities of an account executive?

6. Distinguish among house agency, in-house agency, a la carte agency, and full-
   service agency.

7. What is the usual policy regarding an agency handling competing accounts?
   Why is it this way?

8. What is meant by the "agency of record"?

equipment and for gifts to be given away at quiz shows. Some entrepreneurs got the idea that they would get these goods at very low cost, bartering with stations in exchange for blocks of time on the air—again at a very low rate—and then selling that time to advertisers below card rates, but at a good profit. The Federal Communications Commission has held that bartering for broadcast time is legal.

Firms that handle barter will supply a station anything it needs in barter for time—furniture, equipment, even travel tickets—but the chief subject of barter is program material in the form of films, a constant need of TV stations, which they usually rent from independent film syndicators. Usually included are Hollywood films, films of popular old TV programs, and, more important, films of current popular TV series that the barter houses control. All of this involves no cash outflow for the station.

Some barter houses virtually become brokers or wholesalers of time. They build inventories of time accumulated in various barter deals. These inventories, known as *time banks,* are then available to advertisers or agencies seeking to stretch their TV or radio dollars.

Of course, barter has its drawbacks. Often the weaker stations in a market use it most. Some stations won't accept barter business from advertisers already on the air in the market. Much of the time is poor time (even though it is still good value at the low rate paid). The advertiser or agency does not deal directly with the station; it deals with barter houses, who then deal directly with the station. Problems of make-goods can be sticky. Nevertheless, barter is a flourishing practice, used by many well-known advertisers.

When the advertiser is the seller.   An article in *Television/Radio Age* began:

Barter, timebanking
assumes added dimensions

Whither television barter as a syndicated form? Onward and upward by all indications. . . . Barter is a growing force in TV syndication, and the advertising agency is getting back into programming.

This denotes a big reversal in roles. The agency is not going to the barter house asking if, in their timebank, they have time for some client. Instead, the agency, on behalf of the client, goes to the station and says, "We have prepared a fine syndicate program show for you, for which we won't ask any cash. In this program we have retained four minutes per hour for ourselves, and you can sell three or four minutes to local advertisers." The advantage to the advertiser of *trade-out shows,* as they are often called, is not only a possible saving in TV costs, but more important, it offers the advertiser control over the quality of environment in which the commercial appears. Competitive commercials or commercial overcrowding can be fended off.

The arrangement has proven so successful that a number of agencies have gone into the barter business, creating syndicate shows, bartering time for them

9. What were the reasons behind the development of media services? What are the chief functions of a media service?

10. What are some of the purposes for which advertising research is used?

11. Describe the barter method of buying time. What are its chief advantages? Disadvantages?

12. What are trade-out syndicated programs? What are their advantages for the advertiser? For the station?

READING SUGGESTIONS

"Ad Buy Trends: Flexibility Amid Media Alternatives," *Advertising Age* (October 25, 1976), 1 ff.

COLBERT, JUNE, "How to Get the 'Critical Edge' in Your Agency Presentation," *Advertising Age* (March 22, 1976), 41–42.

DIETZ, STEPHEN, and RODNEY ERICKSON, "How Agencies Should Get Paid: Trend Is to 'Managed' Systems," *Advertising Age* (January 17, 1977), 41–42.

GARDNER, HERBERT S., JR., *The Advertising Agency Business*. Chicago: Crain Books, 1977.

HECKENBACH, ROY A., "You Can—and Should—Audit How Well Your Agency Performs as Your Agent," *Industrial Marketing* (November 1976), 64–68.

IAN, SETH, "The Meeting of the Minds," *Advertising Age* (December 20, 1976), 19–20.

LERNER, AL, "What Agency Type Best Serves Retailers?" *Advertising Age* (November 8, 1976), 56.

MILLER, DONALD B., RICHARD C. CHRISTIAN, ARTHUR W. SCHULTZ, and STUART B. UPSON, *Next Generation of Agency Management*. New York: American Association of Advertising Agencies, 1976.

"The New World of Advertising," *Advertising Age* (Special issue, November 21, 1973).

Standard Directory of Advertising Agencies. Skokie, Ill.: National Register Publishing Company, published annually.

VAUPEN, BURTON, ROBERT F. LYMAN, and THOMAS R. VOHS, *Agency Compensation and Fee Arrangements*. New York: American Association of Advertising Agencies, 1976.

WIND, YORAM and STEPHEN E. SILVER, "Segmenting Media Buyers," *Journal of Advertising Research* (December, 1973) 33–38.

WYMAN, S., and HERBERT MANELOVEG, "Agency Service: a la Carte or Full Fare," *Advertising Age* (February 7, 1972), 49 ff.

22

The Advertiser's Marketing/Advertising Operation

In this chapter, we speak of the marketing/advertising operation, not of just the advertising department. There are two fundamental differences in the way that the consumer advertising operation is handled by various companies: the traditional advertising department way and the newer marketing services approach.

The traditional advertising department

Traditionally, all advertising matters are funneled through the advertising department, headed by an advertising manager or director (the terms vary with each company) who operates under the marketing director. The manager's duties, broadly speaking, are to supervise the entire advertising strategy and operation: budgeting, monitoring the creation and production of the advertising, planning media schedules, and controlling expenditures in line with the budget. The department head works with the sales department and with the agency. As the business grows, and new lines are added, assistant advertising managers, usually known as *product advertising managers*, are appointed to handle the advertising of the different brands of the company, under the supervision of the advertising director.

The marketing services system

The traditional system was the chief one until Procter & Gamble found itself growing, with many new brands, each of which represented its own marketing problems and all of which together (now about 60) make Procter & Gamble America's largest advertiser. P & G developed a new organizational concept, best described as the marketing services system. With variations, it has been widely adopted, especially in the package goods field, for groceries, drugs, cosmetics.

This system has two parts. One is the marketing activity, which begins with the product managers assigned to different brands. The other is a structure of

476

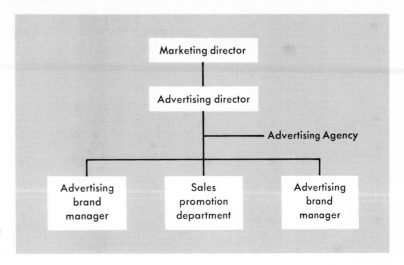

**Simple organization chart
of an advertising department.**

marketing services, representing all the technical talent involved in implementing a marketing plan, including creative services, promotion services, media services, broadcast programming, advertising controls, and marketing research services. These are all available to the product manager, as is the help of the agency assigned to that manager's brand. The product manager can bring together the agency professional and his or her counterpart in the marketing services division, giving the client the benefit of the best thinking of both groups. When different agencies are used, each is assigned to a different group of brands. Each group has a group product manager, who supervises the product managers.

The product manager's job is to plan strategy and objectives, gather information relevant to the brand, coordinate budget developments and control, get recommendations from agencies and others up the line for final discussion and approval as quickly as possible. The product manager is a primary liaison between the marketing department and all other departments, as well as the advertising agency.

The product manager's plans must be approved by the group product manager, who then submits them to the vice-president for marketing, for approval, and finally to the executive vice-president.

Under this system, the advertising department is a branch of the marketing services division. The vice-president for advertising, responsible for the review and evaluation of brand media plans, attends all creative presentations to act as an adviser and is an adviser and consultant on all aspects of the advertising. The vice-president for advertising reports to the senior vice-president-director of marketing.

The biggest difference in this operation is that the advertising does not all come through one huge funnel, with one person in charge of all brands. The great advantage, from the corporate viewpoint, is that each brand gets the full marketing attention of its own group, while all brands get the full benefit of all the company's special marketing services and of the accumulated corporate wisdom. The more important the decision, the higher up the ladder it goes for final approval.

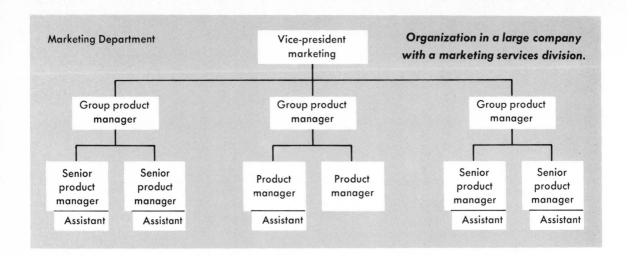

Marketing Department

**Organization in a large company
with a marketing services division.**

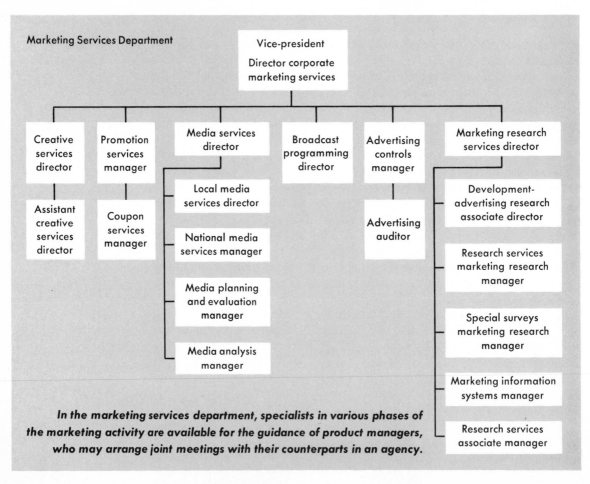

Marketing Services Department

*In the marketing services department, specialists in various phases of
the marketing activity are available for the guidance of product managers,
who may arrange joint meetings with their counterparts in an agency.*

A large advertiser's marketing/advertising operation.

The largest variable expense in most companies is for consumer oriented advertising. Yet with all the technology we can apply to determine how much to spend for advertising, the final decision is a judgmental one. It differs for launching a new product, which is the height of risk taking, and for a company with a steadily growing business and many years background. It differs with the temperament of the top management group. The approach to making a budget is usually along the following lines.

Setting the budget

Percentage of sales.   Companies usually make up their forthcoming budgets in terms of a percentage of sales, with the preceding year as a base. If the rate of growth has been consistent with that of earlier years, they may set the budget percentage higher than last year, in anticipation of continued increase in business and of inflation. If they feel the rate of growth will be slowed, they may lower or maintain the percentage, using the preceding year's sales as a starting figure.

The task method.   By this method, the company sets a specific sales target for a given time, to attain a given goal. Then it decides to spend whatever money is necessary to meet that quota. This might also be called the "Let's spend all we can afford" method, especially in launching a new product. Many big businesses today started that way. Many businesses which are not here today did, too.

The task method is used most widely in a highly competitive environment, as reported in this item taken from the trade press:

Johnson & Johnson Takes on Procter & Gamble. J&J chief Dick Sellars goes after P&G's Pampers (holds estimated 60% share of disposable diaper market) via J&J's Disposable Diaper product. Concentrates advertising efforts in midwest markets. Dick seeks to reach 25% share of each market entered. Earmarks estimated $6 million for advertising campaign to increase awareness of product.[*]

A Gallagher survey asked 111 large advertisers, "What method was used to arrive at the amount set aside for the budget?" Their responses are shown in the next table. The first response reveals a lot about how budgets are often arrived at.

Methods used to arrive at amount set aside for ad budget

Arbitrarily decided by management on basis of available funds	34.6%
Task method combined with percentage of anticipated sales	19.2%
Task method: goals set, then cost of reaching goals determined	17.4%
Compromise between percentage of anticipated new year sales and last year's sales	11.5%
Predetermined percentage of anticipated sales	10.6%
Predetermined percentage of this year's sales	4.8%
Task method combined with percentage of last year's sales	1.9%

Source: Gallagher Report (September 1975).

[*] *Gallagher Report* (September, 1975).

Budgets are under constant scrutiny in relation to sales and usually are formally reviewed quarterly. In addition, budgets are subject to cancellation at any time, except for noncancellable commitments, either because sales have not met a minimum quota, money is being shifted to a more promising brand, or management may want to hold back money to make a better showing on its next statement.

Selecting an agency

No matter which side of the fence you are on, the selection of an agency involves points worth remembering. If you are being chosen, you will be judged with the following points in someone's mind. If you are doing the choosing:

1. Determine what type of services you need from an agency and then list them according to their importance to you. For instance: 1) marketing expertise in strategy, planning, execution; 2) creative performance in television, print, radio, outdoor; 3) media knowledge and clout; 4) sales promotion and/or trade relations help; 5) public relations, corporate or image building ability; 6) market research strength; 7) fashion or beauty sense; 8) agency size; 9) location in relation to your office. Your special needs will dictate many others.

2. Establish a 5-point scale to rate each agency's attributes. A typical 5-point scale would be: 1) Outstanding 2) Very good 3) Good 4) Satisfactory 5) Unsatisfactory. Of course you should give different values or weights to the more important agency attributes.

3. Check published sources and select a group of agencies that seem to fit your requirements and handle accounts about the size of yours. Avoid being the biggest or the smallest account. Also, use your own knowledge or the knowledge of your industry peers to find agencies responsible for successful campaigns or products that have most impressed you. Published sources include the annual issue of *Advertising Age* that lists agencies and their accounts by agency size; the "Red Book" (*Standard Advertising Register*) that lists agencies and accounts both alphabetically and geographically. In case of further doubt, write to the American Association of Advertising Agencies, 200 Park Avenue, New York, New York 10017 for a roster of members.

4. Check whether there are any apparent conflicts with your accounts at the agency. When agencies consider a new account, that is the first question they ask, along with the amount of the potential billings.

5. Now start preliminary discussions with the agencies that rate best on your preliminary evaluation. This can be done with a letter asking if they are interested or a phone call to set up an appointment for them to visit you or for you to visit the agency. Start at the top. Call the president or the operating head of the agency or branch office in your area, who will appoint someone to follow up on the opportunity you are offering.

6. Reduce your original list of potential agencies after first contact. A manageable number is usually not more than three.

7. Now again prepare an evaluation list for rating the agencies on the same 5-point scale. This list will be a lot more specific. It should cover personnel. Who will supervise your account and how will the account team be staffed? Who are the creative people who will work on your business? Similarly, who will service your needs in media, production (television) research, sales promotion, and how will they do it? What is the agency's track record in getting and *keeping* business and in keeping personnel teams together? What is the agency's record with media, with payments? Make sure again to assign a weighted value to each service aspect. If television is most important to you and public relations aid least important, then be sure to reflect this in your evaluation.

8. Discuss financial arrangements. Will your account be a straight 15 percent commission account, a fee account, or a combination of both? What services will the commission or fee cover and what additional charges will the agency demand? How will new product work be handled both from a financial and organizational point of view? What peripheral services does the agency offer and for how much?

9. Do you feel comfortable with them?

10. If your company is an international one, can the agency handle any of your nondomestic business and, if so, how will they do it?

Appraising national advertising

Continuing questions that beset all in national advertising and marketing management are "How well is our advertising working? How well is our investment paying off?" By what yardsticks can one measure national advertising, whose results cannot be traced as easily as those of direct-response advertising?

Advertising goals vs. marketing goals.   Many men have sought an approach to the problem of appraising national advertising in the light of outside influences. Much of the discussion on the subject centers around a report, by Russell H. Colley, prepared for the Association of National Advertisers. The thesis of this study is that *it is virtually impossible to measure the results of advertising, unless and until the specific results sought by advertising have been defined.* When asked exactly what their advertising is supposed to do, most companies have a ready answer: to increase their dollar sales or to increase their share of the market. But these are not *advertising* goals, Colley holds; they are *total marketing* goals. Obviously, national advertising alone is not intended to accomplish this task; but, rather, it is to be used as part of the total marketing effort. The first step in appraising results of advertising, therefore, is to define specifically what the company expects to accomplish through advertising. The report defines an advertising goal as "a specific communications task, to be accomplished among a defined audience to a given degree in a given period of time."

As an example, the report cites the case of a branded detergent. The *marketing goal* is to increase the share of industry from 10 to 15 percent. The *advertising goal* is set as increasing among the 30 million housewives who own automatic washers the number who identify brand X as a low-sudsing detergent that gets clothes clean. This represents a specific communications task that can be performed by advertising, independent of other marketing forces.

The report speaks of a marketing communications spectrum ranging from an *unawareness* of the product to *awareness, comprehension, conviction,* and *action,* in successive steps; and the way to appraise advertising, according to this view, is by its effectiveness in the *communications spectrum,* leading to sales.

Differences of opinion.   Researchers differ on judging the effectiveness of national advertising on a communications yardstick rather than by sales. A report on the subject by the Marketing Science Institute says:

> In general, total sales are not considered a valid measure of advertising effectiveness, because of the presence of other influencing variables. Sales as a criterion may have some validity if advertising is the most prominent variable, or, in the case of mail-order advertising, when it is the only variable.

On the other hand, there are those who "deplore the general acceptance of measures of advertising short of sales or purchases; they frown on communications measures as the sole criterion." Yet even these critics concede that the effectiveness of communications in general is more readily measurable, and for a given expenditure is more reliable, than sales alone. Whatever goal you have selected for your advertising, there are various techniques for finding out how well you have succeeded in achieving it.

Testing for change in awareness.   This is particularly important for testing institutional campaigns, as well as for product advertising. For years the Hartford Insurance Company ran a picture of a graceful stag as a trade character in its ads. A new agency acquired the account and replaced the picture of the

The Hartford's four-legged, antlered trademark is a dramatic part of every visual.

The Hartford casts live stag; tv ads boost trademark awareness by 334%

Courtesy *Advertising Age.*

"Corporate advertising helped us fill an identity void."

—Robert Anderson, President & Chief Executive Officer, Rockwell International

"After our merger with North American Aviation, followed by a series of other mergers and a name change, we needed to establish a clear corporate identity," said Robert Anderson, president and chief executive officer of Rockwell International, in a recent interview.

The situation developed in 1967 when Rockwell Standard, a major automotive parts supplier, merged with North American Aviation. The result was North American Rockwell, a broad-based industrial company that was 70% aerospace and 30% commercial products.

A unified attack on the problem

"The first thing we did was implement a unified advertising, public relations and corporate identity effort, under the direction of H. Walton Cloke, vice president, public relations and advertising," Mr. Anderson continued. To determine the proper direction for this program Rockwell commissioned a research study among businessmen, customers and the financial community. The data confirmed that awareness of Rockwell's stature and product mix was nominal. "In addition to filling the identity void, we wanted to communicate that we were qualified to do extremely complicated technical tasks," Mr. Anderson explained.

To accomplish these two objectives, the advertising campaign was developed to include business and financial publications. Simultaneously a total identification system, including a corporate symbol and logotype, was created and standardized throughout the corporation.

In 1973 Rockwell Manufacturing and Collins Radio were merged with North American Rockwell and a new name, Rockwell International, was adopted to portray the scope of the company. To maintain the recognition that had already been achieved, the name "Rockwell" was retained as part of the new name and the corporate symbol was carried over to the new company.

"Where science gets down to business"

In subsequent years, a number of consumer-oriented products were added to Rockwell's mix—calculators, television sets, stereos, refrigerators, freezers, microwave ovens and power tools—further complicating the identity problem. "It's very difficult to sum up what this company is," said Mr. Anderson. "We were primarily known for putting men on the moon, but the character of the company changed as it grew and diversified."

What's Rockwell done with Collins Radio? Turned up the volume.

In 1971, we acquired a controlling interest in Collins Radio. In 1973 a merger of Collins with Rockwell became effective. Collins' 1974 orders were up 17% over 1973. For more about us and how science gets down to business throughout our multi-industry company, write: Rockwell International, Dept. 815J, 600 Grant Street, Pittsburgh, PA 15219.

Rockwell International
...where science gets down to business

"Now we're about 30% aerospace and 70% commercial, just the reverse of a few years ago." To describe a company that had great technological capability yet was also growing in commercial products, the slogan, "Rockwell International—where science gets down to business," was created and used in all advertising.

As the company's product base broadened, the advertising schedule was increased to include more consumer media—general magazines and television —while continuing a strong campaign in business media.

"We must make the company and its products known to new markets," said Mr. Anderson, "but at the same time we must continue to be attractive to our major customers as well as suppliers, employees and investors. Consequently, we continue to use The Wall Street Journal because it is directed precisely to the audiences we want to reach."

"An additional benefit, of course, is that, with its daily readership of over four million, The Journal gives us a large audience of consumers who are in a position to buy our products."

Commenting on the impact and immediacy of The Journal, Mr. Anderson said, "The Wall Street Journal is the first thing that hits my desk every morning. It's the first thing I read. I think you'd be uninformed from a business point of view if you didn't read The Journal. I'd miss it as much as I'd miss my morning coffee."

Building recognition fast

Since 1968 Rockwell has used research to check the progress of its campaign. A study in September, 1973, showed that Rockwell was clearly better known than many of its major competitors in the commercial and aerospace fields. Even though this was a period in which Rockwell had changed its name and was adding new products, there was marked improvement in recognition of the company's reputation and products.

The report by Yankelovich, Skelly and White, Inc. said of this improvement, "...no other corporation of which we are aware has as effectively communicated its corporate message in such a relatively short period of time."

The survey asked opinions of Rockwell in several important areas. The results below document the increase in positive response:

"We've done probably as good a job as any company in the United States, starting almost from scratch, to become one of the most recognized companies. I think we've made a lot of headway with a relatively small advertising budget," said Mr. Anderson.

Communications Impact Survey, 1968-1973
(Percent of Increase in Positive Response)

Broad Scientific and Technological Base	+ 42%
Respected Reputation	+ 50%
Quality of Products	+ 60%
Good Management	+ 60%

Source: Yankelovich, Skelly and White surveys conducted among customers, the financial community and financial press, 1968 and 1973.

Additional research bears this out. A 1973 Opinion Research Corporation study among security analysts, 6 months after the name change to Rockwell International, showed there was a 70% familiarity with the new corporate name. In another Yankelovich study, security analysts were shown a number of established corporate symbols on a plain sheet of paper. The Rockwell symbol was correctly identified by 40%. Only one other symbol was better known.

Another dividend

A more direct measurement of the success of the program has been requests for additional information offered in all corporate ads. In 1974 Rockwell responded to over 14,000 reader requests.

"Over a period of four years," Mr. Anderson reported, "The Journal has consistently exceeded other publications in generating reader requests for annual reports and additional information about the company. Response has continued to increase to where requests in the first half of 1975 are already ahead of the total for all of 1974."

"We've advertised consistently in The Journal since 1969 and the number of reader inquiries for more information about Rockwell prove that our Journal advertising is being read."

"We've done a big job."

Commenting on the total communications program, Mr. Anderson remarked, "Personally, I think we've done a big job. And, given our objectives, The Wall Street Journal is probably the most effective publication we have in our entire print schedule. It reaches the majority of the people we are seeking."

THE WALL STREET JOURNAL. IT WORKS.

Report of a campaign to change the image of a corporation.

stuffed stag with a live one. More than that, they trained it to be comfortable in scenes with a family; and whenever a Hartford ad appeared, the stag appeared, too, as a living participant in the action. The agency had planned in advance for research to tell the effect of the new stag. They made a tracking test, conducted research before the advertising began and after it had been running.

In a pre-advertising test, research showed that more than 70 percent of the people could not identify Hartford and its trademark. After the first few months, recall and identification of Hartford Insurance Company increased by 72 percent.

An industrial company, Johnson Controls, provides another example of testing for improvement in awareness. Introducing a Total Building Automation System that permits all automatic building systems to be monitored, coordinated, and operated by a single computer, they wanted to reach men who made major decisions regarding building. Johnson ran a campaign in *The Wall Street Journal.* "To check on progress," said the advertising manager, "we set up a research series to objectively measure the results of our total *Journal* campaign. What happened? In just six months, our advertising in *The Journal* increased our top-of-mind awareness by 63%!"

Testing for change of attitude.   In all tests designed to measure changing attitudes, a survey must first be made to see what people think about the product or service before the advertising is run. Those opinions are compared with a corresponding survey made after it has been run. Attitude changes are much more readily observed after exposure to a series of ads in an advertising campaign. Some advertisers also wish to know not only whether a change in attitude has occurred, but whether it is strongly favorable enough to cause the consumer to want the product. The following test shows how this may be done.

TESTING CHANGES IN ATTITUDE WITH A TV COMMERCIAL.   Various methods have been set up for testing attitude changes within the span of a single TV commercial. In one theater testing plan, women are invited to watch a thirty-minute film program, which includes commercials other than the ones being tested. Before the test begins, they are given a list of products and are asked to choose which they would like to take home. After the film showing, they are again asked to prepare a list of what they now want to take home. (The amount of the products is large enough to warrant thoughtful consideration of the brands.) By comparing the "pre-" to the "post-" preferences, the relative effectiveness of the commercial can be weighed. This test can be repeated with other groups, with alternate commercials.

Appraising the campaign before it is run.   There are those who believe that the time to appraise a campaign is before it is run, by testing idea options in different markets. This, of course, is a familiar practice, with one big drawback: it tips off competition to what you are planning to do, and they will try to beat you to it in other markets, especially if it is a new product or is based on a promotion. To meet this problem, cablecasting has come to the rescue.

The increasing use of cable TV for research is based on the fact that thousands of homes get their TV reception via cable. In some cities, cable companies not only relay programs of distant TV stations but can cut in with their own programs, on which they carry spot commercials.

Use of cable TV in testing

AdTel began by selecting one typical test city in which about 50 percent of the homes had cable television. It set up a panel of 2,000 subscribers who were compensated for keeping a diary of their purchases and reporting them each week.

The large advertisers for whom AdTel conducts the tests either already have a TV schedule in that market or can add it to their list. AdTel is able to cut in on the advertiser's own program, replacing their regular commercial with the test commercials, Test Ad A being transmitted to half the homes on the panel, and Test Ad B to the other half. The subscribers see the test ads as regular commercials. From their purchase-diary entries over a period of time, it is possible to compare actual sales to the subscribers who saw Ad A with those to the subscribers who saw Ad B.

This system, which divides a market into two homogeneous test areas—equally subject to the factors that can foul up the usual tests between two different markets—and which gets a weekly diary report of purchases, has been expanded to other test cities. It is being used to check rate of repurchase and alternative promotional efforts like sampling and couponing. It also tests different levels of expenditure, to determine the optimum profit. An advantage to advertisers is that it keeps tests of new products away from the eyes of competitors.

Conditions conducive to research. "As a rule of thumb, in judging whether measurement of results is possible and how comprehensive such measurements can be, the following axioms may be helpful," said the National Industrial Conference Board. To the report, which follows, the writer has added some comments in italics:

Research guidelines

1. The more important advertising is to the sale of a product, the easier it is to appraise results.

   Where advertising plays a minor role in the marketing mix, as in the case of raw materials, even a 100 percent improvement in advertising will not add too much weight to the buying decision.

2. The faster the turnover of a product, the easier it is to appraise the results of advertising.

   The shorter the period of time elapsed between the appearance of an advertisement and the need to make a decision, the better. Fast turnover means early decisions. The price risk of such purchases is usually low.

3. The fewer selling methods employed in moving a product, the easier it is to appraise the advertising.

   If the advertiser is a yarn manufacturer who sells to the weaver of fabric, who sells to a suit manufacturer, who sells to department stores, the results of advertising to the consumer are much harder to trace than are results of mail-order advertising.

4. The less complex the market is (and the less intense the competition), the easier it is to appraise advertising results.

The more competitive a market is, the more business will be done other than by advertising—through deals, promotions, and price changes, obfuscating the effects of advertising and the ability to measure it.

How much testing?   The desirability of conducting extensive testing is a function, first, of the importance of advertising to the company. When advertising is very important to the overall marketing program and a lot of money is spent on it, then extensive research on evaluating ads and campaigns is warranted and necessary. Thus, most major consumer-goods marketers devote much more energy and research money to testing ads than do industrial advertisers.

A second major factor influencing the extent of advertising testing is how major a change in the advertising program is being contemplated. The greater the change, the greater the need for a wide testing base and for in-depth studies. When a previous campaign is being extended with only minor variations, however, partial evaluation will usually suffice.

QUESTIONS

1. We have discussed two fundamental differences in the way that the consumer advertising operation is handled by various companies. Discuss the distinguishing features of each.

2. Explain the major ways of setting the advertising budget.

3. If you were asked how much advertising money you thought would be needed for launching a new brand of a grocery product, how would you go about getting an answer?

4. What is the chapter's suggested 10-step procedure to go about selecting an advertising agency?

5. "Measuring results from national advertising is not easy." Agree or disagree? Why?

6. Discuss the basic idea behind Colley's approach to evaluating advertising.

7. What is meant by the communications spectrum?

8. Describe how cable television is being used for research.

9. What conditions are conducive to appraising advertising campaigns?

10. What are the major factors influencing the extent of advertising testing?

READING SUGGESTIONS

AAKER, DAVID A., "ADMOD: An Advertising Decision Model," *Journal of Marketing Research* (February, 1975), 37–45.

_____, **and JOHN G. MYERS,** *Advertising Management.* Englewood Cliffs, N. J.: Prentice-Hall, 1975.

CLARKE, DAVID G., "Econometric Measurement of the Duration of Advertising Effect on Sales," *Journal of Marketing Research* (November, 1976), 345–57.

DOYLE, PETER, and IAN FENWICK, "Planning and Estimation in Advertising," *Journal of Marketing Research* (February, 1975), 1–6.

ENGEL, JAMES F., HUGH G. WALES, and MARTIN R. WARSHAW, *Promotional Strategy,* Homewood, Ill.: Irwin, 1975.

ENIS, BEN M., and KEITH K. COX, "Ad Experiments for Management Decision," *Journal of Advertising Research* (April 1975), 35–41.

ENNIS, F. BEAVEN, *Effective Marketing Management: Planning and Control Systems for Making Better and Faster Marketing Decisions.* New York: Association of National Advertisers, 1973.

GREYSER, STEPHEN A., and STEVEN DIAMOND, *Consumption and Advertising: A U.S. Management Perspective.* Cambridge, Mass: Marketing Science Institute, 1976.

KRUGMAN, H. E., "What Makes Advertising Effective?" *Harvard Business Review* (March-April 1975), 96–103.

NICKELS, WILLIAM G. *Marketing Communications and Promotion.* Columbus, Ohio: Grid Publishing, 1976.

NICOSIA, FRANCESCO, *Advertising Management, and Society.* New York: McGraw-Hill, 1974.

PRENTICE, ROBERT M., "How to Split Your Marketing Funds Between Advertising and Promotion," *Advertising Age* (January 10, 1977, 41–44.

RISO, O., "Management Bears Chief Responsibility for Ad Costs, Concepts, and Quality," *Industrial Marketing,* (May, 1975), 61–63.

SCHULTZ, R. L., and D. R. WITTINK, "Measurement of Industry Advertising Effects," *Journal of Marketing Research* (February 1976), 71–75.

ZELTNER, HERBERT, "When Should You Market Test? Five Guides Help You Decide," *Advertising Age* (January 17, 1977), 46–48.

23

The Complete Campaign

We are ready to take a new product, place it on the market, and tell the world it is there. This is the moment to take a good, hard look at the chief elements of our advertising campaign.

The product

Is the product good value? Does it work? Does it meet all government requirements covering such merchandise? Will it perform properly in the hands of the consumer? Is there any ingredient in the product that may be affected by its standing on the dealer's shelf? Do you foresee any impediment that may affect your ability to maintain quality production and deliveries?

Does it have a good trademark? If it uses a package, does that have a good design? Is the product ready for the market?

What's the differential? What is the product's reason for existence as far as the consumer is concerned? Why should one buy it? What values does it offer that other products are not already offering? What is its unique advantage? Will the buyer find that this product serves the purpose better, in an important way?

Not only should the product have a significant differential, but that feature should be conspicuous or lend itself to demonstration or dramatization. To differentiate their brand of pantyhose from all the others, the makers of L'eggs linked their brand name with a package shaped like an egg. In speaking of the failure of the Ralston Purina venture into frozen foods, the *Gallagher Report* said, "Marketing me-tooism invites disaster. Lack of product originality leads to failure."

Is the product in step with the times? Changes from many directions, including changes in living styles, affect the sales. In the middle Seventies, so many people began eating at fast-food restaurants such as McDonald's and Burger King, that supermarket sales were appreciably affected.

Is the product being replaced by a new type, better one? (Wooden shingles are being replaced by composition shingles.) All in all, is it part of a growing trend or a waning trend? Is time with it or against it?

It is wise to look at the economic scene for a clue to the way our new product will be received. This reconnaissance will also give us an opportunity to figure out how to present the product so that it *rides with the times.*

Positioning the product.   The decision regarding what you want your product to be known and used for is one of the most important in its success. In one of its own house ads, Ogilvy & Mather, advertising agency, had this to say on the subject:

The marketing program

> The most important decision you will ever make about your advertising is: "How should I position my product?"
>
> Should you position Good Seasons Salad Dressing as a gourmet's delight, for people who appreciate its subtle blend of herbs and spices? Or as a product which competes with bottled salad dressings?
>
> Should you position Shake'n Bake as a new flavor for chicken? Or as an easier way to get old-fashioned "fried-chicken" taste?
>
> The results of your advertising will depend less on how it is *written* than on how it is *positioned.* It follows that the positioning must be decided before the advertising is created.
>
> We positioned Hershey's *oldest* product, Hershey's Milk Chocolate Bar, as the market leader. Familiar, warm, friendly, "the great American chocolate bar."
>
> We positioned Hershey's *newest* product, their new Rally Bar, as "the Hershey-covered hunger-stopper."

Selecting the target market.   Who buys the product? Men, women, teen-agers? What are other significant demographic characteristics of our potential market? Sex? Age? Family size or stage in the life cycle? Income? Occupation? Social class? Is there any part of the country that especially favors this type of product? Do the best prospects have something in common that enables you to reach them as a group?

Who are the heavy users of the product? What distinguishes them from other users? Cereal manufacturers love homes with lots of children; soft drink manufacturers love homes with teen-agers; sporting goods manufacturers love outdoor enthusiasts; lawn seed growers love homeowners with spacious lawns.

A picture of the market.   How large are dollar sales in the prospective market? Which products will be most competitive? What are their particular features? What are their sales (estimated)? Is it a market with a few giant companies having the major share and a long list of small firms dividing the remainder? Will the product be priced competitively? What share of the market are we hoping to get, in what time? Is the product sold through franchised dealers or open trade?

Attitude of trade toward the product.   If our company is well known in the field, salespeople will be welcomed by buyers with a "What's new?" greeting. But if ours is a new company, it will need striking advertising, a good promotion plan, and a good deal, even to get attention. Possibly this is an opportune time for sampling and cents-off offers in newspaper ads, to get the product on the dealers' shelves. This situation also calls for strong trade paper support.

Advertising plan

The budget is established.   We have discussed various yardsticks by which budget figures might be reached. For new products particularly, all formula discussion gives way to the final decision on how much a company wishes to venture on what may become one of their most profitable numbers. But to start an advertising plan, a figure must be set, with the understanding that it is subject to change.

At what stage of the advertising spiral is the product now?   If a product is a new type of article in the pioneering stage, we will have to stress the great advantages now available that were never before available in any form. We will have to change a habit and a life style. We must convince people that previous limitations have been overcome, that this product really works. We might stress a demonstration of the product.

If the product is in the competitive stage, we shall bring out its chief distinctive and significant advantage over other products. We seek to present this benefit as dramatically and conspicuously as we can, only making sure that when a person buys the product it will make good on our claims.

If a product attains a top-of-market share and is in the retentive stage where it is concerned with a holding action, we know it will have to fight off brand substitutes. But the real problem here is not to stand still in that stage, not to rely on continued loyalty of present customers to your product, but to go after new markets with new uses or else to greatly improve the product or add new products to the line. It is time for a new pioneering effort.

Meeting specific selling problems.   In addition to these broad problems affecting a product—based on the stage in which it finds itself—it is reasonable to expect that every product will have its own special marketing problems, ranging from apathy to active prejudice. We now want to plan the total advertising/marketing strategy that will get the desired action.

Among such specific purposes of campaigns, you will recognize those discussed in Chapter 4:

▲ Increase the frequency of use of the product

▲ Increase the variety of uses of the product

▲ Add a new product to a well-known line

▲ Reinforce credibility of important claims

▲ Launch a special promotional campaign

▲ Turn a disadvantage into an advantage

▲ Dispel a misconception

▲ Enhance the image of a company (institutional advertising)

We can recognize the dual usefulness of these objectives. They suggest an entire marketing strategy and provide the theme or even the advertisements themselves, which we now turn over to the creative people.

Creating the advertising.   Once the strategy and the theme of the campaign are set, the creative department can take over the task of preparing advertisements for the print media, the storyboard for TV, and the scripts for radio. While they are working on this, the media department will be busy selecting and buying media.

Selecting and buying the media.   Those who deal with media deal with money. They allocate funds to different media in different proportions. Their decisions determine the number of messages that will be delivered per dollar, to whom, and how often; their judgment directly affects the cost/profit ratio of a marketing program.

There is great opportunity for creative and courageous media selection—not always following the crowd in choice of media, use of space or time, and timing. There is also great variability in what media people can get for their dollars in the purchase of time and space, through negotiation.

The sales promotion plan.   Usually in the first discussions of a campaign for consumer advertising, the sales promotion plans will also be discussed. These plans may involve dealer displays, premiums, cooperative advertising, couponing offers. When the theme of the campaign has been established for consumer advertising, creative work will have begun for sales promotion material, which will be presented along with the consumer advertising material for final approval. At that time, production will be carefully planned so that the sales promotion material will be ready before the consumer advertising breaks.

Getting the campaign approved.   We now have the campaign complete—the advertisements, the media schedule, sales promotion material, and costs for everything spelled out, ready for management's final approval. For that approval, it is wise to present a statement of the company's *marketing* goals. The objectives may be to launch a new product, to increase sales by X percent, to increase the firm's share of the market by Z percent—or whatever the marketing target may be. Next follows a description of the philosophy and strategy of the advertising, with the reasons for believing that the proposed plan will help attain those objectives. Not until then are the advertisements or the commercials presented, along with the media proposal and the plans for coordinating the entire effort with that of the sales department. What are the *reasons* for each recommendation in the program? On what basis were these dollar figures arrived at? On what research were any decisions based? What were the results of preliminary tests, if any? What is competition doing? What *alternatives* were considered? What is the total cost? Finally, how may the entire program contribute to the company's return on its investment? Those who control the corporate purse strings like to have answers to such questions before they approve a total advertising program.

Presenting the campaign to the sales force

The sales force always looks forward to the annual announcement of the company's newest plans. They may gather for the event at a meeting at the home or branch office. There, everything may be set up under wraps on a stage, with all the excitement characteristic of the launching of a new venture. Finally, the new advertising campaign is unfurled, along with the product if it is new to the market.

Sometimes a new campaign is launched through closed-circuit television from the home office to branch-office meetings, to which dealers might be invited. Automobile and household appliance manufacturers, particularly, bring in sales representatives and the main distributors, to give them a theatrical presentation with music. Or it can all be done on a modest scale: the sales representatives are called in to the sales manager's office, and the advertising manager tells of the advertising program.

Usually a kit of the various advertising materials will be given to salespeople, who can show details of the new campaign to the dealers on whom they call.

Summary of the steps

The steps in preparing a national campaign for a consumer product may be enumerated as follows. (The sequence is not the same as that of our previous discussion, but has been rearranged for convenience in surveying the entire problem.)

1. Develop a product that offers good value.
2. Create the trademark.
3. Design the package, if needed.
4. Position the product.
5. Select the target market. Who are the heavy users?
6. Determine the selling price.
7. Determine the form of distribution.
8. Set the appropriation.
9. Establish advertising/marketing strategy and theme.
10. Prepare advertisements and commercials.
11. Choose the media; prepare schedules; order time and space.
12. Create a sales promotion plan for dealer tie-in.
13. Release the plan to salespeople, dealers, and trade publications.
14. Release advertisements to public.
15. Appraise your results.

BACKGROUND

Converse Rubber Company, founded in 1903, is a leading manufacturer of athletic, sports, and leisure footwear, as well as sports equipment and rubber industrial products. Converse sales are nearly $150 million. The company is best known for its line of basketball shoes, specifically the famous "All Star," but Converse tennis shoes and training shoes have achieved a position among leading brands. A quality image has been built on a top quality athletic shoe at a reasonable price. Converse's primary competition comes from brands such as Adidas, Spotbilt, Puma, Nike, Tiger, Keds, and Tretorn.

The Converse Rubber Company is made up of two different sales divisions. The Footwear Division sells only to footwear and department stores. Its line includes Coach athletic shoes for men, Jack Purcell athletic shoes for adults, and P. F. Flyers athletic shoes for children.

The Sporting Goods Division sells to either sporting goods stores or sporting goods departments. Included in this line is the All Star brand, consisting of All Star basketball shoes, All Star training shoes, and Tennis All Stars.

The All Star athletic shoe is the top-of-the-line Converse product. It will never be found in shoe stores or shoe departments, but only in sporting goods or athletic outlets. By selling All Stars *exclusively* through sporting goods outlets, Converse can better maintain its market position against competition and can also maintain the typical 50 percent markup a sporting goods dealer normally requires. The All Star line accounts for about three-fourths of Converse sales.

THE PROBLEM

Increasing competition from aggressive marketers has threatened the Converse position among the leading producers of athletic, sports, and leisure footwear.

HOW DO YOU STEP INTO YOUR BACKHAND SO NICELY, CHRIS?

Chris Evert steps in Chris Evert™ shoes by Converse,® the shoes of the stars. Chris wanted new comfort, new style, and exceptional stress support for the toughest tennis competition in the world. She got what she wanted. Stars and stripes and everything nice.

A perfect testimonial, effectively used.

OBJECTIVES

General. To increase awareness and usage of All Star basketball, tennis, and training shoes, a big advertising campaign was designed, one which would get the story to diverse, potential wearers.

Specific. Magazine and television schedules were designed to reach brand-conscious adult men, adult women, and teen-aged boys and girls.

TARGET MARKETS

For All Star basketball shoes, the target market is the "youth audience," defined by Converse as basketball players from ages 12 through 34. Converse's claim to fame over the years has been the fact that more professional and college basketball players have worn the All Star basketball shoe than those who have worn others. For the most part, rather than using big name endorsements (with the notable exception of Julius Erving, professional basketball's famous "Dr. J"), Converse has taken a more generalized approach to highlighting the product's popularity among people who know; namely, college, pro, and Olympic players. Although the company has an athletic image to uphold with their product, many of the All Stars never see a basketball court, but are worn for casual and leisure dress only. Therefore, the All Star basketball shoe actually has two end-user markets—athletics and casual use.

For the All Star training shoes and the tennis All Stars, aimed at men, women, and teenagers, the target market is somewhat more generalized, because of the wider range of ages enjoying tennis and the various forms of training (e.g., jogging and calisthenics). Like the All Star basketball shoes, many tennis All Stars and All Star training shoes never see a tennis court or a training area. They are used frequently for casual wear alone.

APPEALS

All Star basketball shoes: quality, worn by people who play competitive basketball.

All Star training shoes: style and durability for use in the most rigorous conditioning programs.

Tennis All Stars: comfort, fit, performance, and style for tennis players.

SFX – Tennis sounds, balls thumping, feet running
VO: – Come on, run, stop, run!

SFX – Gardiner shouting instructions
VO: – I'm John Gardiner, and I run a tough tennis ranch.

VO: – People who come here really want to improve their game.
and they work hard to do it!

VO: – And that's why I recommend Converse Tennis Shoes to them.

VO: – They're incredibly comfortable shoes that can take whatever we hand out.

and believe me, we really hand it out around here

VO: – Announcer: Converse could make a difference

Tennis All Stars 30-second television commercial.

Television Schedule

Date	Ad	Program	Network
March			
1	All Star Basketball	NCAA Basketball	TVS
8	All Star Basketball	NCAA Basketball	TVS
15	All Star Basketball	NCAA Basketball Playoffs	NBC
15	All Star Training Shoes	NCAA Basketball Playoffs	NBC
16	All Star Training Shoes	NBA Basketball	CBS
22	All Star Basketball	NCAA Basketball Playoffs	NBC
22	All Star Training Shoes	NCAA Basketball Playoffs	NBC
29	All Star Basketball	NCAA Basketball Playoffs	NBC
29	All Star Training Shoes	NCAA Basketball Playoffs	NBC
31	All Star Basketball	NCAA Basketball Finals – N	NBC
April			
18	All Star Training Shoes	NBA Basketball Playoff – N	CBS
19	Tennis All Stars	World Series of Women's Tennis	ABC
19	Tennis All Stars	World Series of Women's Tennis	ABC
20	Tennis All Stars	World Series of Women's Tennis	ABC
20	Tennis All Stars	World Series of Women's Tennis	ABC
22	All Star Basketball	NBA Basketball Playoff – N	CBS
27	All Star Training Shoes	NBA Basketball Playoff	CBS

8 out of 10 tournament basketball players have one thing in common.

Converse All Stars.®

In every major college and junior college tournament last year, eight out of ten players wore All Stars. That's the way it's been going year after year, tournament after tournament.
Eight out of ten.
Kind of adds up, doesn't it.

★ **converse** ®
When you're out to beat the world

an **Eltra** company

AD NO. 73-40 — As appearing in: Athletic Journal, Coach & Athlete, Jopher, Juco Review, NAIA News, Scholastic Coach, Sports Illustrated, Sport Magazine, Sporting News, Selling Sporting Goods, Sporting Goods Business, Sporting Goods Dealer, Sports Merchandiser

Consumer Magazine Schedule

Month		Magazine	Advertisement
February	**1**	Sporting News	All Star Basketball
	3	Sports Illustrated	All Star Training Shoe
	10	Sports Illustrated	Tennis All Stars
		World Tennis	Tennis All Stars
March	**1**	Sporting News	All Star Training Shoe
	10	Sports Illustrated	All Star Basketball
	15	Sporting News	All Star Training Shoe
		Sport	All Star Training Shoe
		Tennis	Tennis All Stars
		Tennis U.S.A.	Tennis All Stars
		Hot Rod	All Star Training Shoe
		Motor Trend	All Star Training Shoe
		Carcraft	All Star Training Shoe
April	**7**	Sports Illustrated	All Star Training Shoe
	12	Sporting News	All Star Basketball
		Sport	All Star Basketball
May	**10**	Sports News	Tennis All Stars
		World Tennis	Tennis All Stars
		Tennis U.S.A.	Tennis All Stars
June	**2**	Sports Illustrated	Tennis All Stars
	28	Sporting News	Tennis All Stars
		Tennis	Tennis All Stars
July		Tennis U.S.A.	Tennis All Stars
August	**25**	Sports Illustrated	All Star Basketball
		World Tennis	Tennis All Stars
September	**20**	Sporting News	All Star Training Shoe
		Tennis	Tennis All Stars

Converse magazine advertising.

MEDIA SCHEDULE

There were three main approaches to consumers: magazines, television, and point-of-sale. Magazines included *Sports Illustrated, Sport, The Sporting News, Hot Rod, Car Craft, Motor Trend, World Tennis, Tennis,* and *Tennis USA.*

The network television schedule featured commercials on NBA basketball (regular season and playoffs), NCAA basketball (regular season and playoffs), NHL hockey (regular season and playoffs), World Series of Women's Tennis, World Invitational Tennis, World Championship Tennis, Alan King Tennis, Tonight Show, Wimbledon, and Midnight Special.

The point-of-sale promotion consisted of shoe displays, counter cards, sports action posters, wall banners, window streamers, illuminated signs, as well as ad planner kits for Converse dealers.

In addition to the consumer advertising and promotion, Converse All Stars have been advertised in trade publications such as *Sporting Goods Business, Selling Sporting Goods, Sporting Goods Dealer, Sports Merchandiser, Athletic Journal, Coach & Athlete, Scholastic Coach, Black Sports,* and *Tennis Industry.*

Results. Converse judges its All Star advertising campaign to be "extremely successful, effective, and instrumental in helping the company increase its sales by 60 percent in the first two years of the campaign.

THE STORY BEHIND
the national launch of
Gillette TRAC II Shaving System

BACKGROUND

The Gillette Safety Razor Company has been a major manufacturer of blades and razor products since the early 1900s, when King C. Gillette invented the first "safety" razor for his personal use. He wanted something different from the old straight-edge razor used in barbershops. Because he was not a barber and did not have experience in shaving, he wanted a "safety" razor, to guard against nicks and cuts. The concept caught on, and King C. Gillette began manufacturing razors for his friends and neighbors. He founded The Gillette Safety Razor Company in 1903.

Prior to World War I, a myriad of small blade/razor companies stretched across the United States, all making various inventions aimed at providing a consistently close, safe shave. But Gillette increased his business substantially while most of the other companies fell by the wayside because he gave a new safety razor to each serviceman going overseas during World War I. In essence, this was the beginning of sampling as we know it in marketing today. It was continued during World War II, and millions of American servicemen have shaved with Gillette Safety Razor products ever since. Even today, new recruits are given Gillette razors and blades to shave with when they join the armed forces.

Popularity of the new safety razor increased substantially in the post-World War II period, and estimates of the total market for blades and razors reached $100 million in retail sales in the mid-1950s. In 1960, the estimated annual retail blade market was $144 million, and the estimated total razor market was $19 million. This grew to a level of $218 million (blades) and $34 million (razors) in 1967. In terms of market share, Gillette accounted for approximately 55 percent of the blade market and 70 percent of the razor market in 1967, *prior to the launch of the Wilkinson Bonded System.*

THE PROBLEM

Gillette's market share (primarily in the blade category) had been declining for many years prior to the mid-1960s. Carbon steel blades had been very popular in the post-World War II period; and Gillette, virtually the only manufacturer of carbon steel blades, had 80 percent of the market. With the advent of the stainless steel blade, first by Wilkinson, then by Gillette and Schick in the early 1960s, Gillette's market share began to decline.

Wilkinson was a well-respected British manufacturer of double-edge blades and had been doing a considerable amount of experimenting with blade coatings. In the 1960s they developed the stainless steel blade and began exporting them to the U.S. Their advertising message was essentially a quality impression based on hundreds of years' experience in "Wilkinson swords." The fact of the matter from a technical standpoint was that a stainless steel coating provided a substantially improved shave in both closeness and reduced nicks and was readily recognized by the average consumer. As a result, Wilkinson's share increased substantially, predominantly at Gillette's expense. This was truly a product innovation.

Although Gillette quickly followed to introduce a stainless steel blade of its own, Wilkinson already had a good reputation and many customers in the United States. It also introduced a new "bonded" system with claims of unsurpassed shaving performance and especially reduced nicks and cuts. The single stainless steel blade was bonded in a plastic cartridge that eliminated sharp corners and reduced exposure of the blade to the face. This product, too, met with good levels of consumer satisfaction. Market share for Wilkinson kept rising, at Gillette's expense.

Concurrent with the Wilkinson launch of its bonded system, Gillette was developing a twin-bladed bonded system of its own in its research laboratories in both the U.S. and the U.K. This product was designed to take advantage of the bonded principle (similar to Wilkinson's) and also to take advantage of the twin-bladed shaving principle, a combination of closeness and safety superior to the single-blade bonded system. Under normal timing, Gillette would have taken two years to introduce their new system, since all the key machines had to be redesigned. But the combination of Wilkinson's success and the technical superiority of the twin-blade concept in the laboratory led Gillette to speed up. Manufacturing worked around the clock seven days a week for a 16-month period to launch the TRAC II shaving system as soon as possible. This was accomplished in October and was announced on the World Series broadcasts that year. The World Series timing was particularly appropriate, since Gillette has been a sponsor of these broadcasts since 1939, and retailers gave Gillette considerable merchandising support at this time of the year.

ADVERTISING LAUNCH OBJECTIVES

TRAC II's introductory copy had three specific objectives:

1. *Communicate product news* by positioning TRAC II as a revolutionary breakthrough in shaving, in order to stimulate consumer trial.
2. *Clearly identify key features of the product* by emphasizing the unique twin-blade construction of the TRAC II shaving cartridge.
3. *Establish product exclusivity and superiority* by adding the highly preemptive tag line "Gillette made it one blade better."

The key to the success of TRAC II's introductory advertising lay in its ability to create better consumer awareness of how a twin-blade system works. Several different advertising techniques were used to measure the level of consumer understanding. The advertising to be used appeared to be both highly memorable and persuasive.

**TV commercials
in the same
campaign.**

B&B

BENTON & BOWLES
909 THIRD AVENUE
NEW YORK, N.Y.
(212) 758-6200

Client:	GILLETTE CO.
Product:	TRAC II
Length:	30 SECONDS - GSRD2193
Title:	"CONSTRUCTION"

1. ANNCR: Gillette has created a revolutionary new kind of shaving system.

2. First ... to shave you close,

3. we put in our finest blade.

4. Then to shave you even closer ...

5. we put in another one.

6. Two separate blades in a replaceable cartridge.

7. Two blades.

8. To get whisker one blade could miss.

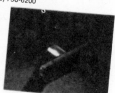

9. The Gillette Trac II -

10. Two bladed shaving system.

11. Gillette made it one blade better.

BENTON & BOWLES
909 THIRD AVENUE
NEW YORK, N.Y.
(212) 758-6200

Client:	GILLETTE CO.
Product:	TRAC II
Length:	30 SECONDS - GSRD1163
Title:	"SILHOUETTE"

1. (DRUMS IN BKGD.) ANNCR: This is a revolutionary new shaving system from Gillette.

2. To shave you close,

3. we put in our finest blade.

4. And then, to shave you even closer ...

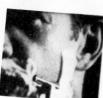

5. (MUSIC BKGD.) We put in another one.

6. Gillette introduces the world's 1st razor with 2 separate blades -

7. the New Gillette Trac II.

8. 2 blades...

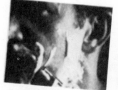

9. to get whisker one blade could miss.

10. The New Gillette Trac II twin blade shaving system.

11. It's one blade better than whatever you're using now.

You may think our 2 blades are too many. Maybe your one blade isn't enough.

Your one blade. Is it enough?

(1) When you shave with your one blade razor,

(2) your whisker is actually stretched out for a moment from the skin.

(3) But after the whisker is shaved, it snaps right back.
And that's that.

Our two blades. It's not too many.

(1) When you shave with the TRAC II,

(2) the 1st blade stretches your whisker out for a moment, just like your one blade razor.

(3) But then, before that extra whisker can snap all the way back,

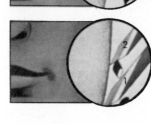

(4) the 2nd blade can shave it again—closer.
And with 2 blades shaving so fantastically close, we could recess them for extra safety. No one blade razor made can match it.

The Gillette TRAC II™ Two Bladed Razor
It's one blade better.

Why the new Gillette 2 bladed razor shaves you better than a one blade razor.

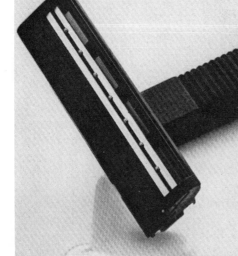

When we set out to develop a razor that would shave you better than a conventional razor, we knew we had a tough job ahead of us.

There were already lots of good razors around.

If we were going to give you a better shave, we needed to develop a better razor.

And so we did.

To shave you close, we put in our finest blade.

And then, to shave you even closer, we put in another one.

With 2 blades you can get whisker one blade could miss.

That's because the 1st blade gets most of your whisker.

And the 2nd blade gets whisker the 1st blade leaves behind.

One more remarkable fact. Despite its extraordinary closeness, our 2 bladed razor delivers one of the safest shaves you'll ever experience.

You see, because 2 blades give you extra shaving efficiency, we've been able to set the blades at a very safe angle, reducing the risk of cuts and irritation.

The new Gillette Trac II 2 bladed razor. It's one blade better.

The New Gillette TRAC II Twin Blade Shaving System

© 1972, The Gillette Company, Boston, Mass.

Ads from an intensive magazine campaign.

The introductory TRAC II copy strategy follows:

Copy objective: to announce the new Gillette TRAC II twin blade shaving system.

End benefit: The TRAC II, with two separate blades, will provide most men with a combination of a closer and safer shave than the system they are now using.

Reason why: The first blade gets most of the whisker; the second gets the whisker that the first blade leaves behind.

Tone: introductory/announcement in nature, in keeping with the "revolutionary breakthrough" aspect of the product.

Accompanying this report are samples of introductory TRAC II TV commercials and magazine print ads—all aimed at communicating these key copy points.

MEDIA PLAN

During the introductory period (September through February), TRAC II aired three 30-second commercials on national TV. Both the spending (in dollars) and the number of announcements were split approximately 50/50 between prime-time programming and sports participations. Three introductory commercials ("Construction," "Silhouette," and "Fusign") were rotated equally so that each had 1/3 of the TV occasions. A follow-up pool of introductory commercials was used during the period January - June, and this also included three different story lines.

Additionally, a series of four different full-page, four-color print ads supported the TRAC II launch. These were run in predominantly male-oriented vehicles averaging two pages per month. To encourage people to try the razor, some ads included coupons to be redeemed. The total dollars allocated for advertising support (excluding sampling effort) during September through August was approximately $4.7 million. Spending was approximately 2/3 during September through February and 1/3 in the March through August period. However, what should also be pointed out is that over $1 million was allocated toward sampling in addition to media spending, and this occurred primarily in the second 6-month period. Sampling did not start earlier because razors were not available. Gillette's total output had been allocated to an early launch.

BUSINESS RESULTS

TRAC II sales have been the most successful in the history of the blade/razor category. At the retail level, sales accounted for over $20 million during the first calendar year. These continued to grow to a total of over $100 million. This translates to nearly 30 percent of the blade dollar market and makes the TRAC II franchise alone larger than the Schick, Wilkinson, and Personna companies. The launch of TRAC II has enabled Gillette to increase its market share to approximately 60 percent of the blade market and 72 percent of the razor market.

At least one package of TRAC II appears in virtually all food, drug, and mass merchandising stores in the United States. A total of 15 million men and more than 12 million women regularly use TRAC II. Roughly 500 million TRAC II blades are sold each year, or approximately 1.4 million blades per day.

Courtesy Stephen A. Shapiro, product
manager—Trac II, The Gillette Company.

THE STORY BEHIND
International Harvester's nationwide
cooperative advertising campaign

Late in the year, International Harvester Company decided to liquidate its Travelall station wagon and Pickup light-duty truck in the coming spring. To do this promptly and efficiently, a cooperative advertising program on a national scale, involving a high degree of dealer participation, was planned, on a 25 percent dealer-share basis. The Ketchum, MacLeod & Grove agency was appointed to handle the assignment. Both advertiser and agency were well aware of the problems inherent in cooperative advertising. With these problems in mind, a new type of campaign was planned, as follows, work beginning immediately.

Actual budgets are confidential, but let us use hypothetical figures and say that $900,000 was set aside for the company's contribution to the fund, with the objective of soliciting an additional $225,000 from the dealers as their 25 percent share of their own advertising. In a joint effort, the IH home office and the agency analyzed all markets, to pick the most efficient sales markets for each of the two vehicles to be liquidated; 103 markets were finally selected. A complete media plan was prepared for each market.

In the meantime, four agency men were selected and trained to act as field representatives of the agency, to work with the International Harvester regional managers.

Concurrently, a creative campaign consisting of print ads, radio commercials, and TV spots was prepared and approved within three weeks. The entire advertising program was ready for presentation to regional meetings on February 10, along with a carefully prepared plan for the complete, yet streamlined, coordination of the entire project among agency, regional managers, and IH home office. Meetings between field representatives and regional management were started. The Cincinnati and Dallas regions were selected for the first tests on how well the program would be received at the regional level. The program was well received and other regional meetings were immediately scheduled.

The entire program, from the development of the marketing plan to the creation and preparation of the ads and commercials, was completed in less than two months. Even more noteworthy than the swiftness of action was the way the entire campaign was sold and administered to approximately 540 dealers, each of whom had to be treated as a separate client. We spotlight some of the significant aspects of this program.

Test drive these Internationals over to a Ford dealer and compare.

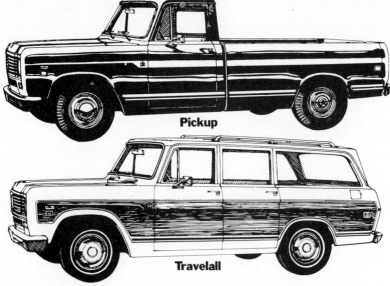

Pickup

Travelall

You're going to be surprised. The new '75 International® Travelall® and Pickup will take you over to any Ford dealer (or Chevrolet dealer) and anywhere else you might want to go.

In fact, you can get a factory-installed towing package on the new '75 Travelall and with the right engine and rear-axle options, you can tow a 5,000-lb. trailer and still carry 6 people in comfort.

The new '75 International Pickup is perfect for pulling a really big travel trailer or a fifth-wheel trailer. For special recreation needs, you can get a camper special package, step bumper or a special towing package. And the new '75 Pickup is as powerful as it is comfortable. Something you really need on long trips.

So take a test drive today. And compare. You'll be surprised.

> dotted line for position only
>
> DROP IN AREA
> (one feature or Safety First Aid Kit)

DEALER NAME AND ADDRESS

INTERNATIONAL HARVESTER

A typical newspaper ad in this campaign, urging readers to visit the showroom and test drive one of the vehicles. Each ad runs above the dealer's name. The square at the bottom right provides space for illustration of a special feature, which the dealer may select from a portfolio.

Travelall Features (500 line)

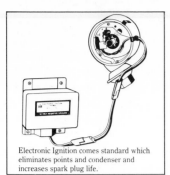

Electronic Ignition comes standard which eliminates points and condenser and increases spark plug life.

Standard Power Front Disc Brakes provide fade-resistant, straight-line braking with low pedal pressure.

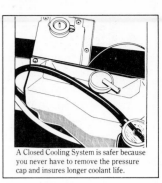

A Closed Cooling System is safer because you never have to remove the pressure cap and insures longer coolant life.

You get up to 120 cubic feet of cargo space in a vehicle that's up to a foot-and-a-half shorter than a conventional wagon.

Add selective 4-wheel drive and you're set for the off-road driving. You're able to maintain control on mud or snow covered roads.

The folding second seat allows for quick easy conversion to cargo hauler. Just fold it flat and load in your gear.

The tilt steering wheel (optional) gives you seven positions for your driving comfort. Just flip the lever.

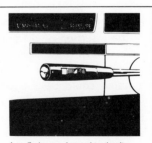

Auto-Cruise speed control (optional) automatically maintains speed at the rate you prefer. Ideal for expressways.

The optional adaptive braking system automatically takes over and prevents rear wheel lockup and skidding to assure safer, straight line stops.

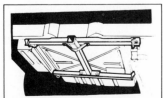

Complete Factory Towing Package... factory built, factory installed to take the guesswork out of ordering your tow wagon. Includes Class IV weight-equalizing trailer-hitch mount, complete wiring and much more.

Take a test drive and get your free International Harvester Safety First-Aid Kit, at participating dealers while the supply lasts.

Take a test drive and get your free International Harvester Safety First-Aid Kit, at participating dealers while the supply lasts.

The dealer problem.   In some markets, dealers had been accustomed to creating their own advertising locally with allowances from IH by prior agreement. In other markets, dealers in an area would conduct a joint campaign. National advertisers who offer to share the cost of cooperative campaigns usually face the problem of dealers who feel that since their money is involved, and since they know their markets better than anyone else, they should make all final decisions on how much to spend on advertising, where to spend it, and how to spend it. As a result, the company usually has only loose control of these expenditures. Dealers very often will have local agencies prepare their ads, with the result that there is diversity in the ads, without any single mass impact. Even worse, advertisements prepared without company guidance could make claims that might cause legal problems.

But this was a different approach. Although cooperative advertising was to be used, it was being planned as a complete, solid, intensive national campaign, with a unified theme for the advertising to run on a preselected and fixed media schedule within a given period of time. Finally, all this had to be presented and sold to the dealers whose participation was desired.

The creative problem.   Flexibility within uniformity was the objective. Advertising must have a unified theme, but it must be adaptable, to suit any dealer in any market.

The theme proposed, ''Test drive an International today,'' was well received by the dealers, because it directly brought people to the showrooms. To make the print advertising adaptable for all dealers, 29 possible variants were supplied. In each basic ad, space was provided for the insertion of a small panel describing one special feature of the Travelall or Pickup, which the dealer could select to suit the needs of his particular market. In addition, there were six one-minute radio spots, on reels, to the end of which the dealer's name could be tagged; also two thirty-second TV commercials, also with a dealer tag. There was a separate series of ads offering a premium of a first aid kit for all who came in for a test drive. This array of material was all put in a portfolio for each dealer. It was well received, and proved very practical in use.

The media problem.   After the agency had made a comprehensive analysis of the total marketing picture, and after reviews of their own markets by the regional managers, a schedule was prepared for each market, with a minimum acceptable weight level for print and broadcast media to reach a target audience of men 25–35 years with $15,000 or more household income.

Regional managers.   The country is divided by IH into regional offices in charge of regional managers, each responsible for the sales in his region, and in this plan responsible also for the final media decisions. Managers were responsible also for selling the program to branches and dealers, including creative and media people. Agency field representatives worked with managers in meeting special problems. The ability to sell the campaign was the crucial factor in this project. This required much person-to-person selling to dealers.

Agency field representatives.   One of the unique features of this operation was the agency's appointment of four people who were trained to spend their time in the field. They worked with regional managers, helping to sell the program to dealers, reviewing media proposals for specific markets and dealers, presenting creative suggestions to dealers within the basic creative framework, and arranging for shipment of production materials on agreed schedules. They also provided management with market summaries for each region.

To organize the total campaign, to keep management fully abreast of the progress of the campaign acceptances, and to keep regional managers posted as to the exact state of the operation in their territory, the agency planned and installed a new overall system suited to the needs of the company, with a minimum of paper work. The plan also permitted quick shifting of funds from markets where they were not being used as planned to other markets where they would be used, because the goal was to have the full force of the advertising run and to sell trucks.

Handling bills and payment.   Since the agency placed all media, local rates were eliminated. However, the control of media placement, timing, daypart (in the case of braodcast), and the resulting efficiencies were deemed more than compensatory for the loss of the difference between local and national rates. The only way to assure local rates would have been to allow the dealers to buy the media, and the risk of losing control and efficiency was considered too great. The agency compensation was on a fee basis.

The results.   Dealers supported the campaign by contributing 94 percent of the $225,000 quota that had been set for their 25 percent participation. Even before the bills for the advertising had been paid in April, the sales results were reported ''Impressive!'' Equally important, was International Harvester's close work with its agency. Together they developed a program to maximize co-op advertising dollar effectiveness in an area of advertising that has been, historically, undisciplined and inefficient.

Co-op administration program

The complete program to launch on-air media was accomplished in less than two months as outlined below.

Step 1	Development of marketing information and selection of 91 SMAs by IH General Office and KM&G	Jan. 20–29
Step 2	Development of media recommendations by KM&G outlining media weights desired by market	Jan. 29–Feb. 5
	Selection and briefing of four agency field representatives	Jan. 22–23
	Development of creative materials by KM&G	Jan. 17–Feb. 5
Step 3	Approval of KM&G media and creative recommendations by General Office	Feb. 7
Step 4	Initial presentation to regions	Feb. 10–18
Step 5	Revision of market selections and media schedules by KM&G, based on regional office input.	Feb. 17–21
Step 6	Further meetings with regions for final approval of media, creative, and budgets. Begin production of creative materials	Feb. 24–28
Step 7	Presentation of program by IH regional personnel to dealers for final approval	Feb. 26–Mar. 7
Step 8	Placement of media schedules upon dealer approval and trafficking of TV film, radio tapes, and newspaper mats, first on-air commercials	Mar. 3–14
Step 9	Payment of media invoices by IH regional offices	Mar. 17–Apr. 30
Step 10	Postanalysis of program performance	April 21

Courtesy The International Harvester Company, Inc.
Advertising agency: Ketchum, MacLeod & Grove, Inc.

QUESTIONS

1. What major steps will you take in developing a complete advertising campaign?

2. Ask some of the important questions that you will need answers to in selecting the target market.

3. A new product is presented to you for your marketing and advertising proposals. What are the chief technical questions you would ask? What would you ask about an existing product for which you will be developing an advertising campaign?

4. Products in the pioneering, competitive, or retentive stage require different kinds of advertising approaches. What direction or approach would you take if you were called upon to advertise different products in each one of the stages?

5. Select three of the specific advertising objectives mentioned in the chapter. For each, discuss a particular current advertisement or commercial that illustrates an approach to dealing with that objective.

6. Describe the areas you, as advertising director, would cover in a presentation to top management for approval of your advertising program and budget.

7. Explain how you would go about presenting your plan for an advertising campaign to the sales force. How would you achieve dealer cooperation?

8. Why is it important to appraise the results of an advertising campaign? What lessons can be learned? How can the information you get from the appraisal be used?

READING SUGGESTIONS

AAKER, DAVID A., and JOHN G. MYERS, *Advertising Management.* Englewood Cliffs, N. J.: Prentice-Hall, 1975.

AULD, D.A.L., and C. SOUTHEY, "Advertising Strategy and the New Theory of Demand," *Southern Economic Journal* (October 1975), 225–30.

CLARKE, DARRAL G., "Econometric Measurement of the Duration of Advertising Effect on Sales," *Journal of Marketing Research* (November 1976), 345–57.

CONSTANTIN, JAMES A., RODNEY E. EVANS, and MALCOLM L. MORRIS, *Marketing Strategy and Management.* Dallas: Business Publications, Inc., 1976.

ENGEL, JAMES F., HUGH G. WALES, and MARTIN R. **WARSHAW,** *Promotional Strategy.* Homewood, Ill.: Irwin, 1975.

FORNELL, CLAES, "Efficiency in Marketing Communication," *Marquette Business Review* (Summer 1975), 80–89.

KOTLER, PHILIP, *Marketing Management,* 3rd ed. Englewood Cliffs, N. J.: Prentice-Hall, 1976.

PERCY, LARRY, "How Market Segmentation Guides Advertising Strategy," *Journal of Advertising Research* (October 1976), 11–22.

ROMAN, KENNETH, and JANE MAAS, *How to Advertise.* New York: St. Martin's Press, 1976.

SEIDEN, HANK, *Advertising Pure and Simple.* New York: AMACOM Div. of American Management Assoc., 1976.

PART SIX

Other worlds of advertising

24

Retail Advertising

The largest part of newspaper advertising is local advertising; the fastest growing part of TV and radio advertising is local advertising; the most important part of local advertising is retail advertising, to which we now proceed.

National advertising is chiefly done by a marketer, to get people to buy his or her branded goods wherever they are sold. *Retail advertising* is done by local merchants or service organizations to attract customers either in person, by mail, or by phone, to buy the goods and services they have to offer.

Some firms do both national and retail advertising. The outstanding example is Sears, which produces and advertises goods under its own name and trademark, and is one of the largest users of national advertising. But its many stores advertise under the Sears name in their communities and thus are local advertisers.

Many franchise operations, like the McDonald's quick food restaurants, use national advertising to spread their reputations around the country, and local advertising to get the business of the immediate neighborhood. The fact that both kinds of advertising are used by a single firm should not obscure the basic differences between the two. In national advertising, the manufacturer says, "Buy this brand product at any store." The retail advertiser says, "Buy this product here. Better come early!"

In national advertising, it is difficult to trace the sales effect of a single insertion of an ad. To trace the effect of a series of ads takes time and is difficult unless the series runs exclusively in one medium. In retail advertising, a retailer can usually tell by noon the day after an ad appeared how well it is doing.

National advertisers speak to a wide and distant audience. Retail advertisers work in the community where they advertise. They know the people, their life styles, their tastes.

Differences between national and retail advertising

515

A woman looks at national advertising whenever she happens to come upon it—in newspapers, magazines, television, or while listening to the radio. She reaches for her newspaper as a ritual to see what the department stores are offering in styles and values and what the supermarkets are featuring.

The national advertiser has chiefly one product or one line of products to sell at a time. The retailer is faced by a relentless river of new styles and offerings to sell within a week, generating a great sense of urgency in the advertising department. It's a fast tempo.

Retail newspaper rates, as we have previously discussed, are generally lower than national rates—one of the factors that have given rise to cooperative advertising, whereby national advertisers share the payment of a retail ad for their product at local rates.

The retail media mix

The problem of selecting local media is a "How best to . . . ?" problem: how best to use the newspapers, radio, television, direct mail—the chief media—alone or in combination with each other, to sell merchandise and to attract store traffic.

Newspapers in retailing. Newspapers continue to be the backbone of retail advertising. They are part of the way of life of a large part of the population. Many a woman gets the paper, glances at the front page, especially for local news, then turns to the department store ads to see what's new, what's the latest style, even though she is not planning right now to buy a new garment. Grocery shoppers turn to see the latest specials the supermarkets are offering. The Sunday edition, with its circulation going to the outlying reaches, brings in many mail orders from the further distances, in addition to store traffic the next day. The use of loose inserts (*preprints*), which we discussed earlier in the newspaper chapter, has grown enormously. It was first thought that many inserts of various shapes and sizes in one issue of a newspaper might cause a reaction to the clutter, as TV does. But the TV watcher has to put up with the promotional clutter, walk out of the room, or turn off the set. The newspaper reader can pick out the interesting inserts and discard the rest.

Radio and television in retailing. Use of the broadcast media has soared in recent years. Radio is a great medium for news. Daytime programs are geared to the housewife and mother; drive time, morning and evening, reaches men. Radio also has a large following among young listeners. A department store may use two or three stations with a young audience to promote a new young men's department, and a different combination of radio stations and times to advertise a ladies' coat sale. Radio seems to reach many people who haven't seen newspaper ads, and it is effective in bringing people to stores to buy high-priced items.

Television was a comparatively slow starter in the retail field, but now that stores have learned of its effectiveness in creating sales, and feel more at home with its creation and production, there has been a dramatic increase in its use.

Another influence in increasing its use has been its greater acceptance by national advertisers for cooperative advertising, since a good checking system, which we describe later, was developed.

TV has brought to retail stores the tremendous power of a personal sales presentation of a piece of merchandise displayed and demonstrated.

Direct mail in retailing.   Practically every form of retail establishment uses direct mail. The small store will mail out a card announcing a sale to its list of customers. The giant store will send out hundreds of thousands of such mailings at one time. Department stores and discount stores use preprinted pages (loose inserts) of special offerings to be distributed through the mail as well as through the newspapers. The best organized retail users of direct mail are the traditional department stores, which we shall soon discuss.

Retailing covers a wide variety of store and service operations. There is much shifting and overlapping among them. Drugstores sell radios, food stores carry garden furniture, and discount department stores sell food. Instead of trying to draw a sharp distinction between stores that could fall into several classifications, we arbitrarily consider just four contrasting types: the discount store, the supermarket, specialty stores, and the traditional department store.

Classes of retail stores

The discount store.   Stores that wish to be known for low prices and bargains in everything they sell operate on a smaller markup than do department stores and make every ad look like a page full of bargains. The ad is not an attempt at elegance; rather, it is designed to give the impression that anything the store sells will be at a good price.

Sears, Montgomery Ward, and J.C. Penney.   Because these firms control their own production, they can plan all their merchandise programs, including special sales and special offerings, far in advance. All the advertising material for each part of the year is prepared centrally—including newspaper ads, radio scripts, TV spots, store signs, and direct mail. It is then available directly from the home office or the regional office, upon requisition by the store. In such operations, the merchandising manager may decide to feature children's apparel during the 30-day period before Easter—and all the advertising will be prepared for that event. Stores located in warmer climates may decide to run this particular children's ad four weeks prior to Easter, while stores in the northern states may prefer to run the ad ten days prior to Easter. Once this decision is made, the advertisement has to be positioned in the local papers, signs and in-store displays have to be requisitioned, and salespeople must be advised, so they will be knowledgeable about the advertised goods.

Although these chains may be national, the stores are billed at the lower local rate—the rule being that if an ad appears over one name only, it is so eligible.

Supermarkets.   Continuous competition makes supermarkets vie with each other not only in price, but in variety of goods and quality of merchandise. Their

Purposely functional, full of a variety of merchandise with prices featured, this ad is similar to many placed by discount houses whose selling strength is based on low price and great variety.

Quality, as well as price, is emphasized in this supermarket advertisement.

chief drawing card is their advertising of weekly price specials, found usually in the Wednesday food sections of newspapers. No supermarket could exist, however, on the patronage of those who come in to buy only the low-priced specials advertised, and they work to acquire a loyal following of steady customers by establishing a distinctive quality or service image for themselves. Stop and Shop does it by featuring the high quality of its own brand of goods, along with low prices.

Specialty shops.   Many stores feature one class of merchandise—women's apparel, household appliances, TV and radio, hardware. There are many regional and national chains of specialty shops that prepare their own advertising, but the majority of them are independently owned and cater strictly to local trade. They use newspapers, circulars, radio, and television. There are television production firms that prepare syndicated TV commercial tapes, which stores can use on television for series of short flights, as, for example, a series of films for jewelers, to advertise jewelry and gifts toward the holiday and wedding seasons. Similarly, there are syndicated services available for use in newspaper advertising. The whole ad, with art work, is prepared in mat form, with space for the local merchant's name. Local stores often use a local agency or a free-lance advertising person to prepare the advertising on a fee basis.

The traditional department store.   These stores usually sell clothing for all members of the family, each store setting its own style and price level. They usually also sell household furnishings, furniture, and household appliances. Merchandise is arranged by departments, with salespeople assigned to each. They emphasize customer service including deliveries, dressing rooms with fitters' services, ease of returning merchandise, restrooms, restaurants—all with a view to creating regular clientele. Much of their business is done on credit, and their lists of charge customers are of great value. Most of these stores began with what is now the "downtown" or main store, then built branches in the suburbs and other cities.

These are the stores we usually have in mind when we speak of "department stores," to distinguish them from discount stores, which have a different advertising outlook and operation.

Types of department store advertising

The kind of advertising done by a traditional department store stems directly from the kind of store the management wishes to operate, the type of trade it seeks, the range of merchandise it plans to offer, and the image it seeks to project. This affects everything connected with the operation—store location, decor, degree of emphasis on latest styles, and types and price range of merchandise. It affects the advertising. All advertising of all stores, however, has these objectives: to sell the specific article advertised, to bring in store traffic, and to project the store image. The advertising may be any of three types or a combination of them.

Promotional advertising is devoted to a specific product, such as dresses, bedspreads, lamps, china. It reflects the efforts of a buyer to make a particularly

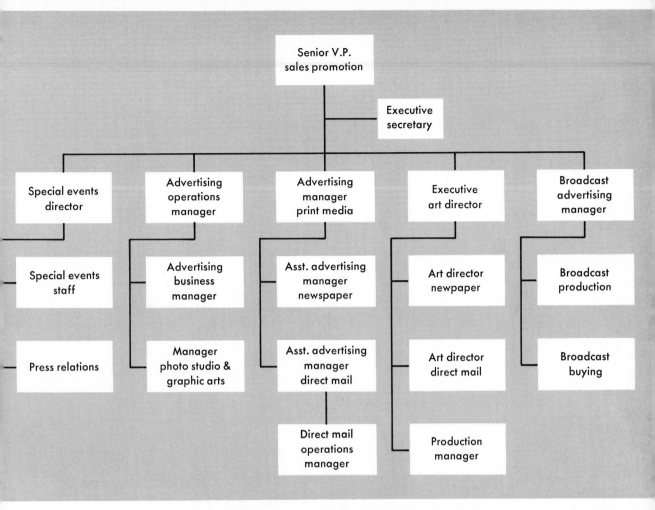

Advertising operation of a large department store. In the department store world, the total sales effort is referred to as sales promotion, of which advertising is a part, just as it is a part of the marketing operation of a national advertiser.

advantageous purchase in terms of style, variety, and price. Promotional advertising can be that of individual items or goods of one particular department. Departmental advertisements are often built around a theme designed not merely to sell the particular items advertised, but to establish that department as a headquarters for such goods.

Next, there is the *advertising of sales,* including storewide special sales events. Most stores have storewide special sales at the end of each season or on some annual or special promotional basis, such as Washington's Birthday, Anniversary Sale, or a Midsummer Sale. Special advertising will be prepared to move merchandise that may be growing stale, to try out new merchandise for the coming season, and above all, to generate traffic. There will also be departmental sales during the year to which advertising will be devoted.

macys

FEBRUARY HOME SALE AND SHOW

Last two days
Saturday and Sunday

Frigidaire heavy duty washer has 2 speeds, 4 wash/rinse temps. **280.00.** Color 10.00 more. Matching elec. dryer. **198.00.** Gas 238.00.

Speed Queen handles everything. Pre-wash, temps, water levels. **290.00.** White only. Matching electric dryer **190.00.** Gas 220.00.

Whirlpool 2-speed 4-cycle washer offers 3 levels, surgilator*, more. **298.00.** Matching elec. dryer **198.00.** Gas 228.00. All in white only.

G.E. 2-speed mini-basket washer is heavy duty. 5-wash-rinse temps. **290.00.** White only. Matching elec. dryer **190.00.** Gas 230.00.

G.E. convertible portable dishwasher is a real Potscrubber®. Power Scrub®. 3 wash levels, soft food disposer. **268.00.** Color 10.00 more.

G.E. built-in dishwasher has Power Saver cycle, normal soil, rinse-hold and short wash cycle. **248.00.** Color 10.00 more.

G.E. Potscrubber¹ features reversible color panels in white, avocado, gold, copper. Power Scrub® cycle and 3 others. Power Saver **289.000.**

KitchenAid dishwasher saves energy. Full cycle and rinse/hold, big random load racks, large silverware basket, **350.00.** Color 10.00 more.

Philco giant 21.9 cu. ft. size offers lots of no-frost refrigeration. 200 lb. freezer. Only 32¾" w., 65⅜" h. **550.00.** Icemaker 60.00 more. Color costs 10.00 more.

Philco 17.1 cu. ft. Cold Guard saves electricity. No frost. many features. 30" wide, 65⅝" high. Reg. 470.00. **430.00.** Color 10.00 more. With icemaker 460.00.

Gibson 19 cu. ft. no-frost refrigerator/freezer is 31" wide, 66" high, adjustable shelves. **450.00.** Color 10.00 more. Automatic icemaker 60.00 more.

G.E. no-frost refrigerator-freezer has 17.6 cu. ft. capacity, power saver switch. **428.00.** Color 10.00 more. Icemaker 60.00 more. 30½" wide 66" high.

Magic Chef 30" continuous clean gas range has 17 great features, including Uni-Burners*, digital clock, oven window and light. **290.00.** 10.00 more for color.

Magic Chef eye level range has two continuous-clean ovens, lets you bake as you broil. 30" wide. Many, many features. **500.00.** 10.00 more for color.

Litton Minutemaster microwave oven has solid state heat control. Oven shuts off when food is done. Microbrowner dish, cookbook included. **498.00.**

G.E. Jet 90 microwave oven cooks by time or temperature. Cook hefty pot roasts, fish and 3½ min. bacon-egg breakfasts quick! Browning dish, cookbook. Reg. 498.00. **468.00.**

This departmental ad featuring home appliances-was a cooperative ad.

522

Major Appliances — all Macy's except Monterey (ordermatic in San Rafael)

ORDER NOW! Call toll-free 24 hours a day: 468-4444 in San Francisco; 800-792-0800 elsewhere in Northern California. Shop all Macy's Sunday noon to 5 p.m.

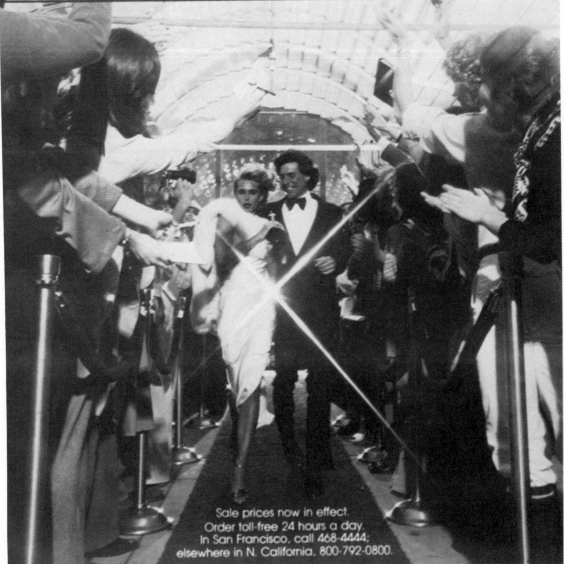

macys
spring sale
starring values for the whole family
at all northern california locations

Sale prices now in effect.
Order toll-free 24 hours a day.
In San Francisco, call 468-4444;
elsewhere in N. California, 800-792-0800.

A storewide sale. Many customers wait for these sales,
which stores usually run between peak selling seasons.

Most traditional department store advertising is a mixture of the foregoing types, featuring either sales or new merchandise.

Then there is *institutional advertising,* designed to give the whole store a lift in the esteem of the public, above and beyond its reputation for good merchandising. It may be to help some community project; it may be something the store is doing to bring pride to the community; it may be some advice to help a woman in her shopping knowledge of products. It makes no specific price offerings of merchandise.

Institutional advertising as a rule is a one-shot ad, created only when there is something to say, although it may be a series of occasional ads devoted to an overall theme. The results are hard to trace. Most stores rely on their range of merchandise and the character of their personnel, service, and advertising to help them establish the image they seek.

Much retail advertising is a blend of the foregoing forms.

Cooperative advertising

Although we have discussed cooperative advertising allowances in the past, chiefly from the manufacturer's point of view, let us review some of its features from the store's viewpoint. Cooperative advertising is so important in retailing that in some departments it may run as high as 50 percent of the total advertising expenditure.

Chief advantages:

▲ Helps the buyer stretch his advertising capability.

▲ May provide good artwork of the product advertised, with good copy, especially important to the smaller store.

▲ Helps the store earn a better volume discount for all its advertising.

Cooperative advertising is best when the line is highly regarded and is a style or other leader in the field.

Chief disadvantages:

▲ Although the store may pay only 50 percent of the cost, that sum may still be out of proportion from the viewpoint of sales and profit.

▲ Most manufacturers' ads give more emphasis to the brand name than to the store name.

Manufacturers' ads cannot have the community flavor and the style of the store ads. Retail stores get far more offers for cooperative advertising than they can possibly use. Everything depends on the importance of the product to the store.

For newspaper advertising, the store sends the vendor a tear sheet of its ad, as evidence that the ad ran, together with its bill for the vendor's share of the cost.

Since there are no tear sheets for radio and TV advertising, a special form has been adopted to assure the vendor that his commercials ran as scheduled. Designed by the Association of National Advertisers, the Radio Advertising Bureau, and the Television Bureau of Advertising, it combines in one form the commercial script, the bill, and an affidavit to be signed by the station. A copy of this

AM: 1600 kHz – .5 kw • FM: 106.7 mHz – 20 kw

POST OFFICE BOX 1600 • ELIZABETHTOWN, PENNSYLVANIA 17022 • 717-367-7700

Client:				For:		

			Begin:	End:	Date:

1

2   INSTRUCTIONS:

3   PLAY ARMSTRONG TAPE NUMBER AKFF-1000. TAG EACH ANNOUNCEMENT WITH:

4   TAG:

5   THIS WEEK ONLY, ACE LUMBER IS MARKING DOWN EVERY ARMSTRONG CEILING

6   10%...SOME EVEN MORE. SO HURRY DOWN TO ACE LUMBER, 444 HIGH STREET,

7   AND CASH IN ON THE GREAT VALUES THIS WEEK. ACE LUMBER, 444 HIGH ST.

This announcement was broadcast _____ times, as entered in the
station's program log. The times this announcement was broadcast
were billed to this station's client on our invoice(s) numbered/
dated _____ at his earned rate of:

$_____each for _____ announcements, for a total of $_____
$_____each for _____ announcements, for a total of $_____
$_____each for _____ announcements, for a total of $_____

_____
Signature of station official

_____   _____   _____
(Notarize above)   Typed name and title   Station

A standard form for use in TV or radio cooperative advertising.

form is sent to the vendor, who then can be sure that the commercial was broadcast as stated on the form containing the station's affidavit. All stores doing cooperative broadcast advertising use such a form. This dependability in billing has undoubtedly led to the greatly increased volume of TV and radio department-store advertising.

There is so much involved in using cooperative advertising, that most stores have a business department inside the advertising department, to make sure the store collects all the money due it.

A Department Store Advertising Department in Action

The entire selling and advertising operation of a department store is reflected in a series of promotional calendars, beginning with an annual one, prepared before the year starts. As the year advances, seasonal calendars—three-month, one-month, and finally weekly—are made up. The budget is usually based on the previous year's events but may be increased somewhat because business grows and so does inflation. These plans are designed to make possible a coordinated effort by all involved.

To anyone entering the department store operating world for the first time, the most impressive thing is the long-range planning under which the store operates and the great amount of lead time set for the preparation of advertising. Also impressive is the large number of people involved, each with a different corporate responsibility. Each store has its own operating plan and titles. The accompanying plan is a typical one—that of Macys California.

Note on plan: A staff of departmental copywriters, who also handle TV and radio commercials, works within the newspaper department. Several are also assigned to direct mail. Not shown on the chart are the store buyers and merchandise administrators (called merchandising managers in many stores), each of whom is responsible for the operation of a series of related buying areas.

Newspaper advertising.   About three months before a season begins, the preliminary seasonal promotion calendar is prepared. All major events are scheduled and entered on this calendar.

Seven or eight weeks in advance of scheduled publication, the monthly plans for advertising are made, to allow time for review and approval by various senior executives. Approved ads can then be in the hands of the advertising department six weeks in advance of publication.

Four weeks in advance of a given week, the production of that week's advertising begins. The advertising department publishes a master schedule for that week, showing the day the ad is to run, the newspapers involved, group number, merchandise to be featured, vendor money, and size of ad.

	SUNDAY	MONDAY	TUESDAY	WEDNESDAY	THURSDAY	FRIDAY	SATURDAY
			SALES PROMOTION CALENDAR			SEASON: FALL	
						MONTH: NOVEMBER	
WEEK 14	OCT 31 HALLOWEEN XMAS HOME CATALOG eff.	1	2 ELECTION DAY	3	4 Z TELEGRAM	5	6
LY	2 Xmas II eff.	3	4 Election Day	5	6 Telegram	7	8
WEEK 15	7	8	9 VETERANS DAY (State)	10	11	12 ECDC	13
Lᵛ	9	10	11 Veterans Day (State)	12	13	14 ECDC	15
WEEK 16	14 ECDC Xmas II eff.	15	16	17	18 WHITE FLOWER DAY	19	20
LY	16 ECDC Xmas II eff.	17	18	19	20 White Flower Day	21	22 Nite Open
WEEK 17	21 C2-G NEWSPAPER INSERT	22	23	24	25 THANKSGIVING	26 POST THANKSGIVING SALE	27
LY	23 Dom/Hswares Insert	24	25	26	27 Thanksgiving	28 Post Thanksgiving Sale	29
WEEK							
LY							

Section of a typical calendar for an annual storewide sales promotion. Made up before the beginning of the year, it is followed by a 3-month calendar and then a weekly one, for the same period.

MACY'S CALIFORNIA ADVERTISING REQUEST

Use separate form for each item to be advertised,
except item listings.

PREPARE IN TRIPLICATE

DATE: _____
DEPT: _____
BUYER: _____
AD NUMBER: _____

Paper	Size	Date	Paper	Size	Date
___	___	___	___	___	___
___	___	___	___	___	___
___	___	___	___	___	___
___	___	___	___	___	___

Has ad run before?_____Which paper(s)_____Date_____(Attach tear sheets)

Can you take mail or phone orders?   Yes ☐ No ☐   Do you need M.O.B. ☐ Phone line ☐ Both ☐

Store listing?   SF   H   BF   VF   STAN   SAC   STK   C   M   SER   E   HT   SR
               (Cross out stores not to be listed in divisional ad)

Essential required merchandise facts: Dept._____Class_____Factory No._____

Style No._____ Shipping Weight:_____Price:_____Quantity for ad ($'s) _____(Pcs.)_____

Comparative price description (check one):

　　　regular ☐　　　formerly ☐　　　originally ☐　　　if perfect ☐

Vendor money: (attach invoice)

　　　Amount_____Vendor requirements_____ Logo?_____

Submit samples to advertising department with this advertising request

The following information must be given for each item: 1. Colors 2. Sizes 3. Dimensions (length, width,
height, weight) 4. Special features 5. Material 6. Styles available 7. Stuffing (where applicable)

1. (feature) _____
_____
_____
_____

2. _____
_____
_____
_____

3. _____
_____
_____
_____

4. _____
_____
_____
_____

5. _____
_____
_____
_____

Special instructions or comments:

F.36-01 3/76   **DISTRIBUTION:**   ORIGINAL TO ADVERTISING DEPT.   **IMPORTANT REMINDER:**
　　　　　　　　　　　　　　DUPLICATE TO MAIL & PHONE ORDER DEPT.   **ORDER SELLING SIGNS NOW!**
　　　　　　　　　　　　　　TRIPLICATE FOR BUYER'S FILE

How to select a major appliance

It's been a long time since you needed the services of an iceman. Or dragged out the wash boiler on Monday morning. Or, weather permitting, clothespinned a basketful of dripping, flapping laundry. Or hand-washed a mountain of dishes, silver and pots after a big family dinner. Hard-working major appliances have taken over these chores. And, each year, there are more things they can do. 1978-model refrigerators act as important tools in helping you get more out of your food dollar, and have such special features as automatic ice cube dispensers. A dishwasher can save you 28 8-hour days a year and get dishes cleaner too. And many multi-cycle clothes washers give specialized highly efficient care to both your pantyhose and the dirtiest work clothes, using two different water levels to save you money. Macy's would like to tell you about the options possible when you select an appliance in any of these categories.

Refrigerator/freezers
First, consider your needs

Refrigerators range in size from 2 cubic feet to 25 cubic feet. But remember, the one you choose isn't just for now. You can plan on using it for from 10 to 14 years, during which time the size of your family may change. Even if you have only 32" of available space in your kitchen, you may still be able to buy for the future. New thinwall insulation makes possible a 19 cubic foot side-by-side refrigerator/freezer which stores as much as 168 lbs. of food in the freezer alone, and lives comfortably in a 32" width.

Unless you choose a very small refrigerator, chances are you'll have some freezer space. All other considerations being equal, you may make your selection on the basis of freezer size. If it has a separate cold control, you can count on unusual economy. Such a freezer can be used as you would use a true freezer which allows you to stock up

How many cycles, how many water levels

A highly sophisticated washer can pay for itself through the years. For example, your clothes will last longer, because the washer will give specialized care to each kind of fabric. How about your water bill? Many washers have three, four, or infinite water level selections. Flexibility is another consideration. Pre-soak cycles assure cleaner diapers, work and play clothes. This feature may be found in the machine with permanent press cycle. There may also be a hand-wash cycle that's as careful as you are with pantyhose and cashmere sweaters. If you have a large family, a really big washer, one that handles up to 18 pounds of laundry, may be an economy. It will mean that many fewer washer loads for you.

A lint removal feature is now standard in many washers and dryers.

Delivery and installation

Find out who pays for delivery. This extra cost could be nearly as much as your saving on the purchase. Installation is almost always extra. It might be worth your while to comparison shop this service. If you're replacing an older appliance in the same space, installation will cost less because special wiring, plumbing and/or cabinet work will already exist.

Color

For about 10.00 more, you can choose your new appliance in gold, avocado, or even poppy red, to coordinate with other appliances or carry out a color scheme in your kitchen. Some dishwashers have special

An institutional ad that is designed to generate goodwill, rather than to sell specific merchandise.

Copy preparation.   Ads are prepared from information and samples submitted by buyers. If a manufacturer is paying part of the cost of the ad, the invoice must be submitted with copy.

Once a week the ad copy, vendor invoice, and the merchandise are presented at a meeting of the merchandise administrator, buyer, layout and copy people, and the advertising manager. The final copy is then written, and the advertising layout is made. A copy of the layout is sent to the merchandise administrator and buyer for review. Sketches or photographs are made of merchandise. The first proof is without art, only copy. The second proof is with art. The final proof is with art and any corrections. The advertising division has final authority on the layout and the presentation of merchandise. It must be consistent with the standards of the store.

Results of ads can be obtained immediately by checking the sales the next day. The sales over normal show the success of the ad.

Broadcast advertising.   There is a regular broadcast budget for store-wide events plus merchandise groups based on last year's (yearly) events. There is a slush fund for special events. The senior vice-president for advertising makes the final decision on slush funds.

The budget request for broadcast is submitted by the buyer, who specifies date of promotion, merchandise description, quantity available, sales plan for period of promotion; also last year's sales, trend for period, expected PON (plus over normal) over trend. This has to be approved by the merchandise administrator, senior vice-president for merchandising, and sales promotion director.

The broadcast department decides whether to use radio, television, or both, according to type of merchandise. Then, based on information from the merchandise buyer, broadcast decides on the target audience (who are the people to go after? women of a certain age? kids? total men? daytime showing? sports?) and what markets are to be covered (San Francisco Bay Area, Sacramento, or Salinas/Monterey). Broadcast also decides when to start the radio or television schedule and how long the spot will run. Radio spots are either 30 or 60 seconds. Television spots are either 10 or 30 seconds. The time spots are determined by the dollars we have and the availability of time. Summertime presents fewer problems than the fall season, with its new programming and higher rates. Media buyers ascertain stations' availabilities and buy the time.

Production handles the concept, script, models, wardrobe, props, type of production—depending on merchandise—location or studio. Script approval is given by the buyer, and the commercial is assembled. Traffic notifies stations of the schedule and gives them the number of the tape or film to run.

Schedules are then made up showing the day and date of television or radio spot, station, length of spot, time of day or night spot will be shown. These are then distributed to all concerned.

Broadcast advertising needs approximately six weeks to put together a television campaign. Radio schedules require less time unless it is a campaign involving custom music and/or specialized production techniques.

A page from a catalog that has outdoor eating as its theme. The copy has less pressure than newspaper ads have; but toll-free ordering, prices, and concise descriptions of merchandise are included to evoke immediate response.

Direct mail.   Direct mail is becoming more and more important as a method of retail advertising. It wasn't long ago that direct mail consisted of 3 to 4 catalogs a year. Now there is a major catalog every month, plus newspaper preprints, bill inserts, and other sale mailers, all direct mail.

The charge account customers are the backbone of direct mail. Their roster has been further refined by the development of a "department of allegiance" list of customers who have shopped a particular department during a given time. For example, a small Father's Day catalog will be sent to all charge customers who have shopped in the men's area in the last six months. Some areas in the store develop their own lists.

The direct-mail coordinator starts with the budget set up at the *pre-season planning* meeting, at which all the advertising events are scheduled. The coordinator figures the approximate cost, including an estimate of what vendor money will be available. After everything is budgeted, a final schedule of mailings is printed by the coordinator and sent to all who are involved.

Putting through the catalogs.   This needs two to three months' lead time, depending on the size of the catalog. The Senior Merchant asks the administrators how many pages each wants. The administrator meets with buyers and a decision is made on which items will be featured. The buyer meets with the advertising department and talks with the art director, copy chief, and copy writers about what is important and what approach should be used. Merchandise is given to the photo studio, which coordinates it. The copy chief and writers set up a page sequence and the emphasis for each page. The copy and merchandise are due in the advertising department approximately *two to four months* in advance of mailing. A layout for every page is made and sent to each administrator for approval. *Five to six weeks* before going to the printer, the writers begin to write their copy. At the same time, the photo studio is shooting pictures of the same merchandise for the catalog. It takes approximately *two to four weeks* to complete copy and photography. As the copy is written, page by page, it is sent to the buyer for approval. Then the layout and copy are sent to typesetting, which will produce camera-ready repro type. Repro type and photos are now pasted up in the production department to fit the exact page size. These are called flats. Buyers once again get the opportunity to look at these pages after everything is completely pasted up and color transparencies are attached. After this approval, the flats are circulated throughout the department for a final proofreading. Then they are sent to the typesetting department for final corrections. Everything is then sent to the printer.

It takes only about one week to print the catalog, collate, and staple it. Some copies are delivered to the store to be dispersed to senior merchants, administrators, buyers, and advertising people. The rest are sent to a jobber who handles labeling and mailing.

The above discussion shows the technique for handling major mailing pieces. For special bill inserts and sale mailers, the procedure is similar, except it is on a smaller scale, with fewer people involved. Many of the small bill inserts are provided by the vendor. These are still handled by the direct-mail department. By the time these inserts are in the mail, work on some new mailing has already been started.

Courtesy Macys California.

QUESTIONS

1. Point out the differences between retail and national advertising.

2. How does the retailer evaluate the effectiveness of advertising?

3. In department store advertising, distinguish among promotional advertising, special events advertising, and institutional advertising.

4. Why do most retailers use their own advertising departments rather than advertising agencies?

5. Discuss the major factors that affect department store advertising budgets.

6. Compare the advertising in the discount store, the supermarket, specialty stores, and the traditional department store.

7. From the retailer's viewpoint, what are the advantages and disadvantages of cooperative advertising?

READING SUGGESTIONS

ABRAHAMS, HOWARD P., *Making TV Pay Off: A Retailers Guide to Television Advertising.* New York: Fairchild, 1975.

BARNES, JAMES G., "Factors Influencing Consumer Reaction to Retail Newspaper Sales Advertising," in *Marketing in Turbulent Times* and *Marketing: The Challenges and the Opportunities,* Combined Proceedings of the American Marketing Association. Chicago: American Marketing Association, 1975.

DICKSON, J. P., "Retail Media Coordination Strategy," *Journal of Retailing* (Summer 1974), p 61–69.

DUNCAN, DELBERT J., and STANLEY C. HOLLANDER, *Modern Retailing Management.* Homewood: Ill.: Irwin, 1977.

FRY, J. N., and G. H. MCDOUGALL, "Consumers Appraisal of Retail Price Advertisements," *Journal of Marketing,* (July 1974), 64–67.

HAIGHT, WILLIAM, *Retail Advertising's Management and Technique.* Morristown, N. J.: General Learning, 1976.

HAUGH, L. J., "Media-Emphasis Changes Appearing in Ad Strategies of Top U.S. Retailers," *Advertising Age* (July 26, 1976), 3 ff.

JAMES, DON L., BRUCE J. WALKER, and MICHAEL J.

ETZEL, *Retailing Today: An Introduction.* New York: Harcourt, 1975.

KRUM, JAMES R., and STEPHEN K. KEISER, "Regulation of Retail Newspaper Advertising," *Journal of Marketing* (July, 1976), 29–34.

LARSON, CARL M., ROBERT E. WIEGAND, and JOHN S. WRIGHT, *Basic Retailing.* Englewood Cliffs, N. J.: Prentice-Hall, 1976.

LERNER, AL, "What Agency Type Best Serves Retailer?" *Advertising Age* (November 8, 1976), 56.

MARKIN, ROM J., JR., *Retailing Management.* New York: Macmillan, 1977.

MASON, JOSEPH BARRY and MORRIS LEHMAN MAYER, *Modern Retailing* (Dallas: Business Publications, Inc., 1978).

MILTON, SHIRLEY F., *Advertising for Modern Retailers.* New York: Fairchild 1974.

PORTER, M. E., "Consumer Behavior, Retailer Power, and Market Performance in Consumer Goods Industries," *Review of Economics and Statistics* (November 1974), 419–436.

ROSENBLOOM, BERT, "The Trade Area Mix and Retailing Mix: A Retailing Strategy Matrix," *Journal of Marketing* (October 1976), 58–66.

25

Advertising to Business

$\mathbf{A}$lthough more money is spent on advertising to consumers than on any other form of advertising, more dollars are involved in sales to business buyers than in sales to consumers. Under "business advertising," the Standard Rate and Data Service includes advertising to

Distributive trades *(trade advertising)*

Manufacturers and builders *(industrial advertising)*

Top officers of other corporations *(management advertising)*

Physicians, dentists, architects, and other professional people *(professional advertising)*

Trade papers

Because most nationally advertised products depend upon dealers for their sales, we give trade paper advertising our first attention. Usually this advertising is prepared by the agency that handles the consumer advertising, and both are prepared at the same time, in any new campaign. The term *trade papers* is applied particularly to business publications for those who buy products for resale, such as wholesalers, jobbers, retailers. Typical trade papers are: *American Druggist, Supermarket News, Chain Store Age, Hardware Retailer, Modern Tire Dealer, Women's Wear Daily,* and *Home Furnishings,* their points of view revealed in their titles.

Hardly a business engaged in distributing goods does not have a trade paper to discuss its problems. Trade papers are the great medium for reporting the merchandising news about products and packaging, prices, deals, and promotions of the manufacturers who cater to their particular industries. The chain store field alone has more than 20 such publications. Druggists have a choice of over 30, while more than 60 different publications are issued for grocers. There are many localized journals, such as *Texas Food Merchant, Michigan Beverage News, Southern Hardware, California Apparel News, Illinois Building News.*

HOW TO MAKE HIGHER PROFITS ON LOWER CALORIES.

STOCK THE LINE FEATURING AMERICA'S NO. 1 DIET FRUIT.

Diet Delight* holds a hefty 60.0% SAMI share of the market. That's a margin of almost 2 to 1 over our nearest competitor!

STOCK THE LINE WITH PROVEN HIGH-VELOCITY POTENTIAL.

In just six days on stack at a special price in a leading New England supermarket chain, Diet Delight fruits showed an increase of *10 times* normal shelf movement.

STOCK THE LINE BACKED BY THE HEAVIEST ADVERTISING.

Diet Delight accounts for over 60% of all consumer advertising done by the three leading full-line diet food brands.

STOCK THE LINE WITH NO REFINED SUGAR ADDED.

Diet Delight is the natural choice for both cosmetic *and* medical dieters, because our products contain *no sugar.* And our strict quality and carbohydrate control has become a standard in the industry.

If *you* want to make higher profits on lower calories, stock Diet Delight: Fruits, Vegetables, Jam & Jellies, Mayonnaise, Syrups, Sweeteners and Specialty Items. We put our reputation on the line for you!

CALIFORNIA CANNERS AND GROWERS
3100 FERRY BUILDING, SAN FRANCISCO 94106

A trade paper ad in a grocery trade paper. Addressed to store buyers, it stresses the high profits a store can make on Diet Delight.
All copy is devoted to the products' attractiveness—both to the consumer and to the dealer. Goal: to induce buyers to stock the line.

Trade paper copy

No matter what the field, all trade papers have a common editorial objective: to tell the dealer how to make more money. Whether the magazine is for sporting goods, hardware, grocery, or service station dealers, articles deal with how to increase stock turnover; how to get the most out of window displays; finding, training, and motivating salespeople; the use of contests to attract new business; how to buy merchandise that will sell; how to get the most out of available selling space; and a host of merchandising ideas designed to increase store profits.

The advertising discusses not how good a product is—that is taken for granted—but how it will help the profit picture of the store. Among the subjects promoted are new aspects of the product, such as a new:

▲ feature of the product

▲ style of packaging

▲ display idea

▲ consumer deal

▲ store deal

▲ plan for a new advertising campaign involving the retailer (couponing)

▲ promotional idea

▲ in-store suggestion for improving sales of the advertised and related products

▲ idea that will help sales and reduce expense

Industrial advertising

As we move into the world of a member of one industry selling its materials, machinery, tools parts, and equipment to another company for use in making a product or conducting operations, we are in an altogether different ballgame—the *industrial marketing* arena.

There are fewer customers than in the consumer market, and they can be more easily identified. The amount of money in making a sale may be large, hundreds of thousands of dollars—maybe even millions. Nothing is bought on impulse. Many knowledgeable executives with technical skills often share in the buying decision. The sales representative has to have a high degree of professional competence in dealing with the industrial market, in which personal selling is the biggest factor in making a sale. Advertising is a collateral help in paving the way for, or supporting, the salesperson; hence, it receives a smaller share of the marketing budget.

Advertising addressed to people responsible for buying goods needed to make products is called *industrial advertising*. It is designed to reach purchasing agents, plant managers, engineers, comptrollers, and others who have a voice in spending the firm's money.

The uniqueness of industrial advertising.   Industrial advertising speaks to people who have their own approach to making business decisions. For example:

▲ Buying is done with a sense of professional responsibility that asks "Will this prove to be the best choice?" A poor decision will be around to haunt all who shared in it.

▲ Buyers purchase to meet predetermined specifications, not on impulse.

Somebody's stealing you, blind!

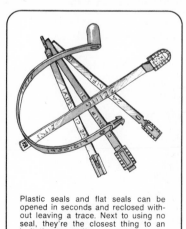

Plastic seals and flat seals can be opened in seconds and reclosed without leaving a trace. Next to using no seal, they're the closest thing to an invitation to steal!

No flat seal ever slowed down a thief who knows his business. Flat-sealed merchandise is his bread-and-butter. And you pay for it, one way or another, when it's you he hits.

The Tyden Seal is tamperproof.

A Tyden Seal on your cargo makes it impossible for thieves to operate undetected. A Tyden Seal keeps you from paying for "lost" or looted-without-proof merchandise, out of your company's pocket.

The Tyden Seal is tamperproof because its job-proven design makes intact removal impossible.

Send now for a free sample of the Tyden Seal. You'll also get an informative brochure that shows how and why the kind of seal you may be using now could be costing you a bundle.

The Tyden Seal is tamperproof. Use it, and be sure.

The Tyden Seal Company
Division of The Viking Corporation
Hastings, Michigan 49058
For more information, circle **No. 122**, Distribution Data Card

An industrial advertisement in an industrial magazine reaching corporate purchasing agents, heads of shipping departments, and other executives in the production area. It discusses not only the seal it is selling, but the problem that the seal helps to remove. Goal: to elicit inquiries that can be followed up by district representatives.

▲ Many people may be involved in a decision—a scientist, a designer, an engineer, a production manager, a purchasing agent, a comptroller—each approaching the problem from a special viewpoint.

▲ Decisions are made after many demonstrations, much inquiry, many meetings.

▲ With so many individuals involved, so many actions to be taken, so much money involved, there is often a big time lag between the moment it was decided to consider a purchase and the final decision.

A report issued by Time Inc., reveals some of the complexity in an industrial buying decision.

An *air-conditioning exhaust system*—the kind found in office buildings and factories, as opposed to a room air-conditioner for home use. The process of purchasing an air-conditioning exhaust system can be very complicated. Some 16 actions were taken by six individuals within the company.

A *case loader*—a packaging machine used for loading small, packaged bottles into corrugated containers. Some 13 actions were taken by 9 individuals or groups of individuals in middle management, top management, and purchasing.

An *encoder drum*—part of an electrical system needed in a Departmment of Defense project. Some 12 actions were taken by 3 individuals within the company. In addition, 4 suppliers were involved, as well as the U.S. government offices concerned with this project.

A *desk calculator*—the kind normally found in offices throughout the United States. It is a lightweight, semiportable, and highly versatile machine small enough to be placed on a desk, as opposed to a special "table" by the desk. Some 8 actions were taken by 4 individuals or groups of individuals within the company.

Carpeting—the kind of floor covering normally found in offices and reception rooms. Some 10 actions were taken by 11 individuals within the company.°

From 3 to 11 people had a say in those final buying decisions. Advertising's problem is to reach all who may be involved.

Effectiveness of industrial advertising.   A number of studies have been made to measure the impact of industrial advertising. Typical study results are reported by the Arthur B. Little Company from its survey of 1,100 studies:

Companies that maintain their advertising in recession years have better sales and profits in those and in later years.

Industrial advertising reaches purchasing influences not normally reached by salesmen.

It reduces the cost per sales dollar by supplementing the salesman's efforts.

Industrial product advertising increases the share of potential buyers who consider the brand.

° Based on a study conducted by Dr. Emanual Demby, Fairleigh Dickinson University. Reprinted through the courtesy of Time Inc.

Industrial advertising reaches prospective purchasers the salesman can't find or does not have adequate time to cover.

Industrial advertising copy.   Industrial advertising speaks to engineers and to other people who are technically trained. They read their trade or professional journals because of a constant challenge to keep informed of the latest developments affecting their field; they have to fight professional obsolescence. They read advertisements with the same critical curiosity with which they read the editorial matter. They are looking for news of products and experiences relevant to their problems, expressed in specific, factual form. They are interested in problems and their solution; they are most interested in case reports showing how some problem was successfully met. They seek confirmation or other proof of all claims made. They will read long copy and welcome any charts or photographs that help explain matters.

Most advertisements make a strong bid to the reader to write for further information. Industrial advertising adheres closely to the copy structure discussed earlier—promise of benefit, amplification, proof, action.

The case history is widely used in industrial advertising as a publicity release, as a fact sheet for salespeople, as direct mail, and as an advertisement.

The following practices relate to trade papers as well as to industrial publications (which have their own special problems to be discussed after this general discussion).

Business publications— general practices

Controlled circulation.   Business publications include *paid circulation* and *controlled circulation.* Controlled circulation is free circulation to a carefully selected list of those who are in a position to influence sales; furthermore, they must annually express in writing a desire to receive, or continue to receive, the publication, in order to qualify for the list. They must also give their title and function. Most business papers are sent out in controlled circulation, but some are paid for. Paid circulations are usually smaller than controlled circulations, but their publishers hold that the paying audience is more select.

Circulation audits.   The leading trade and industrial publications belong to the Business Publications Audit of Circulation, Inc. (BPA), which audits approximately 700 business publications. In their audit of circulation, BPA pays particular attention to the qualifications of all those on the controlled list and when they last indicated they wanted the publication.

In addition to BPA, the Audit Bureau of Circulations (ABC) performs essentially the same function (for over 200 paid circulation publications), although its main effort is in the consumer field. Some publications have both ABC and BPA audits. (Many business publications, especially the smaller ones, do not offer any circulation audit report.)

A third auditing group is the Verified Audit Circulation Company (VAC). Its standards are less strict than those of BPA.

Circulation audit reports provide the business advertiser with information and statistics to use in selecting the best publications for carrying a product's advertising.

Industrial publications— special practices

Vertical or horizontal publications. Industrial publications designed to reach people who make purchasing decisions for industry may be classified as *vertical* and *horizontal*.

Vertical industrial publications discuss problems of a single industry. *Manufacturing Confectioner,* for example, "is intended for management and departmental executives of firms manufacturing confectionery, chocolate, cough drops, nut products, marshmallows, chewing gum, etc. Editorial content covers production, formulation, quality control, materials handling, storage, packaging, shipping, marketing, merchandising, new ingredients, supplies, equipment, business management and others, including association news." *The Glass Industry* "is edited for those who engage in the manufacture of glass from raw materials and those who fabricate finished glass products from purchased glass. It answers technical and manufacturing questions and indicates the trends that the industry is following." Each industry will have several publications devoted to its problems. In the engineering-construction classification in the Standard Rate and Data Service, over 80 publications are listed; the automotive and brewing categories each list more than 60, while there are over 50 publications listed for the grocery classification.

Horizontal publications are edited for people who have similar functions in their enterprises, regardless of industry. Consider *Grounds Maintenance,* "edited for landscape architects and for landscape contractors and grounds superintendents, serving industrial plants, parks, colleges and schools, golf courses, cemeteries, shopping plazas, highways, institutions, public works, and recreational areas. It provides technical and management information about landscape beautification, care of turf, trees, and ornamentals. Articles cover such subjects as plant selection, seeding, planting, transplanting, fertilizing, irrigating, pruning, controlling weeds and pests, selection and service of equipment." *Consulting Engineer* "is edited for engineers in private practice in mechanical, electrical, structural, civil, sanitary, and allied engineering disciplines who have authority over the specifications of products and systems for their firms' projects." *Purchasing* "provides news and ideas for today's purchasing professional."

There are also a large number of state industrial publications. Many of the larger publications have geographic and demographic editions, and some have international editions.

Standard Industrial Classification System (SIC). One thing that greatly facilitates the industrial marketing process is the Standard Industrial Classification System, a numbering system established by the U.S. government. SIC classifies more than 4 million manufacturing firms into 10 major categories further subdivided into more specific groups. The code numbering system operates as follows. All major business activities (agriculture, forestry, and fisheries; mining;

PUBLISHER'S STATEMENT
For 6 Month Period Ending
DECEMBER 19-

BPA

BUSINESS PUBLICATIONS AUDIT OF CIRCULATION, INC.
360 Park Avenue South, New York, N.Y. 10010

No attempt has been made to rank the information contained in this report in order of importance, since BPA believes this is a judgment which must be made by the user of the report.

THE CRITERION

Criterion Publishing Company
360 Park Avenue South, New York, N.Y. 10010
(212) 487-5200

OFFICIAL PUBLICATION OF   None

ESTABLISHED   1931   ISSUES PER YEAR   12

FIELD SERVED

THE CRITERION serves the field of data processing systems and procedures in manufacturing industries, service organizations, finance, insurance companies, government, utilities, retail and wholesale trade and transportation, communication, printing and publishing firms.

DEFINITION OF RECIPIENT QUALIFICATION

Qualified recipients are corporate officials, controllers, data processing and accounting personnel, purchasing and other management personnel in the above field.

Also qualified are a limited number of library addressed copies.

AVERAGE NON-QUALIFIED DISTRIBUTION

	Copies
Advertiser and Agency	443
Non-Qualified Paid	28
Rotated or Occasional	26
Samples	122
All Other	242
TOTAL	861

1. AVERAGE QUALIFIED CIRCULATION BREAKDOWN FOR PERIOD

	Qualified Non-Paid		Qualified Paid		Total Qualified	
	Copies	Percent	Copies	Percent	Copies	Percent
Single	7,007	34.1%	12,917	62.9%	19,924	97.0%
Group	–	–	523	2.5	523	2.5
Association	–	–	–	–	–	–
Gift	–	–	–	–	–	–
Bulk	–	–	100	0.5	100	0.5
TOTALS	7,007	34.1%	13,540	65.9%	20,547	100.0%

U.S. POSTAL MAILING CLASSIFICATION ...... SECOND CLASS

2. QUALIFIED CIRCULATION BY ISSUES WITH REMOVALS AND ADDITIONS FOR PERIOD

19– Issue	Qualified Non-Paid	Qualified Paid	Total Qualified	Number Removed	Number Added	19– Issue	Qualified Non-Paid	Qualified Paid	Total Qualified	Number Removed	Number Added
July	6,936	13,546	20,482	778	533	October	7,049	13,485	20,534	651	684
August	6,696	13,899	20,595	351	464	November	7,286	13,278	20,564	528	558
September	6,857	13,644	20,501	523	429	December	7,215	13,388	20,603	345	384
									TOTALS	3,176	3,052

Publisher's statement, showing paid and nonpaid circulation. Turnover is indicated by numbers removed and numbers added, keeping the list fresh.

construction; manufacturing; transportation, communication, and public utilities; wholesale; retail; finance, insurance, and real estate; services; government) are given a two-digit code number. A third and a fourth digit are assigned to identify more specific activities within each major business category, in much the same way that the Dewey Decimal System works.°

For example:

(2 digits)	25	Manufacturers of Furniture and Fixtures
(3 digits)	252	Manufacturers of Office Furniture
(4 digits)	2521	Manufacturers of Wood Office Furniture
(4 digits)	2522	Manufacturers of Metal Office Furniture

The great value of the SIC system is that it enables the advertiser to identify and locate specific target markets. Industrial publications usually provide an analysis of circulation by SIC classifications. The advertiser can then pick the publication reaching the greatest number of the appropriate classification, or the information can be used in buying lists for direct mailings.

Professional publications

The Standard Rate and Data Service, in its special *Business Publications* edition, includes journals addressed to physicians, surgeons, dentists, architects, and other professionals who depend upon these journals to keep abreast of their professions. Their editorial content ranges from reporting new technical developments to discussing how better to meet client or patient problems, and how to conduct their offices more efficiently and more profitably. These professional people are great influences in recommending or specifying the products their patients or clients should order. Much advertising of high technical caliber, therefore, is addressed to them.

Industrial direct mail

New products, new product features, sales leads, and price changes make their appearance in industrial direct mail, which is used also to follow up calls of salespeople by sending supportive information.

The great problem in industrial direct mail is to send it to those who will be involved in the buying decisions of a forthcoming project. You cannot always determine this responsibility from job titles, since many steps are taken to reach a final buying decision. Top management, department heads, and technical specialists may join in

▲ Determining the need
▲ Establishing specifications
▲ Listing potential buyers
▲ Contacting suppliers

▲ Evaluating suppliers
▲ Selecting suppliers
▲ Placing the order
▲ Evaluating the purchase after it has been made

° The Standard Industrial Classification Manual is available from the Superintendent of Documents, United States Government Printing Office, Washington, D.C.

Manufacturing Firms
By SIC

SIC		Quantity		Price
‡ 2000		27,869	Food & kindred products mfrs. (SIC 2011 to 2099 combined)	$29/M
		26,791	-Rated $ 10,000 & over*	add 5/M
		25,505	-Rated $ 20,000 & over*	add 7/M
		24,002	-Rated $ 35,000 & over*	add 10/M
		9,345	-Rated $ 75,000 & over	add 23/M
		6,697	-Rated $200,000 & over	add 28/M
□ 2011		2,401	Meat packing plants	$38/M
□ 2013		1,288	Sausage & prepared meat products mfrs.	$38/M
□ 2016	■	69	Poultry dressing plants	$38/L
□ 2017	■	41	Poultry & egg processors	$38/L
□ 2021		369	Creamery butter manufacturers	$38/L
□ 2022		786	Natural & processed cheese mfrs.	$38/L
□ 2023		186	Condensed & evaporated milk mfrs.	$38/L
□ 2024		761	Ice cream & frozen dessert mfrs.	$38/L
□ 2026		1,271	Fluid milk plants	$38/M
□ 2032		201	Canned specialties producers	$38/L
□ 2033		1,031	Fruit & vegetable canners	$38/M
□ 2034		174	Dehydrated fruit, vegetable & soup manufacturers	$38/L
□ 2035		499	Pickle, sauce & salad dressing mfrs.	$38/L
□ 2037		527	Frozen fruit & vegetable mfrs.	$38/L
□ 2038	■	64	Frozen specialties mfrs.	$38/L
□ 2041		579	Flour & other grain mill products plants	$38/L
□ 2043		68	Cereal breakfast food mfrs.	$38/L
□ 2044		67	Rice millers	$38/L
□ 2045		117	Blended & prepared flour mfrs.	$38/L
□ 2046		57	Wet corn millers	$38/L
□ 2047	■	70	Dog, cat & other pet foods mfrs.	$38/L
□ 2048		2,258	Prepared feed mfrs., n.e.c.	$38/M

Courtesy National Business Lists, Inc.

Industrial mailing lists by SIC classifications.

INDUSTRIAL DIRECT MAIL GUIDELINES

▲ Find out who your customers really are.

▲ Use a professional list compiled to determine total number of names available for each list classification.

▲ Rate prospect value by percent of customer penetration for each list classification.

▲ Tie your advertising expenditures to prospect value rather than allocating them equally for each list classification. (A prospect list with a 40 percent rating warrants twice the advertising expenditure of a prospect list with a 20 percent rating, for example.)

▲ Learn your "spheres of influence" through studying functional titles, such as systems manager, chief maintenance officer, . . . or any title which will help to get a qualified response. Lists having a high percentage of customer penetration often warrant mailings to more than one title within a firm.

▲ Control your direct-mail support program from the home office.

▲ Settle for nothing less than scrupulous maintenance of your total list, with non-duplication between prospect lists and customer lists.

▲ See that distributors, dealers, and salesmen all have bound copies of the available names receiving promotions in their respective territories. Provide not only firm names and addresses but telephone numbers as well.*

Catalogs and directories

Many industrial producers make parts and equipment that are sold through hardware supply, electrical supply, and other distributive channels. These establishments could not possibly keep on hand an inventory of all the many items for which they get occasional calls. Rather, they maintain a series of loose-leaf binders, for which manufacturers supply the pages in standardized sizes. The issuance of these pages is a large part of the advertising budget.

Every industry will have its directory and buyers' guide, with descriptions of its lines and lists of the various companies selling its products. These directories are a responsible medium for any firm that wishes to have its name before their audiences. *Thomas' Register of American Manufacturers*, a distinguished comprehensive directory and catalog, even has its offerings on microfilm, in a form that can stand on a purchasing agent's desk.

Business shows; publicity

One of the dependable sources of new leads for salespeople is the annual business show staged by many industries. Leading sellers present their products in booths that are visited by interested prospective customers. Business Publications Audit of Circulation, Inc. (BPA), in its Exposition Audit, provides a head count of registered attendance at trade shows and a complete profile of their business or occupation, job title, and function.

A report of a significant contribution to technology is a reliable source of publicity. The developments come from the R&D department; but since noteworthy advances do not occur every month, the resourceful publicity person generates

---

* Leo Gans, president, National Business Lists, in Bob Stone, *Successful Direct Marketing Methods* (Chicago: Crain Books, 1975), p. 15.

Citibank, N.A.   Member FDIC

Across Alaska, worldwide Citibank has played a constructive part in the largest privately-financed construction project in history.

Building the 800-mile trans-Alaska pipeline has called for a peak work force of 23,000 rugged men and women. Plus almost half a billion dollars worth of often remarkable equipment. (These side-boom tractors, for example—used to lay 80′ lengths of 48″ pipe just a dime's thickness apart.)

Together, men and machines have conquered some of the toughest terrain ever pipelined. In temperatures often so low that heavy equipment must be kept running even when not in use—because "warming it up" again could take from four hours to two days, depending on the mercury.

Much of the specialized equipment required, like the tractors above, was provided by a Citibank customer—one of the largest equipment franchise

holders in the country, for whom we are a principal bank, and to whom we extend substantial credits. Additional construction equipment, and many of the construction camps along the pipeline route, were owned and leased by a Citibank affiliate.

Around the world, you'll find Citibank branches, subsidiaries and affiliates providing banking and financing services of exceptional quality and innovativeness. In so doing, they demonstrate our continuing commitment, as a leading international bank, to the best interest of our customers—and the economic vitality of every area we serve.

This industrial ad reaches out to the top financial level of multinational businesses.

news—perhaps reporting the issuance of a new, helpful manual or an informative film. The art of creating publicity is born of having something to say, not merely sending out releases that no editor would accept as news from reporters.

Corporate management advertising

Through institutional advertising, corporations make known their total competence and status in certain fields. Such advertising, addressed to the top officers of other large companies, chiefly discusses major capital investments, as installing a nationwide communications system, or planning financing. This, too, comes under the head of advertising to business—big business. Its media are publications that executives read to keep informed of the world, generally, or the business world, particularly. *Fortune, Business Week, Newsweek, Time, The Wall Street Journal* and other publications carry the advertising messages.

The business end of business advertising

Industrial advertising is usually handled through agencies that specialize in the field. They may have people with scientific training or experience in writing about pertinent subjects. Industrial agencies are usually equipped to handle all phases of an industrial advertiser's promotion needs, including advertising, publicity, brochures, and manuals. Industrial advertisers also use in-house agencies. Medical advertising to physicians has its specialized agencies and writers. Sometimes they are separate divisions of consumer agencies.

Budgets for industrial advertising are much smaller, as a rule, than those for consumer advertising. Industrial sales are consummated by salespersons or, on big projects, by a team of specialists. The role of advertising is mainly to support them. Consumer advertising, on the other hand, attempts to presell products on the shelves. Here, advertising is a smaller percentage of the marketing mix. Through a questionnaire, The Gallagher Report found that 146 industrial advertisers spent an average of approximately $519,000 in 1976. Almost 42 percent of their advertising was done in business publications, 16 percent in catalogs, 10 percent in business shows, 10 percent in direct mail, 4 percent in directories, 4 percent in publicity, and a miscellaneous grouping of media accounted for the rest.*

Consumer advertising often quickly effects sales, but the direct contribution of industrial advertising cannot easily be isolated. Between the first expression of interest and final sale, much time elapses, during which the burden of consummating that sale falls on the sales department. Nevertheless, industrial advertising continues to be an important part of the total selling process.

* The Gallagher Report, XXIV, 48 (November 29, 1976).

QUESTIONS

1. Describe the chief differences between advertising to business and advertising to consumers.

2. Distinguish among trade advertising, industrial advertising, and professional advertising.

3. What is a BPA audit?

4. Compare and contrast the major characteristics of industrial buying decisions and consumer buying decisions.

5. What is the difference between vertical and horizontal industrial publications? Can you give two examples of each type?

6. What is the SIC? How is it useful to industrial advertisers?

7. What are the major features of industrial advertising copy?

8. What are the major features of trade paper copy?

9. Discuss the reasons why an industrial advertiser would undertake an advertising campaign in nonindustrial magazines.

READING SUGGESTIONS

"A Brief Lesson in Writing Copy," *Industrial Marketing,* (February 1976), 43–47.

"Business Advertising Section," *Advertising Age* (June 21, 1976), 43–64.

COREY, E. RAYMOND, *Industrial Marketing,* 2nd ed. Englewood Cliffs, N.J.: Prentice-Hall, 1976.

"Direct Mail Prepares Buyers for Sales Calls," *Industrial Distributor* (November 1974), 76–77.

"Direct Mail Selling Tried by More Industrial Firms," *Industrial Week* (March 31, 1975), 52–53.

FRANK, J. S., and I. L. BEHRENDT, "How to Use a Saturation Sales Campaign to Penetrate New Industrial Markets," *Industrial Marketing* (January 1975), 48 ff.

GRUSSE, W. H., *How Industrial Advertising and Promotion Can Increase Marketing Power.* New York: American Management Association, 1973.

HELFAND, T., "How 16 Leading Industrial Advertisers Are Planning New Marketing Programs," *Industrial Marketing* (June 1976), 98–106.

"Industrial Ad Scene Needs Some Changes, Exec Says," *Advertising Age* (May 10, 1976).

LILIEN, GARY L., ALVIN J. SILK, JEAN-MARIE

CHOFFRAY, and MURLIDHAR RAO, "Industrial Advertising Effects and Budgeting Practices," *Journal of Marketing* (January 1976), 16–24.

McNUTT, GEORGE, "How to Identify Buying Influences in Your Market," *Industrial Marketing* (June 1976), 134–36.

SAWYER, H. G., "Best Strides in Industry Ad Field Were in Media Areas and Graphics; Worst Disappointment in Research," *Industrial Marketing* (March 1976), 56.

STIATA, RAY, "In Good Ad Planning, President Outlines Company Objectives," *Industrial Marketing* (June 1976), 118–24.

SWAN, CHRISTOPHER, "Growth of Industrial Advertising From 1916 to the Present," *Industrial Marketing* (March 1976), 74–75 ff.

TYSON, I. W., "Ad Role Should Change with Industrial Climate," *Industrial Marketing* (March 1975), p. 48.

WILDER, R. P., "Advertising and Inter-industry Competition," *Journal of Industrial Economics* (March 1974), 215–26.

ZIEGENHAGEN, M. E., "Industrial and Consumer Admen Face Common Traps, Chances of Success," *Advertising Age* (March 22, 1976), 44 ff.

Advertising as an institution

26

Legal and Other Restraints on Advertising

When Winston Churchill took his entrance examinations at Sandhurst in 1880, he was given a choice of three essay questions: Riding vs. Rowing; Advertisements, Their Use and Abuse; and The American Civil War. (He chose The American Civil War.) The fact that the use and abuse of advertising was up for discussion nearly a century ago reveals that criticism of advertising is not new.

The fact is that advertising is a technique; techniques have no morality of their own, but reflect the mores of the times and the standards of their users. People who publish claims in an advertisement have to think twice about what they say, because it becomes a matter of public record, for which they can be held accountable.

In most large companies, advertisements go through layers of accuracy checks before they can be released. The only reason that advertising continues to be a viable means of communication is that most people have had satisfactory experiences with most advertised products they have bought. There have always been some advertisers, however, whose products did not live up to their claims. In recent years, even some prestigious firms have been cited by the government for making questionable claims. To protect the public from false and misleading advertising, numerous laws have been passed. Chief among these is the Federal Trade Commission Act, which we discuss first. We shall then touch upon some other federal and state laws affecting advertising, as well as other steps to protect the consumer from misrepresentation in advertising.

When the Federal Trade Commission Act was passed in 1914, Congress held that "unfair methods of competition are hereby declared unlawful." (An example of what was going on in those days, which brought on the act, was cited

The Federal Trade Commission

in Chapter 1.) The law was designed to protect one businessman from another; the consumer was not in the picture.

In time, the Federal Trade Commission (FTC), the enforcing arm of the government under this act, came to consider misleading advertising as an unfair method of doing business, and in this way, the FTC became involved in protecting the consumer from misleading advertising. In 1938, the FTC's power was officially expanded by the Wheeler-Lea Amendments to the original act, to cover "unfair or deceptive acts or practices." This law also gave the FTC specific authority over false advertisements in the fields of food, drugs, therapeutic devices, and cosmetics. Today, the FTC has a wide sweep of power over advertising of products sold across state lines.

Some basic FTC ground rules

Over the years, there have emerged some basic ground rules for applying the FTC law to advertising. Based largely on the rulings of the Federal Trade Commission and on court decisions, these rules include the following important points.

Total impression.   The courts have held that the overall impression an advertisement gives is the key to whether it is false or misleading. Thus, in one case, although the term "relief" was used in an advertisement, the net impression from the entire context was that the product promised a "cure" for the ailment. Similarly, words like *stops, ends,* and *defeats* may improperly imply permanent rather than temporary relief. If an advertisement has even a "tendency to deceive," the FTC may find it illegal.

Clarity.   The statement must be so clear that even a person of low intelligence would not be confused by it. The tendency of the law is to protect the credulous and the gullible. If an advertisement can have two meanings, it is illegal if one of them is false or misleading.

Fact vs. puffery.   The courts have held that an advertiser's opinion of the product is tolerated as the legitimate expression of a biased opinion, and not a material statement of fact. However, a statement that might be viewed by a sophisticated person as trade puffery can be misleading to a person of lower intelligence. Much controversy over misleading advertising hovers around the questions, "When is a statement trade puffery and when is it a false claim?" All factual claims must be supportable. If you say, "This is an outstanding leather case," and the case is made of vinyl, that is misrepresentation. If you say, "This is an outstanding case," that is a subjective matter of opinion and is considered puffery, which is not a legal matter.

The question of taste.   The courts have held, "If the advertisement is not false, defendants have a constitutional right to use it even though its content and blatancy may annoy both the Federal Trade Commission and the general public. The issue is falsity. . . . " Hence, bad taste is not a matter involving the FTC.

Demonstrations.   Demonstrations of product or product performance on television must not mislead viewers. The FTC requires literal accuracy in nutritional ads, both audio and video.

Exaggerations in the impression conveyed may also be found misleading. Mars, Inc., makers of Milky Way candy bars, had a TV spot showing a glass of milk magically changing into a Milky Way bar. The commercial was held misleading because it gave the impression that a whole glass of milk went into a Milky Way bar.

Warranties.   A report on the subject by the FTC says:

"The final disclosure rule . . . applies to written warranties on consumer products . . . costing the consumer more than $15. . . . The warrantor must disclose "in simple and readily understood language," the following items of information, among others:

- what is covered by and, where necessary for clarification, what is excluded from the warranty;
- what the warrantor will do in the event of a defect, malfunction or failure to conform with the written warranty, including a statement of what items or services will be paid for or provided by the warrantor, and, where necessary for clarification, those that will not be; and
- a step-by-step explanation of what the purchaser should do to get the warranty honored.

"Free."   Along with related words, *free* is a popular word in advertising: "Buy one—Get one free," "2-for-1 sale," "Gift," "Bonus," and "Without charge." If there are any terms or conditions for getting something free, they must be stated clearly and conspicuously with the word *free.* If a purchaser must buy something to get something else free, the purchased product must be at its lowest price (same quality, same size) in 30 days. A "free" offer for a single size may not be advertised for more than six months in a market in any twelve-month period.

Lotteries.   Lotteries are schemes for the distribution of prizes won by chance. If a person has to pay to enter a lottery conducted by an advertiser (except government lotteries) the U.S. Postal Service calls it illegal and bans the use of the mail for it. If a lottery is advertised in interstate commerce, the FTC also holds it illegal and will proceed to stop it. Prizes in many sweepstakes (which are a form of lottery) are allowable if money need not be paid to enter the sweepstakes.

Federal Trade Commission guidelines.   The FTC, after consulting with members of over 175 industries, has compiled and published trade-practice rules calling attention to illegal practices in each industry. These rules are offered as guidelines for legal operation. All advertisements containing claims that may come under FTC scrutiny should be submitted to an attorney before the ad is produced. For foods, drugs, and cosmetics, particularly, proof of performance must have been available before the advertisement was run.

Corrective advertising.   In the past, when the commission found advertising false and misleading, it would require the advertiser merely to sign a decree consenting to discontinue such advertising. This *consent decree* permits an offending company to avoid pleading guilty if it agrees not to indulge in such practice again. Any violation thereafter is subject to a $10,000 fine for each offense. Meanwhile, however, damage to the public has been done; and formerly, during the long time required for hearings and the advertiser's appeal, the advertising could continue. It was the intent of the FTC, however, by offering the advertiser the option of signing a consent decree, to put an immediate stop to the false advertising. Now, a new philosophy has been introduced: to counteract the residual effects of the deceptive advertising, the FTC may require the advertiser to run advertising at its own expense "to dissipate the effects of that deception." The commission appears to require corrective advertising chiefly when major advertising themes are the bases for consumers' choices. The first corrective advertising case to face court review was that of Listerine.

The Listerine Case

For over 50 years, Listerine was advertised as a cold and sore-throat remedy, based on tests made long ago showing that Listerine killed the germs causing colds and sore throat. The FTC long had questioned these findings, but Listerine stuck to its advertising. Finally, the FTC was able to prove the invalidity of the tests on which Listerine claims were made. More than that, medical science found that colds are not caused by bacteria, but by viruses that enter through the nose and the eyes, not through the mouth. To the commission, all the evidence was against the Listerine claim, and the court held that during all those years the advertising had been false.

In previous years, the advertiser could have escaped a fine merely by consenting to discontinue the advertising. But now—as a result of the commission's findings and the decisions of the courts, through the U.S. Circuit Court of Appeals—Warner-Lambert, maker of Listerine, is called upon to run language in $10.2 million worth of ads stating that "Listerine will not help prevent colds or sore throats or lessen their severity." Warner-Lambert still has the right to appeal to the Supreme Court.

Meanwhile they have withdrawn the claim they had been making all those years, pending the final outcome of court action.

The Robinson-Patman Act

The Federal Trade Commission, through its antitrust division, enforces another law affecting marketing and advertising, the Robinson-Patman Act. In brief, this law requires a seller to treat all competitive customers on *proportionately* equal terms in regard to discounts and advertising allowances. This is not a law for or against advertising and promotional allowances; it simply says that *if* they are granted to one customer, they must be offered to competing customers on the same proportionate terms in relation to sales. The Federal Trade Commission, which is in charge of the enforcement of this act, offers the following examples of how the law is interpreted:

Example 1: A seller may properly offer to pay a specified part (say 50 percent) of the cost of local advertising up to an amount equal to a set percentage (such as 5 percent) of the dollar volume of purchases during a specified time.

Example 2: A seller should not select one or a few customers to receive special allowances (e.g., 5 percent of purchases) to promote a product, while making allowances available on some lesser basis (e.g., 2 percent of purchases) to customers who compete with them.

Example 3: A seller's plan should not provide an allowance on a basis that has rates graduated with the amount of goods purchased, as, for instance, 1 percent of the first $1,000 purchases per month, 2 percent of the second $1,000 per month, and 3 percent of all over that.

Example 4: A seller should not identify or feature one or a few customers in his own advertising without making the same service available on proportionally equal terms to customers competing with the identified customer or customers.

For advertisers whose dollar allowance is not big enough to run meaningful newspaper space, the manufacturer may offer the dollar equivalent in direct mail bearing the store imprint or some other promomotional offer. Enforcement of the Robinson-Patman Act has been difficult.

In 1978 the FTC proposed that all commercials seen by a substantial number of children under 8 years old be banned, because the children are too young to understand the selling intent of the advertising. It proposed also that the advertising of sugary foods that pose a dental health risk be banned from TV programs reaching substantial numbers of children between ages 8 and 11. It is for the future to reveal what comes of this proposal, a significant change in direction for the FTC.

The widening role of the FTC in advertising

Closely tied to the Federal Trade Commission Act is the Federal Food, Drug, and Cosmetic Act, passed in 1938, giving the Food and Drug Administration broad power over the labeling and branding—as contrasted with the advertising—of foods, drugs, therapeutic devices, and cosmetics. It is under this law that food and drug manufacturers must put their ingredients on the labels.

The Federal Food, Drug, and Cosmetic Act

The term *labeling* has been held to include any advertising of the product appearing in the same store in which the product is sold; it does not have to be physically attached to the package. In the case of one drug preparation, the package itself was properly labeled, but stores also sold a soft-cover book on health, written by the maker of the drug, mentioning it, and making unprovable claims for it. The drug manufacturer was in trouble with the Food and Drug Administration for false labeling and for false advertising.

Other federal controls of advertising

The Federal Trade Commission also exercises control over the advertising and labeling of products under laws affecting specific industries, including:

Wool Products Labeling Act of 1939

Fur Products Labeling Act (enacted in 1951)

Flammable Fabrics Act (enacted in 1953)

Textile Fiber Products Identification Act (enacted in 1958)

The Alcohol Tax Unit of the U.S. Treasury Department.   The liquor industry has a unique pattern of labeling and advertising under both federal and state laws. The federal laws are under the jurisdiction of the Treasury Department, for an interesting historic reason: The first American excise tax was the one levied under Alexander Hamilton, secretary of the Treasury, on alcoholic beverages. That department, through its Alcohol Tax Unit, is interested to this day in the labeling, in standards of size of bottles for tax purposes, and in the advertising of these beverages.

Each state also has its own liquor-advertising laws. In some states you cannot show a drinking scene; in others you can show a man holding a glass, but not to his lips; in another you can picture only a bottle. In few industries does an advertising person need a lawyer more often than in liquor advertising.

The Securities and Exchange Commission.   The SEC is the government agency that controls all advertising of public offerings of stocks or bonds. It insists on full disclosure of facts relevant to the company and the stock to be sold, so that the prospective investor can form an opinion. Its insistence on the facts that must be published—including a statement of negative elements affecting the investment—is very firm and thorough. The SEC never recommends or refuses to recommend a security; its concern is with the disclosure of full information.

The U.S. Postal Service.   The Postal Service has the authority to stop the delivery of mail to all firms guilty of using the mails to defraud—which is enough to put any firm out of business. It deals mainly with mail-order frauds.

State laws relating to advertising

While the pattern of the federal statutory scheme is generally one of broad language that is not essentially confined to specific industries, most states have narrower laws directed at one or more designated practices or industries. The result has been a hodgepodge of state mandates on liquor, bedding, stockbrokers, banks, loan and credit companies, employment agents, business-opportunity brokers, real estate brokers, and a variety of others. Among the laws of many states, as an example, was one that prohibited pharmacies from advertising the price of prescription medicines. In 1976 the Supreme Court held that advertising in general, especially for a commercial product, is entitled to protection under the First Amendment guarantee of free speech, thus invalidating all those state laws and showing the interplay between state laws and federal laws.

The first basic state statute in the regulation of advertising, which still represents a landmark in advertising history, is the Printers' Ink Model Statute drawn up in 1911, attempting to punish "untrue, deceptive, or misleading" advertising. *Printers' Ink* magazine, the pioneer trade paper of advertising, has died, but its model statute, in its original or modified form, exists in 44 states.

Regulation by media

The media are among the oldest continuous controllers of advertising content. National magazines keep a close eye on all ads, especially those of new advertisers with new products, to make sure their readers will not be misled. The greatest number of problems is found in those newer magazines which, anxious to sell space, are not vigilant about some of the mail-order advertisers.

Newspapers also have their codes of acceptable advertising. Most of them exercise control over even the comparative price claims made in retail advertising. A store may be asked to change a headline such as "These are the lowest-price sheets offered," to "The lowest-price sheets we have ever offered." "The greatest shoe sale ever" will be changed to "Our greatest shoe sale ever."

The National Association of Broadcasters, to which many television stations belong, has set up codes for TV and radio, to meet public criticism. Seventy-six percent of the country's television stations, as well as all three networks, are code subscribers and closely follow the station and network code. Taste, a big problem, is hard to define, even in a code. Radio, with 8,000 stations, presents a more difficult problem than TV. Only about 3,000 radio stations are code subscribers. It has been difficult to unite the radio broadcasters behind a code that, among other things, limits the amount of commercial time per broadcast hour.

The code stations do not accept liquor advertising. In addition to enforcing the NAB code, each network has its own clearance department for all commercials. NBC, for example, with its own Broadcast Standards Department, reviews all programs and advertising material, and says of that department:

> It is basically a consumer's advocate. Its object is to protect the public interest, to look at every commercial from the public's point of view, and to strive conscientiously to protect the viewer or listener from deception.

Self-regulation by individual industries

The problem of advertising on children's programs, which has aroused very strong feelings, provides a good example of how the self-regulation by marketers is even more rigid sometimes than that of the media. The Association of National Advertisers, whose members do over 75 percent of national television advertising, has established children's television guidelines that include specifications such as the following, which show the nature of the restrictions.

> Any form of presentation that capitalizes on a child's difficulty in distinguishing between the real and the fanciful should be positively guarded against.
>
> Particular control should be exercised to be sure that:
>
>   *a*) Copy, sound, and visual presentation—as well as the commercial in its total-

ity—do not mislead the audience to which it is directed on such performance characteristics as speed, size, color, durability, nutrition, noise, etc.; or on perceived benefits such as the acquisition of strength, popularity, growth, proficiency, intelligence, and the like.

b) The advertisement clearly establishes what is included in the original purchase price of the advertised product, employing where necessary positive disclosure on what items are to be purchased separately. All advertising for products sold unassembled should indicate that assembly is required.

c) A clearly depicted presentation of the advertised product is shown during the advertisement. When appropriate in assisting consumers to identify the product, the package may be depicted, provided that it does not mislead as to product characteristics or content.

d) Advertising demonstrations showing the use of a product or premium can be readily duplicated by the average child for whom the product is intended.

Many industries have established their own codes of standards of advertising practice. Most of them relate to local advertising of products by their distributors or dealers or franchise owners, especially products such as air conditioners, water softeners, or other products with new or servicing features. Voluntary trade codes usually prove ineffective. The associations lack the power of enforcement because of antitrust laws, which preclude any action that might be regarded as interfering with open competition.

The leading organizations of the advertising industry have created a self-regulating mechanism that avoids conflict with antitrust laws. It uses peer pressure on advertisers whose advertising is questionable, and it has an original and effective system for helping to prevent misleading advertising or, failing that, helping the law to curb it if it is run. It is an offspring of the Better Business Bureau, created by the advertising industry to curb misleading advertising, especially at the local level.

The Better Business Bureaus. In 1905, various local advertising clubs formed a national association that today is known as the American Advertising Federation. In 1911, this association launched a campaign for "Truth in Advertising," for which purpose various vigilance committees were established. These were the forerunners of the Better Business Bureaus, which adopted that name in 1916 and became autonomous in 1926. Today the movement has over 122 separate bureaus operating in major cities, supported by more than 100,000 firms, who contribute over $6.5 million per year. The bureau handles about 2.5 million inquiries and complaints from business and the public, and it shops or investigates more than 40,000 advertisements per year for possible violations of truth or accuracy. It has also produced booklets and films such as "Safeguarding Your Savings," aimed at forestalling questionable advertising and selling practices. Its published service, *Do's and Don'ts of Advertising Copy,* is a standard reference work on the subject.

The Better Business Bureau has worked, until recently, chiefly at the local level. It has no legal power to enforce its findings, but its influence in the community is a force to protect the public. In 1971, however, it assumed a new responsibility and role as part of the National Advertising Review Council.

The National Advertising Review Council.   In response to the many voices of different consumer groups against deceptive advertising, the chief advertising organizations formed the most comprehensive self-regulating apparatus ever established in advertising. Called the National Advertising Review Council, its chief purpose is "to develop a structure which would effectively apply the persuasive capacities of peers to seek the voluntary elimination of national advertising which professionals would consider deceptive." It concerns itself with matters of deception. It consists of the Council of Better Business Bureaus and the three leading advertising groups: the American Advertising Federation, the American Association of Advertising Agencies, and the Association of National Advertisers. The council has two operating arms: (1) The National Advertising Division of the Council of Better Business Bureaus and (2) The National Advertising Review Board.

The National Advertising/Division of the Council of the Better Business Bureaus' full-time professional staff has had a lot of experience working with advertisers on complaints. If a complaint appears valid, personal and private contact is used to get the advertiser to correct the deceptive item.

If that does not work, the case is passed to the National Advertising Review Board, composed of 50 people, five of whom are assigned to a case—like a court of appeals. If they feel the action was justified and the advertiser still does not wish to correct the deceptive element, the whole matter will be referred to the appropriate government agency. The review board will publish the letter or referral, along with any statement the advertiser wishes to make.

In discussing the National Advertising Review Council, we should understand that it cannot

> Order an advertiser to stop running an ad
>
> Impose a fine
>
> Bar anyone from advertising
>
> Boycott an advertiser or a product

What it can do is to bring to bear the judgment of the advertiser's peers, that what is being done is harmful to advertising, to the public, and to the offender. This usually has great moral weight. The situation is also reinforced by the knowledge that if the results of an appeal to the National Advertising Review Board are not accepted, the whole matter will be referred to the appropriate government agency, and that fact will be released to the public, together with any statement the advertiser wishes to make. This step, unique in business self-regulation machinery, avoids any problem of violating antitrust laws, presents

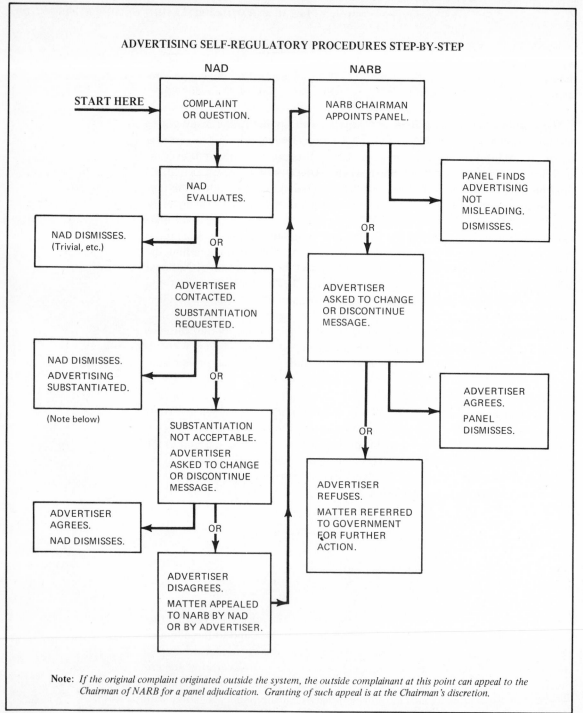

ADVERTISING SELF-REGULATORY PROCEDURES STEP-BY-STEP

NAD

NARB

START HERE → COMPLAINT OR QUESTION.

NARB CHAIRMAN APPOINTS PANEL.

NAD EVALUATES.

PANEL FINDS ADVERTISING NOT MISLEADING. DISMISSES.

NAD DISMISSES. (Trivial, etc.)

OR

OR

ADVERTISER CONTACTED. SUBSTANTIATION REQUESTED.

ADVERTISER ASKED TO CHANGE OR DISCONTINUE MESSAGE.

NAD DISMISSES. ADVERTISING SUBSTANTIATED.

OR

ADVERTISER AGREES. PANEL DISMISSES.

(Note below)

SUBSTANTIATION NOT ACCEPTABLE. ADVERTISER ASKED TO CHANGE OR DISCONTINUE MESSAGE.

OR

ADVERTISER AGREES. NAD DISMISSES.

OR

ADVERTISER REFUSES. MATTER REFERRED TO GOVERNMENT FOR FURTHER ACTION.

ADVERTISER DISAGREES. MATTER APPEALED TO NARB BY NAD OR BY ADVERTISER.

Note: *If the original complaint originated outside the system, the outside complainant at this point can appeal to the Chairman of NARB for a panel adjudication. Granting of such appeal is at the Chairman's discretion.*

Courtesy National Advertising Review Board.

Self-regulation of advertising involves many aspects.

the entire matter to public view, and still leaves the advertiser subject to a Federal Trade Commission ruling on the advertising. The following case report is typical:

> *Complaint*—That Schick, Inc., had engaged in a campaign of comparison advertising claiming superiority for its "Flexamatic" Shaver over electric shavers manufactured by the Remington Shaver Division of Sperry-Rand, North American Philips Corp., and Ronson Corporation.
>
> NAD recommended that Schick discontinue claims that: tests by an impartial laboratory as to the comparative effectiveness of electric shavers established that the Schick "Flexamatic" shaves closer than any or all competitive shavers; and that the Schick "Flexamatic" is the "King of Beards."
>
> Lacking assurance that this would be done, NAD appealed the matter to NARB. Schick requested dismissal without a hearing on grounds that FTC had reviewed the advertising, and because litigation had been started by Remington. Despite these arguments, the panel voted to proceed because of its responsibility to the consumer.
>
> *Decision*—The panel concluded that Schick made a good faith effort to meet the exacting criteria for comparative advertising, but did not think it succeeded. The campaign as a whole was judged false in some details and misleading in its overall implications.

The NAD has been very active in pursuing complaints against advertising.

Courtesy National Advertising Review Board.

NAD STATISTICAL CASE RECORD
As of March 1, 1977

	Cumulative (June 1971 to Present)
TOTAL COMPLAINTS	1174
DISPOSITION	
Dismissed —	
Adequate Substantiation	423
Dismissed —	
Advertiser Modified or discontinued	396
Administratively closed	286
Referred to NARB by NAD	12*
Pending	57

*Other cases appealed to NARB by outside complainants or advertisers.

SOURCES OF COMPLAINTS	
Consumers	184
Consumer organizations	178
Competitors	149
Local Better Business Bureaus	244
NAD monitoring	374
Other	45

NOTE: Since 1971 NAD has logged a total of 69 reviews regarding Advertising to Children.

Advertiser response—Schick stated its objections to part of the panel's report but said that in the interests of self-regulation it would, in future comparative advertising, be guided by the panel's recommendations. It urged, also, that the findings be applied to all comparative advertising by electric shaver manufacturers.°

By the end of 1977, almost 500 of the approximately 1300 national advertising cases reviewed by the NAD resulted in either substantially modified advertising or discontinuance of the advertising claim by the advertiser. The Children's Advertising Unit of the NAD had similar action in over 50 additional cases involving advertising to children.

Comparison advertising.   This term refers to the comparison of a product with a named competitive product. Comparison advertising is not new. In 1930 J. Sterling Getchell, head of an agency bearing his name, introduced the Chrysler car, never on the market before, by inviting comparison with General Motors and Ford cars, using the headline "Try all three." For many years car advertisers would stress a feature or the track record of their cars against other named brands. But the common wisdom of the advertising trade generally was that if you mentioned a competitor's name you were giving him free advertising.

When television came along it provided a valid, demonstrable base for comparing the effectiveness of two products; for example showing the relative absorbency of two brands of paper towels by dipping each into a glass of water. But the TV networks, caught in the middle by the possibility of having competitive comparison advertisers on the same program, initiated the ritual of having all comparisons made against Product X—X being the competitor whom the viewer was supposed to recognize. In 1973, however, the FTC prevailed upon the television industry to drop that restriction, and mentioning names of competitors in ads became acceptable. Today it is a popular technique in all media. There are those who still question its efficacy, but many consider such comparisons helpful in making buying decisions.

Legal aspects of comparison advertising

The Schick case dealt with the question of protecting the public against deceptive advertising and could be settled by an NARB panel. But it also shows the problems involved in comparison advertising. Any time a comparison ad mentions a competitive product by name, the advertiser is subject to a lawsuit if the competitor feels the product has been misrepresented and that its reputation must be protected. This type of legal action between two advertisers does not necessarily protect the public and is not the province of the NARB. When you compare your product with that of a competitor and mention it by name, you must be able to substantiate in court any adverse statement you make about that product. Comparison tests are open ground for inquiry. For example, how was the test conducted? Under whose auspices? Was it conducted in the normal situation for the use of the product? These are crucial questions. Furthermore, if you

° Courtesy The National Advertising Review Board, 1977.

Ban Roll-On
not only keeps you drier
than these sprays,
it keeps you drier...longer.

ban.
ROLL-ON
ANTI-PERSPIRANT
DEODORANT

51
days

The two finest vermouths
in the world.

TRIBUNO
VERMOUTH
DRY
FOR PERFECT
DRY MARTINIS

MARTINI & ROSSI
VINO
VERMOUTH
SECCO

$2.05 $3.25

They're both exceptionally dry.
They both help make unforgettable martinis.
But as you can see, there's a difference.
Tribuno Vermouth costs over a dollar less.
That may not mean much if you're the
Shah of Iran, but for most of us these days, a dollar
difference is quite a difference.
Tribuno Vermouth. Dry, Sweet, or Half &
Half. The taste makes it one of the world's finest.
But the price puts it in a class by itself.

TRIBUNO

▲ (Above): **A product that challenges the field.**

◀ (Left): **A less expensive product equating itself with a more expensive and presumably higher quality product.**

claim superiority over the whole product because you have established your superiority on one feature, how important is that to the consumer? Does the sale of the product hinge on that one feature alone? These are among the questions that the advertiser must be prepared to answer.

A simple test of any comparison ad is to ask yourself: if a competitor said about you what you are planning to say or imply about your competitor, would you be calling your lawyer?

Advertising of legal services.   Two legal restrictions against legal advertising had long prevailed, one imposed by state laws, one by the Bar Associations, which had the power to drop the membership of an attorney who advertised. The state laws have been invalidated by the Supreme Court decision of 1977, which held that forbidding lawyers to advertise violates the First Amendment right of free speech. Advertising by lawyers is now permissible in all states. The Court limited such advertising to "Truthful information on the availability and terms of routine legal services such as uncontested divorce, deeds, adoption papers." Lawyers are now free to advertise their specialities, education, professional honors, and certain fees.

The Bar Associations are now restricted from seeking to impose their own regulations on their members. The problem is still fluid.

FELLOWS, KEE & NESBIT
General Practice of Law
Main Street

David W. Kee, Samuel Nesbitt, Jr., Frank G. Fellows (1914–1975) Reciprocal Wills (Husband and Wife—$85.00. Single Will—$35.00. Simple Trust—$125.00. Deeds—$25.00. Real Estate Title Work—½ of one percent of purchase price plus Registry time. Estates—Fee discussed at First Conference. Divorces (uncontested with simple property agreement—$275.00 plus filing and Sheriff's costs. Adoptions—$125.00 plus filing fees. Industrial Accident Commission—Employer pays fee. Bankruptcy—$275.00 Bill Collecting—¼ of amount collected. Incorporating a Business—$300.00 plus filing fees. Personal Injury Cases—¼ if settled prior to instituting suit. Defending Operating Under The Influence Cases—$300.00. Other Criminal Defense Matters—Fee Discussed at First Conference.

There is no charge for your first conference on any matter. Bank Americard and Master Charge accepted. Other credit arrangements available.

A legal advertisement.

Self-regulation by individual advertisers

The most meaningful of all forms of advertising self-regulation is that of the individual advertiser. It is wholly voluntary, not the result of group pressure. It reflects the policy of top management, its sense of public responsibility, and its

HOW TO IMPROVE A BOTTLE OF CHIVAS REGAL.

As magnificent as even the most prestigious 12 year old Scotches are, some people think they have a smoky, slightly heavy quality that takes a lot of getting used to.

If you're one of these people, you'll find Cutty 12 a lot more satisfying. It's smoother. More polished. With a taste that slips over the palate without a tremor. It makes 12 year old Scotch a lot easier to acquire a taste for.

CUTTY 12.
THE 12 YEAR OLD THAT TASTES EVEN BETTER.

—from Advertising Age

Cutty pours controversial ad down the drain to settle suit

It's not legal to pour a great Scotch into someone else's bottle. We don't recommend it. Instead we suggest you pour Cutty 12 directly into your glass.

DISTILLED AND BOTTLED IN SCOTLAND. SOLE U.S. IMPORTER, THE BUCKINGHAM CORPORATION, NEW YORK, N.Y.

A comparison ad that went too far and ended in a lawsuit between Seagram and Cutty Sark. That ended the campaign.

enthusiasm to survive and grow in a competitive arena where consumer confidence is vital. Almost every sizable advertiser maintains a careful system of legal review and appraisal, backed by factual data to substantiate claims. At Lever Brothers Company, all copy developed by the advertising department and agencies is submitted first to a research and development division, where it is analyzed in the light of records and reports of experimental data. It must then be passed by the legal department, and only after this second approval is it released for publication.

In a statement of corporate responsibility, General Mills said:

> Recognizing the power and importance of such amounts [in the advertising budget] to the corporation and to society, the company through the years has endeavored to produce advertising that is not only truthful, but also informative and educational, that renders a maximum of helpful service, and that, insofar as possible, seeks to expand markets rather than merely to take business away from competitors.

> Any competitive or comparative statement to be made about any product or service must be supported. Each manager responsible for a product is also responsible for the preparation of claims and the development of adequate substantiation for them where necessary.

The Purex Corporation has rules (which are a part of the copy platform) that state:

> Purex advertising shall not claim or promise by implication any product performance or characteristic which is not fully supported by laboratory research, consumer research, or similar factual information.

> Comparative claims for Purex products must be clearly supported by research laboratory or consumer tests vs. competitive products. Such tests are not to be made against inferior brands, but against the best competitive products on the market.

> Purex management is concerned selfishly, because we recognize that without a justifiable confidence in the honesty and sincerity of an advertising message, the value of that message in selling our products is heavily discounted. . . . To contribute to still higher advertising costs through loss of consumer confidence in our advertising is unforgivable.

These statements represent the attitudes that have helped build large businesses and that have given advertising its power.

Legal releases   Before using the name or picture of a living person in an advertisement, it is most important to get the subject's legal release to do so. Each person is protected under the laws of privacy against such use without written permission. In some states, unauthorized use is a misdemeanor, and in all instances it subjects the advertiser to a suit for damages. If the subject is a child, the release must be obtained from the parent or guardian. A rigid house rule usually states: No release, no picture!

Copyrighting has nothing to do with the problems of the legal controls of advertising, which we have been discussing here. But since copyrighting is a legal procedure related to advertising, it seems appropriate to have this discussion join its legal relatives at this point.

Copyrighting advertising

The nature of copyrights.   A copyright is a federal procedure that grants the owner of it the exclusive rights to print, publish, or reproduce an original work of literature, music, or art (which includes advertising) for a specific period of time. *January 1, 1978* marked a memorable day in copyright history, for on that day a new law made *the period of time of copyright protection the life of the author plus 50 years.* (Since 1909 it had been only for a maximum of 56 years.)

A copyright protects an "intellectual work" as a whole from being copied by another; however, it does not prevent others from using the essence of the advertising idea and from expressing it in their own way. Copyrighting does not protect a concept or idea or theme, but only the expression of it. To be copyrightable, an ad must contain a substantial amount of original text or picture. Slogans and other short phrases and expressions cannot be copyrighted, even if they are distinctively arranged or lettered. Familar symbols and designs are not copyrightable.

Copyrighting policy.   Some companies make it a policy to copyright all their publication advertising. Most national advertisers, however, deem copyrighting unnecessary in their publication advertising, unless it contains a piece of art or copy that they think others will use. Retail newspaper advertising moves too fast for the advertiser to be concerned about having it bodily lifted. Direct-response advertisers often copyright their publication and direct-mail advertising; because if an ad is effective, it may be used over a long period of time, and it could readily be used, with minor changes, by another.

How to register a copyright.   Registering a copyright is one of the simple steps that can be handled directly by the advertiser, but it must be followed precisely.

1. Write to the Register of Copyrights, The Library of Congress, Washington, D.C. 20559, for the proper application form for what you plan to protect.

2. Beginning with the *first* appearance of the advertisement, the word *Copyright* or the abbreviation *Copr.*, or the symbol © should appear with the name of the advertiser. Add the year if foreign protection is planned. For a booklet or other form of printed advertising, other than publication advertisements, the copyright notice "shall be affixed to the copies in such manner and location as give reasonable notice of a claim of copyright."

3. As soon as the ad is published, two copies, with the filled-out application form and fee, should be sent to the Register of Copyrights.

QUESTIONS

1. What is the Federal Trade Commission?

2. What are its criteria for considering an advertisement false and misleading?

3. What powers does the FTC have over bad taste in advertising?

4. What special precautions must be observed in (a) using the word *free* and (b) issuing guarantees?

5. The FTC considers lotteries for use in the advertising of products illegal except on one condition. Because of what provision in the law are sweepstakes allowed?

6. What is meant by corrective advertising?
   a) Describe the FTC's powers governing corrective advertising.
   b) How does corrective advertising differ from the consent decree?

7. What does the Robinson-Patman Act have to say about advertising?

8. You are a manufacturer who has been allowing a flat 5 percent advertising allowance on all purchases, regardless of size. A large chain says that if you will allow a 7½ percent allowance, it will increase its order by 15 percent and put on a special advertising campaign for the product. You could use the business and even at that figure make a good profit. Is there any legal reason why you should not allow the 7½ percent? Explain.

9. Besides the FTC, what departments of the federal government are also interested in the labeling and advertising of products?

10. Broadly speaking, how do state laws affecting advertising differ from federal laws?

11. Explain how the media exercise control over advertising content.

12. Describe advertising industry attempts at self-regulation.

13. What is the National Advertising Review Council? What are its powers?

14. What are the chief pitfalls to guard against in comparison advertising?

15. If you were president of a company which spent a lot of money on advertising, what rules would you establish for the content of your advertisements?

16. What is meant by a legal release, and when do you need it?

17. What is the value of a copyright? What steps must you take to get it? When do you take those steps?

READING SUGGESTIONS

ARMSTRONG, GARY M., and FREDERICK A. RUSS, "Detecting Deception in Advertising," *Michigan State University Business Topics* (Spring 1975), 21–31.

BRANDT, MICHAEL T., and IVAN L. PRESTON, "The Federal Trade Commission's Use of Evidence to Determine Deception," *Journal of Marketing* (January 1977) 54–62.

COHEN, DOROTHY, "Concept of Unfairness as It Relates to Advertising Legislation," *Journal of Marketing* (July 1974), 8–13.

Council of Better Business Bureaus, *NAD/NARB Decisions.* Washington: Council of Better Business Bureaus, published monthly.

CUNNINGHAM, WILLIAM H., and ISABELLA C. M. CUNNINGHAM, "Consumer Protection: More Information or More Regulation?" *Journal of Marketing* (April 1976), 63–68.

DAY, GEORGE S., "Assessing the Effects of Information Disclosure Requirements," *Journal of Marketing* (April 1976), 42–52.

DILLON, T. C., "Advertising Is a Reflection of Our Right of Free Speech," *Broadcasting* (July 12, 1976), 10.

DYER, ROBERT F., and PHILIP G. KUEHL, "The 'Corrective Advertising' Remedy of the FTC: An Experimental Evaluation," *Journal of Marketing* (January 1974), 48–54.

GARDNER, DAVID M., "Deception in Advertising: A Conceptual Approach," *Journal of Marketing* (January 1975), 40–46.

GRIFFIN, G., "Truth in Advertising—Does It Pay?" *Graphic Arts Monthly* (December, 1974), 58–61.

HOWARD, JOHN A., and JAMES HULBERT, "Advertising and the Public Interest," *Journal of Advertising Research* (December 1974), 33–39.

JACOBY, JACOB, and CONSTANCE B. SMALL, "Deceptive and Misleading Advertising: The Contrasting Approaches of the FTC and the FDA," *Purdue Papers in Consumer Psychology,* No. 146 (1975).

O'CONNOR, N. W., "To Tell the Truth: Credibility in Advertising," *Vital Speeches* (July 1, 1976), 567–70.

PARTIN, T., "FTC and Image Advertising," *Public Relations Journal* (July 1976), 18–19.

"Product Advertising and Consumer Safety," *Advertising Age* (July 1, 1974), 47–50.

ROSCH, J. THOMAS, "Marketing Research and the Legal Requirements of Advertising," *Journal of Marketing* (July 1975), 69–72.

ROSDEN, GEORGE, and PETER ROSDEN, *The Law of Advertising.* New York: Matthew Bender and Company, 1975.

SAWYER, ALAN G., "The Need to Measure Attitudes and Beliefs Over Time: The Case of Deceptive and Corrective Advertising," *Marketing: 1776–1976 and Beyond,* ed. Kenneth L. Bernhardt. Proceedings of the American Marketing Association. Chicago: American Marketing Association, 1976, pp. 380–85.

ULANOFF, STANLEY, *Comparison Advertising: A Historical Retrospective,* Marketing Science Institute 1975.

WILKIE, WILLIAM L., and PAUL W. FARRIS, "Comparison Advertising: Problems and Potential," *Journal of Marketing,* (October 1975) 7–15.

27

Economic and Social Aspects of Advertising

The most exciting advertising in the years ahead will not result from a clever phrase or commercial. It will start in the research and development department of a company, where someone has an idea in which the company is willing to invest hundreds of thousands of dollars to bring the concept to fruition. Companies agree to invest such sums in ideas for promising new products because they know that if the product is acceptable to the public, they will be able to create a mass market through advertising that will produce profits commensurate with the risk. This confidence in the freedom to advertise reinforces a company's readiness to invest in the development of such products. This is the first impact of advertising upon our economy.

Creative impact of competition

Once a new product shows promise of success, other producers can be expected to come out with their versions, designed to improve upon the original. Soon many others will enter the new market, each offering special features. This pattern is our competitive way of life. Every marketer will advertise improvements that may not seem large, but the total effect is a better product and a wider choice for consumers.

It may be hard to judge the growth of house plants, standing in a row, if comparison is made one with another. But if you compare the growth of the whole row from one time to another, the difference is clear. Similarly, products may seem alike; but if you compare yesterday's product with today's product, the improvement in the entire class will be impressive.

"Even in this period of uncertainty," said a spokesman for the Goodyear Tire and Rubber Company, "the industry, buoyed by the fact that people are continuing to use their automobiles and thus are wearing out tires, remains in a development race that has improved the auto tire more in the past ten years than in the previous fifty."[*]

[*] Goodyear News Bureau, 1977.

Product improvements and variety—response to need and preferences.   A good insight into corporate thinking that leads to new and better products was offered by Procter & Gamble in a United States Senate hearing on the subject. The following extracts are of special interest:

> Consumer needs are discovered through a wide variety of market research techniques before, during, and after the development of a product. . . . It is clear from our research and marketplace experience that different consumers want different products with different benefits, and they are willing to pay different amounts for these benefits. One example of this is provided by our laundry brands which are offered in several different formulations, catering to different consumer interests. Some are soaps and some are detergents; some are high sudsers, others medium or low sudsing; some contain bluing, others a bleach; most are in granular form, one is compressed into tablets; some contain enzymes, another may have special brighteners; each has a distinctive perfume scent. . . .
>
> The flux of brands within the free market system results in a constant process of upgrading. . . . All our brands seek meaningful changes—in performance, aesthetics, cost reduction, and production. All changes are explored within the broad concept of consumer choice—attempting to make products which will appeal to a larger number of people as measured by preferences in the marketplace. . . . °

Each improvement is launched with advertising, because

> Advertising is the way
> to tell many people about a product or service
> in the fastest time
> at the lowest cost per message.

From the consumer's viewpoint, advertising serves as a newscast. It tells what products are available, where to get them, and particularly in the case of retail advertising, what are the prices. Advertising enables people to store information for future use whenever they are ready to buy something in a particular field. All this is possible under our competitive free enterprise system, which creates products for people to select and gives them the freedom to do so. Advertising also helps create jobs on which millions depend.

"Where did you get those good-looking oranges?"   Hedrick Smith, returning from Moscow, reported the following:

> With good reason, Americans growl about the continual bombardment of their senses by ads and commercials on television and in their press. But they might half reconsider if exposed for a while to the consumer blackout in Russia. Lack of the most basic consumer information is one of the most enervating and crippling facets of Russian life. It is the main reason Russian sidewalks are so constantly populated by shoppers earnestly plodding from store to store with their string bags and briefcases,

° D.P. Fitz, vice-president for corporate affairs, Procter & Gamble. *Report Submitted to Committee on Commerce, United States Senate* (Washington, D.C.: U.S. Govt. Printing Office, 1972), pp. 111–12.

From This

General Electric, 1905

Westinghouse, 1908

General Electric, 1913

Hotpoint, 1923

Frigidaire, 1947

Frigidaire, 1963

From Fran Maierhauser, *The Evolution of Electric Appliances. Courtesy Rural Kentuckian Magazine.*

*The creative impact of the competitive system, in which advertising plays
an important part. Advertising makes known the advances in our technology;
and in doing so, it creates markets, spurs competition, stimulates creativity.*

this 5-lb. roast cooked in just 35 minutes!

ROPER

COMBINATION MICROWAVE RANGE

Beautifully browned roasts . . . cooked just the way your family likes them at super speeds . . . is *only one* of the remarkable things your new Roper does. Combination cooking for all foods with regular heat *plus* super-fast microwave energy at the same time cooks up to 75% *faster* . . . saves costly energy, too! The Roper Combination Microwave Range does everything your way . . . in one big oven . . . with no special dishes, no extra elements, no extra finishing. No special recipes needed . . . no complicated time or temperature conversions for combination cooking. The *newest* from the *oldest* name in cooking is so different, so advanced and so easy that you'll just have to try it to believe it.

An American Tradition of Quality for over a Century

three cooking choices!

1 Combination Cooking with regular heat and Microwave at the same time . . . you can even cook a complete meal at one time . . . and up to 75% faster!

2 Super-fast, energy-saving Microwave Only in a big oven . . . plus separate Defrost Cycle.

3 Regular roasting, baking or broiling with regular heat.

PLUS: Self-Cleaning Oven with automatic cycle to clean itself completely. Roll-out Storage Drawer for utensils.

ROPER SALES

KANKAKEE, ILLINOIS 60901

engaged in an unending hit-or-miss lottery, hoping to stumble onto a find or to bump into some strange woman on the street and ask her where she got those good-looking oranges.°

The American consumer learns about the services which advertising performs not from reading about it in books, but by lifelong experience. Nationwide research, under academic auspices, shows that over 70 percent of American consumers think advertising is a good way to learn about what products are available; 77 percent think advertising is a good way to find out about new products; 66 percent regard advertising as a good way to find out where products and services they want are available; and 41 percent think advertising is a good way to find out how much products cost.†

As most price advertising is done by department stores and by supermarkets, the 41 percent who look to advertising as a source of price information are chiefly people who reach quickly for their Wednesday newspapers to see which stores are advertising what products, for how much, and who scan the department store ads daily to see what's for sale and for how much.

Incidentally (if you can call an elephant incidental to the man riding on top of it), advertising makes possible the newspapers and magazines we read. They could not survive without their advertising revenues; nor could commercial TV and radio stations, whose programs we can enjoy without charge.

The Value Goal of a Product and the Cost of Advertising

Granting all the advantages that advertising brings to us, the question still often arises, "Doesn't the consumer have to pay for all that advertising?" The answer is "Yes." The consumer who buys a product has to pay a share of all the costs that go into making and selling the product. But to say that consumers pay for advertising is not the same as saying they are paying more money because of that advertising. The answer to that question depends largely on the *value goal*, which is the value a business plans to offer in a product and the form that value is to take. It is the reason for the product's existence. The value goal may be to produce a dependable product at the lowest possible price, as in the case of Timex watches. Here the whole business was dedicated to that low-price goal— the mechanism of the works, the design, choice of materials, planning of production—everything was aimed at producing the lowest-cost dependable watch. But it took advertising to create the sales to amortize the cost of the special machinery needed and to get the volume of business necessary to keep that production line busy at its cost-saving level. Here it is legitimate to say that advertising helped reduce the cost of the product to the consumer.

° Hedrick Smith, "The Bigger the News, the Smaller the Story," *The New York Times*, November 13, 1975. Magazine section, p. 14.

† Rena Bartos and Theodore F. Dunn, *Advertising and Consumers: New Perspectives* (New York: American Association of Advertising Agencies, 1976), p. 136.

The Talon zipper story: how private enterprise works to make a good idea better.

It all started in 1893, when Whitcomb Judson invented what he called a clasp locker.

Lewis Walker liked the idea and started a company to make it. But it took twenty years of struggle before the company had its first real success—the Hookless Fastener.

Today it's called a Talon zipper—and it started a whole new industry that provides tens of thousands of jobs around the world.

The original "clasp locker," patented by Whitcomb Judson, 1893.

Competition and growth

Last year the Talon Division of Textron sold over a billion zippers. But Talon doesn't have the business all to itself. Since 1913 more than a hundred companies have come into the business to compete with it.

Competition.

That's why Talon makes zippers in hundreds of styles and colors.

That's why it pioneered the nylon zipper.

That's why Talon is working on even better fasteners to help it stay ahead.

That's what private enterprise is all about.

Spreading the word

It's a story that people can understand and maybe even get excited about. So Textron has made it into a television commercial. You can see it on the election coverage programs of the NBC and ABC networks.

Together with other commercials like it dealing with other stories from Textron—about Bell helicopters, Homelite chain saws, Fafnir bearings. And there'll be more. We think stories like these are worth telling. You'll find several of them in our booklet "How Private Enterprise Works at Textron." For a copy, write to: Textron, Providence, Rhode Island 02903.

TEXTRON

573

Or the value goal of the business may be to offer the most luxurious product in its field, like the Piaget watch, which has been advertised as "the most expensive watch in the world." Here everything was planned with one goal in mind: to make the finest watch possible, regardless of cost. Advertising tells people why the watch is worth the money. Certainly, in this case, advertising is not an instrument for reducing cost. The same applies to the luxury or premium end of most product lines—for example, Chivas Regal Scotch Whiskey, a most expensive brand.

Because of the differences in the value goals of various enterprises, it is not possible to make a single sweeping statement about the effect of advertising on the cost of a product to the consumer. The fact does remain that for most products designed for widespread consumer use, the value goal of management is to produce a better product at a lower cost to the buyer.

A point may be reached in mass production, however, where unit costs remain constant. The economy of scale has reached its peak—costs may even go up if production increases—and management control becomes looser. The job of advertising is to help create the volume of orders needed to maintain the optimum level of production, and minimum unit cost.

By the time one manufacturer reaches that point, the chances are that competitors also have, as in the automobile business. The goal of management then becomes to find out how to offer improvements that will give their product advantages over others, at the same price. Low price is only one form of value that a product may deliver. The management of each company decides what form of value it plans to offer through its product, not merely the price.

When we discuss the effect of advertising on the price of a mass-produced product, we must realize that the product might not exist if advertising had not created volume sales for its mass production.

National vs. private brands

How often have we seen signs like these in a supermarket, usually in front of two stacks of similar packages. The "advertised" brand refers to a nationally advertised brand. "Our brand" is the *house brand*, often called a *private brand*, on which the price is always lower. The difference in price fosters the impression

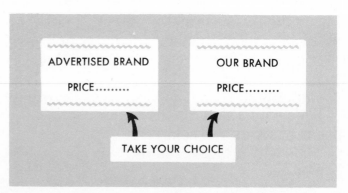

that the higher price of the "advertised" brand is due, not to any difference in quality, but to national advertising costs, overlooking the fact that supermarkets are among the newspapers' largest advertisers. This calls for some definitions.

Nationally advertised brands.   Owned and advertised by the marketer, these are, nevertheless, sold through many outlets.

Nationally advertised private brands.   A marketer's own outlets are the only ones who may sell these brands, which are also owned and controlled by the marketer. The outstanding example is Sears, one of the largest of all advertisers. Most of their advertising is done through their many local stores; however, they also advertise in national magazines and are rated as national advertisers. If their prices are lower, it is not because their merchandise is unadvertised, but because of Sears's method of doing business.

Locally advertised private brands.   Chains, department stores, or independent outlets own some brands that they confine to their respective outlets. These outlets are very large newspaper, local TV, and radio advertisers. Hence, here also, whatever lower prices they offer are possible not because "they don't advertise" (the stores do), but because of their operational pattern.

Private brands owned by wholesalers.   Drug, hardware, grocery, and liquor wholesalers will often package products under their own label and sell them to local retailers. These are seldom advertised except locally in a price ad.

When a salesperson says that a private brand product, such as a refrigerator, is made by the manufacturer of a nationally advertised brand, even when true—and that is sometimes questionable—there is no assurance that the private label product and the nationally advertised brand were made to the same specifications. Most consumers rely on the consistent quality of the nationally advertised brand for a majority of the everyday products they buy.

The more a company has invested in advertising its trademarked product, the more it will protect this asset by guarding its quality. The public knows merely that on the whole it feels safer buying a product with a reputation behind it than it does in buying one that does not have such a reputation. With each purchase, therefore, a buyer has his choice of *risks*, not merely of products. *It is not accurate to say that two products are just the same to the buyer if they differ in the insurance of satisfaction they offer at the time of purchase.*

If national advertisers had not created and launched new types of products and improved them constantly, the private label brands might not even exist. Private brands, however, constantly remind the owners of national brands that it isn't enough to keep in line with each other's prices, for as the prices of nationally advertised goods go up, the number of private brands at lower prices increases. Private label brands serve as a countervailing force, to use Galbraith's term, to the price of nationally advertised brands.

Lower costs through advertising: some dramatic examples

Datril and Tylenol.   For years Tylenol was an over-the-counter drug for people who could not tolerate aspirin, but who wanted the relief that aspirin affords. An effective substitute for aspirin, Tylenol was not advertised, and it sold for $2.85 per 100 tablets.

Datril came along with the identical formula, giving the same results, and was offered at $1.85 for 100 tablets. It was extensively advertised. Tylenol dropped its price, and prices dropped for some time thereafter.

Eyeglasses.   Until recent changes in the law, about three-fourths of the states prohibited opticians and optometrists from advertising. In those states, eyeglasses were at least 25 percent higher than in such states as Texas, Iowa, Utah, Colorado, Minnesota, and others that permitted advertisement of eyeglasses.

> In Texas it is possible to have a prescription for eyeglasses filled at $20. In California, where regulations prohibit an optometrist from advertising the price of eyeglasses, that same prescription most probably will average $30 and up.

> In Texas, an "advertising state," one chain, Lee Optical, sold contact lenses for $69.50. In California or Ohio, nonadvertising states, those same contact lenses sold for $200 and up.

> The markup on eyeglasses and contact lenses is frequently more than 100 percent in states where advertising [is] permitted, and 200 percent in states where it is prohibited.°

Prescription drugs.   "In 1976, in what was regarded as a landmark victory for the consumer movement, the Supreme Court ruled 7 to 1 that states may not forbid pharmacists from advertising prices of prescription drugs. The Federal Trade Commission staff said that lifting restrictions on drug-price advertising could save consumers over $300 million a year."†

It is not always easy to tell the effects of advertising alone in reducing prices, but the foregoing are clear examples of where it has reduced prices.

The role of information in advertising.   Direct-response advertising seeks to crowd into a given amount of space or time all the information about the product that a person might desire before making a decision to buy. But when we speak of national advertising we are speaking of only one step in the buying process, that of acquainting a person with the availability of the product, its chief usefulness and its advantages—in TV that has often to be done in 30 seconds—and encouraging him or her to buy the product or to make further inquiries if necessary. Automobile buyers, for example, are invited to go to a dealer with whatever questions they may have, and even try the car. The buyer of foods or drugs will find further information on the package, much of it required by law.

° *Parade*, January 5, 1975, p. 4.
† *The New York Times*, May 25, 1976.

IF YOU USE TYLENOL:

NEW NON-ASPIRIN DATRIL GIVES YOU THE SAME PAIN RELIEVER, SAME SAFETY AS TYLENOL.

THE DIFFERENCE IS THE PRICE.

Millions of people who are concerned about aspirin side effects take Tylenol instead of aspirin. Tylenol is safer for those who suffer from aspirin side effects, and it's gentler to the stomach. Like aspirin, it relieves pain and works quickly.

Your doctor can tell you Datril® is the same as Tylenol (Reg. TM of McNeil Labs., Inc.). The exact same pain reliever (acetaminophen). The exact same dosage (325 mg. per tablet). The exact same benefits, safety and effectiveness as Tylenol. Yet the 100-tablet size of Datril sells for as much as a dollar less than the same quantity of Tylenol. A dollar less!

Since they are both the same, there is no reason to keep paying more for Tylenol. Ask your doctor about Datril.

DATRIL.	TYLENOL.
Contains no aspirin.	Contains no aspirin.
Easier on the stomach than aspirin.	Easier on the stomach than aspirin.
No other aspirin side effects.	No other aspirin side effects.
Fast, effective pain relief.	Fast, effective pain relief.
Reduces fever of colds or "flu."	Reduces fever of colds or "flu."
Retail price up to **$1.85** 100 Tablets	Retail price up to **$2.85** 100 Tablets

NEW DATRIL FROM BRISTOL-MYERS.

© 1975, Bristol-Myers Co.

The ad that brought down the price of an important unadvertised product. Once Datril appeared, Tylenol reduced its prices and began to advertise. This was the beginning of an active quality competition between the two brands.

For household appliances—such as stoves, refrigerators, laundry equipment—advertising usually supplies enough information to enable the prospective purchaser to decide whether or not to seek further information. Advertising for a service, such as an airline, refers interested persons to a travel agent or possibly invites them to send a coupon for further information. Retail advertising offers products that the customer can examine at the store and can look to the package, label, or salesperson for further facts. Not every advertisement is responsible for supplying all the information buyers might need; it may merely lead them to sources of more information. As a rule, the costlier or more technical a product is, the more information about it is given in the advertising.

The impact of consumerism on advertising.   The demand for more complete and reliable information is one of the main objectives of the consumer movement, which, to quote Greyser, is "the movement to augment the power of buyers versus that of sellers in the marketing system." He continues:

> Consumerism . . . has found advertising to be a prime object of attention because advertising visibly touches Americans virtually all day long. Among the areas in which advertising has been affected in recent years by pressures from consumer activists and the regulatory community are:
>
> ▲ Advertising substantiation, whereby advertising now must have advance substantiation for the factual claims in their advertising;
>
> ▲ Corrective advertising, whereby those advertisers guilty of false and misleading advertising must admit their guilt in a given amount of future advertising;
>
> ▲ Broadening of interpretations of "deception" in advertising, including attacks on brand claims that are truthful but not unique to the advertised brand.°

In another study of the subject, Greyser reports that consumers are highly self-critical:

> Consumers criticize many business practices but also are highly critical of themselves. I hear them saying: "Many of us aren't interested enough to take the trouble to help ourselves in the marketplace."

> Let me remind you of some specific findings from the study results: the public agrees (2 to 1) that "there is generally enough information available for consumers to make sensible buying decisions" and by over 4 to 1 that "most consumers don't use the information available about different products in order to decide to buy one of them; further, they agree by 4 to 1 that "many of the mistakes consumers make are the result of their own carelessness" and by over 5 to 1 that "if people are careful and use good judgment they can still get good value for their money today."†

° Stephen A. Greyser, "Consumerism's Growing Impacts on Advertising," *AdEast* (March 1977).

† Sentry Study, *Consumerism at the Crossroads*, May 1977.

family health magazine

Salutes

The Winners of the 1976
Nutritional Advertising Awards

*In recognition of significant Nutritional Information presented to the
American Consumer through Advertising in Magazines—Newspapers—Radio and Television*

Awards for Excellence

Cereal & Bread Products including Grain
Kellogg Company (2 Print Awards)
Leo Burnett U.S.A.

Fruits & Vegetables
Del Monte Corporation (Print)
McCann-Erickson, Inc.
Florida Department of Citrus (Print)
Dancer, Fitzgerald, Sample, Inc.
The National Potato Board (Print)
Botsford Ketchum, Inc.
Chiquita Brands, Inc. (Print)
Young & Rubicam, Inc.

Oils, Fats & Margarines
Best Foods Division,
CPC International, Mazola (Print)
deGarmo, Inc.

Desirable Food Choices
American Dairy Association (Television)
D'Arcy-MacManus & Masius Advertising
Kellogg Company (Radio/Television)
Leo Burnett U.S.A.

Foods for Special Diets
Foodways New York, Inc. (Print)
Ted Barash & Co., Inc.
Borden Foods, Lite-Line Cheese (Print)
Ross Roy of New York
Miles Laboratories—Morningstar Farms (Radio)
Tatham-Laird & Kudner

General Nutrition Information
Best Foods Division of CPC International, Inc. (Print)
Dancer, Fitzgerald, Sample, Inc.
Safeway Stores, Incorporated (Newspapers)

Honorable Mention

Animal Products
Booth Fisheries (Print)
Draper Daniels, Inc.
Oscar Mayer & Co. (Television)
Clinton E. Frank, Inc.—Chicago

Cereal & Bread Products including Grain
Nabisco, Inc. (Television)
Ted Bates & Company

Dairy Products
Knudsen Corporation (Television)
Grey Advertising

Oils, Fats & Margarines
Pacific Vegetable Oil, Saffola (Radio)
Clinton E. Frank, Inc.—San Francisco

Vegetable Protein Rich Foods
Standard Brands Foods—Planters Peanuts (Print)
Benton & Bowles, Inc.

Foods for Special Diets
Miles Laboratories—Morningstar Farms (Print/Television)
Tatham-Laird & Kudner

The Society for Nutrition Education has one goal—to promote proper nutritional information to all Americans through communication and education-related research. Because of this commitment, they administer the Annual Family Health Magazine Nutritional Advertising Awards program. The awards were created to honor advertisers and their agencies who promote food on the basis of comprehensive nutritional information. This year's awards jury was composed of representatives from:

The Advertising Council
American Dietetic Association
American Home Economics Association

American Institute of Nutrition
Consumer Federation of America
Society for Nutrition Education

Advertising is recognized for its contribution to nutrition education.

Whether to Buy; What to Buy; the Consumer Has the Choice

We bask in our freedom to make choices in the things we can buy, but all of us have made choices that we later regretted. Most such purchases are errors of judgment made on unadvertised products as well as on advertised products.

Under our system of government, we have the responsibility of deciding for ourselves how to spend what remains of our money after taxes, what things are necessary or important to us, and what we want to work for. Would it be reasonable to refrain from telling about a product because some readers or viewers of the ad could not afford it?

A service is performed by the person who shows people how they can live better or get better satisfaction in their way of living. This is not the exclusive province of advertising. Store windows do it. A visit to a friend may do it. A magazine, a book, or a lecture may do it. But advertising not only tells about these satisfactions; it is forever telling how they may be attained more easily, more quickly, and at less cost—the favorite words of advertising headlines.

The price of having choices.   One of the prices we have to pay for living in a society that offers choices to meet different tastes is the responsibility of setting our own scale of values. Which of the goodies you learn about are for you? Which are not? What is your list of priorities? This effort is a small price for having the privilege of choice.

Since 1964, under the direction of an academic review committee, the American Association of Advertising Agencies has been recurrently sponsoring a scientific nationwide survey of what people think about advertising. In the 1964 survey 78 percent of those interviewed thought advertising essential; in 1974 the figure was 88 percent.[*]

Not only is advertising essential, but it is growing more so. John Crichton, the late president of the American Association of Advertising Agencies, said:

> The truth of the matter is that the advertising business in this country keeps growing. There are more advertisers each year, and they spend more money. Given the realities of our market—our retail mechanism—there is no hope for any other kind of selling, other than advertising. One will not see the revival of massive sales forces. One will not see the informed retail sales clerk. What one will see more and more is self-service and automation. The choice will be made by the consumer before he enters the store. His basic information will stem from advertising. All national marketers know this. Increasingly the vast retail chains are putting it into operation. It is not really debatable. The facts are there for anyone to see.[†]

And with this observation we conclude our discussion of advertising. This book has sought to capture the essence of advertising thinking today, a brief moment in the long history of advertising. From the first chapter, we have seen how

[*] Bartos and Dunn, *Advertising and Consumers: New Perspectives*, p. 43.

[†] *Report of the President.* Papers of the Annual Meeting of the American Association of Advertising Agencies, 1976.

OPINIONS ABOUT ADVERTISING: TRENDS

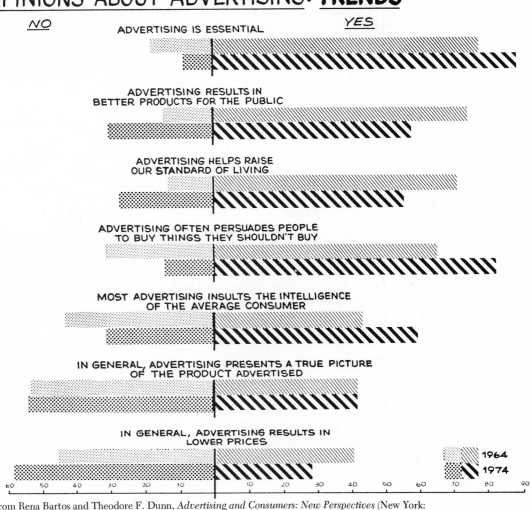

_NO_   ADVERTISING IS ESSENTIAL   _YES_

ADVERTISING RESULTS IN
BETTER PRODUCTS FOR THE PUBLIC

ADVERTISING HELPS RAISE
OUR STANDARD OF LIVING

ADVERTISING OFTEN PERSUADES PEOPLE
TO BUY THINGS THEY SHOULDN'T BUY

MOST ADVERTISING INSULTS THE INTELLIGENCE
OF THE AVERAGE CONSUMER

IN GENERAL, ADVERTISING PRESENTS A TRUE PICTURE
OF THE PRODUCT ADVERTISED

IN GENERAL, ADVERTISING RESULTS IN
LOWER PRICES

1964
1974

60 50 40 30 20 10   10 20 30 40 50 60 70 80 90

From Rena Bartos and Theodore F. Dunn, _Advertising and Consumers: New Perspectives_ (New York: American Association of Advertising Agencies, 1976), p. 43. Reprinted by permission.

**The chart makes it abundantly clear that an increasing number of people consider advertising essential.**

advertising has its roots in the history of the human desire to tell the world about what people have to sell. In our industrialized society, there are many who have products and services to offer, and there are many interested in knowing about such things and able to buy them. In the free world there are media through which people can reach each other. Techniques will change, styles of advertising will change, the forms of advertising will change. But the need for advertising will continue to grow.

QUESTIONS

1. What is meant by the creative impact of the competitive system and how does it relate to advertising?

2. Explain why and how consumer needs and preferences provide the basis for new products and product improvements.

3. If advertising were not used to bring products before the public, what alternatives would there be?

4. What is meant by the "value goal of a product"? Select three products with which you are familiar, and describe what you judge were the value goals in producing them.

5. What is the relationship between mass production and advertising, in terms of cost to the consumer?

6. "The consumer is king." Agree or disagree? Why?

7. How does advertising affect the public's freedom of choice?

8. What, in your opinion, are the things advertising does best? The things it does not do so well and could improve?

9. "This product costs less because we don't advertise." Discuss.

10. What do you think are the social responsibilities of advertising? How well does it fulfill them?

11. Is advertising essential? Why or why not?

READING SUGGESTIONS

BARKSDALE, HIRAM C., and WARREN A. FRENCH, "Response to Consumerism: How Change Is Perceived By Both Sides," *MSU Business Topics* (Spring 1975), 55–67.

BARTOS, RENA and THEODORE F. DUNN, *Advertising and Consumers: New Perspectives.* New York: American Association of Advertising Agencies, 1977.

BLACK, R.H., "Advertising Can Play Important Role During Economic Slump," *Industrial Marketing* (December 1975), 60–61.

BROZEN, YALE, ed., *Advertising and Society.* New York: New York University Press, 1974.

BURKE, M. C., and L. L. BERRY, "Do Social Actions of a Corporation Influence Store Image and Profits?" *Journal of Retailing* (Winter 1974–75), 62–72.

CARTER, DOUGLAS, and others, *Television as a Social Force.* New York: Praeger, 1975.

GOBLE, ROSS LAWRENCE, and ROY T. SHAW, *Controversy and Dialogue in Marketing.* Englewood Cliffs, N. J.: Prentice-Hall, 1975.

GRANFIELD, M., and A. NICOLS, "Economic and Marketing Aspects of the Direct Selling Industry," *Journal of Retailing* (Spring 1975), 30–50.

GREYSER, STEPHEN A., "Understanding and Meeting Consumerism's Challenges," *Harvard Business Review,* reprints series (1977).

HANNA, NESSIM, A. H. KIZILBASH, and ALBERT SMART, "Marketing Strategy Under Conditions of Economic Scarcity," *Journal of Marketing* (January 1975), 63–67.

HOWARD, JOHN A., and JAMES HULBERT, *Advertising and the Public Interest.* Chicago: Crain Books, 1977.

KANGUN, NORMAN, KEITH K. COX, JAMES HIGGINBOTHAM, and JOHN BURTON, "Consumerism and Marketing Management," *Journal of Marketing* (April 1975), 3–10.

KRAUSE, JO REACE, "Consumer Wants," *The Yale Review* (Spring 1976), 392–99.

LAMBIN, J. J., *Advertising, Competition and Market Conduct in Oligopoly Over Time.* Amsterdam, The Netherlands: North-Holland Publishing Company, 1976.

————, "What Is the Real Impact of Advertising?" *Harvard Business Review* (May 1975), 139–47.

LANE, S., "Should Ads Promote Moral Values?" *Advertising Age* (March 10, 1975), 15.

LAZER, WILLIAM, and EUGENE J. KELLEY, *Social Marketing.* Homewood, Ill.: Irwin, 1973.

LEVY, SIDNEY J., and GERALD ZALTMAN, *Marketing, Society, and Conflict.* Englewood Cliffs, N.J.: Prentice-Hall, 1975.

MORRIS, D., "Some Economic Aspects of Large-Scale Advertising," *Journal of Industrial Economics* (December 1975), 119–30.

NELSON, P., "Economic Consequences of Advertising," *Journal of Business* (April 1975), 213–41.

NELSON, R. H., "Economics of Honest Trade Practices," *Journal of Industrial Economics* (June 1976), 281–93.

NICOSIA, FRANCESCO, *Advertising Management, and Society.* New York: McGraw-Hill, 1974.

PARSONS, J. L., "Product Life Cycle and Time-varying Advertising Elasticities," *Journal of Marketing Research* (November 1975), 476–80.

SCHRAMM, R., and R. SHERMAN, "Advertising to Manage Profit Risk," *Journal of Industrial Economics* (June 1976), 295–311.

SWAN, JOHN E., and LINDA JONES COMBS, "Product Performance and Consumer Satisfaction," *Journal of Marketing Research* (April 1976), 25–33.

WEBSTER, FREDERICK E., JR., *Social Aspects of Marketing.* Englewood Cliffs, N. J.: Prentice-Hall, 1974.

WHITE, IRVING S., "The Functions of Advertising in Our Culture," *Journal of Marketing* (July 1959), 8–14.

WOTRUBA, T. R., and P. L. DUNCAN, "Are Consumers Really Satisfied?" *Business Horizons* (February 1975), 85–90.

WRIGHT, JOHN SHERMAN, *Advertising's Role in Society.* St. Paul: West, 1974.

P.S.

On Getting the First Job

There comes a moment in the lives of all students of business when they must come down from the mountaintop where they have been enjoying a sightseer's view of the world and begin their trek toward their own goals.

Although this is an advertising book, we speak here of careers in both advertising and marketing, because they are interwoven. There is much moving from one area to the other. A man or woman who begins as a salesperson in a firm and rises to be a marketing executive in that firm, may leave to become the chief executive of an agency; an assistant account executive may emerge years later as the advertising director of a company with a multimillion-dollar budget.

Consider the first job as a gateway to many opportunities. This is the time to learn all you can about the industry, the company you are working for, its goals, its standards, its marketing problems. Get to know others in the company who have been there a long time. Most important, you will be learning something about yourself: your aptitudes and interests and what your long-term goals might be.

The various fields of advertising

The advertising agency is the most publicized institution in advertising, but it employs only about one-third of all people in the field. Other sources of advertising employment include national, retail, industrial, and direct-response advertisers, television and radio producers, sales promotion services, research companies. A full description of career opportunities in advertising is given in *Advertising, A Guide to Careers in Advertising,* a booklet prepared by the American Association of Advertising Agencies.° It discusses the many different kinds of work done by agencies and by advertisers, the great diversity of talent employed in advertising, and the qualifications needed for the various jobs.

° For a copy, write to American Association of Advertising Agencies, Materials Department K, 200 Park Avenue, New York, N.Y. 10017. There is a nominal charge.

Alfred L. Plant, Vice President—Marketing Services, of the Block Drug Company, Inc., offered the following suggestions:

Breaking into advertising

> There is no sure-fire way to break into advertising. Every year, however, thousands of young men and women somehow get started. Here are a few hints that might be helpful.
>
> 1. *Sell*
> Advertising is part of the selling process. So learn what interests—motivates—influences—and makes people decide to buy. The very best way is by experience. By doing it yourself and watching and listening. It doesn't matter what you sell—doorknobs or doggy bags—the experience of selling will provide a fundamental knowledge that will stand you in good stead.
>
> 2. Get a job where you will be exposed to advertising. If possible, in an advertising department or with an agency. But don't let your pride stand in the way of starting in a lowly position if it will give you the exposure to advertising that is so essential.
>
> This can be the gateway to a real advertising job if you are interested—ambitious—ingenious—and suitable.
>
> 3. Once you have the opportunity to be exposed to advertising, be curious and ambitious. If you are interested in copywriting, talk to some of the young copywriters. Ask them what they are doing and why they are recommending the approach they are taking. Ask if they would mind if you took a crack at writing the ad or the commercial and brought it in for their critique.
>
> If you are interested in the film-making end, ask to see a storyboard and then talk about it and again inquire what the creative talent had in mind. Most people are flattered when you ask for their advice and help.

Breaking into the advertising agency

Agencies that may not have training courses nevertheless often accept beginners to work in various departments. The beginning pay may seem low, but after six months to a year—when beginners have had a chance to reveal their aptitudes—their rise in the agency can pick up momentum. In about two years, beginners suddenly realize how many opportunities are open for those with "about two years' experience." By the time they are in their early 30s, they may well be making far more money than some of their classmates who started in other fields with higher starting salaries but slower potentials for moving up. The advertising agency world is one in which a person who reveals talent and competence is not denied the opportunity of earning good money because he or she is "too young" or because of seniority, as is the case in some other fields.

To the young person embarking on a career in the advertising agency, Ogilvy offers the following advice:

> After a year of tedious training, you will probably be made an assistant executive. The moment that happens, set yourself to become the best informed person in the agency on the account to which you are assigned. If, for example, it is a gasoline account, read textbooks on the chemistry, geology, and distribution of petroleum products. Read all the trade journals in the field. Read all the research reports and mar-

keting plans that your agency has ever written on the product. Spend Saturday mornings in service stations pumping gasoline and talking to motorists. Visit your client's refineries and research laboratories. At the end of your second year, you will know more about gasoline than your boss; you will then be ready to succeed him or her.°

Sidney and Mary Edlund, in their book, *Pick Your Job and Land It!* give good advice on turning your interview into an offer:

▲ Have a clear picture of what the job calls for.

▲ Gather all the facts you can about the firm and its products.

▲ Draw up in advance an outline of the main points to be covered.

▲ Appeal to the employer's self-interest. Offer a service or dramatize your interest.

▲ Back up all statements of ability and achievement with proof.

▲ Prepare some questions of your own in advance. Keep etched in mind the two-way character of the interview: mutual exploration.

▲ Prepare for the questions normally asked.

▲ Anticipate and work out your answers to major objections.

▲ Close on a positive note.

▲ Send a "thank you" note to each interviewer.

▲ And follow up your best prospects.

Don't necessarily do all the talking. If the employer starts talking, listen! Find out what the job is like, what he or she expects from you. Sometimes good listening is as effective in selling as a dictionary full of words. After the interview, follow up your conversation with a letter. Thank the interviewer for the time given you. Try to use something he or she told you about the position to show your special aptitudes. Even if you have been given the job, it is good business to write a "thank you" note.†

Some final words: You may find yourself doing the same kind of work as many others in your department. There is one sure way of standing out in the crowd and being up front when a promotion is open: be the first in the office in the morning! You will get more work done; that's a good reputation. Some morning you will find the boss coming in with you. Some day you will *be* the boss. It happens, and you can't lose by trying.

° Reprinted from *Confessions of an Advertising Man* by David Ogilvy. Atheneum Publishers, 1963, pp. 151–52. Copyright 1963 by David Ogilvy Trustee. Reprinted by permission of Atheneum Publishers, New York, and Longmans, Green & Co. Limited, London.

† See also Melvin W. Donaho and John L. Meyer, *How to Get the Job You Want: A Guide to Résumés, Interviews, and Job-Hunting Strategy* (Englewood Cliffs, N.J.: Prentice-Hall, Inc., 1976). A Spectrum Book.

Appendix

Sources of Information

PERIODICALS

General advertising publications

Advertising Age
740 N. Rush St.
Chicago, Ill. 60611

Journal of Marketing
222 S. Riverside Plaza
Chicago, Ill. 60606

Media Decisions
342 Madison Avenue
New York, N.Y. 10017

Direct Marketing

Direct Marketing
224 Seventh Street
Garden City, N.Y. 11530

Packaging

Modern Packaging
205 East 42nd Street
New York, N.Y. 10017

Research

Journal of Advertising Research
Advertising Research Foundation, Inc.
3 East 54th Street
New York, N.Y. 10022

Journal of Marketing Research
222 S. Riverside Plaza
Chicago, Illinois 60606

Sales promotion

Incentive Marketing
633 Third Avenue
New York, N.Y. 10017

Television and radio

Broadcasting
1735 DeSales St., N.W.
Washington, D.C. 20036

Television/Radio Age
666 Fifth Avenue
New York, N.Y. 10019

REFERENCE BOOKS AND INFORMATION SERVICES

Editor and Publisher Market Guide
850 Third Avenue
New York, N.Y. 10022

Media Market Guide
Conceptual Dynamics
P. O. Box 332
Wakefield, New Hampshire 03598

Newspaper Circulation Analysis (NCA)
Standard Rate & Data Service
866 Third Avenue
New York, N.Y. 10022

N. W. Ayer & Sons Directory of Newspapers and Periodicals (annual)
N. W. Ayer & Son, Inc.
West Washington Square
Philadelphia, Pa. 19106

Standard Directory of Advertisers (The Red Book)
Standard Directory of Advertising Agencies
National Register Publishing Co., Inc.
5201 Old Orchard Road
Skokie, Illinois 60076

ASSOCIATIONS OF ADVERTISERS AND AGENCIES

The Advertising Council
825 Third Avenue
New York, N.Y. 10017

American Advertising Federation (AAF)
1225 Connecticut Avenue, N.W.
Washington, D.C. 20036

American Association of Advertising Agencies (AAAA—the 4A's)
200 Park Avenue
New York, N.Y. 10017

American Marketing Association (AMA)
222 S. Riverside Plaza, Suite 606
Chicago, Illinois 60606

Association of National Advertisers (ANA)
155 East 44th Street
New York, N.Y. 10017

Business & Professional Advertising Association (BPAA)
41 East 42nd Street
New York, N.Y. 10017

International Advertising Association (IAA)
475 Fifth Avenue
New York, N.Y. 10017

National Advertising Review Board (NARB)
850 Third Avenue
New York, N.Y. 10022

National Council of Affiliated Advertising Agencies
6 East 45th Street
New York, N.Y. 10017

SYNDICATED MEDIA RESEARCH SERVICES

Syndicated media research services conduct regular surveys to reveal the publications people read, stations they listen to, advertisements they read, programs they listen to or watch, their reaction to programs and commercials, types of products they use, which brands, and demographic information. Each service focuses on some special phase of the total picture. Since they are continually working to make their output more helpful, no effort is made here to describe the specific services each offers. For latest information communicate directly with them.

The Arbitron Company, Inc.
1350 Avenue of the Americas
New York, N.Y. 10019

Axiom Market Research Bureau, Inc.
420 Lexington Avenue
New York, N.Y. 10017

Broadcast Advertisers Reports, Inc. (BAR)
500 Fifth Avenue
New York, N.Y. 10036

Gallup & Robinson, Inc.
44 Nassau Street
Princeton, N.J. 08541

Leading National Advertisers, Inc. (LNA)
347 Madison Avenue
New York, N.Y. 10017

A. C. Nielsen Company
Nielsen Plaza
Northbrook, Illinois 60062

The Pulse, Inc.
1212 Avenue of the Americas
New York, N.Y. 10019

W. R. Simmons & Associates
Research, Incorporated
1180 Avenue of the Americas
New York, N.Y. 10017

Standard Rate & Data Service, Inc.
5201 Old Orchard Road
Skokie, Illinois 60076

Starch, Inra, Hooper, Inc.
E. Boston Post Road
Mamaroneck, N.Y. 10544

Trendex, Inc.
800 Third Avenue
New York, N.Y. 10017

Glossary

AAAA (4 A's). *See* American Association of Advertising Agencies.

AAF. *See* American Advertising Federation.

ABC. *See* Audit Bureau of Circulations.

ABP. *See* American Business Press.

ACB. *See* Advertising Checking Bureau.

Account executive. Member of the agency staff who is the liaison between advertiser and agency, presenting the advertiser's problems to the agency, and the agency's recommendations and proposed advertisements to the advertiser. Responsible for keeping in close touch with the advertiser's needs and plans and for seeing that approved plans are carried out by the agency.

Across the board. A TV or radio program scheduled for broadcast in the same time period on different days during the week (usually Monday through Friday).

ADI. *See* Area of Dominant Influence.

Adjacency. A program or time period which immediately precedes or follows a scheduled program on a single radio or television station.

Ad lib. To extemporize lines not written into the script or the musical score. Lines or music so delivered.

Advertising. A method of delivering a message impersonally to many people over the sponsor's name.

Advertising agency. An organization rendering advertising services to clients.

Advertising Checking Bureau (ACB). A private organization through which most newspaper publishers send their tear sheets to national advertisers for checking purposes.

Advertising Council. The joint body of the AAAA and the ANA, and media, through which public service advertising is produced and presented.

Advertising network. A group of independently owned, non-competing advertising agencies that agree to exchange ideas and services in the interests of their clients.

Advertising Research Foundation (ARF). An association of research people devoted to furthering the use and effectiveness of marketing and advertising research.

Advertising specialty. An inexpensive gift (limit $4.00, usually much less) bearing the advertiser's name and trademark, given without cost to a selected list.

Advertising spiral. The graphic representation of the stages through which a product might pass in its acceptance by the public. The stages are *pioneering, competitive, retentive.*

Affidavit. A sworn statement. A TV or radio station must make an affidavit that a commercial appeared as stated on invoice.

Affiliate. An independently owned TV or radio station that agrees to carry programs provided by a network.

AFTRA. *See* American Federation of Television and Radio Artists.

Agate line. A unit measurement of publication advertising space, one column wide (no matter what the column width) and one-fourteenth of an inch deep.

Agency. *See* Advertising Agency.

Agency charges (TV). All items, including talent session fees, artwork, commission, taxes, etc., appearing on the television production budget, exclusive of the production studio bid.

Agency commission. Compensation paid by a medium to recognized agencies for services rendered in connection with placing advertising with it. Usually 15 percent. Some media also allow 2 percent of the net (85 percent) as a cash discount for prompt payment. This is passed on to the client for prompt payment.

Agency network. A voluntary affiliation of one agency in a major city to act as local office or provide local service for other members of that network. There are a number of different networks.

Agency of record. The advertising agency designated by the advertiser to coordinate the total media buy and the programming of products in a network buy. It keeps a record of all advertising placed. Used in situations where large advertisers have several agencies handling the advertising of their various divisions and products.

Agency recognition. The acknowledgment by a medium that an organization qualifies under its terms to receive a commission for business placed.

Aided recall. A research technique that uses prompting questions or materials to aid a respondent's memory of the original exposure situation, as "Have you seen this ad before?" In contrast to *unaided* recall: "Which ad impressed you most in this magazine?"

Air check. A recording of an actual broadcast that serves as a file copy of a broadcast, and which a sponsor may use to evaluate talent, program appeal, or production.

A la carte agency. One which offers parts of its services, as needed on a negotiated fee basis; also called *modular* service.

Allocation. The assignment of frequency and power made by the Federal Communications Commission to a broadcasting station.

AM. See Amplitude modulation.

American Academy of Advertising. (AAA) The national association of teachers of advertising in colleges and universities, and of others interested in the teaching of advertising.

American Advertising Federation (AAF). An association of local advertising clubs and representatives of other advertising associations. The largest association of advertising people. Very much interested in advertising legislation.

American Association of Advertising Agencies. AAAA. The 4A's. The national organization of advertising agencies.

American Business Press, Inc., (ABP). An organization of trade, industrial, and professional papers.

American Federation of Television and Radio Artists (AFTRA). A union involved in the setting of wage scales of all performers.

American Newspaper Publishers' Association (ANPA). The major trade association of daily and Sunday newspaper publishers.

Amplitude modulation (AM). The method of transmitting electromagnetic signals by varying the *amplitude* (size) of the electromagnetic wave, in contrast to varying its *frequency* (FM). Quality not as good as FM but can be heard further, especially at night. See Frequency modulation—FM.

ANA. See Association of National Advertisers.

Animation (TV). Making inanimate objects apparently alive and moving by setting them before an animation camera and filming one frame at a time.

Announcement. Any TV or radio commercial, regardless of time length, within or between programs, which presents an advertiser's message or a public service message.

Announcer. Member of a TV or radio station who delivers live commercials or introduces a taped commercial.

ANPA. See American Newspaper Publishers' Association.

Answer print (TV). The composite print of the television commercial with all elements in place.

Antique-finish paper. Book or cover paper that has a rough, uneven surface, good for offset printing.

Appeal. The motive to which an advertisement is directed and which is designed to stir a person toward a goal the advertiser has set.

Approach (copy). The point of view with which a piece of copy is started—factual or emotional.

Approach (outdoor). The distance measured along the line of travel from the point where the poster first becomes fully visible to a point where the copy ceases to be readable. (There is long approach, medium approach, short approach, and flash approach.)

Arbitrary mark. A dictionary word used as a trademark that *connotes nothing* about the product it is to identify, e.g., *Rise* shaving cream, *Dial* soap, *Jubilee* wax.

Area of Dominant Influence (ADI). An exclusive geographic area consisting of all counties in which the home market station receives a preponderance of total viewing hours. Developed by American Research Bureau. Widely used for TV, radio, newspaper, magazine, outdoor advertising in media scheduling. *See also* Designated Market Area (DMA).

Area sampling. See Sample, Sampling.

ARF. See Advertising Research Foundation.

ASCAP. American Society of Composers, Authors, and Publishers. An organization that protects the copyrights of its members and collects royalties in their behalf.

Ascending letters. Those with a stroke or line going higher than the body of the letter—b, d, f, h, k, l, and t—and all capitals. The descending letters are g, j, p, q, and y.

Association of National Advertisers (ANA). The trade association of the leading national advertisers. Founded 1910.

Association test. A research method of measuring the degree to which people correctly identify brand names, slogans, themes.

Audience, primary. TV, radio: the audience in the territory where the signal is the strongest. *Print*: the readers in households that buy or subscribe to a publication.

Audience, secondary. TV, radio: the audience in the territory adjacent to the primary territory which receives the signal, but not so strongly as the latter. *Print*: the number of people who read a publication but who did not subscribe to or buy it. Also called pass-along circulation.

Audience, (TV) share of. The number or proportion of all TV households that are tuned to a particular station or program.

Audience composition. The number and kinds of people classified by their age, sex, income, and the like, listening to a television or radio program.

Audience flow. The TV household audience inherited by a broadcast program from the preceding program.

Audimeter. The device for recording when the television in a household is on, a part of the research operation of the A. C. Nielsen Company.

Audio (TV). Sound portion of a program or commercial. See Video.

Audit Bureau of Circulations (ABC). The organization sponsored by publishers, agencies, and advertisers for securing accurate circulation statements.

Audition. A tryout of artists, musicians, or programs under broadcasting conditions.

Audition record. A transcription of a broadcast program used by a prospective sponsor to evaluate it, generally before the broadcast.

Author's corrections, author's alterations. (AA's) Changes made in proofs (called author's proofs) not printer's errors, chargeable to whoever is paying for composition. Unnecessary expense for this item can be reduced by careful editing of copy before it is sent to the printer.

Availability. In broadcasting, a time period available for purchase by an advertiser.

B

Background. A broadcasting sound effect, musical or otherwise, used behind the dialogue or other program elements for realistic or emotional effect.

Back-to-back. Describes the situation in which two commercials or programs directly follow each other.

Bait advertising. An alluring but insincere retail offer to sell a product that the advertiser in truth does not intend or want to sell. Its purpose is to switch a buyer from buying the ad-vertised merchandise to buying something costlier.

Balloons. A visualizing device surrounding words coming from the mouth of the person pictured. Borrowed from the comics.

Balopticon (balops). A type of TV animation made possible through the use of a Balopticon machine.

Barter. Acquisition of broadcast time by an advertiser or an agency in exchange for operating capital or merchandise. No cash is involved.

Basic bus. A bus, all of whose interior advertising is sold to one advertiser. When the outside is also sold, it is called a basic basic bus.

Basic network. The minimum grouping of stations for which an advertiser must contract in order to use the facilities of a radio or television network.

Basic rate. See Open rate.

Basic stations. TV networks are offered in a list of stations that must be included. These are the basic stations. There is also a supplementary list of optional additions.

Basic weight. The weight of a ream of paper if cut to the standard or basic size for that class of paper. The basic sizes are: writing papers, 17 × 22 inches; book papers, 25 × 38 inches; cover stocks, 20 × 26 inches.

BBB. See Better Business Bureaus.

Bearers. (1) Excess metal left on an engraving to protect and strengthen it during the process of electrotyping. (2) Strips of metal placed at the sides of a type form for protection during electrotyping.

Better Business Bureaus. An organization launched by advertisers, and now with wide business support, to protect the public against deceptive advertising and fraudulent business methods. Works widely at local levels. Also identified with the National Advertising Review Board.

Billboard. (1) Popular name for an outdoor sign. Term not now generally used in the industry. (2) The television presentation of the name of a program sponsor plus a slogan, used at the start or close of a program, usually 8 seconds.

Billing. (1) Amount of gross business done by an advertising agency. (2) Name credits of talent in order of importance.

Bit. A small part in a dramatic program is a bit part, and the performer who plays it is a bit player.

Black and white. An advertisement printed in one color only, usually black, on white paper. Most newspapers are printed black and white.

Blanking area. The white margin around a poster erected on a standard size board. It is widest for a 24-sheet poster, for example; narrower for a 30-sheet poster, and disappears on a bleed poster.

Bleed. Printed matter that runs over the edges of an outdoor board or of a page, leaving no margin.

Blister pack. A packaging term. A preformed bubble of plastic holding merchandise to a card. Used for small items. Also called bubble card.

Block. (1) A set of consecutive time periods on the air; or a strip of the same time on several days. (2) Wood or metal base on which the printing plate is mounted. (3) British term for photoengraving or electrotype.

Blowup. Photo enlargement of written, printed, or pictorial materials; e.g., enlargement of a publication advertisement to be used as a poster or transmitted through television.

BMI. Broadcast Music, Inc. Chief function: to provide music to radio and TV shows with minimum royalty fees, if any.

Boards (outdoor). Poster panels and painted bulletins. Term originated in the period when theatrical and circus posters were displayed on board fences.

Body copy. Main text of advertisement, in contrast to headlines and name plate.

Body type. Commonly used for reading matter, as distinguished from display type used in the headlines of advertisements. Usually type 14 points in size, or smaller.

Boldface type. A heavy line type; for example, the headings in these definitions.

Bond paper. The writing paper most frequently used in commercial correspondence, originally a durable quality used for printing bonds and other securities. The weight in most extensive use for letterheads is 20 lb. ($17 \times 22 = 20$).

Book paper. Used in printing books, lightweight leaflets, and folders, distinguished from writing papers and cover stocks. Basic size: 25×38.

Bounce back. An enclosure in the package of a product that has been ordered by mail. It offers other products of the same company and is effective in getting more business.

Boutique. A service specializing in creating advertisements. Often calls in independent artists and writers. This term is usually applied to small groups. Larger groups refer to themselves as *creative services,* and they may develop into full-service agencies.

Box-top offers. An invitation to the consumer to get a gift or premium by sending in the label or box top from a package of the product (with or without an additional payment).

BPA. *See* Business Papers Audit of Circulation.

Brand name. The spoken part of a trademark, in contrast to the pictorial mark; a trademark word.

Bridge. Music or sound effect cue linking two scenes in a TV or radio show.

Broadcast spectrum. That part of the range of frequencies of electromagnetic waves assigned to broadcasting stations. Separate bands of frequencies are assigned to VHF and UHF television, AM and FM radio.

Brochure. A fancy booklet or monograph.

Bubble card. *See* Blister pack.

Bulk mailing. A quantity of third-class mail that must be delivered to the postoffice in bundles, assorted by state and city.

Bulldog edition. A morning paper's early edition, printed the preceding evening and sent to out-of-town readers on the night trains or planes. If an advertiser does not get copy in early, it will miss this edition.

Buried offer. An offer for a booklet, sample, or information made by means of a statement within the text of an advertisement without use of a coupon or typographical emphasis. (Also called hidden offer.)

Business Papers Audit of Circulation, Inc. (BPA). An organization that audits business publications. Includes controlled or "qualified" free circulation.

Buying services (media). A professional organization that plans and executes media schedules for agencies and advertisers. Also known as *media services,* operating chiefly in broadcast field.

Buying space. Buying the right to insert an advertisement in a given medium, such as a periodical, a program, or an outdoor sign; buying time is the corresponding term for purchase of TV or radio broadcast privilege.

C

Cablecasting. A term used interchangeably with CATV (Community Antenna Television). Built around an antenna at a high neighborhood location, it transmits the program it receives by a cable to the office of a local cablecasting system. The program in turn is carried by cable to local subscribers, who pay a monthly fee for the service. The cablecasting system can also initiate its own programs and transmit them to subscribers without FCC approval because it does not use airwaves. Chief advantages: excellent reception, relatively inexpensive, reaches places where reception is otherwise disturbed by interference. Now used with earth satellite stations to transmit paid TV programs.

Calendered paper. Paper with a smooth, burnished surface, attained by passing the paper between heavy rolls called calenders.

Call letters. The combination of letters assigned by the Federal Communications Commission to a broadcasting station. They serve as its official designation and establish its identity.

Camera light. Pilot light on TV cameras indicating which camera is on the air.

Camera lucinda (Lucy). A device used in making layouts, enabling art-ist to copy an illustration larger, smaller or in the same size.

Campaign. A specific advertising effort on behalf of a particular product or service. It extends for a specified period of time.

Caption. The heading of an advertisement; the descriptive matter accompanying an illustration.

Casting off. Estimating the amount of space a piece of copy will occupy when set in type of a given size.

Cathode ray tube (CRT). Electronic tube used by highspeed photocomposition machines to transmit the letter image onto film, photopaper, microfilm, or an offset plate.

CATV. *See* Cablecasting.

Center spread. The space occupied by an advertisement on the two facing center pages of a publication.

Center-Spread *Print:* An advertisement printed across the two facing middle pages of a publication bound through the center. Otherwise called double-page spread. *Outdoor:* Two adjacent panels using coordinated copy.

Certification mark. A name or design used upon, or in connection with, the products or services of persons other than the owner of the mark, to certify origin, material, mode of manufacture, quality, accuracy or other characteristics of such goods or services; e.g., *Seal of the Underwriters' Laboratories; Sanforized; Teflon II.*

Chain. (1) A group of retail outlets with the same ownership, management, and business policy. (2) A regularly established system of TV or radio stations interconnected for simultaneous broadcasting through the associated stations. (3) A network of TV stations.

Chain break. Times during or between network programs when a broadcasting station identifies itself (2 seconds) and gives a commercial announcement (8 seconds). The announcements are referred to as chain breaks or ID's (for identification).

Channel. A band of radio frequencies assigned to a given radio or TV station or to other broadcasting purposes.

Checking copy. A copy of a publication sent to an advertiser or agency, to show that the advertisement appeared as specified.

Circular. An advertisement printed on a sheet or folder.

Circulation. Refers to the number of people a medium reaches. (1) In publication advertising: *prime* circulation is that paid for by the reader, in contrast to *pass-along* circulation. (2) In outdoor and transportation advertising: people who have a reasonable opportunity to observe display. (3) In TV: usually referred to as audience.

Circulation waste. Circulation for which an advertiser pays, but it does not reach the type of prospect desired.

Classified advertising. Published in sections of a newspaper or magazine set aside for certain classes of goods or services, in columns so labeled. Example: Help Wanted, Positions Wanted, Houses for Sale, Cars for Sale. The advertisements are limited in size and illustrations.

Class magazines. The term loosely used to describe publications that reach select high-income readers, in contrast to magazines of larger circulations, generally referred to as mass magazines.

Clear. (1) To obtain legal permission from responsible sources to use a photograph or quotation in an advertisement or to use a certain musical selection in a broadcast. (2) To clear time is to arrange with a TV station to provide time for a commercial program.

Clear-channel station. A radio station that is allowed the maximum power and given a channel on the frequency bank all to itself. Possibly one or two sectional or local stations may be removed from it far enough not to interfere. (See Local-channel station; Regional-channel station).

Clear time. See Clear.

Clip. A short piece of film inserted in a program or commercial.

Closed circuit (TV). Live, videotape, or film material transmitted by cable for private viewing on a TV monitor.

Closing date; closing hour. (1) The day or hour when all copy and plates or prints must be in the medium's hands if the advertisement is to appear in a given issue. The closing time is specified by the medium. (2) The last hour or day that a radio program or announcement may be submitted for approval to a station or network management to be included in the station's schedule.

Cluster sample. A random or probability sample that uses groups of people rather than individuals as a sampling unit.

CMX (TV). Computer editing, in which the videotape of the TV commercial is edited at a console with two side-by-side monitors.

Coarse-screen halftone. A comparatively low, or coarse, screen, usually 60, 65, or 85 lines to the inch, makes the picture suitable for printing on coarse paper.

Coated paper. Coating gives paper a smooth, hard finish, suitable for the reproduction of fine halftones.

Coaxial cable. In TV, the visual part is sent on AM frequency; the audio part, on FM. Both frequencies are sent through the same cable, the *coaxial* cable.

Coined word. An original and arbitrary combination of syllables forming a word. Extensively used for trademarks, as Acrilan, Gro-Pup, Zerone. (Opposite of dictionary word.)

Collateral services. An agency term, to describe the noncommissionable forms of services different agencies perform, such as sales promotion, research, merchandising, new product studies. Done on a negotiated fee basis, both for clients and nonclients.

Collective mark. An identification used by the members of a cooperative, an association, collective group, or organization, including marks used to indicate membership in a union, an association, or other organization; e.g., Sunkist.

Color proof. Combined impressions from separate color plates.

Column-inch. A unit of measure in a periodical one inch deep and one column wide, whatever the width of the column.

Combination plate. A halftone and line plate in one engraving.

Combination rate. (1) A special space rate for two papers, such as a morning paper and an evening paper, owned by the same publisher. Applies also to any other special rate granted in connection with two or more periodicals. (2) The rate paid for a combination plate.

Comic strip. A series of cartoon or caricature drawings.

Commercial. The advertiser's message on TV or radio.

Commercial program. A sponsored program from which broadcasting stations derive revenue on the basis of the time consumed in broadcasting it.

Community Antenna Television (CATV). A method whereby one antenna placed at an advantageous height can receive many stations and relay programs on a coaxial cable to the TV sets of subscribers. See Cablecasting.

Comparative advertising. See Comparison advertising.

Comparison advertising. Used interchangeably with the term *comparative advertising*, it directly contrasts an advertiser's product with other named or identified products.

Competitive stage. The advertising stage a product reaches when its general usefulness is recognized, but its superiority over similar brands has to be established in order to gain preference. (*Compare* Pioneering stage; Retentive stage.) See Spiral.

Composite print (TV). A 35mm or 16 mm film print of a TV commercial, complete with both sound and picture.

Composition. Assembling and arranging type for printing. (Also called *typography* or *typesetting*.)

Composition (cold). Strike-on or direct-impression typesetting by a typewriter.

Composition (hand). Metal type already molded, picked out of its case by hand, to compose the copy.

Composition (hot). Type molded for the needs of the copy being set, as by a line-casting machine (e.g., the Linotype).

Composition (photo). Type set photographically or electronically onto photosensitized paper or film.

Comprehensive. A layout accurate in size, color scheme, and other necessary details, to show how final ad will look. For presentation only; never for reproduction.

Computerized composition. The use of a stand-alone or built-in computer in phototypesetting (or, rarely, linecasting) equipment for the purpose of justifying and hyphenating, storing (as for telephone directories, price and parts lists, etc.) and typographically manipulating copy after it has been keyboarded, but before it is set into type.

Consumer advertising. Directed to people who will personally use the product, in contrast to trade advertising, industrial advertising, professional advertising.

Consumer goods. Products that directly satisfy human wants or desires, such as food and clothing; also products sold to an individual or family for use without further processing; as distinct from industrial goods.

Contemporary music. Pop music, also called Top 40.

Contest. A promotion in which consumers compete for prizes and the winners are selected strictly on the basis of skill. See Sweepstakes.

Continuity. A TV or radio script. Also refers to the length of time a given media schedule runs.

Continuity department (TV). Determines whether or not a commercial is up to the broadcast standards of the station.

Continuous tone. Shading in a picture that is not formed by screen dots.

Contract year. The period of time, in space contracts, running for one year beginning with the first advertisement under that contract. It is usually specified that the first advertisement shall appear within 30 days of the signing of the contract.

Controlled circulation business and professional publications. Sent without cost to people responsible for making buying decisions. To get on, and stay on, such lists people must state their positions in com-

panies and request annually that they be kept on the list. Also known as qualified circulation publications.

Convenience goods. Consumer goods bought frequently at nearby (convenient) outlets, as distinct from shopping goods, for which a person compares styles, quality, prices.

Conversion table. Table showing what the equivalent weight of paper stock of a given size would be if the sheet were cut to another size.

Cooperative advertising. (1) Joint promotion of a national advertiser (manufacturer) and local retail outlet in behalf of the manufacturer's product on sale in the retail store. (2) Joint promotion through a trade association for firms in a single industry. (3) Advertising venture jointly conducted by two or more advertisers.

Cooperative mailing. Sent to a select list comprising all the inserts of a group of noncompetitive firms trying to reach the same audience. A way of reducing mailing costs.

Copy. (1) The text of an advertisement. (2) Matter for a compositor to set. (3) Illustrations for an engraver to reproduce. (4) Any material to be used in the production of a publication. (5) The original photograph, drawing, painting, design, object, or anything that is in process of reproduction for printing purposes.

Copy approach. The method of opening the text of an advertisement. Chief forms: factual approach, emotional approach.

Copy platform. The statement of the basic ideas for an advertising campaign, the designation of the importance of the various selling points to be included in it, and instructions regarding policy in handling any elements of the advertisement.

Copyright. Legal protection afforded an original intellectual effort. Application blanks for registry are procurable from the Copyright Office, Library of Congress, Washington, D. C. 20559. Copyright notice must appear on advertisements for this protection.

Copy testing. Measuring the effectiveness of advertisements.

Copywriter. A person who creates the text of advertisements and often the idea to be visualized as well.

Corrective advertising. To counteract the past residual effect of previous deceptive advertising, the FTC may require the advertiser to devote future space and time to disclosure of previous deception. Began around the late 1960s.

Cover. The front of a publication is known as the first cover; the inside of the front cover is the second cover; the inside of the back cover is the third cover; the outside of the back cover is the fourth cover. Extra rates are charged for cover positions.

Coverage. The portion of an area, community, or group that may be reached by an advertising medium.

Coverage (TV). All households in an area able to receive a station's signal, even though some may not be tuned in. *Grade A coverage:* those households in the city and outlying counties that receive signals with hardly any disturbance. *Grade B:* those on the fringes of the market area, receiving signals with some interference.

Cover stock. A paper made of heavy, strong fiber; used for folders and booklet covers. Some cover stocks run into the low weights of paper known as book paper, but most cover stocks are heavier. Basic size, 20 × 26 inches.

CPM. Cost per thousand. Used in comparing media cost. Can mean cost per thousand readers or viewers or prospects. Must be specified.

Crash finish. A surface design on paper, simulating the appearance of rough cloth.

Crew (TV). All personnel hired by the production company for shooting a TV commercial.

Cronar film and Cronar plates. A conversion method by which either type of letterpress engraving is transferred directly to film by mechanical means (balls or fingers). This film can then be used to make offset plates, gravure cylinders, or very faithful duplicate letterpress plates.

Cropping. Trimming part of an illustration. Cropping is done either to eliminate nonessential background in an illustration or to change the proportions of the illustration to the desired length and width.

CRT. *See* Cathode ray tube.

CU. Close-up (in television). ECU is *extra close-up.*

Cue. (1) The closing words of an actor's speech and a signal for another actor to enter. (2) A sound, musical or otherwise, or a manual signal calling for action or proceeding.

Cumes (TV). Cumulative audience. The number of unduplicated people or homes reached by a given schedule over a given time period. In network TV this usually is four weeks. In spot TV it is usually one week.

Customer profile. A composite estimate of the demographic characteristics of the people who are to buy a brand and the purchase patterns they will produce.

Cut. (1) The deletion of program material to fit a prescribed period of time, or for other reasons. (2) A photoengraving, electrotype, or stereotype; derived from the term *woodcut.* In England called a *block.*

𝕯

Dailies (TV). All film shot, developed, and printed, from which scenes are selected for editing into the completed TV commercial. The term may also apply to videotape shooting. Also known as *rushes.*

Dayparts (TV and radio). Time segments into which a radio or TV day is divided, from first thing in the morning to the last thing at night. The parts are given different names. The cost of time depends upon the size of the audience at the time of each different daypart.

DB. *See* Delayed broadcast.

Dealer imprint. Name and address of the dealer, printed or pasted on an advertisement of a national advertiser. In the planning of direct mail, space is frequently left for the dealer imprint.

Dealer tie-in. A national advertiser's promotional program in which the

dealer participates (as in contests, sampling plan, cooperative advertising plans).

Deals. A *consumer* deal is a plan whereby the consumer can save money in the purchase of a product. A *trade* deal is a special discount to the retailer for a limited period of time.

Decalcomania. A transparent, gelatinous film bearing an advertisement, which may be gummed onto the dealer's window. Also known as a transparency.

Deckle edge. Untrimmed, ragged edge of a sheet of paper. Used for costlier forms of direct mail.

Deck panels (outdoor). Panels built one above the other.

Definition. Clean-cut TV and radio transmission and reception.

Delayed broadcast. A TV or radio program repeated at a later hour to reach people in a different time belt.

Delete. "Omit." Used in proofreading.

Demographic characteristics. A broad term that refers to the various social and economic characteristics of a group of households or a group of individuals. Refers to characteristics such as the number of members of a household, age of head of household, occupation of head of household, education of household members, type of employment, ownership of home, and annual household income.

Depth interview. A research interview conducted without a structured questionnaire. Respondents are encouraged to speak fully and freely about a particular subject.

Depths of columns. The dimension of a column space measured from top of the page to the bottom, in either agate lines or inches.

Designated Market Area (DMA). A rigidly defined geographical area in which stations located, generally, in the core of the area attract most of the viewing. A concept developed by the A. C. Nielsen Company. *See also* Area of Dominant Influence (ADI).

Diary. A written record kept by a sample of persons who record their listening, viewing, reading, or purchases of brands within a specific

period of time. Used by syndicate research firms who arrange with a selected sample of people to keep such diaries and to report weekly, for a fee.

Die-cut. An odd-shaped paper or cardboard for a direct-mail piece or for display purposes, cut with a special knife-edge die.

Diorama. (1) In point-of-purchase advertising, these are elaborate displays of a scenic nature, almost always three-dimensional and illuminated. (2) In TV, a miniature set, usually in perspective, used to simulate an impression of a larger location.

Direct-mail advertising. That form of direct response advertising sent through the mails.

Direct marketing. Selling goods and services without the aid of wholesaler or retailer. Includes direct-response advertising, and advertising for leads for salespeople. Also direct door-to-door selling. Uses many media, direct mail, publications, TV, radio.

Director. (TV, radio). The person who writes or rewrites, then casts and rehearses a TV or radio program and directs the actual air performance.

Direct process. In two-, three-, and four-color process work, color separation and screen negative made simultaneously on the same photographic film.

Direct-response advertising. Any form of advertising done in direct marketing. Uses all types of media: direct mail, TV, magazines, newspapers, radio. Term replaces *mail-order advertising. See* Direct marketing.

Disc. Circular carrier of negative fonts used in phototypesetting equipment such as Photon or Fototronic.

Disk jockey. The master of ceremonies of a radio program of transcribed music (records).

Display. (1) Attention-attracting quality. (2) Display type is in sizes 18 points or larger. Italics, boldface, and sometimes capitals are used for display; so are hand-drawn letters and script. (3) Display space in newspapers usually is not sold in units of less than 14 column lines; there is no such minimum requirement for undisplay classified advertisements. (4) Window display, interior display, and counter display are different methods of point-of-purchase advertising. (5) Open display puts the goods where they can be actually handled and examined by the customer; closed display has the goods in cases and under glass.

Display advertising. (1) In a newspaper, ads other than those in classified columns. (2) Advertising on backgrounds designed to stand by themselves (as window displays) or mounted (as a tack-on sign).

Dissolve (TV). Simultaneous fading out of one scene and fading in of the next in the TV commercial.

DMA. See Designated Market Area.

DMAA. See Direct Mail Advertising Association.

Dolly. The movable platform on which a camera is placed for TV productions when different angles or views will be needed.

Double-decker. Outdoor advertising erected one above another.

Double-leaded. See Leading.

Double-page spread. Facing pages used for a single, unbroken advertisement. Also called double-spread and double-truck, or center spread if at the center of a publication.

"Down-and-under." A direction given to a musician or sound effects person playing solo in a broadcast. It means "quiet down from your present playing level to a volume less than that of the lines of dialogue that follow."

Drive time (radio). A term used to designate the time of day when people are going to, or coming from, work. Usually 6 A.M. to 10 A.M. and 3 P.M. to 7 P.M., but this varies from one community to another. The most costly time on the rate card.

Drop-in. In broadcasting, a local commercial inserted in a nationally sponsored network program.

Drop-out halftone. See Halftone.

Dry-brush drawing. A sketch made with a brush and extra thick, dry ink or paint.

Dry run. Rehearsal without cameras.

Dubbing. The combining of several sound tracks for recording on film.

Dubbing in. The addition of one TV film to another; e.g., adding the part containing the advertiser's commercial to the part that carries the straight entertainment.

Dubs (TV). Duplicate tapes, made from a master print, sent to different stations for broadcast.

Due bill. (1) In a media barter deal, the amount of time acquired from a station by a film distributor, owner, or producer. (2) An agreement between an advertiser (usually a hotel, restaurant, or resort) and a medium, involving equal exchange of the advertiser's service for time or space.

Dummy. (1) Blank sheets of paper cut and folded to the size of a proposed leaflet, folder, booklet, or book, to indicate weight, shape, size, and general appearance. On the pages of the dummy, the layouts can be drawn. Useful in designing direct-mail advertisements. A dummy may also be made from the proof furnished by the printer. (2) An empty package or carton used for display purposes.

Duograph. A two-color plate made from black-and-white art work. The second color is a flat color and carries no detail. Less expensive than a duotone.

Duotone. Two halftone plates, each printing in a different color and giving two-color reproductions from an original one-color plate.

Duplicate plates. Photoengravings made from the same negative as an original plate or via DuPont Cronapress conversion.

E

Early fringe. The time period preceding prime time, usually 4:30–7:30 P.M., except in Central Time Zone, where it extends from 3:30 to 6:30 P.M.

Ears of newspaper. Boxes or announcements at the top of the front page, alongside the name of the paper, in the upper right- and left-hand corners. Sold for advertising space by some papers.

Earth station. A TV receiving station designed to capture signals from satellites for relay to broadcasting stations or, in time, possibly directly to receiving sets.

ECU (TV). Extreme-close-up in shooting a picture.

Editing (TV). Also known as "completion," "finishing," and "post-production." The second major stage of TV commercial production, following shooting, in which selected scenes are joined together with opticals and titles and sound track into the finished commercial.

Electric spectaculars. Outdoor advertisements in which electric lights are used to form the words and design. Not to be confused with illuminated posters or illuminated painted bulletins.

Enameled paper; enamel-coated stock. A book or cover paper that can take the highest-screen halftone. It is covered with a coating of china clay and a binder, then ironed under high-speed rollers. This gives it a hard, smooth finish, too brittle to fold well. Made also in dull and semi-dull finish.

End-product advertising. Advertising by a firm that makes a constituent part of a finished product bought by the consumer. For example, advertising by DuPont that stresses the importance of Teflon in cooking ware.

English finish (EF). A hard, even, unpolished finish applied to book papers.

Engraving. (1) A photoengraving. (2) A plate in which a design is etched for printing purposes.

Equivalent weight of paper. The weight of a paper stock in terms of its basic weight. See Basic weight.

Ethical advertising. (1) Standards of equitable, fair, and honest content in advertising. (2) Addressed to physicians only, in contrast to ads of a similar product addressed to the general public.

Extended covers. A cover that is slightly wider and longer than the pages of a paper-bound booklet or catalog; one that extends or hangs over the inside pages. Also called overhang and overlap. See Trimmed flush.

Extra (TV). A commercial performer who does not take a major role nor receive re-use payments, or "residuals."

F

Face. (1) The printing surface of type or a plate. (2) The style of type.

Facing text matter. An ad in a periodical opposite reading matter.

Fact sheet, Radio. A page of highlights of the selling features of a product, for use by an announcer in ad libbing a live commercial.

Fade. (TV) *Fading in* is the gradual appearance of the screen image, brightening to full visibility. (Radio): to diminish or increase the volume of sound on a radio broadcast.

Fading. Variation in intensity of a radio or TV signal received over a great distance.

Family of type. Type faces related in design, as Caslon Bold, Caslon Old Style, Caslon Bold Italics, Caslon Old Style Italics.

Fanfare. A few bars of music (usually trumpets) to herald an entrance or announcement in broadcasting.

FCC. *See* Federal Communications Commission.

FDA. *See* Food & Drug Administration.

Federal Communications Commission. The federal authority empowered to license radio and TV stations and to assign wave lengths to stations "in the public interest."

Federal Trade Commission (FTC). That agency of the federal government empowered to prevent unfair competition; also to prevent fraudulent, misleading or deceptive advertising in interstate commerce.

Field intensity map. A TV or radio broadcast coverage map showing the quality of reception possible on the basis of its signal strength. Sometimes called a contour map.

Field intensity measurement. The measurement at a point of reception of a signal delivered by a radio transmitter. Expressed in units of voltage per meter of effective antenna height, usually in terms of microvolts or millivolts per meter.

Fill-in. (1) The salutation and any other data to be inserted in the individual letters after they have been printed. (2) The blurring of an illustration, due to the closeness of the lines or dots in the plate or to heavy inking.

Firm order. A definite order for time or space that is not cancellable after a given date known as a firm order date.

Fixed position. A TV or radio spot delivered at a specific time; e.g., 8 AM.

Flag (outdoor). A tear in a poster, causing a piece of poster paper to hang loose. Plant owner is supposed to replace promptly.

Flat color. Second or additional printing colors, using line or tints, but not process.

Flat rate. A uniform charge for space in a medium, without regard to the amount of space used or the frequency of insertion. When flat rates do not prevail, time discounts or quantity discounts are offered.

Flight. The length of time a broadcaster's campaign runs. Can be days, weeks, or months, but does not refer to a year. A flighting schedule alternates periods of activity with periods of inactivity.

FM. *See* Frequency modulation.

Following, next to reading matter. The specification of a position for an advertisement to appear in a publication. Also known as full position. This preferred position usually costs more than run-of-paper position.

Follow style. Instruction to compositor to set copy in accordance with a previous advertisement or proof.

Font. An assortment of type characters of one style and size, containing the essential 26 letters (both capitals and small letters) plus numerals, punctuation marks, etc. See *Wrong font.*

Food & Drug Administration (FDA). The federal bureau with authority over the safety and purity of foods, drugs, cosmetics; also the labeling of such products.

Forced combination. A policy of allowing advertising space to be purchased only for a combination of the morning and evening newspapers in the community.

Form. Groups of pages printed on a large single sheet. This book was printed in 32s (32 pages to one sheet, or *form*).

Format. The size, shape, style, and appearance of a book or publication.

Forms close. The date on which all copy and plates for a periodical advertisement must be in.

4A's. American Association of Advertising Agencies (AAAA).

Four-color process. The process for reproducing color illustrations by a set of plates, one of which prints all the yellows, another the blues, a third the reds, the fourth the blacks (sequence variable). The plates are referred to as process plates.

Free lance. An independent artist, writer, TV or radio producer, or advertising person who takes individual assignments from different accounts but is not in their employ.

Frequency. (1) The number of waves per second that a transmitter radiates (measured in kilohertz [kHz] and megahertz [MHz]). The FCC assigns to each television and radio station the frequency on which it may operate, to prevent interference with other stations. (2) Of media exposure, the number of times an individual or household is exposed to a medium within a given period of time. (3) In statistics, the number of times each element appears in each step of a distribution scale.

Frequency modulation (FM). A radio transmission wave that transmits by the variation in frequency of its wave, rather than by its size (AM modulation). An FM wave is 20 times the width of an AM wave, which is the first source of its fine tone. To transmit such a wave, it had to be placed high on the electromagnetic spectrum, far from AM waves with their interference and static. Hence, its outstanding tone.

Fringe time (TV). The hours directly before and after prime time. May be further specified as early fringe or late fringe.

FTC. *See* Federal Trade Commission.

Full position. A special preferred position of an advertisement in a newspaper. The advertisement either (1) follows a column or columns of the

by direct-response advertisers who use different mailing lists for the same mailing. Mailing lists are sent to a central merge/purge office that electronically picks out duplicate names. Saves mailing costs, especially important to firms that send out a million pieces in one mailing. Also avoids damage to the good will of the public.

MF. Machine-finish paper.

Milline rate. A unit for measuring the rate of advertising space in relation to circulation; the cost of having one agate line appear before one million readers. Calculated thus:

$$\frac{1,000,000 \times \text{line rate}}{\text{quantity circulation}} = \text{milline}$$

Used in newspaper advertising.

Modern Roman. *See* Old style Roman.

Modular agency. Also called *a la carte agency.*

Month preceding. "First month preceding publication" means that the closing date is in the month that immediately precedes the publication date on the cover of a periodical.

Motivational research. Research without a questionnaire. The respondent is invited to talk freely on a series of selected topics relating to the advertiser's interests or to react to a situation pictured or described. Also called unstructured research.

N

NAD. *See* National Advertising Division.

NARB. *See* National Advertising Review Board.

National advertising. Advertising by the marketer of a trademarked product or service sold through different outlets, in contrast to local advertising.

National Advertising Division (NAD). The policymaking arm of the National Advertising Review Board.

National Advertising Review Board (NARB). The advertising industry's major organization for policing misleading ads.

National brand. A manufacturer's or producer's brand distributed through many outlets; distinct from a private brand.

National plan. Advertising campaign tactics aimed at getting business nationwide, simultaneously. When properly used it is the outgrowth of numerous local plans.

Nemo. Any broadcast not originated in the local studio.

Net audience. The total audience for a schedule in a medium, less duplication.

Network. Interconnecting stations for the simultaneous transmission of television or radio broadcasts.

Next to reading matter (n.r.). The position of an advertisement immediately adjacent to editorial or news matter in a publication.

Nielsen Station Index (NSI). These reports, issued by the A. C. Nielsen Company, provide audience measurement for individual television markets.

Nielsen Television Index (NTI). National audience measurements for all network programs.

Nonilluminated (Regular). A poster panel without artificial lighting.

Nonstructured interview. An interview conducted without a prepared questionnaire. The respondent is encouraged to talk freely without direction from the interviewer.

NSI. *See* Nielsen Station Index.

NTI. Nielsen Television Index.

O

OAAA. *See* Outdoor Advertising Association of America.

O & O stations. TV or radio stations owned and operated by networks.

Off camera. A TV term for an actor whose voice is heard but who does not appear in the commercial. Less costly than being on camera.

Off-screen announcer. An unseen speaker on a TV commercial.

Offset. (1) *See* Lithography. (2) The blotting of a wet or freshly printed sheet against an accompanying sheet. Can be prevented by slip-sheeting. Antique paper absorbs the ink and prevents offsetting.

Old English. A style of black-letter or text type, now little used except in logotypes of trade names or names of newspapers.

Old style Roman (o.s.). Roman type with slight difference in weight between its different strokes, as contrasted with Modern type, which has sharp contrast and accents in its strokes. Its serifs for the most part are oblique; Roman serifs are usually horizontal or vertical.

On camera. A television term for an actor whose face appears in a commercial. Opposite of off camera. Affects the scale of compensation.

One-time rate. The rate paid by an advertiser who uses less space than is necessary to earn a time or rate discount, when such discounts are offered. Same as Transient rate, Basic rate, and Open rate.

Open end. A broadcast in which the commercial spots are added locally.

Open rate. In print, the highest advertising rate on which all discounts are placed. It is also called Basic rate, Transient rate, or One-time rate.

Opticals. Visual effects that are put on a television film in a laboratory, in contrast to those that are included as part of the original photograph.

Out-of-home media. Outdoor advertising; transportation advertising.

Outdoor Advertising Association of America (OAAA). The trade association of the outdoor advertising industry. Oldest advertising association.

Overtime (TV). Television production hours beyond the normal shooting day, when crew costs double, sometimes triple.

P

Package. (1) A container. (2) *In radio or television,* a combination assortment of time units, sold as a single offering at a set price. (3) A special radio or television program or series of programs, bought by an advertiser (for a lump sum). Includes all components, ready to broadcast, with the addition of the advertiser's commercial. (4) In *direct-response* advertising, a complete assembly of everything to be included in the mailing, including the envelope, letter, brochure, return card.

Package insert. A card, folder or booklet included in a package, often used for recipes, discount coupons and ads for other members of the product family. When attached to outside of package, called package *outsert*.

Package plan (TV). Some combination of spots devised by a station and offered to advertisers at a special price. Package plans are usually weekly or monthly buys.

Participation (TV, radio). An announcement within a program, as compared with one scheduled between programs.

Pattern plate. (1) An electrotype of extra heavy shell used for molding in large quantities to save wear on the original plate or type. (2) An original to be used for the same purpose.

Photocomposition (phototypesetting). A method of setting type by a photographic process only. Uses no metal.

Photoengraving. (1) An etched, relief printing plate made by a photomechanical process—as a halftone or line cut. (2) The process of producing the plate.

Photoplatemaking. Making plates (and the films preceding the plates) for any printing process by camera, in color or black-and-white.

Photoprint. The negative or positive copy of a photograph subject.

Photoscript (TV). A series of photographs made at the time of shooting a TV commercial picture based on the original script or storyboard. Used for keeping record of commercial, also for sales promotion purposes.

Photostat. One of the most useful aids in making layouts or proposed advertisements. A rough photographic reproduction of a subject; inexpensive and quickly made (within half an hour if desired).

Phototypesetting. The composition of phototext and display letters onto film or paper for reproduction. Letters are projected from film negative grids and are also stored in a binary form in computer core to be generated through a CRT system. Also called photocomposition.

Phototypography. The entire field of composing, makeup, and processing phototypographically assembled letters (photodisplay and phototext, or type converted to film) for the production of image carriers by platemakers or printers.

Photounit. The print-out or photoexposure unit of a phototypesetting system. When activated by keyboarded paper or magnetic tape, the unit exposes alphanumerical characters onto film or paper from negative fonts, discs, or grids.

PI (per inquiry) advertising. A method used in direct-response radio and television advertising, whereby orders as a result of a commercial are sent directly to the station. The advertiser pays the station on a per inquiry (or per order) received basis.

Pica; pica em. The unit for measuring width in printing. There are 6 picas to the inch. Derived from *pica*, the old name of 12-pt. type (1/6 inch high). A page of type 24 picas wide is 4 inches wide (24 ÷ 6 = 4).

Picture resolution. The clarity with which the television image appears on the television screen.

Piggyback (TV). The joining of two commercials, usually 15 seconds each, back-to-back for on-air use. A practice going out of use.

Pilot film (TV). A sample film to show what a series will be like. Generally specially filmed episodes of television shows.

Pioneering stage. The advertising stage of a product in which the need for such product is not recognized and must be established, or when the need has been established but the success of a commodity in filling those requirements has to be established. *See* Competitive stage; Retentive stage; Spiral.

Plant operator. In outdoor advertising, the local person who arranges to lease, erect, and maintain the outdoor sign and to sell the advertising space on it.

Plate. The metal or plastic from which impressions are made by a printing operation.

Plated stock. Paper with a high gloss and a hard, smooth surface, secured by being pressed between polished metal sheets.

Playback. (1) The playing of a recording for audition purposes. (2) A viewer's or reader's report on what message he or she derived from a commercial or advertisement.

Point; pt. (1) The unit of measurement of type, about 1/72 inch in depth. Type is specified by its point size, as 8 pt., 12 pt., 24 pt., 48 pt. (2) The unit for measuring thickness of paper, one thousandth of an inch.

Point-of-purchase advertising. Displays prepared by the manufacturer for use where the product is sold.

Poll. An enumeration of a sample. Usually refers to sample opinions, attitudes, and beliefs.

Pop (radio). Contemporary music.

POPAI. *See* Point of Purchase Advertising Institute.

Position (magazine). The place in a magazine where an ad or insert appears. Best position is up front or as close to it as possible; right-hand side.

Position (newspaper). Where in paper, on what page, and on what part of page the ad appears.

Position (TV and radio). Where in the program your commercial is placed.

Positioning. Segmenting a market by creating a product to meet the needs of a selective group or by using a distinctive advertising appeal to meet the needs of a specialized group, without making changes in the physical product.

Poster panel. A standard surface on which outdoor posters are placed. The posting surface is of sheet metal. An ornamental molding of standard green forms the frame. The standard poster panel is 12 feet high, 25 feet long (outside dimensions).

Poster plant. The organization that provides the actual outdoor advertising service.

Poster showing. An assortment of outdoor poster panels in different locations sold as a unit. The number of panels in a showing varies from city to city and is described in terms of a 100 showing, a 50 showing, a 25 showing. This identification has no reference to the actual number of posters in a showing, nor does it mean percentages.

Posting date (outdoor). The date on which posting for an advertiser begins. Usually, posting dates are every fifth day starting with the first of the month. However, plant operators will, if possible, arrange other posting dates when specifically requested.

Posting leeway (outdoor). The five working days required by plant operators to assure the complete posting of a showing. This margin is needed to allow for inclement weather, holidays, etc., as well as the time for actual posting.

PPA. Periodical Publishers Association, a group of magazine publishers that passes on agency credit. For newspaper credit, *see* ANPA.

Pre-date. In larger cities, a newspaper issue that comes out the night before the date it carries, or a section of the Sunday issue published and mailed out during the week preceding the Sunday date.

Preemption; preemptible time. (1) Recapture of a time period by a network or station for important news or special program. (2) By prior agreement, the resale of a time unit of one advertiser to another (for a higher rate). Time may be sold as nonpreemptive (NP) at the highest rate, two weeks preemptible (lower rate), or immediately preemptible (IP) the lowest rate.

Preferred position. A special, desired position in a magazine or newspaper, for which the advertiser must pay a premium. Otherwise the advertisement appears in a run-of-paper (ROP) position; that is, wherever the publisher chooses to place it.

Premium. An item, other than the product itself, given to purchasers of a product as an inducement to buy. Can be free with a purchase (e.g., on the package, in the package, or it may be the container itself) or available upon proof of purchase and a payment (self-liquidating premium).

Primary circulation. See Circulation.

Primary service area. The area to which a radio station delivers a high level of signals of unfailing steadiness and of sufficient volume to override the existing noise level both day and night and all seasons of the year, determined by field intensity measurements.

Prime rate. The TV and radio rate for the times when they reach the largest audience.

Prime time. A continuous period of not less than 3 hours per broadcast day, designated by the station as reaching peak audiences. In TV, usually 8:00 P.M. to 11:00 P.M. E.S.T. (7:00 P.M. to 10:00 P.M. C.S.T.).

Principal register. The main register for recording trademarks, service marks, collective marks, and certification marks under the Lanham Federal Trade-Mark Act.

Printers' Ink Model Statute. (1911) The act directed at fraudulent advertising, prepared and sponsored by *Printers' Ink,* which was the pioneer advertising magazine.

Private brand. The trademark of a distributor of products sold by that distributor, only, in contrast to manufacturers' brands, sold through many outlets. Also known as private labels or house brands.

Process plates. Photoengraving plates for printing in color. Can print the full range of the spectrum by using three plates, each bearing a primary color—red, yellow, blue—plus a black plate. Referred to as 4-color plates. *See* Process printing.

Process printing. Letterpress color printing in which color is printed by means of process plates.

Producer. One who originates and/or presents a TV or radio program.

Production. (1) The conversion of an advertising idea into an advertisement, mainly by a printing process. (2) The building, organization, and presentation of a TV or radio program.

Production department. The department responsible for mechanical production of an advertisement and dealing with printers and engravers

or for the preparation of a TV or radio program.

Production director. (1) Person in charge of a TV or radio program. (2) Head of department handling print production.

Professional advertising. Directed at those in professions such as medicine, law, or architecture who are in a position to recommend use of a particular product or service to their clients.

Profile. (1) A detailed study of a medium's audience classified by size, age, sex, viewing habits, income, education, and so on. (2) A study of the characteristics of the users of a product or of a market.

Progressive proofs. A set of photoengraving proofs in color, in which: the yellow plate is printed on one sheet and the red on another; the yellow and red are then combined; next the blue is printed and a yellow-red-blue combination made. Then the black alone is printed, and finally all colors are combined. The sequence varies. In this way the printer matches up inks when printing color plates. (Often called "progs.")

Proof. (1) An inked impression of composed type or of a plate for inspection or for filing. (2) In photocomposition, a proof is made on photographically or chemically sensitized paper. (3) In engraving and etching, an impression taken to show the condition of the illustration at any stage of the work. Taking a proof is "pulling a proof."

Psychographics. A description of a market based on factors such as attitudes, opinions, interests, perceptions, and life-styles of consumers comprising that market. *See* Demographic characteristics.

Public service advertising. Advertising with a message in the public interest. When run by a corporation, often referred to as *institutional advertising.*

Public service announcements. Radio and TV announcements made by stations at no charge, in the public interest.

Publisher's statement. The statement of circulation issued by a publisher, usually audited or given as a sworn statement. All publication rates are based on a circulation statement.

Pulsation. Short bursts of advertising in a few markets at a time (rather than a steady schedule of advertising simultaneously in many markets).

Q

Qualified circulation. The term now being applied to those controlled (free) circulation trade magazines sent only to people who have representative positions in the field and who apply in writing annually for continuation on the free list.

Quarter showing. One fourth of a full showing in outdoor or transportation advertising.

Queen-size poster. An outside transit advertising display placed on the sides of vehicles (usually the curb side). Size: 30″ × 88″. See King-size posters.

R

Randomization. In consumer research, a method of securing random (unbiased) selection of respondents. See Sample; sampling.

Rate card. A card giving the space rates of a publication, circulation data, and data on mechanical requirements and closing dates.

Rate-holder. The minimum-sized advertisement that must appear during a given period if an advertiser is to secure a certain time or quantity discount. It holds a lower rate for an advertiser. Used mostly in local advertising.

Rate protection. The length of time an advertiser is guaranteed a specific rate by a medium. May vary from three months to a year from the date of signing a contract.

Rating point (TV). (1) The percentage of TV households in a market a TV station reaches with a program. The percentage varies with the time of day. A station may have a 10 rating between 6 and 6:30 P.M., and a 20 rating between 9 and 9:30 P.M. (a real hit!). (2) In radio, the percent-

age of people who listen to a station at a certain time. See Gross rating points.

Rating points (outdoor). Used in estimating the number of people to whom an outdoor sign is exposed. Each board is rated in terms of 1 percent of the daily passersby in relation to population. In making up a showing of different sizes in a market, the total number of rating points of those signs is added and referred to as the gross rating point of that showing for that market. The count includes duplication of people who may pass a sign more than once a day.

Reach. The total audience a medium actually covers.

Reading notices. Advertisements in newspapers set up in a type similar to that of the editorial matter. Must be followed by "Adv." Charged for at rates higher than those for regular ads. Many publications will not accept them.

Ream. In publishing and advertising, 500 sheets of paper. Thousandsheet counts now being used as basis of ordering paper.

Recognized agency. An advertising agency recognized by the various publishers or broadcast stations and granted a commission for the space it sells to advertisers.

Reduction prints (TV). 16mm film prints made from 35mm films.

Regional-channel station. A radio station that is allowed more power than a local station but less than a clear-channel station. It is assigned a place on the frequency band set aside for regional-channel stations. See Local channel and Clear-channel.

Register. Perfect correspondence in printing; of facing pages when top lines are even; of color printing, when there is correct superimposition of each plate, so that the colors mix properly.

Registering trademark. In the U.S., the act of recording a trademark with the Commission of Patents, to substantiate claim of first use. The law differs from many in South America and some in Europe. Whoever is the first to *register* a mark is its owner.

One result: trademark pirates in South America and Europe watch for new American trademarks, register them, and thus become owners. Then they wait for American firms to enter their markets. At that time, they may permit use of the trademark, for a price.

Register marks (engraving). Cross lines placed on a copy to appear in the margin of all negatives as a guide to perfect register.

Release. A legally correct statement by a person photographed authorizing the advertiser to use that photograph. For minors, the guardian's release is necessary.

Relief printing. Printing in which the design reproduced is raised slightly above the surrounding, nonprinting areas. Letterpress is a form of relief printing contrasted with intaglio printing and lithography.

Remote pickup. A broadcast originating outside the studio, as from a football field.

Repro proofs, or reproduction proofs. Exceptionally clean and sharp proofs from type for use as copy for reproduction.

Residual. A sum paid to certain talent on a TV or radio commercial every time the commercial is run after 13 weeks, for life of commercial.

Respondent. One who answers a questionnaire or is interviewed in a research study.

Retail advertising. Advertising by a local merchant who sells directly to the consumer.

Retentive stage. The third advertising stage of a product, reached when its general usefulness is everywhere known, its individual qualities thoroughly appreciated, and when it is satisfied to retain its patronage merely on the strength of its past reputation. See Pioneering stage Competitive stage; Spiral.

Retouching. The process of correcting or improving art work, especially photographs.

Reversed plate. (1) A line-plate engraving in which white comes out black, and vice versa. (2) An engraving in which right and left, as they appear in the illustration, are transposed.

Riding the showing. A physical inspection of the panels which comprise an outdoor showing. Also, riding through a market, selecting locations for signs.

Robinson-Patman Act. A federal law, enforced by the FTC. Requires a manufacturer to give proportionate discounts and advertising allowances to all competing dealers in a market. Purpose: to protect smaller merchants from unfair competition of larger buyers.

Roman type. (1) Originally, type of the Italian and Roman school of design, as distinguished from the blackface Old English style. Old style and modern are the two branches of the Roman family. (2) Type faces that are not italics are called roman.

ROP. See Run-of-paper position.

ROS. See Run of schedule.

Rotary plan (outdoor). Movable bulletins are moved from one fixed location to another one in the market, at regular intervals. The locations are viewed and approved in advance by the advertiser.

Rotary press. A printing press having no flat bed, but printing entirely with the movement of cylinders.

Rotogravure. The method of intaglio printing in which the impression is produced by chemically etched cylinders and run on a rotary press; useful in large runs of pictorial effects.

Rough. A crude sketch to show basic idea or arrangement. In making layouts, this is usually the first step.

Rough cut (TV). The first assembly of scenes in proper sequence, minus opticals and titles, in the TV commercial. Also called work print.

Routing out. Tooling out dead metal on an engraving plate.

Run-of-paper (ROP) position. Any location that the publisher selects in a publication, in contrast to preferred position.

Run-of-schedule (ROS). Commercial announcements that can be scheduled at the station's discretion anytime during the period specified by the seller (e.g., ROS, 10 A.M.-4:30 P.M., Monday through Friday).

Rushes (TV). The first, uncorrected prints of a commerical. Also called dailies.

S

Saddle stitching. Binding a booklet by stitching it through the center and passing stitches through the fold in the center pages. Enables the booklet to lie flat. When a booklet is too thick for this method, side stitching is used.

SAG. Screen Actors' Guild.

Sales promotion. (1) Those sales activities that supplement both personal selling and marketing, coordinate the two, and help to make them effective; for example, displays. (2) More loosely, the combination of personal selling, advertising, and all supplementary selling activities.

Sample; sampling. (1) The method of introducing and promoting merchandise by distributing a miniature or full-size trial package of the product free or at a reduced price. (2) Studying the characteristics of a representative part of an entire market, or universe, in order to apply to the entire market the data secured from the miniature part. A probability sample is one in which every member of the universe has a known probability of inclusion. A random sample is a probability sample in which, with a fixed mathematical regularity, names are picked from a list. A stratified quota sample (also known as a quota sample) is one drawn with certain predetermined restrictions on the characteristics of the people to be included. An area sample (or stratified area sample) is one in which one geographical unit is selected as typical of others in its environment. In a judgment sample, an expert's experience and knowledge of the field are employed to choose representative cases suitable for study. A convenience or batch sample is one selected from whatever portion of the universe happens to be handy.

Satellite earth station. A receiving station for domestic satellite transmission, usually to cablecasting systems. (Over 100 such stations in operation in 1978. Number estimated to double in 3 years.)

Satellite station. A term born before we had sky satellites. A small local TV station that has a feeder line running to a distant larger station (a parent station), so that programs can be relayed from the larger station. Not to be confused with earth satellite station.

Saturation. A media pattern of wide coverage and high frequency during a concentrated period of time, designed to achieve maximum impact, coverage, or both.

SC. Single column.

sc. Small caps.

Scaling down. Reducing illustrations to the size desired.

Scatter plan (TV). The use of announcements over a variety of network programs and stations, to reach as many people as possible in a market.

Score. To crease cards or thick sheets of paper so that they can be folded.

Scotchprint. A reproduction proof pulled on plastic material from a letterpress plate or form. Normally used in conversion of color plate from letterpress to offset.

Screen. (Photoengraving). The finely crossruled sheet used in photomechanical plate-making processes to reproduce the shades of gray present in a continuous tone photograph. Screens come in various rulings, resulting in more, or fewer, "dots" to the square inch on the plate, to conform with the requirements of different grades and kinds of printing paper. *TV:* The surface on which a picture is shown.

Screen printing (or silk screen). A printing process in which a stenciled design is applied to a textile or wire mesh screen. A squeegee forces paint or ink through the mesh of the screen to the paper directly beneath.

Script (TV). A description of the video, along with the accompanying audio, used in preparing a storyboard or in lieu of it.

Secondary meaning. When a word from the language has long been used as a trademark for a specific product and has come to be accepted as such, it is said to have acquired a ''secondary meaning'' and may be eligible for trademark registration.

Secondary service area (radio). The area beyond the primary service area where a broadcasting station delivers a steady signal, that signal must be of sufficient intensity to be a regular program service of loudspeaker volume, day and night, all seasons. *See* Primary service area.

SEG. Screen Extras Guild.

Segmentation. *See* Market segmentation.

Seque. (Pronounced segway; Italian, "it follows.") The transition from one musical theme to another without a break or announcement.

Serif. The short marks at top and bottom of Roman lettering. Originally chisel marks to indicate top and bottom of stone lettering.

Service mark. A word or name used in the sale of services, to identify the services of a firm and distinguish them from those of others; e.g., Hertz Drive Yourself Service; Weight Watchers Diet Course. Comparable to trademarks for products.

Sets in use. The number of TV sets and radios turned on at any given time.

Sheet. The old unit of poster size, 26 × 39 inches. The standard-size posters are 24 sheets (seldom used) and 30 sheets. There are also 3-sheet and 6-sheet posters.

Shooting (TV). The first stage of TV production, which covers the filming or videotaping of all scenes up through delivery of the "dailies."

Short rate. The balance advertisers have to pay if they estimated that they would run more ads in a year than they did and entered a contract to pay at a favorable rate. The short rate is figured at the end of the year or sooner if advertisers fall behind schedule. It is calculated at a higher rate for the fewer insertions.

Showing—outdoor. Outdoor posters are bought by groups, referred to as showings. The size of a showing is referred to as a 100 GRP showing or a 75 or 50 GRP showing, depending on the gross rating points of the individual boards selected. There is no relationship between the number of a showing, as 100, and the number

of boards in a showing. Each outdoor plant publishes the number of posters included in a 100 showing.

Showing—transit (interior). A unit for buying card space inside buses and subways. A showing usually calls for one card per bus or per car per market.

Showing—transit (exterior). A unit for buying outdoor space on buses. The cards vary according to size, position, and cost per bus.

SIC. *See* Standard Industrial Classification.

Side stitching. The method of stitching from one side of a booklet to the other. Stitching can be seen on front cover and on back. Used in thick booklet work. Pages do not lie flat. *See* Saddle stitching.

Signal area. The territory in which a radio or TV broadcast is heard. Can be primary, where most clearly heard, or secondary, where there may be more interference.

Signal (TV, radio). The communication received electronically from the broadcast station. One speaks of a "strong signal" or a "weak signal."

Signature. (1) The name of an advertiser. (2) The musical number or sound effect that regularly identifies a TV or radio program. (3) A sheet folded, ready for binding in a book, usually in multiples of 32, but 16's and 8's are also possible. A mark, letter, or number is placed at the bottom of the first page of every group of 16 or 32 pages to serve as a guide in folding.

Silhouette halftone. *See* Halftone.

Silk screen. A printing process in which a stenciled design is applied to a screen of silk, organdy, nylon, Dacron, or wire cloth. A squeegee forces paint or ink through the mesh of the screen to the paper directly beneath.

Simulation (computer). The process of introducing synthetic information into a computer for testing; an application for solving problems too complicated for analytical solution.

Simulcast. The simultaneous playing of a program over AM-FM radio.

SIU. Sets in use (TV).

Sized and supercalendered paper (s. and s.c.). Machine-finish book paper that has been given extra ironings to insure a smooth surface. Takes half-tones very well.

Sized paper. Paper that has received a chemical bath to make it less porous. Paper sized once and ironed (calendered) is known as machine-finish. If it is again ironed, it becomes sized and supercalendered (s. and s.c.).

Skin pack. A packaging method whereby a plastic film is pulled tightly around a product on a card. Used for "card merchandising."

Sky waves. The electromagnetic waves that shoot toward the sky from a station. During the day they all go through the Heaviside electronic layer, which blankets the earth. At night the AM waves bound back at an angle; hence AM broadcasts can be received at night over vast distances. *See* Ground waves.

Slip-sheeting. Placing a sheet of paper (tissue or cheap porous stock) between the sheets of a printing job to prevent them from offsetting or smudging as they come from the press.

Small caps (abbreviated sc or sm. caps). Letters shaped like upper case (capitals) but about two-thirds their size—nearly the size of lower-case letters. This sentence is set with a regular capital letter at the beginning, the rest in small caps.

SMSA. *See* Standard Metropolitan Statistical Area.

Snipe. A copy strip added over a poster advertisement; e.g., a dealer's name, special sale price, or another message. Also referred to as an overlay.

Sound effects. Various devices or recordings used in TV or radio to produce lifelike imitations of sound, such as footsteps, rain, ocean waves.

Space buyer. The official of an advertising agency who is responsible for the selection of printed media for the agency's clients.

Space discount. Given by a publisher for the linage an advertiser uses. *Compare* Time discount.

Space schedule. Shows the media in

which an advertisement is to appear, the dates on which it is to appear, its exact size, and the cost.

Special representative. An individual or organization representing a medium selling time or space outside the city of origin.

Spectacolor. Similar in purpose and method to Hi-Fi color, except color pages come out with registration points to fit newspaper page; no need for continuous design.

Spectacular. An outdoor sign built to order, designed to be conspicuous for its location, size, lights, motion, or action. The costliest form of outdoor advertising.

Spiral (advertising). The graphic representation of the stages through which a product might pass in its acceptance by the public. The stages are pioneering, competitive, retentive.

Split run. A facility available in some newspapers and magazines, wherein the advertiser can run different advertisements in alternate copies of the same issue at the same time. A pretesting method used to compare coupon returns from two different advertisements published under identical conditions.

Sponsor. The firm or individual paying for talent and broadcasting time for a radio or TV feature; the advertiser on the air.

Spot (TV and radio). *(1) Media use:* purchase of time from an independent station, in contrast to purchase from a network. When purchased by a national advertiser it is, strictly speaking, *national spot,* but is referred to just as *spot.* When purchased by a local advertiser it is, strictly speaking, *local spot,* but is referred to as *local* TV or *local* radio. *(2) Creative use:* the text of a short announcement.

Spread. (1) Two facing pages, a double-page advertisement. (2) Type matter set full measure across a page, not in columns. (3) Stretching any part of a broadcast to fill the full allotted time of the program.

Spread posting dates. Division of outdoor posting dates: one-half the panels of a showing may be posted

on one date, the other half later, say 10 or 15 days.

Staggered schedule. Insertions alternated in two or more periodicals.

Standard Industrial Classification (SIC). The division of all industry, by the Bureau of the Budget, into detailed standard classifications, identified by code numbers. Useful in making marketing plans.

Standard Metropolitan Statistical Area (SMSA). An allocation of territories in a metropolitan area as defined by the Bureau of the Budget, brought to county line basis. Used in sales planning and scheduling.

Stand by. Cue that a program is about to go on the air.

Standby space. Some magazines will accept an order to run an advertisement whenever and wherever the magazine wishes, at an extra discount. Advertiser forwards plate with order. Helps magazine fill odd pages or spaces.

Station breaks. Periods of time between TV or radio programs, or within a program as designated by the program originator.

Station clearance. See Clear.

Station satellite. A station, often found in regions of low population density, that is wholly dependent upon another, carrying both its programs and commercials. Purpose is to expand coverage of the independent station and offer service to remote areas. Nothing to do with TV from satellites.

Steel-die embossing. Printing from steel dies engraved by the intaglio process, the sharp, raised outlines being produced by stamping over a counter die. Used for monograms, crests, stationery, and similar social and business purposes.

Stet. A proofreader's term—"Let it stand as it is; disregard change specified." A dotted line is placed underneath the letter or words to which the instructions apply.

Stock footage (TV). Existing film that may be purchased for inclusion in a TV commercial.

Stock music. Existing recorded music that may be purchased for use in a TV or radio commercial.

Storecasting. The broadcasting of radio programs and commercials in stores; usually supermarkets.

Storyboard. Series of drawings used to present a proposed commercial. Consists of illustrations of key action (video), accompanied by the audio part to go with it. Used for getting advertiser approval, also as a guide in production.

Strip. (1) *TV or radio:* a commercial scheduled at the same time on successive days of the week, as Monday through Friday. (2) *Newspapers:* a shallow advertisement at the bottom of a newspaper, across all columns.

Subcaption (subcap). A subheadline.

Substance No. Usually followed by a figure, as Substance No. 16. In specifying paper stock, the equivalent weight of a given paper in the standard size.

Supplements (newspaper). Loose inserts carried in a newspaper. Printed by advertiser. Must carry "supplement" and newspaper logotype to meet newspaper postal requirements.

Surprint. (1) A photoengraving in which a line-plate effect appears over the face of a halftone, or vice versa. (2) Printing over the face of an advertisement already printed.

Sustaining program. Entertainment or educational feature performed at the expense of a broadcasting station or network; in contrast to a commercial program, for which an advertiser pays.

Sweepstakes. A promotion in which prize winners are determined on the basis of chance alone. Not legal if purchaser must lay out money to get it. *See* Contest.

Sworn statement. When a publisher does not offer a certified audited report of circulation (as many small and new publishers do not) it may offer advertisers a sworn statement of circulation.

Syndicate mailings. (direct-response advertising). The mailing pieces a firm prepares for its products but then turns over to another firm to mail out to the latter's lists. Terms are negotiated individually.

Syndicated research services. Research organizations regularly report on what TV and radio programs are being received, what magazines are read, what products are being used by households, where, and other information. Sold on subscription basis.

Syndicated TV program. A program that is sold or distributed to more than one local station by an independent organization outside of the national network structure. Includes reruns of former network entries and movies that are marketed to stations by specialized firms that had a hand in their production.

Syndication, trade-out. See Trade-out syndication.

TAB. See Traffic Audit Bureau.

Tag (TV). A local retailer's message at the end of a manufacturer's commercial. Usually 10 seconds of a 60-second commercial.

Take-one. A mailing card or coupon attached to an inside transit advertisement. The rider is invited to tear off and mail for further information on the service or offering by the advertiser.

Tear sheets. Copies of advertisements from newspapers. Sent to the agency or advertiser as proof of publication.

Telecast. A sound and pictorial image sent by television.

TF. (1) Till-forbid. (2) To fill. (3) Copy is to follow.

Till-forbid; run TF. Instructions to publisher meaning: "Continue running this advertisement until instructions are issued to the contrary." Used in local advertisement.

Time classifications (TV). Stations assign alphabetical values to specific time periods for easier reference in reading rate cards. The values generally extend from A through D. In an average market, the classification might work as follows: AA and A for Prime Time; B for Early Evening and Late News; C for Day Time (afternoon) and Late Night; D for the periods from 1 A.M. until sign-off and from sign-on until noon.

Time clearance. Making sure that a given time for a specific program or commercial is available.

Time discount. Given for the frequency or regularity with which an advertiser inserts advertisements. Distinguished from quantity discount, for amount of space used.

Tint. A reproduction of a solid color.

To fill (TF). Instructions to printer meaning: "Set this copy in the size necessary to fill the specified space indicated in the layout."

Total audience plan (TV, radio). Spot package consisting of a combination that will hit all a station's listeners in a specified time span.

Tr. Transpose type as indicated, a proofreader's abbreviation.

Trade advertising. Advertising directed to the wholesale or retail merchants or sales agencies through whom the product is sold.

Trade character. A representation of a person or animal, realistic or fanciful, used in conjunction with a trademark to help identification. May appear on packages as well as in advertising (e.g., Green Giant).

Trademark. Any device or word that identifies the origin of a product, telling who made it or who sold it. Not to be confused with trade name.

Trade name. A name that applies to a business as a whole, not to an individual product.

Trade-out syndication. A TV program series produced by an advertiser and containing that advertiser's commercials is offered to stations. There are no charges on either side. Stations save the expense of the programs, and advertisers keep other ads away from their own. Stations are free to sell a selected amount of the time at specific points in the program.

Trade paper. A business publication directed to those who buy products for resale (i.e., wholesalers, jobbers, retailers).

Traffic Audit Bureau (TAB). An organization designed to investigate how many people pass and may see a given outdoor sign, to establish a method of evaluating traffic measuring a market.

Traffic count. In outdoor advertising, the number of pedestrians and vehicles passing a panel during a specific time period.

Traffic department. In an advertising agency, the department responsible for prompt execution of work in all departments and getting complete material to the forwarding department for shipment on schedule.

Traffic flow map (outdoor). An outline map of a market's streets scaled to indicate the relative densities of traffic.

Transcription program library. A collection of transcription records from which the radio station may draw. Stations subscribe to various transcription libraries.

Transient rate. Same as one-time in buying space.

Transition time. See Fringe time.

Transparency. Same as decalcomania.

Traveling display. An exhibit prepared by a manufacturer of a product and loaned to each of several dealers in rotation. Usually based on the product and prepared in such a way as to be of educational or dramatizing value.

Trimmed flush. A booklet or book trimmed after the cover is on, the cover thus being cut flush with the leaves. *Compare with* Extended covers.

Triple spotting. Three commercials back to back.

TV week. Sunday to Saturday.

25 × 38-80. Read twenty-five, thirty-eight, eighty. The method of expressing paper weight, meaning that a ream of paper 25 × 38 inches in size weighs 80 lbs. Similarly, 25 × 38-60, 25 × 38-70, 25 × 38-120, 17 × 22-16, 17 × 22-24, 20 × 26-80, 38 × 50-140. Used as a standard for paper sold in any size.

Type face. The design and style of a type letter.

Type family. A group of type designs which are variations of one basic alphabet style. Usually comprising roman, italic, or boldface, they can also vary in width (condensed or extended) and in weight (light to extra bold). Some families have dozens of versions.

Type page. The area of a page that type can occupy; the total area of a page less the margins.

U

Ultra high frequency (UHF). Television channels 14-83, operating on frequencies from 470 MHz to 890 MHz.

Unaided recall. A research method for learning whether a person is familiar with a brand, slogan, advertisement or commercial without giving a cue as to what it is. "What program did you watch last night?" *See* Aided recall.

V

VAC. Verified audit circulation by an auditing organization, which believes every publication selling advertising should have an audit available, whatever the circulation method (paid or free).

Value goal. The amount and form of value a company sets out to offer in a product.

Vertical publications. Business publications dealing with the problems of a specific industry; e.g., *Chain Store Age, National Petroleum News, Textile World. See* Horizontal publications.

Very high frequency (VHF). The frequency on the electromagnetic spectrum assigned to television channels 2-13, inclusive. *See* Ultra high frequency.

Video (TV). The visual portion of a broadcast. *See* Audio.

Videotape (TV). An electronic method of recording images and sound on tape. Most TV shows that appear live are done on videotape.

Videotape recording. A system that permits instantaneous playback of a simultaneous recording of sound and picture on a continuous strip of tape.

Vignette. A halftone in which the edges (or parts of them) are shaded off gradually to very light gray.

Voice-over. The voice of a TV commercial announcer or actor or singer recorded off-camera. Costs less than if delivered on-camera.

VTR (TV). Videotape recording of a commercial.

W

Wait order. An advertisement set in type, ready to run in a newspaper, pending a decision on the exact date (frequent in local advertising).

Warm-up. The 3- or 5-minute period immediately preceding a line broadcast in which the announcer or star puts the studio audience in a receptive mood by amiably introducing the cast of the program or discussing its problems.

Wash drawing. A brushwork illustration, usually made with diluted India ink or watercolor. In addition to black and white, it has varying shades of gray, like a photograph. Halftones, not line plates, are made from wash drawings.

Wave posting (outdoor). Concentration of poster showings in a succession of areas within the market. Usually coincides with special promotions in each of these areas.

Weather contingency (TV). An estimated emergency fund to cover daily pay for union crew and equipment rental if unfavorable weather interferes with scheduled shooting of a commercial.

Web printing. Also called roll-fed printing. In contrast to sheet-fed printing, paper is fed into the press from rolls. This method is used in rotogravure, newspapers, magazine presses, packaging presses, and increasingly in offset. Do not confuse with *wet* printing, though both may take place simultaneously.

Wet printing. Color printing on specially designed high-speed presses with one color following another in immediate succession before the ink from any plate or cylinder has time to dry.

wf. Wrong font.

Widow. In typography, applied to the last line of a paragraph when it has only one or two words.

Wild spot (TV). A commercial broadcast by noninterconnected stations.

Window envelope. A mailing envelope with a transparent panel, permitting the address on the enclosure to serve as a mailing address as well.

Work-and-turn. Printing all the pages in a signature from one form and then turning the paper and printing on the second side, making two copies or signatures when cut.

Work print (TV). *See Rough Cut.*

Wove paper. Paper having a very faint, clothlike appearance when held to the light.

Wrong font (wf). Letter from one series mixed with those from another series or font. *This sentence is the wrong font.*

Z

Zinc etching. A photoengraving in zinc. Term is usually applied to line plates.

Zone plan. Concentration on a certain limited geographical area in an advertising campaign. Also known as local plan.

Zoom (TV). A camera lens action or optical effect that permits a rapid move-in toward, or pull-back away from, the subject being photographed in a commercial.

Index

S

OTTO KLEPPNER

A graduate of New York University, Otto Kleppner started out
in advertising as a copywriter. After several such jobs, he
became advertising manager at Prentice-Hall, where he began
to think that he, too, ''could write a book.'' Some years later,
he also thought that he could run his own advertising agency,
and both ideas materialized eminently. His highly successful
agency handled advertising for leading accounts (Dewar's Scotch
Whisky, I. W. Harper Bourbon and other Schenley brands,
Saab Cars, Doubleday Book Clubs, and others). His book became
a bible for advertising students, and his writings have been
published in eight languages.

Active in the American Association of Advertising Agencies,
Mr. Kleppner has served as a director, a member of the Control
Committee, chairman of the Committee of Government, Public and
Educator Relations, and a governor of the New York Council.
He was awarded the Nichols Cup (now the Crain Cup) for
distinguished service to the teaching of advertising.